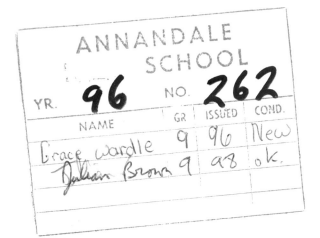

NELSON

SCIENCE

9

NELSON
SCIENCE 9

BOB RITTER
Austin O'Brien High School
Edmonton

ALAN J. HIRSCH
Port Credit Secondary School
Mississauga

DONALD PLUMB
Earl Haig Secondary School
North York
(on secondment to TVOntario)

ELIZABETH WORRALL
Frontenac, Lennox, and Addington
Roman Catholic Separate School Board
Kingston

TED GIBB
London Board of Education
London

Pedagogical Consultant
DOUGLAS A. ROBERTS
The University of Calgary
Calgary

CONTRIBUTING WRITERS
Dr. Larry Bencze
Alex Corry
Roland van Oostveen
Gabriel Roman Ayyavoo

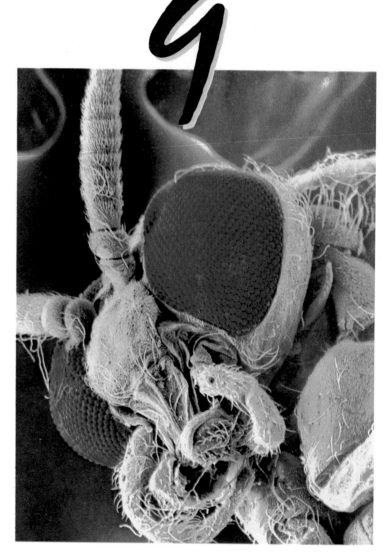

Nelson Canada

I(T)P An International Thomson Publishing Company

Toronto • Albany • Bonn • Boston • Cincinnati • Detroit • London • Madrid • Melbourne
Mexico City • New York • Pacific Grove • Paris • San Francisco • Singapore • Tokyo • Washington

Nelson Science 9 Project Team

Executive Editor: **David Steele**

Project Coordinator: **Colin Bisset**

Assistant Coordinator: **Carolyn Madonia**

Supervising Editor: **Cecilia Chan**

Art Director: **Liz Harasymczuk**

Design/Art Direction: **Stuart Knox**

Assistant Designer: **Julia Hall**

Composition Analyst/Design: **Suzanne Peden**

Manuscript Processor: **Elaine Andrews**

Production Coordinator: **Renate McCloy**

Photo Researcher: **Vicki Gould**

Project Management & Development: **Trifolium Books Inc.**

Development Editors: **Julie Czerneda, Ruta Demery, Trudy Rising, Mary Kay Winter**

Copy Editor: **Rosemary Tanner**

Proofreader: **Kathleen ffolliott**

Illustrators: **Academy Artworks, Inc., Norman Eyolfson, Catherine Farley, illustrious, inc., Martin Lengden, Dave Mazierski, Margo Stahl, Bart Vallecoccia, Kam Yu**

Safety Consultant: **Margaret Redway, Fraser Scientific and Business Services, Richmond, B.C.**

Cover photo: **CNRI/ Science Photo Library.** False-colour scanning electron micrograph of the head of the minute black fly, *Simulium* sp., also known as the buffalo-gnat.

I(T)P ™

International Thomson Publishing
The ITP logo is a trademark under licence

© Nelson Canada,
A division of Thomson Canada Limited, 1995

Published in 1995 by
Nelson Canada,
A division of Thomson Canada Limited
1120 Birchmount Road
Scarborough, Ontario M1K 5G4

The information and activities presented in this book have been carefully edited and reviewed for accuracy and are intended for their instructional value.
However, the publisher makes no representations or warranties of any kind, nor are any representations implied with respect to the material set forth herein, and the publisher takes no responsibility with respect to such material. Publisher shall not be liable for any general, special, consequential or exemplary damages resulting, in whole or in part, from the readers' use of, or reliance upon, this material.

Canadian Cataloguing in Publication Data

Main entry under title:

Nelson Science 9

Includes index.
ISBN 0-17-604725-5

1. Science - Juvenile literature.   I.   Ritter, Bob,   1950-

Q161.2.N45 1995   500   C95-930954-3

Printed and bound in Canada by Metropole Litho Inc.

3 4 5 6 7 8 9 0 /ML/ 4 3 2 1 0 9 8 7 6

Reviewers

Carolyn Anco
Archbishop Romero Secondary School
Toronto

Gillian Bartlett
The National Ballet School
Toronto

David Boag
E.C. Drury High School
Milton

Lynda Bolzon
Birchmount Park Collegiate Institute
Scarborough

Roman Charabaruk
Albert Campbell Collegiate Institute
Scarborough

Jim Dawson
Windsor Board of Education
Windsor

Francine Delvecchio
Holy Cross Secondary School
Kingston

Bob Hartley
Sir Winston Churchill Collegiate Institute
Thunder Bay

Jodie Hauch
Sir Frederick Banting Secondary School
London

Wanis Khouri
Milliken Mills High School
Markham

James Lewko
Thistletown Collegiate Institute
Etobicoke

Michael McMahon
Centennial Secondary School
Belleville

John Sherk
Sir Robert Borden Business and Technical
Institute
West Hill

John van der Beek
Lincoln County Board of Education
St. Catharines

Karen Walker
Port Arthur Collegiate
Thunder Bay

Acknowledgments

Nelson Canada would also like to acknowledge the contribution of Ed Boyd of Wright Environmental Management Inc.

The authors thank the science students of Brampton Centennial Secondary School and their teachers, Vince Hill and David Williamson, for their invaluable aid.

NELSON SCIENCE 9

Table of Contents

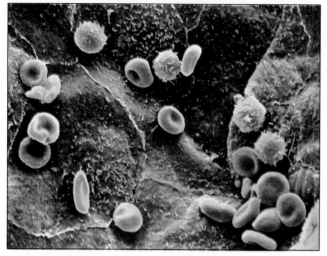

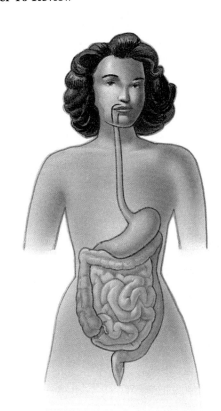

Using Nelson Science 9

N ELSON SCIENCE 9 WILL SUPPORT YOU as you explore science. *Nelson Science 9* will pose questions, ask you to make predictions, and provide you with an opportunity to perform investigations to check your predictions. You will be encouraged to speculate and create explanations for events you observe. All of this is provided in a text you will enjoy using and reading.

Organization

Nelson Science 9 was written and designed using a two-page spread format. Each spread highlights a concept or procedure. Different types of page spreads focus on different aspects of science, technology, and society.

Science and Invention spreads at the beginning of the book introduce you to the basic processes and procedures of science that you will use throughout this program.

▼

Investigations are hands-on experiments. They emphasize data collection and analysis and provide opportunities to solve problems and design your own experiments.

▼

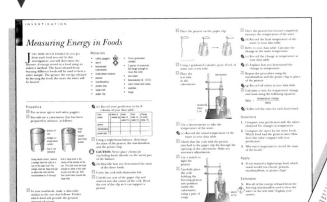

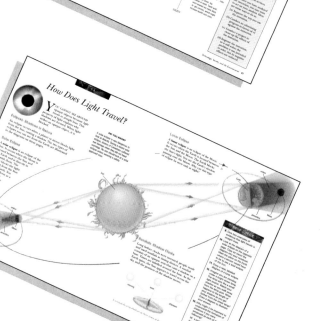

▶ **Topic** spreads throughout every chapter explore key scientific concepts and ideas through the use of clear, readable text and large, colourful graphics, photos, and tables.

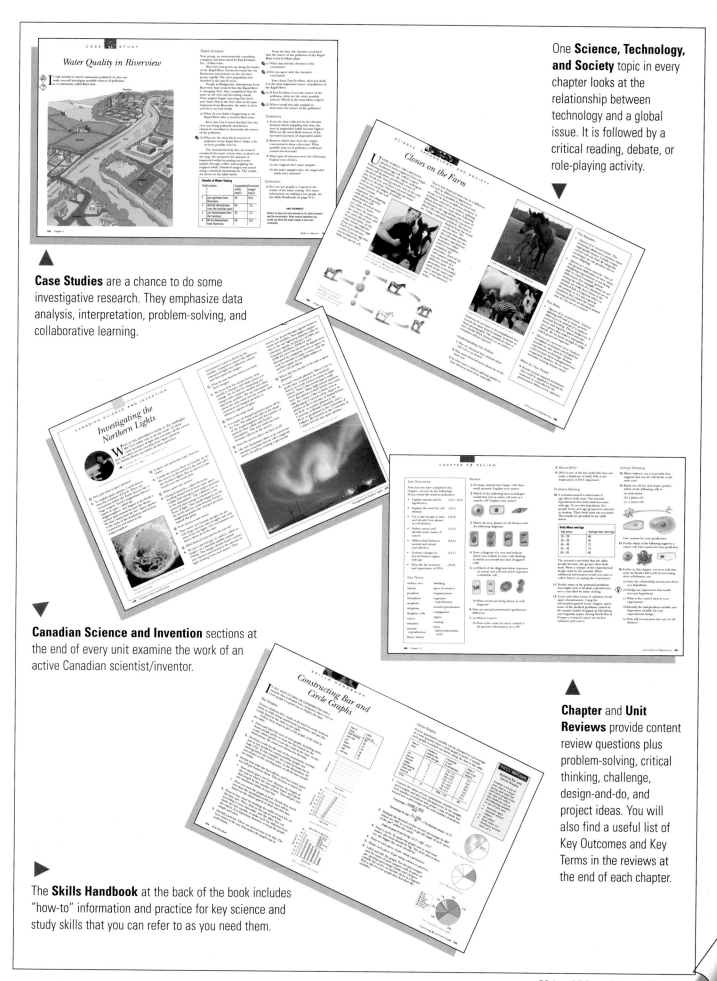

One **Science, Technology, and Society** topic in every chapter looks at the relationship between technology and a global issue. It is followed by a critical reading, debate, or role-playing activity.

Case Studies are a chance to do some investigative research. They emphasize data analysis, interpretation, problem-solving, and collaborative learning.

Canadian Science and Invention sections at the end of every unit examine the work of an active Canadian scientist/inventor.

Chapter and **Unit Reviews** provide content review questions plus problem-solving, critical thinking, challenge, design-and-do, and project ideas. You will also find a useful list of Key Outcomes and Key Terms in the reviews at the end of each chapter.

The **Skills Handbook** at the back of the book includes "how-to" information and practice for key science and study skills that you can refer to as you need them.

Special Features

Throughout *Nelson Science 9* you will find special features. These features will make the science you are learning personally relevant.

Try This features provide shorter activities and experiments that illustrate a key concept or idea.

Skill Builder exercises focus on building specific science skills and are cross-referenced to the corresponding how-to section of the Skills Handbook at the back of the book.

Links connect science to math, technology, careers, history, the environment, and the arts.

Did You Know boxes provide fascinating facts related to a topic.

Key Terms are highlighted in boldface and defined in the text and in the Glossary at the back of the book.

Subtractive Colour Mixing

A CHEMICAL THAT ABSORBS certain colours, but reflects others, is a **pigment**. You have probably mixed two pigments (when working with paints or inks) to produce a third colour. For example, if you mix yellow paint with cyan paint, you get a greenish colour. This process of mixing pigments to obtain new colours is called **subtractive colour mixing** because each of the pigments ab... different colours of light

Subtractive Colour Th...

Three colour ... almost b...

B G R

R

G

Questions

Different types of questions are included in *Nelson Science 9* to help you review, apply, and extend your learning.

SELF CHECK

1. (a) List five physical properties that you can observe simply by using your senses.

   (b) List five properties that you can observe if you do some simple tests.

2. Look again at the photograph of the dinner table on page 46. Choose another one of the materials pictured and describe it, mentioning as many physical properties as you can.

Self Check questions help review ideas presented on every topic spread and help you assess what you have learned.

CHALLENGE

What makes solids, liquids, and gases different from one another? Why does water become hard when it is cooled below 0°C? Discuss these questions with a partner, then write down your explanations.

Challenge questions present problem-solving and critical thinking opportunities, and give you an opportunity to explore a topic in greater detail.

Getting Started at the beginning of a chapter and Ask Yourself questions throughout a chapter provide you with a record of how your thinking is changing as you learn about science, and also some clues about the way you learn.

Investigation and Case Study questions focus on the analysis, application, and extension of ideas developed in the activity.

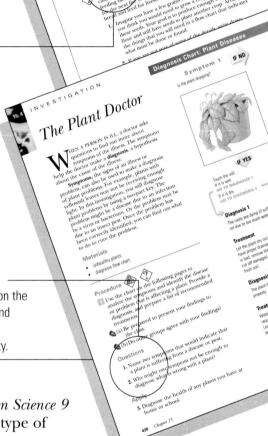

Icons

Icons or symbols are used throughout *Nelson Science 9* to highlight key ideas or indicate a specific type of activity or process.

 The Caution symbol specifies the necessary precautions for a dangerous material or procedure. Make sure you have read and understood all the cautions in a procedure before beginning.

 The Goggles and Apron symbols indicate when protective clothing should be worn.

 The Pencil icon indicates when you should be recording Investigation and Case Study observations or answers in your notebook or journal.

 Opportunities to use problem-solving skills and techniques are highlighted with the Problem Solving icon.

 Opportunities to design your own experiment, a model, or a display are highlighted with the Design icon.

 Opportunities for working together with other members of your class are highlighted with the Working Together icon.

 Opportunities to use a CD-ROM for additional research are highlighted with the CD-ROM icon.

Safety in Science

YOU WILL ENJOY WORKING with *Nelson Science 9* in your continuing discovery of science. When you perform the investigations, you will find them challenging, interesting, and safe. However, you should be aware that accidents can happen. In *Nelson Science 9*, chemicals and procedures that are hazardous are noted with a caution.

 You should always read cautions carefully, and make sure you understand what they mean, before you proceed.

Certain safety hazards exist in any laboratory. You should know about them, and about the precautions you must take to reduce the risk of a safety hazard. In this section, you will identify hazards, find some devices that can help you deal with hazards, and set some safety rules for working in a laboratory.

Materials

- balloons

Procedure

Part 1 *Balloon Safety*

1 In your notebook, make a table like the one below.

Balloon Safety

What we did to the balloon	What the balloon did	Hazards	Precautions
blew it up as far as it would go, then released it			

2 Blow some air into a balloon, and then release it into the air so that it zips around.

(a) In your table, make a note of what you did to the balloon, and what happened.

3 Repeat step 2 three more times, using a different amount of air each time.

4 Repeat step 2 three more times, holding the balloon at a different angle each time you release it.

(b) In your table, give one hazard, and one precaution that might prevent the hazard, for each of the things you did to the balloon.

Part 2 *Safety Scavenger Hunt*

5 Copy the table on page 19 into your notebook.

6 Find each of the safety devices listed in the table. Record the location of each safety device, and any information you found with the device, in your table.

Safety in Science—Precautions and Devices

Hazard	Some precautions	Safety device	Location of device	Secret information
	tie back loose clothing and long hair avoid contact with the flame or the hot part of the burner avoid sudden movements	fire extinguisher fire blanket fire alarm switch		
	wear safety goggles wear an apron avoid sudden movements	safety goggles aprons eye wash station		
	keep glass containers away from edge of counters avoid sudden movements	beaker clamp disposal container for broken glass		

Part 3   *Setting Safety Rules*

7 In groups, or in a large group with your teacher, come to an agreement on answers to the following questions. (You may want to refer to Safety in the Laboratory on page 526.) In your notebook, write down each of the group's decisions.

(c) Must safety goggles be worn for all activities? Explain.

(d) Are normal glasses ever an acceptable substitute for safety goggles?

(e) Should you inform your teacher if you receive a cut or burn during an activity? Why?

(f) What should you do if you have an allergy, medical condition, or physical problem?

(g) Is it acceptable to bring food or drink into the science classroom?

(h) When can you touch, taste, or smell chemicals in a science activity?

(i) What should you do if you accidentally touch chemicals during normal activity?

(j) What special procedure should you follow if chemicals accidentally splash into your eyes?

(k) How should you dispose of chemicals?

(l) How should you dispose of broken glass?

(m) Should you report any damaged or defective equipment to the teacher?

8 In your notebook, draw a map of the route your class should follow when the fire alarm sounds.

9 Note that, in science, **Safety is No. 1!**

Questions

1. Briefly describe the procedure to follow if exposed skin comes in contact with any chemical substance.

2. Do you think it is always safe to pour waste chemicals and solutions down the sink with lots of water? Explain.

3. Why is it important to have a separate container for the disposal of broken glass?

Working Together

SCIENTIFIC DISCOVERIES AND inventions are almost always made by teams of people working together. Scientists share ideas, help each other design experiments and studies, and sharpen each other's conclusions. While working with *Nelson Science 9*, you will spend much of your time doing science as scientists do it—in teams. In this investigation, you will work as a team. After you finish, you will answer questions to help you reflect on how teamwork helped the process.

Materials

- 5 sheets of letter-size paper
- sheet of scrap paper (for design)
- 1 m of tape
- 1 small piece of paper (for flag)
- 1 toothpick
- scissors
- stopwatch
- metre stick or measuring tape
- 100 g Plasticine
- marbles
- sink or pan with water

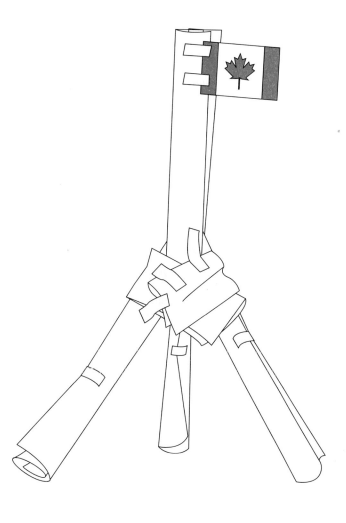

LEARNING TIP

When you work together with other students in a group, follow these tips.
- Encourage all members to contribute to the work of the group.
- Respect everyone's contributions. There should be no put-downs.
- Be prepared to compromise.
- Keep focused on the task at hand.
- Support the group's final decisions.

Procedure

Part 1   *Building a Tower*

1 Your team has three tasks:

- In the time allowed, design and build the tallest possible free-standing tower using five sheets of paper and 1 m of tape.

- Make sure that everyone in your team takes turns and participates equally in the activity.

- Make a flag for the top of your tower that identifies your team.

2 There are several roles in your team, which could include materials manager, designer, cutter, taper-assembler, timer-measurer, and artist. Your teacher may assign roles or let you choose them. Decide in your team how you will make sure that everyone participates equally.

3 The materials manager should obtain a set of materials for the team.

4 The designer should consult with the team and sketch a design, using the team's suggestions. When all team members have accepted the design, they should sign the design sheet.

5 The cutter and taper-assembler should build the tower.

6 The artist should consult with the team to design and produce a flag for the top of the tower.

7 If you think of a better way to build your tower at any point, you may want to start again. (Remember—time's running out!)

8 When the tower is complete, ask the timer-measurer from another team to measure the height of your tower. (The flag does not count as part of the height.) The tower must be free-standing for 30 s to qualify. The timer-measurer should write the height on the design sheet and sign his or her name.

Part 2 *Building a Boat*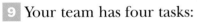

9 Your team has four tasks:

- Make sure everyone in your team has a role and participates in the activity.

- Draw a prototype of a boat capable of carrying a maximum number of marbles.

- Using only 100 g of Plasticine, construct the boat, using your drawing as a plan.

- Carefully place the boat in water and load marbles on one at a time. Record the maximum number of marbles that the boat is capable of carrying.

10 There are several roles available for team members.

- Organizer—will be responsible for assigning roles, organizing equipment, and beginning the discussion.

- Designer—will be responsible for combining ideas presented by team members. The designer must check for team agreement.

- Scrutinizer—will look for other solutions and suggest other ways to make the boat. The scrutinizer will also perform the test of the boat's carrying capacity.

- Artist—will be responsible for drawing the boat and will make any oral presentations to the rest of the class.

- Builder—will be responsible for making the boat.

Questions

1. How well did your team work together?

2. Were there any problems in working together? If so, what were they?

3. How did you overcome the problems?

4. If you were working again on a similar task, how would you change the way your team worked?

5. What did you like most about the team's work? Was there anything you disliked?

6. What did you contribute to the team? If you were working again on a similar task, how could you improve your contribution?

Exploring Cause and Effect

THE MAJOR GOAL IN SCIENCE is to explain the world around us, and the major goal of invention is to improve the world—to create and develop technology. For example, scientists have been trying to explain how mosquitoes find people and animals to bite, while inventors have been trying to find ways to protect us from these pests.

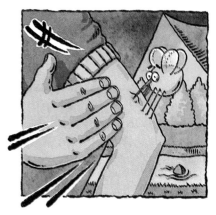

Mosquitoes have no problem finding their next meal ...

Asking Questions

Despite their different goals, both scientists and inventors ask questions about cause-effect relationships. These questions often take the form: "What are the *effects* on a variable if we change another variable?" A **variable** is something that can change (or vary). For example, you may have noticed that balloons stick to walls if you rub them on the wall first. You could ask the scientific question, "What is the effect of increasing *the number of times that a balloon is rubbed on a wall* (a possible cause variable) on *the time that the balloon stays stuck to a wall* (a possible effect variable)?"

... except when we invent something to keep them away.

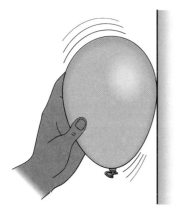 

Scientists call the cause variable the **independent variable**, and the effect variable the **dependent variable**.

Answering Questions

A suggested answer or reason why one variable affects another in a certain way is called a **hypothesis**. It is based on a prediction—an educated guess—about how changing one variable will affect another. Scientists and inventors form a hypothesis so they can test the relationship between variables.

A few examples of predictions and hypotheses are given in the table below.

Sample Predictions and Hypotheses

Prediction of cause-effect relationship

Possible cause (independent variable)	Possible effect (dependent variable)	Hypothesis (possible reason for cause-effect relationship)
As the number of hours that a student watches TV increases, ...	... the student's math scores decrease, ...	... because watching TV keeps a person from practising math, and practice is important in learning to do math.
As the amount of candy that a person eats increases, ...	... the number of tooth cavities increases, ...	... because candy contains sugar that is used for energy by germs in the mouth, and these germs produce an acid that decays the teeth.
As the size of the sail increases, ...	... the top speed of the sailboat increases, ...	... because larger sails trap more air, which then provides a greater force.
As the amount of salt on a road increases, ...	... the amount of rusting of the metal parts of a bicycle increases, ...	... because salt helps oxygen in the air combine with iron in the metal of the bicycle to form rust.

SKILL BUILDER

Testing a Prediction and a Hypothesis

Your group will need one or more balloons and perhaps a metric measuring tape, a protractor, or a stopwatch.

1. Decide which of the following questions your group will test.
   - What is the effect of increasing the size of a sealed balloon on how quickly it falls?
   - What is the effect of increasing the size of an unsealed balloon on how far it travels when it is let go?
   - What is the effect of increasing the angle from a table from which an unsealed balloon is released on how far it travels?
   - What is the effect of increasing the size of an unsealed balloon on how long it takes the balloon to stop losing air?

2. For your question, suggest a prediction and a hypothesis.

3. Design an investigation that would test your prediction. Carry out your test after obtaining your teacher's approval.

4. Sketch a graph to display your results. (For more information on graphing, turn to the Skills Handbook on pages 510–517.)

5. Do your results match your predicted results? If they do, you can conclude that your hypothesis is reasonable.

6. Pick a spokesperson to describe your group's prediction, hypothesis, observations, and conclusions to classmates.

Doing Science: Experimenting

OVER THE CENTURIES, QUESTIONS like "Why do plants grow upward?" have been asked many times. And there have been many different answers. How do you decide what the correct answer is? Science is about testing answers, to find the ones that are not correct. Scientists develop tests to produce evidence that may or may not support an answer. There are two main types of these tests: controlled experiments and correlational studies.

An experiment

Controlled Experiments

A **controlled experiment** is a test in which one variable is *purposely and steadily* changed to find out what (if any) effect occurs. For example, if you think that plants grow toward light, you could shine lights on plants at steadily greater angles to see if the plants will grow toward the lights.

However, if the plants do grow toward the lights, it is possible they are doing so for other reasons. Plants normally grow under the Sun. Perhaps using a lamp changes the *kind* of light that the plant receives, as well as the angle of the light. To be more sure that the angle of the light is a cause of the result, only the angle should be changed.

A better experiment would be to reflect sunlight off a mirror, instead of using an artificial light. Then, the kind of light has been controlled. The prediction and hypothesis might be: "As the angle of light shining on plants steadily increases, the angle of the plants' growth should steadily increase, because plants are attracted to light."

The kind of light is now controlled.

Ways of Controlling an Experiment

One way to control an experiment is to control—keep constant—all known possible causes of the result except one. When changing the angle that the light shines on a plant, you must ensure that the amount of wind, water, heat, etc. is the same for each plant.

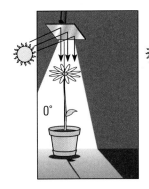 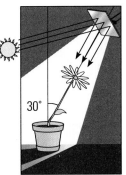 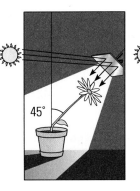 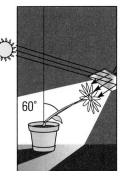 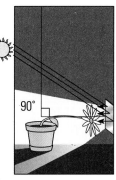

The same experiment with a control group.

You can use a control group as well. In the plant experiment, you could have a plant that has sunlight shining on it from directly above. If the hypothesis is correct, it will not grow at an angle. This plant is the control group for the experiment, and the other plants are the test cases. The control group is set up exactly like the test cases, but in the control group no variable is changed.

Unfortunately, scientists can never be sure that they have controlled all possible causes of the effects. Because of this, they can never be absolutely sure that the conclusions they make are true. However, the more the results match the prediction, the more confident the scientists can be about their hypothesis.

SKILL BUILDER

Experimenting

A model of a swing—called a pendulum—can be used to show how experiments work. You will need string, scissors, several metal washers, a metric measuring tape, something to hang the string from, and possibly a clock with a second hand.

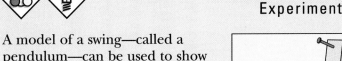

1. Examine the variables in the table below. Pick one variable from each column, and develop a prediction and a hypothesis for the relationship between the two variables.

Possible causes (independent variables)	Possible effects (dependent variables)
length of string	time to complete one cycle (one side to the other)
number of washers	length of time that pendulum continues to swing
distance the washers are pulled back	

2. Plan an experiment in which the independent variable is purposely and steadily changed. Design a control for the experiment, then conduct your experiment.

   (a) Record the results in a table.

   (b) Sketch a graph showing how changes in the independent variable affect the dependent variable. (For more information on graphing, see the Skills Handbook on page 510.)

   (c) Did the results agree with your prediction? Explain. What does that tell you about your hypothesis?

   (d) What steps did you take to control this experiment? Explain.

Designing and Conducting an Experiment

Follow this example of how an experiment is designed and conducted.

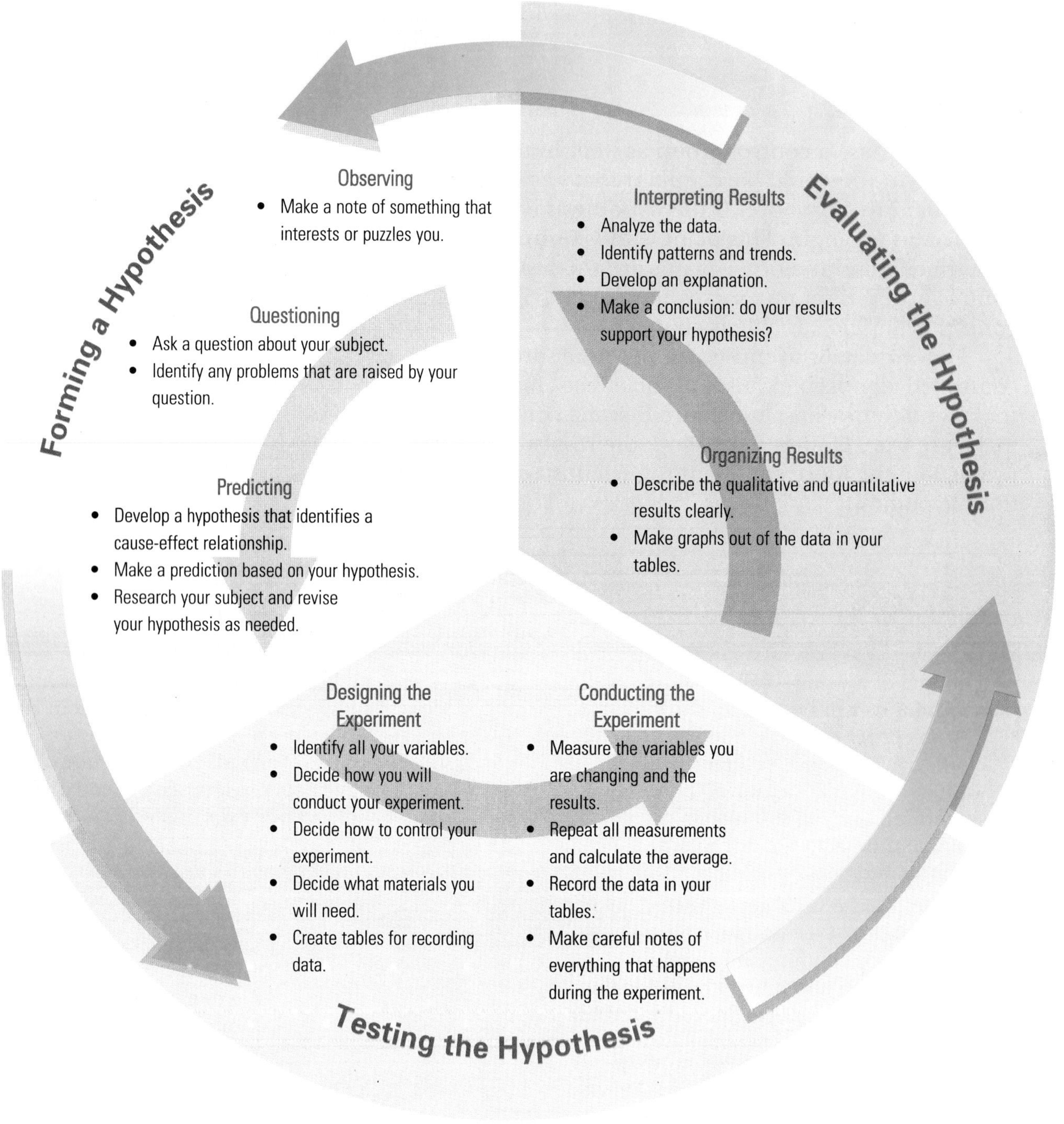

Forming a Hypothesis

Observing
- Make a note of something that interests or puzzles you.

Questioning
- Ask a question about your subject.
- Identify any problems that are raised by your question.

Predicting
- Develop a hypothesis that identifies a cause-effect relationship.
- Make a prediction based on your hypothesis.
- Research your subject and revise your hypothesis as needed.

Evaluating the Hypothesis

Interpreting Results
- Analyze the data.
- Identify patterns and trends.
- Develop an explanation.
- Make a conclusion: do your results support your hypothesis?

Organizing Results
- Describe the qualitative and quantitative results clearly.
- Make graphs out of the data in your tables.

Testing the Hypothesis

Designing the Experiment
- Identify all your variables.
- Decide how you will conduct your experiment.
- Decide how to control your experiment.
- Decide what materials you will need.
- Create tables for recording data.

Conducting the Experiment
- Measure the variables you are changing and the results.
- Repeat all measurements and calculate the average.
- Record the data in your tables.
- Make careful notes of everything that happens during the experiment.

Experimental Checklist

√ CONTROL the experiment.

√ STEADILY change the independent variable.

√ MEASURE the changes in the independent variable AND the results.

√ REPEAT measurements, and calculate the average.

√ MEASURE the dependent variable in more than one way.

√ MEASURE variables other than the results.

SKILL BUILDER

Designing an Experiment

Using the information in this section, your group will design an experiment based on an observation, for example:

- Since we have heard about acid rain, we have noticed that some of our statues and buildings are decaying (losing mass).

- Tennis balls seem to bounce differently when they are wet.

- A candle gets shorter as the flame burns.

- The iron parts of vehicles seem to rust more quickly when salt is put on the roads.

- White paper turns yellow when left in sunlight.

You may have observations of your own that you want to investigate.

Submit your experimental design to your teacher. The design should include the following:

- a title

- the observation

- the variables

- your hypothesis and prediction

- the procedure

- how you will control the experiment

- the materials you will need

- sample data tables

If your procedure is approved, carry out the experiment, following each of the steps in this section. Write a report on your experiment that includes completed data tables, a graph, some suggestions on how the experiment could be improved, and your conclusion. (For more details on making reports, refer to the Skills Handbook on page 520.)

Doing Science: Correlational Studies

I N THE PREVIOUS SECTION, EXPERIMENTATION was described as purposely and steadily changing the independent variable while controlling all other known variables. However, it is often difficult to *know* all the variables, let alone control them. A correlational study is an alternative to a controlled experiment. In a **correlational study**, a scientist examines whether a variable is affecting another variable *without* purposely changing any of the variables. Instead, variables are allowed to change naturally.

When to Use a Correlational Study

Correlational studies are often chosen to test hypotheses that may be unsafe, impossible, or unethical to test with a controlled experiment. For example, scientists could not purposely cause a series of volcanoes to erupt to find out the effect of eruptions on carbon dioxide levels in the atmosphere.

ASK YOURSELF

You are probably more familiar with correlational studies than with experiments. These studies are frequently summarized in newspapers under headlines like "Chemical X Suspected in Heart Disease." Find a headline like this in a recent newspaper, and identify the variables that were studied.

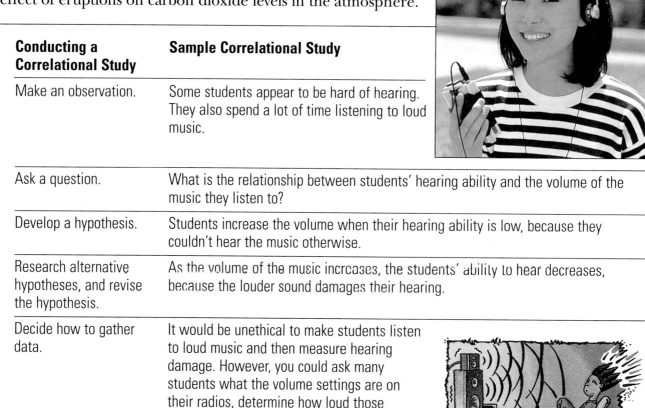

Conducting a Correlational Study	Sample Correlational Study
Make an observation.	Some students appear to be hard of hearing. They also spend a lot of time listening to loud music.
Ask a question.	What is the relationship between students' hearing ability and the volume of the music they listen to?
Develop a hypothesis.	Students increase the volume when their hearing ability is low, because they couldn't hear the music otherwise.
Research alternative hypotheses, and revise the hypothesis.	As the volume of the music increases, the students' ability to hear decreases, because the louder sound damages their hearing.
Decide how to gather data.	It would be unethical to make students listen to loud music and then measure hearing damage. However, you could ask many students what the volume settings are on their radios, determine how loud those settings are with a sound meter, and then test the students' hearing. Correlate the radio volume with each student's hearing ability.

SKILL BUILDER

Conducting a Correlational Study

You will need a metre stick, a pen, and some graph paper to investigate student reaction time. Each student will measure the reaction time of another student. Reaction time will be measured by how quickly the student can catch a ruler dropped between the index finger and thumb. The number of centimetres the ruler drops will be a measure of the reaction rate.

1. Hold the ruler with the 0 mark between the index finger and thumb of the other student.

2. Drop the ruler and say "go" at the same time. Record where the student's finger and thumb are when he or she catches the ruler.

3. Repeat steps 1 and 2 five times for each hand, and average the results.

4. Note the student's sex and age, the time since the student last ate, the number of hours of sleep the student had the night before, and whether the student is right- or left-handed. (Your class may wish to add other variables.)

5. As a class, collect all the data in a table.

6. In groups, choose two variables from the table. Write a hypothesis to state how the two variables are related.

7. Make a graph of the two variables you have chosen, using the data from the class table. (For more information on making and reading graphs, see the Skills Handbook on pages 512–517.)

   (a) Does the graph support your hypothesis? Why or why not?

8. Using your graph, present your findings to the class.

Conducting a Correlational Study	Sample Correlational Study
Gather the data in a table.	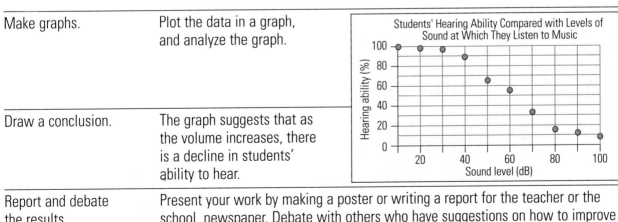

Sample Correlational Study

Student	Radio setting	Volume (dB)	Hearing ability (%) test #1	test #2	average
1	4	80	20	16	18

Make graphs.	Plot the data in a graph, and analyze the graph.

Students' Hearing Ability Compared with Levels of Sound at Which They Listen to Music

Draw a conclusion.	The graph suggests that as the volume increases, there is a decline in students' ability to hear.

Report and debate the results.	Present your work by making a poster or writing a report for the teacher or the school newspaper. Debate with others who have suggestions on how to improve your study, or who have different interpretations of your data.

Designing and Conducting a Correlational Study

As you have learned, correlational studies are sometimes preferred over experiments.

Suppose, for example, we wanted to study the relationship between student lateness and weather conditions. What do you feel would be important in designing and carrying out such a study? You may want to write down some notes.

In the checklist below, you will find what others feel is important in designing a correlational study. By following this format, investigators can do science without doing experiments or field work. Instead, they can use data banks, CD-ROMs, the Internet, and surveys to find relationships between two or more variables. They can also, of course, make their own observations and measurements.

CHALLENGE

Design your own correlational study. You may have made observations that you want to check using a correlational study. List the data and materials you will need, and the detailed steps you will follow in your investigation. Have you taken a similar approach to the checklist below?

Checklist: Designing a Correlational Study

Gather Data

√ Collect data, lots of data, on a large number of possibly related variables in your chosen topic area. The data can be generated by measuring or by taking surveys. You can also use data collected by others, e.g., governments, banks, insurance companies, and scientific organizations.

√ Choose two variables for further study (you are looking for one variable that may have a natural effect on the other). Develop a prediction and a hypothesis about them.

√ Develop or find ways to measure the two variables.

√ Plan to make as many measurements as it takes to get a continuous and wide collection of measurements of the variables.

√ Try to make measurements and observations in the same way each time.

Organize and Display Results

√ Plan appropriate tables to hold your observations.

√ Using the data in your tables, develop graphs in which the two variables you have chosen are plotted against each other.

Analyze Results and Conclusions

√ Describe all results, including observations you made that you could not measure.

√ Describe the strengths and weaknesses of the methods you used.

√ Conclude whether the results support your original hypothesis. If not, suggest a modified hypothesis.

√ Make suggestions for future work on this topic.

Report on the Study

√ Tell others about your work and your conclusions.

Analyzing a Correlational Study

A correlational study attempts to determine the strength of a relationship between two variables. The researcher must be cautious not to link unrelated variables while doing a correlational study.

Student name	Sex (F or M)	Skull size (circumference, mm)	Science test score (%)	Body mass (kg)	Study time (h per night)
Dae-Sung	M	569	75	70	2.2
Delia	F	555	82	50	3.0
Darby	F	520	65	49	0.7
Darren	M	570	89	65	3.2
Diane	F	540	55	55	0.2
Saverio	M	557	72	61	2.0
Stephanie	F	552	92	52	3.3
Sayed	M	570	67	75	2.3
Sylvia	F	522	59	53	0.4

1. Examine the graph showing the relationship between test scores and study time. Is there a relationship between test scores and study time? (For more information on reading graphs, see the Skills Handbook on page 516.)

2. Suggest other factors that may affect test scores.

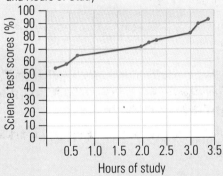

Relationship between Science Test Scores and Hours of Study

3. Examine the graph showing the relationship between test scores and skull size. Is there a relationship between test scores and skull size?

4. Would you agree with the conclusion that people who have larger skulls have bigger brains, and therefore do better on science tests? Explain why or why not.

5. Suggest other factors that might be related to skull size.

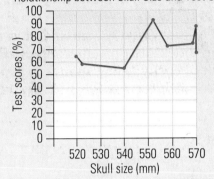

Relationship between Skull Size and Test Scores

6. Construct a graph to investigate the relationship between skull size and body mass by plotting skull size on the y-axis and body mass on the x-axis. (For more information on making a point-and-line graph, see the Skills Handbook on page 512.) What conclusion do you draw from your graph?

7. In general, do larger people have larger skulls?

8. A relationship is not disproved by a single exception. In correlational studies, scientists often report how many times the relationship was observed. For example, after collecting much more data on the subject, a scientist might indicate that 9 times out of 10, a student with an above-average body mass will have a skull size that is also larger than average. This does not mean that increasing body mass causes skull size to increase, only that the relationship occurs 90% of the time. Choose any two variables in the chart above and draw a graph to test the strength of the relationship. Can you identify a pattern?

Inventing

INVENTIONS CAN BE THOUGHT OF as solutions to complaints, irritations, or problems that we observe in our lives. Engineering products such as computers, new materials such as plastic, and new processes such as desalination of sea water, are all technologies that have been invented.

One of the easiest ways to invent is to choose one variable in an existing product and change it a little at a time. The result of each change should be recorded, so the best changes can be determined.

Testing an Invention

The designing and testing of an invention are very similar to the procedures used in experimentation. The example below shows how this might be done with a simple product—an elastic-powered toy car.

Designing a Test of an Invention	Sample Invention Test
Make an observation.	Elastic-powered toy cars travel a short distance.
Define the problem in a question.	Can the distance travelled by elastic-powered toy cars be improved by changing some part of the car?
Suggest a solution, including the independent and dependent variables.	If the number of elastics is increased (independent variable), then the car will travel farther (dependent variable), because there will be more power driving the car.
Research to discover alternative solutions.	Some toy cars are made of a lighter material (plastic). This is difficult to obtain. Some have a spring wind-up mechanism. This is more expensive and more difficult to fix.
Revise your solution.	No change—alternative solutions are not better.

Modifying the Bugscopter

Your team of flight engineers will work to modify an existing technology, the Bugscopter, and then test the new model. You will need scissors, a stopwatch, paper clips, and material to make your Bugscopter. The Bugscopter, a precision flying machine with amazing flight characteristics, is illustrated above.

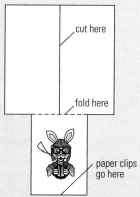

cut here

fold here

paper clips go here

1. Draw a Bugscopter of your own. Cut it out with scissors and fold it as indicated. Paper clips should be added to the bottom of the Bugscopter to keep it stable.

2. Your team must keep the Bugscopter airborne as long as possible, timing flights with a stopwatch. You can change only one variable to do this. (The choice of variable is entirely up to your team.) You will also investigate how changing the variable affects the flight time of the Bugscopter. Remember the importance of controls and repeated trials in the design of your investigation.

3. Your team will submit a report on the experiment that includes the following:

   - the problem on which the test is based

   - your solution to the problem, including the relationship between the variable you chose to change and the dependent variable (flight time)

   - a detailed outline of the steps you followed

   - observations presented in a table and a graph (for more information on drawing a graph, see the Skills Handbook on page 512)

   - a conclusion, based on the data

   (For more detail on making reports, refer to the Skills Handbook on page 520.)

Designing a Test of an Invention	**Sample Invention Test**
Test the solution, using controls.	Starting with one elastic band, gradually increase the number of bands used until there are too many to fit on the hooks available. When testing the elastics, they should all be wound to the same amount (control). The distances the toy travels should be measured with a measuring tape. Each test should be repeated several times to obtain an average. The car should always be run over the same course (control).
Make a table to record data.	The number of elastic bands used and the distances that the car travelled should be recorded in a table.
Use the data to draw a graph.	For each number of elastic bands, the distances travelled should be averaged so that only one value is plotted. 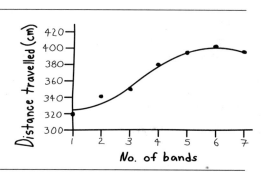
Draw a conclusion.	From the graph, the number of elastic bands that causes the toy car to travel the farthest is six.

Designing an Invention

Even though inventions are intended to solve some problem that we observe around us, there are many ways to invent.

Improving Existing Inventions

The most common method of inventing is to take something that already exists, and make it better. Improvements in car design, new stereos, and new computer systems are all developed this way. But this type of invention isn't limited to high-tech industries—even changing the way you make your favourite sandwich might improve an existing invention!

Combining Inventions

Many inventions are nothing more than combinations of other, existing inventions. An example is shoes that use Velcro as a fastener, which combine the ancient invention of shoes with the more recent Velcro invention. Other examples are cars with telephones and gum that comes in a roll—both are combinations of inventions.

Using Old Inventions in New Ways

Often we use inventions in ways the inventor did not intend. Have you ever cleaned coins with toothpaste or used a wrench or a shoe as a hammer? Sometimes it is cheaper and quicker to use an invention that is available, instead of buying one that is designed for the job. Sometimes the new use arises because people don't want to create waste—for example, empty plastic containers are often used to store nuts and bolts, or as plant pots.

Testing Solutions

Testing the solution to a problem, as with the elastic bands in the toy car, is part of inventing. However, testing an invention should go beyond testing how well it works. You may need to find out whether the product has any harmful side-effects—there is no point in solving a problem by creating a worse problem. You may also want to find out if other people like the product. If nobody else likes your invention, it will not be used.

Testing may be done by measuring the results directly, as in the case of the toy car or the Bugscopter, or indirectly. Indirect testing can be done by measuring the sales of a product, doing market surveys, and by monitoring reactions in newspaper articles and letters to the editor.

The following checklist highlights the things you have to keep in mind when testing an invention. The process is very similar to experimenting.

The car has been improved step by step.

Checklist for Testing Inventions

√ CONTROL the test by keeping all other known variables constant.

√ STEADILY change the variable that determines the performance of your invention, and measure any changes.

√ MEASURE the changes in the performance of your invention.

√ REPEAT each measurement and each test.

√ MEASURE variables other than the performance results.

SKILL BUILDER

Testing an Invention

In the following case study, you can examine how a better toothbrush might be invented.

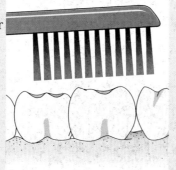

After a poor dental checkup, an inventor decided to improve her toothbrush. The inventor thought the problem with her toothbrush was the length of the bristles—they seemed too short and stiff to penetrate into all the nooks and crannies in her teeth. She decided to try bristles of different lengths in a series of toothbrushes.

1. What method was the inventor using to produce the invention?

To test how well these new toothbrushes worked, she asked 100 people to use each of her brushes for 50 brushings. She tested the volunteers' mouths for cavity-causing bacteria before and after each brushing.

2. What were the independent and dependent variables in the test?

3. If you were the inventor, how would you change the independent variable in a steady way?

4. How was the success of the invention measured?

All of the 100 volunteers ate the same kind and amount of food with every meal, and brushed for the same amount of time.

5. What other variables did the inventor identify? How did she control these other variables?

6. Identify some other variables the inventor missed. How would you control these variables?

After studying her results, the inventor discovered that the best length for the bristles seemed to be 1.5 cm. However, there were still problems with her invention. She had observed that the bristles no longer stood up straight after the 50 brushings, so she tested the strength of the bristles of each toothbrush. She found the bristles were weak. Also, her graph showed that during the last 10 brushings, the toothbrushes were becoming less effective. The number of bacteria in the volunteers' mouths no longer decreased as much after brushing.

7. How else could the inventor improve the toothbrush?

8. Design a test for this improvement.

Communicating Ideas

COMMUNICATION IS AN IMPORTANT aspect of science and invention. Without communication, there would be no knowledge. Things that you know are correct aren't necessarily knowledge. Think of those discussions you have with your friends about who plays the best guitar, or who is the best actor. You know you are right, but the others may not agree. In science, **knowledge** is information that has been communicated and agreed upon by a large number of people.

At one time, a flat Earth was common knowledge.

Three Steps to Knowledge

Without agreement, a piece of information is not knowledge. In order to get agreement, a certain process is followed. The first step is the development of new information or technology by an individual investigator or group. Next, the information or technology must be tested by both the scientist or inventor and colleagues.

Once a group of experts supports the results of the testing, the information or technology must also be accepted by society before it becomes knowledge. This may seem fairly straightforward, but many pieces of information have not been accepted immediately, for a variety of reasons. It took many centuries before the idea that the Earth is spherical, and not flat, was generally accepted.

Who you are may influence whether the information is accepted or ignored. Suppose you make a fascinating new discovery in your high school classroom—are scientists likely to accept your work immediately?

Sometimes, information may be ignored or avoided for social reasons. Certain kinds of information may make the society that generates it uncomfortable. Society also selects what it wants to know, by funding some types of research, but not others. Knowledge even has fashion trends: what is in vogue for research today may not be fashionable in the future.

If you want your work to be accepted, you must communicate it, you must defend it, and you may have to promote it.

ASK YOURSELF

If you wish to share information, what do you do? How do you convince others that you are right? How would you share a discovery with the world? These are problems that all scientists face.

Reporting Your Work

There are other good reasons for telling others about your work and defending your conclusions. Doing the work is valuable, but sharing it with others can help you look at your own work through other people's eyes. Professional investigators communicate their findings by

- giving presentations,
- publishing findings, and
- using professional gatherings to discuss their findings.

Before giving a final report, the investigator works to make the report organized and believable. You can write stronger reports by following the four steps listed below.

- Make a rough draft.
- From the draft, prepare a short presentation for colleagues.
- After making the presentation, debate your ideas with your colleagues.
- With what you learn from the debate, write a final version of your report.

SKILL BUILDER

Reporting

Here's a chance to practise sharing ideas with others. Choose one of the investigations or other science activities you have completed, and prepare a report. Use one of the methods below to share what you learned.

- Write a story, a poem, a letter, or a song.
- Create a concept map or a drawing.
- Organize a debate.

Whichever method you choose, you should include the following:

- the problem, observation, or experience that you wanted to investigate
- the question you asked, or problem you identified, including the independent and dependent variables
- your hypothesis or solution
- the method you chose to test your hypothesis or solution
- the results
- your conclusions
- any problems you encountered in your investigation

Listen to the responses of your classmates as you give your report—they have been working on related investigations and can offer useful insights into your work. Record the feedback, either by taking notes of what they say or passing around blank cards so they can comment. Rewrite your report, including valid changes from the feedback. (For more detail on making reports, refer to the Skills Handbook on page 520.)

Evaluating and Improving Ideas

COMMUNICATING THE RESULTS of your own work is important, but what about the work of others? Understanding and evaluating the works of others is an important part of communication.

Every day you see and hear extraordinary claims about objects and events in newspapers and magazines, and on television and radio. Often science, or the appearance of science, is used as a way of convincing us that the claims are true.

Sometimes this method of reporting is used to get you to buy something. (How many times have you heard that "three out of four dentists say ..." or that "engineers have designed the most comfortable, economic, and sporty model yet"?) Sometimes the claims are reported just to catch interest ("Naturalist spots bigfoot").

But even serious stories on scientific work are sometimes difficult to interpret, especially when they are reported in a way that makes the scientific work sound important, official, and somewhat mysterious.

Evaluating Media Reports

How can you make sense out of media reporting? It takes some practice, but it can be done. Using the ideas you have learned about scientific investigations, you can pick apart claims and figure out if, and how much, you should believe them.

Coffee no risk to heart, study says

Allergies linked to lower gum disease risk

New study adds proof diet affects cancer risk

Lack of exercise cited in heart disease

When you encounter a "scientific" report in the media, analyze the report carefully, and see if you can identify the following:

- the dependent and independent variables in any reported investigation

- the type of investigation that is being reported (experiment, correlational study, or test of an invention)

- the strengths and weaknesses in the design of the investigation

Then, decide if the strengths or the weaknesses are more important, and if you can trust the conclusions.

SKILL BUILDER

Analyzing a Science Report

The article to the right was published recently in *The Toronto Star*. By reading the article and discussing the answers to each of the questions, you can analyze the investigation that is reported in the article. (The "frontal activity" that is mentioned refers to natural electrical charges moving in the front part of a baby's brain. This activity is easily measured in a way that does not hurt the child.)

1. What are the variables studied in this investigation?

2. What type of investigation was used?

3. Was the investigation well done, using scientific standards? Give two reasons that suggest that it was done well or badly.

4. What conclusions did the investigators reach, according to the report?

5. What extra information about the investigation would you need to know before agreeing with the investigator quoted in the story?

6. Now that you have analyzed the article, do you believe the story?

Brain waves provide a sign of baby's personality

SAN FRANCISCO (Special)
A baby's personality—timid and shy or outgoing—may be predicted soon after birth by reading the infant's brain activity, researchers say.

"Infants who show a strong right-sided pattern of frontal activity in their first two years are more likely to be fearful and inhibited, and may be shy and timid as your children," Dr. Nathan Fox, a professor of human development at the University of Maryland involved with the study, said yesterday.

Those who do not show strong right lobe activity tend to be more relaxed and easy-going, and welcome new experiences and new faces, he added.

The conclusions were based on monitoring how the babies' frontal lobes reacted when presented with unfamiliar faces or other stimuli. The tests have been conducted on more than 300 babies over seven years and are continuing.

The new findings were presented at the annual meeting of the American Association for the Advancement of Science.

Technology, Society, and the Environment

INVENTORS HAVE PRODUCED MANY technological innovations that were designed to make our lives easier and more enjoyable—televisions, cars, modern medicine, clean running water, packaged instant food, microwave ovens, aircraft, etc. All of them affect our lives, and the lives of other living things.

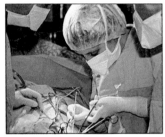
Surgery

Microwave communication

Skis

Hot running water

Science, Technology, Society, and the Environment

The products of invention (technology) often depend on the products of science (laws and theories about natural objects and events). Radios were not invented until science had developed a theory that there are forms of radiation that we cannot detect with our senses. On the other hand, science often needs inventions before knowledge can be advanced. For example, the conclusion that liquids boil at certain temperatures could not be reached without a thermometer.

Similarly, scientists and inventors do not make decisions in a vacuum. Society lets inventors know what kinds of products to develop. Our society wants a cure for cancer, which requires leaps in our scientific understanding of cells and how they work. Society also demands inventions to make lives more enjoyable and convenient. In turn, inventions and scientific knowledge affect society. Time travellers from 2000 years ago would be amazed at modern societies, but they might also be alarmed.

There is a web of relationships between four important ideas— science, technology, society, and the environment.

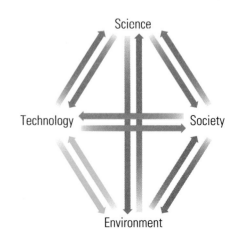

Disposable products, such as diapers, lighters, cameras, pens, and wrappers, are convenient, but they may also be harmful to the environment—our living and non-living surroundings. Canadian society produces more garbage per person than any other society in the world. Some of that garbage contains chemicals that harm other living things. We also produce waste with our cars and factories that pollutes the air and the water. In turn, damage to the environment harms people. Scientists observe the environment to produce their theories. The environment also affects invention—imagine what living in Canada would be like without insulation or parkas!

Judging Effects of Technology on Society and the Environment

Often, products of technology have both good and bad effects on society and the environment. Whether the good outweighs the bad, or the bad outweighs the good, is something that we must all learn to judge.

For example, consider the electric toothbrush. Its effects are analyzed below. Should you use an electric toothbrush?

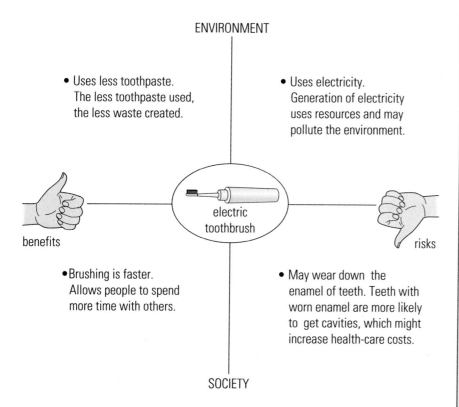

ENVIRONMENT

• Uses less toothpaste. The less toothpaste used, the less waste created.

• Uses electricity. Generation of electricity uses resources and may pollute the environment.

benefits

electric toothbrush

risks

• Brushing is faster. Allows people to spend more time with others.

• May wear down the enamel of teeth. Teeth with worn enamel are more likely to get cavities, which might increase health-care costs.

SOCIETY

SKILL BUILDER

Analyzing Technology

Use the format illustrated on this page to analyze one or more of the following inventions. To complete your analysis, you may need to do some research.

- vitamin pills
- fashionable clothes
- nuclear power
- television
- hair spray
- makeup
- X rays for dentistry and medicine
- packaged snack foods
- cold remedies
- hygiene products
- "instant" foods
- formal education
- window-cleaning liquids
- plant fertilizers
- cigarettes
- music videos
- carbonated soft drinks
- insecticides
- lotteries
- psychological services

Once you have analyzed the invention, you may want to act on your analysis. Here are some ways to do so.

(a) Improve the way you use the invention.

(b) Conduct an advertising program in favour of or against the invention.

(c) Conduct a project to clean up the effects of the invention.

(d) Improve the invention, so it still solves the problem it was intended to solve, but its negative effects are reduced.

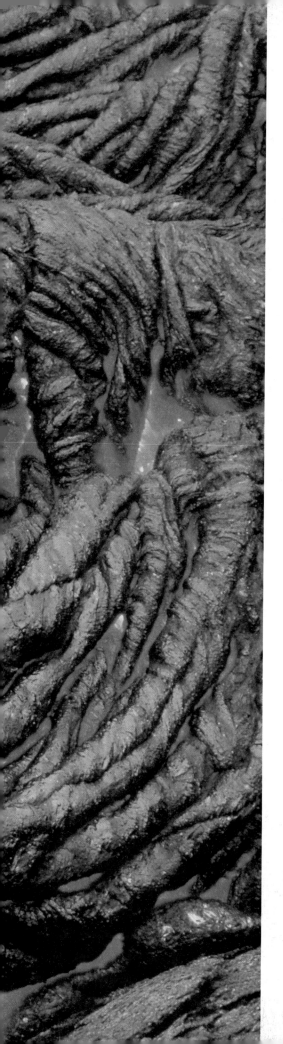

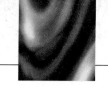

UNIT 1

Structure of Matter

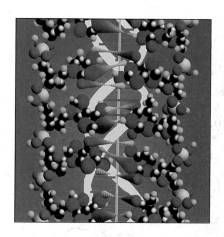

CHAPTER 1

Looking at Matter: Physical Properties

WHAT IS MATTER? Matter is the leather in the ball and the air that is used to inflate it. Matter is the uniforms worn by the players and the shoes protecting their feet. Matter is the liquids consumed by the players to replace body fluids lost through exertion. Matter is the oxygen in the air inhaled by the forward who has just dribbled the length of the field and scored. Matter is the players themselves.

Matter is anything that has mass and takes up space. **Mass** is the measure of the amount of matter an object has. **Volume** is the measure of how much space an object fills.

In this chapter, you will focus on how to

- describe the three states of matter—solid, liquid, and gas,

- measure the mass and volume of matter, and

- use measurements of mass and volume to calculate the density of a material.

 Getting Started

1. In a small group, brainstorm a list of as many different materials as you can from the photograph. Suggest how you would organize or group the materials according to their similarities or differences.

2. Writers, artists, technicians, mechanics, teachers, and chemists all use matter. For different purposes, different descriptions of matter are useful. For example, water could be called "what boats float on," or "crystal clear refreshment," or "a clear, colourless liquid that freezes at 0°C."

   - In your group, select one solid, one liquid, and one gas you use in everyday life. Then brainstorm different ways of describing each material.

   - Trade a few of your descriptions with another group. Can you identify their materials from their descriptions? Can they identify yours?

CHALLENGE

What makes solids, liquids, and gases different from one another? Why does water become hard when it is cooled below 0°C? Discuss these questions with a partner, then write down your explanations.

Properties of Matter

WHEN YOU OBSERVE MATTER—whether you see it, touch it, hear it, smell it, or taste it—you are observing its characteristics, called **physical properties**. To begin, you might describe its state—whether it is solid, liquid, or gas. The state of the material is one of its physical properties.

DID YOU KNOW?

Water is one of the very few substances that can exist in all three states at temperatures commonly experienced on Earth. It can be a solid, a liquid, or a gas, depending on the temperature.

The States of Matter

	Solid	**Liquid**	**Gas**
Example			
Shape	Definite: has a fixed (unchanging) shape	Indefinite: always takes the shape of its container	Indefinite: always takes the shape of its container
Volume	Definite: has a fixed (unchanging) volume	Definite: has a fixed (unchanging) volume	Indefinite: always fills the entire container

Characteristic Properties

Physical Properties Observed Using Your Senses	
colour	is it black, white, colourless, red, blue, greenish-yellow, ...?
texture	is it fine, coarse, smooth, gritty, ...?
odour	is it odourless, spicy, sharp, burnt, ...?
lustre	is it shiny, dull, ...?
clarity	is it clear, cloudy, opaque, ...?
taste	is it sweet, sour, salty, bitter, ...?
state	is it a gas, a liquid, ...?

Pick one of the materials shown here and describe it, mentioning all of the properties listed in the table to the left.

There are other physical properties you might choose to describe. Simple tests and measurements can aid your senses in observing these properties.

Viscosity

Syrup is thicker than water—it flows more slowly than water when you pour it. **Viscosity** refers to how easily a liquid flows: the thicker the liquid, the higher the viscosity.

Hardness

Because they are harder than glass, diamonds are used to cut glass. **Hardness** is a measure of the resistance of a solid to being scratched or dented. How would you rank the following substances by hardness: steel nails, chalk, glass, diamond?

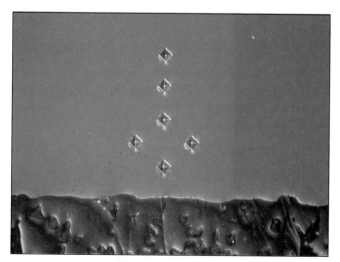

Diamond, the hardest natural material known, is used to measure the hardness of other materials. Here, small diamonds are being fired at a metal. The farther they penetrate, the softer the metal is.

Malleability

Gold can be hammered into thin sheets, so it is said to be malleable. If a solid is **malleable**, it can be hammered into different shapes. What other materials can you think of that are malleable? Many materials, glass for example, are not malleable. Instead of flattening out when hammered, they shatter. **Brittle** objects shatter easily.

Ductility

One of the reasons copper is used for electrical wiring is that it can be drawn out into long, thin wires. If a solid is **ductile**, it can be pulled into wires. What other materials can you think of, besides copper, that are ductile?

Grouping Matter According to Physical Properties

Scientists find it useful to group substances according to similarities and differences. Classification systems are useful because they provide insight into the properties that are most useful in understanding different substances. Examine the picture of the glass of water. How would you group the three materials in the picture into two categories?

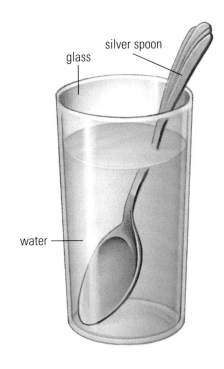

You might group the glass and water together, because both allow light to pass through them. By contrast, the silver spoon does not allow light to pass through. You may have chosen other physical properties to develop a classification system. You might argue that the glass and spoon are most alike, because they do not change shape as easily as the water. Yet another classification system would be to group the spoon and the water together. A chemist could argue that the water and the silver spoon are pure—they are not mixtures of substances—but the glass is composed of a variety of chemicals. The glass is a mixture.

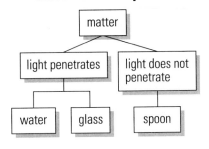

Classification system 1

Classification system 2

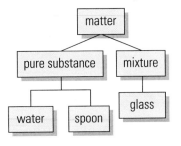

Classification system 3

TRY THIS

Just How Thick—Comparing Viscosity

You will need an apron, safety goggles, rubber gloves, a watch, a marble, and a graduated cylinder to compare the viscosity of water, several different cooking oils, syrups, and liquid detergents.

As a measure of viscosity, you can time how long it takes the marble to fall from the top of the cylinder to the bottom when the cylinder is filled with each of the liquids. (If you use water in your first trial, that will give you a standard for comparing the other liquids.)

- Before you get started, which of the liquids do you think has the highest viscosity? Comment on the accuracy of your prediction: which liquid is the "thickest"?

- Could you identify a liquid based on your data? Try it out: ask a friend to pick a liquid in secret, and then use the marble test to identify the liquid.

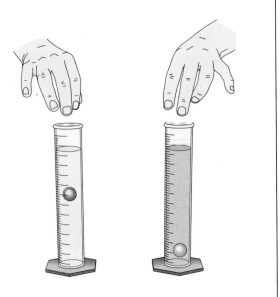

Using the Physical Properties of Metals

Matter can be grouped as metals and non-metals. In this section, you will examine some of the physical properties of different metals that make them suitable for different uses.

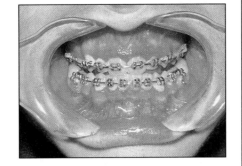

Metals have been used by people for thousands of years, first copper, then bronze, iron, and steel. Now, many different mixtures of metals, called **alloys**, are used. For any purpose, such as airplane parts, the bottoms of cooking pots, or braces for teeth, the metal chosen has properties useful for the job.

The table below shows which metals have properties that make them useful for braces on teeth.

Physical Properties of Some Metals Used in Braces

Metal	Stiffness	Springiness	How easily does it bend?	How easy is it to join?
stainless steel	high	good	fair	fair
gold alloy	medium	fair	fair	easy
nickel/ titanium alloy	low	excellent	poor	difficult

CHALLENGE

Working in groups, design a classification system for the variety of substances provided by your teacher. Group the substances by similar physical properties. A chart similar to the sample below may be useful in constructing your classification system for matter. Note: The number and position of the boxes will differ for each classification system.

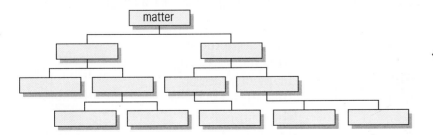

SELF CHECK

1. (a) List five physical properties that you can observe simply by using your senses.

   (b) List five properties that you can observe if you do some simple tests.

2. Look again at the photograph of the dinner table on page 46. Choose another one of the materials pictured and describe it, mentioning as many physical properties as you can.

3. When you identify matter in your everyday life, which physical properties mentioned in this section do you find more helpful?

4. Examine the table of Physical Properties of Some Metals Used in Braces. Rank the materials in the table from best to worst for each of the purposes below.

   (a) Some wires on a brace have to push against teeth to get them to change position. They must be stiff.

   (b) The wires on a brace get moved about when the person eats. It's important that they spring back into place without becoming bent out of shape.

   (c) When the wires of a brace are made, they have to be bent into different shapes.

   (d) The wires on a brace must be joined in places.

5. If you wanted to build a shelter under the surface of the ocean, what properties would be important in the materials you selected? Why?

Identifying Substances

HAVE YOU EVER CONFUSED the salt and sugar in your kitchen at home? Because they have the same appearance, you must use other properties to distinguish between them. In this investigation, you will distinguish among some common substances by examining physical properties and using your general knowledge.

Materials

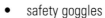
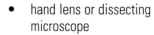

- apron
- safety goggles
- set of numbered samples
- hand lens or dissecting microscope
- spot plate or 2 depression slides
- medicine dropper
- conductivity tester
- copper wire
- carbon rod (from a pencil)
- small beaker with distilled water

CAUTION: When you receive your samples, do not open any closed containers unless your teacher specifically tells you to do so.

Procedure

1. Make a table similar to the one below to record your observations.

Physical Properties and Identification of Samples

Sample number	Appearance	Possible identification	Other properties	Actual identification
1				
2				
3				

2. Put on your apron and safety goggles.

3. Look at one of the samples. Describe its appearance and enter your description in your table.

 (a) Without specific directions from your teacher, which of your five senses is the only one you can use for your observations? Why?

(b) What do you think is in the sample? Record the possible identification in your table.

4. Examine the sample for other physical properties, as directed by your teacher.

(c) Record your observations in the table.

(d) What is the substance? Record your identification in your table.

5. Repeat steps 3 and 4 for each sample.

6. Obtain crystals of salt and sugar from a labelled container. Place a few crystals of each on a piece of paper and examine them with a hand lens or dissecting microscope.

 (e) Which kind of crystals appears larger?

 (f) Compare the shape of the two kinds of crystals. Record any differences you see.

7. Using the hand lens, count out 20 salt and 20 sugar crystals. Place each group of crystals in a different well of the spot plate.

8. Using a medicine dropper, add two drops of water to each well. Observe what happens to the crystals.

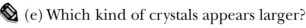
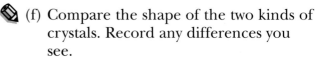

Step 8

(g) Record your observations.

(h) Which kind of crystals mixed with water faster?

9 Obtain a piece of copper wire. Touch one electrode of the conductivity tester to one end of the wire, and the other electrode to the opposite end of the wire.

(i) What evidence suggests that copper conducts electricity?

(j) Predict whether distilled water and the carbon rod from a pencil will conduct electricity.

10 Use the conductivity tester to test distilled water in the beaker. Test the carbon rod with the conductivity tester, just as you did with the copper wire.

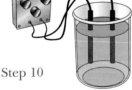
Step 10

(k) Record your observations.

(l) Provide an explanation for your observations.

(m) Based on your explanation, predict whether the sugar mixed with water or the salt mixed with water in the spot plates can conduct electrical current.

11 Use the conductivity tester to check your predictions. Rinse the electrodes with distilled water and wipe them clean after each test.

(n) Record your observations.

(o) Provide an explanation for your observations.

(p) Why were the electrodes cleaned with distilled water after each test?

12 Clean up your work station and wash your hands.

Questions

1. (a) What physical properties do the solid samples share?

   (b) What properties do the liquid samples share?

(c) What properties do the gas samples share?

(d) Are there any samples that you cannot easily classify as being in one of these three states? Why?

2. Which samples are difficult to identify? Explain why.

3. Name two other physical properties you could use to determine the identity of the difficult samples. Explain how using these properties would help your identification.

Apply

4. What laboratory evidence did you collect that supports the idea that salt contains metals?

5. Describe at least two situations where it could be important to be able to identify substances accurately in each case.

   (a) in the science classroom

   (b) in the home

6. Look at the three products in the photograph. What properties could you use to distinguish among them?

Extension

7. At home, collect five samples of white powder. Choose from flour, corn starch, icing sugar, baking powder, cream of tartar, citric acid, powdered milk, coffee whitener. Put each sample in a small bottle and label the bottles A to E. Keep a list of your samples, labelled with the correct letters. Trade samples with a friend, and try to identify each other's samples.

 CAUTION: Do not use your sense of taste when you identify these substances.

Calculating Volume

YOU CAN MEASURE THE VOLUME of a liquid directly, by reading the volume from a measuring container. For a regular solid, you can find the volume by measuring its dimensions and calculating the volume.

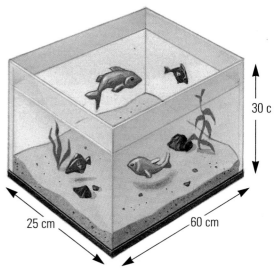

30 c

25 cm   60 cm

Volume of a Rectangular Solid

You can easily calculate the volume of a rectangular solid if you know its length, width, and height.

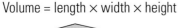

Volume = length × width × height

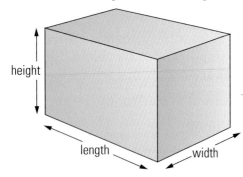

height

length   width

If all the sides are measured in centimetres (cm), its volume will be in cubic centimetres (cm³).

Because the base unit of length in SI is the metre, the unit of volume is the cubic metre (m³). A cubic metre is the space occupied by a cube 1 m × 1 m × 1 m. This unit of volume is used to measure large quantities, such as the volume of concrete in a building. In your investigations, you are more likely to use the cubic centimetre (cm³) to record the volume of a regular, solid object. How many cubic centimetres are in a cubic metre?

Volume and Capacity

Cubic metres and cubic centimetres are **cubic units** of volume. The volume of a liquid is usually measured in **capacity units**, such as litres (L) or millilitres (mL). Capacity units and cubic units are related to each other.

You can easily change from one type of unit to the other. For example, if you calculate the volume of a container (dimensions: 2 cm × 2 cm × 2 cm) to be 8 cm³, you know that it will hold 8 mL of water.

Capacity and Cubic Units	
Capacity unit	Cubic unit
1 mL	= 1 cm³
1 L	= 1000 cm³
1000 L	= 1 m³

SKILL BUILDER

Estimating and Measuring Volume

The volume of many kinds of regular-shaped objects can be calculated from dimension measurements.

- Obtain an object of each of the shapes shown here. Measure each object and calculate its volume. After you have completed Investigation 1.4, Measuring Volume, return to this activity and use the displacement method to determine the volume of each object.

- Which method seems more accurate? Give a reason for your answer.

Volume and Water Conservation

A recent survey showed that Canadians use about 300 L of water per person per day. Visualize what this amount of water might look like. Would it fill the classroom you are sitting in? A swimming pool? How can you get through this much water every day?

Canadian Water Use

Activity	Approximate amount of water used
taking a shower	15 L per minute
taking a bath	200 L
cleaning your teeth	5 L
flushing a toilet	10 L per flush
washing your hands	5 L
running a washing machine	140 L per load
running a dishwasher	42 L per load
washing dishes by hand	15 L
using a garden sprinkler	10 L per minute
using a garden hose	15 L per minute

TRY THIS

Saving Water

Let the kitchen tap at home drip slowly, or find a dripping tap in your home. Estimate, then measure, the amount of water that drips from the tap in five minutes. Calculate how much water would be wasted in one day if the tap continued to drip.

SELF CHECK

6. Examine the diagram of the aquarium on the facing page.
   (a) Calculate its volume in cubic centimetres.
   (b) What is the maximum capacity of the aquarium in litres?

7. (a) Estimate the volume of air in your classroom in cubic metres.
   (b) How much air per person does your classroom contain?

8. Describe three ways to reduce the amount of water you use each day.

9. A toilet dam conserves water by dividing a toilet tank into two halves. Only one half of the tank fills with water. The other half stays empty because of the dam. Devise a method to determine the volume of water normally contained in a toilet tank at home. Assuming an average of 20 flushes per day, how much water would be saved every day by installing a toilet dam?

Measuring Volume

YOU KNOW TWO WAYS TO FIND the volume of a sample of matter.

• For regular-shaped solids, such as a box or a cylinder, you can calculate the volume if you measure the dimensions.

• You can measure the volume of a liquid directly. Using a measuring cup or a graduated cylinder, you simply read the volume from the scale.

But how could you measure the volume of a solid such as a pencil or a piece of rock? In this investigation, you will measure volume a third way, indirectly, by the displacement of water.

Materials
• apron
• beaker
• graduated cylinder
• solid objects, such as nuts and bolts, kitchen utensils, an orange
• overflow can

Procedure

Part 1 *Volume of Liquids*

1 Put on your apron.

2 Pour some water from the tap into a beaker.

(a) Estimate the volume of water in the beaker, and record your estimate.

3 Pour the water into a graduated cylinder and read the volume directly from the scale. For an accurate reading, be sure to have your eye at the same level as the top of the liquid. The upper surface curves downward where it touches the side of the container; this curved surface is called the meniscus. Read the volume at the lowest part of the meniscus.

(b) Record the actual volume.

(c) Compare your estimate and your partner's estimate with the measured volume.

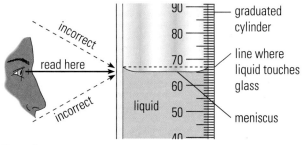

Step 3

Part 2 *Volume of Small, Irregular Solids*

4 Make a table in your notebook like the one below, titled Estimated and Measured Volumes. In the first column, list the small objects of which you will measure the volume.

(d) Estimate the volume of each object and record your estimates in your table.

Estimated and Measured Volumes		
Object	Estimated volume (mL)	Measured volume (mL)

5 Pour some water into the graduated cylinder and measure the volume of the water.

(e) Record the volume of the water in your notebook.

Volume of water and object   =

Volume of water   =

Difference (Volume of object) =

6 Tilt the graduated cylinder slightly and gently slide one of the small objects into it. Return the cylinder to an upright position. If necessary, hold the object beneath the surface of the water with the tip of a pencil. Read the new volume.

 (f) Why is it important to tilt the cylinder?

 (g) Record the combined volume of the water and the object in your notebook.

 (h) Calculate the volume of the object, and record the volume in your table.

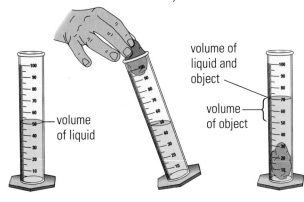

volume of liquid and object

volume of object

volume of liquid

Step 6

7 Repeat steps 5 and 6 for each small object.

Part 3 *Volume of Large, Irregular Solids*

8 Fill an overflow can while holding your finger over the spout. Place the can on a level surface and allow the excess water to drain from the spout into a sink.

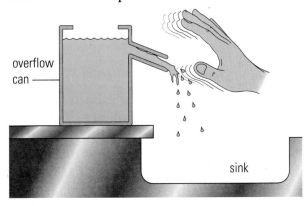

overflow can

sink

Step 8

9 When the can has stopped draining, hold a graduated cylinder under the spout, and carefully lower a large object into the water. If necessary, push it gently under

the surface of the water with the tip of a pencil. Catch all the water flowing from the overflow can in the cylinder. Read the volume of water displaced by the object.

 (i) Record the volume of water. What is the volume of the object?

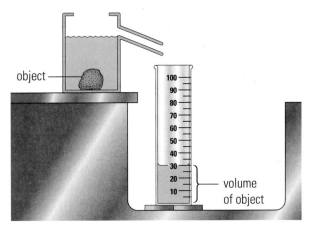

object

volume of object

Step 9

Questions

1. Look at your completed table of Estimated and Measured Volumes.

   (a) How would you assess your ability to estimate volume?

   (b) Rank the objects you measured from the easiest to make a volume estimate to the most difficult. Why is it more difficult to estimate the volume of some objects?

2. What are the possible sources of error when measuring volume by displacement of water?

Apply

3. (a) What problem might arise if you tried to use displacement to find the volume of a piece of soap? What could you do to minimize the problem?

   (b) List at least two other irregular objects for which displacement of water is not a suitable method for determining the volume. Explain your reasoning.

4. Describe two ways to determine the volume of a whole egg.

Relating Mass and Volume

WHICH IS HEAVIER: a kilogram of feathers or a kilogram of lead? Once you think about it, the answer is obvious. But this question points out an important difference between feathers and lead. Equal masses of these two substances have very different volumes.

What about other substances? How are volume and mass related to each other? In this investigation, you will measure mass and volume of some substances, and then draw a graph to discover their relationship.

Materials
- apron
- balance
- 50-mL or 100-mL graduated cylinder
- thread
- large bolt and nut
- centimetre ruler
- graph paper
- sample metals of different sizes (iron, copper, zinc, aluminum, and lead)

Procedure

Part 1 *Mass of Different Volumes of Water*

1 Put on your apron.

2 In your notebook, draw a data table like the one below.

Volume and Mass of Water

Mass of graduated cylinder (g)	Volume of water sample (mL)	Mass of graduated cylinder and water sample (g)	Mass of water sample (g)
	10		
	40		

3 Using a balance, measure the mass of a graduated cylinder.

 (a) Record the mass of the cylinder in the data table.

4 Pour 10 mL of water into the graduated cylinder. (Remember that readings are taken at the bottom of the meniscus.) Using a balance, measure the mass of the graduated cylinder and the 10-mL sample of water.

 (b) Record your measurement in your data table.

 (c) How would you calculate the mass of the 10-mL water sample? Record the mass of the water in your data table.

 (d) Predict the mass of a 40-mL sample of water.

5 Add 30 mL of water to the graduated cylinder. Repeat steps 3 and 4 to determine the mass of 40 mL of water.

 (e) How accurate was your prediction?

 (f) Account for any possible sources of error.

Part 2 *Changing Volume and Mass*

6 Position the graduated cylinder with 40 mL of water on a balance. Tie a nut and bolt to a thread and lower them into the graduated cylinder until the nut and bolt are immersed by water. Do not let go of the thread.

 (g) What happens to the level of the water as the nut and bolt are lowered?

 (h) Does the mass of the graduated cylinder change as the volume increases? Provide an explanation for the results.

(i) Predict what would happen if you were to let go of the string and the nut and bolt settled on the bottom of the graduated cylinder. Give reasons for your prediction.

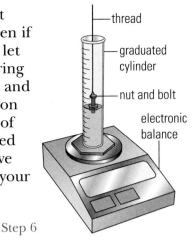

thread

graduated cylinder

nut and bolt

electronic balance

Step 6

7 Gently lower the nut and bolt until they touch the bottom of the graduated cylinder. Let go of the thread.

(j) Does the height of the water in the graduated cylinder change? Provide a possible explanation.

(k) Does the mass of the graduated cylinder change after the thread is released?

Part 3 *Mass to Volume Relationship of Metals*

8 In your notebook, draw a data table like the one below.

Masses and Volumes of Metals

Sample	Mass (g)	Volume (cm³)	Mass/Volume (g/cm³)
metal 1, sample a			
metal 1, sample b			
metal 1, sample c			
metal 2, sample a			
metal 2, sample b			
metal 2, sample c			

9 Your group will receive three different samples each of two metals. Use a balance to measure the mass of each sample.

(l) Record your results in your data table.

10 Use the water displacement technique to determine the volume of each metal sample.

(m) Record your results in your data table.

11 Calculate the mass-to-volume ratio of the metal samples by dividing the mass (g) by volume (mL). This relationship is called density. (Recall: $1 mL = 1 cm^3$)

(n) Record your calculations in the data table.

(o) What do you notice about the densities of the three samples of the same metal?

(p) What do you notice about the densities of the two different metals?

Questions

1. Use the data collected in Part 1 to predict the mass of 100 mL of water and the volume of 50 g of water.

2. Provide an explanation of why the mass of the graduated cylinder changed when the thread was released in step 7.

3. Draw a line graph showing the relationship between mass and volume for the two metals you tested. Plot mass on the vertical or y-axis and volume on the horizontal or x-axis. (For a review of graphing, refer to the Skills Handbook on page 512.)

4. From your graph, what evidence suggests that all samples of the same metal have the same density?

Apply

5. In terms of the relationship between mass and volume, explain the difference between feathers and lead.

6. When rocks from the Moon were brought back to Earth by the Apollo astronauts, they were carefully analyzed and stored. Suppose you are shown a rock that someone claims came from the Moon. You can't do chemical tests on the rock, in case it really is a valuable Moon rock. How might you go about testing whether the rock came from the Moon?

Density as a Characteristic Physical Property

I F YOU ARE COMPARING A METAL such as copper with a material such as wood, you are likely to describe the copper as "heavier." But a tiny piece of copper is not heavy, and a large log can be very heavy indeed. The physical property that you are describing as "heaviness" is really the ratio of mass to volume. If your piece of copper had the same volume as your piece of wood, the copper would have more mass. That is, the mass-volume ratio is greater for copper than for wood.

When you compare the masses of equal volumes of different kinds of matter, you are comparing their densities. **Density** is the amount of matter per unit volume of that matter. This is expressed as grams per cubic centimetre (g/cm^3), or, for very large and heavy objects, usually kilograms per cubic metre (kg/m^3).

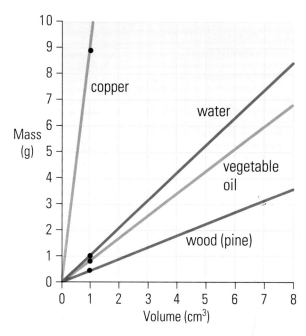

The mass-volume ratio for copper is higher than those of the other substances shown on this graph. You can see that 1 cm³ of copper has a mass of 8.9 g, compared with 1.0 g for water, 0.9 g for vegetable oil, and 0.45 g for pine.

Density as a Property

Density is a physical property of materials; each substance has its own characteristic density. Look at the table on the opposite page to see the densities of some common solids, liquids, and gases.

Density as an Equation

Density can be expressed as an equation:

$$\text{Density } (D) = \frac{\text{Mass } (m)}{\text{Volume } (V)}$$

If you know the value of any two of the three variables (D, m, or V) in this equation, you can solve for the third.

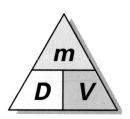

DID YOU KNOW?

The world's largest passenger and cargo aircraft are built using the relatively low-density metals magnesium and aluminum. If the same aircraft were made of other metals, they would be much heavier, requiring more powerful engines and more fuel.

Approximate Densities of Some Common Materials

Substance	Density	
Solids	kg/m³	g/cm³
gold	19 300	19.3
lead	11 300	11.3
silver	10 500	10.5
nickel	8 900	8.90
copper	8 900	8.90
iron	7 900	7.90
aluminum	2 700	2.70
magnesium	1 700	1.70
ice	920	0.92
wood (birch)	660	0.66
wood (western red cedar)	370	0.37
wood (balsa)	120	0.12
Liquids	kg/kL	g/mL
mercury	13 500	13.5
chloroform	1 500	1.50
glycerol	1 260	1.26
sea water	1 030	1.03
distilled water	1 000	1.00
vegetable oil	920	0.92
isopropanol	790	0.79
gasoline	690	0.69
Gases	kg/m³	g/cm³
carbon dioxide	1.98	0.001 98
oxygen	1.43	0.001 43
air	1.29	0.001 29
nitrogen	1.25	0.001 25
helium	0.179	0.000 179
hydrogen	0.089	0.000 089

SELF CHECK

10. (a) Use the graph on the opposite page to find the mass of 5 cm³ of water.

    (b) Check your answer by calculating the mass from the data in the table of densities.

11. (a) From the graph, determine the density of pine wood.

    (b) If a block of wood 5 cm × 10 cm × 3 cm has a mass of 100 g, could it be pine? Explain your reasoning.

12. A magnificent metal piece in the shape of a crown is unearthed at the excavation of an ancient tomb. The mass of the crown is measured to be 17 800 kg and its volume is 2 m³. What is the density of this crown? Use the density table to predict what it might be made of.

13. Of all the materials that are classified as metals, there is only one that is a liquid. From the information on this page, what substance do you think that might be? Explain your reasoning.

14. Why do you think that people use balsa wood rather than birch for making miniature glider airplanes?

15. Refer to the table of densities to find the density of water and of vegetable oil. If vegetable oil and water were in the same container, explain where you would expect to find the vegetable oil: in a layer above the water, in a layer below the water, or mixed with the water.

Finding the Density of a Liquid and a Gas

IN INVESTIGATION 1.5, you determined the density of solid materials. You measured the mass and volume of samples, and found that the mass/volume ratio (that is, density) is constant for all samples of the same substance.

In this investigation, you will find the density of a liquid and a gas. Each of these states of matter presents unique challenges for measuring mass and/or volume.

Materials

- safety goggles
- apron
- 100-mL graduated cylinder
- balance
- liquid, such as glycerol, cooking oil, or isopropanol
- small beaker
- large beaker
- 2 anti-indigestion tablets
- small piece of paper
- glass plate or piece of paper towel

CAUTION: Isopropanol is toxic and flammable.

Procedure

Part 1 *Determining the Density of a Liquid*

1 Put on your apron and safety goggles.

2 Your teacher will provide you with a sample of a liquid.

3 Devise a method to determine the density of the liquid.

✎ (a) What measurements will you need to make?

✎ (b) What equipment will you need to make your measurements?

✎ (c) What calculations will you have to do?

(Hint: You may wish to refer to Investigation 1.5 to help you plan your procedure.)

4 Have your teacher approve your procedure. Then carry out your investigation.

✎ (d) Refer to the table of densities on page 59. What is the liquid in your sample?

5 Return the liquid to your teacher for disposal, and clean up your work station.

Part 2 *Measuring the Mass of a Gas*

6 To measure the mass of each anti-indigestion tablet, put one at a time on a small piece of paper on a balance pan. Read the mass of each tablet. Both tablets should have the same mass (within 0.1 g). You may have to scrape some material from the larger tablet.

✎ (e) Record the mass of the tablets.

7 Half-fill the small beaker with water.

8 Place one of the tablets on the piece of paper, and put the paper, the tablet, and the beaker on a balance pan. (Make sure the tablet remains dry!) Read the total mass.

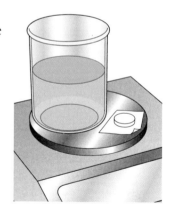

Step 8

✎ (f) Record the total mass.

9 Remove the beaker from the balance pan, then drop the tablet into the beaker.

✎ (g) Record your observations.

10 The tablet releases gas when put in the water, producing a fizzing effect. After the fizzing has stopped, measure the mass of the beaker and its contents again. (Be sure to put the small piece of paper you had

under the tablet in step 8 back on the pan.)

✎ (h) Record the mass.

✎ (i) What is the difference between the masses you measured in step 8 and step 10? Record the difference in mass.

✎ (j) What mass of gas was released from the tablet?

✎ (k) Why is it important to make both mass measurements with the piece of paper on the pan?

Part 3 *Measuring the Volume of a Gas*

11 Because the volume of gas from one tablet may be too large to collect at one time, you must collect half the gas and then the other half. Break your remaining tablet into two halves, being careful not to lose any small pieces.

12 Half-fill a large beaker with water. The beaker must be large enough to hold both your hand and a graduated cylinder.

13 Completely fill a graduated cylinder with water. Place the palm of your hand or a glass plate over the top of the cylinder.

Step 13

14 Turn the cylinder upside down without allowing any water to escape. Quickly lower the inverted cylinder into the large beaker.

Step 14

15 Once the mouth of the cylinder is totally submerged, carefully remove your hand. The cylinder should remain full of water. If there are more than one or two bubbles of air inside the cylinder, repeat steps 13 and 14.

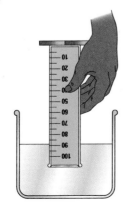

Step 15

16 Drop one half of the tablet into the beaker and immediately cover it with the graduated cylinder.

✎ (l) Record your observations.

17 After the fizzing has stopped, read the volume of gas that has collected in the cylinder.

✎ (m) Record the volume of the gas.

18 Repeat steps 13–17 for the other half of the tablet. Make sure you include any small pieces of the tablet that may have broken off. Try to keep the pieces together, and capture as much of the gas as you can.

✎ (n) Calculate the total volume of the gas released from the tablet.

19 Discard the water into the sink, clean your glassware and your work station, return your materials to your teacher, and wash your hands.

Part 4 *Determining the Density of a Gas*

20 Using your values of the mass and volume of the gas from Parts 2 and 3 of this investigation, calculate the mass/volume ratio of the gas.

✎ (o) Record the result as the density of the gas.

Questions

1. When you measured the mass of the gas, did you make a direct or indirect measurement? Explain.

2. List any difficulties you experienced when measuring the volume of the gas that may have affected the accuracy of your results.

3. (a) Compare your value for the density of the gas with the table of densities on page 59. Which gas do you think was produced by the anti-indigestion tablet?

   (b) Determine the average of all the gas density values obtained by the groups in your class. How does your class average compare with the values in the table on page 59?

Making a Hydrometer

DIFFERENT LIQUIDS have different densities. You can compare the densities of liquids by observing how an object floats in each of them. If the liquid is much denser than the object, most of the object will be above the surface of the liquid. If the liquid is only slightly denser than the object, more of the object will be under the surface.

A hydrometer is a measuring instrument designed to measure liquid density in this way. In the following investigation, you will design your own hydrometer, evaluate the effectiveness of your design, and compare it with those of others.

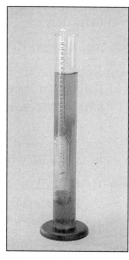

A commercial hydrometer. To determine the density of a liquid using a hydrometer, you float it in the liquid and read the scale at the surface. The reading at the surface of the liquid indicates the density.

Materials
- safety goggles
- apron
- assortment of materials such as drinking straws, Plasticine, sand, pencil with eraser on the end, thumb tacks, 10- to 15-cm piece of wooden
- dowel, short wood screw, plastic single-serving coffee creamer
- graduated cylinder or tall drinking glass
- liquids such as water, salt water, milk, isopropanol, glycerol

CAUTION: Isopropanol is toxic and flammable.

Procedure

1 In your group, design and make a hydrometer. Here are some examples of hydrometers made by other students.

2 Put on your apron and safety goggles. Test your hydrometer in three different liquids with a wide range of densities. As you test, consider the following questions.

 (a) Does your hydrometer float in all three liquids?

(b) Would you have any difficulty putting a scale on your hydrometer?

(c) Is your hydrometer sensitive enough to distinguish two liquids with similar densities?

(d) Will the hydrometer still work accurately after being used many times?

3 Make marks on the side of your hydrometer to show the level at which it floats in each of the three liquids. Use the density table on page 59 and the marks to help you calibrate a scale on your hydrometer showing density in grams per cubic centimetre. (Recall 1 cm³ = 1 mL.)

4 Did you have problems putting the scale on the hydrometer?

(e) What modifications could you make to your design to solve these problems?

(f) Record your modifications, and test them.

5 Clean up your work station and wash your hands.

Questions

1. Did your hydrometer work effectively the first time in all the liquids tested? Did it record a different density for each?

2. If not, what modifications did you make that improved the effectiveness of your design?

3. Of all the hydrometers made by members of your class, which two were the most successful designs? Suggest reasons for this.

Apply

4. A submarine can float or sink. How does the crew control this? A submarine has large ballast tanks. When air is forced into these tanks, the submarine floats to the surface. When the tanks are filled with water, the submarine sinks.

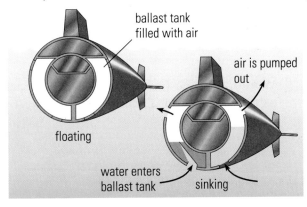

Estimate values for the following, and explain your answers.

(a) The combined density of the submarine and the ballast tanks when the tanks are full of water.

(b) The combined density of the submarine and its ballast tanks when the tanks are full of air.

Extension

5. (a) Make several sugar solutions by dissolving various known amounts of sugar in 1 L of water. Use your hydrometer to find out how density is related to the amount of dissolved sugar in these solutions.

(b) Two bodies of water, the Dead Sea and Great Salt Lake, are much more salty than oceans. Why is it almost impossible for a person to sink below the surface when swimming in these locations?

Swimming in the Dead Sea

6. (a) Divide your class into teams for a competition. Each team will design and make a "ship" using no more than four empty aluminum pop cans. The cans may not be cut, but you may join them together using whatever method you design. The winning ship is the one that can carry the greatest load of sand without capsizing or sinking.

(b) For the winning ship, determine the mass of the ship plus the load of sand. Estimate the volume of the ship. Use these values to determine the overall density of the ship.

7. Ice floats, or does it? Why has the ice cube sunk to the bottom of the isopropanol?

Density and Buoyancy

HAVE YOU EVER NOTICED how much easier it is to lift a heavy person in water? Fluids exert a buoyant force on people in water, making them easier to lift.

Previous sections on density have provided many clues for understanding buoyancy. In this case study, you will apply what you have learned about density to buoyancy. You will be encouraged to use reasoning to make predictions about density and buoyancy. Once the case study is complete, you may wish to test your predictions through experimentation.

Part 1 *A Historical Profile*

The ruler of Syracuse, an ancient Greek city in Sicily, suspected that his new crown was not solid gold, as claimed by the goldsmith. Silver, a cheaper metal, was often added to gold. The object would look and feel like solid gold, but would be much less expensive. Believing that he was being cheated, the ruler asked Archimedes, the great mathematician of his city, to prove that the crown was not solid gold. The task was indeed a difficult one. The purity of the gold had to be determined, but the crown could not be damaged.

(a) Why didn't Archimedes just take a small piece of the metal from an inside surface of the crown and analyze it for gold?

The problem baffled Archimedes for a long time. Then one day, he stepped into his bath, only to have it overflow. Instantly, the answer came to him. He reasoned that the amount of water that overflowed must be equal to the volume of the body part that he inserted.

(b) Explain how this observation could be used to determine the volume of the crown.

(c) Would crowns identical in shape, but different in the type of metal used, occupy the same volume?

gold   gold and silver alloy

(d) Would a crown made from gold displace as much water as a gold brick of the same mass and volume?

Archimedes had blocks of silver and gold of identical volumes prepared. He found the two blocks had very different masses.

Metal	Volume (cm³)	Mass (g)
gold	10	193
silver	10	105

(e) Calculate the density of gold and silver. (Hint: Refer to page 58 for the equation, if you need it.)

Storytellers claim that having made his discovery, Archimedes jumped up from his tub and yelled "Eureka," which means "I've got it." He was so excited that he ran through the streets of Syracuse absolutely naked, until he got to the palace. There he tested his hypothesis. Unfortunately for the goldsmith, the crown turned out to be a blend of silver and gold, and the goldsmith was executed.

Part 2 *Understanding Buoyancy*

When Archimedes put his leg in the bath, he discovered an important idea, which we now call Archimedes' principle. It states that buoyant force equals the weight of the liquid displaced by a submerged object.

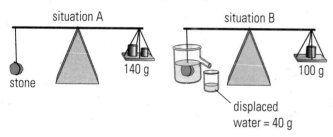

Examine the diagram above that shows a stone and a balance. It is the same stone in situation A and situation B, but it appears to change weight.

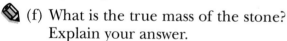 (f) What is the true mass of the stone? Explain your answer.

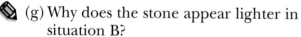 (g) Why does the stone appear lighter in situation B?

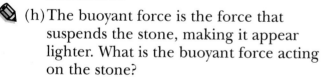 (h) The buoyant force is the force that suspends the stone, making it appear lighter. What is the buoyant force acting on the stone?

(Hint: Buoyant force = weight of the object in air – weight of the object in water.)

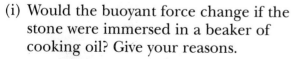 (i) Would the buoyant force change if the stone were immersed in a beaker of cooking oil? Give your reasons.

Questions

1. State Archimedes' principle in your own words.

2. Would Archimedes' experiment have changed if salt water was used instead of fresh water? Explain your answer.

Apply

3. A spring balance is used to measure the weight of a cup. Calculate the buoyant force of an unknown liquid from the following data:

Weight of the cup in air = 500 g

Weight of the same cup immersed in a large beaker of the liquid = 410 g

CAREER-LINK

Geologist

An important part of a geologist's training is learning to identify materials. Geologists recognize rocks and minerals from their physical (and chemical) properties and an understanding of how they were formed. This knowledge helps them predict where valuable minerals might be found. Geologists may work in wilderness areas, study fossils, or assess an area using photographs. Like many other scientists, geologists spend a lot of time analyzing data on computers.

Fool's gold

- A mineral called fool's gold looks like real gold. Find out the scientific name of fool's gold, and how geologists distinguish it from real gold.

- Find out how the following careers are related to the work of geologists: prospector, seismologist, paleontologist, geophysicist, gemmologist. Use a reference book, or if a CD-ROM resource is available, try entering the name of the career you would like to explore.

Balancing Ballast

SHIPBUILDERS HAVE KNOWN for centuries that if a ship is to float, its total density must be less than the density of water. For example, a solid steel sphere sinks, but the same amount of steel made into a hollow sphere floats. Of course, a hollow, floating sphere would make a terrible ship.

Today's ships, the freighters that travel the waterways of the world, are giant floating steel cities. As big as they are, they can still be tossed by waves and pushed by wind, especially when they are empty. This is why ships carry ballast. Ballast is any substance carried in the hold (the empty space in the hull where cargo is carried) or attached to the keel (a part of the hull of a sailboat that is shaped like a fin and sticks down into the water to prevent tipping).

Galleons in the 16th century carried rocks and cannon balls as ballast. Modern sailboats have a strip of dense metal, usually lead, inside their keels. Larger ships, such as tankers and ocean transports, use their cargoes or water for ballast.

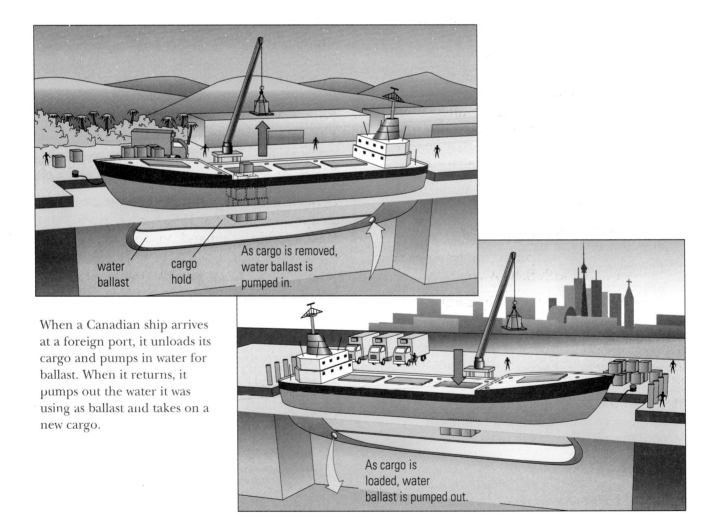

water ballast   cargo hold

As cargo is removed, water ballast is pumped in.

When a Canadian ship arrives at a foreign port, it unloads its cargo and pumps in water for ballast. When it returns, it pumps out the water it was using as ballast and takes on a new cargo.

As cargo is loaded, water ballast is pumped out.

The Problem with Ballast

Every year, ships travel across the world's oceans and into the Great Lakes. These ships carry almost anything you can imagine, from raw materials such as grain and oil to products such as telephones and cars. In each port, as they unload their cargo, these ships take in water for ballast. When they load cargo in the next port, they pump out the water.

The problem is that the dumped ballast often contains more than just water. For example, the zebra mussel arrived accidentally in the Great Lakes in 1985 as part of the ballast in a ship from Europe. The zebra mussels flourished in their new home, where there are no natural predators (organisms that feed on zebra mussels). These hitchhiking mussels are now damaging natural ecosystems and clogging human structures, such as water pipes.

Ballast may also contain oil or other pollutants. In fact, many oil tankers routinely fill their cargo holds with water after they pump out the oil. This water, polluted by the oil that was still in the hold, is later dumped directly into the local waterway when the tanker is ready to be filled with oil again.

Understanding the Author

1. Describe the function of ballast.

2. Large fishing boats pump out water as they fill their holds with fish. Why?

3. How can ballast from a ship entering Canadian waters have an effect on Canadian wildlife?

The Issue

Water ballast pollutes Canadian waters. Following are some solutions to the problem.

(a) Make ships dump their ballast outside Canadian waters.

(b) Make ships dump their ballast into special holding tanks. The water in the tanks could then be used by other ships that need ballast.

(c) Have ships pay to dump their ballast. The money could be used to help clean up any problems.

Benefits

Opinion of a utilities official Zebra mussels are a disaster for electricity generators and municipalities on both sides of the Great Lakes. The technology and labour to keep our water intake pipes clear of mussels is costing hundreds of millions of dollars. That cost is passed on to everyone who uses electricity or water.

Risks

Opinion of a port official Shipping is a very competitive industry. If Canadian ports make too big a demand on shipping companies, they'll just go to other ports. Thousands of Canadian jobs could be lost, and the cost of shipping to and from Canada will increase. Canadian consumers and exporters will have to pay more.

What Do You Think?

4. In your group, consider the three solutions above and any others you can think of. Write a group report on which option is best. Your report should include the effects of your option on safety, ship owners, exporters, consumers, and the environment.

Key Outcomes

Now that you have completed this chapter, can you do the following? If not, review the sections indicated.

- Describe physical properties of substances. (1.1, 1.2)

- Estimate and measure the mass and volume of objects in suitable metric units. (1.3, 1.4, 1.5)

- Define density, and recognize and use the density equation, $D = m/V$, to solve density problems. (1.5, 1.6, 1.7, 1.8)

- Identify substances by measuring/calculating densities and comparing them with known values. (1.7, 1.8, 1.9)

Key Terms

matter

mass

volume

physical properties

viscosity

hardness

malleable

brittle

ductile

alloy

cubic unit

capacity unit

density

Review

1. (a) What is a physical property?

   (b) Give two qualitative physical properties of an earring.

   (c) Give as many quantitative physical properties of your backpack or gym bag as you can.

2. (a) What is meant by the expression displacement of water?

   (b) Describe how water displacement can be used to find the volume of a solid and the volume of a gas.

3. (a) You can float on water, but you can also make yourself sink. Estimate the approximate density of your body.

   (b) Why do you think it is easier to float in the ocean than in a freshwater lake?

4. When comparing two objects, does the object with the larger volume always have the larger mass? Use an example to explain your answer.

5. Explain how the density of materials is important when making surfboards and water skis.

6. A block of steel sinks when placed in water, yet a ship with a steel hull floats in water. Explain.

Problem Solving

7. Plot a mass/volume graph for a particular type of glass, using the data in the table below:

Volume (cm³)	0	40	80	120	160
Mass (g)	0	100	200	300	400

   (a) Use the graph to find the volume of a 160-g sample.

   (b) Find the mass of a 50-cm³ sample of this glass.

(c) What is the mass/volume ratio for this type of glass?

(d) Could another type of glass have the same mass/volume ratio? Explain.

8. Calculate the density in each case:

   (a) $m = 7.2$ g, $V = 3.0$ cm³.

   (b) $m = 5200$ kg, $V = 2.0$ m³.

   (c) $m = 6300$ g, $V = 9.0$ L

9. What is the mass of the air in a classroom that is 10.0 m × 8.0 m × 3.0 m?

10. A metal sample has a mass of 35 000 kg and a volume of 4.0 m³. What is the density of this metal?

11. A stone is placed at the bottom of an empty graduated cylinder. When 35 mL of water is added, the water level reaches the 50-mL mark. If the density of the stone is 3000 kg/m³, what is the mass of the stone?

12. A bar of soap measures 10 cm × 5 cm × 3 cm. If it has a mass of 120 g, calculate the density of the soap. Will it sink or float in your bathtub? Explain.

13. Many fish can adjust the density of their bodies by controlling the amount of gas in a sac-like organ called a swim bladder. How would the amount of gas in the swim bladder change in order for the fish to swim deeper underwater? How would it change so the fish could swim closer to the surface? Explain your answers.

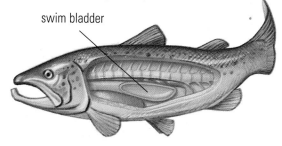

swim bladder

14. A graduated cylinder containing 40 mL of water has a total mass of 60 g. A solid object is carefully lowered into the graduated cylinder. The level of the water in the cylinder rises to the 70-mL mark. The total mass of the cylinder, water, and object is now 95 g. Calculate the mass, volume, and density of the object.

15. (a) Would a 100-mL graduated cylinder hold 120 g of ethyl alcohol ($D = 0.79$ g/mL)?

    (b) Would the same graduated cylinder hold 250 g of mercury ($D = 13.5$ g/mL)?

Critical Thinking

16. What is the difference between a 5-kg weight made from iron and a 5-kg weight made from plastic filled with sand? Would this difference affect you if you were working out with these weights?

17. Hydrogen chloride gas is escaping from a train wreck. Firefighters walking along the tops of the tank cars are not affected by the leaking gas. Firefighters walking in low-lying areas near the wreck are overcome by hydrogen chloride fumes. Explain.

18. A piece of hardwood floats lower in water than a piece of softwood of the same size and shape.

    (a) Use your knowledge of density to explain why this occurs.

    (b) Which would have a greater volume, 1 kg of hardwood or 1 kg of softwood?

    (c) Which type of wood would you choose if you were building a boat? Explain.

19. You and a friend are in a small, inflatable raft in a swimming pool. If your friend jumps out of the raft into the pool, will the water level in the swimming pool rise, fall, or stay the same? Explain.

20. Automobile manufacturers are now using less steel in the bodies, motors, and transmissions of cars, and using aluminum and plastic instead. Why do you think they are doing this?

CHAPTER 2

Changes of State

L OOK CLOSELY AT THE PHOTOGRAPH of Niagara Falls in winter. What changes can you see in the appearance of the water? Torrents of water and splashes of spray touch various surfaces. As the temperature rises and falls, tiny droplets of water (liquid) change to ice crystals (solid), and disappear into vapour (gas). Niagara Falls in winter provides a dramatic example of all six changes of state.

As you know, matter can be a solid, a liquid, or a gas. In this chapter, you will

- focus on the changing states of matter, and

- explore how temperature and other factors bring about these changes.

Changes of state can be used to make art.

 Getting Started

1. In a group, make a list of all the possible changes of state that can occur (for example, solid to gas, liquid to solid). Give an example of each.

2. Take on the role of a group of tourists in Niagara Falls. Imagine yourselves in this photograph. Write an entry in a "travel diary" describing what you see. Mention the changes of state that are going on about you. Suggest possible reasons for those changes.

3. On a hot summer day, why does the air feel cooler next to a body of water?

4. "It's not the cold, it's the humidity." Canadians who live on the Prairies claim that even though the temperature may be very low there in the winter, it does not feel as cold as it does near the Great Lakes. They say that on the Prairies the air is dry. The humidity near the lakes makes you feel colder. Are they correct? How would you test this hypothesis?

CHALLENGE

Which freezes more quickly, hot water or cold water? Make a prediction, then design and conduct a kitchen experiment to test your prediction.

Changes in the State of Matter

IN DAILY LIFE, YOU CAN FIND EXAMPLES of water in all three states. Water is different from most other substances because it changes state with fairly small changes in temperature. You will commonly find other substances in only one state—solid, liquid, or gas. For example, gold is a solid, oxygen is a gas, and oil is a liquid.

But even these substances can undergo a change of state. At high temperatures, gold can be melted down to a liquid in order to create a fine piece of jewellery. When cooled to extremely low temperatures, oxygen becomes a liquid. And oil that is cooled enough becomes solid.

Nitrogen, a gas, is a liquid at low temperatures.

TRY THIS

What Causes Evaporation and Boiling?

Will rubbing alcohol (isopropanol) evaporate faster when placed on your hand or on a piece of paper? (When the change of state from a liquid to a gas occurs slowly from the surface of the liquid, it is called evaporation.)

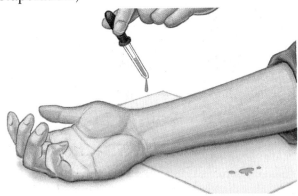

Using a medicine dropper, place a drop of rubbing alcohol on your arm and one on a piece of paper. Record your findings using the following headings.

- Prediction — What do you think will happen?
- Observation — What did you measure and what did you see?

- Explanation — How do you explain your observations? How does the arm differ from the paper, and how does this difference affect the time required for evaporation?

Now try this: Predict which evaporates faster, water or rubbing alcohol. Which liquid feels cooler? Design a procedure to test your prediction. Use the prediction, observation, and explanation headings to record your findings. Would your explanation for the differences in evaporation rates between your arm and a piece of paper be useful in explaining the different evaporation rates of water and alcohol?

Boiling is a much more rapid process than evaporation and requires more heat. When a liquid boils, molecules escape from within the liquid, not just at the surface. Will water boil at a lower temperature than alcohol? Make your prediction and then check the boiling points of both substances by referring to the table on page 80. Would the explanation used to account for evaporation be useful in explaining boiling?

solid to liquid

Melting is the change from solid to liquid. Metals heated to very high temperatures become liquid and can be poured and cast into new shapes.

liquid to solid

Freezing is the change from a liquid to a solid. If this change occurs at temperatures above 0°C, the word **solidification** is often used. Molten lava from volcanic eruptions cools and solidifies, forming solid rock.

liquid to gas

Vaporization is the change of state from a liquid to a gas. When this occurs slowly from the surface of a liquid over a wide range of temperatures, it is called **evaporation**. **Boiling** is a much more rapid process that causes gas to be formed throughout the liquid, not just at the surface. Water in the kettle boils and turns to steam.

gas to liquid

Condensation is the change from a gas to a liquid. This change is also called **liquefaction**. This cold glass of cola is covered with a coating of water droplets that condensed from water vapour in the air.

gas to solid

solid to gas

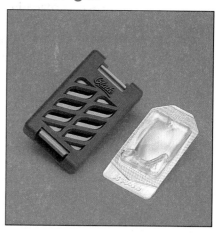

Sublimation is the change of state directly from a gas to a solid, or from a solid to a gas, without going through the liquid state. (Notice that this change has the same name for both directions.) Water vapour in the air sublimes into solid snowflakes on cold days. A solid air freshener gradually changes state into a fragrant vapour, without making any spots of liquid on the furniture.

A Transfer of Heat

What happens when you hold ice in your hand? It begins to melt. As the ice warms and your hand cools, the ice changes state from a solid to a liquid. Heat has transferred from your hand to the ice. All changes of state require such transfers of heat.

To melt ice, heat is added. Melting, the change from a solid to a liquid, requires the *addition of heat,* as shown by the red arrow in the diagram. Which other changes require the addition of heat? As shown in the diagram, vaporization, the change from liquid to gas, also requires the addition of heat.

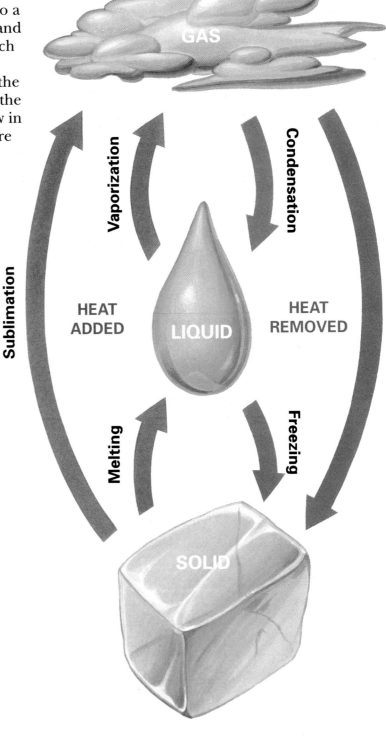

GAS

Vaporization

Condensation

Sublimation

HEAT ADDED

LIQUID

HEAT REMOVED

Sublimation

Melting

Freezing

SOLID

TRY THIS

Cracks and Sizzles

When you drop an ice cube into a glass of liquid, you may hear a few cracks, followed by a sizzling sound. The cracks are the sound the ice makes as it breaks. The warmer liquid is causing a sudden change in temperature on the surface of the ice. As the ice begins to melt, tiny air bubbles trapped in the ice escape and make the sizzling sound. Ice cubes that do not contain air bubbles will only crack, not sizzle!

Try this yourself: Boil some water, then cool and freeze it in an ice cube tray. Put some of these ice cubes in a glass of room-temperature water, and listen carefully. Then put some ice cubes made from cold tap water in another glass of  room-temperature water and listen again. Explain the difference.

In some changes of state, heat is removed. Freezing or solidification, the change from liquid to solid, requires the *removal of heat*, as shown by the blue arrow in the diagram. Condensation, the change from gas to liquid, is another change of state that occurs when heat is removed.

Sublimation is the change of state in which a solid changes directly to a gas or vice versa, with no liquid stage. As shown by the red arrow in the diagram, the change from a solid to a gas requires the addition of heat. The change from a gas to a solid requires the removal of heat, as shown by the blue arrow.

TECHNOLOGY-LINK

Creative State Changes

Technology permits artists to change the state of materials to produce a piece of art. An example is the manufacture of glass objects. Glass is made when solid ingredients, one of which is a substance derived from sand, are melted together at extremely high temperatures. This molten glass can then be shaped by several different methods. One of these is glass blowing.

The artist begins with a large mass of hot, molten glass at the end of a long, hollow tube. By blowing down the tube, the artist makes use of the fluid nature of the material to expand the glass ball into a bubble, and then, as it cools, to shape it as desired. As the glass cools, it loses its ability to flow. It ends up "frozen" in the shape the artist chose, with properties very different from the starting material.

- Predict what would happen if you tried to bend a glass rod. Predict what would happen if you heated the glass rod and then tried to bend it. Ask your teacher to test your prediction.
- Suggest a method for joining two glass rods.

SELF CHECK

1. Copy and complete the following table in your notebook.

Summary of Changes of State

Name of change	From	To	Heat must be ...
melting	solid	liquid	
freezing			
vaporization	liquid		added
condensation		liquid	removed
sublimation	solid	gas	
sublimation	gas		removed

2. List the six changes of state and give one example of each.

3. Refer to the diagram on the opposite page.
   (a) What do the red arrows indicate?
   (b) Which changes of state are indicated with blue arrows?
   (c) Why is sublimation shown as both a red-arrow process and a blue-arrow process?

4. Give six examples of substances, not previously mentioned, that undergo changes of state. For each example, write the following information.
   (a) the initial state
   (b) the final state
   (c) the change of state that is occurring
   (d) whether heat is added or removed

ASK YOURSELF

Return to your answer to question 1 in the Getting Started at the beginning of this chapter. Would you change or add to that answer now?

Cooling a Liquid

IN THIS INVESTIGATION, you will observe what happens as a liquid cools, and make a graph of your observations. The liquid you will study is stearic acid, a substance found in animal fat and vegetable oil. It is used in the manufacture of candles and cosmetics.

You will also learn a technique that is useful in identifying substances. One property of a liquid is the temperature at which it solidifies. Some liquids form crystals as they cool and solidify. The crystal shape of each substance is distinctive, and is also a property of that substance. Knowing the temperature at which a substance solidifies and its crystal shape can help you identify the substance.

Materials

- safety goggles
- apron
- 250-mL beaker (water bath)
- ring stand
- retort stand
- water
- hot plate or other heating device
- thermometer
- test tube with a sample of solid stearic acid
- forceps
- glass slide
- test-tube holder
- test-tube rack
- clock or timing device
- thermometer clamp
- hand lens

Procedure

1 Put on your safety goggles and apron. Then, prepare a liquid sample of stearic acid as follows. Fill a clean beaker with 150 mL of water and place it on a hot plate set on medium-high. Obtain a test tube with a sample of solid stearic acid from your teacher. Gently push the thermometer into the stearic acid in the test tube until the thermometer bulb is in the centre of the sample. Using a test-tube holder, put the test tube into the water bath.

Step 1

2 Make a data table like the one below to record your observations in step 6.

The Solidification of Stearic Acid		
Time (min)	Temperature (°C)	Observations
0		
1		

3 When the stearic acid has partially melted, carefully remove the thermometer from the liquid stearic acid and let it touch a clean, dry slide to transfer a small amount of stearic acid onto the slide. Set the slide aside for future observation with the hand lens. Return the thermometer to the test tube.

Steps 3 and 7

4 When all the solid in the test tube has melted, check the temperature and turn off the hot plate.

(a) Record the temperature of the liquid stearic acid.

5 Using the test-tube holder, carefully remove the test tube from the water bath and place it upright in the test-tube rack.

CAUTION: Do not touch the test tube. The test tube and its contents are hot.

Step 5

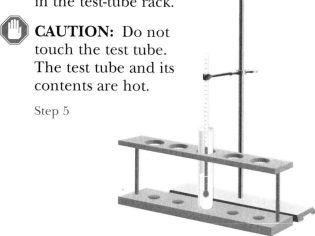

6 Use a retort stand and a thermometer clamp to keep the thermometer in the centre of the liquid. Make observations and temperature readings at 1-min intervals. Read temperatures to the nearest degree. Continue your observations until the temperature falls to 55°C or lower.

(b) Record your observations in your data table.

(c) Why is it important to keep the thermometer away from the sides of the test tube?

(d) What was the temperature as your liquid sample of stearic acid began to solidify?

(e) At what temperature did most of the stearic acid turn into the solid state?

7 Using the hand lens, examine the crystals that have formed on your glass slide.

(f) Describe the characteristics of the stearic acid crystals (colour, shape, etc.).

(g) Draw a sketch of the crystals.

8 Return the stearic acid in the test tube to your teacher. When the water in the water bath has cooled, discard it. Return all materials and clean up your lab station.

Questions

1. (a) Use your data table to plot a temperature-time graph. Plot time in minutes along the horizontal axis and temperature in degrees Celsius along the vertical axis. This graph will illustrate the *cooling curve* for stearic acid as it changes from a liquid to a solid. (For a review of how to make a line graph, see the Skills Handbook on page 512.)

   (b) Describe the shape of your graph.

2. What happened to the temperature of the stearic acid

   (a) in the first few minutes after the sample was placed in the test-tube rack?

   (b) as the stearic acid began to solidify?

   (c) near the end of the experiment?

3. Compare your observations with those of other students. List similarities and differences.

4. On the basis of your results and those of other class members, write a conclusion to summarize your findings in this investigation.

Apply

5. Predict how rapid cooling of the stearic acid might affect crystal formation.

Extension

6. Your teacher has several "mystery" samples of heated liquids. Determine the solidification temperature and crystal shape of each sample, using a method similar to your work with stearic acid. Use the chart of physical properties supplied by your teacher to determine the identity of the unknown samples.

Heating Ice

IN THIS INVESTIGATION, you will slowly heat a sample of ice until it melts and eventually boils. By carefully recording the temperature throughout this experiment, you will establish the *heating curve of water*.

Materials

- safety goggles
- apron
- crushed ice
- 250 mL beaker
- ring stand
- hot plate
- retort stand
- thermometer clamp
- thermometer
- clock or timing device
- stirring rod

Procedure

1 Put on your apron. Half-fill a clean beaker with crushed ice.

2 Set up your equipment. Clamp the thermometer in place, with the bulb at the centre of the ice as shown. Leave the hot plate in the "off" position and allow the temperature of the ice to drop to its lowest level.

Step 2

(a) Why should you place the thermometer in the middle of the sample?

3 While you wait for the temperature reading to stabilize, prepare a data table like the one shown below.

Heating of Ice

Time (min)	Temperature (°C)	Observations
0		
1		

4 Check the temperature of the ice frequently until it stops changing.

(b) What is the minimum temperature reached? Record this minimum temperature at time "0 min" on your data table.

(c) Describe the appearance of the ice.

5 Wearing safety goggles, set the hot plate at medium-low. Do not change this setting from now on.

(d) Why do you think you must control the amount of heat reaching the ice?

CAUTION: The final temperature will be very hot, so remember to wear eye protection and observe safety rules at all times.

Step 5

6 Gently stir the ice/water mixture with a stirring rod.

(e) Record the temperature every minute.

(f) Note any changes in the appearance of your sample (condensation on the beaker, amount of ice remaining, appearance of steam, etc.).

(g) Why is stirring important?

CAUTION: Thermometers are fragile! Stir gently so you don't hit the thermometer.

7 Continue the experiment until the water is at full boil for at least 5 min, then turn off the hot plate.

Step 7

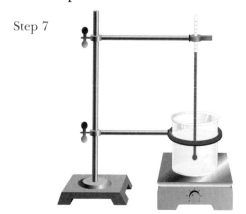

(h) What is the maximum temperature reached?

(i) Name all the changes of state you have observed during this experiment.

8 When the water has cooled, remove the thermometer, pour out the water, return all materials, and clean up your lab station.

Questions

1. (a) What was happening to the sample near the beginning of the investigation, when the temperature remained steady?

   (b) What was the temperature during this time?

2. (a) What was happening to the sample before it began to boil?

   (b) What happened to the temperature during this time?

3. (a) What was happening to the sample near the end of your investigation, when the temperature again remained steady?

   (b) What was the temperature during this time?

4. From your data, determine the temperatures at which ice melts and water boils.

5. (a) Using your data table, plot a temperature-time graph to illustrate what happens as ice is heated from a solid, through the liquid state, to a gas.

   (b) Describe the shape of your graph.

6. Compare your graph of the heating curve for water with those of other students. Suggest reasons for similarities and differences in the shape of your graph and those of your classmates.

Apply

7. Compare your findings with the melting and boiling temperatures of distilled water given in the table on the next page. Suggest reasons for any differences.

8. (a) Make a prediction about which has more energy: solid ice at 0°C or liquid water at 0°C.

   (b) Design an experiment to test your prediction.

Extension

9. How would ice made from salt water affect the results of this investigation? Design a method to test your hypothesis.

CHALLENGE

In some areas, salt is spread on icy roads in winter. Explain why this is done. Sometimes ash, sand, or other materials are used instead. What are the advantages and disadvantages of salt compared with one of the other commonly used materials?

Heat and Changes of State

A S YOU HAVE LEARNED, water changes from one state to another at a certain temperature. Other substances behave the same way, but each substance does so at its own temperatures. These temperatures are important quantitative properties that can be used to identify the substances.

Melting and Boiling Points

The exact temperature at which a substance changes from a solid to a liquid is called its **melting point**. For example, ice melts at 0°C. You could also say water freezes to form ice at 0°C. The **freezing point** of a substance is the temperature at which it changes from its liquid state to its solid state. Each substance has its own melting/freezing point.

If enough heat is added to a liquid, it will begin to bubble rapidly—or boil. The exact temperature at which a liquid changes rapidly to form a gas is called its **boiling point**.

Melting/Freezing Points and Boiling Points of Some Common Substances

Substance	Melting/ Freezing Point (°C)	Boiling Point (°C)
ammonia	−77.7	−33.4
carbon dioxide	−78.5	−78.5
chlorine	−101.0	−34.6
copper	1083.0	2566.0
ethanol	−114.4	78.5
glycerin	20.0	290.0
gold	1064.0	2807.0
iodine	113.5	184.35
isopropanol	−89.5	82.4
mercury	−38.9	356.6
salol	43.0	173.0
sodium chloride	801.0	1413.0
stearic acid	71.5	360
tin	232.0	2270.0
water (distilled)	0.0	100.0

Heating Curve for H_2O

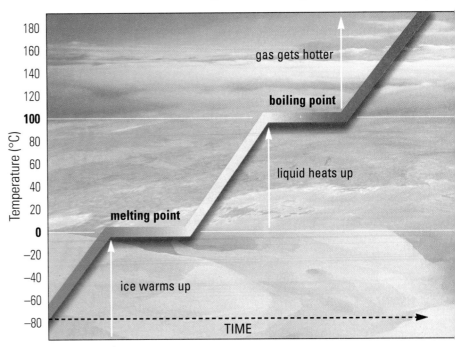

gas gets hotter

boiling point

liquid heats up

melting point

ice warms up

TIME

▲

Heating Curves

Examine the temperature-time graph for the heating of water. Look at the three parts where the graph slopes steadily upward. This tells you that each minute of heating is causing a uniform increase in temperature.

During the times when the water is changing state, the graph has a different appearance; it levels out to form a plateau. These level parts of the graph occur at the melting point of ice and the boiling point of water. As matter changes state, *it does not change in temperature*, even though heat is still being added. It seems from the graph that temperature does not begin to increase again until all the (solid) ice has been melted to become (liquid) water. What is happening to the heat? The heat must be connected with the change of state. In the next chapter, you will learn about a theory that helps explain these changes.

Cooling Curves

When cooled, a gas condenses to form a liquid. The exact temperature at which the gas changes to liquid is called its **condensation point**. With the removal of more heat, eventually the liquid will solidify. The freezing point of any substance is exactly the same temperature as its melting point. Examine the cooling curve for water (shown below) and use it to determine the condensation point and freezing point of pure water. What is happening to the water in the parts of the graph that slope downward? Why do other parts of the graph show plateaus?

Because each pure substance has its own characteristic freezing and boiling points, different substances produce different graphs. What is common to all the graphs, however, is the presence of plateaus. The pattern shows that the temperature remains constant during changes of state.

Cooling Curve for H$_2$O

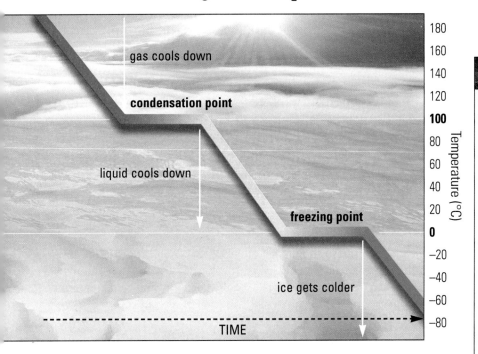

gas cools down

condensation point

liquid cools down

freezing point

ice gets colder

TIME

Temperature (°C)

180
160
140
120
100
80
60
40
20
0
−20
−40
−60
−80

SELF CHECK

5. What happens to the temperature of a substance as it undergoes a change of state?

6. How does the melting point of a substance compare with its freezing point? Explain your answer by referring to the changes of state.

7. Which of the following would require a higher temperature to produce: copper pennies or Olympic gold medals? Explain your answer.

8. Dry ice (solid carbon dioxide) is considered to be better than water ice for keeping foodstuffs cool while being transported over large distances. Suggest reasons.

9. When an infant has a high fever, you can reduce its temperature by giving it a sponge bath of lukewarm water or rubbing alcohol (isopropanol). In terms of what you know about changes of state, explain how this procedure might work.

TECHNOLOGY-LINK

Skating on Water

When you watch a figure skater, it appears as though she is gliding effortlessly across a smooth, glasslike surface of ice. Actually, she is not skating on ice, she is skating on water! As the blades of the skates pass over the surface of the ice, the ice melts, and the blades glide on a thin film of water. The water immediately freezes once the skate blades are removed.

- Predict what will happen if you run the dull side of a table knife back and forth across the surface of an ice cube. Use an ice cube to check your prediction.

Weather and Changes of State

THE CHANGES OF STATE of water are important, not just when you want to play hockey or steam your vegetables. One reason for that importance is the weather, because weather is mostly about water changing state and rising and falling.

Water Up, Water Down

The **water cycle** is the name given to the series of changes of state of water in nature. Water evaporates constantly from lakes, oceans, and moist environments. The evaporated water enters the air, making it humid. When this humid air rises into a cooler region, the water vapour condenses on dust particles to form water droplets. In really cold temperatures, water vapour can sublime, forming ice crystals. These collections of droplets or crystals are called clouds. When the water droplets or ice crystals become too large to be held up in the air, the water returns to earth as **precipitation**: rain, snow, freezing rain, sleet, and hail.

Temperature, air pressure, wind speed, and humidity determine the type of precipitation. Predicting the amount and type of precipitation becomes increasingly difficult at temperatures near 0°C. The same storm may be responsible for rain in the Niagara peninsula, freezing rain in Metro Toronto, sleet at Canadian Forces Base Trenton, and a major snowfall in the Gatineau Hills near Ottawa. The diagram below illustrates what happens when warm air (travelling from west to east) meets cooler air.

Rain

High-altitude clouds heavy with water vapour release precipitation in the form of snow. During its descent through the warm air mass, the snow melts and falls as rain.

Freezing Rain

The snow melts to rain as it falls through the warm air mass. The cold air closer to the ground causes the raindrops to cool rapidly to below-zero temperatures. This super-cooled water instantly solidifies as it strikes the ground.

Sleet

The snow melts and then passes through a broad band of much colder air, causing it to re-solidify and fall as ice pellets.

Snow

In the absence of the layer of warm air, the snow released from the cloud mass falls directly to Earth.

Hail

High winds can carry a raindrop up to a colder region, where it freezes. A frost layer can also be added by sublimation. When the ice pellet falls into a warmer layer, more water can condense on the forming hailstone. Because the hailstone is cold, the water will freeze. The cycle can be repeated many times, and each time the hailstone grows larger.

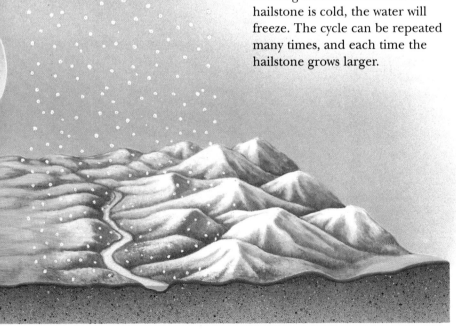

Weather Wisdom

I T IS FRIDAY EVENING at the beginning of March break. Lana is at the airport, with thousands of other holiday travellers, anxiously waiting for her flight to be called. It is going to be terrific to leave the cold and snow behind and enjoy a week of sand and surf.

In the control room on the roof of the airport, computers are constantly providing updated weather information. How these facts are analyzed will play a major role in deciding whether Lana's flight will leave on schedule at 8:32 p.m. It is less than an hour before the flight, and it is time to make the decision.

(a) If you were Lana, what would you hope the decision will be? Should the flight take off as scheduled?

The data below will help you make a decision.

- The most recent report from the orbiting weather satellite indicates that at the cruising altitude of 10 000 m, the air is very cold (–35˚C), but flying conditions are stable, with favorable wind currents.

- There is a cold air mass between 2000 m and 5000 m directly above the airport. Ground instruments and microwave readings indicate this has a very high moisture content.

(b) Why would precipitation be expected?

- Weather balloons show a mass of warm (15˚C) air immediately to the west of the airport. This mass extends from 200 m above ground up to an altitude of 1400 m, and is moving east.

(c) Make a sketch showing weather conditions at and near the airport. Be sure to include the temperature at different altitudes.

- The Sun set several hours ago. Ground temperatures are quickly dropping, with temperatures as low as –10˚C on the metal surfaces of the aircraft.

(d) What type of precipitation might be expected? (Hint: It might be useful to review section 2.5, Weather and Changes of State.)

- In the control room, the traffic controllers are aware of the restlessness of the holiday crowds, and how upset they would be if their flights were delayed or cancelled. They also remember the disastrous consequences of icing, which has been responsible for several major airplane accidents in recent years.

Questions

1. Speculate about why icing is hazardous to taking off.

2. Why would freezing rain on the wings of an airplane be more dangerous than a light layer of snow?

3. What factors must be considered in deciding whether the plane should take off or not?

4. The two diagrams below show different weather conditions that might affect flight. In both situations, a moist warm air mass collides with a cold air mass near the airport.

(a) Identify weather conditions that might be produced.

(b) Speculate what dangers these weather conditions pose for pilots.

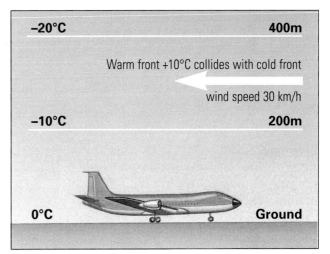

Situation A

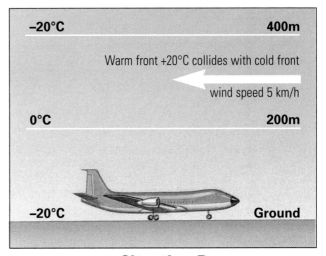

Situation B

Making Use of Changes of State

BECAUSE CHANGES OF STATE either require or release heat, they can be used for heating and cooling indoors, and they can affect the climate outdoors.

The Refrigerator

Basically, any refrigeration system is a closed circuit containing a refrigerant. A **refrigerant** is a substance that readily changes state from gas to liquid and from liquid to gas. The most commonly used refrigerant is freon, although alternatives to freon will be used more often in the future.

What is happening when you hear a refrigerator turn on? Follow the path of the refrigerant as it travels through the circuit of the refrigerator below.

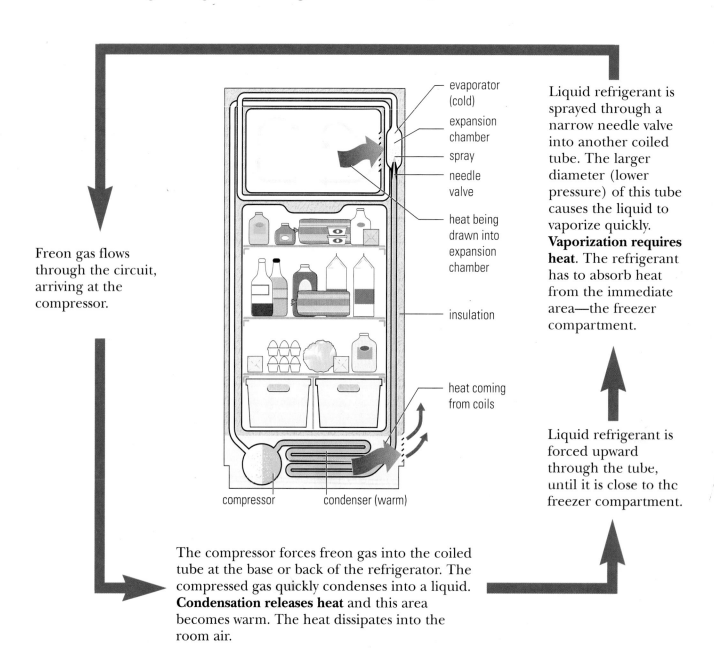

evaporator (cold)

expansion chamber

spray

needle valve

heat being drawn into expansion chamber

insulation

heat coming from coils

compressor

condenser (warm)

Freon gas flows through the circuit, arriving at the compressor.

Liquid refrigerant is sprayed through a narrow needle valve into another coiled tube. The larger diameter (lower pressure) of this tube causes the liquid to vaporize quickly. **Vaporization requires heat**. The refrigerant has to absorb heat from the immediate area—the freezer compartment.

Liquid refrigerant is forced upward through the tube, until it is close to the freezer compartment.

The compressor forces freon gas into the coiled tube at the base or back of the refrigerator. The compressed gas quickly condenses into a liquid. **Condensation releases heat** and this area becomes warm. The heat dissipates into the room air.

The State Outdoors

People who live along the shores of large lakes experience cooler springs and warmer falls than people who live inland.

As the ice on the lake melts in the spring, heat must be drawn from the immediate surroundings. Thus it is noticeably cooler by the lake shore, even if the air is calm and the Sun is shining.

In contrast, during winter as the lake freezes, it gives off heat to the surrounding region. This creates an area of warmer air along the lake shore.

The pitch pine (*Pinus rigida*) is normally found in southeastern North America. Its range extends from Florida to Cape Cod—it cannot survive the harsh winters of northern areas. Surprisingly, there are large stands of these pines on south-facing slopes of many of the Thousand Islands in the St. Lawrence River. The water in the river keeps the area warmer in fall and winter, and allows this rare plant to survive in a northern location.

Protecting Food Crops

As a substance freezes, it releases heat to its surroundings. Fruit farmers use this principle when a frost threatens to damage their crop, especially during blossom season in the early spring.

Farmers spray water on the fruit plants when the temperature is about 1°C and a frost is predicted. The sap within plants is composed of water, plus sugars and other substances. The sugars lower the freezing point of the sap to about −1°C or −2°C. As the temperature drops, the sprayed water freezes first. In doing so, it releases heat. This released heat helps to keep the temperature close to the water from dropping further, and the plant doesn't freeze.

SELF CHECK

13. Why does the outside of a refrigerator feel warm?

14. Describe at least two everyday situations where you utilize changes of state.

15. Imagine you are standing next to a large, unfrozen lake. The radio reports that in most areas the temperature is −20°C. Is the air around you colder or warmer? Why?

16. In pioneer times, large, unglazed pottery crocks were often used to keep drinking water cool. Because these crocks were porous, water would gradually seep through the sides, moistening the outer surface. Use your knowledge of evaporation to explain how these crocks helped to keep the water in them cool in warm weather.

17. Before refrigerators, people kept their vegetables in root cellars. Occasionally, in winter, the temperature would drop so low that even the vegetables in the cellar would freeze. In order to prevent this, people put large barrels of water near the vegetables. Use your knowledge of changes of state to explain why this helped prevent the stored food from freezing.

ASK YOURSELF

Return to the answers you wrote in the Getting Started at the opening of this chapter. Would you change some or any of those answers now?

In Search of Safer Paint

YOU MAY HAVE NOTICED a strong odour in a freshly painted room. This odour means that particles of solvent—the liquid part of the paint—have evaporated into the air and entered your nose.

As the solvent evaporates into the air, the solid components of paint are left behind to coat the wall or other surface. Unfortunately, some solvents evaporate to form fumes that are more dangerous than being simply strong or unpleasant smells. These fumes may burn, or even explode if concentrated in a poorly ventilated room. Many solvents are also toxic and can poison a person who inhales large amounts.

Latex Paints

Water is the major solvent in latex paint, so the fumes from latex paint are safer. However, water is not very good at dissolving resins, the part of paint that provides strength and durability. As a result, latex paint contains less resin than alkyd paint, and is less strong and durable. Latex paints are not as sticky, and so cannot be used on all surfaces. The water in latex paints damages some surfaces. On the other hand, latex paints dry very quickly, and you can use water to clean the brushes.

Inside a Can of Paint

What is in Paint	Comes from	Function		Possible Hazards
pigment	earth, metals, other coloured substances	long-lasting colour		some components harmful if consumed
resin	plant or insect secretions, plastics (alkyds, acrylics, urethanes)	forms hard film that sticks		some components harmful if consumed
solvent	water, mineral spirits, turpentine (from plants)	dissolves other parts of paint		fumes may be toxic fumes may burn easily (combustible) fumes may be explosive

Alkyd Paints

Alkyd paint does not contain water, instead it uses mineral spirits and/or turpentine as the solvent. These solvents are able to dissolve the resins that make this type of paint useful. Alkyd paint is strong and durable. It sticks to metal and other surfaces. But the solvent fumes are hazardous, so very good ventilation is necessary when painting. Cleaning up requires the same solvents, which adds more fumes to the air.

Understanding the Author

1. When is paint most hazardous to human health: while it is in the can, while it is being applied, or after it is dry? Explain your reasons.
2. What parts of paint evaporate? What parts do not?
3. Which paint would you buy for each of the following uses? Explain your choice.

   (a) painting the walls of a hospital

   (b) painting the walls of a school hallway

   (c) painting the window sills in a home

COLOUR DEPOT

NEW

INTERIOR LATEX

ENVIRO-SAFE PAINT
Satin Flat
Scrubbable
Colourfast
Stain Resistant
Solvent Free (No V.O.C.'s)
The Healthy Choice for
Your Home Environment

FANTASTIC VALUE

Enviro-safe Paint

Painters prefer Enviro-safe!
- Environmentally Safe; Better for Your Health
- Completely Solvent Free Paint
- Enviro-safe releases no pollutants into the air you breathe!
- Odour-free
- Available in over 100 pastel shades.
- No V.O.C.'s (volatile organic compounds)
- Easy Cleanup
- Help keep the environment clean with Enviro-safe Paint. Each can covers 25% more wall surface, reducing packaging waste by 20% over other paints.

Interior Latex
(Not suitable for bare wood, metal, or unfinished walls.)

Safe Paint

4. In a group, list the advantages of Enviro-Safe Paint that are claimed in the advertisement.

5. Discuss these claims. Consider the following questions:

   - What evidence has been presented to support each claim?

   - What evidence would you need before you were convinced the claim is accurate?

   - Are there any confusing or incorrect statements in the advertisement? If so, why do you think this has happened?

6. (a) Rank the claims as very important, less important, or not important to health/safety.

   (b) Rank the claims as very important, less important, or not important to the function of the paint (colouring and protecting a wall).

ASK YOURSELF

Would you prefer to use Enviro-Safe Paint or regular latex paint if you were painting your room? Why? If you are not sure, what else would you want to know in order to make this decision?

Key Outcomes

Now that you have completed this chapter, can you do the following? If not, review the sections indicated.

- Classify observed changes of state. (2.1)

- Identify energy changes associated with changes of state. (2.2, 2.3)

- Construct and interpret graphs of changes of state. (2.2, 2.3, 2.4)

- Relate changes of state to weather conditions. (2.5, 2.6)

- Explain technological applications of changes of state. (2.7, 2.8)

Key Terms

melting

freezing

solidification

vaporization

evaporation

boiling

condensation

liquefaction

sublimation

melting point/ freezing point

boiling point/ condensation point

water cycle

precipitation

rain

freezing rain

sleet

snow

hail

refrigerant

Review

1. For each of the following situations, give the initial state and the final state. Then give the name of the change of state that is occurring.

    (a) Hair is dried using a blow dryer.

    (b) Water droplets form on cold water pipes on hot summer days.

    (c) Ice cubes disappear in a frost-free refrigerator.

2. For each of the situations in question 1, say whether heat is being added or removed.

3. Which changes of state require the addition of heat? Which require the removal of heat?

4. Draw a concept map (see the Skills Handbook on page 502) to illustrate your understanding of the three states of matter and how they change with the addition or the removal of heat.

5. Explain the following.

    (a) Dew forms on a still, cloudless summer night.

    (b) Humidity in buildings is usually very low in winter.

    (c) Solid carbon dioxide is often called dry ice.

Problem Solving

6. Carefully examine the warming curve for paraffin wax on the next page. Use the graph to help you answer the following questions.

    (a) What is the melting point of paraffin wax?

    (b) What is the boiling point of paraffin wax?

(c) What is the state of paraffin wax at a temperature of 20°C?

(d) What is the state of paraffin wax at a temperature of 50°C?

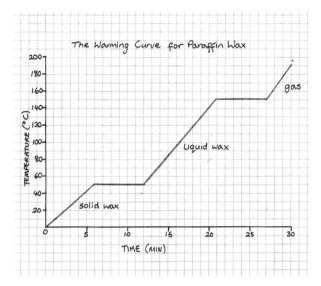

7. Two popular ways to eat potatoes are french fries (boiled in oil) and mashed potatoes (boiled in water). Both methods make use of boiling liquids to provide enough heat to cook the potatoes. But it takes longer to cook similar-sized potato pieces in boiling water than in boiling oil. Why?

8. Ashraf is trying to make popsicles from fruit juice. He becomes curious about how quickly and at what temperature they freeze, so he puts a thermometer in one. Every 10 min he checks the temperature of the popsicles and records the information in a chart.

The freezing of Fruit Juice	
Time (minutes)	Temperature (°C)
0	20
10	14
20	8
30	2
40	−2
50	−2
60	−2
70	−4
80	−10
90	−12
100	−12

(a) Use the temperature readings that Ashraf recorded to construct a temperature-time graph.

(b) At what temperature does a plateau appear on the graph?

(c) What do you think was happening at that temperature?

(d) At what temperature do you infer that the fruit juice froze? Explain your answer.

9. In the past, mercury was frequently used as the liquid inside thermometers. These are some of its properties.

melting point: −38.9° C

boiling point: 356.6°C

density: 13.5 g/mL

appearance: shiny silvery liquid

other properties: a liquid metal, forms highly poisonous compounds, expands when heated

(a) What properties make mercury an appropriate choice for use in thermometers?

(b) Why might schools and hospitals use alcohol (ethanol) thermometers instead of mercury thermometers?

(c) List the characteristics you would find in the materials used in the construction of thermometers.

(d) Alcohol thermometers are preferred in very cold climates, such as near Inuvik. Why?

Critical Thinking

10. Some tropical plants need a warm environment for their leaves, but a cool environment for their root systems. For healthy growth, experts use clay pots rather than plastic ones. Can you suggest why clay pots are preferred?

11. Many schools cannot afford to buy thermometers. Design a thermometer for student use in investigations such as those you carried out in this chapter. After having your design approved by your teacher, try it out.

CHAPTER 3

A Model for Matter

WHEN YOU HAVE A QUESTION you can't answer, or an observation you can't explain, one of the ways to find an answer is to develop a model. A **model** is a mental picture, a diagram, or some other means of representing something. You can use a model to explain things.

Look at the illustrations on these pages. See how observation and measurement, improved technology, and analysis of new information have enabled people to build better and better models of the universe.

In the previous two chapters, you examined matter in detail. You know what matter does, now try to explain why matter behaves as it does. To help you, try building a model of matter.

In this chapter, you will

- develop a model for matter, and
- use this model to explain the characteristics of matter.

 Getting Started

You have made many observations that you can use to help build a model to explain matter. In a group, brainstorm some answers to the following questions.

1. Why does a solid have a definite shape?
2. What happens to a solid when it melts to form a liquid?
3. Why does a liquid take the shape of its container?
4. When liquids boil, why do bubbles rise to the surface?
5. What happens to those bubbles?
6. Why do hot-air balloons rise?

Do the answers fit together in some way? Can you come up with a model that explains them all? Later, as you develop your model, you can revisit these questions.

Early flat
Earth model

Greek Earth-
centred model

Copernicus's Sun-
centred model

Only recently have we been able to make observations from orbit around the Earth, from the Moon, and even from the very edge of our solar system. Our model is now much improved.

The Disappearing Volume

I N THIS INVESTIGATION, you will predict and then measure the total volume as you combine two samples of matter.

Materials

- safety goggles
- apron
- 2 100-mL graduated cylinders
- water
- alcohol
- stirring rod
- sand
- marbles

Procedure

Part 1 *Combining Volumes of Water*

1 Prepare a table, as shown, to record your predictions and findings.

Addition of Volumes

Volume (mL) Substance 1	Volume (mL) Substance 2	Predicted total volume (mL)	Actual total volume (mL)
50 mL water	50 mL water		

2 Put on your apron and safety goggles. Then carefully pour 50 mL of water into each of the two graduated cylinders. Remember to measure at the bottom of the meniscus (the curved surface of the liquid in the cylinder).

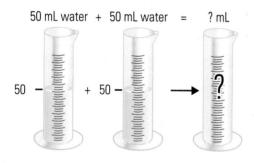

3 When these two samples of water are combined in one graduated cylinder, what do you think the total volume will be?

(a) Record your prediction in the table.

4 Carefully combine the two volumes of water and use the stirring rod to mix thoroughly.

(b) Measure the total volume accurately and record the volume in the table.

5 Was there any difference between your predicted total volume and the measured total volume? Discuss possible reasons for this.

6 Drain the graduated cylinder by pouring the water down the sink.

Part 2 *Combining Alcohol and Water*

7 Fill one graduated cylinder with 50 mL of water, and the second with 50 mL of alcohol.

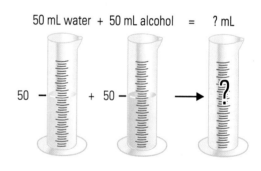

8 With your partners, discuss and predict the total volume that will result when these two samples of different liquids are combined in one graduated cylinder.

(c) Record your prediction in the table.

9 Carefully combine the alcohol and water in one graduated cylinder and use the stirring rod to mix thoroughly.

(d) Measure and record the total volume.

10 Was there any difference between your predicted total volume and the measured total volume? Discuss possible reasons.

11 Pour the alcohol/water solution into the waste container. Rinse and dry the graduated cylinders.

Part 3   *A Model for Changing Volumes*

12 Using two clean, dry graduated cylinders, measure 50 mL of sand and 50 mL of marbles.

✎ (e) Can this be done accurately?

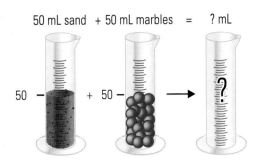

50 mL sand + 50 mL marbles = ? mL

13 With your partners, discuss and predict the total volume that will result when these two samples are combined in one graduated cylinder.

✎ (f) Record your prediction in the table.

14 Carefully combine the sand and marbles in one graduated cylinder. Cover the top of the cylinder with your hand and invert several times to mix thoroughly.

✎ (g) Measure and record the total volume.

15 Was there any difference between your predicted total volume and the measured total volume? Discuss possible reasons.

16 Pour the sand/marble mixture into a collection beaker. Clean the graduated cylinders, return all materials to your teacher, and clean up your work station. Wash your hands.

Questions

1. Is the total of 50 mL + 50 mL always 100 mL? Explain.

2. Which substances used in this investigation showed a loss of volume when combined?

Apply

3. In the case of alcohol and water, compare your prediction of total volume with the actual result. In what way do the marbles and sand provide a model for understanding what happens when the alcohol and water are combined?

Extension

4. What do you predict about the combined mass of 50 g of water and 50 g of alcohol? Design and conduct an investigation to test your prediction. Be sure to wear an apron and safety goggles when conducting your experiment.

5. What will happen if vinegar is added to a solution containing baking soda? Record your prediction. Put on your apron and safety goggles. Mix 10 g of baking soda in 100 mL of water. Pour 10 mL of your baking soda solution into a graduated cylinder. Add approximately 2 mL of dilute acetic acid (vinegar), and observe what happens.

(a) What caused the combination of the two solutions to change in volume?

(b) Predict the volume of the combined solutions 24 h later. Will the volume change?

(c) Observe the combined solutions 24 h later. Measure the volume of the combined solutions. Provide an explanation for your observations.

The Particle Theory and the Three States of Matter

M ORE THAN 2000 YEARS AGO in Greece, a philosopher named Democritus suggested that matter is made up of tiny particles too small to be seen. He thought that if you kept cutting and cutting a substance into smaller and smaller pieces, you would eventually come to the smallest possible particles.

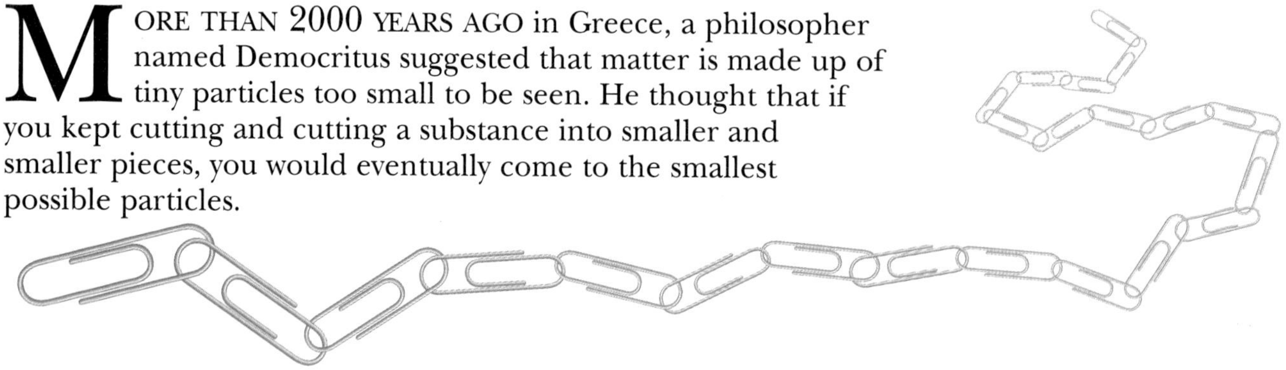

Democritus called these tiniest particles *atomos* (meaning indivisible), from which we have the English word atom. The idea of tiny particles first suggested by Democritus is called a hypothesis. A **hypothesis** is an attempt to explain observations made in the natural world.

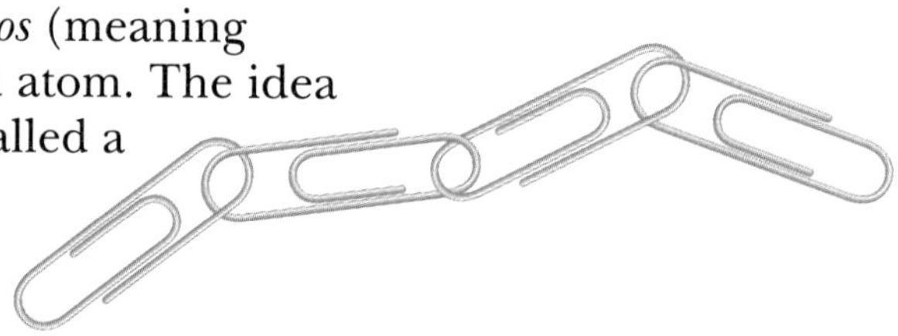

A chain of paper clips can be used to illustrate the hypothesis of Democritus. Each paper clip represents one particle.

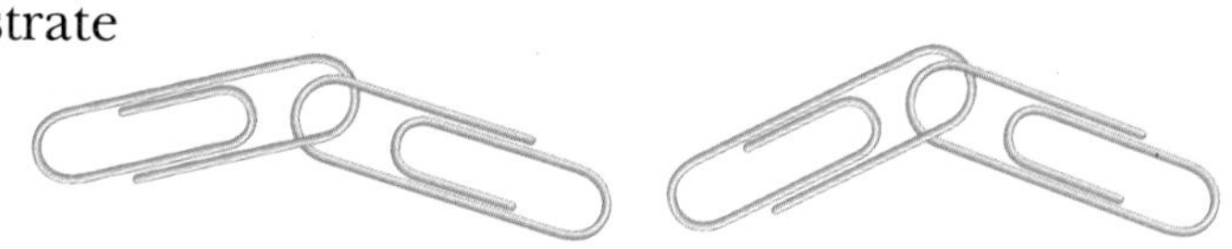

You can divide the chain into two chains, which can then be divided into smaller chains. Eventually the chain will be divided into individual paper clips.

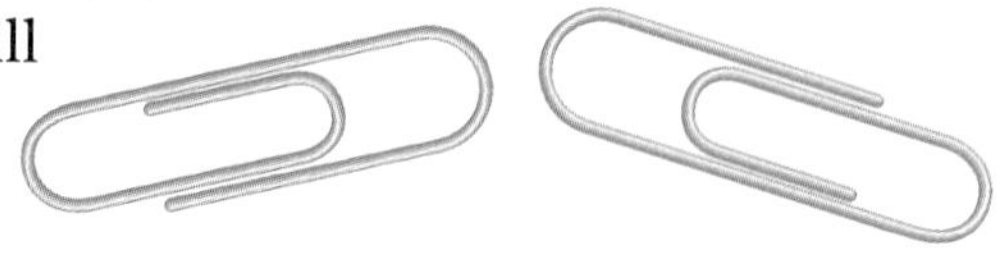

If you break a paper clip, it no longer has the characteristics of a paper clip. Similarly, there is a limit to how far matter can be subdivided and still retain the characteristics of that type of matter.

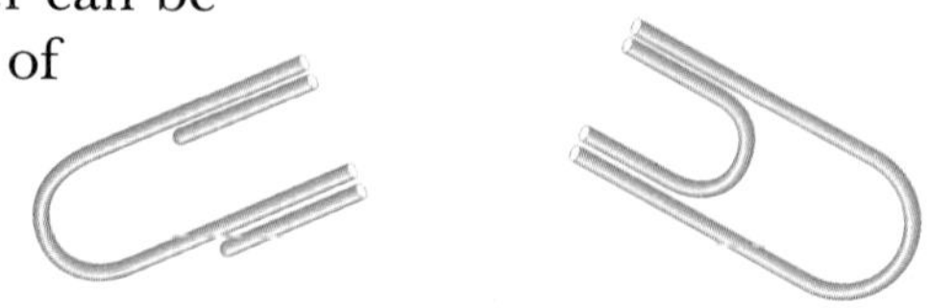

The Particle Theory

Over the centuries, scientists have carried out many investigations of matter. So far, the hypothesis of Democritus is still useful in describing the characteristics of matter and in predicting how it will behave. A hypothesis or a set of related hypotheses that is supported again and again by experimental results is called a **theory**. The theory that matter is made up of tiny particles is now widely accepted. Called the **Particle Theory of Matter**, it is summarized in the diagram on the next page.

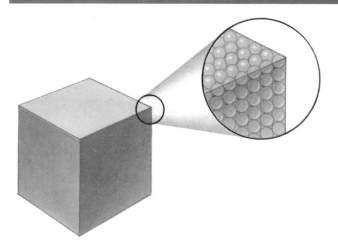

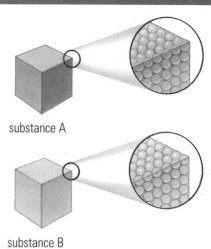

substance A

substance B

1. All matter is made up of tiny particles.

2. All particles of one substance are the same. Different substances are made of different particles.

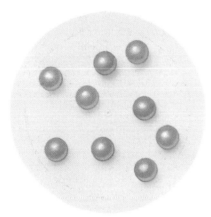

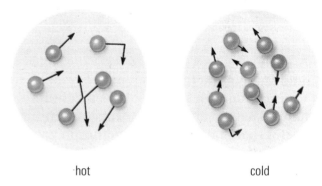

hot   cold

3. There are spaces between the particles.

4. The particles are always moving. The more energy that particles have, the faster they move.

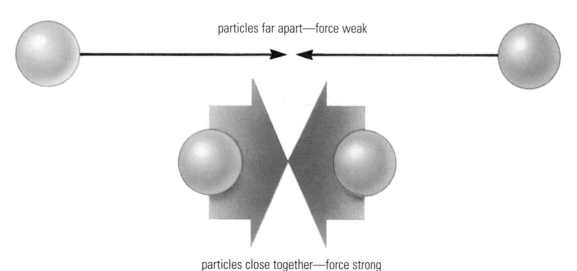

particles far apart—force weak

particles close together—force strong

5. There are attractive forces among particles. These forces are stronger when the particles are closer together.

Particles and the Three States of Matter

You can use the particle theory to explain the differences among solids, liquids, and gases. Consider the characteristics of matter in each of the three states. How do you explain them in terms of each point of the particle theory?

Solids

Solids have a definite shape and volume. In the particle theory, solids are made up of an orderly arrangement of particles. Strong attractive forces hold the arrangement together. Particles can vibrate a little, but otherwise they stay in fixed positions. When a solid is heated, the particles gain energy. They vibrate more rapidly, but still around the same fixed point.

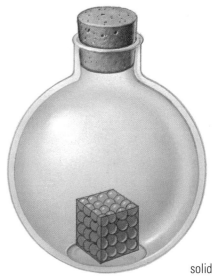

solid

Liquids

Liquids have no definite shape (they take the shape of their container), but they have a definite volume. The particle theory explains that the particles in liquids are held together in groups that are less orderly. Because the particles are farther apart than the particles in a solid, the weaker attractive forces permit the particles to move around one another. When a liquid is heated, the speed of the particles increases.

liquid

Gases

In a gas, the particles have even more energy and move rapidly throughout the container. Gases have no definite shape or volume. They fill whatever container they are in. The particle theory explains that the attractions among the particles of gases are so weak that individual particles are quite far apart, with a lot of space around them. This leaves the particles free to move in any direction. Gas particles move constantly and randomly.

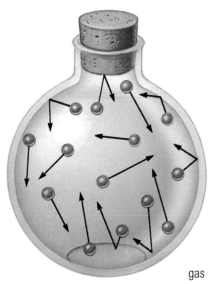

gas

Scientific Notation

Experiments have shown that the particles that make up matter are incredibly small. An average drop of rain contains about 30 000 000 000 000 000 000 000 particles of water! That number is larger than the total number of people who have ever lived on Earth.

You will find it convenient to use scientific notation for very large and very small numbers. Each number is written as the product of a number between 1 and 10 and a power of 10.

For example, the scientific notation of the number 123 000 is 1.23×10^5, and of the number 0.000 012 3 is 1.23×10^{-5}.

Rewrite the following in scientific notation:

- the number of particles in a drop of rain
- the mass of a single water particle (estimated as 0.000 000 000 000 000 000 000 029 9 g)

Distances between Particles in a Gas and a Liquid

How can you show that the distances between the particles in a gas are greater than those in a liquid?

Place two test tubes in an ice bath for 10 min. Using a graduated cylinder, add 6 mL of cold soda pop to each of the test tubes. Mark the original level of the fluid in each test tube with a wax pencil. Quickly place balloons over each test tube and then shake one of the test tubes.

- Record your observations.
- In which balloon did you find more gas?

After approximately 5 min, measure the fluid levels in each of the test tubes.

- What evidence suggests that a gas takes up more space than a liquid?
- What does this suggest about the spaces between the particles of a gas compared with those of a liquid?
- Suggest a method for determining the amount of gas collected in each of the balloons.
- Using a similar design, investigate how temperature affects the rate at which gases leave liquids. Submit your procedure to your teacher for approval before beginning your experiment.

1. In your notebook, copy each of the following statements and write whether the statement is consistent with the Particle Theory of Matter. Explain why or why not.
   (a) Matter is made of particles.
   (b) All substances are made up of the same kind of particles.
   (c) The particles of matter are in motion.
   (d) Cooling speeds up the motion of particles.
   (e) Particles all move in the same direction.
   (f) The particles of matter are separated by air.
   (g) The spaces between the particles get smaller as matter is heated.
   (h) Particles of matter are attracted to each other.
   (i) Cooling matter weakens the attractions between particles.
   (j) As matter is cooled, the particles shrink.

2. In your notebook, copy and complete the summary chart on the left.

The States of Matter and the Particle Theory

	State of matter		
	Solid	Liquid	Gas
Particle motion		slower	
Particle spacing			farthest apart
Particle attraction		weaker	

The Dissolving Process

A GOOD, GENERAL THEORY explains as many observations as possible. In this investigation, you will examine the dissolving process. Does the Particle Theory of Matter explain what happens when you put sugar in water?

 CAUTION: Never leave a hot plate or a Bunsen burner unattended.

Materials

- apron
- safety goggles
- sugar (icing sugar, sucrose, glucose, brown sugar, sugar cubes, etc.)
- water (ice water and tap water)
- glassware (stirring rod, test tubes, beakers, graduated cylinder)
- scoop
- thermometer
- measuring spoons
- timing device (stopwatch, clock, etc.)
- balance

What Factors Affect the Dissolving Process?

In this investigation, you will study how to speed up or slow down the dissolving process. Many factors could be studied; the choice is yours. You could heat or cool the solution, stir it or shake it, put it in the dark or in the light, transfer it to a larger or smaller container, grind up the sugar or use large lumps, try different brands of sugar, ... whatever factors you think might affect the rate of the dissolving process.

Terms You Should Know

Sugar **dissolves** in water: it mixes with the water so thoroughly that the parts of the mixture can't be distinguished. The water-sugar mixture is called a solution. **Solutions** are made up of a solvent and one or more solutes. A **solute** is the material that dissolves. A **solvent** is the material into which the solute dissolves. In the sugar-water solution, sugar is the solute and water is the solvent.

As you proceed with this investigation, remember to design a controlled experiment, so your results can be used or repeated by others. (See pages 22–27 for more information on forming hypotheses and designing experiments.)

In this investigation, you will time sugar dissolving in water.

Procedure

1. With your partner, choose a factor that might make sugar dissolve faster or slower in water.

✎ (a) What is the independent variable in your investigation?

✎ (b) Write down a hypothesis on how the factor will affect the rate at which sugar dissolves, based on the particle theory.

2. Design an investigation that will test your hypothesis. It is important to plan a method that will allow you to accurately time how long it takes to completely dissolve the sugar in a given amount of water.

✎ (c) What is the dependent variable in your investigation?

✎ (d) List all the factors that you will control (keep the same) in your investigation.

✎ (e) Write a list of the materials you will need, the safety precautions you will take, and the steps of your proposed method. Include a diagram of the equipment set-up.

3. Discuss your procedure (and theirs) with another lab group, sharing ideas to improve the safety, reliability, and accuracy of both of your designs.

4. Have your revised method approved by your teacher. Collect the necessary equipment and carry out your investigation, using all appropriate safety precautions.

✎ (f) What are the results of your investigation?

✎ (g) How do your results compare with your hypothesis?

✎ (h) Do your results support the Particle Theory of Matter? Explain.

5. Clean up your work station and return all cleaned equipment. Wash your hands.

6. Help make a summary table of the class results.

✎ (i) List each factor that was tested by the class and its effect on the rate of dissolving.

✎ (j) Discuss whether each of the class results supports the Particle Theory of Matter.

✎ (k) Make a concluding statement based on the results of the entire class.

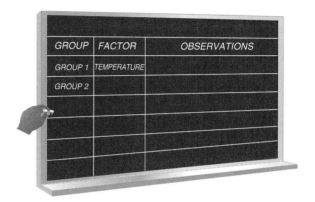

Questions

1. Which factors speed up the dissolving process?

2. Which factors slow down the dissolving process?

3. Name any factors that do not seem to affect the dissolving process.

4. Which results did you feel were more reliable: the results from your own investigation, or the results collected from the entire class? Explain.

5. Which of the class results did you find most informative: those that were quantitative, qualitative, or both? Explain.

6. (a) State two reasons why the method you proposed was appropriate.

   (b) Name a source of error that could have affected the results of your investigation.

   (c) Suggest a way (other than correcting any sources of error) to improve your investigation.

The Particle Theory and Changes of State

THE PARTICLE THEORY explains the three different states of matter. But can the particle theory explain changes in the state of matter? Matter can change state, and does so at specific temperatures (the melting point and the boiling point). All changes of state involve the transfer of heat. Can the particle theory explain water changing from solid ice to a liquid, and then to a gas?

The Warming Curve for Pure Ice

When you heat an ice-water mixture and graph your results, you observe a pattern similar to the diagram on these pages. The particle theory can explain the features of the graph.

Melting

According to the particle theory, when particles of a substance are heated, they absorb energy and increase their motion. Because of this motion they take up more space, and the solid expands. If the particles vibrate quickly enough, they will break free from the fixed pattern and the substance becomes a liquid.

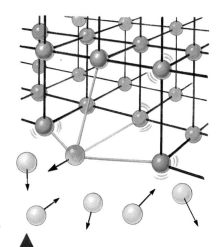

At the melting point, particles start to break free of the solid structure.

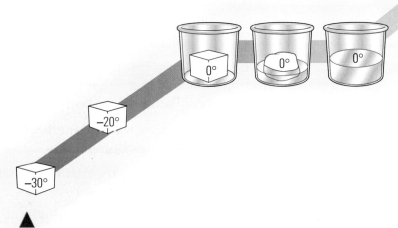

According to the particle theory, particles of water are in a fixed arrangement between −30°C and 0°C. As the temperature approaches 0°C, the particles absorb more heat and vibrate more, but not enough to break free from one another.

At 0°C, some particles absorb enough energy to vibrate so much that they break out of the fixed arrangement. As heating continues, the particles absorb more energy, so more and more of them increase their motion. The attractive forces cannot maintain the solid state. This process continues until all the particles are in the liquid state.

Vaporization

Particles in the liquid state also absorb energy as the temperature rises. The particles move faster and the space between them increases. Because the attractive force is weaker when the particles are farther apart, particles with enough energy (particularly those near the surface) can escape from the liquid. These particles are now gas particles: they have evaporated. When enough heat has been added, all the particles will have enough energy to vaporize into the gas state.

150°

120°

100°

100°

100°

100°

100°

100°

◀ All the particles have now changed their state to gas. Any additional heat will increase the speed of the particles, causing a rise in temperature.

▲
By 100°C, the energy of the particles is much higher. They are moving very rapidly. Some particles have enough energy that they can actually break away from the liquid. They have entered the gas state.

◀ At 100°C, every addition of energy permits more particles to break free. Sometimes the number of particles escaping is so large that you can see groups of them rising to the surface in the form of bubbles—the liquid is boiling.

▶
At the boiling point, particles of the liquid are moving fast enough to escape.

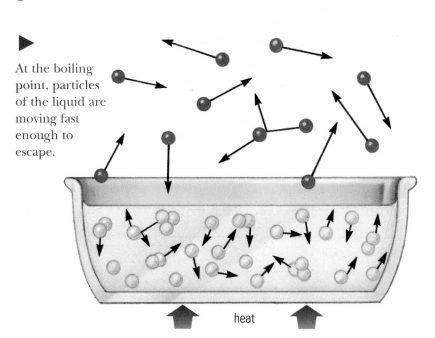

heat

SELF CHECK

Use the particle theory to answer the following questions.

3. How do bubbles form when liquids are boiled?

4. What is the difference between evaporation and boiling?

5. Why does the temperature of ice water remain constant during melting?

6. Why does the volume of water expand between 10°C and 90°C?

7. What happens when steam particles from a pot of boiling water strike cold air?

8. Which has more energy: ice at 0°C or water at 0°C? Explain.

Making Crystals

WHEN A SOLUTE is added to water, it dissolves, forming a solution. Is it possible to get the solute back out of the solution? In this investigation, you will study the process of evaporation of a solution, and you will have the opportunity to grow crystals.

CAUTION: Bluestone is toxic if ingested and a strong irritant. Report any spills to your teacher.

Materials

- safety goggles
- apron
- beaker
- hot water
- 30 g crushed bluestone (copper sulphate crystals)
- scoopula
- stirring rod
- evaporating dish
- crystal of bluestone
- saturated solution of bluestone (from Part 1)
- 10-cm thread
- plastic wrap

Procedure

Part 1   *Evaporating a Solution*

1 Put on your safety goggles and apron.

2 Pour about 30 mL of hot water into your beaker.

(a) Why is hot water used?

3 Slowly add a small amount of the bluestone to the water, using a scoopula. Stir with a stirring rod.

(b) Why is stirring important?

(c) Describe the appearance of your solution.

Step 3

4 Continue adding bluestone, while stirring, until no more dissolves. You have prepared a saturated solution. A **saturated solution** is one in which no more solute will dissolve.

(d) What evidence do you have that no more solute can dissolve?

5 Obtain a clean, dry evaporating dish and label it. Carefully pour some of the saturated bluestone solution into the dish. Do not completely fill the dish. (Keep the rest of your solution. You will need the beaker of solution for Part 2 of this investigation.)

(e) What makes this dish suitable for studying evaporation?

Step 5

6 Allow the solution to evaporate over the next few days.

(f) Could you speed up the process of evaporation? How?

(g) Record daily observations as the solution in the dish evaporates.

Part 2 *Growing Crystals*

7 Tie one end of a piece of thread around a small crystal of bluestone. Tie the other end around a stirring rod. Leave the thread long enough so you can suspend the crystal in the middle of your saturated bluestone solution in the beaker.

Step 7

(h) Why is it important to use a saturated solution?

8 Lay the stirring rod across the top of the beaker, immersing the crystal in the middle of the solution. Cover the top of the beaker with plastic wrap.

Step 8

(i) Record your daily observations of the solution and the crystal in a data table. Include a sketch to illustrate the colour, estimated size, and shape of the crystal.

9 Label your beaker and store it where it will not be disturbed. Examine it each day for several days. Wash your hands before leaving the laboratory.

(j) Record your daily observations in your table.

Questions

1. In Part 1 of the investigation, what part of the solution evaporated? What happened to it?

2. What was left behind in the dish? Explain.

3. In terms of the particle theory, explain why stirring and using hot water were important in this experiment.

4. The starter crystal of bluestone that you used in Part 2 is often called a seed crystal. Suggest why this name is appropriate.

5. Could you keep growing your bluestone crystal in the same beaker of solution indefinitely? Explain.

6. In terms of the particle theory, explain how the crystal grew in size and shape.

7. As your crystal grew, what changes did you notice in your solution? Explain your observations in terms of the particle theory.

8. How did the shape of your crystal compare with that of other crystals grown by your classmates? Suggest reasons for similarities and differences.

Extension

9. Devise a method for growing a very large bluestone crystal.

10. Have you ever been in a cave that has stalactites (deposits that hang from the ceiling)? The following procedure may help you understand how these deposits are formed in nature. Put on your apron and safety goggles. Prepare a saturated solution of Epsom salts. Pour the solution into two medium-size beakers or jars. Tie two washers together with a piece of string and place them into the beakers, as shown in the diagram. Research how stalactites are formed in nature.

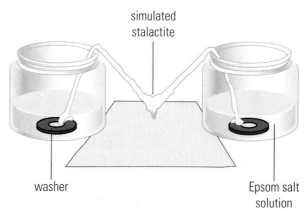

simulated stalactite

washer

Epsom salt solution

The Great Diffusion Race

IF YOU OPEN A BOTTLE OF PERFUME near the back of your classroom, the students near you will soon notice, and eventually everyone in the room will smell the scent. This is an example of diffusion. **Diffusion** is the gradual spreading of a substance from an area where it is highly concentrated to an area where the concentration is lower.

The Race Is On

Imagine a Great Diffusion Race that has three particle contestants: Solid, Liquid, and Gas. The winner is the one who crosses the finish line first. Each contestant attempts to travel through water, but the water is in different states.

Solid attempts the ice course; Liquid tries to drift through the water course; and Gas gets set to roar through the vapour trail. Who wins? Who doesn't even leave the starting block?

The Great Diffusion Race

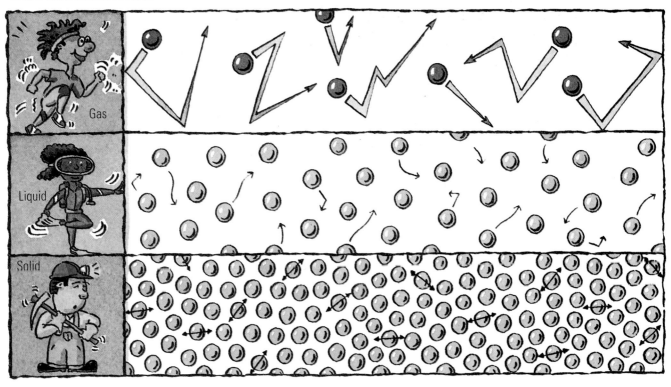

Diffusion in Gases

If you picked the gas as a winner you're absolutely right! In the vapour state, there are lots of spaces between the water particles, which means fewer obstacles in the way. The particles are not strongly attracted to each other because they are far from each other and moving quickly, so a gas particle is not greatly influenced by surrounding particles. Gas particles travel at high speed—they have lots of energy and cover great distances in a very short time. When collisions occur, the particles react like billiard balls, bouncing off one another at high speed.

Diffusion in Liquids

In the liquid state, there is reasonable room for movement in the spaces between particles. Lots of collisions frequently change the direction of travel of a particle. There is rolling and tumbling motion, with moderate energy and speed. Overall, liquids show a slow and steady movement pattern.

Diffusion in Solids

The very features that give solids their definite shape and volume also make diffusion very difficult. The attraction between the particles is so strong that they simply vibrate, held in a fixed structure. The space between the particles is not enough to let other particles through easily. Diffusion occurs in solids with great difficulty.

TRY THIS

Particle Size and Diffusion

Using a medicine dropper, place two drops of vanilla in a balloon. (Be careful not to get any vanilla on the outside of the balloon or on your fingers.) Hold the balloon downward, so the vanilla does not touch your mouth, and begin inflating the balloon. Tie the end of the balloon. Move the balloon progressively closer to your lab partner until she or he can detect the smell of vanilla.

- How does the smell get outside the balloon?

  Repeat the procedure using scented oils and perfumes.

- Which of these particles move through the balloon?

- How would the size of the particle affect diffusion through the balloon?

SELF CHECK

9. What is diffusion? Give two examples.
10. How does diffusion differ in the three states of matter?
11. You wake up one morning to the smell of freshly brewed coffee, but the only coffee in your home is in the kitchen. Explain this observation in terms of the particle theory.
12. Propane gas is clear, colourless, and almost odourless. Why is an easily smelled substance usually mixed with propane?

Diffusion of Potassium Permanganate

HOW DOES TEMPERATURE affect the rate of diffusion? In this investigation, you will compare the rate at which a solution of potassium permanganate spreads throughout a petri dish filled with water, at two different temperatures.

CAUTION: Potassium permanganate stains skin and clothes. Handle it with tweezers.

Materials

- safety goggles
- apron
- petri dish
- thermometer
- tweezers
- 2 similar crystals of potassium permanganate
- grid paper (5 sheets)
- timing device (stopwatch, clock, etc.)

Procedure

1 Prepare a data table as shown, with time increasing by 30 s in each row until you reach 600 s.

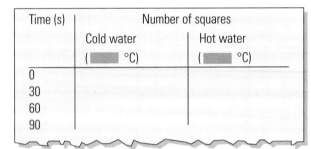

Time (s)	Number of squares	
	Cold water (___ °C)	Hot water (___ °C)
0		
30		
60		
90		

2 Put on your apron and safety goggles. Half-fill a petri dish with cold water. Dry the bottom of the petri dish with a paper towel.

3 Use a thermometer to measure the temperature of the water in the dish.

(a) Record the starting water temperature in the data table.

Step 3

4 Take two sheets of grid paper and make a dot at the centre of each. Place the petri dish on one sheet, centred on the dot. Keep the other sheet for your contour map.

(b) Label your contour map "Diffusion in Cold Water."

5 As a team, discuss how you will conduct the experiment accurately and efficiently. Every 30 s, you are to count the number of squares covered by the dye, and sketch the contour pattern on the second sheet of grid paper. While you are working, you will have to be careful not to move the dish. Touching the dish or brushing against the desk could disturb the water.

(c) How could disturbing the water affect your investigation?

6 After waiting until the water is still, use tweezers to gently place a single crystal of potassium permanganate in the water directly above the dot on the grid paper. Begin your timed observations for your contour lines as soon as the crystal hits the surface of the water (time = zero), and every 30 s for 10 min.

(d) Each 30 s, record in the second column of your data table the number of squares covered by the coloured solution.

(e) Each 30 s, draw on your contour map the area covered by the solution.

Step 6

7 Dispose of the contents of the dish in the sink and rinse the dish with running water.

8 Repeat the experiment using the same petri dish, half-filled with hot water, and a crystal of potassium permanganate similar in size to the one you used earlier. As before, put a sheet of grid paper with a centre dot below the petri dish, and keep a fresh sheet ready for your contour map. Record your observations in the third column of the data table.

(f) Note the starting temperature of the hot water before you place the crystal in the water. Then record observations as you did before.

9 Clean and return all equipment. Wash your hands.

10 Prepare a line graph of time and diffusion using the results of this experiment. Graph the results for hot and cold water on the same sheet of grid paper. (For more information on drawing line graphs, see the Skills Handbook on page 512.)

Questions

1. (a) At which temperature did the permanganate diffuse more quickly?

(b) How is this shown in the contour maps that you produced? How is it shown in the line graphs?

2. Make a concluding statement for this investigation.

Apply

3. What were two sources of error in this investigation? Could you have corrected them? How?

4. How can the particle theory help to explain your results?

Extension

5. Put on your apron and safety goggles. Prepare a gelatin solution (follow directions on the package) and pour the solution into two petri dishes. Allow the gelatin to set for 24 h. Once the gelatin is firm, use a cork punch to remove a small piece from the centre of the petri dishes. Using a medicine dropper, add a single drop of methylene blue indicator to each of the holes.

CAUTION: Methylene blue is toxic. If there is a spill, wear gloves to clean it up, and wash the area of the spill with water.

Replace the lids on each of the dishes. Place one petri dish in a cupboard and the other in a refrigerator. Predict and sketch what you might observe in each dish after 24 h. Examine the dishes 24 h later.

(a) Does the methylene blue move in all directions equally?

(b) Provide a possible explanation for your observation.

(c) Compare the petri dishes maintained at different temperatures. How are they similar? How are they different?

(d) Draw a conclusion from your comparison.

(e) Compare the rate of diffusion between the potassium permanganate in water and the methylene blue in gelatin. Provide a possible explanation for the differences that you observed.

A Global Environmental Hazard

WHAT GIVES THAT SHARP, tangy smell to the air after a thunderstorm? What protects you whenever you step into sunlight? Ozone—a gas you wouldn't want to breathe and yet you can't live without.

What is Ozone?

Ozone is a pale blue gas that is formed by the action of sunlight on oxygen. Ozone is also formed by lightning and as a side effect of pollutants released from automobile engines.

Ozone and Sunlight

Sunlight contains ultraviolet (UV) radiation. UV radiation causes skin cancer, decreases the body's resistance to diseases, and can blind unprotected eyes. It also harms plant life. Fortunately, less than 10% of the Sun's UV radiation passes through the atmosphere. The reason is ozone.

The Ozone Killer

Chlorofluorocarbons (CFCs) seemed safe when they were invented in the 1930s—they didn't break down and they weren't harmful to living things. CFCs were used to clean, to cool, and to dissolve other substances. The first CFC, Freon, is probably the coolant in your refrigerator at home.

Slowly, CFCs worked their way up through the atmosphere. After 60 years, the first CFCs reached the ozone layer, where an unexpected reaction took place. UV radiation released chlorine particles from the CFCs. And each chlorine particle broke apart 100 000 particles of ozone. An ozone killer was on the loose. Could it be stopped?

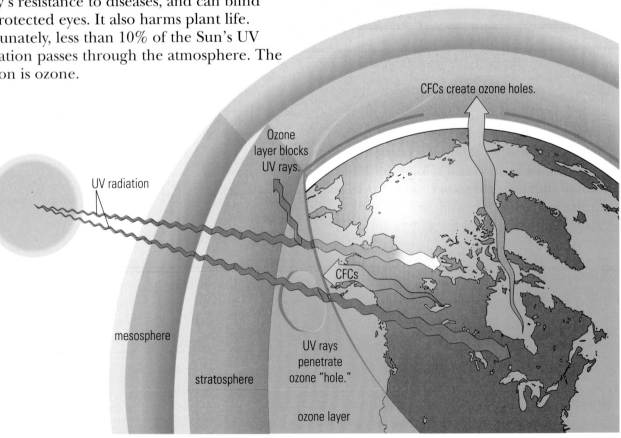

CFCs create ozone holes.

Ozone layer blocks UV rays.

UV radiation

CFCs

mesosphere

stratosphere

UV rays penetrate ozone "hole."

ozone layer

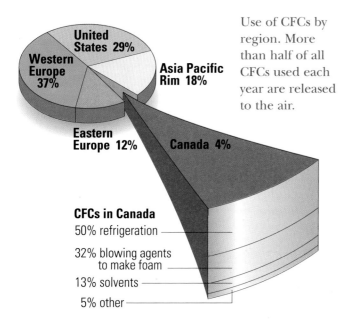

Use of CFCs by region. More than half of all CFCs used each year are released to the air.

United States 29%

Western Europe 37%

Asia Pacific Rim 18%

Eastern Europe 12%

Canada 4%

CFCs in Canada

50% refrigeration

32% blowing agents to make foam

13% solvents

5% other

The Montréal Protocol

Recognizing the need to stop CFCs from reaching the ozone layer, over 100 countries signed the Montréal Protocol—agreeing to stop making CFCs by January 1996. Equipment that already contains CFCs was not banned, because of the expense, because the technology to completely replace CFCs is not developed yet, and because the technology that depends on CFCs, especially the refrigeration of food and medicine, is too important to people's lives to just shut down.

For some equipment, there is no perfect replacement for CFCs. A short-term solution is to use a less harmful substance. By modifying existing equipment, HFCs (hydrofluorocarbons) can be used. HFCs are less harmful to the ozone layer than CFCs, but they are dangerous to living things. So they must be handled carefully and kept from entering the atmosphere.

Understanding the Author

1. What is the effect of ozone in the upper atmosphere? How does this effect benefit living things?
2. Why are CFCs now considered dangerous?
3. Why did it take so long for people to recognize the dangers of CFCs? What does this mean for the CFCs being released into the atmosphere today?

Issue

CFCs should be banned by 2000. All refrigerators, air conditioning systems, manufacturing uses, etc., must be converted to some other substance.

Benefits

Opinion of an atmospheric scientist If we ban CFCs, damage to the ozone layer may stop getting worse within a few decades, instead of over a century.

Opinion of a dermatologist The sooner CFC use is ended, the less the damage to the health of people. The rate of skin cancer may keep on climbing unless we do something now.

Risks

Opinion of a consumer group If there is a ban, many people who can't afford it will have to buy new fridges and air conditioners. Besides, how do we know that the substitutes for CFCs are any safer? We used to think CFCs were safe.

Opinion of a highrise owner Each of my apartment buildings has a large air conditioner. Each one uses half a tonne of CFCs every year, and about 10% of that escapes into the air. But it would cost $200 000 to replace each one. I'd have to raise the rent for all my tenants.

What Do You Think?

4. Should Canada ban CFCs? Should Canada stick to the Montréal Protocol? Is there another alternative? Here are some questions you may want to consider.

- Old equipment is being replaced with equipment that doesn't use CFCs as it breaks down. Is this adequate? Should the switch happen more quickly?

- Should we wait for a better replacement for CFCs?

Key Outcomes

Now that you have completed this chapter, can you do the following? If not, review the sections indicated.

- Show an understanding of how models and theories are helpful in science. (3.1)

- List the main points of the particle theory. (3.2)

- Design and safely perform a controlled experiment as a member of a cooperative team. (3.3, 3.5, 3.7)

- Use the particle theory to explain the properties of each of the three states of matter. (3.2)

- Use the particle theory to explain dissolving, changes of state, crystal formation, and diffusion. (3.3, 3.4, 3.5, 3.6, 3.7)

Key Terms

model

hypothesis

theory

Particle Theory of Matter

dissolve

solution

solute

solvent

saturated solution

diffusion

Review

1. Name the five main points of the Particle Theory of Matter.

2. From the diagrams below, choose the best diagram to illustrate each point of the particle theory.

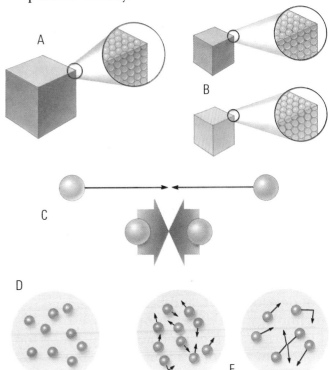

3. Name the following states of matter.

    (a) This state has a rigid arrangement of particles.

    (b) This state has the greatest amount of particle movement.

    (c) This state has the least distance between particles.

Problem Solving

4. Use the particle theory to answer the following questions.

    (a) Why is salt left behind during the evaporation of salt water?

    (b) Why do crystals have characteristic shapes?

5. When Celine was preparing a pitcher of lemonade for her friends, she added 25 mL of lemon powder mix to 1000 mL of very cold water and tasted the mixture. She then poured out glasses for her friends, serving herself last. Then she added ice cubes to each glass. She noticed several things, listed below. Explain each of her observations in terms of the particle theory. Include a small diagram with each answer.

   (a) Before tasting, the total volume of lemonade was 1005 mL. Celine had expected to get 1025 mL.

   (b) The lemon powder dissolved slowly at first, but more quickly when she stirred the lemonade.

   (c) When she drank from her glass, the lemonade was sweeter than when she first tasted it.

   (d) The ice cubes that she added to each glass floated to the top of the glass.

6. Consider a kernel of popcorn before and after it has been popped. Compare its shape and volume before and after popping. Account for the similarities and differences using the particle theory.

7. Ramon dropped a small amount of potassium permanganate into a graduated cylinder, and the same amount of quartz into another cylinder. The cylinders held equal amounts of water, at room temperature. Twenty minutes later, Ramon drew the two cylinders.

potassium permanganate quartz

(a) What is happening in the cylinder on the left? Use the particle theory to help you answer the question.

(b) Explain how the particles of the two solids must be different.

Critical Thinking

8. Draw a concept map to illustrate your understanding of the particle theory. Put "matter" in the centre.

   (For a review of how to make a concept map, see the Skills Handbook on page 502.)

9. In terms of the particle theory, explain the following statements.

   (a) Solids have a hard, rigid shape.

   (b) Liquids boil.

   (c) Liquids freeze.

   (d) Gases always fill their containers.

   (e) A liquid can be poured.

10. Can the particle model boldly go where no one has gone before? Write a brief science fiction story to explain the technology behind the Star Trek transporter unit in terms of the particle model, or a better model of your own design.

ASK YOURSELF

Return to the Getting Started at the beginning of this chapter. Now that you have a model for matter, review each of your answers. How does the Particle Theory of Matter compare with the model for matter that you first created?

Trapping CFCs

DUSANKA FILIPOVIC is the co-founder of a new company, Halozone Technologies Inc., based in Mississauga. Her understanding of the properties of matter led to her pioneering work on the capture and recycling of CFCs (chlorofluorocarbons).

◀ Dusanka Filipovic won the prestigious Association of Ontario Engineers Award for the development of the Blue Bottle technology.

Q. Where did you grow up and go to school?

A. I graduated in engineering from the University of Belgrade, in the former country of Yugoslavia. After arriving in Canada about 20 years ago, I began working for Union Carbide. Eventually, I became manager of new business development.

Q. How did you become interested in CFC recycling?

A. I love solving problems. That's how I discover most of my new product ideas. When the information came out that CFCs were damaging the ozone layer of the atmosphere, I knew that here was a problem I wanted to do something about. What could be done right now to stop more CFCs from being released into the atmosphere?

Q. What was your approach?

A. I worked with a team of other researchers. We wanted to develop a technology similar to the blue box used in many towns and cities for recycling glass, newspaper, and other wastes from homes. The blue box is easy for people to use, which is very important, and it collects materials that are valuable. The result of our work was our trademark "Blue Bottle"—a way to collect and recycle CFCs from all sorts of cooling equipment.

Q. Why would you want to recycle CFCs?

A. New CFCs will not be made in most countries of the world, because their governments have agreed to this. But over $200 billion of equipment still needs CFCs in order to work. For example, there are CFCs in every old air conditioner and refrigerator. When these devices are repaired, the CFCs are removed. Fresh CFCs are added once the repairs are done. Using our Blue Bottle technology, the CFCs that are removed during the repairs can now be collected and reused.

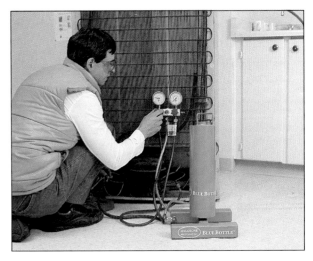

In order to repair a refrigerator, the CFC coolant must be removed and fresh CFC added. In the past, about 10% to 20% of the old CFC escaped into the air. Using the Blue Bottle, none of the CFC escapes.

Q. How does the Blue Bottle work?

A. The bottle is filled with a substance that looks like tiny beads. Each bead contains microscopic holes that are exactly the right size to trap CFC particles. The beads work so well that essentially all of the CFCs can be collected.

Q. How can you tell when the bottle is full?

A. First, the bottle warms up, because the CFCs release a little heat as they enter the "trap." The second way is to monitor the mass of the bottle. We know how much mass will be added by the CFCs.

Q. What happens then?

A. Distributors pick up the bottles, just as blue boxes are picked up by recycling trucks. The CFCs are flushed out of the bottles and collected. The bottles can be used again—and we have fresh CFCs ready for whoever needs them.

Q. Why did you form your company Halozone?

A. I realized we had something quite special on our hands. I negotiated with Union Carbide to form my own company to market the Blue Bottle process. With help from the Canadian government, we built a pilot plan and began trying the product. It worked even better than we hoped! Now I'm travelling around Canada and the world telling people about the Blue Bottle process. No one who uses CFCs wants to harm the environment, but very few companies can afford to change equipment until it wears out. They can see that the Blue Bottle is a great solution to their problem. It's tremendously satisfying.

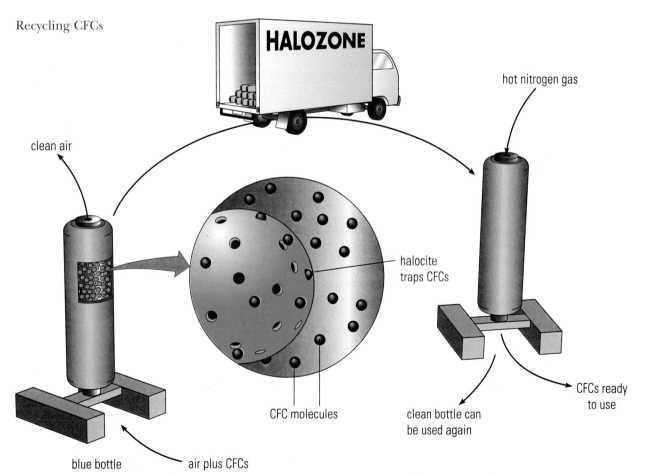

Recycling CFCs

clean air

HALOZONE

hot nitrogen gas

halocite traps CFCs

CFC molecules

CFCs ready to use

clean bottle can be used again

blue bottle   air plus CFCs

"If all goes well, within 20 years there will be no CFCs to recycle. We designed the Blue Bottle process so it can also be used to recycle the new substances being developed to replace CFCs."

NOW THAT YOU HAVE COMPLETED Chapters 1, 2, and 3, you can assess your understanding of the Structure of Matter by trying these questions.

Before you begin, you may find it useful to return to the Chapter Review. There, you will find lists of Key Outcomes and Key Terms. Read these to ensure that you understand the main points and the important vocabulary of the chapters. If necessary, look back at the appropriate sections in the text, which are listed with the Key Outcomes.

Write your answers to the questions in your notebook.

True/False

For each of the following, write T if the statement is true. If the statement is false, rewrite it to make it true.

1. If you measure the length of an object in centimetres, you have made a qualitative observation.

2. The density of a substance increases as the size of a sample gets larger.

3. Wood floats because its density is greater than that of water.

4. The volume of a liquid in a graduated cylinder should always be read from the bottom of the meniscus.

5. The freezing point of all substances is 0°C.

6. Melting and condensation are two changes of state that require energy.

7. Sugar dissolves faster in hot water than in cold water.

8. If a liquid has a measured density of 1.2 g/mL, the liquid is probably water.

Completion

Copy the following sentences, filling in each blank with the word or phrase that correctly completes the sentence. Use words from this list: added, condensation, crystals, freezing, gas, stronger, weaker, different, same, liquid, mass, melting, motion, particles, qualitative, quantitative, solid, space, spaces, volume. (You will not need to use all of the words.)

9. Matter is anything that has ▇ and occupies ▇.

10. Matter occurs in three states: ▇ , ▇ , and ▇.

11. ▇ observations involve measurements.

12. Density is a measurement of the mass per unit ▇ of a substance.

13. The change of state from a liquid to a solid is called ▇.

14. The particle theory suggests that:

- All matter is made up of ▇.

- Different substances are made of ▇ particles.

- There are ▇ between particles.

- Particles are always in ▇.

- Attractions between particles are ▇ when the particles are closer together.

15. In order for a change of state to occur, energy must be ▇ or removed.

Matching

Copy the numbers of the descriptions given below. Beside each number, write the word from the right column that best fits the description. (You will not need to use all of the words.)

16. characteristic used to describe or identify a substance

17. keeps its volume and shape when placed in a different container

18. the amount of material in a substance relative to the volume of space it occupies

19. the process that causes particles to spread evenly throughout another substance

20. absorbed or released when a substance changes state

21. the change of state from a solid directly to a gas

A density

B matter

C boiling

D condensation

E energy

F sublimation

G property

H diffusion

I solid

Multiple Choice

Write the letter of the best answer for each of the following questions. Write only one answer for each.

22. Substance X has a definite mass and a definite volume, but takes the shape of its container. What is the most likely state of substance X?

    A solid   **D** solid or liquid

    B liquid   **E** liquid or gas

    C gas

23. Refer to the table on page 59. Which of the following will sink in water?

    A an ice cube   **D** vegetable oil

    B magnesium   **E** balsa wood

    C gasoline

Use the following graphs to answer Questions 24–26.

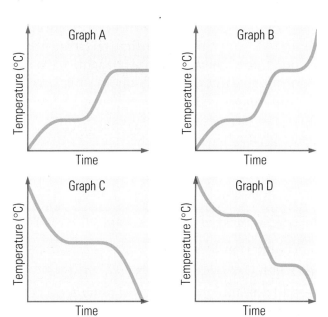

24. Glycerin has a melting point of 18°C and a boiling point of 90°C. If you warmed glycerin from 0°C to 400°C, the graph of the results would have a shape similar to

    A graph A.   **D** graph D.

    B graph B.   **E** none of the above graphs.

    C graph C.

25. If you cooled steam from 200°C to –100°C, the graph of the results would have a shape similar to

    A graph A.   **D** graph D.

    B graph B.   **E** none of the above graphs.

    C graph C.

26. If you warmed a block of ice from –100°C to 100°C, the graph of the results would have a shape similar to

    A graph A.   **D** graph D.

    B graph B.   **E** none of the above graphs.

    C graph C.

Short Answer

Write a sentence or a short paragraph to answer each of the following questions.

27. Why do you think quantitative rather than qualitative physical properties are preferred when identifying an unknown substance?

28. List the equipment you would need to determine the following.

(a) the volume of a block of wood

(b) the volume of a stone

(c) the mass of a large crystal

(d) the density of cola

29. A dry golf ball was placed on a balance and a reading of 115 g was obtained. When the golf ball was submerged in an overflow can, 50 mL of water overflowed. What is the density of the golf ball?

30. Explain the following events using the particle model.

(a) A balloon expands when heated.

(b) Substances diffuse faster when heated.

(c) Solids keep a rigid shape in any container.

(d) When heated, a solid melts into a liquid.

(e) A balloon filled with carbon dioxide sinks to the floor.

31. Explain how a solid air freshener works, in terms of diffusion and changes of state.

32. Describe the following substances, including at least four of their physical properties.

(a) maple syrup   (d) water

(b) brown sugar   (e) oxygen

(c) dry ice

Problem Solving

33. Explain why it is easier to open the metal lid on a pickle jar after the lid has been held under running hot water.

34. An Erlenmeyer flask has a mass of 15.2 g when empty, and 47.6 g when full of water. The same flask has a mass of 39.8 g when completely filled with liquid X.

(a) What is the mass of water in the flask?

(b) What is the volume of the flask?

(c) What is the density of liquid X?

35. The table below shows the data recorded when a sample of an unknown solid was heated from −40°C to 120°C. Of the following substances, which is most likely to be the unknown substance: ethanol, brine (a solution of salt in water), water, or glycerin? Give reasons for your answer.

Time (min)	Temperature (°C)	Time (min)	Temperature (°C)
0	−40	9	60
1	−20	10	80
2	0	11	100
3	0	12	100
4	0	13	100
5	0	14	100
6	0	15	100
7	20	16	120
8	40		

Challenge

36. Have you ever noticed that honey, once it starts to crystallize, rapidly becomes solid? It may remain liquid for months, then solidify in a week. Explain why solidification happens so quickly.

37. A glass of water contains billions of water molecules, and you will drink many thousands of glasses of water in your lifetime. Could you drink the same molecule twice? Write a short story or poem explaining why or why not.

38. Modern materials have some useful qualities. For example, Gortex fabric has openings that allow water vapour to pass through, but not ice pellets or liquid droplets. This makes it ideal for rainwear. Design a fabric for each of the following uses, giving a list of the properties of your material.

(a) a fabric that firefighters could wear

(b) a fabric that could be used by athletes in a winter sport

(c) a material that could be used to build a kayak

39. Examine the diagram of the water cycle.

(a) Where does the energy for evaporation come from?

(b) What causes water vapour to condense in the atmosphere?

(c) Why do you think rain falls from some clouds but not from others?

40. Water is unusual: its solid state is less dense than its liquid state. In most substances, the solid state is denser than the liquid state. If ice were more dense than water, how do you think this would affect plants, animals, humans, and the climate in Canada?

Design and Do

41. Design an energy-efficient refrigeration unit for a recreational vehicle used for summer camping trips.

Project Ideas

42. Design and conduct an experiment to compare a porous clay pot, an ice bucket, and a styrofoam sleeve for keeping various substances cool over a given length of time.

43. In a group, design and conduct an experiment to determine the density of dairy products (skim milk, 2% milk, whole milk, chocolate milk, whipping cream, ice cream, sour cream, cream cheese, butter, etc.). Create a display for your findings. (You may want to use a computer.)

The water cycle

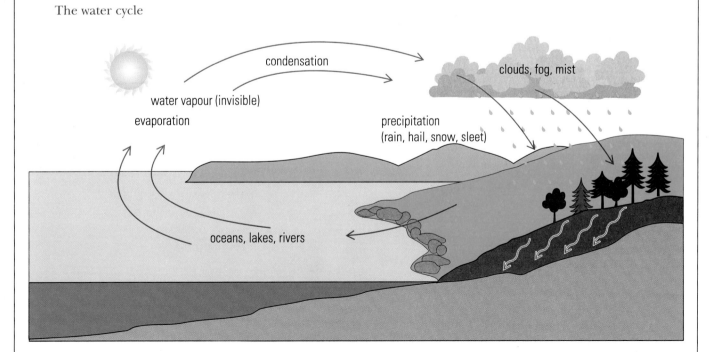

UNIT 2

Changes in Matter

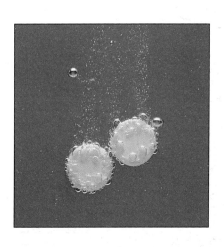

CHAPTER 4

Matter in Mixtures

WATER DRIPS SLOWLY IN AN UNDERGROUND cave, as it has for thousands of years. Each drop carries more than water alone. It is a mixture of water and dissolved substances from the soil and rock above the cave.

As each drop slides down the rock, some of the water gradually evaporates into the air. As it evaporates, the substances carried in the water are left behind. They cling, solid, to the surface of the rock, forming more of the rock itself.

Under a waterfall the same process works, only in reverse. There, rock gradually erodes away as it dissolves into the water.

Such cycles happen everywhere in nature. Liquids, solids, and gases are constantly mixing and separating.

In this chapter, you will

- classify matter as either pure substances or various kinds of mixtures,

- learn how different mixtures can be formed and how they can be separated into their components, and

- discover how to apply these methods to solve problems, including that of providing clean water.

 Getting Started

1. Suppose you take a pail, lower it into a lake or a river, and lift it out full of water. What do you think you have in the pail besides water? In a small group, list as many substances as you can think of that might be in the water. Put your list in one column of a table. In the second column, indicate whether your group thinks that the substance is harmful or harmless to human health.

2. How could you make this water safe to drink? Discuss how you might separate the substances on your list from the water in the pail. In the third column of your table, describe how you think each substance could be removed.

Pure Substances and Mixtures

WHY ARE CLASSIFICATION systems needed? If you keep your school subjects in separate notebooks, you are using a classification system. Classification systems are ways of organizing things so they are easier to understand or use.

In a similar way, a classification system can help you better understand the variety of matter around you. One simple system is to classify a sample of matter as being either a pure substance or a mixture.

Pure Substances

A **pure substance** contains only one kind of particle. For example, a piece of aluminum foil contains only aluminum particles. Sugar is a pure substance. It contains only sugar particles. A scoop of sugar made from Canadian sugar beets contains exactly the same kind of particles as a scoop of sugar made from Australian sugar cane.

pure substance

Mixtures

A **mixture** contains at least two pure substances, or two different types of particles. When you drink a glass of milk or eat bread, you are consuming mixtures of different substances. Most common substances are mixtures.

pure substance

Making Mixtures

By mixing different substances, people can take advantage of the properties of each substance. For example, table salt is a mixture. It is mainly a pure substance called sodium chloride. But it also has a small amount of potassium iodide added, to prevent a disease called goitre.

mixture

Pure substances have only one type of particle; mixtures have two or more types of particles.

Changing the Properties of a Mixture

The properties of any mixture can be changed by varying the amount of each substance in the mixture. Some substances are dangerous, but the same properties that make them dangerous may also make them useful in a mixture. For example, benzoyl peroxide can harm skin. But skin medications may contain small amounts of benzoyl peroxide mixed with other substances. Why? Because in small amounts, benzoyl peroxide kills the bacteria that cause acne, without damaging the skin.

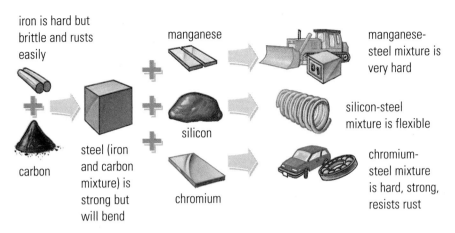

iron is hard but brittle and rusts easily

carbon

steel (iron and carbon mixture) is strong but will bend

manganese

manganese-steel mixture is very hard

silicon

silicon-steel mixture is flexible

chromium

chromium-steel mixture is hard, strong, resists rust

Adding pure substances to a mixture changes the properties of the mixture.

TECHNOLOGY-LINK

Just the Right Mix

What do bone and the pole being used by the athlete in this photograph have in common? Each combines strength with the ability to resist breaking.

The fibreglass in the athlete's pole is strengthened with fibres of graphite. Similarly, the bone in your body is a mixture of calcium phosphate with protein fibres scattered throughout to help prevent the bone from breaking. Predict what might happen to bone if the calcium is removed.

- Clean all the meat from a chicken or turkey leg bone. Try to bend the bone without breaking it.

- Place the bone in a glass jar and add enough vinegar to cover the bone. Put a lid on the jar. Change the vinegar in the jar every few days.

- After two weeks, try to bend the bone again. Explain your observations. What has the vinegar removed? (If you wish, you can continue this procedure until you can tie the bone into a knot.)

SELF CHECK

1. Explain, with an example, the difference between a pure substance and a mixture.

2. Describe, with a reason, whether each of the following is a pure substance or a mixture.
   (a) lettuce and tomato salad
   (b) air
   (c) wood
   (d) tap water
   (e) chalk

3. Practise classifying matter by looking at the labels of products in your home. Make a list of 10 products you find in your home. Which products are pure substances? Which products are mixtures? Which of the products contain a substance that might be dangerous on its own?

4. By changing the amount of a substance in a mixture, the properties of the mixture can also be changed. Match each mixture from Column A with the appropriate type of clothing from Column B. Use these clues:
   - Cotton absorbs moisture and is a good insulator, but wears out quickly.
   - Nylon does not absorb moisture and is a poor insulator, but it is very strong and long-lasting.

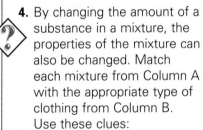

Column A:	Column B:
20% cotton, 80% nylon	socks
	fall jacket
50% cotton, 50% nylon	T-shirt
80% cotton, 20% nylon	

Looking at Mixtures

S O FAR, YOU HAVE BEEN CLASSIFYING matter as either a pure substance or a mixture. But how would you classify mixtures that appear to be different? In this investigation, you will examine several different mixtures and develop a classification system of your own.

Materials

- safety goggles
- apron
- small scoop
- white beans
- sugar
- clay
- pieces of paper (10 cm × 10 cm)
- hand magnifier
- 10 test tubes
- test-tube rack
- water
- 4 stirring rods or stir sticks
- laundry starch
- cooking oil
- stopper
- liquid detergent
- medicine dropper

Procedure

1. Put on your apron and safety goggles.

2. Make a table for your observations like the one below.

Mixtures

Substances mixed	Observations before mixing	Observations after mixing
1. beans and water		
2. sugar and water		
3. clay and water		
4.		

3. Place a small scoop (about 0.5 g) each of beans, sugar, and clay onto separate pieces of paper. Use a hand magnifier to look closely at each of the substances.

   (a) Record your observations in your table.

Step 3

4. Half-fill three test tubes with water. Add the beans to one test tube, the sugar to another, and the clay to the third. Stir each for about 30 s. Observe each of the mixtures, noting how the substances mix and the appearance of the mixture.

   (b) Record your observations in your table.

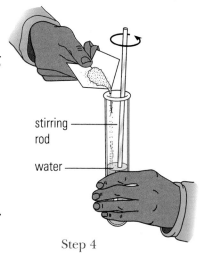

stirring rod

water

Step 4

5. Put a small scoop of dry laundry starch on a piece of paper and examine the starch with a hand lens.

   (c) Record your observations of the starch in your table.

6 Add dry laundry starch to a depth of about 1 cm to a clean, dry test tube. Add enough water to half-fill the test tube. Stir thoroughly.

(d) Record your observations of the mixture in your table.

— 1 cm of dry starch

Step 6

7 Put two other clean, dry test tubes in the rack. Put water in one to a depth of about 1 cm. Put the same amount of cooking oil in the second tube, and observe the oil.

(e) Record your observations in your table.

8 Pour the cooking oil into the test tube holding the water.

(f) Record your observations in your table.

9 Stopper the tube with the oil and water and shake the contents for 30 s. Allow the contents to settle.

(g) Record your observations in your table.

10 Remove the stopper and add a few drops of liquid detergent. Return the stopper to the tube and shake the mixture.

(h) Record your observations in your table.

(i) What effect did the detergent have on the mixture?

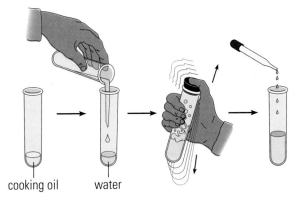

cooking oil   water

Steps 7 to 10

11 Dispose of your materials as directed by your teacher. Clean and return glassware and clean up your work station. Wash your hands.

Questions

1. After being stirred, which mixture or mixtures had the following physical properties?

(a) clear (transparent)

(b) cloudy (opaque)

(c) made up of separate components

2. In your group, decide on a simple system that allows you to classify and describe all the different mixtures you encountered in this investigation.

Apply

3. If possible, classify the following mixtures using your group's classification system.

(a) cheese and pepperoni pizza

(b) orange juice

(c) air

4. If any of the mixtures in question 3 cannot be classified in your system, how would you change your classification system so you can include them?

Extension

5. Try making mixtures of water with salt, cocoa, gelatin powder, and coffee in separate test tubes. Record your observations. Classify each mixture.

ASK YOURSELF

Think about how you could separate the substances from each mixture you made in this investigation. Rate each mixture as "easy to separate," "difficult to separate," or "probably cannot be separated." Explain why you rated each mixture as you did. You will have an opportunity later in this chapter to check your ideas.

Classifying Mixtures

IMAGINE YOU HAVE BEEN ASKED to identify an unknown sample of matter. You know that matter can be either a pure substance or a mixture. You are fairly certain that your sample is a mixture. But what type?

Classifying Matter

Pure Substances

A pure substance contains only one kind of particle.

Mixtures

If the particles mix very well with one another—so well that you can see only one phase—the mixture is called a **solution**. You say that one substance dissolves in another.

If the particles do not mix well with one another, you will see more than one phase. This type of mixture is called a **heterogeneous mixture**.

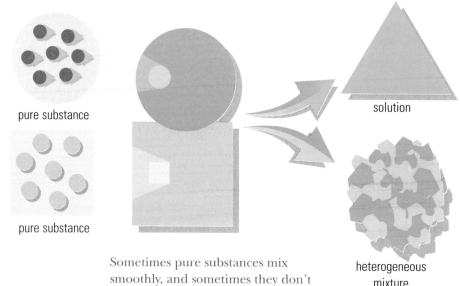

pure substance

pure substance

Sometimes pure substances mix smoothly, and sometimes they don't mix well.

solution

heterogeneous mixture

Solutions

Perhaps your mixture of matter is a solution, like sugar and water. If you add a small amount of sugar to water and stir, eventually the sugar will dissolve. You will be able to see only the water. The substance that dissolves (in this case sugar) is called the solute. The substance in which the solute dissolves (in this case water) is called the solvent.

A solution may be made up of liquids, solids, or gases. A solution is transparent if it is a gas or a liquid; if it is a solid, it looks the same throughout. Air is a solution of gases, and it is transparent if unpolluted. In air, nitrogen is the solvent and the other gases, such as oxygen, are solutes. Perfumes are liquid solutions; they are also transparent. A perfume is made of an alcohol base (the solvent) and fragrances (the solutes).

A solid solution of metals is called an alloy. The gold used in gold jewellery is actually a solution of metals, with gold as the solvent and copper and silver as the solutes. The gold alloy in jewellery looks the same throughout. Both big and small pieces of the alloy have the same properties.

Heterogeneous Mixtures

Your sample of matter may be a heterogeneous mixture, like Italian salad dressing. If you put salad dressing on lettuce, the oil, vinegar, and spices may be mixed together, but each part can be easily seen. There are other examples all around us. Garden soil, with its stones, sand, clay, and humus, is a heterogeneous mixture. So is garbage (plastic, metal, wood, cloth ...). Even air can be, if it is polluted with soot or is carrying dust.

What type of mixture is being produced? How do you know?

DID YOU KNOW?

A dry cleaning machine is like a regular washing machine, except that it does not use water. A different liquid solvent is used that is less likely to make clothing shrink. This solvent is better than water at dissolving grease and oil, but it is very expensive. Dry cleaners recycle and reuse the same solvent as long as possible.

TRY THIS

Analyzing Observations

Read the page of the student's notebook shown below, and then answer the following questions.

- Was the blue liquid in the dish a heterogeneous mixture, a solution, or a pure substance? Give a reason for your answer.
- What has happened to the liquid? Explain, using the particle theory in your explanation.

Investigation 1-1

On Friday we were given a clear blue liquid.

We poured some of the liquid into a shallow dish, and left it on the windowsill. On Monday there was

no liquid left, but the dish had some solid bright-blue

stuff in it.

SELF CHECK

5. Explain the difference between a solution and a heterogeneous mixture, using examples.

6. Make a chart in your notebook with the headings "Solution" and "Heterogeneous Mixture." Sort the following examples by writing each in the appropriate column.
   (a) soy sauce
   (b) grape juice
   (c) cottage cheese
   (d) toothpaste
   (e) hand soap
   (f) paper clip
   (g) styrofoam container

7. Give an example of a heterogeneous mixture that consists of the following.
   (a) a solid and a liquid
   (b) two liquids
   (c) two solids

8. Think about one of your favourite foods. Is it a pure substance, a heterogeneous mixture, or a solution? How do you know?

Looking at Some "In-Between" Mixtures

A CLASSIFICATION SYSTEM THAT DIVIDES all mixtures into solutions and heterogeneous mixtures runs into a problem. What do you call mixtures that are a bit like both? For example, milk appears to have only one phase. Is milk a solution, then? If you look at milk through a microscope, you see that it has two phases—a liquid part and tiny particles of cream. The particles are not mixed as completely as a solution, but are mixed better than a heterogeneous mixture. Such "in-between" mixtures are called suspensions, colloids, and emulsions.

Suspensions

A **suspension** is a mixture that appears to be one phase, but actually contains suspended solids that cause a cloudy appearance. The pieces of solid in a suspension are large enough that they will eventually settle out. Suspensions are common in the home. To find one, look in the refrigerator for tomato juice or in the medicine cabinet for any container that reads, "Shake well before using."

▲ Does anything in this microscopic view of milk suggest to you that milk is not a solution?

TECHNOLOGY-LINK

Suspensions and Light

Laser light at rock shows is visible only because of smoke, dust, and water droplets suspended in the air. When tiny bits of solid or liquid are in the path of light, the light is scattered in all directions and the beam becomes visible. This scattering is called the Tyndall effect.

This effect can help you identify a suspension. When a beam of light is shone through a suspension or a colloid, the light in the beam is scattered and the beam becomes visible.

Try this for yourself. Turn down the lights and use a flashlight to detect the Tyndall effect in a glass of water, before and after adding a small amount of flour.

CHALLENGE

Look back at your table of observations from Investigation 4.2. Predict which of the mixtures you tested would show a Tyndall effect. After you have received your teacher's approval, test your predictions. How would you classify these mixtures now?

Colloids

A **colloid** is a mixture in which pieces of solid or drops of liquid are suspended but they are so small that if conditions remain the same they will not settle out of the mixture, even if you wait for months. Fog is a colloid in which tiny drops of water are mixed with air. The drops are too small to fall as rain, but large enough to feel as a mist on your skin.

Emulsions

An **emulsion** is a type of colloid in which tiny liquid droplets are mixed in another liquid. Milk is an example of an emulsion, in which drops of cream are mixed with water. An emulsifier is any substance that helps keep other substances from separating out of a mixture. For example, the egg yolk in cake batter prevents the separation of oil and water.

In this colloid, what substance is being held suspended as droplets in the air?

TRY THIS

Using an Emulsifier

Use the following materials: salad oil, vinegar, egg yolk, and either two test tubes with stoppers or two small jars with lids. (The foodstuffs are the main ingredients of a common emulsion: mayonnaise.)

Pour equal volumes of oil and vinegar into two test tubes or small jars. To one container only, add two drops of egg yolk. Put stoppers into the tubes or lids on the jars and shake to mix the contents thoroughly.

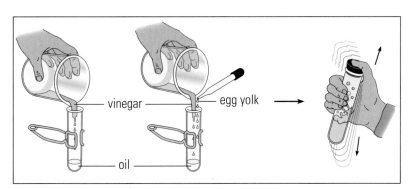

- What happens after you shake each container?
- Sketch the containers and their contents. Colour and label your sketch to show any differences.
- Repeat this experiment, using different proportions of each material. What happens?

SELF CHECK

9. Classify each of the following mixtures as a solution, a colloid, a suspension, or an emulsion by the clue given. (In some cases, more than one answer is possible.)

   (a) The liquid is transparent.

   (b) When light is passed through the liquid, a beam can be seen.

   (c) Some bits of solid settle out when the mixture is allowed to stand.

   (d) When light is passed through the liquid, no beam is seen.

   (e) Some solid particles in the liquid are large enough to be seen.

   (f) The bottle containing the liquid displays the instruction, "Shake well before using."

10. Egg yolk and gelatin are common emulsifiers. In your kitchen at home, find five products that contain these emulsifiers. List these products in your notebook. Which ingredients of the product do you think the emulsifier works on?

Water Mixtures and the Environment

W ATER IN THE ENVIRONMENT is a mixture of substances. Some occur naturally, but human activities add many substances to our lakes and rivers. Salt used to melt ice on a bridge may get into the river below. Other chemicals may come from household or industrial waste.

▶ Human activities add substances to water.

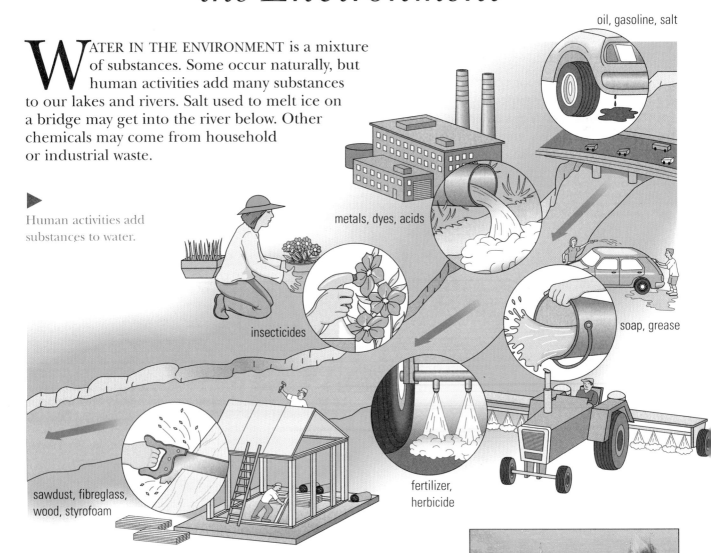

oil, gasoline, salt

metals, dyes, acids

insecticides

soap, grease

sawdust, fibreglass, wood, styrofoam

fertilizer, herbicide

Oxygen in Solution

One of the most important substances that dissolves in water is oxygen. You breathe air to obtain oxygen, but most aquatic organisms must obtain oxygen from water.

If you measure the amount of dissolved oxygen in several rivers, you will probably find that the amounts are different. Swiftly moving water dissolves more oxygen, just as stirring two substances in a beaker causes them to mix better. Warm water has less dissolved oxygen than cold water, because gases dissolve better in colder water. You can demonstrate this by letting a glass of cold tap water warm up to room temperature. As the water warms, dissolved gases come out of solution and form bubbles on the sides of the glass.

Fish need oxygen to live, but they do not breathe as you do. They use gills to remove dissolved oxygen from the water.

Waste produced by agriculture or industry can also affect levels of dissolved oxygen. If waste from human activities gets into the water, organisms like bacteria or fungi that feed on the waste may use up the oxygen in the water. When there is not enough oxygen left for the fish, they die.

In which of these bodies of water would you expect to find the most dissolved oxygen?

Suspended Solids: A Heterogeneous Mixture

Have you ever seen a river after a rainstorm? When soil is washed into a river, most of it does not dissolve. A heterogeneous mixture is formed. Sewage or industrial waste can also produce such mixtures.

Cloudy water can cause problems for the organisms living in the water. The suspended solids block sunlight, preventing it from reaching deep into the water. As a result, aquatic plants may die.

Measuring Mixtures

The concentration of a substance in water is measured in milligrams per litre (mg/L). This measurement is sometimes called parts per million (ppm). The amount of each substance in the water can be measured by a test material that reacts to the substance, or by separating the substance from a water sample.

LEARNING TIP

When you are studying a new topic, make notes in your own words on any information you discover. You will find this improves your understanding.

ASK YOURSELF

Look back at your table from the Getting Started activity at the beginning of this chapter. Expand your table by adding any new information you have learned.

CAREER-LINK

Interested in the Environment?

Do you like to work outdoors? Are you interested in the environment? Maybe a career in environmental science is for you. Find out more about careers related to the environment. Your school library or counselling department can help you get information on such careers. Look in the blue pages of the telephone book to find government agencies that deal with the environment, and ask them for information.

SELF CHECK

11. Describe three ways in which human activities may affect water in lakes and rivers.

12. What kinds of mixture are the following?
    (a) distilled water and dissolved oxygen
    (b) distilled water and suspended soil

13. Use an example to explain how the amount of dissolved oxygen in a river could affect the number of fish that live there.

14. Most organisms living in water need oxygen levels at about 5.0 mg/L of water. A water-quality inspector measures dissolved oxygen in four lakes. Which of the four show enough oxygen for aquatic organisms?

    Lake 1   4 mg/L
    Lake 2   7 mg/L
    Lake 3   8 ppm
    Lake 4   8 mg dissolved in 2 L of water

CASE STUDY

Water Quality in Riverview

IS THE WATER IN YOUR community polluted? In this case study, you will investigate possible sources of pollution in a community called Riverview.

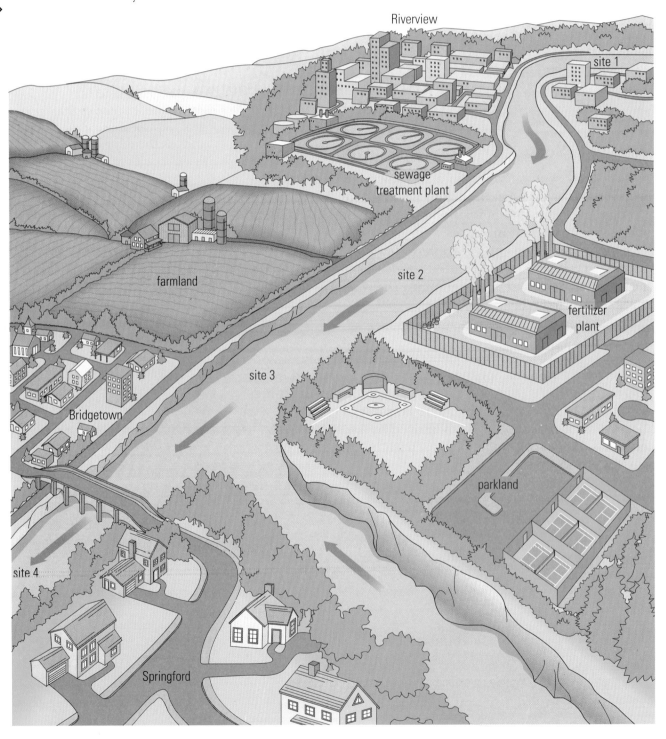

Riverview

site 1

sewage treatment plant

farmland

site 2

fertilizer plant

site 3

Bridgetown

parkland

site 4

Springford

Rapid Analysis

Your group, an environmental consulting company, has been hired by Fast Fertilizer Inc., of Riverview.

Riverview has grown up along the banks of the Rapid River. Farms surround the city. Businesses and industry in the city have grown rapidly. The city's population has doubled in the last 25 years.

People in Bridgetown, downstream from Riverview, have noticed that the Rapid River is changing. First, they complained that the water in the river was becoming cloudy. Then anglers began reporting that there were fewer fish in the river than in the past. Upstream from Riverview, the water is clear and there are lots of fish.

(a) What do you think is happening to the Rapid River after it reaches Riverview?

Riverview City Council decided that the river was being polluted, and hired a chemical consultant to determine the source of the pollution.

(b) What are the most likely sources of pollution of the Rapid River? Make a list of these possible sources.

The chemist hired by the city council examined the water at four sites, as shown on the map. He measured the amount of suspended solids by passing each water sample through a filter and weighing the trapped solids. Dissolved oxygen was tested using a chemical measuring kit. The results are shown in the table below.

Results of Water Testing

Site	Location	Suspended solids (mg/L)	Dissolved oxygen (mg/L)
1	just upstream from Riverview	50	10.0
2	directly downstream from the fertilizer plant	65	3.5
3	just downstream from the farmland	70	2.2
4	60 km downstream from Riverview	56	8.0

From his data, the chemist concluded that the source of the pollution of the Rapid River is the fertilizer plant.

(c) What data led the chemist to this conclusion?

(d) Do you agree with the chemist's conclusion?

Your client, Fast Fertilizer, does not think it is the most important source of pollution of the Rapid River.

(e) If Fast Fertilizer is not the source of the pollution, what are the other possible sources? Which is the most likely culprit?

(f) Where would you take samples to determine the source of the pollution?

Questions

1. From the data collected by the chemist, between which sampling sites does the level of suspended solids become higher? What are the most likely sources of the increased amounts of suspended solids?

2. Between which sites does the oxygen concentration show a decrease? What possible sources of pollution could have caused this decrease?

3. What types of mixtures were the following? Explain your choices.

   (a) the original river water samples

   (b) the water samples after the suspended solids were removed

Extension

4. Plot two bar graphs to represent the results of the water testing. (For more information on making a bar graph, see the Skills Handbook on page 514.)

ASK YOURSELF

Reflect on what you have learned so far about mixtures and the environment. Write several questions you would ask about the water supply in your own community.

Brainstorming Separation Methods

IF YOU HAVE BEEN ON A HIKING TRIP, you have probably eaten trail mix. Making trail mix is easy—you combine raisins, seeds, and different kinds of nuts to make a high-energy heterogeneous mixture. Separating the components from one another is not too difficult either, because the parts are so large. If you like eating the raisins first, you can pick them out with your fingers.

Fossils and bones must be carefully separated from the surrounding soil and rock for analysis.

But think about a pail of lake water. This mixture contains water, bits of soil and algae, and dissolved substances, including gases. How would you separate these components? In this investigation, you will decide on different ways to separate mixtures.

Materials

- safety goggles
- apron
- lab equipment as required

- 6 beakers each containing one of the following mixtures:

marbles and styrofoam balls

soil and water

iron filings and sand

oil and water

salt and pepper

wood chips and pieces of brick

Procedure

1 Put on your apron and safety goggles. Examine the six beakers.

(a) List the substances in each mixture in your notebook.

(b) Beside each substance, list as many physical properties of that substance as you can. For example, does the substance sink or float in water? Does the substance dissolve?

2 In your group, combine your individual lists so that you have as many physical properties as possible.

3 Brainstorm ways to separate the parts of each of the six mixtures. For example, could you separate the parts with forceps? Would a magnet attract one of the substances? Try to think of more than one method for each mixture.

(c) Make a list of the separation methods suggested by the group.

4 Choose one method you think would be best for each mixture, and write a procedure for each one.

5 After your teacher has approved your procedures, carry them out.

(d) Record your observations in each step of your procedure.

6 Return all materials and clean up your work station. Wash your hands.

Questions

1. For each separation method, identify the properties of the substances that made the separation possible.

2. Evaluate the effectiveness of each of your separation procedures. Were you able to completely separate the substances in each mixture? How would you improve your procedures?

Apply

3. Describe how you could use kitchen utensils to separate each of the following mixtures.

   (a) Smarties, caramels, and chocolate chips

   (b) sugar, toothpicks, and rice

4. List the separation techniques you use at home. To begin your list, explore your kitchen and look for different kinds of filters.

Extension

5. You will be given 500 mL of birdseed that contains several different substances. In your group, design a method to find out the amounts of each kind of seed. Describe the amounts in mass or volume units. After your teacher approves your experimental design, do the activity and write a brief report on your findings.

6. Design a filter you could make at home that would allow you to separate a mixture of uncooked rice, macaroni, and egg noodles.

7. Organic chemicals (chemicals that contain carbon) often give drinking water an unpleasant taste or smell. What type of filter is most effective at removing food colouring (an organic chemical) from drinking water? Set up the apparatus as shown in the diagram below.

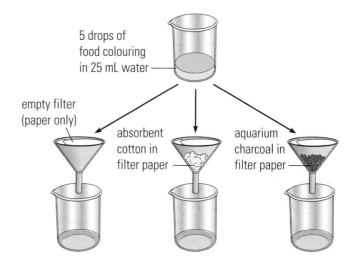

5 drops of food colouring in 25 mL water

empty filter (paper only)

absorbent cotton in filter paper

aquarium charcoal in filter paper

   (a) Predict which filter will be the most effective.

   (b) Check your prediction. Which filter works the best?

   (c) The separation process used with the charcoal filter is referred to as adsorption. Look up the meaning of adsorption and provide an explanation for how this separation technique works.

Using Properties to Separate Mixtures

YOU HAVE SEEN THAT SUBSTANCES in mixtures can be separated from one another if their physical properties are different. There are several ways to take advantage of these differences.

Magnet
Steel and tin cans are pulled out by a magnet.

Shaker and Screens
Small objects, such as broken glass and bottle caps, fall through screens.

Air Classifier
A blast of air separates low-density objects, such as aluminum cans and plastic bottles, from the heavier glass.

▶ When the trucks roll in, many recycling operators are faced with a large separation problem.

Current Separator
An electromagnet charges the aluminum cans. The cans are repelled by the magnet, separating them from the plastic bottles that remain.

Settling

Settling as a method of separation depends on the different densities of the substances in the mixture. Denser substances will tend to settle to the bottom of any container, and less dense substances will float to the top. For example, most solids suspended in water settle if the water is allowed to stand. This is the basis of "panning" for gold.

▶ A prospector adds water to a mixture of river gravel, and gently swirls the mixture in a shallow pan. The less dense bits of gravel are washed over the edge, leaving the denser pieces of gold in the bottom of the pan.

Chapter 4

Filtration

The process of **filtration** can separate particles from either a gas or a liquid. A **filter** is a device that allows part of a mixture to pass through, but traps another part. The trapped substance is called the **residue**. The substance that passes through is called the **filtrate**.

Paper filters are common in science laboratories—they trap solids and let liquids through. Filters also remove solid particles from the gases in industrial smokestacks and from the air in hospital operating rooms. Window screens are filters, preventing the entry of annoying insects but allowing in fresh air. Workers who spray paint or pesticides wear face masks so they do not breathe in droplets of poisonous liquid. Tea bags keep tea leaves out of tea, and coffee filters keep coffee grounds out of coffee. Car engines contain filters to remove solids from air, fuel, and oil. Filtration is also a key step in cleaning wastewater before it is returned to the environment.

MATH-LINK

Crude Calculations

Chemical engineers and environmental chemists use mathematics to help them make decisions about separating mixtures. Use your knowledge of mathematics to solve the following problem.

Crude oil is a mixture of valuable substances that must be separated before each substance can be refined and processed. In an oil refinery, a process called fractional distillation uses heat to separate the different parts, or fractions. Each fraction boils and condenses at a different temperature. First the oil is heated to vaporize most of the fractions, then each of the fractions is separated out by gradual cooling.

An oil refinery has received a shipment of 6000 m³ of crude oil. An engineer analyzes this oil, and discovers that it contains 15% gasoline and 10% kerosene (jet fuel).

(a) Calculate the volume of gasoline that the refinery might be able to separate from the crude oil.

(b) After all of the gasoline has been removed, what percentage of the mixture left behind will be kerosene?

CHALLENGE

Make a mixture to represent wastewater by combining water, coffee grounds, sugar, tea leaves, and salt. Design and build a model wastewater treatment plant to separate and "treat" this water. Test your model using your mixture.

SELF CHECK

15. Match each method of separation listed with the physical property that makes it work. (You can use the same property more than once.)

Method of separation:	Physical property:
settling	size of particles
floating	
evaporation	boiling point
filtration	density

16. If you are in a room where other people are smoking cigarettes, you are breathing in dissolved gases and suspended particles of tar from the smoke. What separation technique(s) could you use to help protect your lungs? Which substances would be the most difficult to protect yourself against?

Separating a Heterogeneous Mixture

IMAGINE THAT YOU ARE WORKING part-time at a local store. One day, you accidentally drop three bags on the floor. The bags contain table salt, sand, and sawdust. All the bags break and the contents mix together. You would rather not pay to replace these substances. But how could you separate the substances? In this investigation, you will try for yourself.

Materials

- safety goggles
- apron
- a mixture of solids (salt, sand, and sawdust)
- 2 250-mL beakers
- stirring rod
- plastic spoon
- paper towel

- funnel
- support stand
- ring clamp
- piece of filter paper
- evaporating dish
- hot plate
- pair of tongs
- hot pad

Procedure

Part 1 *Settling*

1 Put on your apron and safety goggles.

2 Add about two spoonfuls of the mixture of solids to a beaker containing about 50 mL of water. Stir gently. Allow a few minutes for settling to take place. Use the spoon to skim off any material that floats, and place it on a piece of paper towel to dry.

(a) Describe the mixture of the three substances. What kind of mixture was it?

(b) Describe the appearance of any separated substance. What is it?

Step 2

Part 2 *Filtration*

3 Set up a support stand, a ring clamp, a funnel, and a beaker as shown in the illustration.

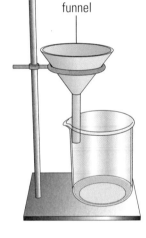

funnel

Step 3

4 Prepare the filter paper by folding it twice and then shaping it into a cone.

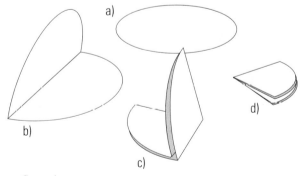

a)

b)

c)

d)

Step 4

5 Wet the funnel and fit the cone of filter paper into it. Wetting the funnel will help the paper stick to it.

6 Stir the remaining mixture. Pour the mixture slowly and carefully into the funnel, directing the flow with the stirring rod.

✎ (c) Why is it important to stir the mixture before filtration?

✎ (d) What is in the beaker?

✎ (e) Describe the appearance of any residue in the filter paper. What is it?

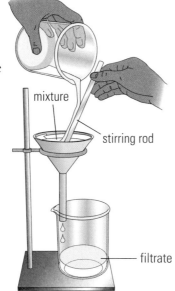

Step 6

7 Carefully remove the filter paper and residue from the funnel, and set them aside to dry.

Part 3 *Evaporation*

8 Pour the filtrate from the beaker into the evaporating dish. Place the evaporating dish on the hot plate, and heat the mixture gently until most of the water has evaporated. Leave the dish to cool.

✎ (f) Describe the appearance of any residue in the evaporating dish. What is it?

Step 8

✋ **CAUTION:** The solution may start to "spit" toward the end of the heating. Be prepared to remove the dish from the hot plate with a pair of tongs if this occurs. Place the dish on a hot pad on the desk.

9 Return the separated substances to your teacher and clean up your work station. Wash your hands.

Questions

1. What property of sawdust enabled you to separate it from the sand?

2. What property of salt enabled you to separate it from sand?

3. What were the residue and filtrate in Part 2 of this investigation? What was the residue in Part 3?

4. Give an example, from this investigation, of a pure substance, a solution, and a heterogeneous mixture.

5. Were all the substances pure after separation? Explain. How would you improve the separation?

Apply

6. Filtration is one of the methods used in water treatment plants to produce cleaner water. What kinds of mixtures can be separated using this technique? What kinds of mixtures cannot be separated? Give some examples of substances in lake water that can and cannot be separated from water by filtration.

Extension

7. In a group, brainstorm different ways that you could separate each of the following mixtures:

(a) water, copper sulphate, and sand

(b) water, flour, and marbles

(c) split peas, salt, and water

Once your procedures are approved by your teacher, perform the actual separations. Be sure to wear your apron and safety goggles.

✋ **CAUTION:** Copper sulphate is toxic. Report any spills to your teacher.

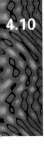

Separating a Solution

HETEROGENEOUS MIXTURES can often be separated using filtration and settling. And you can separate salt from a water solution by evaporation. But how can you separate several substances that are in the same solution? You can use other properties of these substances.

One very useful property is based on the way water moves through paper. You can observe this by putting one end of a paper towel in water and watching how the water gradually soaks the paper. Substances dissolved in the water will also move through the paper, but some will move more easily

than others. This is the basis of **paper chromatography**—separation of different solutes from a solvent.

In the following investigation, you will use paper chromatography to separate dyes in ink and candy.

Materials

- apron
- 2 strips of chromatography paper (or filter paper)
- scissors
- black marker pen with washable ink
- 2 large paper clips
- 2 large beakers or Mason jars
- candy-coated chocolates

Procedure

Part 1   *Marker Chromatography*

1 Put on your apron.

2 Cut the bottom of a strip of chromatography paper to form a "V." Using a black marker pen, draw a thin horizontal line across the width of the paper about 3 cm from the bottom.

3 Straighten the paper clip. Push it through the top of the paper in two places. Test that your paper is the right length by suspending it in the dry beaker. The paper should hang just above the bottom of the beaker. If the paper is too long, remove the strip from the beaker and cut some paper from the flat end. If the paper is too short, begin again with a new strip.

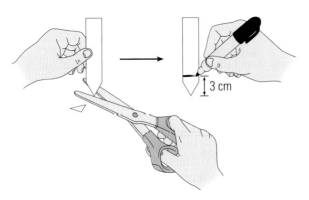

Step 2

Step 3

4 Remove the paper strip from the beaker. Pour water into the beaker to a depth of 1 to 2 cm. Carefully hang the paper in the beaker. The end of the paper should be in the water, but the pen line must be above the surface of the water.

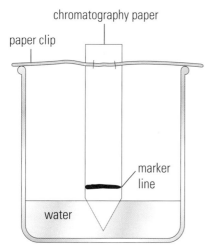

chromatography paper

paper clip

marker line

water

Step 4

5 Observe what happens as the water rises up the filter paper.

 (a) Record your observations in your notebook.

6 Just before the water reaches the paper clip, remove the paper and hang it in an empty beaker to dry.

(b) What colours do you observe?

(c) Draw a sketch of the results, or attach the dried paper to your notebook page.

(d) Why is it better to wait until the water almost reaches the paper clip? What would happen if you took the paper strip out early?

Part 2   *Candy Chromatography*

7 Prepare a new strip of chromatography paper. Obtain a brown candy. Moisten the candy with water and use it to paint a line on the chromatography paper. Paint another line over the first. Repeat steps 3 to 6 with this strip of chromatography paper.

(e) Draw a sketch of the results or attach the dried paper to your notebook page.

(f) How many different substances are in the candy coating?

8 If time allows, repeat the process using different coloured marker pens or candies.

Questions

1. (a) Which colour in the black marker moved the greatest distance through the paper?

(b) Which colour in the black marker moved the shortest distance through the paper?

(c) What do these results suggest about these two substances?

2. Were the substances in the brown candy different from those in the marker? Use your observations to explain.

Apply

3. As a food chemist, you have been asked to determine whether a fast-food restaurant is using an illegal red food colouring in its cherry pie. You have samples of 20 different red dyes, some of which are legal for use in food, and some of which are illegal. The cherry pie colour is one of those 20 dyes. How would you test the cherry pie?

Extension

4. Obtain from your teacher a piece of chromatography paper on which a mystery black marker line has been drawn. Given more chromatography paper and three different brands of black marker, design and perform an experiment to determine which of the three is the mystery marker.

5. Make your own chromatography paper at home using a paper filter, such as the kind used in coffee makers. Use the paper to separate the different solutes in fruit juices, cola, tea, or any other coloured solution.

Applying Separation Techniques: The Canatech Challenge

IMAGINE THAT YOUR GROUP IS the engineering team in a waste-processing company. Your company is trying to get a contract to process the waste mixtures from Canatech Industries, a local manufacturer. In order to get the contract, your team must demonstrate the ability to solve a problem involving separation of substances from wastewater. How would your engineering team separate, identify, and recover several pure substances? Canatech has given you a mixture of three substances in water, along with small samples of the pure substances. It wants back your report and your separated substances.

Materials

- safety goggles
- apron
- sample of each pure substance (one per class)
- unknown mixture (one per group)
- laboratory apparatus as required

CAUTION: Treat all unknown substances as being potentially hazardous.

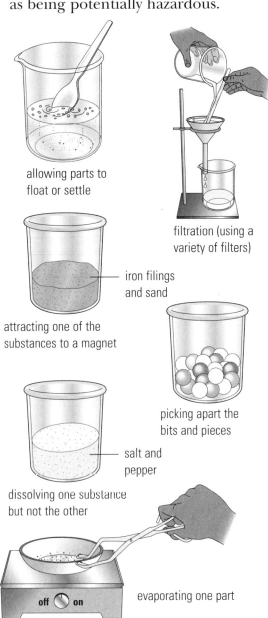

allowing parts to float or settle

filtration (using a variety of filters)

attracting one of the substances to a magnet

iron filings and sand

picking apart the bits and pieces

dissolving one substance but not the other

salt and pepper

evaporating one part

Separation techniques

LEARNING TIP

If you wish to refresh your memory concerning any of these methods, take a moment to look back in this chapter.

- ✓ dissolving one substance but not the other
- ✓ filtration (using a variety of filters)
- ✓ attracting one of the substances to a magnet
- ✓ picking apart the bits and pieces
- ✓ allowing parts to float or settle
- ✓ evaporating one part

Procedure

1. Put on your apron and safety goggles.

2. Examine each sample of the pure substances. You may wish to test the physical properties of small amounts of each sample.

✎ (a) Draw a table describing each of the substances and listing all the properties of each substance that you may find useful in your separation.

3. Brainstorm some ideas for separating the substances from a 150-mL sample of your mixture. Then, narrow down your list by gradually eliminating any ideas that are not practical.

4. Develop and write a clear, detailed procedure to describe how you would separate the substances in your mixture. Your procedure should be in the form of numbered sentences that are clear enough for a grade 8 student to follow. Use labelled diagrams to show how to use the apparatus, what to observe to help you identify the unknown substances, and what safety procedures to follow.

5. Submit the procedure to your teacher for approval.

6. Once your procedure is approved, carry it out, recording observations as you go. Be sure to note the appearance of your mixture at each step. Recover the three solid substances. Wrap each in plastic, and tape the wrapped solids to a sheet of paper. Note on the paper which solid is contained in the wrapping. Hand them in to your teacher with your report.

7. Wash your hands.

Questions

1. What physical property enabled you to separate the iron filings?

2. What physical properties enabled you to separate the other solids from the water?

3. If you had any "high-tech" apparatus that you wanted, how might you use it to separate the mixture?

Apply

4. A tanker has broken apart on rocks off Nova Scotia, but the oil it was carrying has been contained in an inflatable, circular boom. Your team is flown in to supervise the separation of the oil from the seawater.

(a) First you must determine how much oil was spilled. If the diameter of the boom is 200 m and the oil is 0.5 m deep inside the boom, how much oil was spilled? (The oil in the boom is in the shape of a cylinder, and the volume of a cylinder has the formula $V = \pi r^2 h$.)

(b) If you could have any equipment you needed, how would you make sure that all of the oil was removed from the water?

Extension

5. Decide on a name for your waste-processing company, and design a company logo and letterhead you can use in a brochure advertising your company. Include a list of the separation techniques your company offers.

6. Find out what electrostatic precipitators and scrubbers are. How do industries use these devices to separate harmful substances from exhaust gases? How effective are they?

7. Find out about a recent oil spill—where, when, and how it happened. What damage was done? How did people try to repair the damage to the environment?

SCIENCE, TECHNOLOGY, AND SOCIETY

Wastewater to Clean Water

HAVE YOU EVER WONDERED where the water goes after it flows down the drain? Depending on your community's wastewater treatment system, the water may be treated by some or all of the methods described below.

Primary treatment

The water is first filtered by passing it through screens that trap large objects, such as tree branches. Other solids, such as feces, sand, and bits of metal, are allowed to settle to the bottom of a holding tank.

Secondary treatment

Water (and sometimes sludge) from primary treatment is held in tanks. Bacteria are used to decompose the biological waste that did not settle in primary treatment. The bacteria need oxygen, so air is bubbled through the tanks.

Tertiary treatment

This process takes water from secondary treatment and uses chemical reactions to remove dissolved nitrates, phosphates, and suspended solids. If they are not removed, the dissolved chemicals act as nutrients that promote the growth of algae in lakes and rivers. Tertiary treatment is expensive. It is used only by industries, and communities with particular water problems.

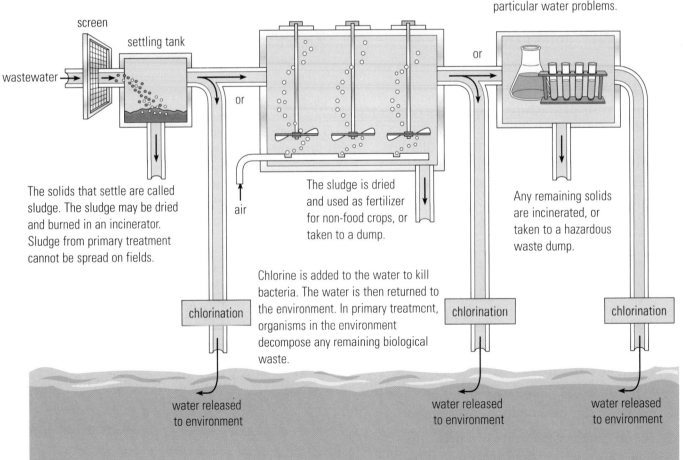

screen

settling tank

wastewater →

or

air

The solids that settle are called sludge. The sludge may be dried and burned in an incinerator. Sludge from primary treatment cannot be spread on fields.

The sludge is dried and used as fertilizer for non-food crops, or taken to a dump.

Chlorine is added to the water to kill bacteria. The water is then returned to the environment. In primary treatment, organisms in the environment decompose any remaining biological waste.

or

Any remaining solids are incinerated, or taken to a hazardous waste dump.

chlorination

chlorination

chlorination

water released to environment

water released to environment

water released to environment

Local Beach Closed; Water Supply Threatened

A child was admitted to hospital after swimming in Neville Lake, and Neville town officials have closed the beach and alerted local residents to possible contamination of the lake.

The child who was admitted to hospital is suffering from nausea, fever, and ear infections. Other swimmers have reported stinging eyes and red, itchy rashes on their arms and legs.

Cottage owners who draw their water directly from Neville Lake are advised to boil their water for 20 minutes before using it, until further notice. Boiling will kill disease-causing bacteria in the water.

Understanding the Author

1. Why was the beach at Neville Lake closed?

2. At which stage of water treatment are each of the following removed? Do any substances return to the environment?

- household ammonia cleanser
- road salt
- weeds
- industrial acids
- insecticides
- pop cans
- biodegradable soap
- feces
- urine
- toothpaste
- vegetable scraps
- fruit juice
- shampoo
- phosphate detergent
- grass fertilizer
- nitrates
- car engine oil
- paint
- turpentine
- dissolved lead
- gum wrappers
- soil

Proposal

All communities surrounding Neville Lake should help pay to construct a new wastewater treatment plant for the tourist community of Neville.

The Supporters

Opinion of a doctor from Neville We must be aware of the potential health risks posed by the town's aging wastewater treatment plant. The plant was not able to cope with recent heavy rain and released some untreated sewage into the lake, probably introducing disease-causing bacteria into our water as well.

Opinion of a motel owner from Neville We need to keep the lake clean in order to keep attracting tourists. The condition of the lake now is creating more algae growth that tourists don't like. This town cannot survive without the tourists!

The Opponents

Opinion of a mayor of a neighbouring city Our city has excellent wastewater treatment, because we put the resources into it. We had to sacrifice to clean up our mess, now we're being asked to sacrifice again to clean up somebody else's.

Opinion of a worker at a financially distressed factory The company I work for cannot afford to pay any more taxes. We have already had major cutbacks at work, and I'm afraid that I will lose my job, or the factory will even close, if the company is asked to pay more taxes.

What Do You Think?

3. Should the towns and businesses surrounding Neville Lake help pay for the clean-up?

Key Outcomes

Now that you have completed this chapter, can you do the following? If not, review the sections indicated.

- Define and classify substances as mixtures or pure substances. (4.1, 4.2)

- Define and classify mixtures as heterogeneous mixtures or solutions. (4.3)

- Define and recognize suspensions, colloids, and emulsions. (4.4)

- Design and use methods, including filtration and chromatography, to separate a given mixture. (4.7, 4.8, 4.9, 4.10, 4.11)

- Describe how human activities can affect water mixtures in the environment, and how such mixtures can be cleaned. (4.5, 4.6, 4.12)

Key Terms

pure substance

mixture

solution

heterogeneous mixture

suspension

colloid

emulsion

settling

filtration

filter

residue

filtrate

paper chromatography

Review

1. Copy the terms in Column A into your notebook. Match each term with the most correct description from Column B.

   Column A:
   mixture
   solvent
   suspension
   solution
   filtrate
   residue
   solute
   chromatography
   filtration
   dissolve

   Column B:
   passes through filter paper
   left behind on filter paper
   a way to separate solutions
   a mixture that will separate itself
   two or more pure substances in the same container
   a mixture with only one phase
   dissolves in something else
   something in which a substance dissolves
   mix together very well
   a way to separate some mixtures

2. State, with a reason, whether each of the following is a heterogeneous mixture or a solution.

   (a) hotdog relish
   (b) clear lemonade
   (c) soda water
   (d) apple juice
   (e) granola
   (f) vegetable soup

3. State, with a reason, whether each of the following is a solution or a suspension.

   (a) a mixture of clay and water
   (b) a mixture of salt and water
   (c) tomato juice

4. Make a table in your notebook with the following headings: Filter, Likely Residue, Desired Filtrate. List as many examples as you can of filters used in your daily life. For each filter, complete the table.

5. A person investigating water quality usually measures the amount of suspended solids.

(a) Explain two ways in which human activities can increase the amount of suspended solids in water.

(b) How could a large amount of suspended solids affect aquatic algae and plants?

6. The water in Tumble Creek is fast-moving and clear. The creek is known to be a good place to catch trout. The water in Placid Creek flows very slowly, is cloudy, and has almost no trout. What dissolved substance in the water might affect the numbers of trout? Where does the substance come from? Why is there more of it in Tumble Creek than in Placid Creek?

Problem Solving

7. Suggest a method to separate each of the following mixtures. Make a list of the equipment needed.

(a) sand, salt, and bird seed

(b) sugar, flour, and pennies

(c) water and cooking oil

(d) iron filings, salt, and iron nails

8. Imagine you are industrial chemists. Part of your job is to think of new and useful mixtures your company can make. Using the following list of substances and their properties, brainstorm three mixtures you would make, and invent a use for each one.

Substance	Useful Property
A	sticks to plastic
B	is bright blue
C	boils at 20°C
D	smells like bananas
E	is elastic
F	glows in the dark
G	conducts electricity
H	bends without breaking
I	repels insects

9. A forensic scientist is investigating a robbery at a lumber store. The criminals tried to hide the loot by mixing it in a large bin with several other substances. If you were the forensic scientist, what separation methods would you use to recover the stolen items from the mixture?

Items reported stolen: paper money, coins, and steel wood-working tools.

Substances in the mixture: sawdust, pieces of copper wire, plastic cups, pop cans, fertilizer, and bits of wood.

10. Imagine that you have spilled a very expensive perfume into the bath. It contains a pure oil made from a rare flower, and you can see this oil floating on the water. Describe the steps that you would take to recover as much of it as possible.

Critical Thinking

11. The filters in cars must be replaced regularly, or the efficiency of the engine decreases. Why do you think this happens?

12. "A chemical leaking from a container onto the ground is potentially more dangerous if it dissolves in water, than if it cannot dissolve." Do you agree with this statement? Explain.

13. Imagine that you have invented a device that will cheaply separate gold nuggets from rocks. Write an advertisement to promote it, explaining how it works.

14. Explain why separation by evaporation is important to each of the following products' function.

(a) The liquid in paint evaporates.

(b) The liquid in a pain-relief cream evaporates. (Hint: How does your skin feel when a drop of water on it evaporates?)

CHAPTER 5

Matter and Change

IMAGINE YOU ARE SITTING AROUND A CAMPFIRE with some friends. You put a pot of water near the fire. When the water begins to bubble and steam, you add some powdered hot chocolate mix and stir until the powder dissolves.

Meanwhile, the others are toasting marshmallows. Suddenly, one marshmallow catches fire, burning brightly for an instant. Your friend blows out the flame and frowns at the black crispy chunk left on the stick.

Several changes took place around this imaginary campfire. Some water changed state from a liquid to a gas. You made a mixture of several substances with water that would taste quite different from water alone. But are these the same kinds of changes as happened to the marshmallow?

The marshmallow did not change state—it was still a solid at the end. No mixing took place. Instead, the marshmallow seemed to become something else: a black substance. There was a change in the chemical makeup of the marshmallow itself.

In this chapter, you will

- recognize chemical changes,
- differentiate between physical and chemical changes,
- observe how changes in matter can lead to useful technology, and
- learn about the impact of technology on air quality.

 Getting Started

You are familiar with dozens of changes in matter. In a small group, brainstorm a list of as many of these changes as you can. Use a different action word for each change (for example, concrete *hardens*, wood *rots*, snow *melts*, paper *yellows*, fireworks *explode*). Put a check mark (✔) beside changes in which you think a new substance is formed. Put an asterisk (*) beside changes that might add materials to the air.

  CHALLENGE

Add one spoonful of baking soda to a glass holding two spoonfuls of vinegar. Use what you observe to design an apparatus that can blow up a balloon without using your breath!

Chemical Magic

THE STUDY OF MATTER and its changes is **chemistry**. Some of these changes make substances seem to disappear, as if by magic. Other changes make new substances appear that have very different properties from the original substances.

In this investigation, you will perform some chemical magic of your own, by making some new substances. If you observe some change in the physical properties, such as a new colour, you will know that you may have made a new substance.

CAUTION: Solutions A–D are corrosive. Spills of any of these solutions on the skin, in the eyes, or on clothing should be washed immediately with cold water. Inform your teacher of any spills.

Materials

- safety goggles
- apron
- 2 small test tubes
- test-tube rack
- 4 labelled medicine droppers
- 2 mL distilled water
- indicator solution (phenolphthalein) in a dropper bottle

- 2 mL of Solution A (0.5% sodium hydroxide)
- 2 mL of Solution B (0.5% sulphuric acid)
- 2 mL of Solution C (2.0% calcium chloride)
- 2 cm² aluminum foil
- graduated cylinder
- 2 mL of Solution D (copper(II) chloride)

CAUTION: Phenolphthalein is harmful if ingested and flammable. Inform your teacher of any spills.

Procedure

1. Put on your apron and safety goggles.

2. Obtain a test tube and put it in a test-tube rack. Use one of the medicine droppers to add 5 drops of water to the test tube. Then add two drops of indicator solution to the water.

   (a) Record your observations.

   (b) Is there any evidence that a new substance was produced? Explain.

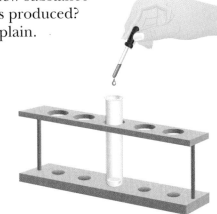

Step 2

3. Use a second dropper to add 5 drops of Solution A to the water/indicator solution.

    (c) Record your observations.

   (d) Is there any evidence that a new substance was produced? Explain.

4. Use a third dropper to add 5 drops of Solution B to the solution.

   (e) Is there any evidence that a new substance was produced? Explain.

5. Use the fourth dropper to add 5 drops of Solution C to the solution.

   (f) Is there any evidence that a new substance was produced? Explain.

6. Crumple a small piece of aluminum foil and place it in a test tube. Place the test tube in a rack. Using a graduated cylinder, measure 2 mL of Solution D and add it to the test tube.

(g) Describe the initial colour of Solution D.

(h) Describe the colour of the solution after 3 min.

(i) Describe the change in the aluminum foil.

(j) Other than any colour changes, what evidence do you have that a chemical change has occurred?

7 Dispose of the contents of your test tubes and put away your materials as directed by your teacher. Clean up your work station. Wash your hands.

Questions

1. How could you tell when a new substance was produced?

2. Describe two properties of substances that changed during this activity.

3. Two students have different hypotheses on what happened in the test tube in step 6. One student speculates that copper metal was produced after the copper chloride solution was poured onto the aluminum. The second student hypothesizes that both copper and aluminum disappeared. Based on your observations, which hypothesis seems more likely? Give your reasons.

Apply

4. List all the changes you can think of that might occur in a kitchen. Do any of the products of these changes have new properties? Explain.

5. Imagine you are a magician and want to design a new magic trick to amaze your audience. You go to a magician's supply store and discover three new products, illustrated below. Describe how you could use any or all of these products to create a magic trick.

explosive powder; strike sharply for loud but harmless explosion with lots of smoke

brilliant red dye; turns colourless after 1 min in air

just mix the two liquids to produce a very sticky substance

Extension

6. The kitchen is a chemical laboratory in which many changes in matter occur. Obtain samples of the following substances: salt, water, baking soda, baking powder, vinegar. Try mixing together combinations of small amounts of the substances. Create a table like the one below to record your results.

CAUTION: Some household chemicals form dangerous products when mixed together. Ask your teacher before mixing any substances other than those listed.

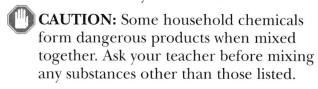

Mixing Kitchen Chemicals		
Substances mixed	Observations	Evidence of a new substance?
salt and water		

Physical and Chemical Change

YOU CAN DISCOVER A GREAT DEAL about how matter can change simply by watching a burning candle. Think about all the changes you can observe.

Physical Change

In a **physical change**, the substance involved remains the same substance, even though it may change state or form. When the candle wax has melted or vaporized, it is still wax.

Changes of state—melting, boiling, freezing, condensing, sublimation—are physical changes. You can see a physical change when you pour melted chocolate over ice cream. Liquid chocolate forms a thin, even coating over the ice cream. The chocolate becomes solid as the ice cream cools it, but it tastes the same in both states because its particles have not changed.

Dissolving is also a physical change. When you dissolve sugar in water, the sugar particles spread out, but they are still there, as sugar particles. You can reverse the process by evaporating the water and collecting the sugar.

Chemical Change

In a **chemical change**, the original substance is changed into a different substance that has different properties.

As the wax in a candle melts and vaporizes, some of the wax particles join up with oxygen from the air. The result of this chemical change is the formation of water vapour, carbon dioxide gas, heat, and light. The wax particles that seem to disappear are actually changing into something else. Burning, cooking, and rusting are all examples of chemical changes.

wax → carbon dioxide, water, and energy
chemical change

solid → liquid
physical change

liquid → solid
physical change

The wax of this candle is undergoing both physical and chemical changes. Which change results in new substances? Which does not?

ASK YOURSELF

Go back to your list from the Getting Started on page 150. Write beside each change on your list whether it is chemical or physical. If there are any you are not sure of, just leave a blank space. You can return to your list as you work through this chapter.

Chemical or Physical?

You can't see the chemical change in the wax just by looking at a burning candle. So how can you tell if a chemical change has occurred? The clues listed below can help you decide. But do not jump to conclusions too quickly. All of these clues *suggest* that a new substance has been produced, but any one of them could also accompany a physical change. You must consider several clues in order to determine what type of change has taken place.

Clues That a Chemical Change Has Happened	
A new colour appears.	
Heat or light is given off.	
Bubbles of gas are formed.	
A solid material (called a precipitate) forms in a liquid.	
The change is difficult to reverse.	

The power needed to drive this jet ski was produced through chemical changes in the fuel of its engine.

SELF CHECK

1. Explain, with a reason, whether each of the following involves a physical or a chemical change.
   (a) garbage rotting
   (b) cutting up carrots
   (c) a silver spoon turning black
   (d) making tea from tea leaves
   (e) bleaching a stain
   (f) boiling an egg

2. List three examples (not mentioned in these pages) of a physical change and three examples of a chemical change.

3. During a power failure, Blair lit four identical candles. He placed three candles very close together on a table, and one on a different table. When the power came back on an hour later, Blair was surprised to see that the candles in the group were much shorter than the one by itself. There was also more melted wax around the base of each of the three candles. Account for Blair's observation.

(a) In the fuel injector, on top of the engine, changes occur as gasoline evaporates and mixes with air.

(b) Inside the engine cylinders, the explosion of the gasoline-air mixture produces hot exhaust gases, including water vapour, carbon dioxide, and nitrogen oxides.

(c) The exhaust gases pass through the catalytic converter, where some harmful gases are changed into safer new gases.

(d) The exhaust passes out the tailpipe. On a cold day, steam from the exhaust condenses into a white cloud.

(e) As the steel of the car is exposed to air and water, a crumbly reddish-brown substance forms: the steel has changed into rust.

Operating a car involves many changes. Which of the changes are chemical, and which are physical?

Observing Physical and Chemical Changes

SOME EARLY CHEMISTS, called alchemists, knew that if they put substances together, they sometimes produced a new substance. They experimented with chemical changes, trying to find, for example, a way to change a less valuable substance— lead—into a very valuable substance—gold. Changing lead into gold is still beyond current technology, but in this investigation, you will perform experiments to learn more about physical and chemical changes.

 CAUTION: Copper sulphate is poisonous. Report any spills to your teacher.

Materials

- safety goggles
- apron
- 4 test tubes
- test-tube rack
- distilled water
- 2-mL measuring spoon
- copper sulphate
- test-tube stopper
- iron (steel wool; a piece about 1 cm x 1 cm x 2 cm)
- stirring rod
- dilute sodium hydroxide
- dilute hydrochloric acid
- magnesium ribbon (2-cm strip)
- tongs

CAUTION: Both sodium hydroxide and hydrochloric acid are corrosive. Any spills on the skin, in the eyes, or on clothing should be washed immediately with cold water. Report any spills to your teacher.

Procedure

Part 1 *Copper Sulphate and Water*

1. Put on your apron and safety goggles.

2. Make a table similar to the one below to record all your observations.

Physical and Chemical Changes

Part	Starting substances		Observations after mixing	Inference Physical? Chemical?	Evidence
	Name	Properties			
1	water				
	copper sulphate				
2					

3. Obtain a small amount of copper sulphate in a test tube. Put the test tube in the test-tube rack. Obtain some distilled water.

 (a) In your table, describe the water and the copper sulphate.

4. Pour distilled water into the test tube containing the copper sulphate, to a depth of about 6 cm. Put a stopper in the test tube to seal it. Take the tube out of the rack and mix the contents by turning the tube upside down several times. Return the test tube to the rack.

 (b) Was there a change? Record your observations.

(c) Make an inference based on your observations: if there was a change, was it physical or chemical? How do you know? Record your inference and the evidence to support it.

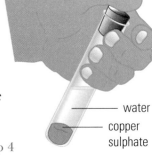

Step 4 — water, copper sulphate

Part 2 *Copper Sulphate and Iron*

5. Into another clean, dry test tube in the rack, pour some of your mixture of copper sulphate and water, to a depth of about 4 cm. (Save the remainder of your copper

sulphate mixture to use in Part 3.) Obtain a piece of steel wool (iron).

(d) Describe the steel wool and the solution before you continue.

6 Using a stirring rod, push the steel wool into the copper sulphate mixture.

(e) Record your observations.

(f) Was there a physical or a chemical change? What is the evidence?

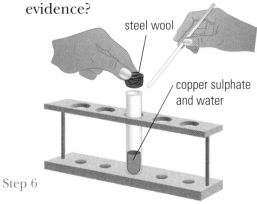

steel wool

copper sulphate and water

Step 6

Part 3   *Copper Sulphate and Sodium Hydroxide*

7 Into another clean, dry test tube pour sodium hydroxide solution, to a depth of about 2 cm.

(g) Describe the sodium hydroxide solution and the remainder of your copper sulphate mixture.

8 Pour one solution into the other.

(h) Record your observations.

(i) Was there a physical or chemical change? What is the evidence?

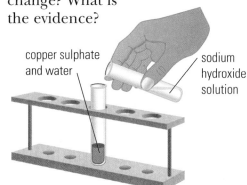

copper sulphate and water

sodium hydroxide solution

Step 8

9 Dispose of the mixtures in the test tubes as instructed by your teacher.

Part 4   *Hydrochloric Acid and Magnesium*

10 Into a clean, dry test tube, pour dilute hydrochloric acid to a depth of about 4 cm. Obtain a small piece of magnesium ribbon.

(j) Describe the dilute hydrochloric acid and the magnesium.

11 Using tongs, carefully add the magnesium ribbon to the test tube without splashing.

(k) Record your observations.

(l) Was there a physical or chemical change? What is the evidence?

12 Dispose of the mixtures in the test tubes as instructed by your teacher. Wash your hands.

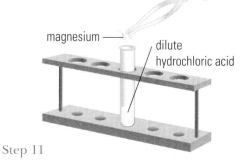

magnesium

dilute hydrochloric acid

Step 11

Questions

1. What kind of change took place when you mixed the substances in each part of the investigation? What evidence do you have?

2. In a chemical change, the new substance may have a different colour, state, texture, or other property. In each part of this investigation, what properties changed?

Apply

3. If you wanted to test more properties of a new substance formed in Part 2, how could you separate it from other materials in the test tube?

Testing for Gases

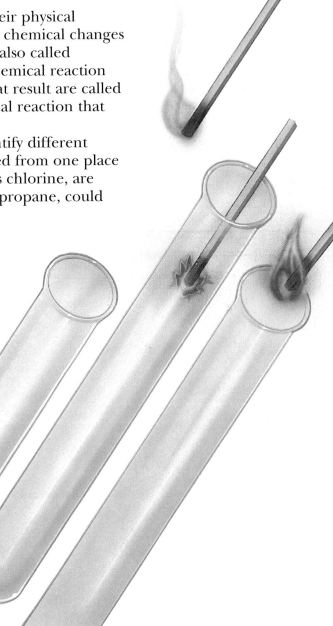

Oxygen—the glowing splint test

WHILE CLEANING UP A SPILL in a laboratory, a chemical technician discovers that the labels of three gas cylinders have been damaged. The technician knows that the cylinders contain carbon dioxide, oxygen, and hydrogen. All of these gases are colourless, odourless, and tasteless. How can the technician determine which gas is in which cylinder?

Chemical Reactions and Tests

When substances cannot be distinguished by their physical properties, you can often tell them apart by the chemical changes they will undergo. These chemical changes are also called **chemical reactions**. The substances used in a chemical reaction are called **reactants**, and any new substances that result are called **products**. A **chemical test** is a distinctive chemical reaction that allows you to identify an unknown substance.

It is extremely important to be able to identify different gases, especially when they are being transported from one place to another. Some commonly used gases, such as chlorine, are poisonous, while others, such as hydrogen and propane, could explode or burn in the presence of oxygen.

Oxygen—The Glowing Splint Test

One common chemical reaction is combustion (burning). Oxygen must be present for combustion to take place. Substances such as wood and oil burn readily in air, which is about 20% oxygen. In pure oxygen, they burn much more intensely.

This chemical property of oxygen— supporting combustion—allows you to identify it. If you suspect that a clear, colourless gas may be oxygen, you can carry out the following test.

- Light a wooden splint.
- Blow out the flame, but leave the splint glowing.
- Hold the glowing splint in a small amount of the unknown gas.
- **If the splint bursts into flame, the gas is oxygen.**

Hydrogen—The Burning Splint Test

Hydrogen burns explosively. This chemical property of hydrogen allows you to identify it. If you have a clear, colourless gas and you suspect that it may be hydrogen, you can carry out the following test.

CAUTION: This test should be attempted only on a small amount of gas in an open-mouthed, shatter-proof container. It should be done only under teacher supervision. Safety goggles should always be worn.

- Light a wooden splint.
- Hold the burning splint in a small amount of the unknown gas.
- **If you hear a loud "pop," the gas is hydrogen.**

CHALLENGE

The gases hydrogen and helium are both less dense than air. This means that either gas may be used in lighter-than-air ships. Use a reference to find out what properties hydrogen and helium have in common, and in what ways these two gases differ. From this information, infer why modern blimps are filled with helium gas instead of hydrogen.

DID YOU KNOW?

Natural gas is a common home heating fuel. It is safe and efficient when used properly, but it is odourless. This means that you might not be able to detect a leak of pure natural gas before a dangerous amount has been released. To solve this problem, gas companies add tiny amounts of a strong-smelling substance before the gas is piped to consumers. This turns the human nose into a detector sensitive enough to warn of escaping gas, well before the amounts in the air become dangerous.

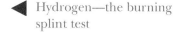

Hydrogen—the burning splint test

Carbon Dioxide—The Limewater Test

Carbon dioxide does not burn and does not allow other materials to burn. If you put a burning splint into carbon dioxide, the flame will go out. But some other clear, colourless gases behave in the same way. So, performing a burning splint test could tell you that the gas is not hydrogen or oxygen, but it would not prove that the gas is carbon dioxide.

The chemical test for carbon dioxide uses a liquid called limewater, a clear, colourless solution of calcium hydroxide in water. Carbon dioxide reacts with the dissolved calcium hydroxide, producing a precipitate. A **precipitate** is a solid, insoluble material that forms in a liquid solution. The precipitate causes the limewater to appear cloudy or milky. If you suspect that a clear, colourless gas is carbon dioxide, you can carry out this test.

- Bubble the unknown gas through the limewater solution, *or*
- Add a few drops of the limewater solution to the gas and swirl it around.
- **If the limewater turns cloudy or looks milky, the gas is carbon dioxide.**

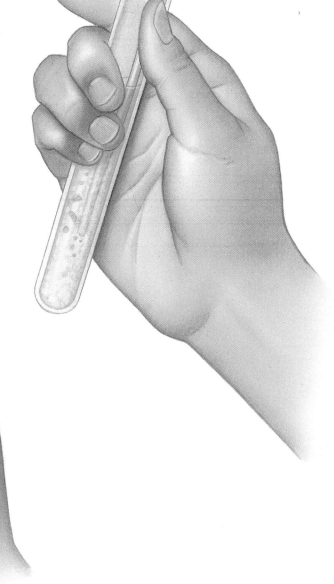

Carbon dioxide—the limewater test

Water Vapour—The Cobalt Chloride Test

Water is a liquid at room temperature, but many chemical reactions produce water vapour as a product. When water vapour touches a cold surface, it condenses to liquid water. To test for the presence of water, you can use the following test.

- Hold a cold surface near the suspected water vapour.
- Touch a piece of blue cobalt chloride paper to any liquid that condenses.
- **If the paper changes from blue to pink, water is present.**

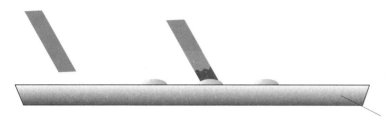

cold plate

Water vapour—the cobalt chloride test

TECHNOLOGY-LINK

Breath Analyzer

In Canada, too many automobile accidents can be linked with the misuse of alcohol. Alcohol affects the coordination and judgment of drivers. Breath analyzers are used by police officers to monitor the blood-alcohol levels of drivers.

A breath analyzer measures the alcohol content in the air exhaled by a person. There are several types of breath analyzers. The following description indicates how a fuel-cell breath analyzer works. As the driver exhales, air from the lungs enters a fuel cell. If the person has consumed alcohol, the mixture of alcohol and air creates an electric current in the fuel cell. The higher the alcohol content, the stronger the electrical current, and the farther the needle on the gauge moves. The police officer reads the gauge to determine the blood-alcohol level.

- A police officer must be able to defend the reliability and accuracy of the readings in a court of law. How do the officers ensure that their results are reliable?
- Survey different age groups about their opinions on the use of breath analyzers. Do they believe that the technology has been effective in reducing drinking and driving?

SELF CHECK

4. Copy and complete this table.

Tests for Gases		
Gas	How to test for the gas	What is observed if gas is present
oxygen		
hydrogen		
carbon dioxide		
water vapour		

5. At the start of this section, a technician was wondering how to identify what was in three cylinders of gas. Write down the steps you would follow to identify which cylinders hold hydrogen, oxygen, and carbon dioxide. Try to be as efficient as possible, so that you do not have to perform every test on each gas.

6. How would you test for the gas produced in each of the following, and what observations would you expect to make?

   (a) A can of pop fizzes. (Hint: the label says "carbonated drink.")

   (b) A nail added to a strong acid produces a very combustible gas.

   (c) When potassium chlorate is heated, a gas that supports burning is produced.

7. (a) If you placed a glowing splint in a test tube full of a clear, colourless gas, and the glowing stopped, what gas is most likely present in the test tube?

   (b) How could you be sure you had correctly identified this gas?

8. Explain the warning on oxygen tanks that cautions against cigarette smoking when the tank is in use.

Identifying Mystery Gases

YOU HAVE LEARNED how to use chemical tests to detect oxygen, hydrogen, and carbon dioxide gases. In this investigation, you will observe some chemical reactions and use those tests to infer which gas is produced.

CAUTION: Hydrochloric acid is corrosive. Any spills on the skin, in the eyes, or on clothing should be washed immediately with cold water. Report any spills to your teacher.

CAUTION: Hydrogen peroxide is poisonous and a strong irritant. Report any spills to your teacher.

Materials

- safety goggles
- apron
- 4 test tubes
- test-tube rack
- hydrogen peroxide (3%)
- toothpick
- manganese dioxide powder
- lighter

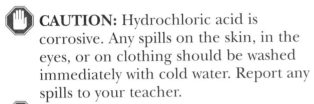

- 3 wooden splints
- hydrochloric acid (10%)
- zinc
- tongs
- limewater solution
- sodium bicarbonate (baking soda)
- test-tube stopper

CAUTION: Manganese dioxide is toxic. Report any spills to your teacher.

Procedure

Part 1 *Hydrogen Peroxide and Manganese Dioxide*

1 Put on your apron and safety goggles.

2 Make a table to record your observations.

3 Put a clean, dry test tube in the test-tube rack. Pour about 4 mL of hydrogen peroxide solution into the test tube. Obtain some manganese dioxide powder on the end of a toothpick.

(a) Record your observations of the two substances in your table.

4 Add the manganese dioxide to the hydrogen peroxide. Allow the reaction to proceed for 15 s, noting any changes. Light a splint and bring the burning splint close to the mouth of the test tube. If no reaction occurs, blow out the flame, and insert the glowing splint halfway into the test tube.

(b) Record your observations of the reaction.

(c) Record the results of the splint test for a gas.

(d) What gas was produced in the reaction?

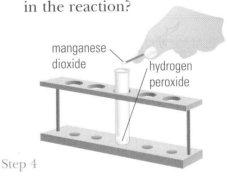
manganese dioxide

hydrogen peroxide

Step 4

Part 2 *Hydrochloric Acid and Zinc*

5 Put another clean, dry test tube in the rack. Carefully pour about 4 cm of hydrochloric acid solution into the test tube. Obtain a small lump of zinc.

(e) Record your observations of the reactants.

6 Use tongs to add the zinc carefully to the acid, to avoid splashing. Allow the reaction to proceed for 15 s, noting any changes.

Bring a burning splint close to the mouth of the test tube. If no reaction occurs, blow out the flame, and insert the glowing splint halfway into the test tube.

✎ (f) Record your observations of the reaction.

✎ (g) Record the results of the splint test for a gas.

✎ (h) What gas was produced in the reaction?

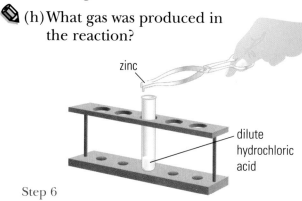

zinc

dilute hydrochloric acid

Step 6

Part 3 *Hydrochloric Acid and Sodium Bicarbonate*

7 Put two clean, dry test tubes into the rack. Pour about 4 mL of fresh limewater into the first test tube. Pour about 4 mL of water into the second tube, then add about the same amount of hydrochloric acid. On a piece of paper, obtain a small amount (about enough to cover a penny) of sodium bicarbonate.

✎ (i) Record your observations of the reactants.

8 Slowly add the sodium bicarbonate to the test tube containing the hydrochloric acid. After about 5 s, put a burning splint close to the mouth of the test tube. If there is no reaction, blow out the splint and insert the glowing end into the tube.

✎ (j) Record your observations of the reaction in the test tube.

✎ (k) Record the result of the splint test for gas.

9 If the splint went out, carefully pour the product gas from the reaction tube into the limewater tube.

✋ **CAUTION:** Be careful—do not allow any of the liquid to pour from the reaction tube.

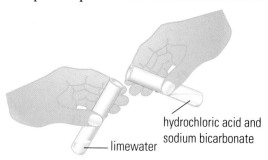

hydrochloric acid and sodium bicarbonate

limewater

Step 9

10 Put a stopper into the limewater tube to seal the tube. Mix the limewater and gas by turning the tube upside down several times.

✎ (l) What gas was produced in this reaction? Do you know for certain? Explain.

11 Dispose of the mixtures in your test tubes as directed by your teacher. Clean up your work station. Wash your hands.

Questions

1. Why did you record your observations of the reactants before proceeding with each chemical reaction?

2. What gas(es) were you testing for with

   (a) the burning splint?

   (b) the glowing splint?

3. (a) What gas were you testing for with the limewater?

   (b) What other indication did you have that this gas might be present?

4. (a) What kinds of changes occurred in each part of the investigation?

   (b) What evidence do you have that new substances were produced?

Apply

5. In a group, discuss the procedures in this investigation. List any problems you encountered and suggest ways to improve the procedure to eliminate the problems.

Word Equations

CHEMICAL REACTIONS may be quick and spectacular, as in fireworks, or too slow to see immediately, as in rusting. They may occur constantly, as in the growth of your body, or only once in a while, as in the changing colour of leaves in the fall. How can you describe such a wide range of reactions? For convenience, chemists use a word equation. A **word equation** is a short way of representing a chemical reaction: it tells you simply what is used up and what is produced.

Writing Word Equations

The left side of a word equation lists the names of all the reactants, and the right side lists all of the products. An arrow points from the reactants to the products.

all of the reactants → all of the products

The reactants, as well as the products, are separated by a plus sign (+).

reactant 1 + reactant 2 → product 1 + product 2

Word Equations for Some Chemical Reactions

When hot steel wool (iron) is plunged into a bottle of oxygen, a spectacular chemical reaction occurs. The reactants are iron and oxygen. The product is iron oxide. Written as a word equation, this reaction is:

iron + oxygen → iron oxide

When a food containing sugar (such as a marshmallow) burns, it reacts with oxygen from the air to produce carbon dioxide and water. The burning of the marshmallow can be represented as a word equation:

sugar + oxygen → carbon dioxide + water

When a coil of copper wire is placed in a beaker of colourless silver nitrate solution, a furry deposit of silver metal forms on the coil. The solution also turns blue as a copper nitrate solution forms. The word equation for this chemical reaction is:

copper + silver nitrate → silver + copper nitrate

Iron oxide forms as steel wool and oxygen react.

The sugar in a burning marshmallow reacts with oxygen to form carbon dioxide and water vapour.

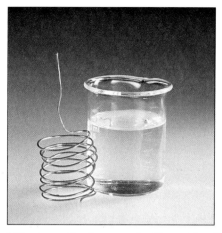  

When a coil of copper is dipped in silver nitrate solution, the copper develops a furry coat, and the solution turns blue. The products of this reaction are silver and copper nitrate.

The three chemical reactions observed in Investigation 5.3 can be represented in the following word equations. Read each equation, and identify the reactants and the products.

copper sulphate + iron → iron sulphate + copper

sodium hydroxide + copper sulphate →
sodium sulphate + copper hydroxide

magnesium + hydrochloric acid → hydrogen + magnesium chloride

---

TRY THIS

Completing Word Equations

Chemists use word equations to summarize what they observe. Copy and complete the word equations that describe the following observations from Investigation 5.5.

(a) Hydrogen peroxide changes to form two products: water and a gas. (The manganese dioxide powder is not written in the equation because it does not take part in the reaction. It is used to speed up the reaction, but is not changed itself.)

hydrogen peroxide → ? + water

(b) Zinc and hydrochloric acid react to form an explosive gas and zinc chloride.

zinc + hydrochloric acid → ? + zinc chloride

(c) Baking soda (sodium bicarbonate) and hydrochloric acid react to form water, sodium chloride, and a gas that turns limewater milky.

sodium bicarbonate + hydrochloric acid →
water + sodium chloride + ?

(d) In the test for carbon dioxide, a chemical reaction produces calcium carbonate (the precipitate) and water. Write a word equation for this reaction.

SELF CHECK

9. Examine the following word equation describing a chemical reaction.

    propane + oxygen →
        carbon dioxide + water
        + energy (light and heat)

    (a) List all of the reactants in this reaction.

    (b) List all of the products in this reaction.

    (c) What is the purpose of the arrow in the word equation?

10. Write a word equation for getting your homework finished, using these terms: time to study, textbook and notes, completed assignment, better marks.

11. Write word equations to represent the following chemical reactions.

    (a) Sodium and water react to form hydrogen gas and sodium hydroxide.

    (b) In a chemical reaction, water forms two gases, one that can be used as a fuel and one that you need to breathe.

    (c) Carbon dioxide and water are produced in cell respiration. The reactants are sugar and a gas.

Combustion

WHAT CHEMICAL REACTION occurs in the gas furnace that heats your home? What kind of chemical reaction occurs when you light a match? What causes a forest fire? All of these changes are examples of an important type of chemical reaction called combustion. In **combustion**, a substance reacts rapidly with oxygen to release energy. The energy is observed as heat and light. Many substances, such as wood, kerosene, and diesel oil, burn readily in air, which is only about 20% oxygen. This makes them useful as fuels.

Fossil Fuels and Combustion

Coal, oil, natural gas, and gasoline are all fuels. They are called **fossil fuels** because they were formed from organisms that lived millions of years ago. When these organisms died, they did not decompose completely. Instead, their bodies were buried by sediments, and the chemical energy in their bodies remained "locked up."

Human technology developed over the centuries depends on these long-buried organisms. Their stored energy powers homes, industries, and various means of transportation.

When any fossil fuel burns, the main products of the reaction are carbon dioxide and water vapour. The particles that make up fossil fuels are called **hydrocarbons**. Thus the word equation for the combustion of fossil fuel can be written as:

hydrocarbon + oxygen ⟶ carbon dioxide + water + energy

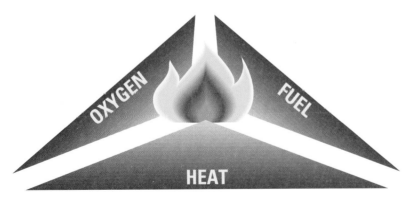

The fire triangle is a convenient way to remember the components of any combustion reaction. There are always three: fuel, oxygen, and heat. Removing any one of these components makes the triangle incomplete, and puts out the fire.

Some combustion reactions are destructive. Forest fires consume thousands of hectares of trees every year in Canada.

The quick reaction of magnesium metal with oxygen is combustion. Magnesium is often used as a component of emergency flares, which produce a bright light even in rain or snow.

Fires raged for months as oil wells in Kuwait burned out of control in 1991. The fires were extinguished one at a time using explosives and other methods that sealed the leaking oil. Which component of the fire triangle was removed to stop the fire?

Combustion and Air Pollution

Under ideal conditions, the combustion of hydrocarbons produces carbon dioxide and water. But ideal conditions rarely exist. Fossil fuels are not pure hydrocarbons, but rather are mixtures of many different substances. Also, the chemical reaction of combustion can be less efficient if there is not enough oxygen or heat. The products of the combustion of gasoline in a car engine, for example, include carbon monoxide, smaller hydrocarbons, sulphur dioxide, and nitrogen oxides, all of which can harm the environment. In fact, combustion is the major source of air pollution in the environment.

CHALLENGE

The wax of a candle is a hydrocarbon. This hydrocarbon is the fuel burned to release stored energy, observed as light and heat. Design a procedure to test for the two major gases produced in the combustion of a candle. Check with your teacher before performing your investigation.

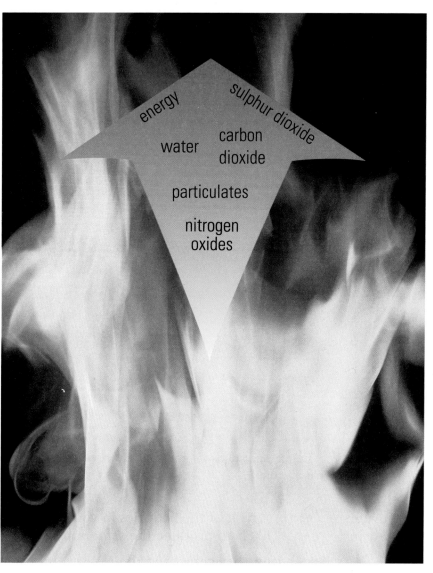

Chemical change happens when any fuel burns. As coal, oil, or gasoline is burned, new substances are produced, and some of these are released into the air.

SELF CHECK

12. Which part of the fire triangle is removed when each of the following methods is used to stop combustion?

    (a) Closing the valve on a propane tank that supplies propane to a barbecue.

    (b) Dropping and rolling if your clothing catches fire.

    (c) Pouring water on a campfire.

    (d) Pouring baking soda on a grease fire.

    (e) Blowing on a flaming marshmallow.

13. (a) List three fossil fuels.

    (b) When each burns, what is the other reactant?

    (c) What are the two main products of this combustion?

14. Write a word equation for the combustion of butane in a lighter.

15. Explain why building codes require an external source of air for fireplaces in new homes.

16. Why should you never operate a gas barbecue inside a building?

Air Quality: Two Students' Experiments

LEE GOES TO SCHOOL IN A LARGE CITY in southern Ontario, and Toni's school is in a rural area 200 km to the north. Lee and Toni exchange information using their schools' computers and the Internet link. They try to leave each other an electronic message at least twice a week.

One day in fall, Lee's message began with a comment about an unpleasant smell in the air outside his school. Toni was surprised, since the air outside her school had no unusual smell. The two decided to compare the air quality outside their schools over the next few weeks. Their results are summarized below.

- The air sometimes has a strong smell of bus and car fumes. Other times, it leaves a metallic taste in my mouth.
- When it's not windy, I can see a brownish colour in the sky in the distance. It starts above the buildings and hangs in a layer. The sky above it is blue.
- The air temperature outside our school is usually warmer than the air temperature reported for the airport, just outside the city.
- Even on clear days, sunsets are often very spectacular, with lots of red and orange in the sky.
- Some days, there is a fine black grit on the cars and sidewalks. It seems to be most common when the wind is blowing toward the school from the steel mills.

These observations were made by Lee outside a school in a large city.

-I don't usually notice much of a smell to the air, except when the farmers near the school are spreading manure on the fields. Then there is a pretty strong odour for a few days.
-When it's clear, the sky is always very blue.
-Our air temperature is usually similar to other areas nearby. Sometimes it is colder by a few degrees at night.
-If there are some clouds in the sky, we get pinks, blues, and some reds at sunset. If there are no clouds, there is very little colour.
-In the spring, especially if it is windy, there can be a lot of brown dust in the air. It seems that all summer and fall, I'm sweeping pollen and leaves off the porch.

These observations were made by Toni outside a rural school.

(a) In a group, list several human activities that could add substances to the air in the rural area where Toni goes to school.

(b) Next, list several human activities that could add substances to the air in the urban (city) area where Lee goes to school.

(c) Which of the activities in your lists are likely to produce the same substance?

After they compared their observations of the air around their schools, Toni and Lee decided to perform two experiments on air quality.

Lee's Experiment

Lee had read that rubber reacts with ozone and other polluting gases. He suggested exposing new rubber bands to the air inside and outside each school. Lee and Toni each found a shady spot outside, and hung some rubber bands on a coat hanger. They also put some bands in sealed containers in the dark. Two weeks later they compared the bands left outside to the bands in the container. Lee and Toni's results are shown below.

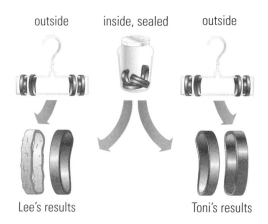

(d) Which of the two sets of bands left outside was most affected?

(e) What would you infer about the difference between the air at Toni's school and the air at Lee's school?

(f) What factors did Lee and Toni control? What factors did they not control?

(g) How would you improve the procedure of Lee's experiment?

Toni's Experiment

Toni was curious about the amount of dust and pollen in the outside air. To find out more, she suggested coating a piece of clean filter paper with petroleum jelly to see what would stick. Both students left a coated paper outside for a day, and then compared it with paper they had put in a sealed jar. Their results are shown in the next column.

(h) What might be the sources of the matter caught by each disk?

(i) What factors were controlled in Toni's experiment? What factors were not controlled?

(j) How would you improve on Toni's experiment?

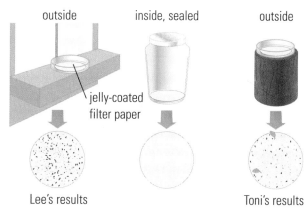

On the basis of their experiments, Lee and Toni concluded that the air outside Toni's school was less polluted than the air outside Lee's school.

(k) Do you agree with their conclusion? If you were to repeat Lee's and Toni's experiments at your school, what results do you think you would obtain?

Questions

1. The air filter in an automobile removes dust and other particles from the air before it enters the engine. Based on the observations in this case study, predict which family car, Lee's or Toni's, would need a new filter more often. Explain your prediction.

2. Substances suspended in the air will cut down the distance you can see. For example, compare the two photographs on page 168. In which photograph can you see farther? What might be suspended in the air in each photograph?

Extension

3. Repeat the experiments described in this case study to test air quality in your area, with the improvements suggested by your group, after you have your teacher's approval.

Fireworks: Combustion with a Difference

HAVE YOU EVER WONDERED how spectacular fireworks are produced? Each fireworks explosion is a carefully controlled series of chemical changes that occur at just the right times.

The history of fireworks (pyrotechnics) began in China 1000 years ago with the discovery of black powder, or gunpowder, a mixture of potassium nitrate (saltpetre), charcoal, and sulphur. People at the time used saltpetre to preserve meat. They may have found by chance that a mixture of charcoal, iron, and saltpetre produced sparks when sprinkled into a fire. When this mixture burns, it produces large amounts of gases and energy in the form of heat and light.

A modern firework shell contains black powder that burns to propel the firework up into the air. The shell also contains separate packages of chemicals that produce special effects, such as bursts of colour, flashes, and sound. Some of these materials are described in the table on the facing page.

 CAUTION: Making fireworks is hazardous and should be attempted only by well-trained professionals.

Inside a Firework Shell

Suppose a technician had the job of making a firework shell that would rise 50 m, produce a red burst of fire, and then a loud bang and a flash. The technician would have to make three different explosive mixtures—one to lift the shell into the air, and then one for each of the two special effects.

The first and most dangerous step is mixing the ingredients. Just as in other combustion reactions, the ingredients needed in fireworks are a fuel, a source of oxygen (called an oxidizer), and a source of heat to start the reaction (a burning fuse). Typical oxidizers are potassium nitrate, potassium chlorate, potassium perchlorate, and ammonium perchlorate. Each mixture also contains binders like red gum, paraffin oil, or dextrin. The binders act as fuel and hold the mixture together. The technician then wraps each mixture in a cardboard package and links the packages with fuses.

The technician who lights a firework shell ignites a complicated set of fuses.

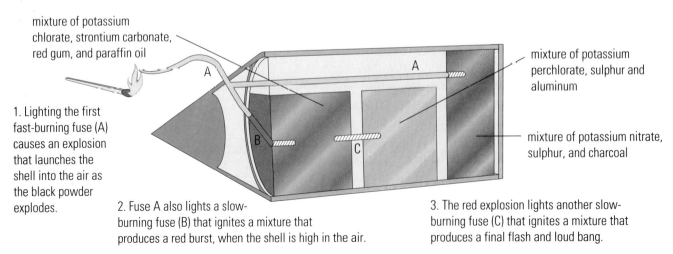

mixture of potassium chlorate, strontium carbonate, red gum, and paraffin oil

mixture of potassium perchlorate, sulphur and aluminum

mixture of potassium nitrate, sulphur, and charcoal

1. Lighting the first fast-burning fuse (A) causes an explosion that launches the shell into the air as the black powder explodes.

2. Fuse A also lights a slow-burning fuse (B) that ignites a mixture that produces a red burst, when the shell is high in the air.

3. The red explosion lights another slow-burning fuse (C) that ignites a mixture that produces a final flash and loud bang.

Some Chemicals Used for Special Effects

Material	Special effect
magnesium metal	white flame
sodium oxalate	yellow flame
barium chlorate	green flame
cesium (II) sulphate	blue flame
strontium carbonate	red flame
iron filings and charcoal	gold sparks
potassium benzoate	whistle effect
potassium nitrate and sulphur	white smoke
potassium perchlorate, sulphur, and aluminum	flash and bang

For displays in theatres and indoor stadiums, fireworks mixtures must be carefully chosen and used in small amounts.

Understanding the Author

1. What is the composition of black powder?

2. In the firework described in the diagram, what is the purpose of each of the following?

   (a) strontium carbonate

   (b) paraffin oil

   (c) potassium chlorate

3. Should fireworks be exploded inside stadiums and theatres? Explain your answer.

CHALLENGE

Design and draw a diagram of a firework you think would be suitable for Canada Day. Explain why you chose your design.

 CAUTION: Do not test your design. Fireworks are extremely hazardous.

Proposal

No one should be allowed to buy or use fireworks at any time within city boundaries.

Point

- Fireworks are dangerous mixtures of chemicals. When ignited, they can explode in unpredictable ways. Children have been injured through the unsafe use of fireworks.

- Fireworks displays pollute the environment. The reactants involved can produce nitrogen dioxide and sulphur dioxide, both of which are poisonous gases and produce acid rain. Noise pollution is also created.

- Fireworks are very expensive, considering they last for only a few seconds. The community would be better off using the money to celebrate special occasions in other ways.

Counterpoint

- Fireworks are a traditional way of celebrating for some cultures. The move to prevent fireworks could be seen as working against those groups.

- People who want to use fireworks will just continue to do so outside the city. In wooded areas or abandoned farmlands far from emergency services, the risk of fire or accident would be greater.

- Fireworks displays to mark special events promote tourism and bring economic benefits to the community.

What Do You Think?

4. Research the issue further, expand upon the points provided, and develop or reflect upon your position. Prepare for the class debate.

Key Outcomes

Now that you have completed this chapter, can you do the following? If not, review the sections indicated.

- Define and distinguish physical and chemical changes. (5.1, 5.2, 5.3)

- Describe and use tests for oxygen, carbon dioxide, and hydrogen gases, and water vapour. (5.4, 5.5)

- Use word equations to describe chemical reactions. (5.6, 5.7)

- Use a word equation to describe the products of the combustion of hydrocarbons, and relate this to different methods of extinguishing fires. (5.7)

- Be aware of the major sources of air pollutants in Canada. (5.7, 5.8)

Key Terms

chemistry

physical change

chemical change

chemical reaction

reactant

product

chemical test

precipitate

word equation

combustion

fossil fuel

hydrocarbon

Review

1. For each of the following, replace the description with one or two words.

   (a) the starting substances in a reaction

   (b) the substances formed in a reaction

   (c) a change in which a new substance is produced

   (d) a change in which no new substance is produced

2. The sentences in the list below contain errors or are incomplete. In your notebook, write your complete, correct version of each sentence.

   (a) A physical change produces a new substance.

   (b) The formation of frost is a chemical change.

   (c) A chemical change may produce a new substance called a predominate.

   (d) A new colour indicates a physical change.

   (e) When a burning splint goes out, it indicates hydrogen gas is present.

   (f) A burning splint tests for carbon dioxide gas.

   (g) Limewater tests for oxygen gas.

   (h) A chemical change is a change of state or form.

   (i) When a glowing splint goes out, it indicates oxygen gas is present.

   (j) When limewater turns red, it indicates carbon dioxide gas is present.

3. Suggest five clues you could consider before deciding whether a change is physical or chemical.

4. Indicate whether each of the following is a physical or a chemical change. Give a reason for each.

   (a) water freezing on a pond

   (b) soap removing grease from hands

   (c) an electric bulb glowing

   (d) a cake baking

   (e) wood burning

   (f) kitchen scraps composting

   (g) a paper clip bending

   (h) dynamite exploding

5. A friend tells you that an antacid tablet bubbling in water is a chemical change, but the water bubbling in a kettle and turning to steam is not. Do you agree? Explain.

6. Copy the tests in Column A into your notebook. Match each test with the appropriate gas from Column B.

Column A	Column B
limewater test	water vapour
cobalt chloride test	hydrogen gas
glowing splint test	oxygen gas
burning splint test	carbon dioxide gas

7. Name four major sources of air pollution and the types of pollutants produced.

8. Make a concept map to summarize the material that you have studied in this chapter. Start with the word "changes."

Problem Solving

9. When carbon dioxide is ejected from the nozzle of a fire extinguisher, the carbon dioxide is so cold that it changes to "snow."

   (a) Is this a physical or chemical change?

   (b) The carbon dioxide snow, when applied to a burning object, is said to smother the flame. What kind of chemical change is the carbon dioxide snow preventing? How does the carbon dioxide stop the fire?

10. Write word equations to represent the following reactions:

    (a) Potassium and water produce potassium hydroxide and a very flammable gas.

    (b) Calcium carbonate and hydrochloric acid produce calcium chloride, water, and a gas that turns limewater milky.

    (c) Potassium chlorate produces potassium chloride and a gas that causes a glowing splint to burst into flame.

11. The photograph shows a welder using heat from the combustion of acetylene (a fossil fuel) to weld steel plates together.

    (a) Name all the physical changes that occur during and after this process.

    (b) Write a word equation for the chemical change that produces the heat the welder needs.

Critical Thinking

12. Name four materials or pieces of equipment that you have used in your last three investigations to ensure lab safety. Explain the function of each.

13. You and your group are advisors to the Minister of the Environment, and you must come up with ways to reduce the amount of air pollution.

    (a) Brainstorm as many ways as possible to reduce the amount of air pollution from vehicles, industries, and power plants.

    (b) Record all your ideas in a table. Be sure to include benefits, drawbacks, and cost.

CHAPTER 6

Elements and Compounds

HOW CAN YOU EXPLAIN the explosion of a burning car? You know that a chemical change has occurred because new substances are produced and large amounts of heat and light are released. But what happens to the particles of gasoline and oxygen when they react?

When a fossil fuel like gasoline burns in the presence of oxygen, the reactants usually form carbon dioxide—the same gas that you exhale with every breath. But the same two reactants, under certain conditions, can produce carbon monoxide—a poisonous gas that kills people every year. How can the same reactants produce different products?

In this chapter, you will

- learn more about pure substances and the particles that make them up,
- extend the particle model into atomic theory,
- use atomic theory to explain chemical reactions, and
- investigate atoms and molecules in the environment.

 Getting Started

1. In a small group, make a list of at least 20 pure substances that you know about. Include everyday substances, such as water, copper, and gold. Also be sure to include substances you have used in the laboratory. Remember that pure substances can be solids, liquids, or gases, and their names can have one word or more than one word in them.

2. Scientists have found that chemical changes can split the particles in some pure substances into smaller particles. Other pure substances cannot be broken down. In your group, discuss your list of pure substances. Which ones do you think can be split?

Chemical changes occur in many industrial processes. If the products of these reactions are released, they may travel through air or water and may affect environments hundreds or even thousands of kilometres away.

Another Look at Pure Substances

YOU HAVE EXPLAINED many properties of matter using the particle theory—the idea that all matter is made up of tiny particles. But what are these particles? To answer that question, you need to look more closely at water, a pure substance.

Since water is a pure substance, it is made up of only one kind of particle. However, as you will find from the experiment in the Try This, water particles can be broken down. It appears that water is made of hydrogen and oxygen, and that there is twice as much hydrogen as oxygen.

$$\text{water} \xrightarrow{\text{electrolysis}} \text{(2) hydrogen} + \text{(1) oxygen}$$

Building Blocks of Matter

Two hundred years ago, scientists already knew of thousands of pure substances, and the number being discovered was constantly growing. It was a never-ending task to learn all the properties of these substances. Scientists hoped that by breaking down these substances, they would discover the building blocks of matter. Once they knew all the building blocks, they believed they would be able to predict the properties of a pure substance from the properties of the "blocks" it was made of.

Using equipment like this, scientists of several centuries ago conducted experiments on matter.

TRY THIS

Separating Water with Electrolysis

Set up the apparatus as shown in the diagram at right. Add a pinch of salt to the water and observe the electrodes (paper clips). The electric current from the battery is used to cause a chemical change. This process is called electrolysis.

- Speculate about what gases are being formed as the water breaks down.
- Do equal amounts of gas appear to evolve at the electrodes? Provide an explanation of why or why not.
- When a glowing splint is put into the gas collected at the left electrode, the splint bursts into flame. The gas collected at the

right electrode produces a loud pop when tested with a burning splint. What conclusions could you draw from these observations? Give your reasons.

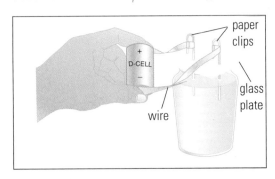

As a result of these efforts, scientists now know of over 110 of these building blocks, which they call elements. **Elements** are pure substances that cannot be broken down into simpler substances.

Water, which is formed from two of these elements (hydrogen and oxygen), is a compound. **Compounds** are pure substances that contain two or more elements in a fixed proportion. For example, in water, there is always twice as much hydrogen as there is oxygen.

The system for classification of matter that you developed in Chapter 4 can be expanded to include compounds and elements.

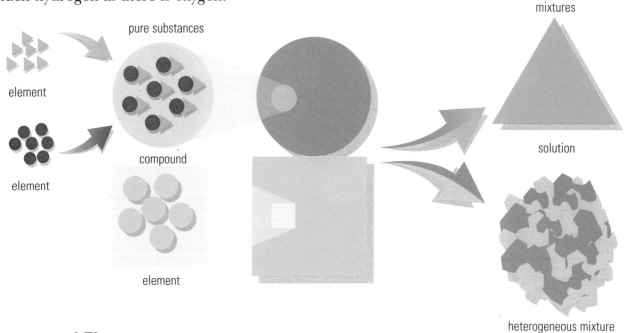

pure substances

element

element

compound

element

mixtures

solution

heterogeneous mixture

Atoms and Elements

How can elements and compounds be explained using the particle theory? Once again, water provides a clue. When water is broken down, there is always twice as much hydrogen as oxygen. A water particle is formed from the particles of two elements: two particles of hydrogen and one particle of oxygen. Scientists call these particles of elements **atoms.** Since there are more than 100 elements, there are more than 100 kinds of atoms.

Molecules

Atoms join together in combinations. When two or more atoms join together, a **molecule** is formed. Molecules can contain two atoms or many thousands of atoms. The atoms in a molecule can all be the same kind of atom, or they can be of two or more kinds of atoms.

Water molecules are made of hydrogen and oxygen atoms. The water particles you used to explain changes of state are actually molecules.

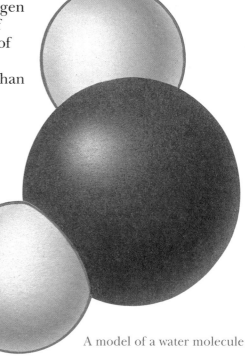

A model of a water molecule

Models of Molecules

Examine the models of molecules shown below. The first shows a molecule that contains two atoms of oxygen. This is a molecule of the element oxygen. The other two show molecules of compounds.

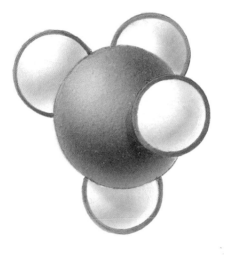

(a) Atoms of the element oxygen join together in pairs, forming oxygen molecules.

(b) In the compound methane (the main component of natural gas), each molecule contains one carbon atom and four hydrogen atoms.

(c) In acetic acid (vinegar), each molecule has eight atoms: two carbon atoms, two oxygen atoms, and four hydrogen atoms.

Different Molecules from the Same Elements

In compounds, atoms of one element join together in a fixed ratio with atoms of other elements. For example, when hydrogen and oxygen combine in the ratio of 2:1, the compound they form is always water. What happens if hydrogen and oxygen combine in a different ratio? The result is a different compound with different properties. In nature, there is only one other compound that contains only hydrogen and oxygen—hydrogen peroxide. In hydrogen peroxide, hydrogen and oxygen are in a 1:1 ratio.

An atomic model of hydrogen peroxide. A hydrogen peroxide molecule has two hydrogen atoms and two oxygen atoms. Compare this model with the model of water on page 177.

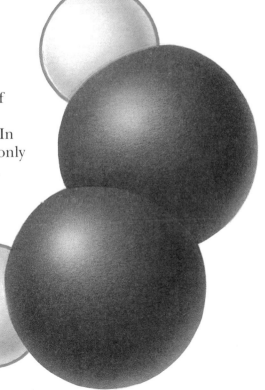

The properties of water and hydrogen peroxide are very different. Water is everywhere on Earth, part of all living things. Hydrogen peroxide is a much more reactive compound. It can be used to kill bacteria and other organisms that might cause infections.

A hydrogen peroxide solution bubbles as blood is added. Hydrogen peroxide is used in antiseptics. It bubbles when it touches dirt and blood in cuts or scrapes. Water in a similar situation does not react.

Other elements can also be combined in different ratios to produce different compounds. For example, acetic acid (vinegar) contains atoms of hydrogen, oxygen, and carbon. These same elements also combine to form sugars and fats.

CAREER-LINK

Quality Control Technician

When you open a new bottle of ketchup, you expect it to taste and look exactly the same as the last bottle of ketchup you used. The job of a quality control technician is to make sure that every batch of food (or other product) is made the same way. For ketchup, the technician would make sure that the same proportions of the ingredients are used each time. This technician would also check details such as cooking temperature. What industries hire quality control technicians? Look in the yellow pages of your phone book under "laboratory" or under "quality control." Make a list of the industries mentioned. If any of these interests you, contact the company and find out more about the importance of quality control.

SELF CHECK

1. (a) What is an element?

   (b) What is a compound?

2. State whether each of the following pure substances is an element or a compound. Explain your reasoning.

   (a) A clear, colourless liquid that can be broken down into two gases with different properties.

   (b) A yellow solid that always has the same properties and cannot be broken down.

   (c) A colourless gas that burns to produce carbon dioxide and water.

3. How is it possible that there are millions of pure substances, even though there are only about 100 different elements?

4. Examine the models on these pages showing water, oxygen, methane, acetic acid, and hydrogen peroxide molecules. For each, state:

   (a) the total number of atoms per molecule, and

   (b) the number of atoms of each type per molecule.

5. In your own words, describe the difference between the terms in each pair.

   (a) element and atom

   (b) compound and mixture

   (c) atom and molecule

   (d) molecule and compound

LEARNING TIP

One of the best ways to understand something is to build models. Your teacher may have model kits available that you can use to build models of molecules. You can also use household materials to construct models.

Finding out about the Elements

WHAT DO YOU ALREADY KNOW about elements? You are probably familiar with the properties of elements such as gold, silver, and oxygen. However, elements like barium and cobalt may be just names to you. In the entire universe, there are only 92 elements that are known to occur naturally. Some are common, and some are extremely rare. Some are quite safe, others are explosive, radioactive, or poisonous. At room temperature, two are liquids, and the rest are solids and gases. Each element has a unique set of properties.

Scientists have created new elements in devices called nuclear reactors, so that there are now over 111 known elements. Some of these elements are so new that their names have not yet been finalized. For example, Element 106 was known briefly as seaborgium (after American Glenn Seaborg), but in August, 1994, the name was changed to rutherfordium (after New Zealander Ernest Rutherford). In this investigation, you will find out more about elements.

Materials

- index cards, each with the name of one element on it
- reference materials, including the periodic table on page 534.

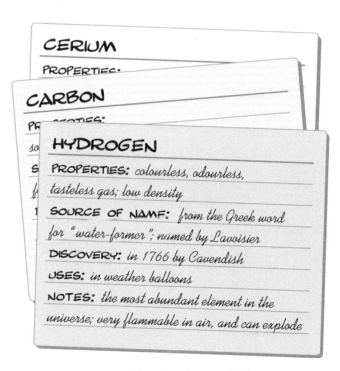

- How common is this element on Earth or in living things?

- Is it dangerous (explosive, radioactive, poisonous)?

Procedure

1 Use the periodic table to pick some elements you are interested in. Use references to find out interesting facts about the elements you have chosen. Write the information on cards. Among the things you could find out are:

- What are the element's most obvious properties?

- Where did it get its name?

- When was it discovered?

- What is it used for?

A completed card for the element hydrogen

Hydrogen burns without creating pollution—the only product is water. This makes it a desirable fuel. Automakers are developing hydrogen-fuelled cars.

2 As a class, use the element cards to make a file of reference material about the elements, or post the cards on the bulletin board.

Questions

1. Examine the element cards.

   (a) Which elements were named after countries or other geographical areas?

   (b) Which elements appear to have been named after people?

   (c) Which elements are poisonous?

   (d) Which elements are present in air or water pollutants?

Apply

2. Copy the following list of compounds into your notebook:

   ethanol (alcohol)

   sodium bicarbonate (baking soda)

   nitrogen dioxide

   calcium carbonate (chalk)

   sodium phosphate

   sodium hydroxide (drain cleaner)

   sucrose (table sugar)

   water

Beside each compound, write the names of the elements you think it might contain. Use the class element cards for information. (Hint: "bi-" means hydrogen is also present and "-ate" means oxygen is also present.)

3. Elements are often classified as metals or non-metals.

   (a) In a reference book, find out the differences between the properties of metals and non-metals. List the properties of each in your notebook.

   (b) In your notebook, make a table with two columns, headed "metals" and "non-metals." List at least 10 familiar elements in each column.

4. On a large piece of paper, create a collage of cut-out pictures and drawings to represent the most interesting characteristics of one of the elements you chose. Include the chemical symbol that represents that element somewhere in your design.

Extension

5. The atoms that make up elements combine to form compounds. You can use table tennis or Styrofoam balls, a marker, Velcro tape, and a paper bag to show how this happens.

   • Mark an O on about one-third of the balls and stick two pieces of rough Velcro on opposite sides of each of these balls. Mark an X on the other balls and stick one piece of smooth Velcro on each of these balls.

   • Drop all the balls into the paper bag, close it, and shake the contents for a few minutes.

   • Open the bag, and describe what has happened. What "molecules" have formed?

Chemical Symbols and Formulas

A CANADIAN CHEMICAL COMPANY that hopes to sell its product in China may need to hire an interpreter to communicate with potential customers. But the interpreter will not need to translate the names of any chemicals. That is because all countries use the same chemical symbols to represent elements and compounds.

Some Modern Symbols for Elements	
calcium	Ca
carbon	C
chlorine	Cl
copper	Cu
hydrogen	H
lead	Pb
mercury	Hg
nitrogen	N
oxygen	O
sodium	Na
sulphur	S
phosphorus	P
tin	Sn
zinc	Zn

Chemical Formulas

Just as single symbols are used to represent elements, combinations of these symbols are used to represent compounds. A **chemical formula** is the combination of symbols that represents a particular compound. The chemical formula indicates which elements are in the compound and in what proportion they are present.

In the Middle Ages, alchemists tried to change lead into gold. They did not succeed, but their use of symbols to represent substances has endured.

DID YOU KNOW?

The names and symbols for elements come from many sources. Hydrogen comes from the Greek word for "water-former." Mercury was named after a Roman god, but its symbol, Hg, comes from the Latin word hydrargyrum for "liquid silver." Sodium was named for sodanum, a headache remedy, and its symbol, Na, came from the Latin word natrium.

Chemical Formulas

You will be using chemical formulas in future science courses. You may also encounter this chemical shorthand in newspaper or magazine articles. This activity will give you practice in using and understanding chemical formulas.

- For each of the compounds in the table Some Examples of Chemical Formulas below, state the number of different types of elements present and the number of atoms of each element. How many atoms are present in one molecule?

- Write a chemical formula for the following.

  (a) a molecule of hydrogen gas that is made up of two atoms of hydrogen

  (b) a molecule of propane gas that is made up of three atoms of carbon and eight atoms of hydrogen

Each symbol of a formula represents an atom of an element. If only one atom is represented, no number is included. If there is more than one atom of that element in the compound, the symbol is followed by a number written below the line. This number (called a subscript) tells how many atoms there are in one molecule. For example, the formula for water—H_2O—tells you that the elements are present in the ratio of two atoms of hydrogen to one atom of oxygen. The formula for sodium bicarbonate—$NaHCO_3$— tells you that the elements are present in a ratio of one atom of sodium to one atom of hydrogen to one atom of carbon to three atoms of oxygen.

Some Examples of Chemical Formulas

Name of substance	Formula
sodium bicarbonate (baking soda)	$NaHCO_3$
calcium carbonate (chalk)	$CaCO_3$
sodium nitrate (fertilizer)	$NaNO_3$
calcium phosphate (fertilizer)	$Ca_3P_2O_8$
sodium chloride (salt)	$NaCl$
acetylsalicylic acid (ASA or aspirin)	$C_9H_8O_4$

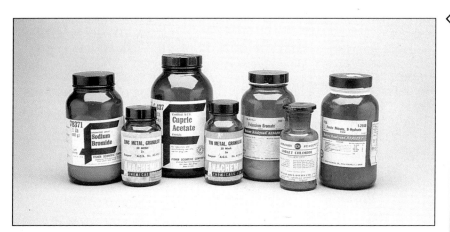

Chemists rely on symbols and formulas to help them keep track of chemicals.

SELF CHECK

6. Why are symbols useful in describing chemicals?

7. The chemical formula for water is H_2O.

   (a) What does each of the symbols in this formula represent?

   (b) What does the number represent?

8. Molecules of nitrous oxide contain two atoms of nitrogen and one atom of oxygen. Write the chemical formula for nitrous oxide.

9. State the types of atoms and the numbers of each type that are present in the following molecules: copper phosphate (Cu_3PO_4) and sodium nitrate ($NaNO_3$).

10. Customs officials investigating a crate shipped from Central America wanted to know what it contained before allowing the crate into Canada. Although the labels were in Spanish, the following chemical formulas were printed on the crate: $NaHCO_3$, $NaNO_3$, $Ca_3P_2O_8$. Would you recommend that the officials allow the crate to continue or should they call the shipping company to ask for more information? Explain your reasoning.

Measuring Masses in Chemical Changes

YOU KNOW ABOUT atoms and molecules, but what exactly happens when they undergo a chemical reaction? Matter changes, but does the amount of matter also change? In this experiment, you will measure masses of reactants and products to find out.

CAUTION: Calcium chloride is toxic. Report any spills to your teacher.

Materials

- safety goggles
- apron
- 250-mL Erlenmeyer flask
- stopper for the flask
- small test tube
- sodium carbonate solution
- calcium chloride solution
- paper towel
- balance

Procedure

1 In a group, discuss how a chemical reaction might affect the total mass of reactants and products.

(a) Write a hypothesis comparing the mass of the reactants and the products.

2 Your group should split into teams to test the hypothesis. Each team should make a data chart like the one below.

Measuring Masses in a Chemical Reaction

Total mass of reactants and apparatus (g)	
Predicted mass of products and apparatus (g)	
Measured mass of products and apparatus (g)	

3 Put on your apron and safety goggles.

4 Check that your test tube is the correct size for your flask. The test tube should be small enough to fit inside the flask with the stopper in, but large enough that it does not lie flat.

Step 4

5 Remove the test tube from the flask. Pour sodium carbonate solution into the flask to a depth of about 1 cm.

6 Fill your test tube about 3/4 full with calcium chloride solution. Carefully dry off the outside of the test tube with a paper towel. Gently place the test tube in the flask, being careful not to spill the calcium chloride solution.

Step 6

calcium chloride solution

sodium carbonate solution

7 Put the stopper firmly in the flask. Check that the outside of the flask is dry. If it is not, dry it off.

8 Determine the total mass of the reactants and their containers.

(b) Record your description of the reactants.

(c) Record the mass of the reactants and their containers.

(d) Record your prediction of what the final mass will be, following the chemical reaction.

Step 8

9 Holding the stopper firmly in place, gently invert the flask. This will mix the calcium chloride from the test tube with the sodium carbonate from the flask.

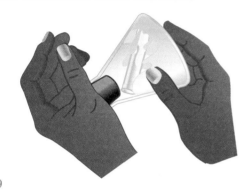

Step 9

10 Observe the reaction that occurs. Measure the mass of the flask and its contents, using the same balance you used for the first measurement.

✎ (e) Record your description of any products of the reaction.

✎ (f) Record the mass of the products and containers.

11 Dispose of the contents of your flask as directed by your teacher. Clean the glassware and return it to storage. Wash your hands.

12 Compare your team's results with those of the rest of your group.

✎ (g) What was the change of mass recorded by each team?

✎ (h) Total all of the mass changes from each team and calculate the average mass change.

Questions

1. Explain why the measurement of the mass of the products might differ for each team. Does this indicate that one of the teams made a mistake?

2. Explain why an average change in mass was calculated and used in observation question (h).

3. What evidence do you have that a chemical reaction occurred in your flask?

4. The products of the reaction are calcium carbonate and sodium chloride. Write a word equation for this reaction.

5. Which product(s) could you see in the flask after the reaction? Explain your answer.

Apply

6. Did the group's results support your hypothesis? Explain your group's results, using what you know about atoms and molecules.

7. List possible factors that might explain why the mass of the products is not equal to the mass of the reactants.

Extension

8. Repeat this investigation using a different pair of reactants: iron(III) chloride solution and sodium hydroxide solution. Before you begin, predict the products of this reaction, and write its word equation.

✋ **CAUTION:** Iron(III) chloride is a strong irritant, corrosive, and toxic. Any spills on the skin, in the eyes, or on clothing should be washed immediately with cold water. Report any spills to your teacher.

✋ **CAUTION:** Sodium hydroxide is corrosive. Any spills on the skin, in the eyes, or on clothing should be washed immediately with cold water. Report any spills to your teacher.

Finding the Missing Mass

W HAT HAPPENS TO MASS when gases are produced in chemical reactions? In this investigation, you will compare the mass of reactants with the mass of products after a burning reaction.

 CAUTION: Hydrochloric acid is corrosive. Any spills on the skin, in the eyes, or on clothing should be washed immediately with cold water. Report any spills to your teacher.

Materials

- safety goggles
- apron
- test tube
- dilute hydrochloric acid
- 250-mL beaker

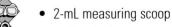
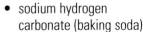

- 2-mL measuring scoop
- sodium hydrogen carbonate (baking soda)
- balance

Procedure

1 Put on your apron and safety goggles.

2 Be sure that the test tube and beaker are clean and dry before you begin. Pour dilute hydrochloric acid into the test tube to a depth of about 5 cm. Put one scoop of sodium hydrogen carbonate into the beaker. Place the test tube in the beaker.

(a) Record your observations of the reactants.

(b) Record the total mass of the reactants, tube, and beaker.

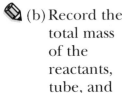

Step 9

3 Remove the beaker from the balance. Slowly pour the acid from the test tube into the beaker.

(c) Record your observations.

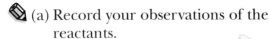
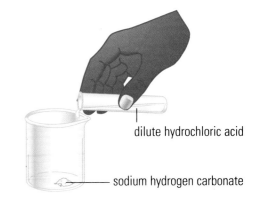

Step 3

dilute hydrochloric acid

sodium hydrogen carbonate

4 Put the test tube back in the beaker and measure the total mass of the beaker, test tube, and products.

(d) Record the total mass.

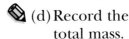

Step 4

5 Dispose of the contents of your beaker as directed by your teacher. Clean up your work station. Wash your hands.

Questions

1. What evidence do you have that a chemical change took place after you poured the dilute acid into the beaker?

2. (a) What were the reactants?

   (b) What was the difference in mass between the reactants and the products?

   (c) What might account for any difference in mass you observed?

3. (a) What were the products of this reaction?

   (b) How could you test the products to be certain?

4. (a) To make a fair comparison between this investigation and Investigation 6.4, how would you modify your procedure?

   (b) How might this modification be dangerous?

   (c) What property of which product causes the potential danger?

5. Suggest why you were told to remove the beaker from the balance before mixing the two reactants.

Apply

6. A senior science student carried out an experiment to examine the burning of magnesium. She determined the mass of a piece of magnesium ribbon. Then she burned it, being careful to collect all the pieces of white ash. Finally, she determined the mass of the ash. Look at her results, and explain them. (Hint: First write a word equation for the reaction. There are two reactants and one product.)

BURNING OF MAGNESIUM	
Mass of magnesium ribbon	3.0 g
Mass of ash	4.8 g
Difference	1.8 g

7. Examine the following recipe.

Blueberry Muffins

Ingredients

300 g all-purpose flour	200 g milk
125 g sugar	10 g melted butter
25 g baking powder	one egg (50 g)
5 g salt	175 g blueberries

Directions

Stir together dry ingredients. Add blueberries. Combine egg, milk, and melted butter. Add to flour and blueberry mixture. Stir until just moist. (Do not beat.) Divide batter evenly in muffin tin (8-muffin size). Bake at 190°C for 20 min.

(a) Calculate the mass of the reactants (ingredients).

(b) Predict the mass of the products (muffins).

(c) What did you assume about the products in order to make your prediction? Is your assumption valid? Explain.

(d) What would you need to know in order to check your prediction?

(e) What is the mass of one muffin?

(f) A bakery sells 120 muffins a day, seven days a week. Calculate the mass of each ingredient the bakery must buy in order to make a week's supply of muffins.

Extension

8. Design an apparatus that would allow you to compare the mass of reactants with the mass of products when wood burns.

Conserving Mass

WHAT HAPPENS in a chemical reaction when one of the reactants or products is a gas? Do the reactants and products still have the same mass? For more than 200 years, scientists tried to devise methods to trap the gases that are used or produced in reactions and to find ways to measure their masses. After years of experimenting, in which the masses of all the reactants and all the products were determined, scientists agreed that mass is neither gained nor lost in any chemical reaction. This conclusion is stated as a law. A **scientific law** is a general statement that sums up the conclusions of many experiments.

The Law of Conservation of Mass

In a chemical reaction, the total mass of the reactants is always equal to the total mass of the products.

If the mass of the products is always the same as the mass of the reactants, what does this tell us about the atoms that make up the reactants and products? Again, experiments have shown that atoms in a chemical reaction are not changed—the number of each kind of atom is the same before and after a reaction. In chemical reactions, the atoms of the reactants are simply rearranged. Molecules may be broken apart and new ones may be formed, but the atoms in the products are the same ones that were in the reactants.

▶

Atoms are not destroyed in a chemical reaction, just rearranged.

If you combine the Law of Conservation of Mass with what you know about atoms and elements, you can expand the Particle Theory of Matter. The expanded theory, called the Atomic Theory, is made up of four simple statements:

The Atomic Theory

- **All matter is made up of tiny particles, called atoms.**
- **Atoms of any one element are like one another and are different from atoms of other elements.**
- **Atoms may combine with other atoms to form larger particles, called molecules.**
- **Atoms are not created or destroyed by any ordinary means.**

An Environmental View

If all of the atoms present at the beginning of a chemical reaction are there after the reaction, what does this mean for the environment? Think about engines that use fuels like gasoline as a source of energy. People want only the energy released during the chemical reaction of combustion. But since mass is conserved, all of the mass of the fuel is still around in some form after combustion occurs. From the point of view of protecting the environment from pollutants, all of the products of any chemical reaction must be considered.

MATH-LINK

Calculating Mass

Knowing the Law of Conservation of Mass makes it possible to calculate the mass of a product or reactant indirectly, without having to use a balance.

For example, when magnesium metal is burned in oxygen gas, the word equation is:

magnesium + oxygen $\longrightarrow$ magnesium oxide

When 60 g of magnesium react, 100 g of magnesium oxide result. Since the total mass of reactants must equal the total mass of product:

mass of magnesium + mass of oxygen

= mass of magnesium oxide

60 g + mass of oxygen = 100 g

mass of oxygen = 100 g – 60 g

= 40 g

Since the ratio of the number of atoms is always the same in any chemical reaction, the ratio of masses is also always the same. In the above example, you can calculate the mass ratio as follows:

$$\frac{\text{mass of magnesium}}{\text{mass of oxygen}} = \frac{60}{40} = \frac{6}{4} = \frac{3}{2}$$

Use ratios to solve the following problems.

- How many grams of magnesium would react with 20 g of oxygen?
- How many grams of oxygen would react with 45 g of magnesium?

Magnesium, a shiny silver metal, burns in oxygen to form a dull, white solid.

Atoms, Molecules, and the Atmosphere

S LOWLY BREATHE in a lungful of air. As you do, think about the billions of molecules that you are inhaling. Air is mostly nitrogen and oxygen, but you are breathing in a mixture that contains other gases as well. In this section, you will learn about some of the gases found in air.

Nitrogen (N_2)

Two atoms of the element nitrogen combine to form the gas nitrogen. Nitrogen makes up the bulk of the atmosphere. It is not very reactive, although under certain conditions, such as in a car engine, nitrogen gas will react with oxygen to produce nitrogen dioxide.

Argon (Ar)

Argon atoms do not form molecules, even with each other. As a result, argon gas is composed of single atoms of argon. Almost all of the argon in the atmosphere has leaked out from inside the Earth.

Oxygen (O_2 and O_3)

Atoms of the element oxygen can combine to form two different molecules. The most common of these molecules contains two atoms of oxygen. This is the form that makes up about 21% of the air you breathe.

The less common oxygen molecule is called ozone (O_3). It contains three atoms of oxygen. Ozone is formed naturally in the upper layers of the atmosphere. It is very important to life on Earth because it absorbs most of the ultraviolet radiation from the Sun. If all of this radiation reached the surface of the Earth, it would harm all living things exposed to it.

Unfortunately, air pollutants such as chlorofluorocarbons (CFCs) have been destroying the ozone layer at an alarming rate. Worldwide measures to stop this pollution have begun, but it will be years before the risk to the ozone layer is past. Because of damage to the ozone layer, more ultraviolet light is reaching the surface of the Earth. Ultraviolet light damages skin. As a result, scientists now

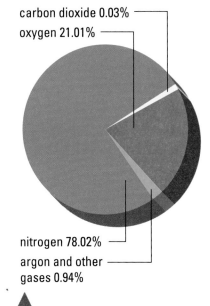

carbon dioxide 0.03%
oxygen 21.01%
nitrogen 78.02%
argon and other gases 0.94%

Gases in the Earth's atmosphere

Nitrogen molecule

Argon atom

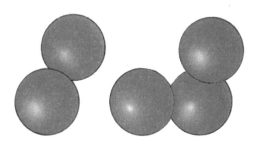

Molecular oxygen   Ozone molecule

encourage people to use sunscreen for skin protection when they go out in the sun.

The ozone several kilometres up in the upper atmosphere is necessary for life. On the other hand, ozone at ground level is hazardous to living things. It can damage plants and causes respiratory problems in people and other animals. It is produced when certain gases, produced mainly by automobiles, react with one another and with the more common O_2 molecule.

Carbon Dioxide and Carbon Monoxide (CO_2 and CO)

Two atmospheric gases contain only atoms of carbon and oxygen. One, carbon dioxide, is necessary for life on Earth. The other, carbon monoxide, is extremely poisonous to living things.

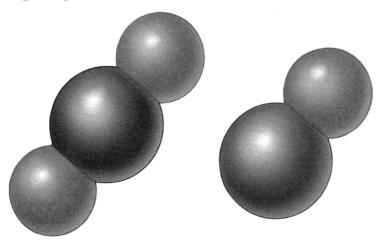

Carbon dioxide molecule   Carbon monoxide molecule

Carbon dioxide and carbon monoxide are both produced during the combustion of fossil fuels. You recall that the two main products of combustion are carbon dioxide and water. However, if there is a shortage of oxygen during combustion, carbon monoxide is also produced.

How can the supply of oxygen be limited? If you burn propane indoors, in a gas barbecue or heater, for example, you might use up most of the oxygen from the air in the room. The same might happen if you run an automobile engine in a closed garage.

The carbon monoxide molecule (CO) is similar to the oxygen molecule (O_2). This similarity makes carbon monoxide poisonous. When carbon monoxide molecules enter the lungs, the body's red blood cells treat CO molecules as if they were O_2 molecules and carry them, instead of oxygen, throughout the body. The cells of the body are supplied with carbon monoxide instead of the oxygen they need. Death can result.

TECHNOLOGY-LINK

Auto Safety

Auto mechanics frequently test car engines indoors while the engine is running. Normally, this would result in carbon monoxide building up inside the garage. Visit a garage.

- What device is used to prevent any buildup of carbon monoxide inside the garage?
- How is fresh air brought into the garage?
- How would fresh air reduce the amount of carbon monoxide produced by cars?

SELF CHECK

14. Write the chemical formulas of each of the following molecules.
    (a) carbon dioxide
    (b) carbon monoxide
    (c) oxygen
    (d) ozone
    (e) nitrogen

15. Carbon dioxide and carbon monoxide each contain carbon and oxygen.
    (a) Which of these molecules is a dangerous substance to breathe?
    (b) Why is it dangerous?

16. (a) How is ozone formed at ground level?
    (b) What effect does this ozone have on living things?

17. (a) What is happening to ozone in the upper atmosphere?
    (b) How could this affect living things?

Analyzing Phosphates and Oxygen in Rapid River

WHEN AN INDUSTRY USES a chemical reaction to make a desirable product, less desirable products may also be produced. Some of these become pollutants and may affect human health as well as the environment.

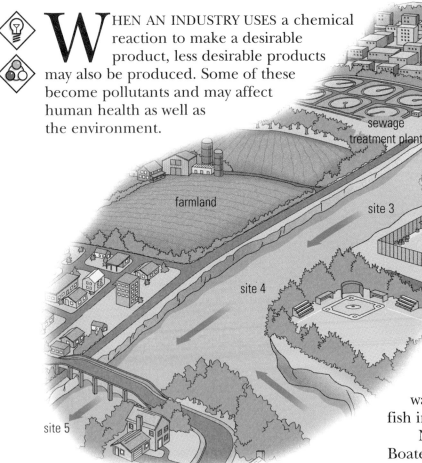

Riverview

site 1

sewage treatment plant

site 2

farmland

site 3

fertilizer plant

site 4

site 5

Pollution in the Rapid River

The problems of residents near the Rapid River are the same as those faced by most river communities. Substances released into the river may be polluting the environment. Earlier, your environmental consulting company was hired by Fast Fertilizers Inc. to investigate pollution of the Rapid River. The fertilizer firm was being blamed for polluting the Rapid River.

Evidence of pollution in the Rapid River was seen in the complaints from people living downstream from the growing city of

Riverview. The complaints, as you learned on page 135, were that the water is very cloudy and the number of fish in the river is declining.

Now a new complaint has surfaced. Boaters and canoeists say water plants clog their motors and paddles, and a green scum is growing on sections of the river. Too much algae and too many water plants are growing in some parts of the river. Anglers say that the number of fish in these areas is very low.

A model of a phosphate molecule

The City Council of Riverview suspects that phosphates are entering the river, and once again blames Fast Fertilizers. **Phosphates**, which contain the elements phosphorus and oxygen, are fertilizers that encourage the growth of plants. In water, fertilizers cause rapid growth of algae and water plants. When the algae and plants die, the oxygen concentration is affected. The bacteria that decompose the dead algae and plants use up dissolved oxygen in the water. That oxygen is no longer available to fish. A chemical test is available that will tell how much phosphate is dissolved in water.

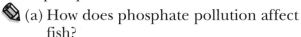 (a) How does phosphate pollution affect fish?

(b) How would you recognize a river or lake that was being polluted by phosphates?

The fertilizer firm is being blamed, but there are other possible sources of phosphates. They could be coming from farm fields. Excess fertilizer can dissolve in water and be carried from fields into local rivers. Phosphates could be entering the river from the wastewater plant. Many detergents used to clean clothes contain phosphates, and the plant may not be treating the wastewater from homes properly.

(c) In your group, discuss the sources of phosphate. If the phosphates in the Rapid River come from the fertilizer plant, where would you expect to find a big increase in the amount of phosphate in the water? If the phosphates come from the wastewater plant or from farms, where would the increase be?

(d) Using the map of the Rapid River, discuss where your company would test for phosphates.

Testing for Phosphates

To discover the source of the phosphates, your company took water samples from five sites and tested for phosphates and dissolved oxygen. The results of the tests are given below. (A normal concentration of phosphates for the area around Riverview is about 10 mg/L of water.)

Results of Rapid River Testing

Site	Location	Phosphates (mg/L)	Dissolved oxygen (mg/L)
1	just upstream from Riverview	10.0	10.0
2	directly downstream from the wastewater plant	22.0	4.0
3	directly downstream from the fertilizer plant	25.0	3.5
4	directly downstream from farmland	28.0	2.2
5	60 km downstream from Riverview	18.0	8.0

(e) At which site does the largest change in the concentration of phosphates occur?

(f) At which site does the largest change in concentrations of dissolved oxygen occur?

(g) What evidence is there that phosphate pollution has been produced by the wastewater plant? By the fertilizer plant? By runoff from farmland?

(h) Which source of phosphate pollution is the most significant?

Questions

1. Plot two bar graphs to represent the results of the water testing.

2. The last time your company was called to Riverview, it tested the river for suspended solids at the same five sites. Which factor, suspended solids or phosphates, do you think had the greater effect on the amount of dissolved oxygen in the river? Explain your answer.

Suspended Solids in Rapid River

Site	Suspended solids (mg/L)
1	50
2	60
3	65
4	70
5	56

The Riverview Public Hearing

FROM CASE STUDY 6.8, you have become aware of the pollution problem in the Rapid River. You have developed opinions about the source of that water pollution—the fertilizer plant, city residents (the wastewater plant), runoff from farm fields, or all three. You have also learned about wastewater treatment, and about how chemical changes can affect the environment.

In this public hearing, you will use what you have learned to help decide whether Riverview should upgrade its wastewater treatment plant. If action must be taken, you will decide who should pay and how much they should pay.

The Hearing

1. Your class will be divided so that each of the roles below is represented by a small group.

   agricultural researchers

   environmental consultants

   farmers/ranchers

   fishing guides

   local environmental group

   management of fertilizer plant

   representatives of downstream towns

   taxpayers

   wastewater treatment technologists

   workers from fertilizer plant

2. Decide whether your group is for, against, or neutral about spending money to upgrade the Riverview wastewater plant to tertiary treatment. Together, develop your presentation to the City Council. Select one person from your group to make the presentation.

3. Set up your classroom for the hearing. All students not speaking become members of Council. Councillors can ask questions and make comments.

4. As the group representatives make their presentations, record your observations and conclusions. Use this summary to help you decide what course of action the city should take.

5. Council must decide what sources are responsible for the phosphate pollution; if the wastewater plant is to be upgraded; or if there are other ways to deal with the problem; and if the plant is upgraded, which group (or groups) should pay.

Sample Opinions

Here are some sample opinions, to get you started in your groups:

Opinion of a taxpayer I won't pay more tax. Our taxes are among the highest in the country. We're a growing city and money is already being taken to pay for roads and schools. We have to clean the water we take from the river. Other communities should do the same.

Opinion of a representative from downstream towns Our water is cloudy and tastes bad. Our towns are small and we cannot afford to improve our water-filtering plants. Our tourism businesses are suffering because of the polluted river.

Opinion of the manager of the fertilizer plant We do release some phosphates into the river. If the city upgrades its wastewater plant, then we can send our effluent to the plant to be cleaned. We'd be willing to pay a fee for this—but we can't afford to build our own system. If you try to force us to, we will have to close the plant.

Opinion of a worker from the fertilizer plant I can find no other work in Riverview. If this plant closes down, I, and many of my fellow workers, would have to leave the city and look for work somewhere else.

Opinion of a wastewater treatment technologist We can remove phosphates from wastewater by adding a chemical such as aluminum sulphate or magnesium sulphate. However, this is expensive. The equipment and its installation will cost about $50 million. The chemicals alone will cost about $3 million per year.

Opinion of an agricultural researcher Phosphate pollution from farms can be reduced by such things as using smaller amounts of fertilizer, leaving vegetation between the fields and river to trap runoff, and diverting runoff into holding basins.

Opinion of a Riverview councillor I don't think we have to spend millions upgrading our treatment plant. Why can't we just take action against each source of phosphates?

Opinion of a fishing guide Ten years ago we used to be very busy here in the summer. People came from all over the country. Now, I take out very few fishing parties because there are fewer fish.

Opinion of an environmental consultant The amount of algae downstream from Riverview has increased to almost four times what it was 25 years ago. Phosphate input from wastewater alone has increased from 190 to 600 tonnes per year. These figures do not include phosphate added directly to the river by industry or washed from fields.

Opinion of a farmer/rancher We need to use all of that fertilizer on our fields to make them productive for crops, and so that we can harvest enough feed for our livestock in the winter. We want to make sure people in the city have enough to eat. It costs money to change farming practices—first to explain the new methods to everyone, and then to actually do it.

What Do You Think?

1. Do you agree with Council's decision? Why or why not?

2. Was there any attempt at compromise made at the hearing? Explain your answer.

ASK YOURSELF

Look in your local newspaper for articles about water quality issues in your area. Compare the concerns and possible solutions to what you heard during this hearing. Did any ideas come up in your class that might be helpful in your community?

Key Outcomes

Now that you have completed this chapter, can you do the following? If not, review the sections indicated.

- Classify substances as (6.1) heterogeneous mixtures, solutions, elements, or compounds.

- State the basic ideas of the (6.1, 6.6) Atomic Theory, and use them to explain elements and compounds.

- Explain how chemical (6.3) symbols and formulas are used to represent elements and compounds.

- Use examples to show how (6.1, 6.3) different combinations of atoms produce molecules of different properties.

- Define and apply the Law (6.4, 6.5, of Conservation of Mass.   6.6)

- Recognize how science and (6.8, 6.9) technology can provide explanations of and possible solutions to environmental problems.

Key Terms

element

compound

atom

molecule

chemical formula

scientific law

Law of Conservation of Mass

Atomic Theory

phosphate

Review

1. Use a sketch to show two different compounds whose molecules contain only atoms of carbon and oxygen.

2. Match the description on the left with one term on the right. Use each term only once.

Description	Term
A smallest particle of an element	1 oxygen
B required for combustion	2 element
C a poisonous gas	3 ozone
D destroy ozone in atmosphere	4 carbon dioxide
E substance containing only one type of atom	5 carbon monoxide
	6 atom
F substance in plant fertilizer	7 molecule
G blocks ultraviolet radiation in upper atmosphere	8 CFCs
H a major product of combustion	9 phosphate
I particle made of two or more atoms	

3. Describe two compounds that contain atoms of the same elements, but in different proportions.

4. What are the four main ideas of the Atomic Theory?

5. (a) What elements are present in phosphates?

   (b) Describe two ways phosphates can enter lakes and rivers.

   (c) How can phosphates harm fish?

6. Examine the molecules in the diagram below.

(a) What substances could the drawings represent?

(b) Write a word equation for the reaction.

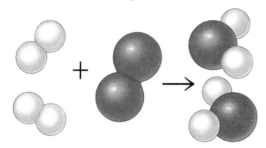

7. Make a concept map to help you summarize the material that you have studied in this chapter.

Problem Solving

8. In an experiment, 24 g of magnesium react with 73 g of hydrogen chloride to produce a gas and 95 g of magnesium chloride.

(a) Does this data prove the Law of Conservation of Mass? Explain your answer.

(b) What gas do you think was produced? How much of the gas do you think was produced?

9. A list of mysterious letters and numbers was discovered in the pocket of a coat left behind at a crime scene. The detective is certain this list hides a secret message that could be an important clue to the identity of the criminal. Is the detective right in looking for a hidden message? Do you think the list is a clue? Explain your reasoning.

$NaHCO_3$

$CaCO_3$

$NaCl$

$C_9H_8O_4$

$Ca_3P_2O_8$

Critical Thinking

10. An inventor is trying to sell an idea to protect people from ultraviolet radiation: a headband that releases a cloud of ozone around a person's head. Write a letter to this inventor explaining whether it is a good idea or not.

11. The graphs below show the elements that are present in the Earth's crust and in the human body, by mass.

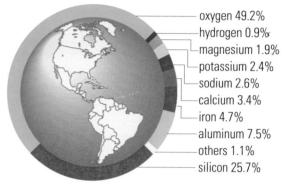

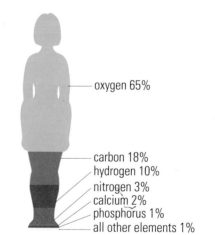

(a) What similarities can you see?

(b) What element makes up a large part of the crust of the Earth, but less than 1% of the human body?

(c) What element makes up a large part of the human body, but less than 1% of the Earth's crust?

12. Suppose you have been asked to present a display, including a poster, that explains the classification of matter. What would you include in such a poster, and what simple props could you use to get your message across?

Managing Chemical Change

NORTH AMERICANS PRODUCE 200 million tonnes of organic waste each year. It was this massive waste that prompted Jim Wright, along with his partner, Bert Baillie, to develop a machine called the Wright In-Vessel Composter that would compost food wastes efficiently and cost-effectively.

◀ Jim Wright, left, and his partner Bert Baillie have developed an award-winning composter.

Q. Just what is composting? We hear a lot about composters today but I'm not sure everybody understands the process.

A. When living things die, microorganisms break them down by a series of chemical reactions. Composting is a way of speeding up the chemical process using controlled amounts of heat, water, and oxygen.

It doesn't take too much work to compost lawn and garden wastes. But food wastes, especially bones, meat, and fat, are harder to break down. And they cause two major problems: they produce smelly gases, and they attract rats, raccoons, bears—any creatures that like to eat meat.

Q. What makes your composter unique?

A. First of all, our composter controls odours. The composting itself takes place inside a thick-walled stainless steel container, or vessel, so that other creatures can't get in. Secondly, the whole process is very simple to operate and maintain.

Q. What has been the reaction to the Wright In-vessel Composter?

A. Experts from around the world are really impressed with its efficiency. Our composters are being used in government buildings, hospitals, correctional institutions, and on military bases. But we can build them to suit any size, from just 45 kg to hundreds of tonnes of waste a day.

Q. How did you and your partner get involved in working together in the first place?

A. Bert and I grew up together in Belfast, Ireland. We often worked on projects together in science and math classes. We moved to Powell River in B.C. at about the same time and began work in the pulp and paper industry.

Q. How did this lead to the Wright Composter?

A. Bert was experimenting with using wood chips to grow mushrooms: I made the machine to chip the wood to just the right size. He moved on to composting sludge from the pulp mill and over the next 20 years became quite an expert at the process. When I said how wonderful it was to turn sludge into a useable product, he said he could compost household garbage. All I said to him was, "Let's do it."

Q. What difficulties did you experience in developing this composter?

A. We looked at a lot of existing systems, but there were obvious problems with each one. It took us 10 years to develop this composter. Along the way, we produced a lot of stupid systems that just didn't work. They didn't add water properly or they trapped too much heat that stopped the chemical change from happening.

Q. What sort of future do you see for this process?

A. Our throwaway world really bothers me. I don't want to leave the world a sewer for my grandchildren. And I think many people feel the same way. Composting is a sunrise industry: there's a real future for people who work in environmental science. We're already scheduled to put a greenhouse on top of one of our composters. The excess heat and moisture from composting can be used to complete the natural cycle and produce plants. My intention is to develop this into a unit that could be used in space stations.

How the Wright In-Vessel Composter Works

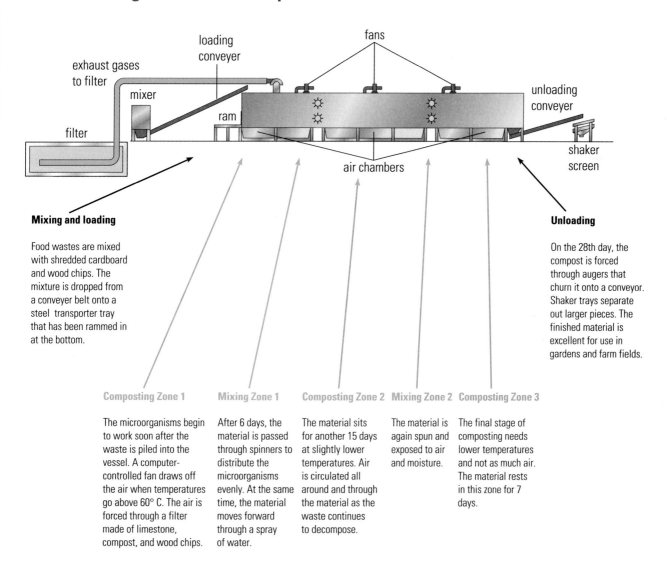

Mixing and loading

Food wastes are mixed with shredded cardboard and wood chips. The mixture is dropped from a conveyer belt onto a steel transporter tray that has been rammed in at the bottom.

Unloading

On the 28th day, the compost is forced through augers that churn it onto a conveyor. Shaker trays separate out larger pieces. The finished material is excellent for use in gardens and farm fields.

Composting Zone 1

The microorganisms begin to work soon after the waste is piled into the vessel. A computer-controlled fan draws off the air when temperatures go above 60° C. The air is forced through a filter made of limestone, compost, and wood chips.

Mixing Zone 1

After 6 days, the material is passed through spinners to distribute the microorganisms evenly. At the same time, the material moves forward through a spray of water.

Composting Zone 2

The material sits for another 15 days at slightly lower temperatures. Air is circulated all around and through the material as the waste continues to decompose.

Mixing Zone 2

The material is again spun and exposed to air and moisture.

Composting Zone 3

The final stage of composting needs lower temperatures and not as much air. The material rests in this zone for 7 days.

All the processes coloured in green occur inside the composting vessel. Only the mixing and loading, the filtering, and the unloading happen outside the vessel.

NOW THAT YOU HAVE COMPLETED Chapters 4, 5, and 6, you can assess how much you have learned about Changes in Matter by trying these questions. Before you begin, you may find it useful to return to the Chapter Reviews. There, you will find lists of Key Outcomes and Key Terms. Read these to ensure that you understand the main points and the important vocabulary of the chapters. If necessary, look back at the appropriate sections in the text, which are listed with the Key Outcomes.

Write your answers to the questions in your notebook.

True/False

For each of the following, write T if the statement is true. If the statement is false, rewrite it to make it true.

1. Distilled water is a pure substance.

2. Soda pop is a heterogeneous mixture.

3. The filtrate is the substance that passes through the filter paper.

4. A salt and sand mixture can be separated by using chromatography.

5. A new substance is produced in a physical change.

6. Melting is a chemical change.

7. A burning splint is used to test for hydrogen gas.

8. Another word for burning is combustion.

9. An element contains only one type of atom.

10. Carbon dioxide is a compound.

11. Lemonwater is used to test for carbon dioxide gas.

Completion

Copy the following sentences, filling in each blank with the word or phrase that correctly completes the sentence. Use the words from this list: residue, filtrate, homogeneous, heterogeneous, glowing, burning, chemical, physical, element, compound, colloid, formula, symbol, chromatography. (You will not need to use all of the words.)

12. A mixture that is intermediate between a solution and a heterogeneous mixture is a ▢.

13. The solid material left in the filter paper after filtration is the ▢.

14. A technique called ▢ can be used to separate coloured dyes in pen inks.

15. Another name for solution is ▢ mixture.

16. To test for oxygen gas, a ▢ splint is used.

17. A new substance is produced in a ▢ change.

18. A pure substance containing two or more kinds of atoms is a ▢.

19. The chemical ▢ of water is H_2O.

20. A change of state or form is a ▢ change.

Matching

Copy the numbers of the descriptions given below. Beside each number, write the word from the right column that best fits the description. (You will not need to use all of the words.)

21. mixture of substances in which separate phases are visible

22. tiniest particle of matter

23. particle made of several atoms

24. pure substance containing more than one type of atom

25. pure substance containing one type of atom

26. the substance that dissolves

27. a mixture made up of two liquids

28. material that goes through a filter paper

29. compound containing only hydrogen and oxygen atoms

A element
B compound
C phase
D water
E atom
F molecule
G solute
H heterogeneous
I residue
J emulsion
K filtrate
L solution

Multiple Choice

Write the letter of the best answer for each of the following questions. Write only one answer for each.

30. Hydrogen is a(n)

A element.   D heterogeneous mixture.
B compound. E emulsion.
C solution.

31. Distilled water is best classified as a(n)

A element.   D heterogeneous mixture.
B compound. E emulsion.
C solution.

32. Sodium chloride is a(n)

A element.   D heterogeneous mixture.
B compound. E emulsion.
C solution.

33. Which of the following is a chemical change?

A wax melting D dry ice subliming
B ice freezing E frost forming
C food rotting

34. Which of the following is a physical change?

A dynamite exploding D grass growing
B gasoline evaporating E bread toasting
C steel rusting

35. Which of the following is a physical change?

A silver tarnishing   D fireworks igniting
B snow melting   E muffins baking
C eggs cooking

36. Which of the following is a compound?

A silver   D hydrogen
B sugar   E mercury
C brass

37. Which of the following is an element?

A chlorine   D carbon dioxide
B tap water   E steel
C smog

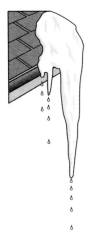
(a) icicle melting

(b) rocket taking off

(c) wood rotting

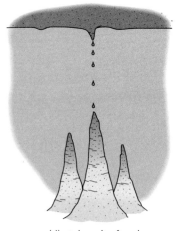
(d) stalagmite forming

Short Answer

Write a sentence or a short paragraph to answer each of the following questions.

38. For each situation illustrated above, decide whether the change is physical or chemical. Give your reasons in each case.

39. (a) What do all chemical reactions have in common?

(b) Give four examples of differences among chemical reactions.

40. Hydrochloric acid reacts with sodium hydroxide to produce sodium chloride and water. Identify the reactants and products of this reaction and write a word equation.

41. Hydrogen peroxide gradually decomposes, forming water and oxygen. Identify the reactants and products and write a word equation for this reaction.

42. Carbon dioxide and water are produced in our bodies. These are the end products of a series of reactions involving sugar and oxygen. Identify the reactants and products of the reaction, and write a word equation.

43. (a) What is an atom?

(b) How are molecules related to atoms?

44. "The untreated water that enters a water treatment plant is a heterogeneous mixture, but the water that leaves the plant is a pure substance." Do you agree with all of this quotation, part of it, or none of it? Explain your reasoning.

Problem Solving

45. Most organisms cannot live in polluted water, but some kinds of worms thrive in polluted conditions. Would you expect these worms to be more numerous than usual in each of the following locations? Explain your answers.

(a) in a river, downstream from a sewage treatment plant

(b) in a river, upstream from a large industrialized city

(c) in a river with a high dissolved oxygen concentration

(d) in a river with a low phosphate concentration

46. A black material is heated. A gas is released and a white substance remains. Was the original material an element or a compound? Explain your answer.

47. During a flood one spring, a truck became stuck in a ditch that empties into a pond. In order to get the truck out of the ditch, the driver had to dump the load. The following summer, there were more algae in the pond than ever before. The next year, there were almost no fish in the pond, although it used to be a favourite fishing hole. What was in the load? Explain what was happening in the pond.

48. After 28 g of nitrogen gas and 10 g of hydrogen gas are mixed to produce ammonia (NH_3), 4 g of hydrogen are left unchanged. How much ammonia was produced?

49. You have a mixture of iron pellets, salt, sand, and marble chips. You are provided with a screen, a magnet, and filter paper. Design an experiment to separate and recover these substances.

50. A colourless, odourless gas is produced when an antacid tablet is added to water. Design an experiment to determine what the gas is.

Challenge

51. Look around your home and find three situations where chemical reactions are occurring. For each, explain how you know it is a chemical reaction. Name the reactants and the products and write a word equation for each.

52. It is easy to lose sight of the benefits of technology when studying the environmental problems that result from a particular technology. For example, automobile exhausts emit nitrogen oxides, which contribute to acid rain, and carbon dioxide, which contributes to the greenhouse effect. List three positive effects that the automobile has had on people's lives. For each benefit, list how it might be achieved without the automobile in the future.

53. Give one benefit and one drawback of each of the following possible actions to reduce acid rain.

(a) By law, industry must reduce sulphur dioxide emissions.

(b) A limit is put on the amount of fuel each household can burn.

(c) Gasoline for cars and trucks is rationed.

(d) All industries and generating stations must build very high smokestacks.

Project Ideas

54. How does your community obtain drinking water? What substances are present in the water before it is purified? How is it purified before it flows out of your tap at home? What substances are added, and why? Write a report on your findings, or prepare a class presentation.

Design and Do

55. Can you control how quickly a reaction happens? Study the diagram below. How much Alka-Seltzer tablet must you add to make the lid blow off in exactly 60 s? Design and carry out an experiment that will allow you to make a prediction. Test your prediction.

 CAUTION: The cap can come off at great speed.

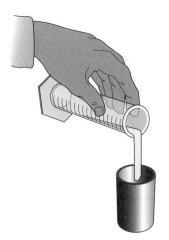

1. Pour water into container until 2/3 full.

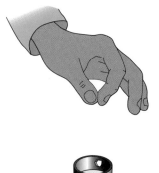

2. Add Alka-Seltzer fragment.

3. Quickly, put lid on.

4. Lid blows off.

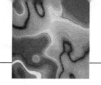

UNIT 3

Light
&
Colour

CHAPTER 7

Light and Its Sources

CHAPTER 8

Reflection of Light

CHAPTER 9

Colour

CHAPTER 7

Light and Its Sources

WITHOUT LIGHT, YOU CAN'T SEE anything at all. But light does more than just let you see. Without light, there would be no life on Earth. Light from the Sun allows plants to grow and provides warmth. And light sent through the fine glass threads of fibre optic cables delivers information quickly by telephone and television. As well, light is used in learning and entertainment: laser shows, fireworks displays, video games, photographs and videos of events in your life, ...

What is light? Is it something that you can touch or taste? Can you find the mass of light? Can you see light? A simple definition is that **light** is a form of energy that you can detect with your eyes. Light energy comes from other forms of energy. The photographs here show light that has come from chemical energy, electrical energy, and nuclear energy.

In this chapter, you will

- explore different sources of light,

- learn how light gets from one place to another, and

- find out what happens to light when it strikes certain objects.

 Getting Started

1. Look at the photographs on these pages. What form of energy do you think is being transformed into light energy in each case?

2. Make a list of all the light sources that you can think of, both inside and outside your classroom. Beside each source in your list, write what you think is the type of energy that has been changed into light energy.

3. Light has many uses. To see how many uses you can think of, complete this statement: Without light, it would not be possible to ....

4. Write several things you know about taking photographs with a camera.

CHALLENGE

If light is energy, it must be able to do work. Devise a way to show that light can do work. For example, can you make light move something?

Where Does Light Energy Come From?

LIGHT ENERGY CAN COME from many different sources, both natural and artificial. The Sun is the most important natural light source. Artificial sources of light are those produced by humans. Objects that emit (give off) their own light are said to be **luminous**. The Sun is luminous; a switched-on flashlight is also luminous.

Objects that do not emit light are said to be **nonluminous**. When a flashlight is switched off, it becomes nonluminous.

In luminous objects, some form of energy changes into light energy. The forms of energy that commonly change into light energy are chemical energy, electrical energy, nuclear energy, and thermal energy.

Light from Incandescence

Things that are extremely hot become luminous. At high temperatures, they begin to emit light. The process of emitting light because of a high temperature is called **incandescence**.

Electrical energy changes into heat and light energy in an incandescent light bulb. A fine metal wire (the tungsten filament) attached to the electrical connections becomes very hot when the bulb is turned on.

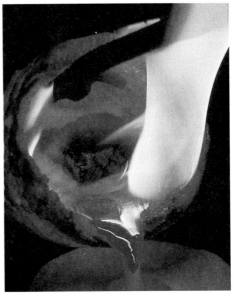

Thermal energy can heat a metal to such a high temperature that it emits light.

Chemical energy changes into heat and light energy.

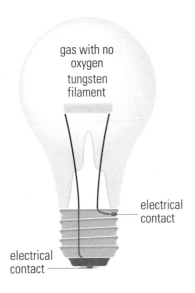

gas with no oxygen

tungsten filament

electrical contact

electrical contact

Light from Electric Discharge

When electricity passes through a gas, the gas particles can emit light. This process of emitting light because of electricity passing through a gas is called **electric discharge**.

Lightning is an example of electric discharge in nature. The electricity discharges through the air, from one cloud to another, or from a cloud to the Earth.

Electric discharge also occurs when electricity is passed through tubes filled with gases. Neon gas gives off a red-orange colour. Mercury vapour gives off a blue colour. Other gases emit other colours.

CHALLENGE

Work in groups to improve on the light bulb design in the Technology-Link. Try using other filaments for a light source, test tubes or other containers, and different combinations of batteries. Predict which light source will provide the greatest illumination.

 CAUTION: Be sure to have your teacher approve your design.

TECHNOLOGY-LINK

Designing a Light Source

Have you ever wondered how light bulbs work? The design shown below will provide you with a light bulb.

Push two thin finishing nails through a cork stopper and attach a fibre of steel wool to the ends. Place the cork in a flask.

- Predict what will happen when you attach wires from a 6-V battery to the ends of the finishing nails, as shown in the diagram. Attach the wires to the battery and observe what happens.

- Using what you know about light, explain what happened.

Light from Phosphorescence

Certain materials, called phosphors, will give off light for a short time after you shine a light on them. One example is the painted luminous dials on some watches and clocks. The process of emitting light for some time after receiving energy from another source is called **phosphorescence.** The colour of the light and the time it lasts depend on the material used.

Light from Fluorescence

Fluorescence is the process of emitting light while receiving energy from another source.

Fluorescent tubes are used in schools, offices, and sometimes in homes. The diagram to the right shows how a fluorescent tube works. Two energy changes occur. First, electricity hits the molecules of mercury vapour, causing them to emit ultraviolet (UV) energy. Then the ultraviolet energy hits a phosphor coating on the inside of the tube. This causes the coating to emit light that you can see.

Light from Chemiluminescence

Chemiluminescence is the process of changing chemical energy into light energy with little or no change in temperature.

Safety lights or "cool lights" produce light by chemiluminescence. In these lights, a thin wall separates two chemicals. When this wall is broken, the chemicals react to produce a light until the chemicals are used up.

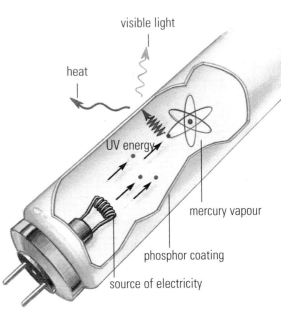

visible light

heat

UV energy

mercury vapour

phosphor coating

source of electricity

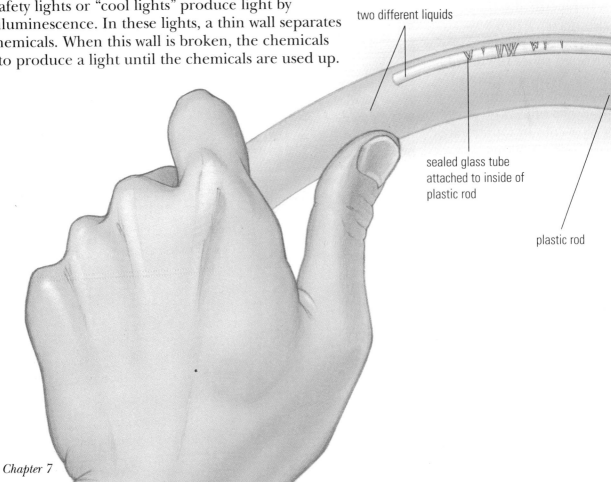

two different liquids

sealed glass tube attached to inside of plastic rod

plastic rod

Light from Bioluminescence

In nature, some living creatures can make themselves luminous by using a chemical reaction similar to chemiluminescence. This process is called **bioluminescence**. Fireflies, glow-worms, and many types of fish, squids, bacteria, and fungi display bioluminescence. If you want to see fireflies (they are actually beetles), your chances are much higher in rural areas than in a city.

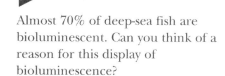

Almost 70% of deep-sea fish are bioluminescent. Can you think of a reason for this display of bioluminescence?

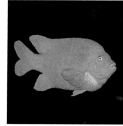

Getting in Light's Way

ONCE LIGHT IS EMITTED from a source, it travels until something gets in its way. Some materials block light, other materials let light pass through. **Transparency** is a measure of how much light can pass through a material. A material can be transparent, translucent, or opaque, as shown in the photographs below. As you read about the photographs, try to think of other examples.

A **transparent** material allows light to pass through easily and allows a clear image to be seen through it. Examples are glass, air, and thin layers of some plastic or water.

A **translucent** material allows light to pass through, but it scatters the light so a clear image cannot be seen through it. Glass bricks, frosted glass, and clouds are examples.

An **opaque** material does not allow any light to pass through it. All the light energy is either absorbed or reflected. Wood, stone, and brick are opaque.

TRY THIS

Classifying the Transparency of Objects

Set up a table with three columns titled *Transparent Objects, Translucent Objects, Opaque Objects*. Beneath each title list several examples. Choose from objects you can see in your classroom, including any set up by your teacher. After you have made your lists, describe any difficulty you might have had in classifying certain objects or materials.

Reflecting Surfaces

The way light acts when it strikes a material depends not only on the material's transparency, but also on the material's colour, sheen (shininess), and texture. Dark, dull, rough surfaces reflect very little light. Instead, they absorb the light energy and transform it into thermal energy. White, shiny, smooth surfaces reflect most of the light that hits them, instead of absorbing it.

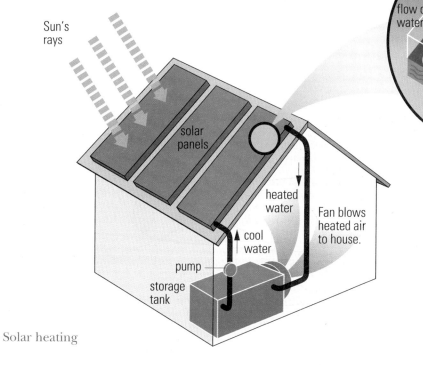

Solar heating

A dark, dull, rough surface absorbs light readily, like a sponge absorbs water. This property of black surfaces is used in solar heating. Light from the Sun is absorbed by black material, where it is transformed into thermal energy. The thermal energy is used to heat water. The hot water can then be used to heat a building.

Plants and animals are adapted to the lighting conditions that surround them. The quiver tree in the picture, found in the Namib Desert in Africa, has a very light-coloured, shiny, smooth bark that reflects light. This adaptation helps make it possible for the quiver tree to survive in a region of intense sunlight.

Blocking Light

A SHADOW IS AN AREA where light has been blocked by an opaque object. The dark part of a shadow is called the **umbra**; no light reaches there. The lighter part of a shadow is called the **penumbra**; some light reaches there. In this investigation, we will use the umbra and the penumbra to reveal an important property of light.

Materials

- ray box
- rubber stopper (or similar opaque object)
- pencil
- ruler

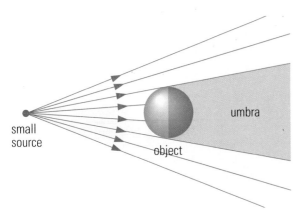

Light from a small source spreads out in all directions, but the opaque object blocks some of the light. The path taken by the light energy is called a ray. It is represented by a line with an arrow to show the direction the light is travelling. Of all the light rays shown, which two rays only would be needed to show the umbra?

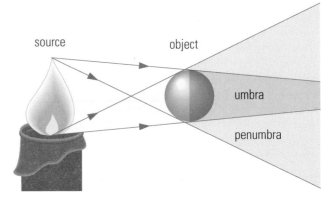

If the light that produces a shadow comes from a large source (or from more than one source), both an umbra and a penumbra are produced. In this case, four light rays are needed to show the outlines of the umbra and penumbra.

Procedure

1. Put a rubber stopper on a piece of paper. Draw the outline of the stopper on the paper. Place the ray box about 5 to 10 cm away from the stopper, and aim a light beam toward the stopper.

2. Use a pencil and a ruler to draw the outside edges of the shadow behind the stopper. Shade the diagram and use arrows to show the direction the light travelled. Label the light source, opaque object, and umbra.

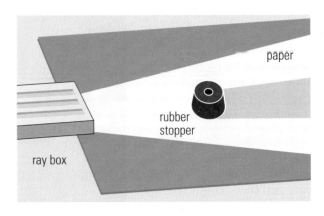

Step 1

3 Start a new diagram, with a fresh piece of paper. Aim light beams from two directions toward the stopper. (You will have to share ray boxes with another group to do this.) Make sure that the beams travel on both sides of the stopper.

4 Draw and shade the shadow behind the stopper. Label the light sources, opaque object, umbra, and penumbra.

Steps 3 and 4

5 Have your teacher check your diagrams before you put the apparatus away.

Questions

1. What property of light is illustrated in this activity?

2. Look at the diagrams on the facing page showing shadows produced by small and by large sources. Compare those diagrams with the diagrams you drew for this activity by answering these questions.

   (a) Does light from a single ray box act like light from a small source or from a large source? Explain your answer.

   (b) Repeat (a) for light from two ray boxes.

Apply

3. With the room lights out, one student stands in front of and facing a large screen. A second student aims one of the following light sources toward the first student. Predict the kind of shadow produced by the following.

   (a) a bright flashlight

   (b) a fluorescent desk lamp

4. If you went to buy plants at a nursery, you might find them labelled "full sunlight," "partial shade," and "full shade." How would a knowledge of shadows help you decide which plants to buy?

Extension

5. Predict the number of each kind of shadow you would obtain if you repeated procedure step 3 with light coming from three sources. Then proceed with the experiment. Is your prediction correct? Explain, using a diagram, why there are different shades of penumbras when three sources of light produce a shadow.

6. Gobos are special discs placed in front of lights to cast shadows on a theatre stage. Design a gobo on thick paper, then cut it out and try it, using a ray box or flashlight.

A typical gobo

How Does Light Travel?

YOU CANNOT SEE AROUND opaque objects because *light travels in straight lines.* This property of light explains why shadows are formed. When light strikes an opaque object, it is blocked.

Eclipses: Shadows in Nature

An eclipse occurs when a planet or moon blocks light from the Sun, casting a shadow. The two types of eclipses you can see from the Earth are illustrated in the diagrams on these pages.

Solar Eclipse

A **solar eclipse** is an eclipse of the Sun. It occurs when the Moon is located between the Sun and the Earth and is directly in line with them. The Moon blocks the light coming from the Sun to the Earth. You see the Moon as a dark circle passing over the Sun.

▼

DID YOU KNOW?

A solar eclipse is very dangerous to look at directly. During a recent solar eclipse, dozens of Canadians suffered eye damage when they did not heed warnings. No one should look at a solar eclipse unless wearing a safety-approved visor.

Sun

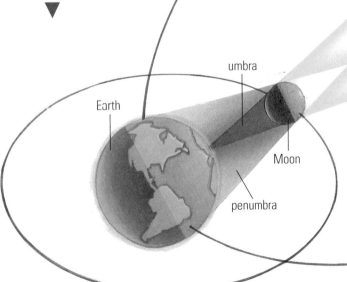

Earth

umbra

Moon

penumbra

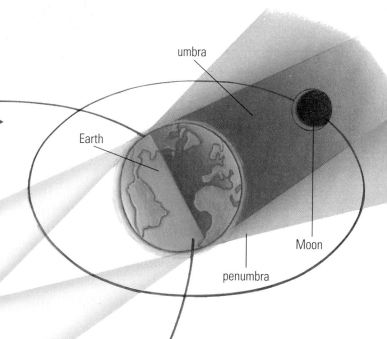

Lunar Eclipse

A **lunar eclipse** is an eclipse of the Moon. It occurs when the Earth is located between the Sun and the Moon. The Earth blocks the Sun's light. You see the Earth's shadow passing over the Moon. Why can this type of eclipse be seen only at night?

umbra

Earth

Moon

penumbra

SELF CHECK

9. Give two examples of evidence that light travels in straight lines.

10. Look at the diagram of a solar eclipse on the opposite page. Draw a similar diagram in your notebook. Mark the place on the Earth where a person would have to be to see a total eclipse of the Sun.

11. Draw a neat, labelled diagram of a lunar eclipse.

12. Imagine you are standing under a bright street lamp. The lamp acts like a small light source. Watch your shadow as you walk away from the lamp post. What happens to the length of your shadow as you get farther from the street lamp? Draw a diagram to illustrate your answer.

13. Why might it be important to understand the formation of shadows if you were employed as each of the following?
    (a) a portrait photographer
    (b) a city planner
    (c) a police officer
    (d) an artist

Sundials: Shadow Clocks

Long before clocks were invented, people made and used sundials as timing devices. A sundial consists of an opaque arm that casts a shadow on a base. Times are labelled around the base. As the Earth spins, the Sun appears to travel across the sky, and the position of the shadow moves.

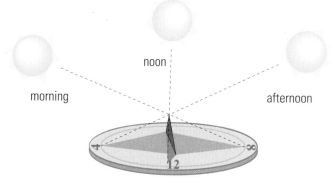

morning

noon

afternoon

A sundial showing shadows at three times of day

Forming Images

W HAT DO YOU SEE when you look into a mirror? You see an image of yourself. You are the object, what you see in the mirror is the image, and the mirror is an optical device. An **image** is the likeness of an object.

Images can be described by four main characteristics, listed in the table below. The diagram shows a description of an image.

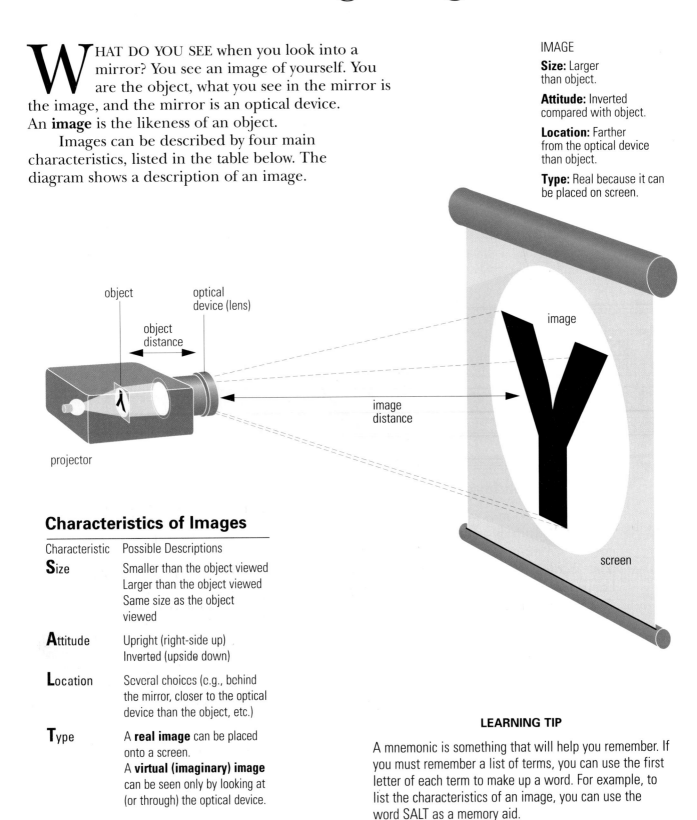

IMAGE

Size: Larger than object.

Attitude: Inverted compared with object.

Location: Farther from the optical device than object.

Type: Real because it can be placed on screen.

Characteristics of Images

Characteristic	Possible Descriptions
Size	Smaller than the object viewed Larger than the object viewed Same size as the object viewed
Attitude	Upright (right-side up) Inverted (upside down)
Location	Several choices (e.g., behind the mirror, closer to the optical device than the object, etc.)
Type	A **real image** can be placed onto a screen. A **virtual (imaginary) image** can be seen only by looking at (or through) the optical device.

LEARNING TIP

A mnemonic is something that will help you remember. If you must remember a list of terms, you can use the first letter of each term to make up a word. For example, to list the characteristics of an image, you can use the word SALT as a memory aid.

The Pinhole Camera

A **pinhole camera** is a box with a tiny hole at one end and a viewing screen at the other end. You can use a pinhole camera to study characteristics of images (as described in the next investigation). A pinhole camera can be small, like a shoe box or a coffee can. It can be large enough for a person to stand inside, like a box for packing a new refrigerator. (In such a large pinhole camera, you could stand inside the box to view the images!) The diagram below shows how a pinhole camera can be made using an ordinary box, such as a shoe box. You can also take photographs with a pinhole camera.

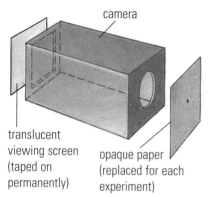

camera

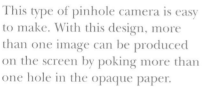

translucent viewing screen (taped on permanently)

opaque paper (replaced for each experiment)

pinhole in opaque paper

This type of pinhole camera is easy to make. With this design, more than one image can be produced on the screen by poking more than one hole in the opaque paper.

When it is completed, this is how you will use the pinhole camera: point toward the object you want to view.

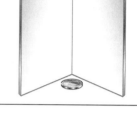
CAREER-LINK

Photographer

Photography can be a hobby or a rewarding career. Professional photographers may work in the following areas:

fashion photography

advertising for magazines, billboards, television, …

portrait photography

travel photography

nature photography

news reporting

television or movie studios

photo developing

business and sales

If you want information about this exciting and creative field, talk to your school counsellor and people who work in the photographic industry. As well, read photography magazines, and try taking your own photos or videos.

SELF CHECK

14. When a slide is placed in a slide projector upside down, the image on the screen is right-side up. Describe the other characteristics of the image of this slide.

15. Based on the definitions of real and virtual images given in the table on the opposite page, do you think the image seen in a pinhole camera is real or virtual? Why?

16. In a pinhole camera used to view images, the screen must be translucent rather than transparent or opaque. Why?

17. An image can be either real or virtual, not both at the same time. But in games with "virtual reality," computer-controlled images appear to be real. Do you think "virtual reality" is a good name for images? Why or why not?

18. List and define three words or phrases (other than optical device) that stem from the word optic. Use your own experience, or look in a dictionary.

Viewing Images in a Pinhole Camera

IN THIS INVESTIGATION, you will use a pinhole camera to study images. First, you can look at images in the camera. Then, you can apply your skill in drawing diagrams to help you understand your observations.

CAUTION: If you use a candle, make sure that you keep the pinhole camera at least 20 cm away from the flame. Check the location of a fire extinguisher and a fire blanket before beginning.

Materials

- pinhole camera with a translucent viewing screen
- tape
- small piece of opaque paper, or aluminum foil
- pin
- luminous object (such as a candle flame, or a small electric light bulb)
- ruler
- thin magnifying lens (optional)

Procedure

Part 1 *Using One Pinhole*

1 Use tape to attach the opaque paper or aluminum foil over the opening of the camera. With a pin, poke a hole in the middle of the paper.

CAUTION: Exercise care when using a pin.

2 With the pinhole about 20 cm away from the object, aim the camera straight toward the object, as shown below.

(a) Describe the four characteristics of the image you see on the screen. (Remember SALT: size, attitude, location, and type.)

3 Move the camera so it is about 40 cm away from the object, and view the image.

(b) Describe what happened to the size and brightness of the image.

Part 2 *Using More Than One Pinhole*

4 Poke a second pinhole about 1 cm above the first one. View the object from the same distance you used in step 2.

(c) Describe what you observe on the screen.

5 Poke 4 or 5 more holes in the paper to form a neat letter F.

(d) Predict what you will see when you view the object through the camera. Then look through the camera and draw a diagram of the pattern you observe.

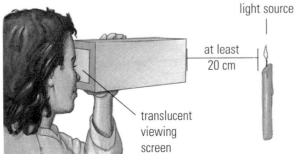

Step 2

Step 5

Questions

1. The diagram below shows the image produced in a pinhole camera using a candle flame as the object. (Notice that the two light rays shown start from the top and bottom of the flame. These rays cross each other at the pinhole.) Describe the four characteristics of the image in this diagram.

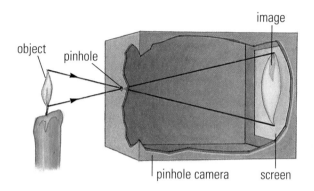

2. This activity provides more evidence that light travels in straight lines. Look at the ray diagram above and explain why the image is inverted.

3. Copy the two diagrams below into your notebook. Use a ruler to draw the cameras, and be sure all sizes and distances are as shown. Then draw the rays needed to find the image in each case. How do these diagrams relate to your observations in the investigation?

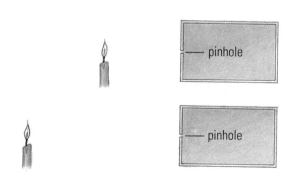

4. Draw a ray diagram to illustrate how images form when a camera has two pinholes.

Apply

5. You can use a pinhole camera to take a photograph if you replace the translucent screen with photographic paper or film. Because a pinhole is so small, the image may not be bright enough to create a picture on the paper or film. What could you do to increase the total amount of light that reaches the film?

Extension

6. Use the opaque paper with several holes in it (such as you made for the letter F) for the pinhole camera. Hold a thin magnifying lens in front of the holes, as shown below. Move the lens back and forth until you get a clear image. Describe what you discover.

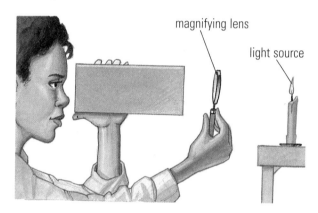

7. Obtain a standard photographic camera that has no film inside. Open the camera.

   (a) Where does the light enter?

   (b) What part of the camera acts as the pinhole?

CHALLENGE

The human eye can be compared to a camera. When you look at an object, an image of the object forms at the back of your eye. As in the pinhole camera, this image is inverted, yet you see the object as upright. How do you think this happens?

Taking Photos with a Pinhole Camera

 SARAH AND MARIO investigated how to take photographs with a pinhole camera. They did several things to get ready to take some photos.

They built a pinhole camera using a coffee can, as shown below. They designed a cover for the camera using the plastic lid of the can. Mario painted the inside of the can black. By piercing a piece of thin brass (bought at a hardware store), they made a pinhole. They used tape to make sure no light could get in except through the pinhole. Sarah designed a simple support stand to hold the camera steady.

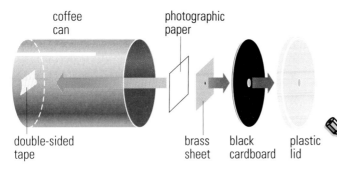

coffee can — photographic paper

double-sided tape — brass sheet — black cardboard — plastic lid

Sarah and Mario helped students in other groups set up the chemicals needed for developing the photos.

They discussed with the other groups what to take pictures of and how to get the best picture.

In a darkened room with only a red safety light on, Mario cut some photographic paper into squares, each measuring about 4 cm on each side. For the first photo, Sarah taped one of the squares to the inside back wall of the camera. Then she put the cover on the camera. Before leaving the darkened room, Sarah placed her thumb tightly over the pinhole.

Mario and Sarah were then ready to take some photos. Sarah wrote the following notes about their investigation.

Photo #1

It was a sunny day, and we set up the camera to take a photo of a white car from the side. The car was about 5 m away. The Sun was behind us. I took my thumb off the pinhole for 5 s, then covered it up again. We developed the picture in the dark room.

The darkness of the car did not surprise us, because we were using photographic paper. This paper is normally used with negatives, rather than in a camera. But the picture also has many light areas that would turn out too dark in a positive picture.

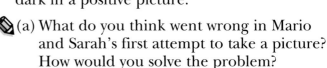

(a) What do you think went wrong in Mario and Sarah's first attempt to take a picture? How would you solve the problem?

Photo #2

We used a similar setup for this picture, but this time we uncovered the pinhole for 10 s.

When we developed this photo we got a clear image of the car, with a good balance of light and dark areas. But the car is on a funny angle, and the picture looks boring.

(b) How would you solve the problems of the second picture?

Photo #3

We set up the camera to take a photo of more of the car, so some of the darker areas would show up. We moved farther away from the car, but used the same exposure time. The lighting conditions were the same. This time we had been more careful putting the paper in the camera, making sure the paper was horizontal.

This photo looks good, except the pavement in the foreground looks too bright in the negative, and it isn't very interesting.

(c) Why would the pavement be too bright in a negative picture?

(d) How would you make the picture more interesting?

Photo #4

This time we put a pop can on the pavement and set up the camera so the can was in the foreground and the white car was in the background. We used the same exposure time (10 s).

(e) What do you think was different when Sarah and Mario took this picture? How should they fix the problem?

Photo #5

This time we tried a pop can in the foreground with a house and trees in the background. We kept the Sun at our backs, and we used the 10-s

exposure time again.

The picture looks good, but the printing on the pop can looks a little blurry.

(f) What caused the blur in the printing on the pop can? How would you prevent this from happening in the next picture?

Photo #6

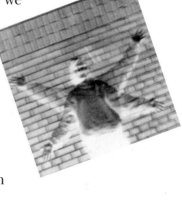

This was the last photo we had time for. We decided to try for a double-exposure photo of a student standing against the school wall. We carefully supported the camera so it was still while he held his arms down for 7 s, then held them up for 7 s.

Photo 6 is interesting, but it doesn't have as much contrast between light and dark areas as some of our other photos.

(g) Why do you think Mario and Sarah decided to increase the exposure time for this photo?

(h) What do you think caused the contrast problem?

Questions

1. List the factors that Sarah and Mario controlled in their investigation.

2. Sarah and Mario didn't have time to take more than six photos in their investigation. Suggest two other pictures they could try to take with their camera in their next investigation. What kinds of problems would you expect them to encounter when they take the extra pictures? How would you solve them?

Apply

3. What lessons that Sarah and Mario learned about pinhole photography could be applied to taking photographs with regular cameras?

7.8

City Lights

A BEAUTIFUL CITY AT NIGHT — its bright lights glow, attracting tourists to its theatres, clubs, and restaurants. But that's not all the bright lights attract.

Migrating Birds

Many birds spend their summers in the north, and fly south for the winter. As they migrate in spring and fall, huge flocks may form. In a single hour, as many as 15 000 blackbirds may pass overhead on their way north or south.

No Stars to Fly By

Most small birds migrate at night, so how do they know which way to fly and if they are on the right course? Experiments have shown that on clear nights they navigate using the light from stars.

On cloudy nights, when they cannot see the stars, migrating birds often get confused, and are attracted to the bright lights of skyscrapers, towers, and lighthouses. Every migration season, thousands of birds collide with buildings and towers and are killed. After one overcast October night in the southern United States, 50 000 birds were found dead or dying at the base of an airport tower.

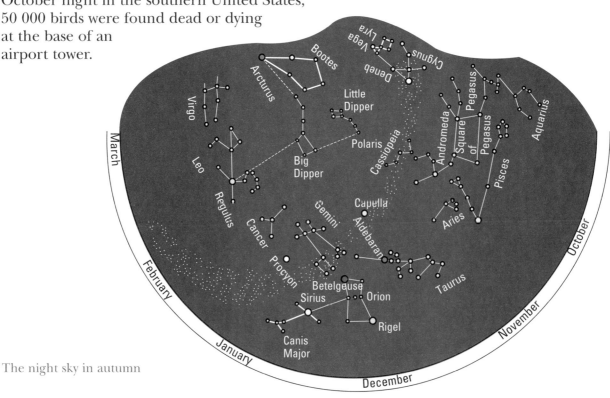

The night sky in autumn

Magnolia warbler   Red-eyed vireo

Small songbirds such as the magnolia warbler and the red-eyed vireo migrate at night. They are among the many species of small birds often found dead at the base of skyscrapers.

The death toll is higher in the autumn than in the spring. This is because there are about four times more birds after the summer reproductive season. Also, nights are cloudiest at that time of year.

Many birds are not killed outright when they fly into lighted windows, but flutter against the windows until exhausted or injured. They then die when they fall to the ground.

Some birds get confused by being at the bottom of "canyons" among the tall buildings. It may be like being trapped inside a deep well.

Understanding the Author

1. During what weather conditions does the greatest number of songbird deaths occur? Why?

2. In what direction are the birds migrating when the greatest numbers are found dead? Explain why.

What to Do?

Proposal to city council Turn off the lights on as many tall buildings as possible, particularly on the south side of east-west streets during the autumn.

Benefits

Opinion of an energy conservation officer Approximately 20% to 25% of the energy consumed in North America can be accounted for by lighting. Reducing the amount of external lighting would lead to tremendous savings.

Opinion of an amateur astronomer Light from roadways, buildings, and neon signs is scattered over the skies, making it impossible to see many of the stars. Any control over night lighting would be an improvement.

Opinion of a bird watcher I have noticed fewer songbirds in the city over the past few years. If we are not careful, all birds will eventually disappear.

Risks

Opinion of a pilot The trend in airport safety is for more and better lighting, not less. The safety of birds should not compromise the safety of air travel.

Opinion of a restaurant owner My restaurant is on the south side of the street. I need a sign that attracts people. My competitors on the north side of the street have a bright sign. This could destroy my livelihood.

Opinion of a police officer I worry about crime. Will the reduction in lighting create a crime wave?

What Do You Think?

3. Should city council pass the proposal?

Key Outcomes

Now that you have completed this chapter, can you do the following? If not, review the sections indicated.

- Recognize the properties of luminous objects and describe examples of them. (7.1)
- Compare and give examples of transparent, translucent, and opaque objects. (7.2)
- Describe factors that affect the amount of light absorbed by or reflected from an object. (7.2)
- Describe evidence that light travels in straight lines. (7.3, 7.4, 7.6)
- Draw and label ray diagrams to illustrate the formation of shadows and eclipses. (7.3, 7.4)
- Define the four main characteristics (SALT) of images. (7.5)
- Describe the construction and use of a pinhole camera. (7.5, 7.6, 7.7)
- Illustrate how an image is formed in a pinhole camera. (7.6)

Key Terms

light	translucent
luminous	opaque
nonluminous	shadow
incandescence	umbra
electric discharge	penumbra
phosphorescence	solar eclipse
fluorescence	lunar eclipse
chemiluminescence	image
bioluminescence	real image
transparency	virtual image
transparent	pinhole camera

Review

1. In your notebook, match the object with the process that makes it luminous.

   A incandescence   **1** glow-worm

   B electric discharge through a gas   **2** neon sign

   C phosphorescence   **3** glow-in-the-dark key chain

   D bioluminescence   **4** toaster heating element

2. Are the following objects transparent, translucent, or opaque? Copy the list into your notebook, and write the answers.

   plastic food wrap
   your hand
   your skin
   the classroom window
   sunglasses
   a frosted light bulb
   your desk
   stained glass

3. What are the names of the main parts of a shadow? How is each part formed? (Make a sketch if this helps.)

4. Briefly describe three demonstrations that show light travels in straight lines.

5. What type of image cannot be placed on a screen? What do you have to do to see this type of image?

6. A pinhole camera is held several metres away from a bright luminous object. What are the four characteristics of the image you would see on the camera screen?

7. Explain why an incandescent lamp is a less efficient light source than a fluorescent lamp.

8. Why can you not see through an opaque object?

Problem Solving

9. The diagram below shows a light source and two opaque objects. Copy the diagram into your notebook. Then draw, label, and shade a ray diagram showing the shadows behind the objects.

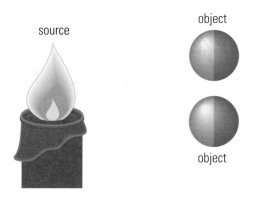

source

object

object

10. Describe how you would use a flashlight or a ray box (representing the Sun) and a pen to show how a sundial works. (You might try this in class.)

11. Imagine a bright light source covered with an opaque piece of paper that has a cutout shaped like the letter L. Imagine you are looking at the resulting L-shaped light with a pinhole camera (one pinhole). Draw a diagram showing what you would see.

12. Which type of lamp, an incandescent lamp or a fluorescent lamp, is more efficient at changing electrical energy into light energy? What happens to the wasted energy?

13. Explain why the insides of many optical instruments have a dull, black finish.

14. In a group, brainstorm ways in which transparent and translucent materials are used in practical applications. Consider home, school, automobiles, clothing, packaging of groceries and cosmetics, interior decorating, and any other areas you can think of. Make two lists of examples of transparent materials and translucent materials.

15. In areas that receive a lot of sunlight, why do people paint their roofs and houses white?

Critical Thinking

16. Draw a concept map, with light energy at the centre, to illustrate several ways in which various types of energy can be changed into light energy. (For a review of concept maps, see the Skills Handbook on page 502.)

17. A manufacturing company wants to hire a student for a summer job designing lamps that have a special feature: the switch that is used to turn the lamp on and off must be visible in the dark, and it must not consume any electrical energy directly.

(a) If you were hired for this job, what design would you use?

(b) How would you test your design to see how effective it is?

18. In order to have artificial light, energy must be used. Split your group into two, then debate the conflict between the need to produce light and the need to conserve energy.

19. Sundials make use of shadows to tell time. What factors must be considered when constructing a sundial? Design a sundial suitable for use at your school. Indicate where you would locate the sundial.

ASK YOURSELF

Go back to the questions at the beginning of this chapter. Add more detail or change your answers if needed. Are there any questions you have that have not been answered? Take the time to have them answered now.

CHAPTER 8

Reflection of Light

THE MANAGER OF A VIDEO ARCADE wanted to be able to see several locations in the arcade while seated in her office. To do this, she hung mirrors on the wall of the arcade, as shown in the diagram. A video camera, hung from the ceiling, can view several games directly. But it can also view other locations by aiming at one of the flat mirrors. If the manager pushes button M1 in the office, the camera aims toward mirror M1 and gets a picture of one location. (Can you guess which one?) Thus, the manager can see several different locations, one at a time, by choosing the right camera direction.

You can see an image in a mirror because light reflects easily off its smooth, shiny surface. In this chapter, you will

- find out how light reflecting from a mirror can produce an image,
- investigate common flat mirrors, as well as less common curved mirrors, and
- learn how light reflects off surfaces of other objects, such as ceilings.

Getting Started

1. The diagram of the video arcade shows six mirrors (M1 to M6) and a video camera hung from the ceiling. Which mirror do you think the camera should point to in order to view each of the following locations: the main entrance, the fire exit, the change counter, the pop machine, and game A? Draw a diagram to help you explain your choices.

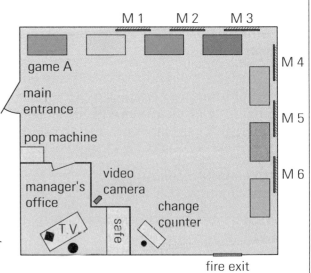

2. Hide a book behind a box or a desk so no one can see the book. Get some flat mirrors from your teacher. Set these up around the room so as many people as possible can see the hidden book by looking at reflections in the mirrors.

3. List as many places as you can where you have seen flat mirrors being used.

4. List as many places as you can where you have seen curved mirrors being used.

CHALLENGE

Draw a circle on a sheet of paper and place it in front of an upright mirror. Stand a book on its edge so that you cannot see the paper, but can still see the mirror. Looking at the mirror, try to trace the circle on the paper. Explain what happens.

Reflecting Light off Regular Surfaces

IF YOU BOUNCE A BASKETBALL off a gymnasium floor, you can predict how the ball will bounce. This is because the floor is a "regular" (flat) surface. If you draw a diagram showing where the ball travelled, you could draw straight lines to represent the path of the ball.

When a ray of light hits a regular surface, it acts like a ball hitting a regular surface. It reflects in a way you can predict. You can draw a diagram to show the path of the light ray.

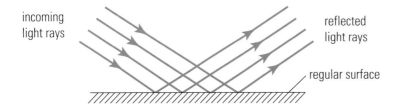

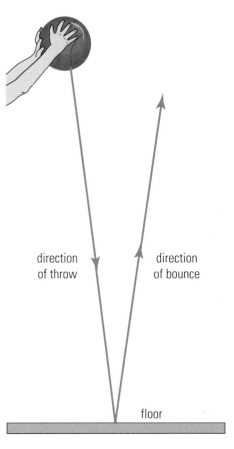

Regular Reflection

You've learned that a smooth, shiny surface reflects light better than a rough, dull surface. The reflection of light off a smooth, shiny, regular surface is called **regular reflection**. When light reflects in this way, you can see an "image." Regular reflection occurs off mirrors, shiny metal, and smooth water surfaces.

Which way is up? Turn the book upside down and see if that helps you decide.

Ray Diagrams

In your investigations of regular reflection, you can draw ray diagrams to help explain what you see. The ray diagram below shows several definitions related to the reflection of light. The light rays are drawn as straight lines, to represent light as it travels. Ray diagrams illustrate the ray model of light.

An **incident ray** is a ray of light that travels toward a reflecting surface.

A **reflected ray** is a ray of light that bounces off a reflecting surface.

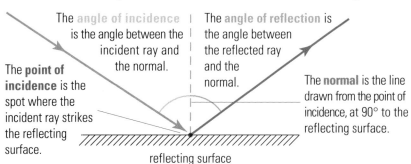

The **angle of incidence** is the angle between the incident ray and the normal.

The **angle of reflection** is the angle between the reflected ray and the normal.

The **point of incidence** is the spot where the incident ray strikes the reflecting surface.

The **normal** is the line drawn from the point of incidence, at 90° to the reflecting surface.

reflecting surface

Measuring Angles in a Ray Diagram

Your skill in using a protractor to measure angles is useful in drawing ray diagrams. Angles are measured in degrees. An important angle to recognize is the right angle, which is 90°. As shown in the ray diagram above, the angle between the normal and the mirror is a right angle. Whenever you measure an angle, always estimate its value first, so you can check that the result of your measurement makes sense.

TECHNOLOGY-LINK

Applying Ray Diagrams

One of the most successful links between science and technology is the use of ray diagrams in light. For hundreds of years, scientists have used the "ray model" of light to help explain what they see with optical devices. But the ray model can also be used to predict what will happen when a new optical device is designed. Optical technologists draw ray diagrams when they design and build such devices as mirrors, binoculars, telescopes, cameras, and eyeglasses.

* What do you think the expression "ray optics" means?
* How did you use the ray model of light to explain the image in a pinhole camera (page 220)?

SELF CHECK

1. What is meant by the term regular reflection?

2. Refer to the ray diagram on this page. Estimate the number of degrees in each of the following.
   (a) angle of incidence
   (b) angle of reflection

3. Use a protractor to measure the two angles in question 2 above. How good were your estimates?

4. Use a protractor to draw the following angles: 90°, 105°, 75°, 45°, 355°, and 5°. Label each angle.

5. In your notebook, draw a ray diagram showing a mirror, a normal, and an incident ray. Make the angle of incidence 37°. Then, draw the reflected ray.

6. What do you think is the largest possible angle of incidence for a light ray travelling toward a mirror? Why couldn't the angle be larger? What do you think is the smallest possible angle of incidence? Why couldn't the angle be smaller?

Reflecting Light off a Plane Mirror

SCIENTISTS CALL THE REGULAR, flat mirrors that you use every day plane mirrors. (Here, the word plane means a flat, two-dimensional surface, just as it does in mathematics.) In this investigation, you will study how light reflects from a plane mirror.

Materials

- ray box with a single-slit window
- plane mirror that can stand by itself
- ruler
- fine-tip pen or sharp pencil
- plain paper
- protractor

Procedure

1 Aim a ray of light from the ray box toward the mirror. Try out different angles of incidence. See how moving the incident ray changes the position of the reflected ray. Predict how the angle of incidence compares with the angle of reflection when a light ray reflects off a plane mirror.

2 Draw a straight line, AB, on a piece of paper. The line should be longer than the width of your mirror. Mark a point near the middle of AB for your point of incidence. Place the plane mirror so its reflecting surface (not the glass surface) lies along AB, as shown.

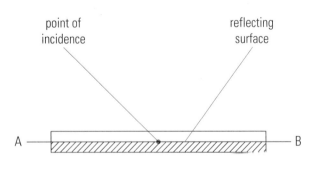

Step 2

3 With the room lights dim, aim a light ray at the point of incidence. Move the ray box until the reflected ray is in line with the incident ray. Draw at least three small dots along the middle of the ray.

(a) Remove the ray box and the mirror, and use a ruler to draw a broken line connecting the dots and the point of incidence. What is this line? Label it.

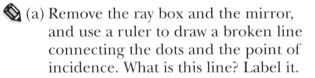

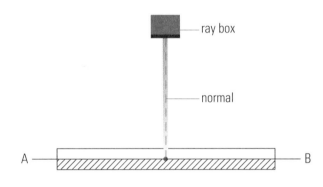

Step 3

4 Replace the mirror and use the ray box to aim a single ray toward the point of incidence. Make the angle of incidence large. Mark several small dots along the middle of the incident and reflected rays.

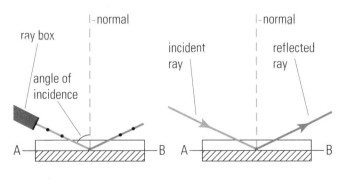

Step 4

Remove the mirror and the ray box, and use a ruler to draw a fine, straight line joining the dots of each ray to the point of incidence.

(b) Label the rays and show their directions with arrows.

5 Use your protractor to measure the angle of incidence and the angle of reflection in your diagram.

(c) Label the sizes of these angles in degrees.

6 Start a new diagram on a fresh piece of paper. Repeat steps 3 to 5, but this time use a smaller angle of incidence.

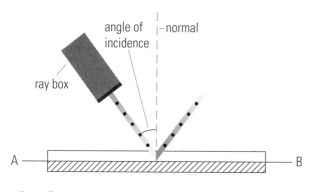

Step 6

ASK YOURSELF

Go back to the diagram of the video arcade on page 228 and trace the diagram. Use your discovery about angles of incidence and reflection to predict where the camera should be aimed to see the main entrance and the other locations listed. Compare your answers now with what you wrote before.

Questions

1. For each ray diagram that your group has drawn in this investigation, compare the angle of incidence with the angle of reflection.

2. Comment on the accuracy of your prediction in step 1.

3. (a) Where is the reflected ray when the incident ray travels along the normal to a plane mirror?

   (b) What are the angles of incidence and reflection in this case?

4. The Law of Reflection compares the angle of incidence with the angle of reflection for light rays hitting a mirror. What do you think this Law of Reflection says?

5. How could you improve the accuracy of your results in this investigation?

Apply

6. Draw lines to represent a plane mirror and a normal.

   (a) Without using a ray box, draw an incident ray with an angle of incidence of 26°, and its reflected ray.

   (b) Repeat step (a), but this time use an angle of incidence of 78°.

7. Billiards is a game where angles of incidence and reflection play an important role. Explain this role. Name any other games or sports in which knowing about angles of incidence and reflection would be useful.

Extension

8. (a) A car with its headlights on is following another car. Draw a ray diagram to show how the light from the headlights of the following car strikes the rear-view mirror of the car ahead and reflects into the driver's eyes.

   (b) Glare from headlights can create a serious vision hazard for nighttime drivers. Examine the rear-view mirror in a car. What feature of the mirror can be used to prevent the glare of headlights from reaching the driver's eyes? How does it work?

Reflecting Light off Irregular Surfaces

WHILE SHOOTING SOME HOOPS outdoors with a friend, have you ever found yourself trying to bounce the ball on the lawn next to the driveway? The ball does not bounce in a direction you can predict, the way it does off the driveway or off a gymnasium floor.

Light hitting an irregular surface does not reflect in a regular way. Look at what happens when light hits white paper, like the paper used in this book. The paper feels smooth, and the surface looks regular. But you cannot see yourself if you look "into" the paper. There is no regular reflection because the paper is not as smooth and shiny as a mirror.

This is paper magnified several hundred times. What seems smooth and regular to fingertips is not smooth and regular to light.

Diffuse Reflection

When light hits an irregular surface such as non-glossy paper, you see **diffuse reflection**. The irregular surface diffuses, or scatters, the incident light, so the reflected light bounces off in many directions.

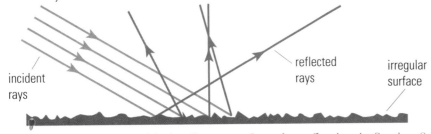

incident rays

reflected rays

irregular surface

Compare this diagram with the diagrams of regular reflection in Section 8.1.

TRY THIS

Regular and Diffuse Reflection

Predict what will happen when you shine a flashlight on the aluminum foil, as shown. Set up the materials, and make observations. You will see the effect best if the room is dark. Explain your observations using a diagram.

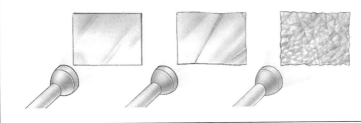

Using Diffuse Reflection

Diffuse light is easy on the eyes. Homes, schools, and places of work are designed with this in mind. For example, ceilings are often coated with an irregular surface, such as stucco, that causes diffuse reflection. Lamps often have "frosted" bulbs that diffuse the light. Lamp shades diffuse light even more.

Indirect lighting also helps diffuse the light in a room. In indirect lighting, the light bulbs cannot be seen. The light from the bulbs reflects off the ceiling or walls before it reaches your eyes.

How many examples of diffuse reflection and regular reflection of light can you find in this photograph? Are there any examples of indirect lighting?

TRY THIS

Mirror Tricks

You can play tricks with a mirror. Practise this one, then try it on someone you know. Prepare two sheets of paper as shown. Show these sheets to another person and say, "Did you know that words printed in blue are always reversed in a mirror, but words printed in red never are?" The other person will probably not believe you. Then hold the first sheet (with the words horizontal) up to a mirror—but hold it upside down. The red "COOKIE" is not reversed! You can then hold the other sheet up to the mirror. Again, the two red words are unchanged, but the blue "COOKIE" is reversed!

WHAT A COOKIE

W
H
A
T
A
C
O
O
K
I
E

- How does this trick work?

SELF CHECK

7. Look around the room you are in and list five examples of diffuse reflection.

8. How can something that feels as smooth as paper cause diffuse reflection of light?

9. A gymnasium floor is "regular" for a basketball, yet it is "irregular" for light. Why do you think this is so?

10. How might a knowledge of diffuse reflection benefit an interior designer? Give examples.

Locating Images in a Plane Mirror

WHEN YOU LOOK AT yourself in a plane mirror, you are the object and what you see is the image. Recall that an image can be described by four characteristics: size, attitude, location, and type (SALT). In this investigation, you will study how an image is formed in a plane mirror, and what the characteristics of the image are.

Materials

- large plane mirror
- ruler
- fine-tip pen or sharp pencil
- plain paper
- ray box with single-slit window
- small plane mirror

Procedure

1 Discuss with your partners what each image characteristic (SALT) means. You may want to look back at page 218.

2 Look into a large plane mirror.

(a) What is the size of your image compared with you, the object?

(b) What is the attitude of your image?

3 On a piece of paper, draw a straight line as long as the small mirror. Label this line *mirror*. Place the reflecting surface of the mirror along this line. Draw a solid dot about 2 or 3 cm in front of the mirror. Label this dot *object*. Get down level with the mirror so you can see the image of the dot. Look at the image from several viewpoints.

(c) How do you explain why the image appears where it does?

4 You can use the ray box and light rays to account for the image you see. Aim an incident ray from the ray box through the dot. Draw both the incident and reflected rays.

5 Move the ray box, and aim a second ray through the object. Again, draw the incident and reflected rays.

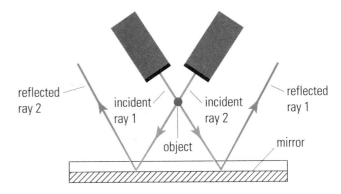

Steps 4 and 5

6 You can now use the rays to explain where the image is located. Use a ruler to draw broken lines extending the reflected rays back behind the mirror. Mark a dot at the point where these extended rays meet. Label this dot *image*.

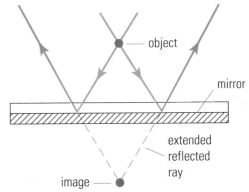

Step 6

Any time you want to find the location of an image, extend the reflected rays back behind the mirror. That is where the rays *appear* to come from. Any lines extended behind a mirror are drawn as broken lines, because the light does not actually travel through the mirror.

7 On your diagram, measure the shortest distance from the mirror to the object. (This is the *object distance.*)

✎ (d) Record the object distance.

8 Measure the shortest distance from the mirror to the image. (This is the *image distance.*)

✎ (e) Record the image distance.

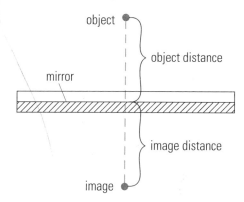

Steps 7 and 8

9 On another piece of paper, draw a line and label it *mirror*. Draw an arrow in front of the mirror, as shown below. Label this arrow *object*. Look at the mirror to see the image of the arrow.

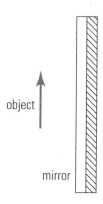

Step 9

10 Use the ray box to help explain what you see. Start by finding and drawing incident and reflected rays from the top of the arrow. Then do the same for the bottom of the arrow. When you are finished, your diagram should have four incident rays and four reflected rays. Remove the mirror. Use the technique you learned in step 6 to find points marking the top and bottom of the image.

11 Join the top and bottom of the image, then label the image.

12 On your diagram from step 9, measure and label the object distance and the image distance.

✎ (f) Record your measurements.

13 On the same diagram, measure and label the height of the object and the height of the image.

✎ (g) Record your measurements.

Questions

1. Refer to your measurements in steps 7, 8, and 12. How does the image distance compare with the object distance? Did your partners get similar results?

2. How does the size of the image compare with the size of the object?

3. Describe how you use light rays to show where an image in a plane mirror is located.

Apply

4. A real image can be seen on a screen. Are the mirror images you worked with in this investigation real or virtual? (You can check your answer. Put a piece of paper where the image seems to be located. If you can see the image on the paper, it is real. If you cannot see the image, it is virtual.)

5. Summarize the results of this investigation by stating the four characteristics (size, attitude, location, and type) of the image in a plane mirror.

Using Diagrams to Explain Images in Plane Mirrors

R AY DIAGRAMS ARE A WAY of thinking about how light travels, so they help explain what you see when you look in mirrors.

The Law of Reflection

For light rays hitting a plane mirror, *the angle of incidence equals the angle of reflection.* This is the **Law of Reflection**. The following shows how you can apply this law.

Applying the Law of Reflection

- From the top of the object, draw two incident rays toward the mirror.

- Draw normals and reflected rays. Make sure that each angle of reflection equals its corresponding angle of incidence.

- Use a similar procedure for the bottom of the object.

- To draw the image, you must make the reflected rays meet. You must therefore extend them (with broken lines) behind the mirror. Where the reflected rays *appear to come from* is the location of the image.

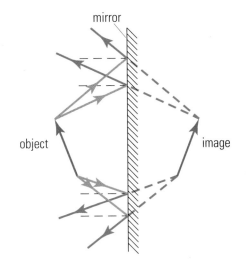

Once the image is drawn, you can describe its four characteristics:

SIZE   The image is the same size as the object.

ATTITUDE   The image is upright. In other words, it is the same way up as the object.

LOCATION   The image is behind the mirror. It is the same distance behind the mirror as the object is in front of the mirror.

TYPE   The image is virtual. If you place a screen behind the mirror at the location of the image, you will not be able to see the image on the screen.

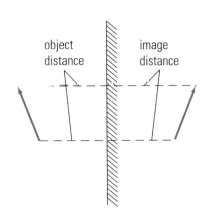

In a plane mirror, the object distance equals the image distance.

How the Eye Sees an Image

When you look in a mirror, you see an image that seems to be behind the mirror. But you know it is just an image you see, not an actual person. Reflected light rays allow you to see the image. To show how this happens, a ray diagram similar to the one at right can be used.

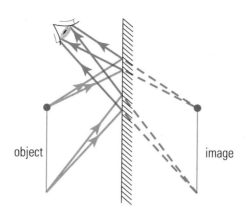

object

image

Another Way of Using a Diagram

You have found that the image distance (behind a plane mirror) equals the object distance (in front of the mirror). This observation provides a convenient way of drawing diagrams to explain images in plane mirrors. The following describes this technique.

- Draw one ray from the top of the object perpendicular to the mirror. Notice that this ray is actually a normal. Extend this ray with a broken line the same distance behind the mirror.

- Repeat from the bottom of the object.

- Draw and label the image.

If the object is more complicated, such as the letter F, you draw rays from several points on the object.

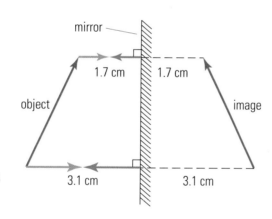

mirror

1.7 cm   1.7 cm

object   image

3.1 cm   3.1 cm

Curved Mirrors

B OTH PHOTOGRAPHS SHOWN HERE are of an object in front of a curved mirror. Like plane mirrors, curved mirrors are usually made of glass with a thin layer of shiny metal for the reflecting surface. The images you see in a curved mirror look different from those you would expect in a plane mirror. Can ray diagrams be used to help explain what you see in a curved mirror? Yes, they can, but they are a little more complicated than the ray diagrams you drew for plane mirrors.

A concave mirror

Classifying Curved Mirrors

Curved mirrors can be either concave or convex.

A **concave mirror** has the reflecting surface on the inside of the curve. It is caved in (remember concave), like the inside of a spoon.

A **convex mirror** has the reflecting surface on the outside of the curve. It is bulged outward, like the back of a spoon.

A convex mirror

Curved mirrors can be further classified as either cylindrical or spherical.

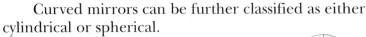
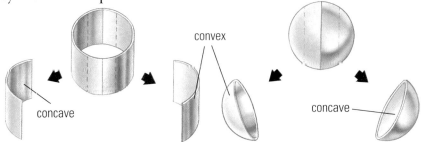

A cylindrical mirror appears to have been cut out of a cylinder, such as an ordinary can. When seen from above, a cylindrical mirror looks like part of a circle.

A spherical mirror appears to have been cut from a large hollow sphere or ball.

Defining Terms Used with Curved Mirrors

The diagrams of concave and convex mirrors below illustrate some definitions related to curved mirrors.

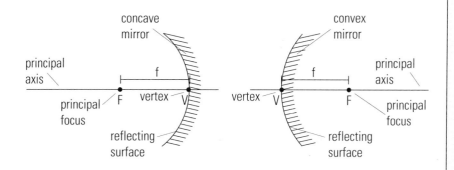

Point V is at the middle of the mirror, and is called the **vertex**.

Point F is called the **principal focus**, which you will define in the next investigation. (You can find the location of F experimentally).

The distance f (from the vertex to the principal focus) is called the **focal length**.

The line that passes through the principal focus and the vertex is called the **principal axis**.

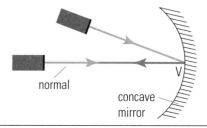

Reflecting Light in Concave Mirrors

I N THIS INVESTIGATION, you will study a concave mirror and the images it forms. Then you will use a ray box to help you draw ray diagrams to explain the images you see.

Materials

- concave mirror
- ray box with multiple-slit window and single-slit window
- concave mirror for use with the ray box
- plain paper
- sharp pencil
- ruler

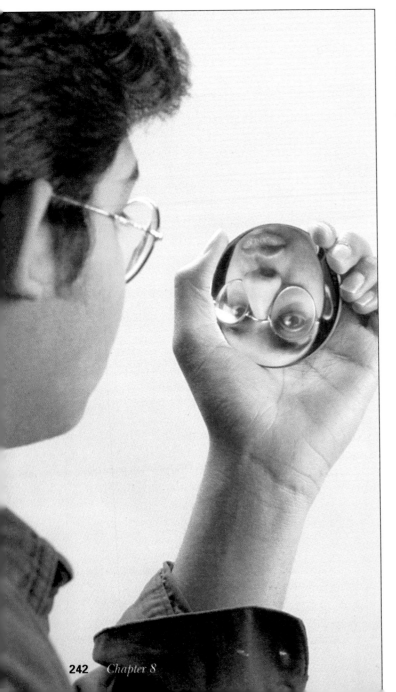

Procedure

Part 1 *Viewing Images in a Concave Mirror*

1 Hold the concave mirror 10 to 15 cm in front of you.

(a) Note the attitude of the image and compare its size with the size of the object (yourself).

2 Repeat step 1, but have the mirror at least 2 m away from you. (You will need someone to hold the mirror.)

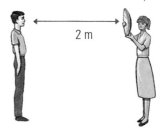

2 m

Step 2

Part 2 *Finding the Principal Focus and the Focal Length*

3 Put the multiple-slit window in the ray box. With the room lights dim, turn on the ray box light and make sure the rays coming from the box are parallel. You can do this by holding a sheet of paper in the path of the rays about 20 cm from the ray box.

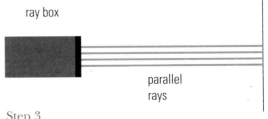

ray box

paper

parallel rays

Step 3

4 Place the concave mirror edge-down on a piece of paper. Use a sharp pencil to trace the reflecting surface of the mirror. Label the mirror on the tracing.

5 Aim the parallel rays from the ray box toward the mirror. Move the ray box until the middle ray reflects onto itself. (Once the mirror is in place, try not to move it. If the rays are not bright enough to see clearly, move the ray box closer to the mirror.) Label the point on the paper where the middle ray strikes the mirror. This is the vertex (V).

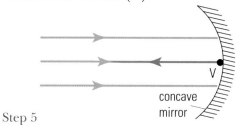

Step 5

6 Draw small dots along each of the incident and reflected rays. Remove the mirror and ray box, and draw straight lines through your dots. Show the directions of all rays.

✎ (b) What do you notice about all the reflected rays?

7 The point where all the reflected rays come together is the principal focus (F). Label F, and use your ruler to measure the distance from the principal focus (F) to the vertex (V).

✎ (c) Record your measurement.

✎ (d) What is this distance called? Label this distance on your diagram.

Part 3 *Finding Rules for Drawing Ray Diagrams*

8 Predict where the incident rays shown in the two diagrams below will reflect.

✎ (e) Write down your prediction.

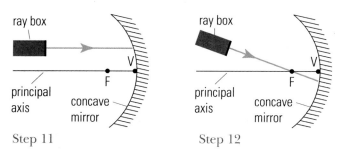

Step 11   Step 12

9 Place the concave mirror edge-down on another piece of paper and trace its reflecting surface. Put the single-slit window in the ray box. Aim a single ray toward the mirror so the ray reflects onto itself. Draw a line along this ray. Label the mirror, the vertex (V), and the principal axis on your diagram.

10 Use your measurement from step 7 to draw and label the principal focus (F).

11 Position the ray box so you can aim a single ray parallel to the principal axis and about 10 mm from it toward the mirror. Draw the incident and reflected rays.

✎ (f) Does the reflected ray travel as you predicted it would?

12 Aim a single ray through the principal focus at a small angle to the principal axis. Draw the incident and reflected rays.

✎ (g) Does the reflected ray travel as you predicted it would?

Questions

1. State the attitude and approximate size of the image in a concave mirror when
  (a) the object is close to the mirror.
  (b) the object is far from the mirror.

2. How does the focal length you measured compare with that found by other members of your group?

3. Write a definition of the principal focus of a concave mirror.

4. Copy the following rules for concave mirrors and complete them.

  (a) An incident ray parallel to the principal axis reflects …

  (b) An incident ray through the principal focus reflects …

Apply

5. Do you think the focal length of a concave mirror would increase, decrease, or stay the same if the mirror were made flatter? Explain your answer, using ray diagrams.

Reflecting Light in Convex Mirrors

IN THIS INVESTIGATION, you will study how images are formed by convex mirrors. A useful observation to remember as you are carrying out the investigation is that reflected rays that spread apart must be extended behind the mirror to find out where they meet.

Materials

- convex mirror
- ray box with multiple-slit window and single-slit window
- convex mirror for use with the ray box
- plain paper
- sharp pencil
- ruler
- protractor (optional)

Procedure

Part 1 *Viewing Images in a Convex Mirror*

1 Hold the convex mirror in front of you. Look at your own image when you are close to the mirror.

✎ (a) Note the attitude of the image and compare the size of the image with the size of the object (yourself).

2 Determine what happens to the image seen in a convex mirror when the object is far from the mirror.

✎ (b) Describe what you discover.

Part 2 *Finding the Principal Focus and the Focal Length*

3 Put the multiple-slit window in the ray box. With the room lights dim, turn on the ray box light and make sure the rays coming from the box are parallel.

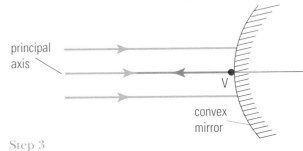

principal axis

V

convex mirror

Step 3

4 Plan a procedure for finding the principal focus of the convex mirror. Have your teacher approve your procedure, then locate the principal focus.

5 Use your ruler to measure the focal length, f, from the principal focus (F) to the vertex (V). Label this distance on your diagram.

✎ (c) Record your measurement.

Part 3 *Finding Rules for Drawing Ray Diagrams*

6 Predict where the incident rays shown in the two diagrams below will reflect. Discuss your predictions with the other members of your group.

✎ (d) Write down your prediction.

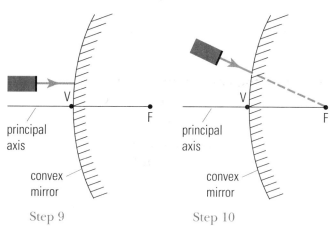

Step 9   Step 10

7 Place the convex mirror edge-down on a piece of paper and trace its reflecting surface. Put the single-slit window in the ray box. Aim a single ray toward the vertex of the mirror so the ray reflects onto itself. With your pencil, extend this ray behind the mirror as a solid line. Label the vertex (V), the mirror, and the principal axis.

8 Use your measurement from step 5 of this investigation to draw and label the principal focus, F.

9 Position the ray box so you can aim a single ray parallel to the principal axis, and about 5 to 10 mm from it, toward the mirror. (See the diagram for step 9 to see how.) Draw the incident and reflected rays. What must you do to the reflected ray to complete the diagram?

10 Remove the mirror from the diagram, then aim a single ray at a small angle to the principal axis, toward the principal focus as shown in the diagram for step 10. Carefully replace the mirror in its original position. Draw the incident and reflected rays. What must you do to the incident ray to complete the diagram?

CHALLENGE

Curved mirrors can be classified as converging or diverging, depending on how light acts when it reflects off them. Is a convex mirror a converging or diverging mirror? (*Converge* means to come together and *diverge* means to spread apart.)

Questions

1. What are the attitude and approximate size of the image in a convex mirror when the object is

   (a) close to the mirror.

   (b) far from the mirror.

2. Compare the focal length you measured with that found by other members of your group. Should they all be the same?

3. Write a definition of the principal focus of a convex mirror.

4. Copy the following rules for convex mirrors and complete them.

   (a) An incident ray parallel to the principal axis reflects ...

   (b) An incident ray aimed toward the principal focus reflects ...

5. Comment on the accuracy of your prediction in step 6.

Extension

6. Devise and carry out procedure steps to determine if the Law of Reflection applies to a convex mirror. Refer to the Try This on page 241.

Using Diagrams to Find Images in Curved Mirrors

WHEN YOU SEE YOURSELF in a curved mirror, you can easily tell whether the mirror is giving an upright image or an inverted image. You can also tell whether the image is smaller or larger than you (the object).

To learn how curved mirrors produce various images, you can draw ray diagrams. These diagrams also help you determine the location and type of image formed. The steps for drawing ray diagrams for a concave mirror start below.

The steps for a convex mirror start on page 248.

Drawing Ray Diagrams for a Concave Mirror

Suppose you have to find the image of a 15-cm high object, located 60 cm from a concave mirror, that has a focal length of 25 cm. The following steps show you how to solve the problem. Notice that the final step is to state the four characteristics (SALT) of the image. (See the top of page 247.)

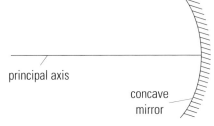

Use a ruler to draw a straight line on a page. This line represents the principal axis of the mirror. Use a compass or circular object to trace the reflecting surface of the mirror. (If you draw the curve so it has a radius twice as big as the focal length, the diagram will work out well.) Label both the principal axis and the mirror.

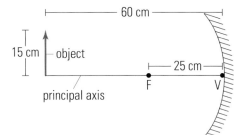

Mark and label the principal focus (F) and the vertex (V). Remember that the focal length is 25 cm. Draw the object so it sits on the principal axis, 60 cm from the vertex. Use an arrow as an object so you can tell the difference between the top and the bottom. The arrow should be 15 cm high in this case.

Stating SALT Characteristics of an Image in a Concave Mirror

Once you have drawn the image, you know three of its four characteristics (Size, Attitude, and Location). Now you must decide if the image is real or virtual. Remember that if you can project an image on to a screen, the image is real. For any mirror, only images that are in front of the mirror can be placed on a screen. If the image is behind the mirror, it cannot be placed on a screen, so it is virtual. In the example below, then, the characteristics are:

Size: smaller than the object

Attitude: inverted

Location: in front of the mirror, closer to the mirror than the object is

Type: real

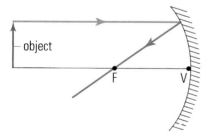

Start at the top of the object. Use a ruler to draw the first incident ray. Remember the first rule for ray diagrams for a concave mirror: *an incident ray parallel to the principal axis reflects through F.*

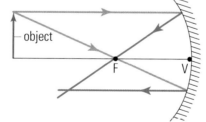

Start again at the top of the object. Draw another incident ray. Remember the second rule for a concave mirror: *an incident ray through F reflects parallel to the principal axis.*

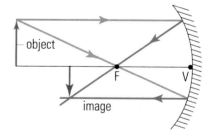

Find the point where the reflected rays meet. This is the image of the top of the object. Join this point to the principal axis, and draw the image.

Drawing Ray Diagrams for a Convex Mirror

Suppose you have to find the image of an object located 30 cm from a convex mirror, of focal length 25 cm. The object is 15 cm high. The steps below show how to solve this problem.

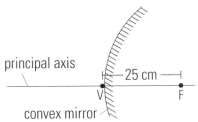

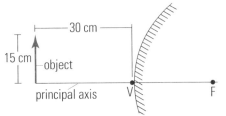

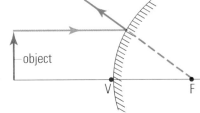

Use a ruler to draw the principal axis of the mirror, and use a compass or circular object to draw the mirror. Locate the principal focus and the vertex. (Remember that the principal focus is behind the mirror.) Label the diagram.

Draw the object so it sits on the principal axis. In our example the object is 30 cm from the vertex and its height is 15 cm.

Start at the top of the object. Use a ruler to draw the first incident ray. Remember the first rule for ray diagrams for a convex mirror: *an incident ray parallel to the principal axis reflects in line with* F. Notice that you must extend the reflected ray straight behind the mirror to show where it appears to come from. Draw this as a broken line because light does not travel behind the mirror.

Stating SALT Characteristics of an Image in a Convex Mirror

Before you can state the four characteristics of the image, you must decide whether the image is real or virtual. You can recognize a virtual image in a mirror because it is always behind the mirror, and it cannot be placed on a screen. Also, a virtual image in a mirror is always upright. For a convex mirror, the four characteristics of an image are:

Size: smaller than the object

Attitude: upright

Location: behind the mirror

Type: virtual

Making a Real Image

You have seen that a concave mirror can produce a real image if the object is far away from the mirror. You can demonstrate this by using the setup shown in the diagram below. The "object" can be a classroom window or a bright light such as the flame of a candle. Do you think you could get an image on the screen if the object were really close to the mirror, or if you used a convex mirror? Find out.

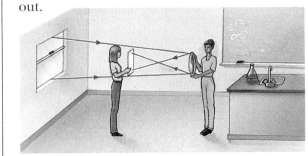

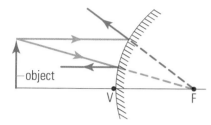

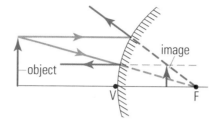

Start again at the top of the object. Draw another incident ray. Remember the second rule for a convex mirror: *an incident ray aimed toward F reflects parallel to the principal axis.* Draw the incident ray behind the mirror with a broken line because light does not actually travel there.

Find the place where the reflected rays meet. In this case, the reflected rays are spreading apart, so you must extend them straight behind the mirror. (Remember to use a broken line for extended rays.) Join the point of intersection to the principal axis, and draw the image. The image is upright because the reflected rays (extended behind the mirror) meet above the principal axis. Complete the labelling on the diagram.

TECHNOLOGY-LINK

Using Lenses

Lenses are used in cameras, microscopes, telescopes, binoculars, and eyeglasses. A concave lens acts like a convex mirror, because it produces a virtual image that is smaller than the object and upright. Fish-eye lenses, used in door peep-holes, are concave.

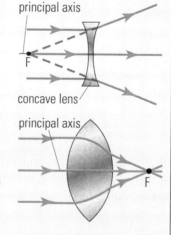

A convex lens, such as a magnifying glass, acts like a concave mirror. When the object is close, the image is larger than the object, upright, and virtual. When the object is farther away, the image is inverted and real.

- Examine the diagrams of concave and convex lenses shown here. Where does a ray that is parallel to the principal axis travel in each case?

- The main lens in a camera must be convex. Why do you think this is so?

Using Curved Mirrors

PEOPLE HAVE FOUND MANY USES for concave and convex mirrors. Funhouse mirrors have various concave and convex shapes to make people look tall or short, skinny or fat, and generally distorted.

▶

Can you tell which parts of the mirror are concave and which are convex?

Using Concave Mirrors

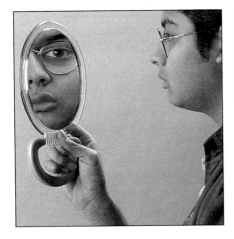

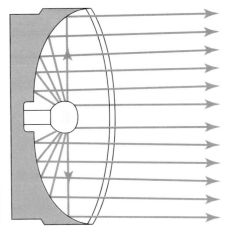

Some cosmetic mirrors are concave. Such a mirror produces an upright, enlarged image when the person using it is closer to the mirror than the principal focus.

In hot, sunny climates, some people use concave mirrors to collect the Sun's energy and use it for cooking. What would be the best location for the cooking pot in this type of solar collector?

Concave reflectors are used in devices that send out light in a beam. In this flashlight, for example, the filament of the light bulb is near the principal focus of the concave mirror behind it. The rays that reflect off the mirror are nearly parallel. This produces a beam of light, as shown in the diagram. What other common light sources use a concave mirror in this way?

Using Convex Mirrors

A convex mirror always produces an upright, virtual image that is smaller than the object. Such a mirror gives a much wider view than any other kind of mirror. Because of their wide-angle view, convex mirrors have several useful applications.

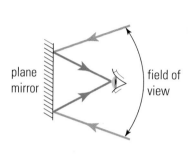 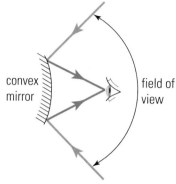

The reflection in a convex mirror gives a much larger view than the reflection in a plane mirror of similar size.

A convex mirror on the front of a school bus allows the driver to see children both beside and in front of the bus. What other vehicles have you seen that use convex mirrors?

Convex mirrors are often used in stores as surveillance devices to prevent theft.

TECHNOLOGY-LINK
Making a Solar Cooker

The middle photograph at the bottom of the opposite page shows a solar cooker.

- In a group, discuss how you would design and construct a solar cooker. If your teacher approves your design, carry out the construction.
- On a sunny day, test your cooker.
- After testing your design, make some suggestions on how to improve it.

The Hubble Space Telescope

IMAGINE HAVING VISION so powerful you could see a bee on a flower in Australia! That is the equivalent of what the world's most powerful telescope can do. The Hubble Space Telescope (right) can see things 10 times as far away as any telescope on Earth.

Earth-based telescopes are often built on mountain tops so they are above much of the cloud cover and part of the atmosphere. This helps get a clearer view of outer space. The telescope shown below is the Canada-France-Hawaii telescope, which is on top of an extinct volcano in Hawaii. However, even the top of the tallest mountain is still inside the atmosphere. The Hubble Space Telescope travels in an orbit around the Earth about 600 km above the Earth's surface, a height that puts it above the Earth's atmosphere.

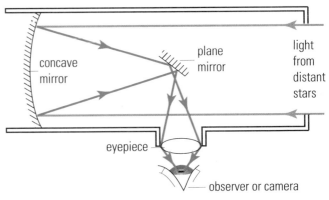

The image on the left was obtained by a large telescope on a mountain top. The detailed image on the right was obtained by the Hubble Space Telescope.

The Reflecting Telescope

Although the Hubble Space Telescope is the most complex telescope ever built, its design is based on reflecting telescopes invented more than 300 years ago. A concave mirror is an important part of a reflecting telescope. It must be ground to an exact shape and polished very smoothly. The mirror gathers light from distant objects, and produces an image that can be seen or photographed.

concave mirror

plane mirror

light from distant stars

eyepiece

observer or camera

A reflecting telescope

Why Build Expensive Telescopes?

Millions of dollars are spent on building telescopes to view outer space. What are the purposes of these telescopes?

- A good telescope can see far into space. This helps scientists learn how our universe began and how it grew.

- Scientists use telescopes to solve mysteries about exploding stars, black holes, and how planets form.

Hubble Controversy

The Hubble Space Telescope required nearly 20 years to build and cost more than $2 billion by the time it was launched in 1990. Despite all the time and money spent developing the telescope, it was flawed, and the flaw was not discovered until after launch. The flaw, which prevented the telescope from obtaining clear images, was in a concave mirror that was not perfectly shaped.

Many people wondered why so much money was spent on a telescope that did not provide advantages over the cheaper, Earth-based telescopes.

Fixing the Flaw

About three years after the flaw was found, it was corrected by astronauts on a shuttle mission. The Canadarm, a robotic arm designed and built in Canada, held on to the telescope while the repairs were being made.

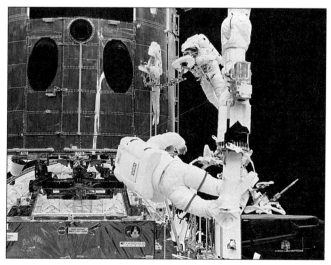

Astronauts repair the Hubble Space Telescope.

Preparing for the Hearing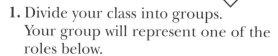

1. Divide your class into groups. Your group will represent one of the roles below.
   - astronomers who study distant stars and galaxies
   - companies that built the telescope and the Canadarm
   - astronauts who have spent thousands of hours training for shuttle missions
   - medical workers who want to improve health care
   - social workers who work with the homeless
   - scientists who aren't astronomers and need more money to do their research
   - taxpayers

2. Decide whether your group is for or against spending money on the Hubble Space Telescope. Develop a presentation to the panel. Select one person from your group to make the presentation.

3. Set up your classroom for the hearing. All students not speaking become government panelists. They can ask questions and make comments during the presentations.

4. As the group representatives make their presentations, record your observations and conclusions. Use this summary to help you decide what the panel should do.

5. The panel decides, after a discussion, if it should spend $2 billion on the telescope, on other projects, or not at all.

What Do You Think?

1. Do you agree with the panel's decision? Why or why not?

2. What attempts at compromise were made at the hearing? Explain your answer.

Key Outcomes

Now that you have completed this chapter, can you do the following? If not, review the sections indicated.

- Define and give examples of regular and diffuse reflection. (8.1, 8.3)

- State the Law of Reflection and prove it experimentally. (8.2, 8.5)

- Locate an image in a plane mirror both experimentally and by using a ray diagram. (8.2, 8.4, 8.5)

- Classify curved mirrors as either concave or convex. (8.6)

- Experimentally determine the focal length of a curved mirror. (8.7, 8.8)

- Draw ray diagrams using the rules to find images in curved mirrors. (8.9)

- State the four characteristics of an image found in any type of mirror. (8.5, 8.9)

- Describe uses of plane mirrors, concave mirrors, and convex mirrors. (8.5, 8.10, 8.11)

Key Terms

regular reflection	Law of Reflection
incident ray	concave mirror
reflected ray	convex mirror
point of incidence	vertex
normal	principal focus
angle of incidence	focal length
angle of reflection	principal axis
diffuse reflection	

Review

1. Describe the difference between regular and diffuse reflection. Give an example of each type of reflection.

2. Copy each diagram below into your notebook. Then complete the diagrams to find the image of each object.

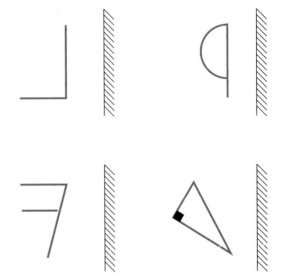

3. If an image is behind a mirror, is it a real image or a virtual image? State three different situations in which this occurs.

4. A girl is standing 40 cm from a plane mirror, looking at her image. Her head is 20 cm long. Draw a ray diagram to locate the image of her head. (Use an appropriate scale so the diagram fits on the page.)

5. Describe how you would experimentally find the principal focus of the following.

   (a) a concave mirror

   (b) a convex mirror

6. A candle flame, 1.5 cm high, is used as an object to demonstrate images in curved mirrors. For each of the following situations, draw a ray diagram to locate the image. List the four characteristics of each image.

   (a) The flame is 8.0 cm from the vertex of a concave mirror. The mirror has a focal length of 2.5 cm.

(b) The flame is three times the focal length from the vertex of a convex mirror. The mirror has a focal length of 2.5 cm.

7. Draw a concept map showing all the ways you can think of that light can reach your eyes. (For example, light can go from a bulb to a concave mirror, then to a screen, and then to your eyes.) Put yourself at the centre of the map.

Problem Solving

8. A boy, standing 2.7 m from a plane mirror, wants to photograph his image. At what distance should he set the focus of the camera to obtain a clear view of his image?

9. The lettering on the front of some emergency vehicles is backward, as on this ambulance. Why is this done?

10. A reflecting telescope with a concave mirror is aimed at the Moon. The focal length of the mirror is 6.0 m.

(a) Where will the image of the Moon be?

(b) List the characteristics of the image.

11. How would you use a curved mirror to start a campfire on a sunny day in the summer? Draw a diagram to illustrate your answer.

12. Draw a top-view diagram to show how you would place a mirror that would allow you to see around a corner.

13. A kaleidoscope is a tube containing two plane mirrors placed at an angle. Bits of

paper or plastic between the mirrors produce a pattern. The angle at which the mirrors are placed determines the number of identical images that you can see at one time.

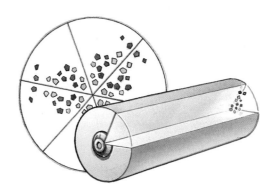

When the mirrors are placed at 90°, you can see three images. At 60°, you can see five images; at 45°, you can see seven images; at 30°, you can see eleven images.

(a) Find an equation that relates the number of images to the degrees at which the mirrors are placed. (Hint: Recall that there are 360° in a complete circle.)

(b) Use the equation to determine the number of images seen if the angle between the mirrors is 40°.

(c) Use two plane mirrors to study multiple images.

Critical Thinking

14. Describe how your life, and life on Earth in general, would be different if there were no mirrors or lenses.

15. It has been suggested that the Earth could receive more energy by reflecting the Sun's light off huge mirrors orbiting above the atmosphere. Draw a diagram of how this could work. What harmful effects might you expect if this were done?

ASK YOURSELF

Go back to the answers you wrote to the Getting Started questions in the chapter introduction. Would you change what you wrote? Make any additions you can think of to your answers.

CHAPTER 9

Colour

COLOURS CANNOT EXIST WITHOUT LIGHT, but the colours you see are both a property of light and a response of your eyes and brain to light. In this chapter, you will

- investigate colour,

- learn how white light can be split into many colours, and

- discover how colours can be added or subtracted to give other colours.

This information will help you understand such things as colour vision and colour television.

 Getting Started

1. When you look at the pattern of coloured dots at right, do you see a number? Write down the number. Do any members of your group see something different?

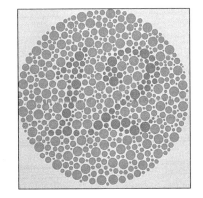

2. Copy (or trace) the outer box and black square of the rectangle below. Stare at the black square between the coloured shapes on this page for at least 45 s. Then stare hard at the black square in your copy for about the same length of time. What do you see in your copy? Mark down on your copy of the rectangle which colours you saw, and roughly where they appeared. What colours did other people in your group see?

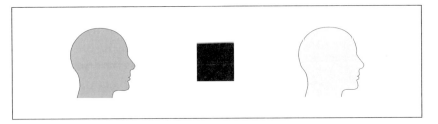

CHALLENGE

A colour television needs only three colours of dots on the screen to produce all the colours you see. List what you think those colours might be.

Splitting Light

HAVE YOU EVER SEEN colours when light hits a transparent object like a crystal glass, a diamond ring, or a crystal chandelier? In this investigation, you will create that effect, and make white light split to form various colours. The glass, the diamond, and the crystals on the chandelier all act like prisms. A **prism** is a solid, transparent piece of glass or plastic.

Materials

- two solid triangular prisms (glass or plastic)
- sheet of white paper
- ray box with a window about 4 to 6 mm wide
- coloured markers
- pencil
- ruler

Like a prism, a diamond has an interesting effect on white light.

Procedure

Part 1   *Investigating White Light*

1 Place the prism (triangle side down) on a sheet of white paper and trace its outline. With the room lights dim, aim a beam of white light from the ray box toward the prism.

Step 1

2 Move the ray box to adjust the position of the beam, until you obtain the brightest possible pattern of colours.

✏ (a) Draw a diagram of your observations. Include the white light beam and the colours. (You can also draw any light that reflects off the surfaces of the prism.)

3 Predict what you will see when you place a second prism in the path of the colours coming from the first prism.

✏ (b) Record your prediction.

4 Position the second prism as shown in the diagram below.

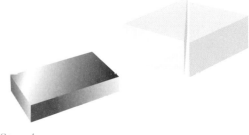

Step 4

✏ (c) Draw a diagram of what you observe.

✏ (d) How accurate was your prediction?

✏ (e) Try to explain what you see.

Part 2 *Viewing Light Sources Through a Spectroscope*

5 Look at the patterns in the picture below. They are what you would see if you looked at various light sources through a spectroscope. The first pattern was a white light source. The other sources of light were gases in electric-discharge tubes.

(f) How does the pattern of the white light source compare with what you saw in Part 1 of this investigation?

(g) What colour do you think you would see if you looked directly at the sodium light source?

Questions

1. List, in order starting with red, the colours produced when white light is split by a triangular prism.

2. State which of the colours changed direction the most when it left the prism, and which changed direction the least.

3. Predict what you would observe if you aimed light of one colour (such as red) at the prism instead of white light.

4. Predict what you would see if you looked through a spectroscope at street lights that looked yellowish.

Apply

5. How do you think an astronomer might use a spectroscope to discover what gases are on the surface of a star?

6. You have probably heard of ultraviolet light and infrared light, which are invisible to humans. Add these two forms of light where you think they belong in your diagram. (Hint: *Ultra* means above or higher than, and *infra* means below or lower than.)

Extension

7. Tape paper in the pattern of colours you observed in this investigation onto the metal lid of a frozen juice container. Poke two small holes near the centre. Run a long piece of string through the holes and tie the string in a loop. Wind up the string, then make the disk spin by pulling at both ends of the string. Look at the pattern in bright white light and describe what you see. Try to explain your observations.

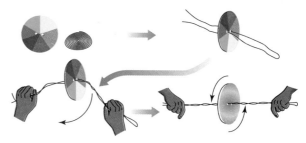

8. Use a spectroscope to compare the light from a variety of light bulbs found in school or at home. Try incandescent lights, various types of fluorescent lights (including grow lights used for plants), halogen lights, etc. Describe what you observe.

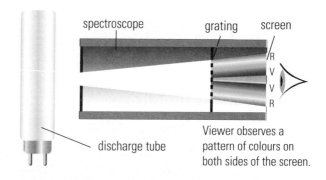

A spectroscope can be used to study light from various sources.

The Visible Spectrum

THE COLOURS OF THE RAINBOW are in the same order as the colours you saw when you shone white light through a triangular prism. To produce a rainbow, light from the Sun acts like the light from a ray box. Water droplets in the atmosphere act like the prism.

The band of colours visible to the human eye is called the **visible spectrum**. The visible spectrum has six main colours, called the spectral colours.

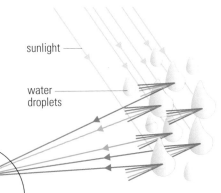

sunlight

water droplets

Formation of a rainbow. A different colour of light reaches our eyes from each layer of water droplets.

TRY THIS

Creating Your Own Rainbow

On a clear day, you can create your own rainbow. With your back to the Sun, spray a fine mist of water from a garden hose into the air. Change the angle of the spray until you see a rainbow.

To see a rainbow, you must have the Sun behind you and the water droplets (in the rain and the clouds) in front of you. Starting with red, the spectral colours seen are red, orange, yellow, green, blue, and violet.

The Discovery of the Composition of White Light

Hundreds of years ago, scientists thought they could see colours in diamonds or glass crystals because the crystals added the colours to the white light. They did not consider that the colours might come from the light itself. Then, in the year 1666, an important discovery was made. A brilliant scientist named Isaac Newton hypothesized that light from the Sun might be made up of several colours. He tested his hypothesis experimentally by passing a beam of sunlight through a triangular glass prism (like the one you used in Investigation 9.1). Newton discovered that white light is made up of the spectral colours, red through violet.

Those who opposed Newton's explanation were quick to argue that the different colours were produced by the prism. They reasoned that the colours must be inside the glass. The light merely allowed the colours to escape.

Recombining the Visible Spectrum

The controversy was put to rest when Newton positioned a second prism to collect the separate colours of light. As Newton predicted, when the six colours were added together once again, the light became white. Newton's experiment is shown in the diagram below.

Newton's experiments provided evidence that the prism does not add colour to light. White light is composed of colours, and each colour must act differently inside the prism. Many years following Newton's discovery, scientists found that the colours of light travel at different speeds in the prism, with violet light travelling the slowest.

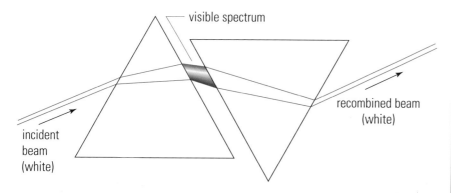

Newton's two-prism experiment

SELF CHECK

1. List as many ways as you can of seeing the visible spectrum.

2. Consider these two explanations of rainbows:

   Statement A: White light is made up of the spectral colours. These colours appear when light passes through water droplets.

   Statement B: Water droplets add colour to white light to produce the spectral colours.

   Write a short paragraph to explain the statement you believe to be correct.

3. (a) What does the expression "recombining the visible spectrum" mean?

   (b) What do you observe when this is done?

Mixing Light Colours

NEWTON'S DISCOVERIES (that white light can be split into spectral colours, and that spectral colours can be added to produce white light) led to other questions about light and colour. One of those questions is the focus of this investigation: What colours are produced when only two or three colours of light are added together?

NOTE: The names of two colours you will see in this investigation may not be familiar to you. *Cyan* (pronounced SIGH-an) is a greenish-blue or turquoise colour. *Magenta* (ma-JEN-ta) is a pinkish-purple colour.

cyan ⬤   ⬤ magenta

Watch for the following as you do this investigation.

- The **primary light colours** are the three light colours that, when added together, produce white light.

- The **secondary light colours** are the colours produced when pairs of primary light colours are added together.

- **Complementary light colours** are any two light colours that add together to produce white light.

Materials

- 3 ray boxes or 3 projectors
- 6 colour filters (red, green, blue, yellow, cyan, and magenta)
- white screen

Procedure

1 Set up a table like the one below.

Mixing Light Colours

Trial	Colours of light added together	Colour produced	
		Predicted colour	Observed colour
A	green and red		
B	green and blue		
C	blue and red		
D	red, blue, and green		
E	blue and yellow		
F	red and cyan		
G	green and magenta		

2 In your table, write your predictions for trials A, B, and C. (If your predictions are only a guess, don't worry! Your skill at figuring out what you will see in this investigation will improve with each step.)

3 Place a green filter in one ray box and a red filter in a second ray box. With the room lights dim, aim one of the coloured lights toward a nearby white screen. Note the size of the spot on the screen. Turn off the first ray box, and aim the second box at the screen. Focus the ray from the second box so the spot produced is the same size as that produced by the first box.

4 Aim both ray boxes so the two coloured spots are in the same location on the screen.

✏️ (a) In your table, record the colour you observe.

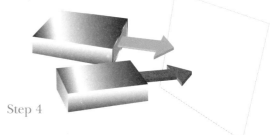

Step 4

5 Repeat step 4 for trials B and C. (You may want to change your prediction before you try adding these colours.)

(b) Record the colours you observe.

6 Predict the result of trial D. Then use three ray boxes to add red, blue, and green lights.

(c) Record your observation.

7 Look carefully at the results you have obtained so far in this investigation. Based on your observations, you may now be able to predict the results of trials E, F, and G. After you have made your predictions, aim the lights as before.

(d) Record your results.

8 Draw three overlapping circles, as shown below, to represent the addition of light colours. Label the colours of the light in the overlapping parts of the diagram. This diagram is called the additive light colour chart.

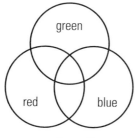

Step 8

Questions

1. Name the three primary light colours that, when added together, produce white light.

2. List the three secondary light colours produced when pairs of primary light colours are added together.

3. State three pairs of complementary light colours that add together to produce white light.

Apply

4. The lighting crew for a rock band uses red, green, and blue spotlights. What colour lights should the lighting crew use to make a white outfit appear red? to make it appear magenta?

Extension

5. A group of three students decides to work in pairs. In how many different ways could they pair up? Make a diagram to show this. The diagram you have drawn is a tree diagram. Such diagrams are useful in problem-solving. Try using tree diagrams to solve the following problems.

- Starting with the three primary light colours, show that you can get only three secondary light colours.

- A group of four students decides to work in pairs. How many different ways can they pair up?

- How many different pairs could be formed from a group of six students working together?

Coloured spotlights change what you see on stage.

Additive Colour Mixing

THINK ABOUT SOME OF THE observations you have made about colour so far in this chapter.

Observations of Light Colours

What You Have Observed	Possible Conclusions
White light can be split into the spectral colours.	White light is made up of the colours of the visible spectrum.
White light is produced when the spectral colours are recombined.	Light is made up of the visible spectrum.
blue light + green light + red light = white light	Evidently there are three primary light colours that add to produce white light.
green light + red light = yellow light	Pairs of the primary light colours can be added to produce secondary colours.
blue light + red light = magenta light	Pairs of the primary light colours can be added to produce secondary colours.
blue light + green light = cyan light	

The process of adding light colours together to produce other colours is called **additive colour mixing**.

The Additive Light Colour Chart

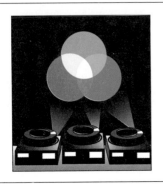

Adding any two primary light colours produces a secondary light colour. Adding all three primary light colours produces white.

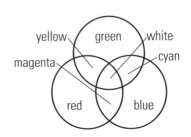

You can use the additive light colour chart to help you understand applications of colour, including colour vision and colour television.

Colour Vision

Think back to the introduction to this chapter on page 256. What happened that made you "see" coloured shapes in your copy of the rectangle? Try staring intently at a blue shape for about a minute. Then look at a white surface. You see a shape that looks like the blue shape, but it is yellow in colour. How does this happen?

Colours and Cones

Lining the inside of your eyes are millions of cells. Some of these, called rod cells and cone cells, are sensitive to light. Scientists hypothesize that there are three types of cone cells: one type sensitive to red light, one to blue light, and one to green light.

The back of the human eye contains millions of specialized nerve cells. The cells that are sensitive to colours are called cones. They look a little like ice-cream cones. (For more about cells, see Chapters 10, 11, and 12.)

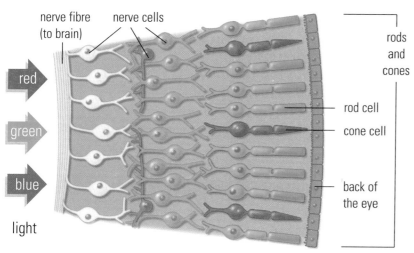

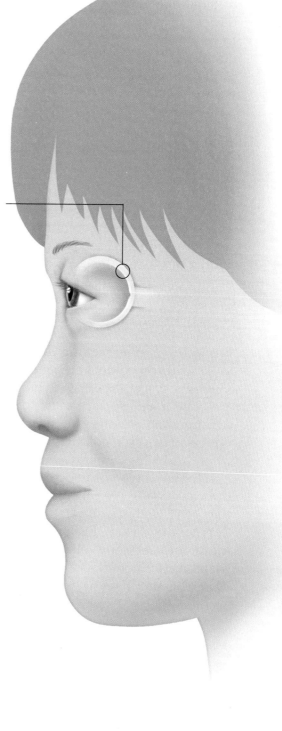

When you stare at a blue object for a long time, the cones sensitive to blue become tired. If you then look at a white surface, the tired, sensitive-to-blue cones do not react to the blue in the white light. However, the cones sensitive to red and green do react, resulting in you seeing yellow instead of white. Remember that yellow is the complementary light colour to blue.

You can predict what colour you would see after staring at any primary light colour and then at a white surface. Refer to the additive light colour chart. Staring at a green object will produce a magenta "after-image" (blue + red = magenta). Staring at a red object will produce a cyan after-image (blue + green = cyan).

Next, consider what happens if you stare at a secondary light colour, such as yellow (yellow = red + green). The cones sensitive to red and green become tired, so when you then look at a white surface, the red and green cones do not react. But the blue cones do, and you see blue. Again, use the additive light colour chart. What colour would you see after staring at any secondary light colour and then at a white surface?

Human Vision and the Visible Spectrum

Think of what the following light sources have in common: fog lights on cars, flashing lights on some highway maintenance vehicles, warning lights at intersections, and street lights in areas where mist or fog is common. These lights are usually yellow. Yellow is used for many safety devices because the human eye is more sensitive to yellow than to other colours. This means that if a blue light and a yellow light of equal strength were the same distance away, the blue light would appear fainter to you than the yellow light.

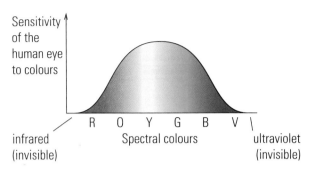

The human eye is not sensitive at all to infrared or ultraviolet light. The eye is most sensitive to the colours in the middle of the spectrum.

Colour Blindness

A person with colour blindness is not blind to colours, but is unable to distinguish certain shades of colour clearly. Some of the cones at the rear of the person's eye do not respond to the light received. One example is red-green colour blindness. A person with this condition may have difficulty seeing something red against a green background from a distance. The coloured-dot pattern you saw on page 256 is one of the tests for red-green colour blindness.

Colour Television

From the average viewing distance, the image of a person's face on TV looks as if the colours are smooth and unbroken. However, if you magnify part of the image, you will see many individual dots.

The inside surface of a TV screen contains thousands of dots. Arranged in sets of three, the dots are made of phosphors that emit one of three colours of light (red, green, or blue) when hit by high-energy electrons. Three electron guns, one for each type of phosphor, are located near the back of the TV tube. At certain instants, they send high-speed electrons toward the dots on the screen. Each dot that is hit by the electrons gains energy, then emits much of that energy in the form of visible light.

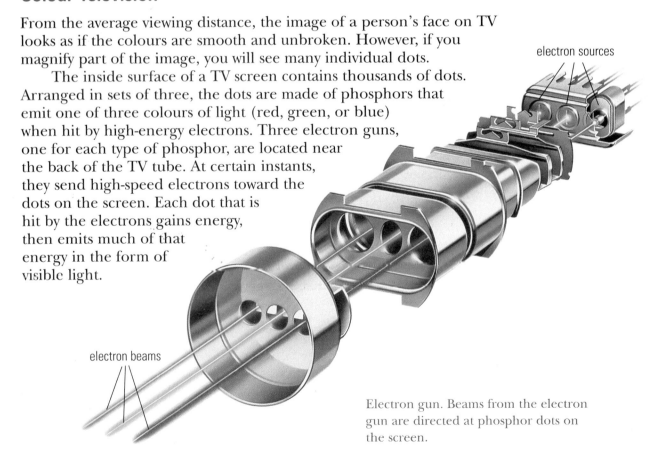

Electron gun. Beams from the electron gun are directed at phosphor dots on the screen.

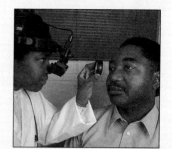
To produce red light on the TV screen, only the phosphors that emit red are hit by the electrons. To produce yellow light, the phosphors that emit green and red are hit. To produce white light, all three types of phosphors are hit. By controlling which phosphors are hit and the number of electrons hitting them, all the colours visible to the human eye can be produced.

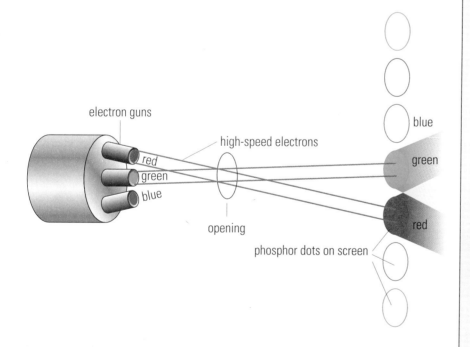

electron guns
high-speed electrons
red
green
blue
opening
phosphor dots on screen
blue
green
red

ASK YOURSELF

Some experienced artists and interior decorators can remember and describe colours very clearly, even when they are not looking at the colours. Do you or other students in your class have this talent? How do you feel about your ability to distinguish colours?

SELF CHECK

4. Use the additive light colour chart to list the following.
   (a) the primary light colours
   (b) the secondary light colours

5. State the complementary light colour of the following.
   (a) red   (d) magenta
   (b) green   (e) yellow
   (c) blue   (f) cyan

6. Which cones in the human eye must be activated in order to see the following colours?
   (a) yellow
   (b) cyan
   (c) white

7. (a) If you stare intently at a bright green square, then look at a white surface, you see a magenta square. Explain why this happens.
   (b) What do you see when you repeat this experiment using a bright cyan square? Why?

8. How does the operation of colour television compare with human colour vision?

Colours of Opaque Objects

WHY IS A WHITE SHIRT WHITE, a black jacket black, and a red tie red? When light hits an opaque object, some of the light is absorbed, or "subtracted." Any light left over reflects off the object. It is this reflected light that gives an opaque object its colour. For example, a white shirt reflects all the colours of the spectrum, so it appears white. A black jacket absorbs all the colours of the spectrum, so it appears black. And a red tie reflects red light.

Predicting Reflected Colours

To learn how to predict the colour that you will see when light reflects off an object, use the additive light colour chart. This chart can also be used to predict the resulting colour when subtraction of light occurs!

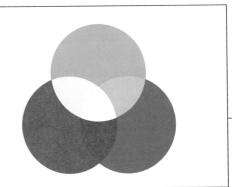

If you look at a red rose in white light, the white light (R + G + B) hits the rose, and the rose reflects the red. But the red rose absorbs the other primary light colours, green and blue.

If you look at a red rose in magenta light, the magenta light (R + B) hits the red surface, which reflects the red but absorbs the blue. Thus, the rose appears red.

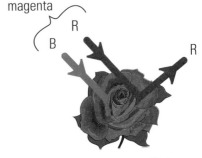

If you look at a yellow rose in white light, the white light (R + G + B) hits the rose, which reflects yellow (R + G). The blue light is absorbed.

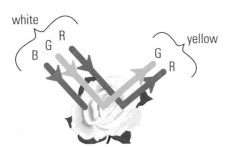

If you look at a yellow rose in magenta light, the magenta light (R + B) hits the rose, which reflects the red but absorbs the blue. Thus, the yellow rose appears red.

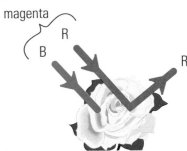

Explaining Reflected Colours

- An object that is a primary light colour *reflects* that colour (e.g., red reflects red).
- An object that is a primary light colour *absorbs* the other primary light colours (e.g., red absorbs blue and green).
- An object that is a secondary light colour *reflects* the light colours it is made up of as well as its own colour (e.g., yellow reflects red and green, and therefore also reflects yellow).
- An object that is a secondary light colour *absorbs* its complementary colour (e.g., yellow absorbs blue).

If you look at a red rose in green light, the rose does not reflect the green light, so the rose appears black.

If you look at a yellow rose in green light, the rose reflects the green light, and the rose appears green.

Using Filters to Subtract Light Colours

EVEN IN SMALL THEATRES, lighting technicians use as many as 150 different lights to illuminate a show. Different coloured filters can be slipped in front of these lights. In this way, the stage lighting can represent a certain time of day or year, a certain kind of weather, or even a certain mood. Lighting designers work closely with the other theatre designers to make sure that the coloured filters they use will react correctly with the colours chosen for the scenery, costumes, and makeup.

A filter "filters out," or subtracts, some light. It makes sense that what you learned about light being absorbed or reflected when it hits opaque objects also applies to filters.

So, you can predict that a filter that is a primary light colour transmits (lets through) light of its own colour, but absorbs the other primary light colours. A filter that is a secondary light colour transmits light of its own colour and light of the colours it is made up of. It absorbs its complementary light colour.

Materials

- seven coloured markers (red, green, blue, yellow, cyan, magenta, and black)
- six colour filters (red, green, blue, yellow, cyan, and magenta)
- six colour splotches (red, green, blue, yellow, cyan, and magenta) on page 271

Lighting designers choose coloured filters, which they call gels, by looking through them at electric light.

Additive light colour chart

| | colour of object in white light | colour of filter | | | | | |
		red	green	blue	yellow	cyan	magenta
	red	red					
	green	black					
	blue						
	yellow						
	cyan						
	magenta						

Procedure

1. In your notebook, draw a table like the one to the right above.

2. Predict what colours you will see in each case. Compare your predictions with those of other students. If you wish to make changes in your predictions, do so now.

(a) Write your prediction in the top triangle of each square, and mark the top triangle of each square with the appropriate coloured marker.

3 To check your predictions, view each of the colour splotches on this page through the red filter.

(b) Use coloured markers to record your observations in the lower triangle of each square of your table.

4 Repeat step 3 with the other filters, one at a time.

(c) Record your observations in your table with coloured markers.

Colour Splotches

cyan

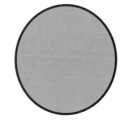

green

red

yellow

blue

magenta

Questions

1. Compare your observations with your predictions. How good were your predictions?

2. Try to explain why the colours you saw in some cases may not be the same as the predicted colours.

3. (a) How do the colours absorbed by a red filter compare with the colours absorbed by a red opaque object?

   (b) How do the colours absorbed by a cyan filter compare with the colours absorbed by a cyan object?

4. Describe any patterns you can see in your data table.

Apply

5. Imagine you are creating a scenery backcloth for a school play. The backcloth must include a circle that will represent the Sun in one scene and the Moon in a later scene. If you were the set designer, which colours would you use to paint the circle? During the play, what colour of filter should you use on the stage lights so the circle looks like the Sun? like the Moon?

Extension

6. Water acts like a filter. The more water that light must pass through, the more of the light is filtered out. Water absorbs light in the order of the spectrum—red is filtered out first, then orange, and so on. An underwater photographer uses beef as bait to attract large fish deep beneath the surface of the ocean. The meat reflects nearly all of the red light that hits it and some of the other colours. Predict what colour the meat will appear. Explain your reasoning.

Subtractive Colour Mixing

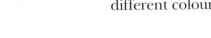

A CHEMICAL THAT ABSORBS certain colours, but reflects others, is a **pigment**. You have probably mixed two pigments (when working with paints or inks) to produce a third colour. For example, if you mix yellow paint with cyan paint, you get a greenish colour. The process of mixing pigments to obtain new colours is called **subtractive colour mixing**, because each of the pigments absorbs (subtracts) different colours of light.

Subtractive Colour Theory

Three colour pigments can be mixed to obtain black (or almost black). These three pigments are yellow, cyan, and magenta. Each of these pigments absorbs one colour from white light, as shown in the diagrams to the right. A pigment that absorbs only one primary colour of light is called a **primary pigment**.

When any two primary pigments are mixed, a secondary pigment colour results. The secondary pigment colours are red, green, and blue. A **secondary pigment** absorbs two primary light colours, but reflects only one.

Notice the difference between light colours and pigment colours. The primary light colours (red, green, and blue) are the secondary pigment colours; and the secondary light colours (yellow, cyan, and magenta) are the primary pigment colours.

Yellow pigment absorbs blue light. It reflects red and green light, and so appears yellow.

Magenta pigment absorbs green light. It reflects red and blue light, and so appears magenta.

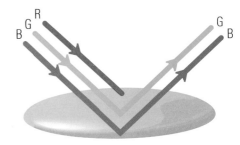

Cyan pigment absorbs red light. It reflects green and blue light, and so appears cyan.

A mixture of yellow, magenta, and cyan absorbs blue, green, and red light. No colour is reflected, so the mixture appears black.

The three primary pigments combine to make a black pigment.

Colour Printing

The theory of the subtraction of light colours is applied in many situations, including colour photography and colour printing. For example, the colour printer of a computer uses three colours of ink—yellow, cyan, and magenta—to produce colours. Using these three colours and black, the printer is able to produce more than a million different shades of colours.

- Why do you think printers need only three colours and black to produce so many shades of colour? Give some examples of colours that can be produced from these four inks.

Use a microscope or a hand lens to examine some colour pictures in a magazine or in this book.

- How are colours created in a magazine? What is the difference between how a magazine printer creates colours and how a painter creates colours?

- Use a CD-ROM resource to research the technology of colour printing.

A magnified view of the picture on the cover.

Mixing Pigments

Get some water-based paints or a set of water-colour marker pens. Predict what you will get when you mix them. For example, mix yellow and cyan, yellow and magenta, cyan and magenta, then yellow, cyan, and magenta. Then try mixing sets of primary and secondary pigments together, such as cyan and red. You can record your predictions and observations in a table like the one on page 270.

---

13. What colours are produced when the following pigments are mixed?
    (a) Y + C
    (b) Y + M
    (c) M + C

14. Use a series of diagrams to show that mixing yellow, cyan, and magenta pigments produces black pigment.

15. What colour results when magenta and green pigments are mixed? Use diagrams to show why.

16. What do you think is meant by complementary pigment colour? List three sets of these colours.

Screens

WHEN YOU THINK of a colour video screen, do you think of a hand-held video game with a colour screen? Do you think of the large, heavy television sets found in many homes? Or do you think of a TV the size of a wrist watch, or a flat TV that hangs on a wall like a framed painting? Perhaps you think of virtual reality, in which a visor pulled over your eyes has a screen that makes you think you are looking at a TV screen as wide as a wall. And maybe you have seen a TV you can write on with a special pencil or with your finger. These are all examples of colour video screens. They all apply what you have learned in this chapter.

Colour video screens are used for virtual reality programs and in video games.

Flat-Screen Televisions

Televisions that do not rely on electron guns can be made as thin as a few centimetres. They have some advantages over electron-gun TVs: they occupy a small space, they weigh much less, and they use much less electrical energy. However, they are hard to make, so they are expensive. (Electron-gun TVs were described on pages 266–267.)

One type of flat-screen TV uses liquid crystal diodes (LCDs) to control the light. In this type of TV, light comes from behind the screen and then must pass through the screen to the front. On the way through the screen, however, the light can be controlled at over a million tiny locations called pixels. These pixels have electronic switches that either block the light or let it through. Any light that gets through the pixels then passes through one of three colours of filter: red, green, or blue. The pixels, electronic switches, and filters are all held together like a sandwich between two flat glass plates.

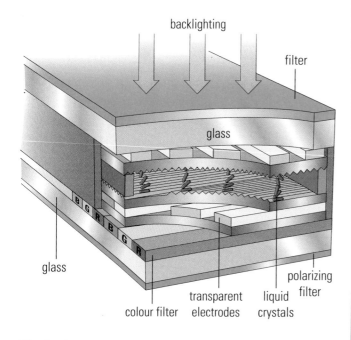

The basic structure of a flat-screen TV made with liquid crystals

Understanding the Author

1. What are LCD screens?

2. How do LCD screens differ from conventional television sets?

The Benefits

LCD screens are safer than electron-gun screens, because they require less voltage. They are also more environmentally friendly, because they use less energy.

As technology advances and prices go down, flat-screen televisions will become more common. The following are a few products that you may see in the near future:

- small television sets placed in airplanes, automobiles, buses, and trains to provide travellers with entertainment, travel schedules, and weather reports

- television sets that provide maps in cars

- screens for advertising messages that will fit in almost any space

- portable note pads that can be used for banking, paying bills, and booking airplane flights

The Risks

LCDs could make televisions more common and accessible than they already are. Is this necessarily a good thing?

- Children will be able to watch more television and see more advertising than they already do.

- What will happen to the old televisions that will no longer be needed? The average North American home has more than two television sets.

- Computers can be joined with your televisions to produce interactive television. However, when you are watching, someone else may be watching back—collecting information on what you watch, read, and buy.

What Do You Think?

3. Will flat-screen television sets be beneficial?

Key Outcomes

Now that you have completed this chapter, can you do the following? If not, review the sections indicated.

- Describe how to demonstrate that white light is made up of many colours.   (9.1)
- Define the visible spectrum and name its colours in order.   (9.2)
- List the primary light colours and state the colours that result when they are added.   (9.3, 9.4)
- List the secondary light colours and describe how they result by adding primary light colours.   (9.3, 9.4)
- State the complementary light colours of the primary and secondary light colours.   (9.3, 9.4)
- Predict what colours an opaque object or filter will reflect or transmit.   (9.5, 9.6)
- Predict the resulting colour when two pigments are mixed.   (9.7)
- Describe applications of the topic of colour, such as colour vision and television.   (9.4, 9.8)

Key Terms

prism

visible spectrum

primary light colours

secondary light colours

complementary light colours

additive colour mixing

pigment

subtractive colour mixing

primary pigment

secondary pigment

Review

1. Draw and label a diagram to show how a triangular prism is used to split light into its spectral colours. Label the colours in the correct order.

2. Name the three primary light colours. What is produced when all three overlap?

3. For each diagram below, name the colour of light that is missing. (Refer to the additive light colour chart if necessary.)

   (a) blue light + ? = magenta light

   (b) blue light + ? = white light

   (c) green light + red light = ?

   (d) green light + ? = white light

4. State the complementary light colour of the following.

   (a) red

   (b) yellow

   (c) magenta

5. (a) What is the colour of a blue shirt in white light? Explain.

   (b) What do you see if you look at a blue shirt in green light? Why?

   (c) What is the colour of a blue shirt in cyan light? Explain your answer using a diagram.

6. List the primary pigment colours. How do they compare with the light colours?

7. For each diagram below, name the pigment colour that is missing.

(a) magenta pigment + ? = blue pigment

(b) cyan pigment + ? = green pigment

(c) red pigment + cyan pigment = ?

8. Describe the similarities between colour vision and colour television.

9. Make up a concept map summarizing what you have learned in this chapter. Put WHITE LIGHT at the centre of the map.

Problem Solving

10. A yellow light source is placed at the front of a classroom. You have two coloured filters, one red and the other green. Explain, using a diagram in each case, what you will observe when viewing the light source through each filter separately and both filters placed one over the other.

11. A singer on a stage is wearing a yellow outfit. Which of the three coloured spotlights, red, green, and blue, would the lighting crew use to make the outfit appear each of the following colours?

(a) yellow

(b) green

(c) black

12. A chef wants a red dye to decorate a cake, but the only food dyes available are blue, yellow, cyan, green, and magenta. How will the chef obtain red?

13. Photographers often use colour filters to improve the colour of their subjects under certain lighting conditions. At sunrise and sunset, for example, the sky can appear reddish. What colour filter can a photographer use to obtain a sky colour that appears more bluish? Explain your answer.

Some of the filters used by photographers

Critical Thinking

14. Think of a room in which colour and lighting are very important. Some places to choose from are: a room in your home, the eating area in a fast-food restaurant, a photographer's studio, a clothing store, the produce department of a food store, etc. Describe ways in which colour and lighting are used to affect the people in the room.

ASK YOURSELF

Go back to your answer to the Challenge on page 257. How would you change your answer now that you have completed this chapter?

Investigating the Northern Lights

WHAT IS THE MYSTERIOUS GLOW in the midnight sky? Is it visible only in the far north? Do these eerie streamers of light that scientists call the aurora have any effect on our everyday lives? Space physicist Dr. Debbie Hearn can answer all these questions.

◀ Dr. Debbie Hearn is a space physicist at the University of Calgary.

Q. First, just what is space physics?

A. To explain space physics, I need first to describe a feature of Earth. There are formations within the Earth that act like a huge magnet. Earth's magnetism affects a region in space, called the magnetosphere, that begins at the Earth's surface and extends far past the Moon. We don't know how far yet! Space physics is the study of the movement and actions of particles and waves in the magnetosphere.

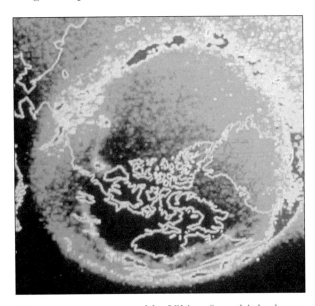

The aurora, as mapped by Viking from high above northern Canada

Q. Is there one particular topic that you study?

A. I study the aurora. Here in Canada, we see the aurora in the northern sky and call it the northern lights. But an aurora is also found near the south pole.

Q. What causes the aurora?

A. Charged particles, called electrons, hurtling toward Earth from outer space, collide with nitrogen and oxygen particles in the atmosphere. The collisions are so powerful that energy is released in the form of light. This usually happens in the far north and far south because Earth's magnetism guides the charged particles toward the poles.

Q. Is an aurora a rare event?

A. They seem rare because people can see only large auroras, only at night, and only away from city lights. Our instruments can detect them all of the time.

Q. What kind of instruments do you use?

A. We put a special type of camera, called an imager, on a Swedish satellite named Viking. This imager divides Earth's surface into squares and measures the amount of light coming from each square. That information is sent to Earth by the satellite. Computers convert the different amounts of light into different colours and then print the images.

Q. What do you discover when you study these images?

A. We learn how the aurora forms, how quickly it changes, and what causes it to change. We do this by comparing our images with computer models and other data from satellites. We use information about the solar wind and the number and movement of charged particles in different regions of space.

Q. What is the solar wind?

A. It is made of charged particles given off by the Sun. The solar wind affects the shape of the magnetosphere and the number of particles that collide with Earth's atmosphere. The solar wind can have dramatic effects on the aurora.

Q. Does the aurora affect our lives at all?

A. Oh, yes! Sometimes there is an enormous amount of activity that we call a magnetic storm. As well as creating a spectacular aurora, the storm disrupts signals between Earth and satellites. You might compare this to the way lightning disturbs radio or television signals. In January of 1994, two Canadian satellites, ANIK E1 and ANIK E2, were lost because all signals were disrupted by a magnetic storm in space. It took six months to make contact with the satellites again. It cost $200 million to correct the problem.

Q. When did you decide to become a space physicist?

A. It wasn't exactly planned. When I was in grade nine, I wanted to be a medical doctor so I took science courses in high school. Then I discovered that I really loved physics. Many high school students hear that physics is hard before they even take the course; I like to think of it as challenging! I earned a B.Sc. degree in physics at the University of Saskatchewan, an M.Sc. in nuclear physics at the University of British Columbia, and a Ph.D. in geophysics at the University of Calgary. My research at the University of Calgary led me into space physics.

The aurora, seen from the ground

NOW THAT YOU HAVE COMPLETED Chapters 7, 8, and 9, you can assess how much you have learned about Light and Colour by trying these questions.

Before you begin, you may find it useful to return to the Chapter Reviews. There, you will find lists of Key Outcomes and Key Terms. Read these to ensure that you understand the main points and the important vocabulary of the chapters. If necessary, look back at the appropriate sections in the text, which are listed with the Key Outcomes.

Write your answers to the questions in your notebook.

True/False

For each of the following, write T if the statement is true. If the statement is false, rewrite it to make it true.

1. A fluorescent light source emits light because it has a high temperature.

2. Lightning is an example of an electric discharge in nature.

3. A phosphorescent light source emits light only during the time it receives energy from another source.

4. The penumbra is the part of a shadow where no light falls.

5. The angle of incidence for a light ray hitting a mirror is the angle between the incident ray and the normal.

6. The image in a plane mirror is always upright and virtual.

7. The image in a concave mirror is always inverted and real.

8. If a red light source overlaps a green light source, white light is observed.

9. A magenta filter can transmit magenta light as well as red light and green light.

Completion

Copy the following sentences, filling in each blank with the word or phrase that correctly completes the sentence. Use words from this list: real, virtual, type, attitude, location, solar, lunar, mirror, normal, principal focus, principal axis, plane, concave, convex, red, orange, yellow, green, blue, violet, cyan, magenta, black, white. (You will not need to use all of the words.)

10. A ▮ image is an image that cannot be placed onto a screen.

11. The ▮ of an image describes whether it is upright or inverted.

12. In a mirror, the angle of reflection is the angle between the reflected ray and the ▮.

13. Light rays parallel to the principal axis that hit a concave mirror reflect toward the ▮.

14. A ▮ mirror can produce both real and virtual images.

15. The cone cells at the back of the human eye are sensitive to these three colours: ▮, ▮, and ▮.

16. The complementary light colour of cyan is ▮.

17. If you look through a green filter at a magenta object, you would observe the colour ▮.

Matching

Copy the numbers of the descriptions given below. Beside each number, write the word from the right column that best fits the description. (You will not need to use all of the words.)

18. a material through which images can be seen clearly

19. the type of image located behind a mirror

20. the mixing of colour pigments

21. a line drawn perpendicular to a mirror

A virtual image

B normal

C focal length

D subtractive mixing

E transparent

F real image

G additive mixing

H opaque

22. Examine the diagram below. Match each object in front of the mirror with the image that has the correct size and attitude.

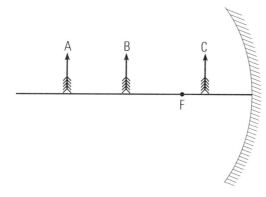

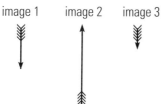

Multiple Choice

Write the letter of the best answer for each of the following questions. Write only one answer for each.

23. All of the following objects are luminous except one. Which is it?

    A fireflies   **D** the Sun

    B a lit candle   **E** the Moon

    C lightning

24. During a solar eclipse,

    A the Moon is between the Earth and the Sun, and the Earth's shadow falls on the Moon.

    B the Moon is between the Earth and the Sun, and the Moon's shadow falls on the Earth.

    C the Earth is between the Sun and the Moon, and the Earth's shadow falls on the Moon.

    D the Earth is between the Sun and the Moon, and the Moon's shadow falls on the Earth.

    E the Sun is between the Earth and the Moon.

25. When an object is far away from the pinhole in a pinhole camera, in comparison with the object, the image on the screen is

    A smaller, inverted, and real.

    B smaller, upright, and real.

    C smaller, inverted, and virtual.

    D larger, inverted, and real.

    E larger, upright, and virtual.

26. An incident light ray aimed along the normal of a plane mirror

    A has an angle of incidence of 0°.

    B has an angle of reflection of 0°.

    C is perpendicular to the mirror.

    D reflects back onto itself.

    E all of the above are true.

27. The image seen in a convex mirror, in comparison with the object, is always

    A smaller, upright, and virtual.

    B larger, upright, and virtual.

    C smaller, inverted, and virtual.

    D smaller, inverted, and real.

    E larger, upright, and real.

28. The three secondary light colours are

    A red, yellow, and blue.

    B red, green, and blue.

    C magenta, yellow, and cyan.

    D yellow, green, and magenta.

    E red, green, and cyan.

29. Which of the following additions of light will not produce white light?

    A red light + blue light + green light

    B red light + cyan light

    C blue light + yellow light

    D red light + blue light

    E green light + magenta light

30. If you stare at a bright green object, then stare at a white surface, the after-image you see is

    A green.   **D** yellow.

    B magenta.   **E** black.

    C white.

31. A mixture of red pigment and cyan pigment produces

    A black.   **D** cyan.

    B white.   **E** magenta.

    C red.

Short Answer

Write a sentence or a short paragraph to answer each of the following questions.

32. State the main difference between each of the pairs of objects named.

    (a) a phosphorescent light source and a fluorescent light source

    (b) a transparent object and a translucent object

    (c) a real image and a virtual image

    (d) primary light colours and primary pigment colours

33. State one use of each of the following items.

    (a) a chemiluminescent light source

    (b) diffuse reflection

    (c) a concave mirror

    (d) a convex mirror

34. (a) In the diagram below, what are the names of lines A, B, and C?

    (b) What is the angle of incidence?

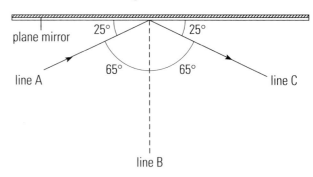

35. Describe factors that affect the amount of light absorbed by or reflected from an object.

36. Describe evidence that light travels in straight lines.

37. What does the memory aid SALT mean?

38. Describe ways in which a person can view the visible spectrum.

39. What are two rules that you can use when you draw ray diagrams to show where an image is located in a concave mirror?

Problem Solving

40. A lunar eclipse lasts a few hours, but a solar eclipse lasts only a few minutes. Draw a diagram explaining why there is such a difference.

41. Determine the colour you would see in each numbered part of the diagram below.

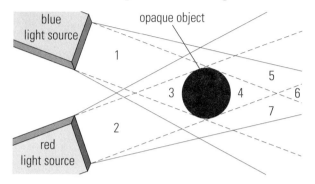

42. Meteoroids are nonluminous chunks of rocky material travelling through space. Meteoroids that fall into the Earth's atmosphere become meteors, also called "shooting stars." Why are meteors luminous?

43. Material X absorbs 80% of the light that hits it and reflects 20%. Material Y absorbs 20% and reflects 80%. What do you think these materials look like?

Challenge

44. Sometimes the image in a concave mirror is upright and sometimes it is inverted.

(a) Where must you be to see an upright image of yourself in a concave mirror? Where must you be to see an inverted image of yourself?

(b) Is it possible for an object to produce an upright and an inverted image at the same time? Demonstrate your answer with a diagram and with a concave mirror.

45. Communication signals act like light. Satellite dishes are used to gather signals from communication satellites that circle the Earth. The signals are then focused onto a receiver.

(a) What is the best shape for a satellite dish? At what position should the receiver be placed?

(b) Draw a diagram showing the path of the signals received from the satellite.

Design and Do

46. Shoppers sometimes complain that the colour of something they bought in a store looks different when viewed in sunlight. This happens because stores often use fluorescent lights that emit a bluish light but lack reddish light. How would the type of lighting in stores affect the colours of such items as clothing, cosmetics, and decorating supplies? Design a system that would avoid this problem.

47. In a group, design, build, and install a sundial. How did you ensure that your sundial would be accurate? Observe how accurately your sundial keeps time over a few months. How do you explain your observations?

48. Design and build your own pinhole camera and use it to take photographs outdoors.

49. Using water-soluble marker pens, illustrate the subtractive mixing of pigment colours to a younger student.

Project Ideas

50. Find out about the different kinds of street lights that are used in towns and cities, on highways and bridges, and in tunnels. Compare lights on the basis of cost (installation and upkeep), brightness, attractiveness, safety, and popularity with the public.

51. Design and build your own reflecting telescope. (You may find sample designs in astronomy reference books.) Test your telescope by looking at the Moon, planets, and stars.

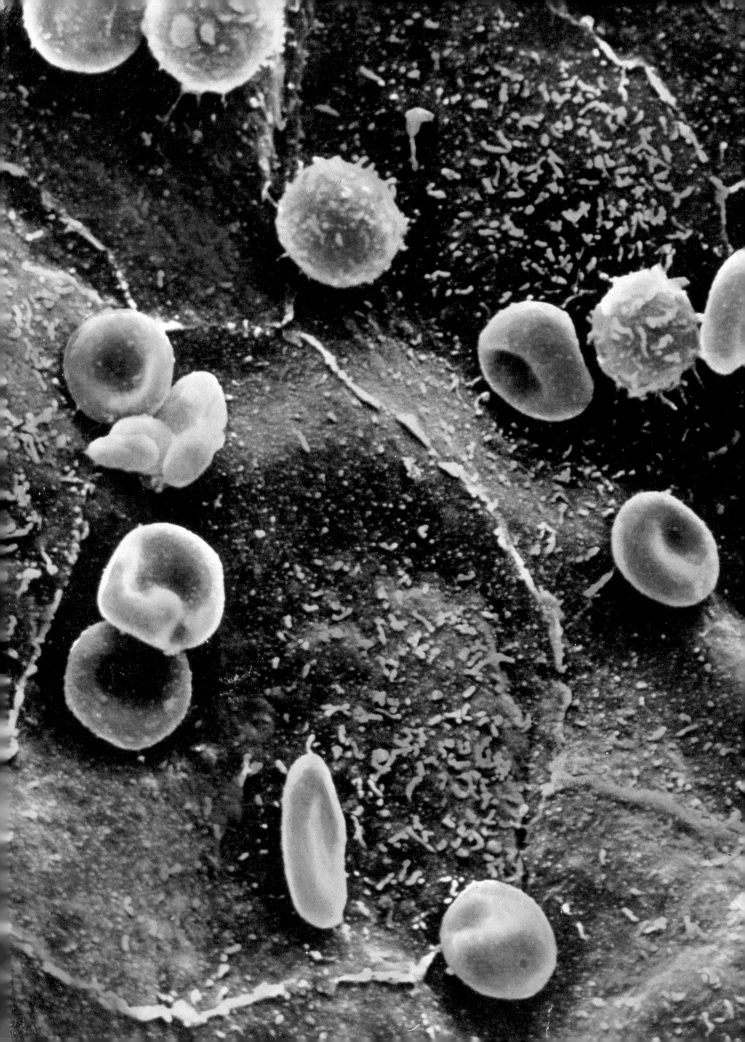

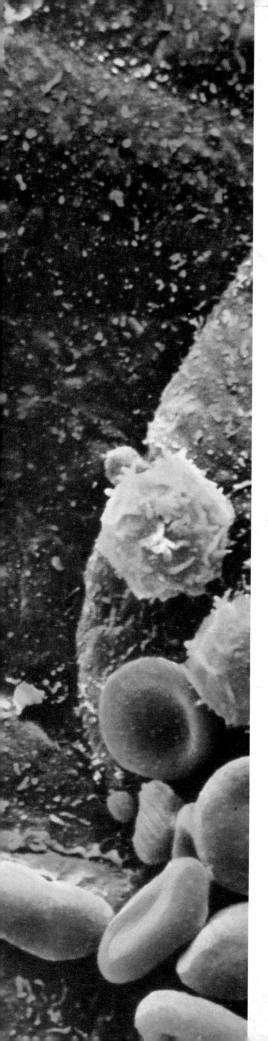

UNIT 4

Cells

CHAPTER 10
Viewing Cells

CHAPTER 11
Cells and Their Environment

CHAPTER 12
Cell Growth and Reproduction

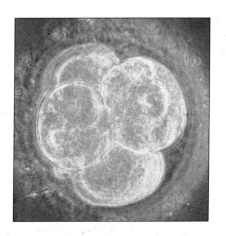

CHAPTER 1 0

Viewing Cells

IMAGINE WHAT A DIFFERENT WORLD you would see if your eyes could magnify images as microscopes do. A glance at yourself in a mirror would reveal not only your hair colour, skin complexion, and style of clothing, but also a landscape of skin cells with treelike hairs and cavelike pores.

New details can be seen with each level of magnification. Using a hand lens, the skin appears like a rough surface covered with hair. The light microscope reveals that the skin, like all living things, is composed of many small, separate units called **cells**. Under the powerful electron microscope, the skin cells in the outer layer look something like corn flakes—all twisted and bent out of shape as they dried.

If you could peer into the pores between the skin cells, you would see spherical, single-celled organisms called bacteria. Most of these bacteria are harmless, and occur naturally on your skin. Pushing up out of the landscape of skin cells are towering pillars, the shafts of hair. At the base of these hairs is another common organism: yeast. A variety of harmless yeast cells lives off dead cells and skin oils.

Just what are cells, and how do they keep us all functioning? In this chapter, you will

- develop microscope skills, and
- investigate cells using a microscope.

 Getting Started

1. Imagine meeting some extra-terrestrials. How would you explain to them how living things differ from nonliving things?

2. Describe what you think cells are. Use a diagram to show what a typical cell might look like.

3. Are all cells the same? Speculate about how the cells of animals differ from the cells of a plant.

4. During the 1700s, telescopes and microscopes were often displayed by amateur scientists as symbols of their learning. What instruments of science and technology do you think have replaced the microscope as symbols of knowledge?

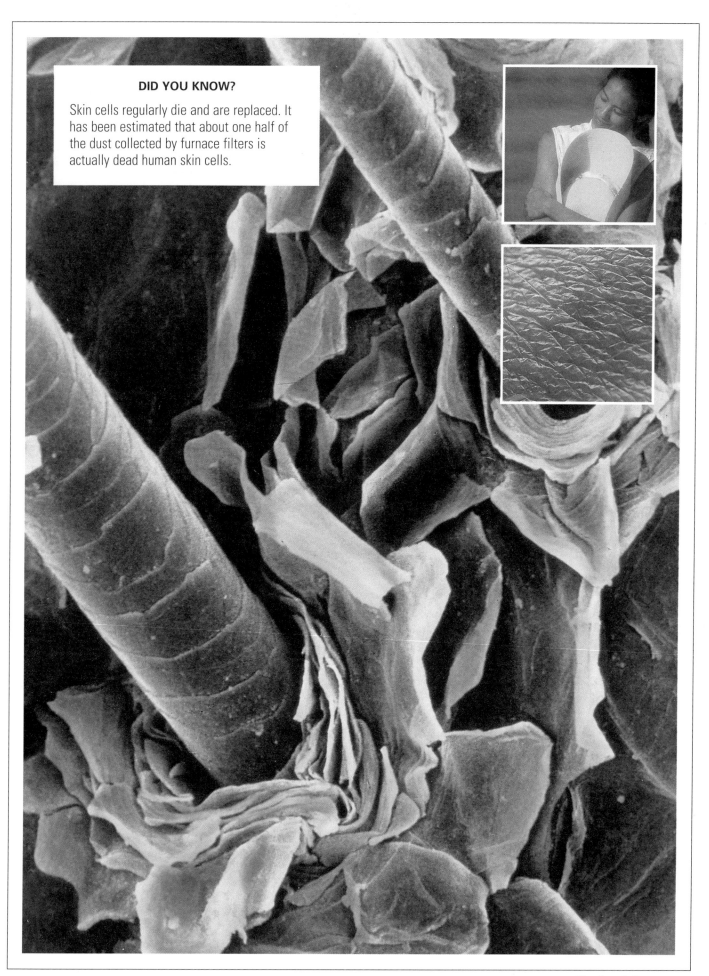

Characteristics of Living Things

HOW DO YOU KNOW if something is alive? What do you look for in living things that tells you they are alive? For example, is a volcano alive? You would probably say "no," but the lava flowing down the sides of a volcano moves, just as some living things do. Is movement enough to identify living things?

In time, the volcano may get larger. Is this growth? Is change in size a characteristic of living things?

A close examination reveals that gases burst from the top of the volcano. Human beings breathe out gases too. Does this emission of gases mean that the volcano is alive?

To answer these questions, you must examine the characteristics of living things. Before a thing can be classified as living, it must show all of these characteristics.

LIVING THINGS ARE COMPOSED OF CELLS.

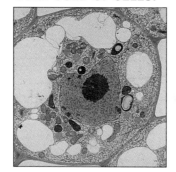

Typical plant cell.

LIVING THINGS GROW AND REPRODUCE.

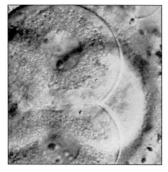

Cells reproduce by dividing in two.

LIVING THINGS REQUIRE ENERGY.

Animals obtain the energy they need by eating plants or by eating other animals that got their energy from plants.

LIVING THINGS RESPOND TO THE ENVIRONMENT.

The response might be to another organism or to many other factors.

The Cell Theory

By looking closely at living things, scientists have compiled a great deal of evidence to support what they call the **cell theory**: *all living things are composed of cells and all cells come from pre-existing cells.* The cell theory has proven very powerful in helping scientists understand how the human body and the bodies of other animals and plants work. By viewing cells, you will increase your understanding of living things.

ASK YOURSELF

A student drops a little water on a hot plate and records the following.

Observation
The water drop splits in half and the two droplets move to opposite sides of the hot plate. After a few seconds, the two droplets disappear.

Interpretation
Either the water drop or something living in the water reproduces. Then it dies because it is exposed to extreme heat.

- Would you accept the interpretation? Give your reasons.

LIVING THINGS HAVE A LIFE SPAN.

Living things exist for only a limited period of time.

LIVING THINGS PRODUCE WASTES.

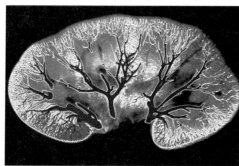

The human kidney filters wastes from the blood.

LIVING THINGS PRODUCE OFFSPRING LIKE THEMSELVES.

Offspring inherit traits from their parents.

SELF CHECK

1. What are the important differences between living and nonliving things?
2. Name at least one characteristic of living things shown by each of the following examples.
   (a) A plant bends toward the light.
   (b) A tadpole develops into a frog.
   (c) Human lungs eliminate carbon dioxide.
   (d) A blue jay feeds on sunflower seeds.
   (e) A cat gives birth to kittens.
3. Make a table listing the seven characteristics of living things in one column. In the second column of the table, next to each characteristic, suggest a nonliving thing that would be classified as alive if only that characteristic applied.
4. Are volcanoes alive? Why or why not?

Learning about the Microscope

BECAUSE CELLS ARE SMALL, you must make them appear larger than they really are in order to see and study them. To view cells closely, you will use a **compound light microscope**. It employs two lenses and a light source to make the object appear larger. The object is magnified by a lens near your eye, the ocular lens (sometimes called the eyepiece), and again by a second lens, the objective lens, which is just above the object. The comparison of the actual size of the object with the size of its image is referred to as **magnification**.

DID YOU KNOW?

Do you have difficulty imagining what 100× magnification looks like? The wing of a small butterfly, increased 100×, would cover two cars. If it were increased to 1000×, it would cover four houses.

Parts of the Microscope

Structure	Function
1 Stage	Supports the microscope slide. Clips are used to hold the slide in position. A central opening in the stage allows light to pass through the slide.
2 Diaphragm	Regulates the amount of light reaching the object being viewed.
3 Objective lenses	Magnify the object. Usually three complex lenses are located on the nosepiece immediately above the object or specimen. The smallest of these, the low-power objective lens, has the lowest magnification, usually four times (4×). The medium-power lens magnifies by 10×, and the long, high-power lens by 40×.
4 Revolving nosepiece	Rotates, allowing the objective lenses to be changed. Each lens clicks into place.
5 Tube	Contains ocular lens; supports objective lenses.
6 Ocular lens	Magnifies the object, usually by 10×. Also known as the eyepiece, this is the part you look through to view the object.
7 Coarse-adjustment knob	Moves the tube up or down so you can get the object or specimen into focus. It is used with the low-power objective lens only.
8 Fine-adjustment knob	Moves the tube to get the object or specimen into sharp focus. It is used with medium- and high-power magnification. The fine-adjustment knob is used only after the object or specimen has been located and focused under low-power magnification using the coarse adjustment.
9 Condenser lens	Directs light to the object or specimen.

MATH-LINK

Calculating Magnification

Two different lenses, the ocular lens and the objective lens, each magnify the object you are viewing. The total magnification of the image is determined by multiplying the two magnifications. For example, a magnification of 10× by the ocular lens and 4× by the objective lens would result in a magnification of the object of 40× (4 × 10).

- If an object is viewed through a 15× ocular lens and 10× objective lens, calculate the total magnification.

- Find the magnification of the ocular and objective lenses on the microscopes used in your classroom. Calculate the magnification of an object viewed under low, medium, and high power.

SELF CHECK

5. Examine the microscope that you will be using in your classroom. Find each of the parts. Describe any way that your microscope is different.

6. Make a list, in order, of all the parts of the microscope that the light passes through, from the lamp to your eye.

7. Why should you not allow the objective lenses to touch the slide?

8. If you are viewing an organism with a 60× objective lens and a 10× ocular lens, what is the magnification of the image you see?

Working with the Microscope

I N THIS INVESTIGATION, you will learn some basic techniques of using a microscope. You will then be able to use the microscope to study cells.

Materials
- newsprint with lower-case letter f
- scissors
- microscope slide
- cover slip
- compound microscope
- pencil
- compasses or petri dish
- ruler

Procedure

Part 1 *Positioning Objects Under the Microscope*

1 Find and cut out a lower-case letter f from a sample of newsprint.

2 Place the letter in the centre of a microscope slide.

3 Hold a cover slip between your thumb and forefinger. Place the edge of the cover slip to one side of the letter. Gently lower the cover slip onto the slide so that it covers the letter. This method of preparing a microscope slide is called a **dry mount**, because no water is used.

Step 3

4 Make sure the low-power objective lens is in place on your microscope. Then put the slide in the centre of the microscope stage, with the top of the letter away from your body. Use the stage clips to hold the slide in position. Turn on the light source.

Step 4

5 View the microscope stage from the side. Using the coarse-adjustment knob, bring the low-power objective lens and the object as close as possible to one another. Do not allow the lens to touch the cover slip.

Step 5

6 View the f through the eyepiece. Slowly move the coarse-adjustment knob so the objective lens moves away from the slide, to bring the image into focus.

(a) In which direction is the f facing?

(b) Using compasses or a petri dish, draw a circle in your notebook to represent the area you are looking at through the microscope. This area is called the **field of view**.

(c) Look through the microscope and draw what you see. Make the letter fill the same amount of area in your diagram as it does in the microscope.

7 While you are looking through the microscope, slowly move the slide away from your body.

✎ (d) In what direction does the letter appear to move?

8 Move the slide to the left while viewing the f.

✎ (e) In what direction does the letter appear to move?

9 Rotate the nosepiece to the medium-power objective lens. Use the fine-adjustment knob to bring the letter into focus.

✋ **CAUTION:** Never use the coarse-adjustment knob with the medium- or high-power objective lenses.

✎ (f) Does the width of the letter appear to change? How?

✎ (g) Draw a new diagram of what you see, showing the field of view under medium-power magnification.

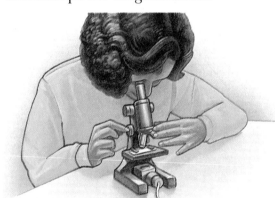

Step 9

10 Adjust the letter so that it is directly in the centre of the field of view. Rotate the nosepiece to the high-power objective lens. Use the fine-adjustment knob to focus the image.

✎ (h) Do you see more or less of the letter than you did under medium-power magnification?

✎ (i) Under which magnification does the image seem closer to the eye?

✎ (j) Draw the field of view and what you see under high-power magnification.

Part 2 *Estimating Size*

11 Return the nosepiece to the low-power objective lens. Position the letter f in the centre of the field of view.

12 Estimate the number of fs that could fit across the field of view.

✎ (k) How many letters will fit across the field of view?

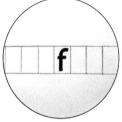

13 Devise a way to estimate the size of the letter f.

✎ (l) Describe the method you used to estimate size.

Questions

1. Explain why a microscope should be stored with its low-power objective lens in position.

2. Why should the coarse-adjustment knob not be used with a high-power objective lens?

3. Which magnification would be most suited for scanning a slide to find a certain object?

4. Based upon your investigation with the letter f, explain why inexperienced biologists often have difficulties using a microscope to follow tiny organisms as they move about in a drop of pond water on a microscope slide.

Apply

5. The cell shown below is viewed under low-power magnification. When you rotate the nosepiece to high-power magnification, you are not able to see an image, no matter how much you try to focus.

(a) Why have you lost the image?

(b) Suggest a technique that would help eliminate this problem.

Using the Microscope

I N THIS INVESTIGATION, you will learn more microscope techniques. These will give you an understanding of how and in which situations the microscope can be used.

Materials

- thread, in two colours
- scissors
- microscope slide
- cover slip
- compound microscope
- lens paper
- transparent ruler

Procedure

Part 1 *Investigating Depth of Field*

The **depth of field** is the amount of an image that is in *sharp focus* when it is viewed under a microscope.

1 Cut two pieces of thread of different colours.

2 Make a temporary dry mount by placing one thread over the other in the form of an X in the centre of a microscope slide. Cover the threads with a cover slip.

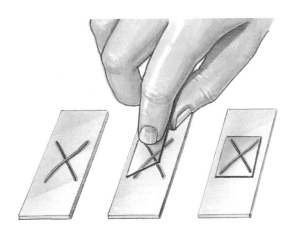

Step 2

3 Place the slide on the microscope stage and turn on the light.

4 Position the low-power objective lens close to, but not touching, the slide.

5 View the crossed threads through the ocular lens. Slowly rotate the coarse-adjustment knob until the threads come into focus. You may wish to adjust the diaphragm for better light.

✎ (a) Can you bring both threads into sharp focus at the same time?

6 Rotate the nosepiece to the medium-power objective lens. Focus on the upper thread by using the fine-adjustment knob.

✎ (b) Describe what you see.

✋ **CAUTION:** Never use the coarse-adjustment knob with the medium- or high-power objective lenses.

7 Repeat step 6 for the high-power objective lens.

✎ (c) Under which magnification is the bottom thread clearest when you focus on the top thread?

✎ (d) As you move from the low- to the high-power objective lens, how does the light intensity change?

✎ (e) Which objective lens is the best for showing the most detail in a thread?

8 Return the microscope to the low-power objective lens. Remove the slide and discard the threads. Clean the slide and cover slip and return them to their appropriate location.

Part 2 *Determining the Field of View*

Recall that the circle of light seen through the microscope is called the field of view. It is the area of a slide that you can observe.

9 With the low-power objective lens in place, put a transparent ruler on the stage. Position the millimetre marks on the ruler immediately below the objective lens.

10 Using the coarse-adjustment knob, focus on the marks on the ruler.

11 Move the ruler so that one of the millimetre markings is just at the edge of the field of view.

✎ (f) Note the diameter of the field of view, in millimetres, under the low-power objective lens.

12 Using the same procedure, measure the field of view for the medium-power objective lens.

✎ (g) Indicate the diameter of the field of view, in millimetres, under the medium-power objective lens.

13 Most high-power lenses provide a field of view that is less than one millimetre in diameter, so it cannot be measured with a ruler. Follow these steps to calculate the field of view of the high-power lens.

Calculate the ratio of the magnification of the high-power objective lens to that of the low-power objective lens.

$$\text{Ratio} = \frac{\text{magnification of high-power lens}}{\text{magnification of low-power lens}}$$

Use the ratio to determine the field diameter (diameter of the field of view) under high-power magnification.

$$\text{Field diameter (high power)} = \frac{\text{field diameter (low power)}}{\text{ratio}}$$

✎ (h) Calculate the field diameter of the high-power lens. Show your calculations.

14 Convert your measurements and calculations of the fields of view from millimetres (mm) to micrometres (μm). (Remember that 1 mm = 1000 μm.)

✎ (i) Record your answers in a table.

15 Rotate the nosepiece to the low-power objective lens and return the microscope to the storage area.

Questions

1. What happens to the depth of field as you move from a lower to a higher magnification?

2. What happens to the diameter of the field of view as you move from a lower to a higher magnification?

3. Explain why the dimensions of objects viewed under high-power magnification are usually recorded in micrometres.

Apply

4. If you were trying to study the detail of a specimen that was very thick, what problems might you have?

5. A scientist wishes to examine a drop of pond water to find a small animal. Which magnification would you suggest? Explain your answer.

6. How would you estimate the size of an object you are viewing, based on field diameter? Construct an equation that would give a good estimate.

Extension

7. Based on your investigation, predict which objective lens would be best suited for viewing Velcro. Place a small piece of Velcro on a slide, view it under low-power magnification and comment on the accuracy of your prediction.

Life from Nonliving Things?

I N THIS CASE STUDY, you will look at some of the early ideas about life, and investigate experiments that helped lead to changes in those ideas.

Life from Rain

Thousands of years ago, scientists noticed that when a pond dried up during a long period of drought, no living frogs or fish were found in the mud. The following spring, rain began to fall and the pond filled with water. The scientists observed that the pond now contained many fish and frogs. Some concluded that the fish and frogs must have fallen to earth during the rainstorm.

(a) What observations can you make to challenge the belief that fish and frogs fall during rainstorms?

It's raining fish and frogs!

Aristotle's Proposal

Aristotle, who lived in Greece in the fourth century B.C., rejected the hypothesis that life came from rain. He proposed that the fish and frogs came from the mud, a nonliving thing. Aristotle also believed that flies came from rotting meat because he had always

observed flies on rotting meat. Aristotle's theory, known as **spontaneous generation**, persisted for nearly two thousand years. Spontaneous generation is the theory that proposes that nonliving things can be transformed into living things without any external causes.

(b) What observations can you make to support Aristotle's theory?

(c) What observations can you make to challenge Aristotle's theory?

Redi or Not

In 1668, Francesco Redi designed an experiment to test the theory that rotting meat is transformed into flies. Redi placed bits of meat in an open jar. He placed similar pieces of meat in another jar, which he sealed. The open jar was designated the control, while the closed jar was designated experimental.

(d) Before you read on, predict what happened in both jars. Provide your reasons.

after 2 weeks

maggots found in open jar

no maggots found in sealed jar

Redi's experiment

Apparently, flies were attracted to the meat in the open jar and began laying eggs on the food supply. The eggs hatched into maggots and the maggots became flies. Redi concluded that flies come from other flies, not from rotting meat!

Next Came Needham

Although Francesco Redi helped defeat the theory of spontaneous generation for larger organisms, many continued to accept the theory for microorganisms (organisms that can be seen only with the aid of a microscope). John Needham (1713–1781) was one of these scientists. The following diagram outlines Needham's experiment to test the theory of spontaneous generation for microorganisms. From the results of this experiment, Needham concluded that microorganisms came from nonliving things in the beef broth!

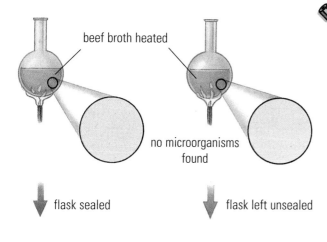

beef broth heated

no microorganisms found

flask sealed

flask left unsealed

after 2 weeks

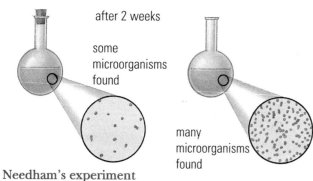

some microorganisms found

many microorganisms found

Needham's experiment

(e) Do the results of Needham's experiment mean that the broth had spontaneously generated microorganisms? Give your reasons.

(f) How is it possible to check for microorganisms immediately after boiling the broth and not find any, but find so many two weeks later?

(g) What changes would you make to Needham's experiment, and what results would you expect?

Spallanzani the Spoiler

Lazzaro Spallanzani (1729–1799) repeated Needham's experiment, but he boiled the flasks longer and used a tighter seal.

(h) How might a longer boiling time affect the experimental results?

(i) How might making a more airtight seal on the flask affect the experimental results?

(j) Predict the results of Spallanzani's experiment. Justify your prediction.

Spallanzani found no microorganisms in the tightly sealed flask of broth.

(k) What conclusion would you draw from Spallanzani's experiment?

Questions

1. What was the variable that Redi was attempting to control in his experiment?

2. What were two major differences between Needham's and Spallanzani's experiments?

3. Examine Needham's experiment. After two weeks of storage, why were more microorganisms found in the unsealed flask than in the sealed flask?

Apply

4. The modern cell theory states that all cells come from pre-existing cells. Cells do not come from nonliving things. What evidence have you seen on these pages to support this theory?

5. Critics of Spallanzani said that sealing the flasks prevented the "active principle," which was in the air, from reaching the broth. They argued that fresh air must reach the broth in the flask before the microorganisms could be created. What problem is created when fresh air gets into the flask?

Extension

6. Research Louis Pasteur and his swan-necked flask. How did the swan-necked flask finally silence Spallanzani's critics?

Plant and Animal Cells

CELLS VARY IN SIZE, SHAPE, AND FUNCTION. After many hours of peering through microscopes, scientists have determined that there is no single common cell, but all plant and animal cells have certain features in common.

Examining Animal Cells

The entire animal cell is surrounded by a cell membrane. Inside the cell membrane, generally near the centre of the cell, is the nucleus. The nucleus is surrounded by a fluid called the cytoplasm.

The **cell membrane** is the outermost edge of the animal cell. Composed of protein and lipid (fat) molecules, the cell membrane connects the cell to the outside environment. The membrane holds the contents of the cell in place and regulates the movement of materials into and out of the cell.

The **cytoplasm** is the area of the cell in which the work is done. Nutrients are absorbed, transported, and processed within the cytoplasm.

As the cell processes nutrients, waste products build up. The cytoplasm stores the waste until it can be disposed of.

Some animal cells have a **flagellum** (plural is flagella), a whiplike tail to help them move.

The **nucleus** is the control centre of the cell. It stores the information that tells the cell what to do and when. This hereditary or genetic information is organized into threadlike structures called **chromosomes**. Each chromosome contains many different units. These units, called **genes**, determine the specific traits of an individual. Every cell in an organism contains the same genes. The nucleus is also involved in cell division.

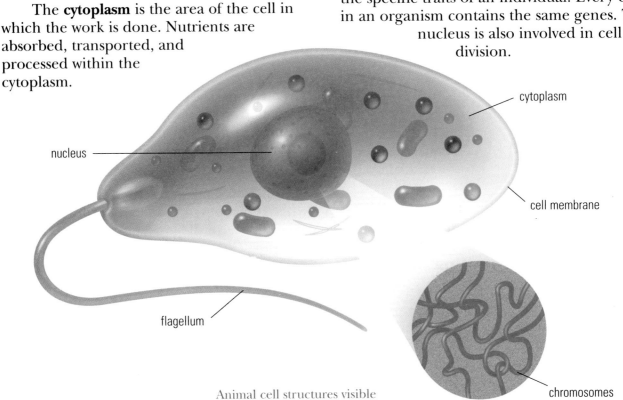

nucleus

cytoplasm

cell membrane

flagellum

chromosomes

Animal cell structures visible with the light microscope

Identifying Plant Cell Structures

Plant cells also have structures not found in animal cells. The cell membrane of a plant cell is surrounded by a cell wall. Composed of cellulose, the **cell wall** protects and supports plant cells. Gases, water, and some minerals can pass through small openings in the cell wall.

Unlike animal cells, plant cells can make their own food. Specialized organelles, called **plastids**, are associated with the production and storage of food. (An **organelle** is any structure found in the cytoplasm that has a specific form and function.) Plastids are chemical factories and storehouses for food and colour pigments. **Chloroplasts** are plastids that contain the green pigment chlorophyll, which is used in photosynthesis. **Photosynthesis** is the process by which plants combine carbon dioxide from the air with water to make sugar and release oxygen.

A large part of the cytoplasm of a plant cell consists of a fluid-filled space. This space is a called a **vacuole**. The vacuole is filled with water, sugar, minerals, and proteins. Animal cells may have vacuoles, but they are much smaller.

DID YOU KNOW?

Cells vary greatly in size and shape. An ostrich egg is the largest single cell, at about 75 mm in diameter. A human nerve cell can be as long as 1000 mm, but the same cell is only 0.01 mm in diameter.

SELF CHECK

9. What are the functions of the nucleus and the cytoplasm of the cell?

10. Where would you find the genetic information in a cell?

11. List two ways in which plant cells differ from animal cells.

12. (a) What is the function of the chloroplasts?

    (b) Why are chloroplasts not found in animal cells?

13. Predict what might happen to a cell if the cell membrane were replaced by a plastic coating that allows nothing to get through. Explain your prediction.

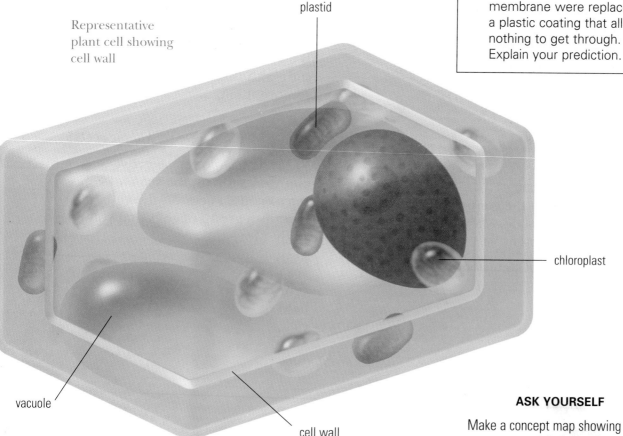

Representative plant cell showing cell wall

plastid

chloroplast

vacuole

cell wall

ASK YOURSELF

Make a concept map showing cell structures and their functions.

Comparing Plant and Animal Cells

IN THIS INVESTIGATION, you will look at some of the differences and similarities between plant and animals cells. Keep in mind, however, that there are also differences among different types of plant cells and different types of animal cells. In Part 3 of this investigation, you will view human epithelial cells. These cells cover, protect, and support many parts of the body.

Materials

- onion
- tweezers
- microscope slide
- cover slip
- medicine dropper
- light microscope
- iodine stain (Lugol's)
- paper towel
- lens paper
- prepared slide of human epithelial cells
- water in a dropper bottle

 CAUTION: Be careful when using Lugol's iodine solution. It is toxic and an irritant. It may stain skin and clothing. Use rubber gloves when cleaning up spills, and rinse the area of the spills with water.

Procedure

Part 1 *Preparing a Wet Mount of Onion Cells*

1 Obtain a small section (about 2 cm²) of an onion from your teacher.

2 Using tweezers, remove a single layer from the inner side of the section of onion. If the layer you removed is not translucent, try again.

Step 2

3 Using tweezers, place the onion skin in the centre of a microscope slide. Make sure the onion skin does not fold over.

4 Place two drops of water on the onion skin.

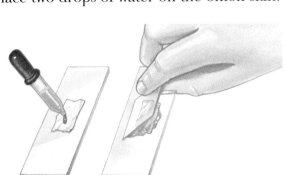

Steps 4 and 5

5 Holding the cover slip with your thumb and forefinger, touch the edge to the surface of the slide at a 45° angle. Gently lower the cover slip, allowing the air to escape. Your slide of the onion skin is called a **wet mount**.

6 If air bubbles are present, gently tap the slide with the eraser end of a pencil to remove them.

Part 2 *Examining the Wet Mount of Onion Cells*

7 With the low-power objective lens in place, clip your slide on the stage of your microscope. Focus on the cells and identify a group of cells that you wish to study. Move the slide so that those cells are in the centre of the field of view.

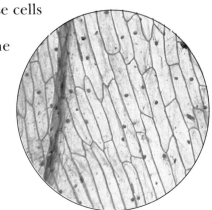

8 Rotate the nosepiece of the microscope to the medium-power objective lens and view the cells. Using your fine-adjustment knob, bring the cells into clear focus.

🖉 (a) Draw and describe what you see. (Refer to the Skills Handbook on page 518 for information about making scientific drawings.)

9 Slowly decrease the light intensity by adjusting the diaphragm of the microscope.

🖉 (b) What level of light reveals the greatest detail?

10 Rotate the nosepiece to the low-power objective lens, and remove the slide from the microscope. Place a drop of iodine at one edge of the cover slip. Touch the opposite edge of the cover slip with a small piece of a paper towel. This will draw the stain across the slide under the cover slip.

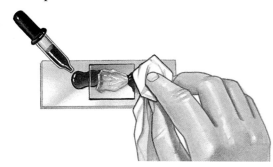

Step 10

11 Select a section of the onion skin with the low-power objective lens and view the cells under the medium-power objective lens.

🖉 (c) What effect did the iodine have on the cells? Why was it used?

12 Rotate the nosepiece to the high-power objective lens. Using the fine-adjustment knob, focus on a group of cells.

🖉 (d) Draw a four-cell grouping and label as many cell structures as you can see.

13 Use the field diameter of the high-power objective lens and the number of cells in view to estimate the diameter of one of the cells.

🖉 (e) What is the diameter of an onion cell?

14 Rotate the nosepiece back to the low-power objective lens and remove the slide. Dispose of the onion skin as directed by your teacher and clean the slide and cover slip with lens paper.

Part 3 *Examining Human Cells*

15 Place the prepared slide of human epithelial cells on the stage of the microscope. Using the coarse-adjustment knob, locate and focus on a group of the cells.

🖉 (f) How does the arrangement of plant and animal cells differ?

16 Rotate the nosepiece to the medium-power objective lens and focus using the fine-adjustment knob.

🖉 (g) Draw three cells and label the cell structures that are visible.

17 Rotate the nosepiece to the high-power objective lens and focus using the fine-adjustment knob.

🖉 (h) Draw and label what you see.

18 Use the same procedure you used for the onion cells to calculate the diameter of a human cell.

🖉 (i) Compare the diameter of the onion and human cells.

Questions

1. In what ways do the onion cells differ from the human cells?

2. Predict the function of the onion cells that you observed under the microscope. What cell structures were prominent that would justify your prediction?

3. Explain why the cells of the onion bulb do not appear to have any chloroplasts. (Don't all plant cells have chloroplasts?)

Apply

4. A student viewing onion cells just sees large, dark circles. What might have caused the dark circles? Did anyone in your class experience this difficulty?

Development of the Microscope

S OME OF THE BEST of the earliest microscopes were made by Anton van Leeuwenhoek in the 1660s. His microscopes had only a single lens that magnified things 10 or more times.

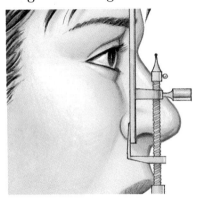

Leeuwenhoek's microscopes used a single lens mounted between two brass plates to magnify objects.

Magnification Needed to Create a 1-mm Image	
Object	Magnification
fish egg	none
human egg	10×
plant cell	20×
animal cell	50×
bacterium	1 000×
mitochondrion	1 000×
large virus	10 000×
ribosome	40 000×
cell membrane	100 000×
hydrogen atom	10 000 000×

As you have discovered in your own investigations, an important advance in the development of the microscope came when scientists added a second lens. An object magnified 10× by the first lens and 10× by the second lens gives an image that is 100× larger.

In order to make images even larger, the lenses must get thicker. But as lenses become thicker, the images they produce become more blurred. Eventually a point is reached where the image is so blurred that no detail can be seen.

Even the most sophisticated lenses limit the light microscope to about 2000× magnification. In order to see very tiny viruses, or the detail within a human cell, greater magnification is required. That's where the electron microscope comes in.

Viewing with the Transmission Electron Microscope

Today's **transmission electron microscopes** are capable of 2 000 000× magnification. Instead of light, the electron microscope uses a beam of electrons. Electrons are tiny particles that travel around the nucleus of an atom. However, electron microscopes have two major limitations. First, specimens that contain many layers of cells, such as a blood vessel, cannot be examined. The electrons are easily deflected or absorbed by a thick specimen. Therefore, very thin sections of cells must be used. These thin sections are

Light microscope

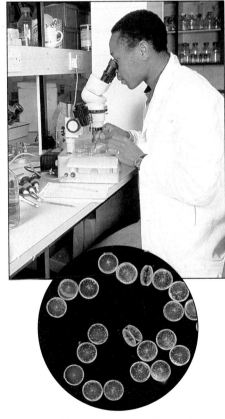

Algae cells seen through a light microscope

obtained by encasing the object in plastic, and then shaving very thin layers off the plastic. But mounting cells in plastic kills them, which means that only dead cells can be observed — the second limitation. Although it is ideal for examining the structures within a cell, the transmission electron microscope does not allow you to examine the details of a many-celled insect eye, or a living cell as it divides.

Viewing with the Scanning Electron Microscope

The **scanning electron microscope** provides a method for investigating thicker specimens by reflecting electrons from their surface. The reflected electrons are magnified onto a TV screen, where they produce a three-dimensional image. The scanning electron microscope lacks the magnification and the high resolution of the transmission electron microscope, but it provides greater depth of field.

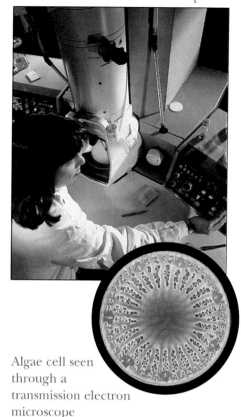
Transmission electron microscope

Scanning electron microscope

Algae cell seen through a scanning electron microscope

Algae cell seen through a transmission electron microscope

TECHNOLOGY-LINK

Arthroscope

An arthroscope is a surgical instrument that combines fibre optics with microelectronics. This instrument has changed the way surgery is done. No longer are large cuts required. The objective lens can be inserted into a joint, such as the knee. The glass fibre in the probe transmits images to a video 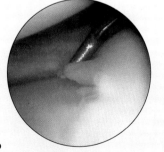 camera, allowing the surgeon to view the inside of the joint (see the picture above). Using tiny surgical instruments, the surgeon can perform the surgery while watching a monitor.

• Do research to find out more about how an arthroscope works. As a project, you might want to design and present a model that shows the science of its operation.

SELF CHECK

14. Give one advantage of using a compound light microscope over a single-lens microscope.

15. Give one advantage of using the light microscope over a transmission electron microscope.

16. Which microscope do you think would be best for viewing each of the following? Give reasons for your choice.

  (a) a virus

  (b) a hair mite

  (c) the detailed structure of a cell's nucleus

  (d) a living microorganism

17. Why is it important to include the magnification beside a picture or a diagram of an object viewed under a microscope?

Parts of a Cell Seen with the Electron Microscope

T HE CYTOPLASM, THE WORKING AREA OF THE CELL, contains specialized structures called organelles. Many of these tiny structures are visible only when viewed with a transmission electron microscope. The organelles described below are found in both plant and animal cells, although the large diagram on this page is of an animal cell.

Mitochondria

Tiny, oval-shaped organelles, called **mitochondria** (singular is mitochondrion), provide cells with energy. Mitochondria are often referred to as the "power house" of the cell, because the mitochondria are the centres of cell respiration. In **respiration**, sugar molecules are combined with oxygen to form carbon dioxide, water, and energy that the cell can use.

Mitochondria are the largest of the cytoplasmic organelles in animal cells.

An electron micrograph of a mitochondrion.

Ribosomes

Ribosomes are the organelles that put proteins together. Proteins are the molecules that form cell structures. Proteins also help many chemical reactions occur in cells. Cell growth and reproduction require continuous supplies of proteins. The nucleus provides the information for the type of protein needed.

Endoplasmic Reticulum

A series of "canals" carries materials throughout the cytoplasm. The canals, composed of parallel membranes, are referred to as **endoplasmic reticulum**. The membranes may be rough or smooth. Endoplasmic reticulum is said to be rough when it has many ribosomes attached to its outside surface.

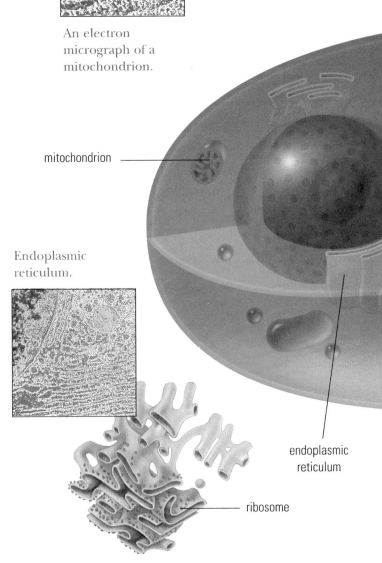

mitochondrion

Endoplasmic reticulum.

endoplasmic reticulum

ribosome

Golgi Apparatus

This structure appears like a stack of pancakes. Protein molecules are stored inside the **Golgi apparatus**. When it is packed with protein, the organelle moves toward the cell membrane. Once the Golgi apparatus attaches itself to the cell membrane, it can release small packets of proteins, called vesicles. Proteins packaged this way can be used inside or outside the cell.

Lysosomes

Formed by the Golgi apparatus, **lysosomes** are saclike structures that contain proteins that can break down large molecules and other cell parts. The smaller molecules produced by the lysosome proteins can be re-used as building material. Damaged or worn-out cells are destroyed by their own lysosomes.

Lysosomes are also an important part of the human body's defence mechanism. For example, white blood cells can engulf invading bacteria. Inside the cytoplasm, the lysosomes of the white blood cell cluster around the bacterium and release their proteins. The proteins destroy the bacterium.

The Golgi apparatus was named after its discoverer, Camillo Golgi.

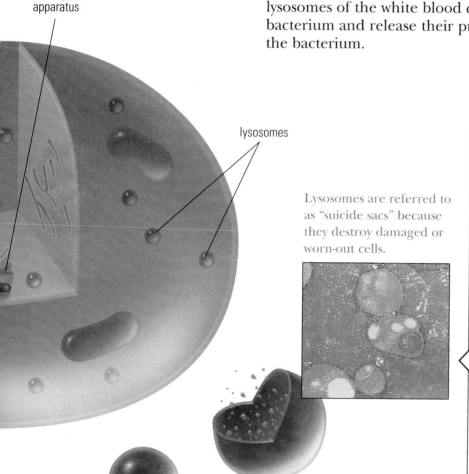

Golgi apparatus

lysosomes

Lysosomes are referred to as "suicide sacs" because they destroy damaged or worn-out cells.

SELF CHECK

18. What are organelles?

19. Refer to the concept map you made earlier in this chapter showing cell structures and their functions. Add the organelles that are visible with an electron microscope.

20. Predict what would happen to a cell if its mitochondria stopped working.

21. Cells lining the stomach release enzymes that aid digestion. These cells have many Golgi apparatuses. Explain why you think so many Golgi apparatuses are found in stomach cells. What do you think the stomach enzymes are made of?

Structure and Function of Cells

IMAGINE THE DIFFICULTIES that you would have if specialists did not exist! Could you build your own television, grow your own food, and provide adequate medical attention for your family? Single-celled organisms do not function as specialists: they have to do everything for themselves. But multicellular organisms, such as you, benefit from **cell specialization**. Multicellular organisms have cells that come in a variety of sizes and shapes, each designed to carry out a special function. Bone cells, for example, are designed to provide support and protection and to help you move. Nerve cells provide information about your environment, and allow you to respond to the information. Cells of your kidney are specialized to help remove wastes from the blood.

Procedure

In this activity, you will design a cell to carry out a special function, and explain why you designed it as you did.

1. You will work in groups, and your teacher will select one of the cell tasks on page 307 for each group.

2. Consider the number and type of organelles you will put into the cell. For example, a cell designed to secrete a specific substance should have ribosomes and Golgi apparatus.

   (a) Identify the organelles that you will include.

3. Consider the size and shape of the cell.

   (b) Sketch a preliminary diagram of your cell design.

4. Consider the reasons for selecting your design. Remember, there is no right or wrong design. However, you must be able to justify the design that you choose.

   (c) Record your reasons for selecting your design.

5. Be prepared to present your design to the class. Can you explain how your cell shape complements its function?

Example

Here is a sample that might help you organize your thoughts.

Cell Task

Movement, and the delivery of genetic material to another cell.

Sample Design

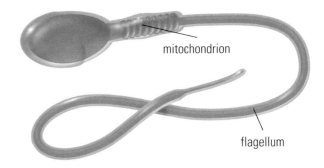

Reasons for the Design Features

The cell has a streamlined shape, which helps it move. The reduced amount of cytoplasm also helps the cell move because it reduces the mass of the cell. The mitochondrion, the organelle that releases energy, is next to the flagellum, the structure that needs energy.

Cell Tasks and Functions

Cell Task	Description of Required Functions
Covers body parts	This cell must provide maximum coverage. The cell must be capable of dividing rapidly, because it is worn down quickly. The cell must provide protection for the more delicate cells that it covers.
Secretes fluids	This cell must make and secrete large amounts of stomach fluids. Its surroundings are highly acidic and it may need some type of protection.
Supports cells	This cell must support other cells. The cell must be rigid.
Absorbs nutrients	This cell lines the small intestine. Food that has been broken down into small molecules moves from the small intestine into the bloodstream through these cells. These cells must have a large surface area to help absorption.
Moves limbs	This cell allows the limbs to move by contracting. When the cell contracts, it becomes shorter. The cell requires a great amount of energy to contract.
Communicates information	This cell allows cells in one part of the body to communicate with other cells. Some of this communication occurs over great distances.
Carries oxygen to other cells	This cell is packed with a special substance that carries oxygen. It must be able to move through small tubes.

Questions

1. What is cell specialization?

2. What advantages does a multicellular organism have over a single-celled organism?

3. Give an example of how cell function influences cell shape.

Extension

4. When viewing cells through the microscope and in the textbook, you have been looking at two-dimensional images. However, cells are three-dimensional. Cells have length, width, and depth. A model allows you to represent cells as they exist in nature. Construct a three-dimensional model of the cell you designed. Before starting, think carefully about the materials you will need.

5. Choose a company that produces a product in a factory. Compare each part of the cell to a part of the factory.

Cells that Work Together

A GROUP OF CELLS SIMILAR IN SHAPE AND FUNCTION is called a **tissue**. For example, when many different nerve cells work together, they are referred to as nerve tissue. Muscle tissue, bone tissue, and cartilage are other tissues that are found in your body. The tendons that attach your muscles to your bones are made up of a tissue called connective tissue. A covering tissue, called epithelial tissue, covers both the outside and the inside surfaces of your body. This tissue provides support and protection for your body structures.

Tissues, in turn, can be organized into larger structures called **organs**. Many organs are composed of several different types of tissue. For example, your heart is composed of nerve tissue, muscle tissue, and epithelial tissue.

Organ systems are groups of organs that have related functions. For example, the circulatory system includes the heart, arteries that carry blood from the heart to the tissues, capillaries where nutrients and wastes are exchanged, and veins that carry blood and wastes from the tissues back to the heart. In addition, blood and nerve tissue are found in the circulatory system.

In Chapter 14, you will study how plant cells are organized into tissues and systems.

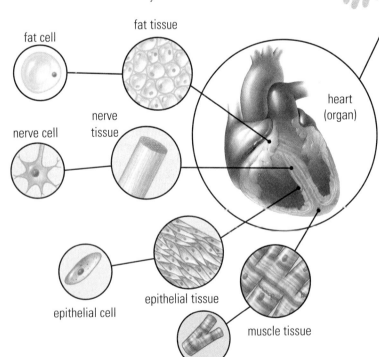

fat cell

fat tissue

nerve cell

nerve tissue

epithelial cell

epithelial tissue

muscle cell

muscle tissue

heart (organ)

Circulatory system

Levels of Cell Organization in the Human Body

Organ system	Major organs in the system	Major tissues in the system
Nervous	brain, spinal cord, eyes, ears, nerves to and from body parts	nerve, connective, epithelial
Excretory	kidneys, bladder, ureters, urethra, liver	epithelial, nerve, connective, muscle
Circulatory	heart, arteries, capillaries, veins	epithelial, nerve, connective, muscle
Digestive	esophagus, stomach, intestines, liver	epithelial, nerve, connective, muscle
Reproductive	testes and vas deferens, or ovaries, uterus, and fallopian tubes	epithelial, nerve, connective, muscle
Respiratory	lungs, windpipe, blood vessels	epithelial, nerve, connective, muscle
Endocrine	pancreas, adrenal glands, pituitary gland	epithelial, nerve, connective

CAREER-LINK

Medical Technologists

Medical technologists provide much of the information needed for proper diagnosis and treatment of diseases or injuries. If you enjoy working with technical equipment, and are interested in helping people, you may wish to consider this rewarding career.

- Ask your guidance counsellor for information about medical technologists. Prepare a list of questions you would like answered.

SELF CHECK

22. Define tissue, organ, and organ system.
23. Explain why the skin is referred to as an organ.
24. Organize the following structures from smallest to largest and give an example of each: organ system, tissue, cell, organelle, organ, molecule.
25. Compare the levels of cell organization with the levels in a familiar organization, such as a sports organization.

ASK YOURSELF

Choose one of the organ systems described in this section and construct a concept map. Arrange structures from the smallest to the largest in your concept map.

Putting Cells to Work

RESEARCHERS THROUGHOUT THE world are looking for ways to put cells to work in beneficial ways. In Canada, for example, scientists at Queen's University in Kingston have modified cells so they churn out antibodies to fight diseases such as cancer, leprosy, and tetanus. (Antibodies are the body's defence against foreign invaders. They attack bacteria, viruses, and other substances that the body identifies as harmful.)

Scientists from McGill University, in Montreal, have fused normal white blood cells to cancer cells. Referred to as hybridomas, these cells also produce huge amounts of antibodies for defence against disease.

Imagine large vats of these cells, producing antibodies on an industrial scale. The antibodies can be sold as drugs, making money for the manufacturers. These cells are of great economic value.

Other Cells

Tissue cultures, groups of cells grown in laboratories, have other exciting applications. When Alyssa Smith was admitted to hospital with a poorly functioning liver, doctors used cells from her mother to give her a second chance. Doctors removed a section of her mother's liver, grew the cells in a tissue culture, and then placed small groups of these cells in Alyssa's failing liver. These small groups of cells continue to divide and grow, until they form a normal liver.

These vats contain cells growing in substances rich in nutrients.

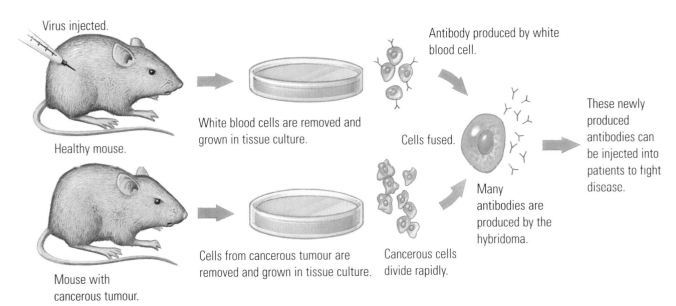

Virus injected.

Healthy mouse.

White blood cells are removed and grown in tissue culture.

Antibody produced by white blood cell.

Cells fused.

These newly produced antibodies can be injected into patients to fight disease.

Mouse with cancerous tumour.

Cells from cancerous tumour are removed and grown in tissue culture.

Cancerous cells divide rapidly.

Many antibodies are produced by the hybridoma.

A hybridoma is a fusion of a cancer cell with a white blood cell. Like a cancer cell, it divides rapidly. Like a white blood cell, it produces antibodies.

Similar methods have been developed for skin cells. As a result, burn victims may soon be able to have new skin from cells grown in tissue cultures. A bad burn will destroy all of the skin tissue in an area. Currently, surgeons replace the burned skin by taking pieces of skin, called grafts, from unburned parts of the patient's body. The grafts grow in the new location, but the area from which the skin was taken must also grow new skin cells. This process can be painful.

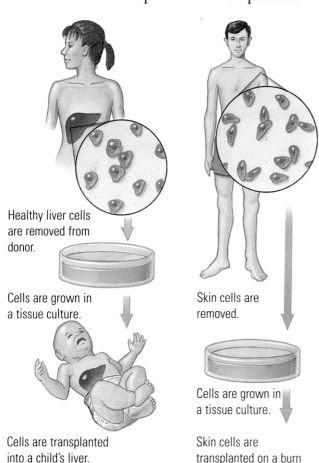

Healthy liver cells are removed from donor.

Cells are grown in a tissue culture.

Cells are transplanted into a child's liver.

Skin cells are removed.

Cells are grown in a tissue culture.

Skin cells are transplanted on a burn area.

Using tissue cultures

Understanding the Author

1. Why are white blood cells fused with cancer cells to produce hybridomas? (Hint: Think of what is special about each cell.)

2. Describe three different situations in which cells grown in tissue cultures may be used.

3. Where do scientists obtain the cells that are grown in tissue cultures?

4. What does the author mean by "These cells are of great economic value?"

The Issue

John Moore had a rare form of leukemia (a cancer of the blood). To treat the disease, a team of doctors removed his spleen. At the time of the operation, Moore signed the standard forms that allow removed tissues to be disposed of. However, Moore's spleen was not disposed of. The doctors found that his spleen cells could be made to produce large amounts of rare substances that could be used in medical research. The cells are worth a considerable amount of money. When he found out what had happened, Moore demanded a share of the profits. Should Moore share in the profits?

Point

- Moore should have been grateful that his life was saved. The fact that his cells were of medical use should not concern him.

- Moore signed the forms allowing for the removal of the cancerous tissue. What would happen to medical research if scientists had to worry about being sued every time they used discarded cells?

Counterpoint

- Doesn't Moore own his cells? If another research company had taken the cells from the doctors, the company would be charged with theft. Why doesn't the same rule apply to the spleen cells taken from Moore's body?

- Moore did not have any idea that his cells might be used in research when he signed the forms. The doctors did not provide Moore with information about how much his cells could be worth and how they could be used.

What Do You Think?

5. Research the issue further, and expand on the points above. Develop or reflect upon your opinion. Prepare for the class debate.

Key Outcomes

Now that you have completed the chapter, can you do the following? If not, review the sections indicated.

- State the cell theory. (10.1, 10.5)
- Demonstrate a knowledge of the function of the parts of a microscope and a skill in microscope techniques. (10.2, 10.3, 10.4, 10.7)
- Distinguish between plant and animal cells and describe the structure and function of the features of plant and animal cells. (10.6, 10.7 10.9, 10.10)
- Outline the levels of cell organization in a multicellular organism, and give an example of each. (10.11)

Review

1. What are the two main statements of the modern cell theory?

2. Your teacher will give you a diagram of a microscope. Label the parts indicated and state the function of each part.

3. List four points you should follow to care properly for your microscope.

4. Describe the steps you would take to focus an object under the medium-power objective lens.

5. List two differences between a compound light microscope and an electron microscope.

6. Set up a table using the headings below. Complete the table. Put a check mark beside the features that are present in plant and animal cells.

Feature	Function	Plant cell	Animal cell
cell membrane			
cell wall			

Key Terms

cell
cell theory
compound light microscope
magnification
dry mount
field of view
depth of field
spontaneous generation
cell membrane
cytoplasm
flagellum
nucleus
chromosome

gene
cell wall
plastid
organelle
chloroplast
photosynthesis
vacuole
wet mount
transmission electron microscope
scanning electron microscope
mitochondrion

respiration
ribosome
endoplasmic reticulum
Golgi apparatus
lysosome
cell specialization
tissue
organ
organ system

7. Copy this table into your notebook.

Organ system	Organs contained	Tissues contained

Write the following words in your table. Some words may be used more than once.

respiratory, esophagus, epithelial, intestines, heart, digestive, lungs, circulatory, blood vessels, connective, stomach, muscle, windpipe, nerve

8. If you wished to view the objects indicated below, which of the magnifying devices studied in this chapter would you use?

(a) a leaf, magnified 15×

(b) a computer chip, magnified 200×

(c) a sugar crystal, magnified 100 000×

(d) the surface of an insect's eye, magnified 1000×

9. Make labeled diagrams to show the structure of the following.

(a) a cell of the skin of an onion

(b) a human epithelial cell

10. What is the difference between the items in each pair?

(a) cell wall and cell membrane

(b) cytoplasm and vacuole

(c) chloroplast and chlorophyll

11. What happens to the size of the field of view and the brightness of illumination as you move to higher magnifications?

Problem Solving

12. Give three possible reasons for seeing only darkness when you first look in a microscope.

13. Draw each of the following letters and numbers as they would look when viewed through the low-power objective lens of a compound microscope: 7, 8, C, B, S, 9, f, h.

14. A sugar crystal is viewed through a compound microscope. If the objective lens is 10× and the eyepiece is 15×, how much larger does the crystal appear to be?

15. Determine the actual size of the fruit fly shown in the diagram if the diameter of the field of view is 6 mm.

Critical Thinking

16. In previous studies, you learned about the characteristics of living things. What characteristics apply to life for a single cell?

17. You are viewing a single-celled animal under the medium-power objective lens of the microscope. The animal appears to be moving in the direction indicated by the arrow. In order to keep the animal within the field of view, indicate by letter which direction you should move the slide on the stage.

18. Identify the cell in each of the following photographs as either a plant or an animal cell. Give reasons for your choices.

(a)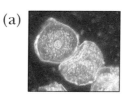

(c)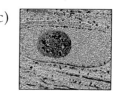

(b)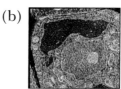

(d)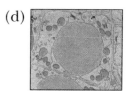

19. Pick one plant cell and one animal cell from the pictures above and draw a diagram of each. Label as many structures as you can.

20. You are viewing the cells shown in the diagram under low-power magnification. If the nosepiece is rotated to the medium-power objective lens, which cell would you expect to see in the field of view?

CHAPTER 11

Cells and Their Environment

HOW IS YOUR HEALTH? Are you, or is someone sitting close to you, fighting off a cold? Most of us have grown accustomed to occasionally coping with some type of infection. Your sniffles or puffy eyes may not even be due to cold germs. You may have allergies. Allergies occur when your body recognizes a basically harmless thing, such as dust or pollen grains, as being dangerous.

The cells of all living organisms must adjust to an ever changing and sometimes hostile external environment. Usually, your cells can maintain a stable internal environment, despite the external changes.

Humans are not the only organisms that must adjust to a changing environment. Most Canadians are familiar with the dramatic story of the salmon returning from the ocean to the streams they were born in. How do they survive the change in environment? If you were to place most salt-water organisms in fresh water they would soon bloat and die. Drinking only salt water would result in death for you. How can the salmon live in both fresh and salt water? To answer this question, you must begin by considering how materials move in and out of cells.

In this chapter, you will

- learn how substances enter and leave a cell,

- observe how plant and animal cells respond to changes in their environment, and

- examine single-cell organisms to observe their responses to environmental changes.

 Getting Started

1. In your group, brainstorm a list of substances you think must enter and leave a cell. Make a separate list of substances you think a cell would need to keep out.

2. Discuss how substances might enter and leave a cell. Write a short description of how you think the process works.

Transporting Materials across Cell Membranes

IMAGINE IF YOU HAD TO LIVE inside a sealed, plastic container. How could you survive? First, there would have to be a way for oxygen to enter the container. Then, you would need a supply of water and food. Even this would not be enough. You would also require a way of removing wastes, such as carbon dioxide and urine.

In some ways, a cell is like a sealed, plastic container. However, the cell membrane is much more than a plastic envelope that holds the organelles in place. Cell membranes are living membranes.

Cell Membranes

Cells allow some materials to enter or leave, but not others. They are said to be permeable to some materials and impermeable to others. **Permeable** means permitting passage, and **impermeable** means not permitting passage. How does the cell know which materials to take in, and which ones to allow out?

In general, small molecules pass easily through the cell membrane, medium-sized molecules move through less easily, and large ones cannot pass through at all. Because it allows certain substances to enter or leave but not other substances, the cell membrane is said to be **selectively permeable**.

The cell membrane appears as two layers of fat (lipid) interspersed with protein molecules.

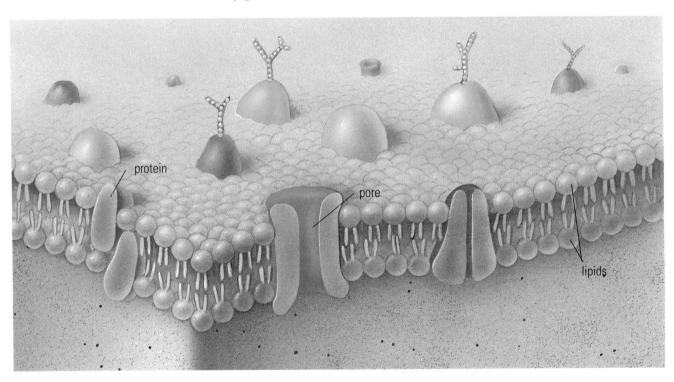

protein

pore

lipids

Diffusion

How do substances move from one place to another? Study the three pictures on this page. Why doesn't the ink remain as a small blob? What causes it to move outward? Recall your study of diffusion in Chapter 3. Molecules are constantly moving and colliding with other molecules. When they collide, they bounce off each other. This causes molecules concentrated in one area to spread outward. Diffusion is the movement of molecules from an area of high concentration to an area of lower concentration.

Diffusion is one of the ways substances move into and out of cells. Substances that a cell uses, such as oxygen, are found in low concentrations inside the cell. When the concentrations of these substances are higher outside the cell, the molecules will diffuse across the cell membrane into the cell. Diffusion will continue until the concentration is the same both inside and outside the cell. When waste products, such as carbon dioxide, become more concentrated inside the cell than outside, they diffuse out of the cell.

Ink diffusing in water

TRY THIS

Models of Membranes

Look at the setup shown.

*   Compare the permeability of the three materials—glass, a screen, cloth—covering the jars. What would happen if you poured water, sugar alone, and the sugar-water solution over each jar? Which jar cover is impermeable to all three substances? Which is permeable to all three substances? Which is impermeable to some substances but permeable to others?

*   Name two other materials that are permeable to some of the substances shown, but impermeable to others. Test the permeability of the substances for yourself.

sugar-water solution

water

sugar

SELF CHECK

1. Define diffusion.
2. Explain what is meant by an impermeable material, a permeable material, and a selectively permeable material.
3. What type of membrane do cells have: impermeable, permeable, or selectively permeable?
4. Draw and label a diagram of a cell membrane.

Osmosis

How can you make limp celery crisp again?

A CASUAL OBSERVATION OF THE WORLD around you can show you just how important water is to living things. Have you ever gone to the refrigerator to snack on some crisp vegetables, only to find a limp stalk of celery? As it loses water, celery becomes limp. If water is returned to the celery, it will become crisp again, as the water moves into the cells of the vegetable.

Water moves across cell membranes easily, by diffusion. The diffusion of water through a selectively permeable membrane is called **osmosis**. In a normal situation, water molecules are constantly passing through the cell membrane, both in and out of the cell. If there is an imbalance, more water will move in one direction than in the other. The direction of the water movement depends entirely on the concentration of water inside the cell compared with the concentration outside the cell.

A Model of Osmosis

Consider the system shown in the top diagram to the right. The membrane is permeable to water, but impermeable to the larger protein molecules. The protein molecules are too large to move through the pores. The concentration of protein on side B is greater than the concentration of protein on side A. Which side has the greater concentration of water? There are fewer protein molecules on side A, but many more water molecules. Side A has a greater concentration of water. Water will diffuse from side A, the area of higher water concentration, to side B, the area of lower water concentration.

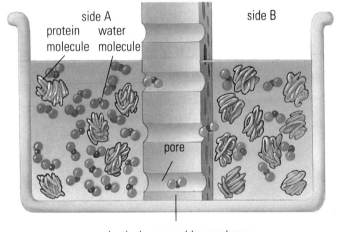

selectively permeable membrane

The bottom diagram to the right shows what happens when water moves from side A to side B. As water moves from side A to side B by osmosis, the protein on side B becomes less concentrated. Eventually, the concentrations of protein and water on sides A and B will become equal.

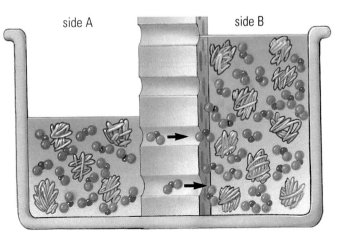

Cells in Solutions of Different Concentrations

The movement of water into and out of living cells is vital to life processes. Ideally, cells are bathed in solutions in which the solute concentration outside the cell is equal to that inside the cell. (Recall from Chapter 2 that solutes are substances that are dissolved in another substance.) In cells, salt and sugars are common solutes, and water is the solvent.

The diagrams below show three different environments in which cells may be found.

A

In situation A, the concentration of solute molecules outside the cell is equal to the concentration of solute molecules inside the cell. This means that the concentration of water molecules inside the cell is also the same as the concentration outside the cell. There is no overall movement of water into or out of the cell, although individual molecules of water will pass both ways. The shape and size of the cell do not change.

B

In situation B, the concentration of solutes outside the cell is less than that found inside the cell. This means that the concentration of water molecules is greater outside the cell than inside the cell. More water molecules move into the cell than out of the cell. The cell increases in size, and in the case of an animal cell, it may eventually burst.

C

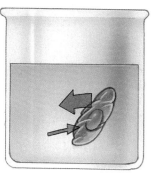

In situation C, the concentration of solutes outside the cell is greater than that found inside the cell. This means that the concentration of water is greater inside the cell than outside the cell. More water molecules move out of the cell than into the cell. The cell decreases in size.

Turgor Pressure

Water pressure, referred to as **turgor pressure**, pushes the cytoplasm of a normal plant cell against the cell wall. The rigid cell wall prevents the plant cell from bursting. Turgor pressure causes plants to stay rigid.

   Have you ever noticed that when salt is used on sidewalks and roads during the winter, the surrounding grass may wilt or die in the spring? In the spring, the salt from the road dissolves in water from the snow. This sets up a situation in which the concentration of the salt solution outside the grass cells is higher than that inside the cells. The result is that water moves out of the grass cells by osmosis. As water leaves the grass cells, the cells shrink and their cytoplasm pulls away from the cell wall. This causes the grass to wilt. If the water in the grass cells is not restored, the grass will eventually die.

CHALLENGE

How heavy can you make an egg? Work with a partner or in a group. Measure the initial mass of an egg, then immerse it in a solution of your choice. Measure the final mass of the egg. Repeat using different eggs in various solutions.

 CAUTION: Check your procedures with your teacher before you begin.

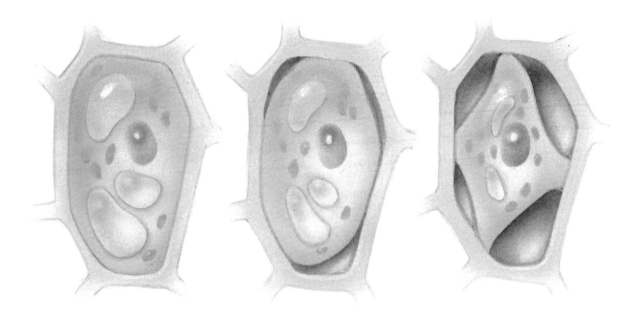

As the plant loses turgor pressure, it begins to wilt.

An Egg as an Osmosis Meter

- Place an uncooked egg, with its round end downward, in a small jar that will hold it as shown in the figure below. Note how far down the bottom of the egg is.

- Remove the egg and add enough vinegar to the jar to the level previously reached by the bottom of the egg. Return the egg and allow it to sit in the vinegar for 24 h. (The vinegar will dissolve the tip of the egg's shell.)

- Remove the egg and rinse it with cold water.

- Dispose of the vinegar as directed by your teacher. Rinse and refill the jar with distilled water.

- Using a kitchen knife, gently crack the pointed end of the egg and remove a small section of shell, without breaking the membrane underneath.

- Insert a glass tube through the small opening, penetrating the membrane. Seal the area around the tube with candle wax, as shown in the diagram.

- Place the egg in the jar filled with distilled water.

- Predict what will happen to the level of water in the glass tube.

- Observe the apparatus 24 h later.

- Explain your observations.

5. How are osmosis and diffusion different? How are they the same?

6. What determines the direction of water movement in or out of cells?

7. What is the structure that prevents a plant cell from bursting when it is full of water?

8. What is turgor pressure?

9. Based on what you have learned about osmosis, explain why grocery stores spray their vegetables with water.

10. Explain why animal cells are more likely to rupture than plant cells when placed in distilled water.

11. People who exercise often lose a tremendous amount of salt as well as water when they perspire. Following extreme exertion on a very hot day, a person who drinks only water to replace lost fluid may become ill. An examination of the person's blood after drinking the water would reveal that many red blood cells have become swollen and that some have ruptured. Why would the red blood cells rupture?

Observing Diffusion and Osmosis

T HIS INVESTIGATION will give you an opportunity to observe osmosis, the diffusion of water through a selectively permeable membrane. You will use dialysis tubing as a model of a cell membrane. The dialysis tubing is a nonliving, selectively permeable, cellophane material.

CAUTION: Be careful when using Lugol's iodine solution. It is toxic and an irritant. It may stain skin and clothing. Use rubber gloves when cleaning up spills, and rinse the area of the spills with water.

Materials

- apron
- safety goggles
- microscope slide
- 3 medicine droppers
- distilled water in wash bottle
- starch solution (4%)
- iodine (Lugol's solution)
- dialysis tubing
- scissors
- 3 250-mL beakers
- 100-mL graduated cylinder
- funnel
- paper towels
- large watch glass
- balance
- clock or stopwatch

Procedure

1 Put on your apron and safety goggles.

2 Place a drop of water on one end of a microscope slide. Using a medicine dropper, place a drop of starch solution on the other end of the slide.

3 Add a small drop of iodine solution to each of the drops on the microscope slide.

✏ (a) Record your observations.

✏ (b) Iodine is used as an indicator. Which substance can be identified by the iodine?

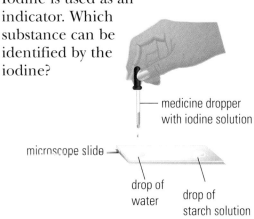

medicine dropper with iodine solution

microscope slide

drop of water

drop of starch solution

Step 3

4 Read the steps of the procedure for this investigation. Decide what data you will need to record. Construct a table in your notebook to record your data.

5 Measure the mass of the empty watch glass.

✏ (c) Record the mass.

6 Cut two strips of dialysis tubing (each about 25 cm long) and soak them in a beaker of tap water for approximately 2 min.

7 Rub the end of each strip of dialysis tubing between your fingers to find an opening (much as you would open a flat plastic bag). Tie a knot near the other end of each piece of tubing.

8 Using a graduated cylinder, measure 15 mL of the starch solution. Pour the solution into the open end of one of the dialysis tubings. Use the funnel to help you with the transfer.

15 mL starch solution

Step 8

9 Twist the open end of the dialysis tubing and tie it in a knot.

10 Rinse the outside of the dialysis tubing with distilled water, to remove any fluids that may have leaked out during the tying procedure.

11 With a paper towel, gently blot excess water from the dialysis tubing containing the starch solution. Place the tubing in the watch glass and measure its mass. Place the tubing in an empty beaker after weighing.

12 Repeat steps 8–11 using the other dialysis tubing and filling it with distilled water.

(d) Record your measurements.

(e) Calculate the initial mass of the dialysis tubing with distilled water and the dialysis tubing with starch solution.

13 Add 100 mL of distilled water to each of the two beakers holding the dialysis tubings.

14 Add 20 drops of iodine to the water in each beaker and observe closely for colour changes.

(f) Record your observations.

(g) Predict what you think will happen to the mass of each dialysis tubing. Justify your prediction.

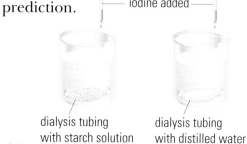
— iodine added —

dialysis tubing with starch solution

dialysis tubing with distilled water

Step 14

15 After 10 min, remove the dialysis tubings from the beakers. Gently blot off any excess water. Place each tubing on the watch glass and measure its mass. Replace the tubings in the beakers, and begin timing for another 10 min.

(h) Record your observations in your data table.

(i) Calculate the mass of each dialysis tubing.

16 Repeat step 15 after 20 min.

(j) Record your results in your data table.

17 Dispose of the substances used in the investigation as directed by your teacher. Clean up your work station and wash your hands.

Questions

1. Account for any colour change you observed in step 14.

2. How did the iodine move into the dialysis tubing? Did it move into both tubes?

3. Does starch move through dialysis tubing by diffusion? How do you know this?

4. Which dialysis tubing acted as a control?

5. Did either dialysis tubing show a change in mass? If so, did it gain or lose mass?

6. Explain any changes in mass of the dialysis tubings that you observed. What process was involved in this change of mass?

Apply

7. Scientific models can be used to describe living things or parts of living things. In this investigation, dialysis tubing was used as a model for the cell membrane.

   (a) Explain why the dialysis tubing provides a good model for the cell membrane.

   (b) Outline some limitations of dialysis tubing as a model for the membrane of a living cell.

8. Predict which of the dialysis tubings below would increase or decrease in mass. Provide your reasons.

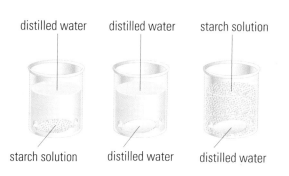
distilled water   distilled water   starch solution

starch solution   distilled water   distilled water

Discovering the Effects of Osmosis on Cells

I N THIS INVESTIGATION, you will look at what happens to plant cells when they are placed in solutions of different concentrations. As you observe the effects of osmosis, remember that plant cells are surrounded by rigid cell walls.

 CAUTION: Be careful when using Lugol's iodine solution. It is toxic and an irritant. It may stain skin and clothing. Use rubber gloves when cleaning up spills, and rinse the area of the spills with water.

Materials

- apron
- safety goggles
- tweezers
- piece of onion
- microscope slide
- 2 medicine droppers
- iodine solution
- cover slip
- light microscope
- dilute salt solution (5%)
- paper towels
- forceps
- distilled water in wash bottle
- 150-mL beaker
- lens paper

Procedure

1 Put on your apron and safety goggles.

2 Your teacher will provide you with a small section (about 2 cm²) of an onion.

3 Using tweezers, remove a single layer from the inner side of the onion. If the layer you removed is not translucent to light, try again.

Step 3

4 Using tweezers, place the onion skin in the centre of a microscope slide. Make sure the onion skin does not fold over.

5 Place a drop of iodine on the onion skin.

6 Holding the cover slip with your thumb and forefinger, touch it to the surface of the slide at a 45° angle. Gently lower the cover slip over the onion skin, allowing the air to escape. If air bubbles are present, gently tap the slide with the eraser end of a pencil to remove them.

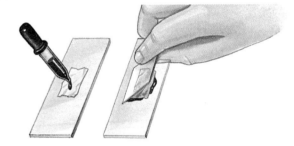

Steps 5 and 6

7 Place the slide on the microscope stage and attach the stage clips. Focus the cells with the low-power objective lens in place.

8 Rotate the nosepiece of the microscope to the medium-power objective lens and view the cells. Using your fine-adjustment knob, bring the cells into clear view. You may wish to adjust the light level.

(a) Draw a group of four cells and label the following parts (if they are visible): cell wall, cell membrane, vacuole, nucleus. Remember to draw only what you see. (Refer to the Skills Handbook on page 518 for information about making scientific drawings.)

9 Rotate the nosepiece to the low-power objective lens, and remove the slide from the microscope. Place a drop of salt solution at one edge of the cover slip. Touch the opposite edge of the cover slip with a small piece of paper towel. This will draw the salt solution across the slide under the cover slip. Using a paper towel, carefully blot excess salt solution from the slide.

CAUTION: Salt solution is corrosive to your microscope. Be sure that no part of your microscope comes in contact with the solution.

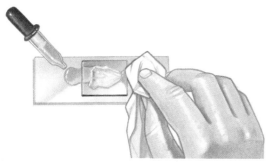

Step 9

10 Return the slide to the microscope stage, and focus first under the low- and then the medium-power objective lens.

(b) Draw a group of four cells. Label the following parts (if they are visible): cell wall, cell membrane, vacuole, nucleus.

(c) Describe any changes in the cell structure you observed in step 8.

(d) Predict what would happen if you washed the onion cells with distilled water.

11 Rotate the nosepiece to the low-power objective lens and remove the slide from the stage. Place the slide over a beaker, and gently remove the cover slip with forceps. Thoroughly wash the cells with distilled water.

150 mL beaker

Step 11

12 Straighten up your piece of onion skin and replace the cover slip. Return the slide to the microscope stage, and focus

under low- and medium-power objective lenses.

(e) Describe and draw what you see. How accurate was your prediction?

13 Rotate the nosepiece back to the low-power objective lens and remove the slide. Dispose of the onion skin as directed by your teacher. Clean the slide and cover slip with lens paper. Wash your hands.

Questions

1. How do you think the response of an animal cell would be different from the response of the onion cells? How would it be the same?

2. Which of the following diagrams shows a plant cell placed in distilled water? The arrows represent water movement into and out of the cell. Explain your answer.

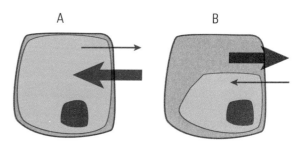

A

B

Cytoplasm takes in water and pushes against the cell wall, creating turgor pressure.

Cytoplasm loses water and shrinks away from the cell wall, decreasing turgor pressure.

Apply

3. Using the information gathered from this investigation, explain why irrigating land plants with sea water would be harmful.

Extension

4. Design an experimental procedure to test what concentration of salt solution would be harmful to grass.

Using Energy to Move Materials across Cell Membranes

AS YOU HAVE SEEN, when there is a difference in concentration of substances inside and outside the cell, materials move across the cell membrane by diffusion and osmosis. The end result is an equal concentration of substances inside and outside the cell. Diffusion and osmosis occur without the cell using any energy. Moving materials into and out of a cell without the use of energy is called **passive transport**.

But cells cannot always rely on passive transport. Cells require some materials in higher or lower concentrations than would be found outside the cell.

For example, the cells in a plant root need more minerals inside the cell than they can get from the soil by diffusion. How do the root cells acquire a greater concentration of minerals than is present in the surrounding soil?

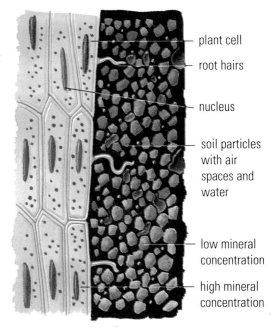

plant cell

root hairs

nucleus

soil particles with air spaces and water

low mineral concentration

high mineral concentration

Moving Large Molecules

How do cells absorb large molecules? Some molecules do not fit through the pores of the cell membrane. One way the cell solves this problem is with a process called **endocytosis**. The cytoplasm of the cell is extended around large particles, forming a cup that is then closed into a pouch. The particles are trapped within the pouch, or vacuole. Endocytosis is not passive transport—it requires energy.

The process of endocytosis can be seen through a microscope.

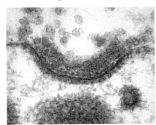

(a) The cell membrane begins to fold around some large molecules.

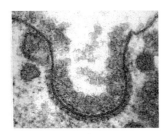

(b) The molecules become trapped within the membrane.

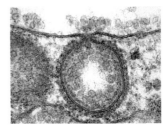

(c) The two parts of the cell membrane come together and a vacuole is formed.

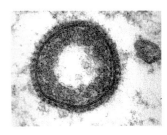

(d) The large molecules are now contained within a vacuole.

Active Transport

Cells that require greater or lower concentrations of substances inside the cell than outside must use energy to achieve the unequal concentrations. You can think of this as a car on a hill. No addition of energy is required for the car to roll down the hill (from high to low). However, to move the car up the hill (from low to high), energy is needed. The movement of materials from an area of low concentration to an area of higher concentration is referred to as **active transport**. Active transport always requires the use of energy.

Moving Specific Molecules

Recall that the cell membrane is made up of two layers of fat (lipid), with protein molecules suspended within the membrane. The protein molecules aid in active transport by acting as carriers to transport molecules into or out of the cell. To do this, they require energy. The diagram below shows how the structure of a protein molecule is well suited for trapping and then transporting a molecule of a specific substance.

SELF CHECK

12. How does active transport differ from diffusion and osmosis?

13. Why must cells use active transport?

14. How do carrier protein molecules move substances into a cell?

15. What is endocytosis?

A model of how a carrier protein might transport a molecule into a cell.

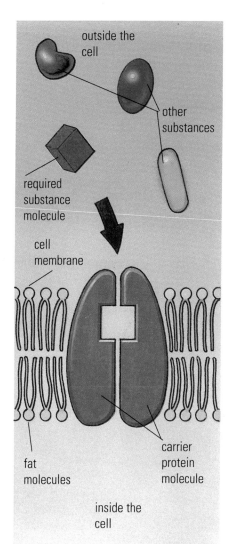

outside the cell

other substances

required substance molecule

cell membrane

fat molecules

carrier protein molecule

inside the cell

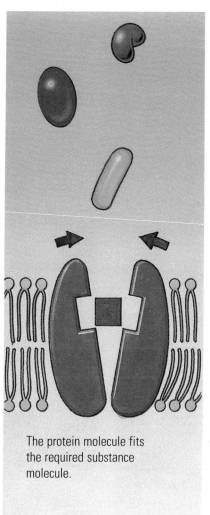

The protein molecule fits the required substance molecule.

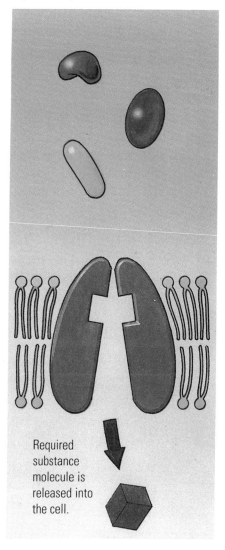

Required substance molecule is released into the cell.

Observing Living Organisms in Pond Water

U P TO THIS POINT, you have learned about cells by viewing them with a microscope in artificial environments. By removing cells from surrounding cells, and by adding dyes, as you did in preparing the slide of onion cells, you can change the cells' shape and greatly reduce movement. In this investigation, you will study microscopic organisms in pond water. Some of these organisms are composed of a single cell, while others are multicellular and have specialized tissues.

Materials
- light microscope
- lens paper
- microscope slide
- medicine dropper
- pond water
- cover slip
- paper towels

Procedure

1 Use lens paper to clean all the objective lenses and the microscope slide.

2 Using a medicine dropper, place a drop of pond water on the centre of a microscope slide.

3 Holding the cover slip with your thumb and forefinger, touch it to the surface of the slide at a 45° angle at the edge of the drop of water. Gently lower the cover slip, allowing the air to escape.

4 Blot excess water from the slide with a paper towel.

5 Place the slide on the stage of the microscope and view it with the low-power objective lens. (You may wish to reduce the light striking the slide by closing the diaphragm of the microscope.)

6 Scan the entire slide under low-power magnification.

(a) Where are more organisms found, along the edges of the cover slip or in the middle?

7 Rotate the revolving nosepiece to the medium-power objective lens. Identify some of the organisms in the pond water. (Note: You may need high-power magnification to identify some single-cell organisms.) The pictures on these pages should help you identify some of the organisms.

(b) Draw at least three different organisms you can see in the pond water. Label each organism and indicate its size. (You can refer to pages 292–295 to review how to estimate the size of an object under a microscope.)

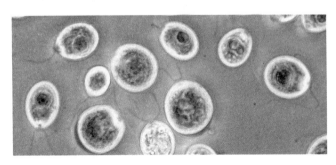

Chlamydomonas, a single-cell animal

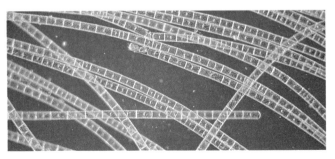

Filamentous algae, a plant-like organism

8 Dispose of your slide as directed by your teacher. Return your microscope to storage and clean up your work station. Wash your hands.

Questions

1. Classify the organisms you viewed as either single-cell or multicellular.

2. Are the single-cell organisms you viewed plant-like or animal-like? Do some have characteristics of both plants and animals? Explain your answer.

3. Describe at least two different methods of movement used by the organisms you observed.

Apply

4. Suggest a procedure for determining the number of organisms in a water droplet.

Extension

5. Periodically, over the next few weeks, test the water sample by viewing drops of the water. Do the numbers and types of organism change over time? Hypothesize about the reasons for some of the changes.

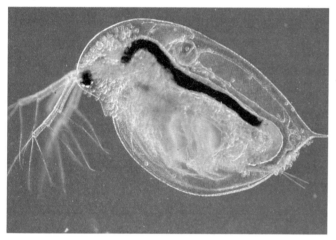

Daphnia, a multicellular animal

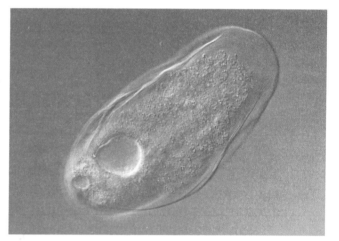

Amoeba, a single-cell animal

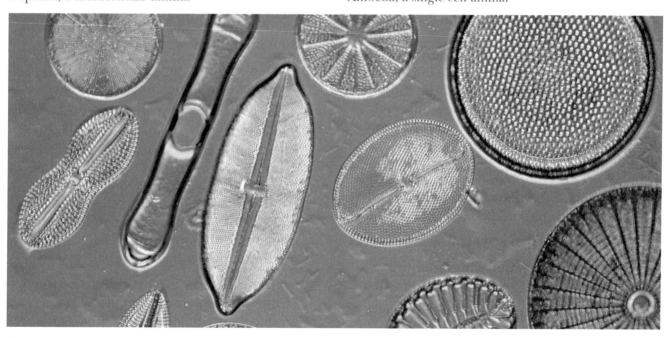

Several varieties of diatoms—a form of algae

CHAPTER 12

Cell Growth and Reproduction

THE 100 TRILLION or so cells that make up your body are truly awe-inspiring, when you think that they all started from one fertilized egg. They stand as proof of the ability of human cells to grow and reproduce. However, your size and the ability of your cells to divide are dwarfed by that of other organisms. The blue whale is about 18 times longer than the average human, and the giant sequoia tree is three times longer than the massive whale. Yet even they are not the largest organisms on Earth. The record holder is a quaking aspen tree.

Quaking aspen trees

How can the small aspen tree contain more cells than the giant sequoia? It was recently discovered that each individual tree is not what it appears. All the aspens in the picture have a common root system. The trees develop from runners, horizontal roots that grow above or below the ground. All the trees share the same genetic information. They are identical — they are the same organism.

Whether an organism is large or small, its cell growth and cell reproduction are very similar. In this chapter, you will explore

- how cells grow, and
- how they reproduce more cells like themselves.

 Getting Started

1. Do you have any questions about cell growth and cell division? Together with two or three classmates, write down the questions you have.

2. Following are a few of the questions you will examine in this chapter.
   - Why are large animals composed of many small cells instead of a few very large cells?
   - Why are some cells in your body larger than other cells?
   - How do cells divide?
   - Do all cells divide at the same rate?

Write down what you think are the answers to these questions.

DID YOU KNOW?

The largest known living organism, a quaking aspen grove, covers 43 hectares and has an estimated mass of 6.4 million kilograms.

The Need for Cell Division

ALL LARGE PLANTS AND ANIMALS, including yourself, are composed of many small cells rather than one large cell. Why?

Is Smaller Better?

Think about how far chemical messages travel in a large cell compared with a small cell. Before the nucleus can tell the organelles in the cytoplasm what to do, it must first receive and then respond to messages about the cell's surroundings. Cells must be small enough for these chemical messages to quickly reach the control centre, the nucleus.

Cells need a constant supply of nutrients to work well. Waste products must also be removed from the cell. Remember that molecules enter and pass out of cells through the cell membrane. If the amount of cell membrane is relatively large, the cell can take in nutrients and eliminate waste efficiently. Because of this, the amount of cell membrane relative to cell size is important. The amount of cell membrane can be described in terms of the surface area of the cell.

> For chemical messages to travel between the nucleus and the cytoplasm efficiently, distances must not be too great. What would happen if it took a long time for the nuclear message to reach the ribosomes?

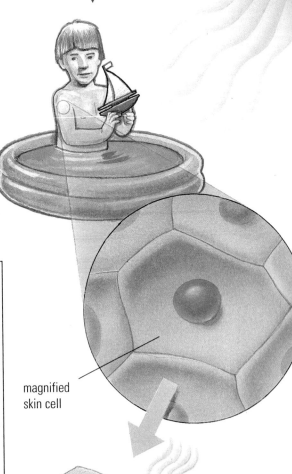

magnified skin cell

Sunlight triggers message that travels to nucleus.

MATH-LINK

Surface Area

The total area of all the faces of an object is called the **surface area**. To calculate surface area, you find the area of each face, and then find the sum of the areas.

  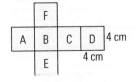

Find the area of face A by multiplying the length by the width.

Area of A = length × width

To find the surface area of the cube, you find the sum of the areas of A, B, C, D, E, and F. Since all six faces of a cube are the same, to find the surface area you can multiply the area of A by six.

Surface area = 6 × area of A

What is the surface area of the cube shown above?

Comparing the Surface Areas of Small and Large Cells

Predict whether you think small or large cells are more effective at exchanging nutrients and wastes. See if you agree with your prediction after you have completed the activity.

1. Measure the length and width of a sugar cube in millimetres. The cube represents a small cell.

2. Calculate the surface area of a single sugar cube. (Refer to the Math-Link.)

3. Multiply the surface area of the single cube by eight. This gives the surface area of eight individual sugar cubes.

4. Arrange eight sugar cubes to form a large cube. This block of sugar cubes represents one large cell.

5. Measure the length and width of the large cube. Calculate the surface area of the large cube.

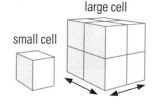

- Compare the surface area of the eight individual small cubes with that of the large cube. Which is greater?

- Which has the greater area of cell membrane through which nutrients and waste materials can pass, one large cell or eight small cells?

Some Big, Some Small

Some cells in your body are larger than others. Do you know why? If you compare the sizes of cells and their functions, you will find that active cells are usually smaller than cells that are not as active. The more active a cell is, the more nutrients it requires to function properly, and the more wastes it produces. Many small cells together are more efficient at exchanging nutrients and waste than one large cell. This is because many small cells together have a greater surface area of cell membrane than a single large cell. (Refer to the results of the Try This.)

Melanin, a dark protein, blocks sunlight.

Nucleus sends message to ribosomes to build melanin.

1. Explain which size of cell is most efficient at transporting messages from its surroundings to its nucleus.

2. What is surface area?

3. Which size of cell would be more efficient at transporting nutrients in and waste materials out—big or small?

4. Explain why highly active cells, such as muscle cells, tend to be small in size.

5. In (a) and (b) below, which cell has the greater surface area if their volumes are the same?

   (a) a cell shaped like a sphere or a cell shaped like a cube

   (b) a cell with a smooth cell membrane or one with many projections

Cell Division

R EPRODUCTION, ON A CELLULAR LEVEL, is one cell becoming two. As you have read, all the cells of your body began from a single, fertilized egg. This fertilized egg cell divided into two cells. Then each of these divided into two cells, and so on, until they formed the multicellular organism that is you. Incredible as it may sound, many of your cells will continue to divide throughout your lifetime. For example, red blood cells die and are replaced by cell division at a rate of one million every second. By the time you complete this science course, you will have totally replaced all of the mature red blood cells that are currently in your body.

ASK YOURSELF

Draw a sketch of the human body. Below the sketch, list areas of the body in which you think cell division is most rapid. Why do you think cells in these areas divide most rapidly? Check these ideas after completing the chapter.

Dividing and Duplicating

Despite the great differences among living things, most cells show remarkable similarities in the way they divide. Cell division occurs in single-celled forms of life, such as bacteria, as well as in multicellular organisms, such as humans. In all cases, the initial cell divides into two identical cells.

The division involves the division of nuclear materials and the division of cytoplasm. For the two new cells to carry on the activities necessary for life, they require the genetic information contained in the original nucleus. During cell division, the genetic information, present as duplicate strands in the chromosomes, divides and moves to opposite ends of the cell. This process of dividing nuclear material is called **mitosis**. Then cell division continues with the separation of cytoplasm into equal parts. This includes organelles like mitochondria, chloroplasts, ribosomes, and lysosomes, which are needed by both new cells. The process of cell division repeats itself millions of times each day, permitting organisms to grow or to replace worn-out cells with new ones.

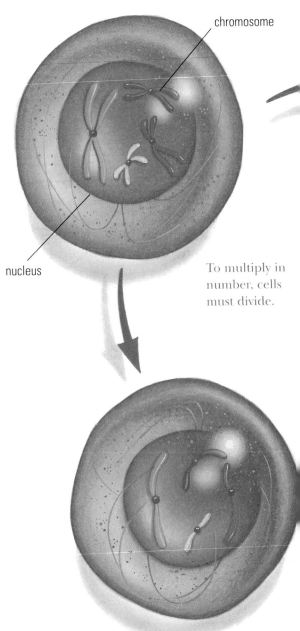

chromosome

nucleus

To multiply in number, cells must divide.

Cells for Different Jobs

Not all cells in the human body have the same shape and carry out the same functions. As cells grow, they develop into differently sized and shaped cells with special functions. But all cells in a human body come from the same fertilized egg, and they all have the same genetic information.

One of the most puzzling questions for scientists who study cells is why cells become different. What makes a cell become a nerve cell, able to conduct nerve impulses? And what makes other cells become muscle cells? After all, nerve cells contain all of the genetic information to be muscle cells, and muscle cells contain all of the genetic information to be nerve cells. The complete answers to these questions are yet unknown.

Cell divides into two identical cells.

Each cell has the same number of chromosomes.

Viewing the Phases of Cell Division

The diagrams on these pages show an animal cell dividing. Although plant cells look different, the process of cell division is basically the same in plant and animal cells. To help describe the events of cell division, scientists have divided the process into several phases. However, the process is a continuous one. Think of each phase as a snapshot taken at a particular point in cell division.

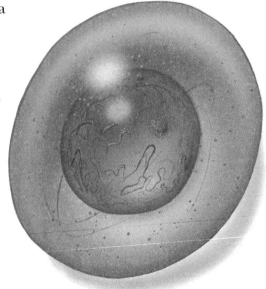

Cell before division

The cell grows and carries on activities necessary for life. It also prepares for cell division.

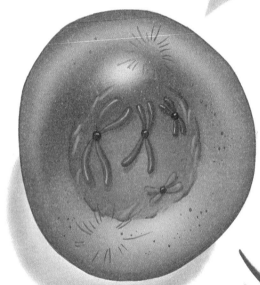

Prophase

The individual chromosomes, each containing two strands of genetic information, become visible.

Metaphase

Chromosomes containing double strands of genetic information line up in the middle of the cell.

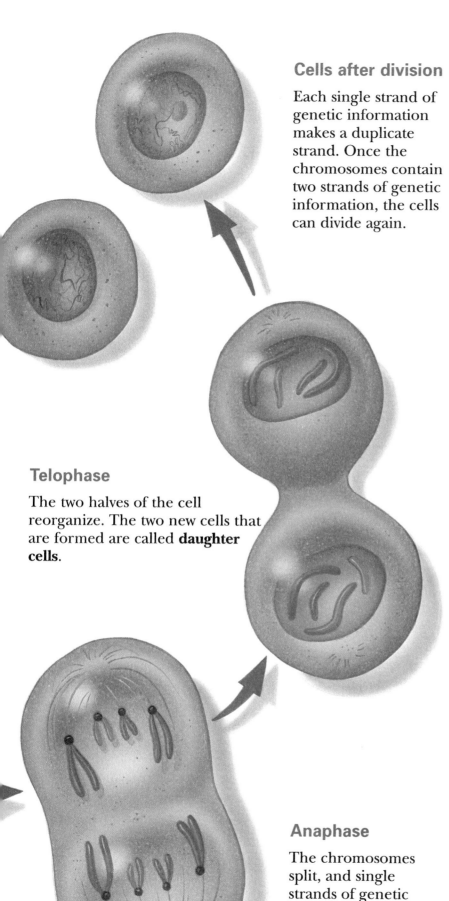

Cells after division

Each single strand of genetic information makes a duplicate strand. Once the chromosomes contain two strands of genetic information, the cells can divide again.

Telophase

The two halves of the cell reorganize. The two new cells that are formed are called **daughter cells**.

Anaphase

The chromosomes split, and single strands of genetic information move to opposite ends of the cell.

Observing Cell Division

IN THE PREVIOUS SECTION, you learned about how cells divide. In this investigation, you will have an opportunity to view and compare plant and animal cells during mitosis. Because you will be looking at prepared slides, you will see the dividing cells of the onion root tip and the whitefish embryo as if they were frozen in time as they were dividing. (The term embryo refers to the very early stages of an animal's development.)

Materials

- microscope
- prepared microscope slide of an onion root tip
- lens paper
- prepared microscope slide of a whitefish embryo

Procedure

1 Obtain an onion root tip slide and place it on the stage of your microscope.

2 View the slide under low-power magnification. Focus using the coarse-adjustment knob. Observe the cells near the root cap. This is the area of greatest cell division for the root.

3 Centre the root tip and then rotate the nosepiece to the medium-power objective lens. Focus the image using the fine-adjustment knob. Identify a few dividing cells.

(a) How can you tell if the cells are dividing?

4 Rotate the nosepiece to the high-power objective lens. Use the fine-adjustment knob to focus the image. Locate and observe cells in each of the phases of mitosis. Use the photographs of dividing cells to help you. Don't be concerned if what you see does not look exactly like the photographs.

(b) Draw and title each of the phases that you see. Label chromosomes if they are visible. It is important to draw and label only the structures that you see under the microscope. (Refer to the Skills Handbook on page 518 for information on making scientific drawings.)

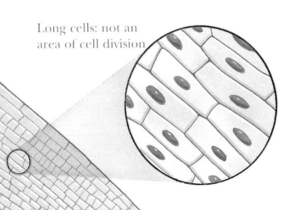

Long cells: not an area of cell division

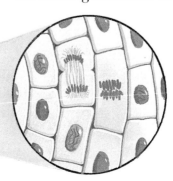

Smaller cells: an area of rapid cell division

root cap

Onion Cells in Mitosis

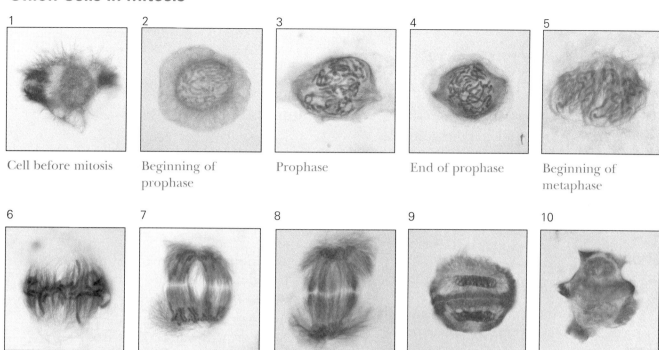

1 — Cell before mitosis
2 — Beginning of prophase
3 — Prophase
4 — End of prophase
5 — Beginning of metaphase
6 — Metaphase
7 — Anaphase
8 — Telophase
9 — End of telophase
10 — Cells after mitosis

5 Return your microscope to the low-power objective lens and remove the slide of the onion.

6 Place the slide of the whitefish embryo on the stage. Focus the slide using the coarse-adjustment knob.

7 Repeat steps 3 and 4 for the whitefish cells.

(c) Draw and title each of the phases that you see. Label the chromosomes if they are visible.

(d) Compare your diagrams with those of other students in your class. Assist each other in locating phases or cell structures.

8 Return your microscope to the low-power objective lens and remove the slide of the whitefish embryo. Put away your microscope, and return the slides to your teacher.

Questions

1. Why were plant root tip cells and animal embryo cells used for viewing cell division?

2. Explain why the cells that you viewed under the microscope do not continue to divide.

3. Compare the appearance of the dividing animal cells with that of the dividing plant cells. You may wish to make a table to list the differences and similarities.

4. If a cell has 10 chromosomes, how many chromosomes will each daughter cell have following cell division?

Apply

5. Predict what might happen to each of the daughter cells if all of the chromosomes move to only one side of the cell during anaphase.

Extension

6. Working in a group, suggest a technique that would allow you to study cell division without killing the cells. Be creative with your answer. You may wish to suggest how you would build a specialized machine for your technique.

Determining the Rate of Cell Division

DO SOME PARTS OF AN ORGANISM have more rapid cell division than others? Using prepared slides, you will be able to find out for yourself.

Materials

- microscope
- prepared microscope slide of an onion root tip
- lens paper
- prepared microscope slide of a whitefish embryo

Procedure

Part 1   *Onion Root Cells*

1 Obtain an onion root tip slide and place it on the stage of your microscope.

2 View the slide under low-power magnification. Focus using the coarse-adjustment knob. Locate the area of cell division, immediately above the root cap.

3 Centre the root tip and then rotate the nosepiece to the medium-power objective lens. Focus the image using the fine-adjustment knob.

4 Count 20 cells that are next to one another in the onion root tip. Determine which of those cells are dividing.

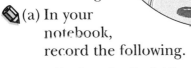

🖎 (a) In your notebook, record the following.

   Number of cells dividing = ▓
   Number of cells not dividing = ▓

🖎 (b) Calculate the percentage of cells dividing.

$$\frac{\text{Number of cells dividing} \times 100\%}{20} = ▓\,\%$$

5 Examine two other areas of the onion root tip to determine if the growth rate is the same in those areas.

🖎 (c) Construct and title a table to record the growth rate of the three areas of the root tip.

🖎 (d) Draw a small diagram of the onion root tip and show the approximate location of each of the areas you selected.

6 Return your microscope to the low-power objective lens and remove the slide of the onion root tip.

Part 2   *Whitefish Embryo Cells*

7 Place the slide of the whitefish embryo on the stage. (Remember, embryo refers to the very early stages of an animal's development.) Focus the slide using the coarse-adjustment knob.

🖎 (e) Predict whether the onion root tip or the whitefish embryo will have a greater percentage of actively dividing cells. Justify your prediction.

8 Centre the whitefish embryo and then rotate the nosepiece to the medium-power objective lens. Focus the image using the fine-adjustment knob. Under medium-power magnification, repeat step 4 for the whitefish cells.

9 Return the nosepiece to the low-power objective lens, and remove the slide of the whitefish embryo.

Part 3 *Making a Cell Division Clock*

10 Replace the slide of the onion root tip under your microscope, and focus using the coarse-adjustment knob.

11 Under high-power magnification, locate 50 cells that are dividing. Identify the phase each of the cells is in. (Do not count cells between divisions.) You may have to search for enough dividing cells by moving the slide.

(f) Make a chart like the one below, and enter the number of cells you found in each phase.

(g) Calculate the percentage of cells that are in each phase of division. For example, if you found 20 cells in prophase:

$$\text{Percentage of cells in prophase} = \frac{20}{50} \times 100\% = 40\%$$

Phase	Number of cells	Percentage of total in phase
prophase		
metaphase		
anaphase		
telophase		

12 With your data, you can now construct a clock for cell division. It actually takes between 12 and 16 h to complete one cycle of mitosis, but for the sake of simplicity, assume it takes 12 h.

(h) Calculate the number of hours spent in each phase by multiplying the percentage of cells in each phase by 12. If you found 40% of the 50 cells in prophase, for example:

Time spent in prophase = 40% × 12 h = 4.8 h

(i) Draw a clock and indicate the amount of time spent in each phase of cell division.

Questions

1. Which areas of the onion root tip have the fastest growth rate?

2. (a) Which has the greater percentage of dividing cells, the whitefish embryo or the onion root tip?

   (b) What does this indicate about the growth rates of the plant root tip and the animal embryo?

3. Why might someone be interested in determining the growth rate of a plant or animal?

Apply

4. Mitosis is described in phases because this makes it easier to talk about. But the cells do not stop between each of the phases. What observations have you made that suggest that mitosis is an ongoing process?

5. Herbicides are chemicals designed to kill weeds. Herbicides like 2,4,D and 2,4,5,T make the cells in plants divide faster than normal. Why would this kill the weeds? (Hint: Think about what cells do when they are not dividing.)

Extension

6. Choose one of the growth rates you calculated in this investigation. Draw a pie graph showing the percent of cells involved in cell division and those not involved. (For more information, see Constructing Bar and Circle Graphs in the Skills Handbook on page 514.)

Cell Division and Cancer

CELL DIVISION NORMALLY PROCEEDS at a rate that keeps an organism healthy. However, cell division can go out of control. When it does, we call it cancer. **Cancer** is the name for a broad group of diseases associated with the uncontrolled, unregulated division of cells. Unlike most diseases, which can be described in terms of cell or tissue death, cancer can be described as too much life. Cancer cells divide much more quickly than normal cells.

When Normal Cells Divide

As you know, the single, fertilized cell from which you began divided to produce many cells. These cells then specialized, becoming muscle cells, nerve cells, blood cells, and so on. Once you have grown to your full size, the cells in your body divide mainly to replace damaged cells. A healthy body maintains a balance between cell destruction and cell replacement.

This balance is controlled by communication. Cells "communicate" information about their changing needs and condition to other cells in the body. This information can cause other cells to divide. For example, take the growth of a callus on your hand after hours of paddling a canoe. The skin cells in your hand divide to replace the damaged cells, but the division also continues beyond that, until the number of cells in the protective layer of the skin has increased. This layer shields the delicate nerve and blood vessels that occupy the inner layer of the skin. If your hand is exposed to more hours of paddling, it is now less likely to be damaged.

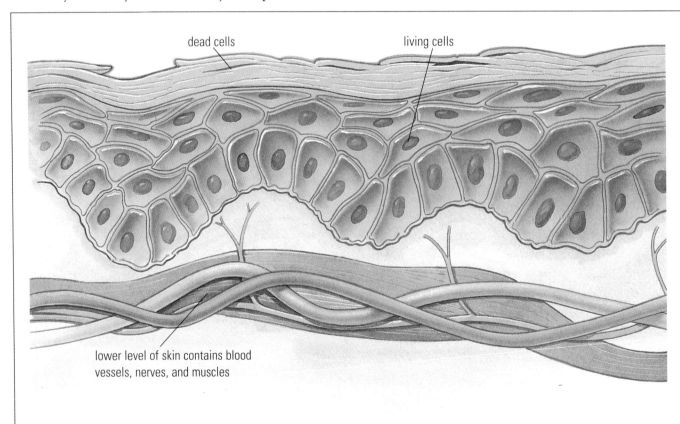

dead cells

living cells

lower level of skin contains blood vessels, nerves, and muscles

Cancer Cells vs. Normal Cells

Normal human cells cannot divide when isolated from one another. Cell-to-cell communication is essential for normal cell division. But cancer cells can divide in isolation. Some cancer cells grown in an artificial culture are capable of dividing once every 24 h. At this rate of division, a single cancer cell would generate over one billion descendants in a month. Fortunately, cancer cells do not reproduce that quickly in the body of an organism. However, their growth does crowd out other cells.

It has been estimated that there are about 100 different types of cells in the human body. Each cell type has a unique shape that enables it to carry out a special function. Unlike normal cells, cancer cells do not change shape and specialize as they mature. Therefore, another threat arises. Because the cancer cells cannot carry out some of the functions of normal cells, they are inefficient. They use up energy and the resources of the body to grow and divide, but they do not do the same work as normal cells.

◀ A cancer cell can often be identified by an enlarged nucleus and reduced cytoplasm. Why do you think a cancer cell might have a large nucleus?

MATH-LINK

Rapid Cell Growth

Not all rapid cell growth is cancerous. A certain virus causes skin cells to divide quickly, producing a wart. Imagine what would happen if a normal cell divided every hour. How large would the growth become? Make a table similar to the one below and fill in the blanks. What pattern do you see in the number of cells?

Time (h)	Number of cells
0	1
1	2
2	4
3	
4	16
5	

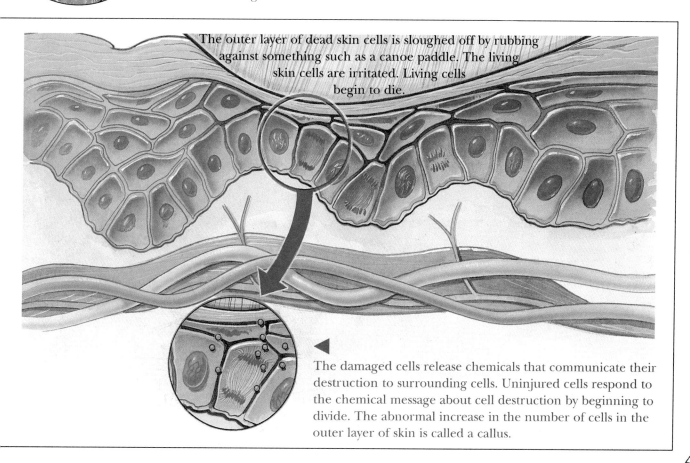

The outer layer of dead skin cells is sloughed off by rubbing against something such as a canoe paddle. The living skin cells are irritated. Living cells begin to die.

◀ The damaged cells release chemicals that communicate their destruction to surrounding cells. Uninjured cells respond to the chemical message about cell destruction by beginning to divide. The abnormal increase in the number of cells in the outer layer of skin is called a callus.

What Causes Cancer?

Many different things appear to cause cancer. Some cancers are caused by viruses. Some types of cancer of white blood cells (leukemia) have been associated with viruses. Radiation has been linked to other types of cancer. Skin cancer, for example, has been linked to ultraviolet radiation from the Sun. A third type of cancer is associated with exposure to harmful chemicals. A variety of cancer-causing substances is found in cigarettes.

Whatever the initial cause, scientists agree that all cancers result when the genetic information of a cell is changed. A change of a cell's genetic information is called a **mutation**.

One type of mutation occurs when a chromosome is broken and repaired incorrectly.

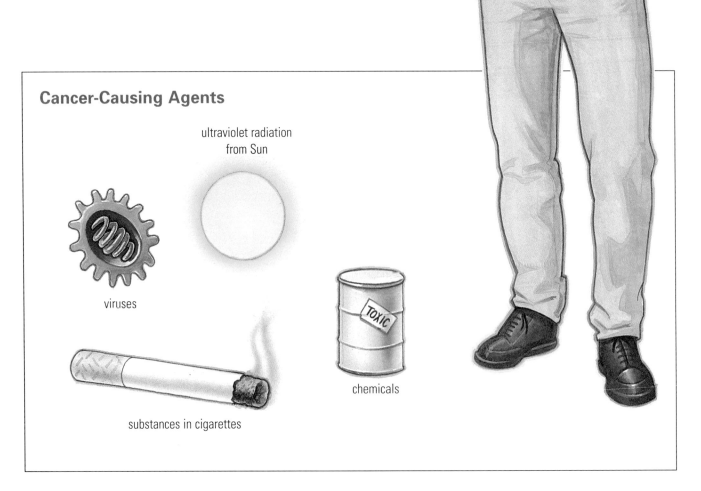

Cancer-Causing Agents

viruses

ultraviolet radiation from Sun

chemicals

substances in cigarettes

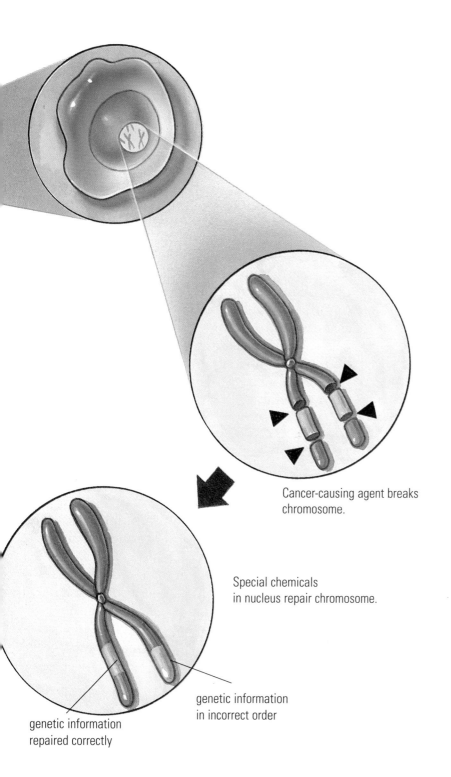

Cancer-causing agent breaks chromosome.

Special chemicals in nucleus repair chromosome.

genetic information in incorrect order

genetic information repaired correctly

Cancer in Other Organisms

Cancer is not found in humans alone. It is found in plants and animals alike. Sunflowers and tomatoes often display a form of cancer called a gall. These plant tumours are caused by invading viruses, bacteria, fungi, or insects. Evidence of cancerous tumours has been found in dinosaur bones, and in cells found in the linen wrapping of ancient mummies.

SKILL BUILDER

Research Paper

Choose one type of cancer and prepare a science report that considers the following points:

- What causes this type of cancer (e.g., virus, chemicals, radiation, unknown)?

- What treatments are available?

- How dangerous is the cancer?

For ideas on how to prepare a science report, turn to the Skills Handbook on page 520.

SELF CHECK

12. What is cancer?

13. What is a mutation?

14. In what ways do cancer cells differ from other cells?

15. Give two examples of abnormal cell growth that are not cancer.

16. Cancerous cells often have a large nucleus and reduced cytoplasm. Why would they have less cytoplasm than normal cells?

17. Cancer cells tend to be warmer than normal cells. This allows a technology called thermography to detect cancerous tumours. Using a special heat-sensitive material, the thermograph finds "hot spots" inside the body where tumours are growing. Why do you think cancer cells might be warmer than normal cells?

Reproducing Asexually and Sexually

ORGANISMS OF ALL SPECIES reproduce. They may reproduce asexually or sexually. In asexual reproduction, a single cell divides into two cells. The cells of the human body, other than those found in male testes or female ovaries, reproduce asexually by mitosis. Most single-cell organisms and some multicellular organisms use asexual reproduction to produce offspring.

Asexual Reproduction

In **asexual reproduction**, the parent cell does not exist after the cell divides. The parent cell becomes two daughter cells. Before a cell divides asexually, the cell duplicates its genetic information. It does this by building double-stranded chromosomes from single-stranded chromosomes. During the division, each daughter cell receives one of the strands of genetic information. Because each of the cells contain the same genetic information, the two cells are identical to each other.

Types of Asexual Reproduction

Binary fission

The organism splits into two equal-size offspring.

Budding

The offspring begins as an outgrowth from the parent. Budding occurs in single-cell organisms, such as yeast, and in multicellular organisms, such as hydra. Eventually, most buds break off from the parent.

Spore formation

The organism undergoes cell division to produce smaller, identical cells, called spores. The spore is usually housed within the parent cell. Many types of spores have a tough, resistant coating that helps them to survive.

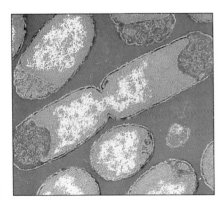

Binary fission is a common type of reproduction in single-celled organisms such as bacteria.

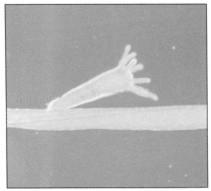

Hydra with a bud.

The penicillium mould reproduces by spores.

Sexual Reproduction

For **sexual reproduction**, two parents are required. There are two general types of sexual reproduction. The first is called **conjugation**: two cells come together and exchange small bits of genetic information. A new offspring is not produced immediately, but when the cells divide, their daughter cells contain the shared information.

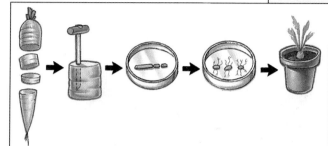

The second form of sexual reproduction is most common among multicellular organisms. Each of the parents produces specialized sex cells that contain genetic information. The sex cells, one from each parent, unite to form a fertilized egg, called a **zygote**. Because the offspring contains genetic information from both parents, it is not identical to either parent.

TECHNOLOGY LINK

Cloning Carrots

Cloning is the process by which identical offspring are formed from a single cell or tissue. Because their characteristics are always predictable, cloned plants are important in agriculture. Some clones can be produced from a few cells taken from an organism. Use the information in the diagram and additional reference materials to grow a carrot clone.

Fragmentation

A part of the organism breaks off from the parent and forms a new organism. Fragmentation can occur with many types of algae, and some plants and animals.

If a starfish is cut through the central disk, both sections will develop into new starfish that contain identical genetic information.

Vegetative reproduction

A section of a plant is used to grow a new plant. The section does not need to be removed from the original plant. Spider plants and strawberries send runners from the original plant.

Each of the runners may develop into another plant with identical genetic information.

ASK YOURSELF

Make a concept map that shows sexual reproduction and another one that shows asexual reproduction. Compare the maps to see how they differ.

SELF CHECK

18. What are the differences between asexual and sexual reproduction?
19. Name and briefly describe five different types of asexual reproduction.
20. How is conjugation different from the type of sexual reproduction that occurs in multicellular animals?
21. What is a clone?
22. Orchids and McIntosh apple trees are examples of plants that are cloned. Indicate one benefit of cloning these plants.

Investigating Patterns of Growth

NOW THAT YOU HAVE STUDIED why and how cells divide, you can investigate patterns of growth in humans. Unlike cancer cells, which divide at an accelerated rate, normal cells divide at a regulated, systematic rate. This ensures that the various parts of your body develop in proportion, and that cells that are destroyed are replaced as needed. In many respects, an understanding of growth and aging stems from an understanding of cell division.

Have you ever noticed how big a puppy's paws and ears are relative to its body size?

Some people try to determine how large a puppy will grow by the size of its paws. If you have a pup with big paws, you may soon have a very large dog. Is the same true for humans? We don't usually look at babies' feet to see how tall they are going to become. But it is true that body proportions of human infants and those of adults are also quite different. This is because parts of human bodies grow at different rates.

1. Examine the diagram of the infant and adult below. The two diagrams are not drawn to the same scale.

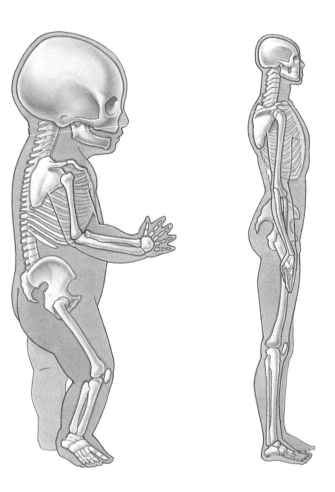

(a) Which parts of the body appear to grow the most between infancy and adulthood?

(b) Which parts of the body grow the least?

(c) Speculate why the infant's head is so large in comparison with the rest of its body.

2. Examine the graph below showing the rate of growth of the brain, heart, and body. The graph shows that at age two, the masses of the brain and heart have doubled, whereas the mass of the body is four times the mass at birth.

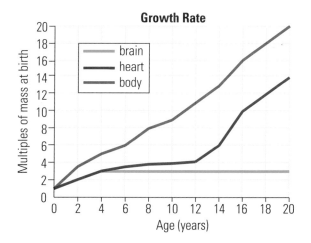

Growth Rate

(legend: brain, heart, body)

X-axis: Age (years)
Y-axis: Multiples of mass at birth

✎ **(d)** How many times the mass at birth is the mass of the body by age 19? How many times has the heart grown?

✎ **(e)** At approximately what age does the brain reach its maximum mass?

✎ **(f)** How does the growth of the heart compare with that of the brain?

✎ **(g)** Would you expect the heart and body to continue to grow at the same pace after 19 years of age? Explain your answer.

3. Examine the graph showing changes in two body functions between the ages of 30 and 70.

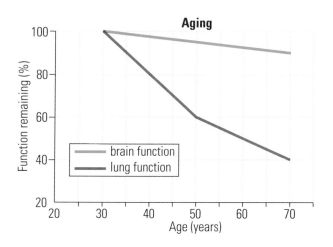

Aging

(legend: brain function, lung function)

X-axis: Age (years)
Y-axis: Function remaining (%)

✎ **(h)** Compare the decline of lung function and brain function.

✎ **(i)** Between what ages is the deterioration of lung function most rapid?

Questions

1. Based on the information provided, state one conclusion about the growth and function of your brain.

2. What evidence can you draw from your own growth patterns that suggests that not all parts of your body grow at the same rate?

Apply

3. The graph that examines aging draws data from many people. Some individuals will not show a rapid deterioration in lung function. What factors might slow the decline of lung function?

4. In which area of your body would you expect to see the greatest amount of cell division? Explain your answer.

Extension

5. How large would the picture of the adult be if it were drawn to the same scale as the picture of the infant? Assume that the head of the adult is approximately twice that of the infant.

The following steps may be helpful to get you started.

Use a ruler to take a horizontal measurement of each head in the picture, and write the results in your notebook.

Size of infant's head in the picture = ■

Size of adult's head in the picture = ■

Size of adult's head, if drawn to same scale as infant = ■

A Closer Look at Chromosomes

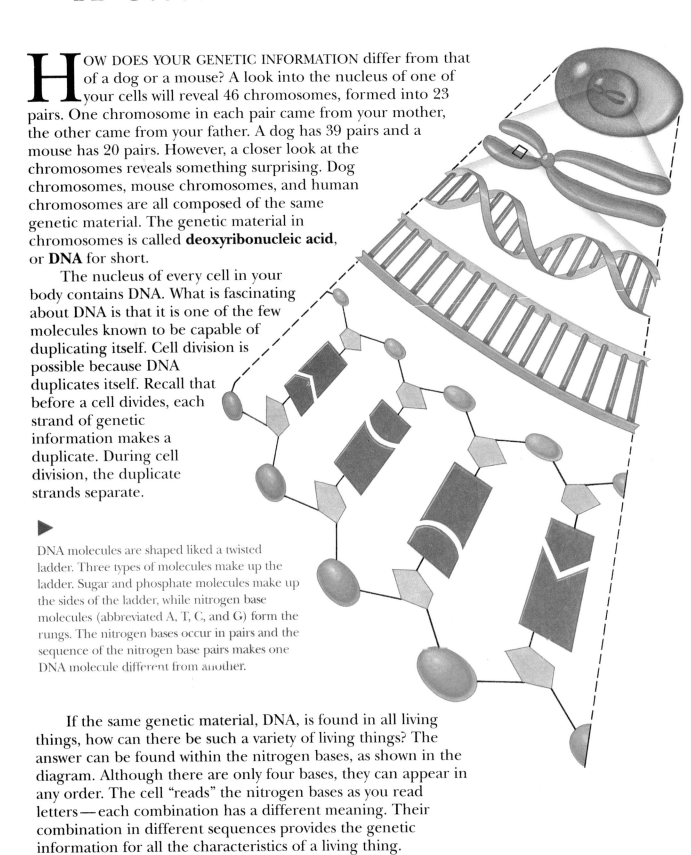

HOW DOES YOUR GENETIC INFORMATION differ from that of a dog or a mouse? A look into the nucleus of one of your cells will reveal 46 chromosomes, formed into 23 pairs. One chromosome in each pair came from your mother, the other came from your father. A dog has 39 pairs and a mouse has 20 pairs. However, a closer look at the chromosomes reveals something surprising. Dog chromosomes, mouse chromosomes, and human chromosomes are all composed of the same genetic material. The genetic material in chromosomes is called **deoxyribonucleic acid**, or **DNA** for short.

The nucleus of every cell in your body contains DNA. What is fascinating about DNA is that it is one of the few molecules known to be capable of duplicating itself. Cell division is possible because DNA duplicates itself. Recall that before a cell divides, each strand of genetic information makes a duplicate. During cell division, the duplicate strands separate.

▶

DNA molecules are shaped liked a twisted ladder. Three types of molecules make up the ladder. Sugar and phosphate molecules make up the sides of the ladder, while nitrogen base molecules (abbreviated A, T, C, and G) form the rungs. The nitrogen bases occur in pairs and the sequence of the nitrogen base pairs makes one DNA molecule different from another.

If the same genetic material, DNA, is found in all living things, how can there be such a variety of living things? The answer can be found within the nitrogen bases, as shown in the diagram. Although there are only four bases, they can appear in any order. The cell "reads" the nitrogen bases as you read letters—each combination has a different meaning. Their combination in different sequences provides the genetic information for all the characteristics of a living thing.

DNA Fingerprints

DNA has found its way into the courtroom. A technique called DNA fingerprinting can be used to identify an individual. Each person's DNA is unique, just as a fingerprint is. A blood sample, hair, or any other tissue containing cells can be used to yield DNA to make a "fingerprint."

▶

Carolyn Krausher works in the RCMP's forensic laboratory.

Simplified DNA Fingerprinting Technique

1. DNA is removed from the nuclei of the cells.

2. Special chemicals are used to cut the DNA into segments. In many ways the chemicals work like scissors.

3. The segments of DNA are placed on a gel and pulled across the gel by an electric current. Different segments are pulled at different rates, forming bands of DNA on the gel.

4. These bands of DNA are the fingerprint—they can be matched to known samples. For example, do the DNA bands formed by blood found on the clothing of a suspect match the DNA bands of the victim's blood? In this example, suspect B and suspect C both had blood on their clothes. Can you identify the suspect whose clothing is stained with the victim's blood?

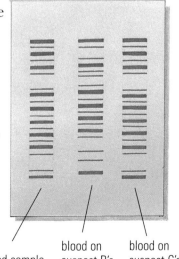

blood sample from victim

blood on suspect B's clothes

blood on suspect C's clothes

SELF CHECK

23. What is the genetic material?

24. What are the three major molecules that make up the much larger DNA molecule?

25. If there are only four different nitrogen bases found in DNA (A, T, C, and G), why are organisms so different? How do you "code" for so many different organisms with only four bases?

26. Briefly outline the technique used for DNA fingerprinting.

27. Give one practical application for DNA fingerprinting.

Clones on the Farm

UNDER NORMAL CIRCUMSTANCES, identical twins originate from a single, fertilized egg cell, called a zygote. Following fertilization, the zygote undergoes many cell divisions, producing a mass of identical cells. During mitosis, one of the cells may break free, and then a second embryo begins to develop. This splitting can occur only in the early stages of embryo development. If the cell masses remain separated, two offspring with identical genetic information will develop. Identical twins are nature's clones. They have the same sex, the same fur colour, and the same blood type. Fraternal twins, on the other hand, originate from two different eggs. Each fraternal twin comes from an egg that was fertilized by a different sperm cell.

That is why fraternal twins can be a different sex and be different in appearance.

How is it possible for identical twin horses to be born to different mothers? A technique referred to as embryo splitting allows scientists to create twins. Following fertilization, the egg divides into a mass of about 100 cells surrounded by a protective sac. Using a salt-water solution, this mass is flushed from the womb of the mare. The scientist then divides the cell mass into two. Another reproductive technique, called embryo transplant, completes the procedure. Each of the cell masses is placed into the womb of a different mare. If the procedure is successful, each of the mares will carry and give birth to one of the identical twins.

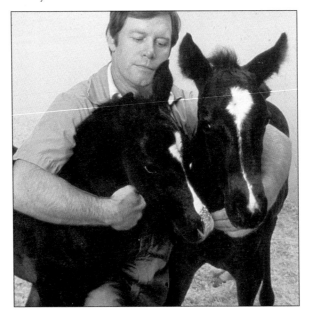

The colts in the picture are identical twins born to different mares. Biologist Ed Squires created twins from a single, fertilized zygote.

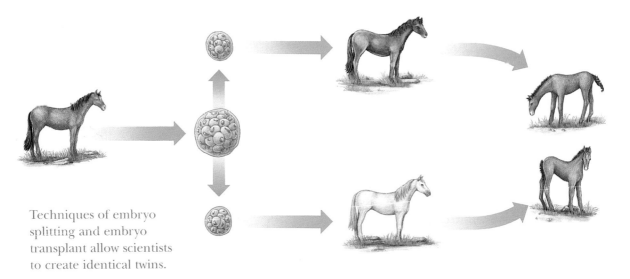

Techniques of embryo splitting and embryo transplant allow scientists to create identical twins.

A mule is nuzzled by her foal, a young horse.

A quarterhorse is shown with her foal, a zebra.

Embryos do not have to be transplanted into exactly the same kind of animal, as shown in these photographs. The animals do have to have similar DNA, however, or an embryo transplant will be rejected.

Understanding the Author

1. Why are identical twin animals often referred to as clones?

2. Why must identical twins always be of the same sex?

3. In what ways is embryo splitting similar to how identical twins form naturally?

The Benefits

- *Opinion of an animal breeder* The technique allows us to produce many high-quality horses. Usually a mare carries only one foal. By using this technique, we can produce two or more offspring.

- *Opinion of a science researcher* One of the greatest difficulties we face, when designing experiments, is not being able to control animals' genetic differences. For example, when we are testing the effects of a chemical on an animal, we really don't know if the chemical had a long-term effect on the animal, or if it was a genetic weakness that caused the result. Cloning provides an identical animal that we can use as a control.

The Risks

- *Opinion of an animal breeder* Embryo splitting will lead to fewer genetic differences in animals if it replaces normal breeding. This is dangerous. A horse with superior speed may also carry genes that make it susceptible to disease. Do we know enough to judge which genes are superior?

- *Opinion of a concerned citizen* Embryo transplant techniques developed for animals are also used for human reproductive technology. Human embryos have been transplanted into nongenetic mothers. Do we want scientists creating human twins?

What Do You Think?

4. Should animal research techniques that could be applied to humans be restricted or controlled by the government? What is your opinion?

Key Outcomes

Now that you have completed this chapter, can you do the following? If not, review the sections indicated.

- Explain the need for cell division. (12.1,)

- Explain mitosis and its significance. (12.2)

- Use a microscope to view and identify four phases of cell division. (12.3)

- Define cancer and identify some causes of cancer. (12.5)

- Differentiate between asexual and sexual reproduction. (12.6)

- Evaluate changes in several human organs with age. (12.7)

- Describe the structure and importance of DNA. (12.8)

Key Terms

surface area

mitosis

prophase

metaphase

anaphase

telophase

daughter cells

cancer

mutation

asexual reproduction

binary fission

budding

spore formation

fragmentation

vegetative reproduction

sexual reproduction

conjugation

zygote

cloning

DNA (deoxyribonucleic acid)

Review

1. Do large animals have larger cells than small animals? Explain your answer.

2. Which of the following sizes and shapes would best suit an active cell such as a muscle cell? Explain your answer.

3. Match the four phases of mitosis with the following diagrams.

4. Draw a diagram of a root and indicate which area is likely to have cells dividing. In which area would you find elongated cells?

5. (a) Which of the diagrams below represent an onion root cell and which represent a whitefish cell?

   (b) What events are being shown in each diagram?

6. How are asexual and sexual reproduction different?

7. (a) What is cancer?

   (b) How is the cause of cancer related to the genetic information of a cell?

8. What is DNA?

9. DNA is one of the few molecules that can make a duplicate of itself. Why is the duplication of DNA important?

Problem Solving

10. A scientist wanted to determine if age affects body mass. The scientist hypothesized that body mass increases with age. To test this hypothesis, five people from each age group were selected at random. Their body mass was recorded. The results are provided in the table below.

Body Mass and Age	
Age group	Average body mass (kg)
20 – 29	60
30 – 39	65
40 – 49	72
50 – 59	75
60 – 69	68

The scientist concluded that the older people become, the greater their body mass. Write a critique of the experimental design used by the scientist. What additional information would you want to collect before accepting the conclusion?

11. Predict some of the potential problems that might arise if all plant reproduction were controlled by tissue cloning.

12. X-rays and other forms of radiation break apart chromosomes. Using the information gained in the chapter, assess some of the medical problems caused by the atomic bombs dropped on Hiroshima and Nagasaki, Japan, during World War II. Prepare a research report on nuclear radiation and cancer.

Critical Thinking

13. What evidence can you provide that suggests that not all cells divide at the same rate?

14. Based on cell size and shape, predict which of the following cells is

  (a) least active.

  (b) a plant cell.

  (c) a nerve cell.

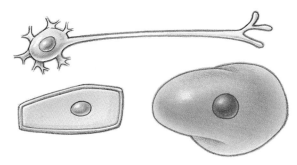

Give reasons for your predictions.

15. Predict which of the following might be a cancer cell. Give reasons for your prediction.

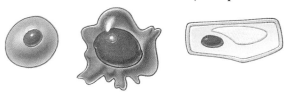

16. Earlier in this chapter, you were told that some herbicides kill weeds by increasing their cell-division rate.

  (a) State the relationship mentioned above as a hypothesis.

  (b) Design an experiment that would test your hypothesis.

  (c) What is the control used in your experiment?

  (d) Identify the independent variable and dependent variable for your experimental design.

  (e) How will you measure the rate of cell division?

How Cells Respond to Stress

STRESS! Everyone faces it sooner or later. If we learn how to manage it, we become stronger emotionally. When we exercise, or stress, our muscles, they become stronger physically. Did you know that even cells manage stress? Dr. Manju Kapoor studies cells to learn how they cope with stress.

◀ Dr. Manju Kapoor is a molecular biologist at the University of Calgary.

Q. What kinds of stress do cells encounter?

A. Cells must endure changes in temperature, changes in the amount and kind of nutrients available, and possibly the presence of harmful chemicals in their environment.

Q. Do you study one particular type of stress?

A. Yes, we study the effects of heat. Cells from most organisms grow best at a certain temperature. If we raise the temperature, the cells will become stressed.

Q. What type of cells do you study?

A. In most of our experiments, we use the fungus *Neurospora crassa*. It is small and easy to handle, yet the cells are very much like those in plants and animals. The results we see using *Neurospora* are very similar to the results other researchers see when studying different species.

Q. How *do* the cells respond to heat?

A. Scientists have discovered that the cells, under heat stress, make special proteins that are not normally present. We call them heat shock proteins or stress proteins.

Q. How do you know that these proteins are helping the cells cope with the heat?

A. Let me describe some experiments to answer this question. *Neurospora* grows very well at 30°C. When we suddenly raise the temperature to 52°C, the organism dies. If we raise the temperature to only 48°C, the fungus survives and its cells make the stress proteins. If we later raise the temperature to 52°C, this organism survives the additional heat.

Q. How does heat kill cells?

A. Cells contain thousands of different proteins and each carries out a special task, necessary for the survival of the cell. Proteins are made of long strands that must be folded in a very precise pattern in order to function. Heat causes the strands to unfold and denatures the proteins. As a result, the cells die.

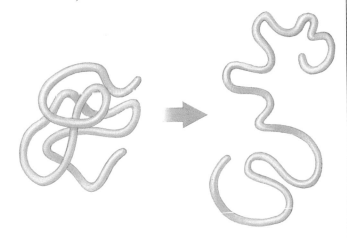

Proteins are long, thin molecules that must fold in a specific way in order to carry out their task. Heat kills cells because it causes proteins to unfold.

Q. How do the stress proteins protect the cells from heat?

A. We have isolated two stress proteins that slow the unfolding of other proteins at high temperatures. They also help proteins to fold again after the temperature is lowered. We call these stress proteins "chaperones" because they guard and protect other proteins. We have also found stress proteins that break down certain harmful chemicals.

Q. How did you become a molecular biologist?

A. In high school, I wanted to be a chemist but when I attended the University of Delhi, in India, I became interested in biology. There, I earned an honours B.Sc. and an M.Sc. in botany, the study of plants. I received my Ph.D. degree in botany from the University of Manitoba. While working on my Ph.D., I studied molecules in wheat cells. That led me into molecular biology.

Q. What would you say about the future of molecular biology?

A. It's where the action is. Molecular biologists now have the tools to study each of the many thousands of genes in all organisms, including humans. It will take many years and many researchers to even begin to answer all of the questions. Molecular biology has applications in medicine, the environment, agriculture, and nutrition.

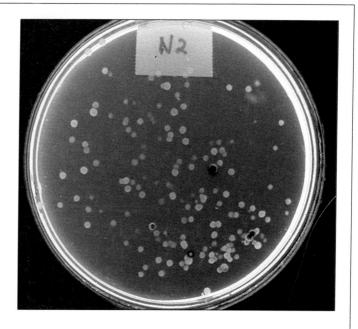

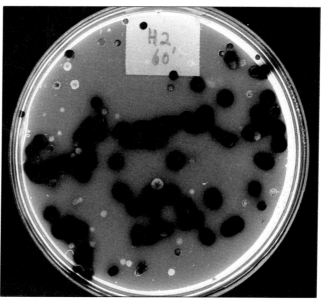

Dr. Kapoor studies this fungus called *Neurospora crassa*. You may know it as bread mould. The colonies at top have not been exposed to high temperatures, while those below have been subjected to heat. The dark brown colour reveals the presence of the stress protein that breaks down harmful chemicals.

NOW THAT YOU HAVE COMPLETED Chapters 10, 11, and 12, you can assess how much you have learned about Cells and Cell Processes by trying these questions.

Before you begin, you may find it useful to return to the Chapter Reviews. There, you will find lists of Key Outcomes and Key Terms. Read these to ensure that you understand the main points and the important vocabulary of the chapters. If necessary, look back at the appropriate sections in the text, which are listed with the Key Outcomes.

Write your answers to the questions in your notebook.

True/False

For each of the following, write T if the statement is true. If the statement is false, rewrite it to make it true.

1. All living things are composed of cells.

2. The light microscope allows scientists to view cells, molecules, and atoms.

3. Images seen through a light microscope appear upside-down and backward.

4. Animal cells can be differentiated from plant cells, because animal cells are always larger.

5. The nucleus acts as the control centre of the cell.

6. A group of cells of similar shape and function is referred to as a tissue.

7. If an onion cell is placed in a concentrated salt solution, water will move out of the cell.

8. All bacteria are harmful.

9. Larger cells are more effective at absorbing nutrients and getting rid of wastes.

10. Cancer is associated with the uncontrolled division of cells.

Completion

Copy the following sentences, filling in each blank with the word or phrase that correctly completes the sentence. Use words from this list: mitosis, DNA, chloroplast, nucleus, mitochondrion, osmosis, diffusion, cell membrane, surface area, active transport. (You will not need all of the words.)

11. The ▒ is the control centre of the cell.

12. Chromosomes are composed of a substance called ▒.

13. ▒ is a form of asexual cell division.

14. The ▒ surrounds the cytoplasm of plant and animal cells.

15. A ▒ is an organelle that contains the green pigment chlorophyll, used for photosynthesis.

16. The movement of water through a semi-permeable membrane is called ▒.

17. The greater the folding of the cell membrane of a cell, the greater is the amount of cell ▒.

18. Cells lining the surface of roots move solutes across cell membranes by using energy in a process called ▒.

19. If you begin to peel an orange, molecules associated with its scent move from the orange through the air by ▒.

Matching

Copy the numbers of the descriptions given below. Beside each number, write the word or phrase from the right column that best fits the description. (You will not need to use all of the words.)

20. the circle of light seen through the microscope in which the image is viewed

21. thread-like structures that carry genetic information, found inside of the nucleus

22. cytoplasmic organelles often called the "power plants" of the cell, the site of cell respiration

23. the organelles where proteins are made

24. a structure composed of many different tissues that work together

25. a cell membrane that allows small molecules to penetrate, but prevents the passage of large molecules

26. the stage of cell division in which the chromosomes line up along the middle of the cell

27. a form of asexual reproduction

28. the theory that living things could arise from nonliving things

29. this microscope is ideally suited for looking at ribosomes and very small structures within the cytoplasm

A   chromosomes
B   spontaneous generation
C   field of view
D   organ
E   ribosomes
F   budding
G   transmission electron microscope
H   selectively permeable
I   mitochondria
J   metaphase
K   diffusion

Multiple Choice

Write the letter of the best answer for each of the following questions. Write only one answer for each.

Use the diagram below to answer the next two questions.

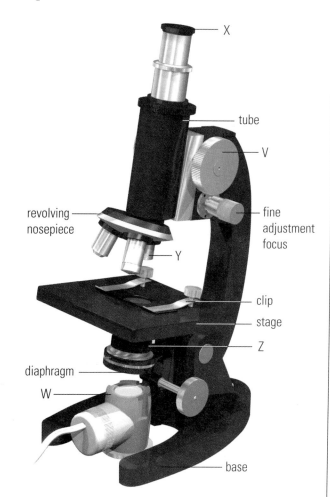

30. Which order traces the movement of light from the source through the microscope to the eye of the observer?

A   W, Z, Y, X   D   X, Z, Y
B   W, X, Z, Y   E   None of the above
C   X, Y, Z, W

31. To calculate the total magnification of the object viewed, you need to know the magnification provided by

A   V and W.   D   Y and V.
B   W and Z.   E   Z and X.
C   X and Y.

Use the diagram below to answer the next three questions.

Cell Type A

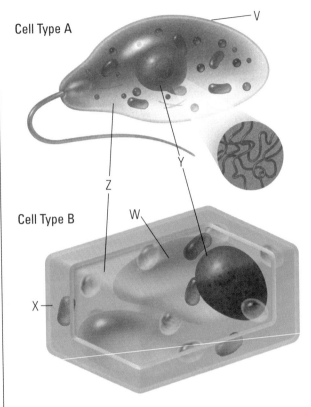

Cell Type B

32. The cell membrane can be identified as structure(s)

A V.

B W.

C X.

D V and X.

E Z and Y.

33. The nucleus can be identified as structure(s)

A V.

B X.

C Y.

D V and X.

E Z and X.

34. The plant cell is cell type

A A, because it has chromosomes and a nucleus.

B B, because it has cytoplasm and a nucleus.

C A, because it has a flagellum and a cell membrane.

D B, because it has chloroplasts and a cell wall.

E A and B, because both types are plant cells.

Short Answer

Write a sentence or a short paragraph to answer each of the following questions.

35. How does the light microscope differ from the electron microscope?

36. Suggest one limitation of the transmission electron microscope for viewing living things.

37. What is the function of the following cytoplasmic organelles?

(a) mitochondria

(b) endoplasmic reticulum

(c) Golgi apparatus

(d) ribosomes

(e) lysosomes

(f) chloroplasts

38. How do plant cells differ from animal cells?

39. What are selectively permeable membranes?

40. A large amount of fertilizer is spilled on a lawn. The grass turns brown and dies. Why does the grass die?

41. How is active transport different from osmosis and diffusion?

42. Explain why a scientist might be interested in monitoring the population of microorganisms in a milk sample.

43. Draw animal cells in the following phases of mitosis and briefly describe each phase.

(a) prophase   (c) anaphase

(b) metaphase   (d) telophase

44. Are larger animals composed of larger cells? Explain your answer.

45. A human cell usually has 46 chromosomes. How many chromosomes would you expect to find following mitosis?

46. In what ways do cancer cells differ from normal cells?

Problem Solving

47. The microorganism below was viewed under high-power magnification. The field diameter is 400 µm. Calculate the size of the organism.

48. Athletes lose salt and water as they perspire. The hotter the conditions, the greater the amount of fluid they lose. If only water is replaced following extreme exercise, the concentration of solutes in the blood will decrease and cells will take up more water. Fragile cells, such as red blood cells, can burst if too much water moves into the cells.

    (a) Suggest why the cells take up more water.

    (b) Design an experiment that will allow you to determine how much solute should be added to the water that an athlete drinks following exercise.

Challenge

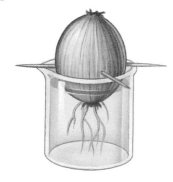

49. Place the lower section of an onion bulb in a beaker of water, as shown in the diagram above. Support the onion bulb on the sides of the beaker by sticking toothpicks into the bulb. The bottom tip of the bulb must touch the water. Once small rootlets begin growing from the onion, remove a single rootlet and prepare a slide by carefully pressing the rootlet between two slides. Press down on the top slide until the rootlet is squashed. The technique is referred to as the squash technique. Remove the upper slide. Add one drop of acetocarmine stain to the squashed rootlet and place a cover slip on the specimen.

    (a) Observe cells in mitosis.

    (b) Find cells in prophase, metaphase, anaphase, and telophase, and draw a diagram of each cell.

    (c) Select four different sections of the root tip. Calculate the rate of cell division in each section.

50. Are large cells more active than small cells? Design an experiment that would allow you to investigate this question.

Design and Do

51. Using only convex lenses, a light source, tape, and a cardboard tube, design a microscope that allows you to view cells in a prepared slide. Move the ocular and objective lenses to create a sharp focal point. Draw a blueprint of your microscope, recording the position of the lenses and length of the tube, then construct the microscope.

52. Build a model of a DNA molecule.

Project Ideas

53. Visit a biotechnology company. What type of work does the company do? What qualifications do staff members require? What are the career prospects? Prepare a poster showing some of the ways the company uses cells to make commercial products.

54. Research how DNA fingerprinting has been used in Canada. List various uses for this new technology.

CHAPTER 13

The Importance of Plants

Trees prevent erosion.

CAN YOU IMAGINE a world without plants? It would certainly be less beautiful. However, the importance of plants extends far beyond their beauty. Plants supply much of the world's oxygen and food. All animals rely either directly or indirectly on plants for energy. In addition, plants help change barren rock into soil, prevent soil erosion, and influence weather patterns. Humans depend on plant fibres for clothing, rope, paper, and building materials. Plant extracts are used to make rubber, dyes, and medicines. Indoors, plants are used to improve the quality of the air in homes, schools, and offices.

In this chapter, you will

- learn how plants use photosynthesis to convert energy from sunlight into food energy,

- learn about the interdependence of plants and animals, and

- discover how carbon dioxide, oxygen, and water are exchanged between living things in the environment.

 Getting Started

Your group is forming a self-sufficient space colony, but you will not be allowed to use plants. In your colony, all of the things that plants do on Earth must be done by machines.

1. Make a list of important functions that are carried out by plants on Earth. (Consider the ways people use plants in homes, offices, schools, factories, and sport.)

2. Think of a machine that could be used instead of plants for each of the functions on your list. Explain how your machines might work. Produce a poster showing the machines you would need.

DID YOU KNOW?

The rosy periwinkle, a plant native to Madagascar, has provided an important medicine for treating various types of leukemia, a form of cancer.

Plants as Food

Although an estimated 80 000 species of plants exist, fewer than 20 species produce 90% of the food humans eat. What is it about these particular plants that makes them a good source of food?

Plants use sunlight energy to make simple sugars. Inside the cells of plants these simple sugars are joined together to make long-chain **starch** molecules, the primary food source of plants. In this investigation, you will test for the presence of starch in various plant products using an iodine solution.

 CAUTION: Be careful when using Lugol's iodine solution. It is toxic and an irritant. It may stain skin and clothing. Use rubber gloves when cleaning up spills, and rinse the area of the spills with water.

Materials

- apron
- safety goggles
- medicine droppers
- depression plate (or small test tubes)
- distilled water
- starch suspension
- sugar solution
- Lugol's iodine solution in dropper bottle
- non-food plant materials (such as paper, cotton fibre, rope)
- plant materials used as food (fruits such as apples, bananas, peaches; seed products such as corn starch, wheat flour, soya flour, oat flour, rice flour; potato flour)
- rubber gloves
- bean seeds (extension)
- beaker (extension)
- potting soil and tray (extension)

Procedure

1. Make a table like the one below to record your observations.

Test for Starch

Substance tested	Predicted results	Observed results
distilled water		
starch suspension		

2. Put on your apron and safety goggles.

3. Using a medicine dropper, add one drop of distilled water to the first well on a clean depression plate. (If you do not have depression plates available, use a clean, dry test tube for each test.) Add one drop of Lugol's iodine to the distilled water.

(a) Record your observations in your table.

Step 3

4. Rinse the medicine dropper. Add one drop of starch suspension to the next clean well on the depression plate. Add one drop of Lugol's iodine to the starch.

(b) Record your observations in your table.

5. Repeat step 4, using the sugar solution instead of the starch.

(c) Record your observations in your table.

(d) Write a sentence to describe how Lugol's iodine can be used as a test for starch.

6 Predict whether each of the plant materials you test will contain starch.

(e) Record your predictions in your table.

7 Place a small amount of each plant material in each of the depression wells and add a drop of Lugol's iodine solution.

(f) Record your observations in your table.

8 Dispose of excess plant materials as directed by your teacher. Clean up your work station. When cleaning the depression plate, be sure to wear rubber gloves. Wash your hands.

Questions

1. Why did you rinse the medicine dropper after each test?

2. Which test acted as a control?

3. What evidence do you have that Lugol's iodine solution is a specific test for starch?

4. (a) What would you conclude about the presence of starch in plant materials that humans do not use for food?

   (b) What would you conclude about the presence of starch in plant materials that humans do use for food?

Apply

5. In the list of materials for this investigation, there is a caution warning that iodine will stain clothing. Explain why iodine would stain a cotton shirt.

6. Iodine is added to two unknown solutions. Both solutions turn blue-black, but the first solution is much darker. Provide a possible explanation for the difference in shade.

7. Provide an explanation for any of the differences you found between your predictions and your results in this investigation.

8. List three different foods you eat that do not contain starch. Why do you think there is no starch in them?

Extension

9. Soak six bean seeds for 24 h in a beaker of water. Split one of the seeds and test it for the presence of starch. Draw a diagram to show where you found any starch. Plant your remaining seeds and observe their growth. (You may wish to use your bean plants in upcoming investigations.)

You can grow bean seeds in soil, or find out how to grow your seeds hydroponically, without using any soil at all.

10. Make and record observations about the growth of your bean plants over the next 10 classes. Make as many quantitative observations as possible.

11. You can grow your own plants in a closed system, called a terrarium. To assemble a terrarium, use any container you like, as long as it is transparent, big enough for your plants, and will hold moisture. Choose small plants, such as moss, ferns, or lettuce. Start with a layer of fine gravel or coarse sand. This will provide proper drainage. Then add about twice as much potting soil. Plant your seeds, and water well. Cover the mouth with a lid or plastic wrap. If your terrarium clouds over with moisture, remove the stopper or lid for half an hour to allow the excess water to evaporate. Your terrarium will probably not need any more water.

Plants in the Ecosystem

Y OU ARE AWARE of the importance of plants as a source of food for humans. Plants are also a source of food energy for other animals.

Producers and Consumers

Animals depend upon plants. This becomes most clear when plants and animals are studied within ecosystems. **Ecosystems** are composed of communities of living things and their physical and chemical environment.

Within any ecosystem, energy and matter move from one group of organisms to other groups.

This movement forms a **food chain**. Food chains begin with energy from the sun. The first organisms in the chain are plants. Plants convert solar energy into chemical energy, or food. Thus, plants are called the **producers** in the ecosystem.

Animals, unlike plants, cannot make their own food. Organisms that must eat other organisms to obtain food energy are called **consumers**.

Decomposers, such as fungi and many bacteria, also serve an important function. They break down the complex molecules in dead organisms. The smaller molecules return to the soil, where plants can use them for growth.

These organisms live within the same ecosystem. Which organisms produce food? Which organisms consume other organisms for food?

Photosynthesis is the Key

Photosynthesis is a series of chemical reactions that plants use to convert light energy into the chemical energy stored in food. During photosynthesis, carbon dioxide and water are combined to make a product—sugar. Oxygen is released as another product. The word equation for photosynthesis is:

carbon dioxide + water + light energy → sugar + oxygen

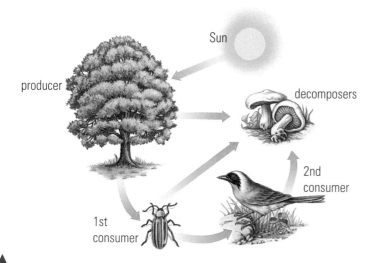

The tree is the source of stored energy in this ecosystem. Light energy from the sun is converted to chemical energy by photosynthesis. The tree stores the energy as starch (sugar molecules joined together).

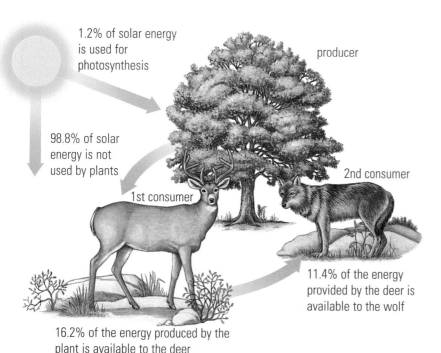

As energy moves through the food chain, some of it is used by living things for motion and other activities. For this reason, at each link in the chain there is less energy available than at the previous link.

MATH-LINK

Energy Pyramid

The data below represent what happens as chemical energy is transferred from producers to consumers. Use the data below to draw a pyramid to represent the amount of energy lost at each level.

Classification in food chain	Energy available $(kJ/m^2/year)$
Producers	85 000.0
First consumers	14 000.0
Second consumers	1 600.0
Third consumers	88.0

- Use the area within each rectangle to represent the energy consumption.
- Select a scale to represent the size of each energy level. (e.g., $100 \ kJ/m^2/year = 10 \ mm^2$.)

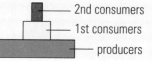

- Colour code each energy level.

Sample energy pyramid

SELF CHECK

1. (a) Why is photosynthesis important to plants?

   (b) Why is photosynthesis important to animals (including humans)?

2. Write a word equation to describe photosynthesis.

3. What is the first organism in a food chain?

4. Explain this statement: Even wolves rely on plants.

Is Light Necessary for Photosynthesis?

Y OU HAVE LEARNED THAT green plants make their own food, and store it in the form of starch. The process by which plants make the food is called **photosynthesis**. The word photosynthesis is composed of two terms: *photo*, meaning light, and *synthesis*, meaning to make or build. In this investigation, you will find out if light is necessary for the process of photosynthesis.

 CAUTION: Be careful when using Lugol's iodine solution. It is toxic and an irritant. It may stain skin and clothing. Use rubber gloves when cleaning up spills, and rinse the area of the spills with water.

Materials

- apron
- safety goggles
- geranium plant
- piece of foil or cardboard (4 cm × 4 cm)
- paper clip
- 250-mL beaker
- pair of beaker tongs (or oven mitts)
- hot plate

- ring stand
- forceps
- large test tube
- test-tube rack
- ethanol
- test-tube holder
- petri dish or watch glass
- Lugol's iodine solution
- rubber gloves

 CAUTION: Ethanol is highly flammable. Never place ethanol near an open flame.

Procedure

1 Obtain a geranium that has been kept in a dark cupboard for 48 h. Use a paper clip to attach two pieces of foil or cardboard to both sides of one leaf. Leave the plant where it will receive bright sunlight for two days.

Attach foil to leaf.

Leave in sunlight.

Remove plant from dark.

Step 1

2 Put on your apron and safety goggles.

3 Pour 100 mL of water into a beaker. Using beaker tongs or oven mitts, place the beaker on the hot plate. Turn on the hot plate and heat the water to boiling.

4 Remove the paper clip and foil from the leaf. Gently remove the leaf from the plant. Using forceps, carefully dip the leaf into the boiling water for 2 s, or until it becomes slightly limp.

 CAUTION: Steam from boiling water will scald skin. Do not put your hand directly above the beaker, and be careful not to touch the beaker.

(a) Describe the colour of the water.

Step 4

5 Shake any water off the leaf, roll it up, and place it in a large test tube. Use the forceps to push the leaf to the bottom of the test tube. Cover the leaf with ethanol.

Step 5

✎ (b) Describe the appearance of the ethanol.

6 Use a test-tube holder to place the test tube containing your leaf in the boiling water bath. Leave it in the boiling water until you observe the ethanol boiling.

✎ (c) Describe the appearance of the ethanol.

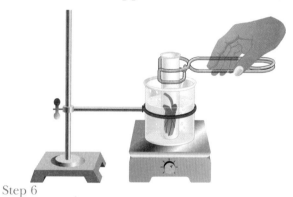

Step 6

7 Use the test-tube holder to remove the test tube from the boiling water bath. Allow the test tube to cool in the test-tube rack. Turn off the hot plate and use beaker tongs (or mitts) to remove the beaker.

8 When the ethanol is cool, dispose of it in the container provided by your teacher. Using the forceps, remove the leaf from the test tube and spread it out in a petri dish or a watch glass. Rinse with a gentle stream of water.

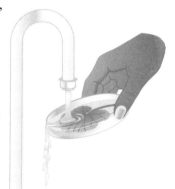

Step 8

9 Make sure you drain any excess water from the leaf. Test for starch by adding enough iodine to cover the leaf.

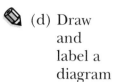

Step 9

✎ (d) Draw and label a diagram showing the distribution of starch in the leaf.

10 Dispose of the leaf as instructed by your teacher. Wear rubber gloves while cleaning the dish and your work station. Wash your hands.

Questions

1. Write a hypothesis for this investigation.

2. Why did you test the leaf for the presence of starch?

3. What change happened to the ethanol when you boiled the leaf in it? What do you think caused this change? Why was this step necessary in this investigation?

4. Why was the plant placed in the dark for 48 h before you attached the foil to the leaf?

5. What would have happened if you had tested the leaf for starch immediately after it was removed from the dark?

6. Is light necessary for photosynthesis? Explain your answer using the results of this investigation.

Extension

7. Sunlight is composed of many different colours: red, orange, yellow, green, blue, and violet (see Chapter 9). Design a procedure that uses the techniques from this investigation to determine which colour of light works best for photosynthesis.

Is Chlorophyll Necessary for Photosynthesis?

IN CHAPTER 10, you learned that plant cells have chloroplasts. Chloroplasts contain a green pigment, called **chlorophyll**, which is used to trap light energy. Inside the chloroplast, light energy is converted into chemical energy.

In this investigation, you will find out if chlorophyll is necessary for photosynthesis by examining this process in a plant with a multicoloured leaf. Green areas of the leaf are rich in chlorophyll, while areas of the leaf that are not green have other pigments and contain little or no chlorophyll.

 CAUTION: Ethanol is highly flammable. Never place ethanol near an open flame.

Materials

- apron
- safety goggles
- hotplate
- ring stand
- 250-mL beaker
- water
- coleus or variegated geranium plant
- beaker tongs (or oven mitts)
- forceps
- large test tube
- test-tube rack
- ethanol
- test-tube holder
- petri dish or watch glass
- Lugol's iodine solution
- rubber gloves

 CAUTION: Be careful when using Lugol's iodine solution. It is toxic and an irritant. It may stain skin and clothing. Use rubber gloves when cleaning up spills, and rinse the area of the spills with water.

Procedure

1 Put on your apron and safety goggles.

2 Prepare a boiling water bath by pouring 100 mL of water into a beaker and placing the beaker on the hot plate. Turn the hot plate on.

3 While the water bath is heating, obtain a leaf from a coleus or variegated geranium that has been kept in a well-lit area.

✎ (a) Draw and label a diagram showing the location of the different colours in your leaf.

4 Using forceps, dip the leaf into the boiling water bath for about 2 s.

 CAUTION: Steam from boiling water will scald skin. Do not put your hand directly above the beaker, and be careful not to touch the beaker.

✎ (b) Describe the colour of the water.

Step 4

5 Roll up the leaf and place it in the large test tube. Using forceps, push the leaf to the bottom of the test tube. Add ethanol to the test tube until the leaf is covered.

Step 5

6 Use a test-tube holder to place the test tube in the boiling water bath. Leave the tube in the bath until the ethanol boils.

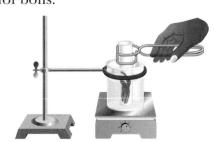

Step 6

7 Once the ethanol boils and becomes coloured, use the test-tube holder to remove the test tube from the hot water bath. Allow the test tube to cool in a test-tube rack. Turn off the hot plate and use beaker tongs (or mitts) to remove the beaker.

(c) Describe the colour of the ethanol.

8 Dispose of the ethanol in the container provided by your teacher.

9 Use forceps to remove the leaf from the test tube and spread it out in a petri dish or a watch glass. Rinse with a gentle stream of water. Make sure you drain any excess water, then add enough iodine solution to cover the leaf.

(d) Draw and label a diagram showing the distribution of starch in the leaf.

Step 9

10 Dispose of the leaf as instructed by your teacher. Wear rubber gloves while cleaning the dish and your work station. Wash your hands.

Questions

1. Based on your observations from this investigation, where does photosynthesis occur?

2. Why did you put the leaf in boiling water?

3. Why did you put the leaf in boiling ethanol?

4. Chlorophyll is the substance responsible for the green colour in a leaf. Based on your results, what is the relationship between chlorophyll and photosynthesis?

Apply

5. A plant called *Iresine* has bright red pigment in its leaves. When tested, these leaves are found to contain starch. How is this possible? What does this result suggest about chlorophyll and photosynthesis?

Extension

6. Leaves are green because chlorophyll reflects the green part of the spectrum of light while it absorbs all other parts. Predict what would happen to a plant exposed only to green light. Design an experiment to test your prediction.

7. The first dyes used on cloth came from plants, and many still do. For example, the blue colour of jeans comes from a dye made from the indigo plant. Try this activity to make and use a plant dye of your own.

- Boil 1/4 head of purple cabbage in water until the water is a rich purple colour.

- After cooling the water, use a colander or sieve to remove the cabbage leaves from the water. (The leaves can be composted or eaten!) The purple water is your dye.

- Experiment with different fabrics. Dip pieces of cotton, nylon, wool, or other cloth into the dye and allow them to dry. Which fabric absorbed the dye the best? Can you wash the dye out again?

- Add a few drops of vinegar to some of your purple dye. What happens? How could you use this change?

LEARNING TIP

Refer to page 299 to learn more about plant cells and where the green pigment, chlorophyll, is located.

Living Together

AS PLANTS PERFORM photosynthesis, they produce food for themselves, and for the animals that eat plants. They also produce the oxygen that animals breathe. But do animals help plants? Experiments to answer this and other questions were conducted over 200 years ago by an English clergyman named Joseph Priestley.

Priestley's First Experiment

Priestley used three heavy glass jars to create almost airtight environments. One of the jars was placed over a mint plant. The second was placed over a mouse. The third was placed over a mint plant and a mouse.

✎ (a) The mouse in Jar B died first. Why do you think the mouse died?

✎ (b) After some time, the mint plant in Jar A died. Why do you think the plant died?

✎ (c) In Jar C, both the mouse and the plant lived longer than they had in the other jars. Why do you think they lived longer?

Photosynthesis and Respiration

Priestley's experiment showed that plants and animals do help each other. But how? You have discovered that plants use water and carbon dioxide from the air to make sugars. Oxygen is released in the process. The word equation for photosynthesis is:

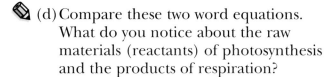

carbon dioxide + water + light energy →
sugar (chemical energy stored in food) + oxygen

Organisms such as yourself and Priestley's mouse use oxygen to release the energy stored in food. Carbon dioxide and water are released as sugars are broken down. The process is known as respiration. The word equation is:

sugar (chemical energy stored in food) + oxygen →
energy (available for use) + carbon dioxide + water

✎ (d) Compare these two word equations. What do you notice about the raw materials (reactants) of photosynthesis and the products of respiration?

Jar A

Jar B

Jar C

Priestley's first experiment

A Critical Balance

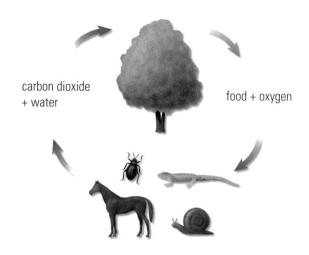

carbon dioxide + water

food + oxygen

In the environment, a balance of oxygen and carbon dioxide is maintained. During photosynthesis, plants take in carbon dioxide and produce oxygen; during respiration, organisms take in oxygen and produce carbon dioxide. The processes of photosynthesis and respiration support each other.

Note that the term "organism" was used in the paragraph above, rather than "animal." This is because plants also perform respiration in order to use the energy they store as food. Does this mean that plants could exist without animals? In Priestley's experiment, the plant that was alone in Jar A died. Plants can produce all the oxygen they need for respiration. But photosynthesis requires more carbon dioxide than a plant alone can release. So animals help plants to survive.

Priestley's Next Experiment

Priestley performed another experiment using airtight jars. In one jar, he placed a burning candle. In a second jar, Priestley placed a mint plant. A short time later, he added a burning candle. The candle by itself went out after three minutes. The candle with the plant continued to burn for five minutes.

(e) What gas is produced as a candle burns?

(f) Why do you think the candle by itself stopped burning first?

(g) In what ways are the experiments with the burning candle and plant similar to Jar C (the mouse and the plant) in Priestley's first experiment?

(h) Do you think you could change how long the candle burned in the jar with the plant by changing the size of the candle? Give reasons for your answer. (Hint: Review the word equation for combustion of a substance by looking at page 166.)

DID YOU KNOW?

If Priestley were alive to conduct similar experiments today, he would not need to sacrifice the plant or the mouse. Instead, he would use sensitive instruments to accurately monitor the concentration of gases in the air.

Questions

1. Construct a hypothesis for Priestley's first experiment.

2. In what ways are the mouse in Jar B of Priestley's first experiment and the candle in his second experiment alike?

3. Using only Priestley's apparatus, how could you test for the presence of oxygen in Jar B?

4. How could you test for the presence of carbon dioxide in Jar A?

ASK YOURSELF

Make a concept map to summarize what you have learned so far, using the terms photosynthesis, respiration, chlorophyll, plants, and animals. If you have studied animal and plant cells, add the terms mitochondria and chloroplasts to your map.

The second Priestley experiment

Is Carbon Dioxide Necessary for Photosynthesis?

PRIESTLEY DISCOVERED THAT GASES were being exchanged between plants and animals. In this investigation, you will find out how the carbon dioxide released from animals is used as a raw material by plants during photosynthesis.

You will use bromothymol blue as a test for carbon dioxide. Bromothymol blue turns yellow-green in the presence of carbon dioxide.

Materials

- apron
- safety goggles
- hot plate
- 250-mL beaker
- beaker tongs (or oven mitts)
- large test tube
- bromothymol blue solution in dropper bottle
- 3 straws
- 2 pieces of a water plant, such as cabomba, or Myriophyllum
- 4 test tubes with stoppers
- test-tube rack
- wax pencil

Procedure

Step 4

1. Put on your apron and safety goggles.

2. Pour 150 mL of water into a 250-mL beaker and bring it to a boil on a hot plate. Turn off the hot plate. Use beaker tongs (or mitts) to remove the beaker and allow 5 min for the water to cool.

3. While the water in the beaker is cooling, half-fill a large test tube with tap water. Add 5 drops of bromothymol blue solution.

4. Over a sink, place a straw in the test tube and blow into the straw slowly. Be careful not to allow the bubbles to cause the solution to spill. Dispose of the straw immediately after this step is complete.

   (a) Record any colour change in the test tube.

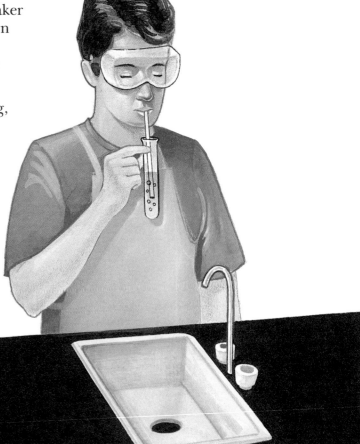

5 Make a table like the one below to record your observations.

Testing for Carbon Dioxide

Test tube	A	B	C	D
Colour at start				
Color after blowing through straw	—	—		
Colour after 24 h				
Other observations				

6 Label four test tubes A, B, C, and D. Fill each test tube with the cooled water from step 2 and place it in the test-tube rack. Add a piece of water plant to test tubes A and C.

7 Add 5 drops of bromothymol blue solution to each of the test tubes.

(b) Record the initial colour of the test tubes in your table.

Steps 6 and 7

8 Using a straw, blow gently into test tubes C and D until you observe a colour change.

(c) Record the colour change you observe.

Step 8

9 Seal all four test tubes with rubber stoppers and place them in a bright place (but not in direct sunlight). Observe the test tubes 24 hours later.

(d) Record any colour changes you observe after 24 h.

10 Clean up your work station and wash your hands.

Questions

1. How did you confirm that bromothymol blue is a test for carbon dioxide?

2. What controls did you use in this investigation?

3. Why did you blow into tubes C and D?

4. Identify the independent variable and the dependent variable in your experiment.

5. What can you infer from the colour changes you observed?

6. What can you infer from any tubes that did not change colour?

Apply

7. In this investigation, you boiled the water to remove any dissolved gases. What evidence do you have that suggests carbon dioxide was removed by boiling?

8. Suppose that you had placed your four test tubes in the dark instead of the light. What observations would you expect? Provide reasons for your predictions.

Exploring Photosynthesis and Respiration

I N CASE STUDY 13.5, you learned that photosynthesis and respiration support each other. In this section, you will learn more about the chemical processes of photosynthesis and respiration.

More about Photosynthesis

You have learned that plants convert light energy into food or chemical energy. Although the word equation seems a simple, one-step process, photosynthesis is actually a series of chemical reactions. You can think of this series as having two main parts.

In the first part of photosynthesis, light energy is absorbed by chlorophyll. This energy is used to split water molecules into their components: hydrogen and oxygen. The oxygen is released into the atmosphere, and the hydrogen is used in the second part of photosynthesis.

light energy + water (H_2O) → oxygen (released) + hydrogen

During the second part of photosynthesis, carbon dioxide molecules are linked with each other and with hydrogen from water. The result is the energy-rich simple sugar, **glucose**:

hydrogen (from water) + carbon dioxide → glucose

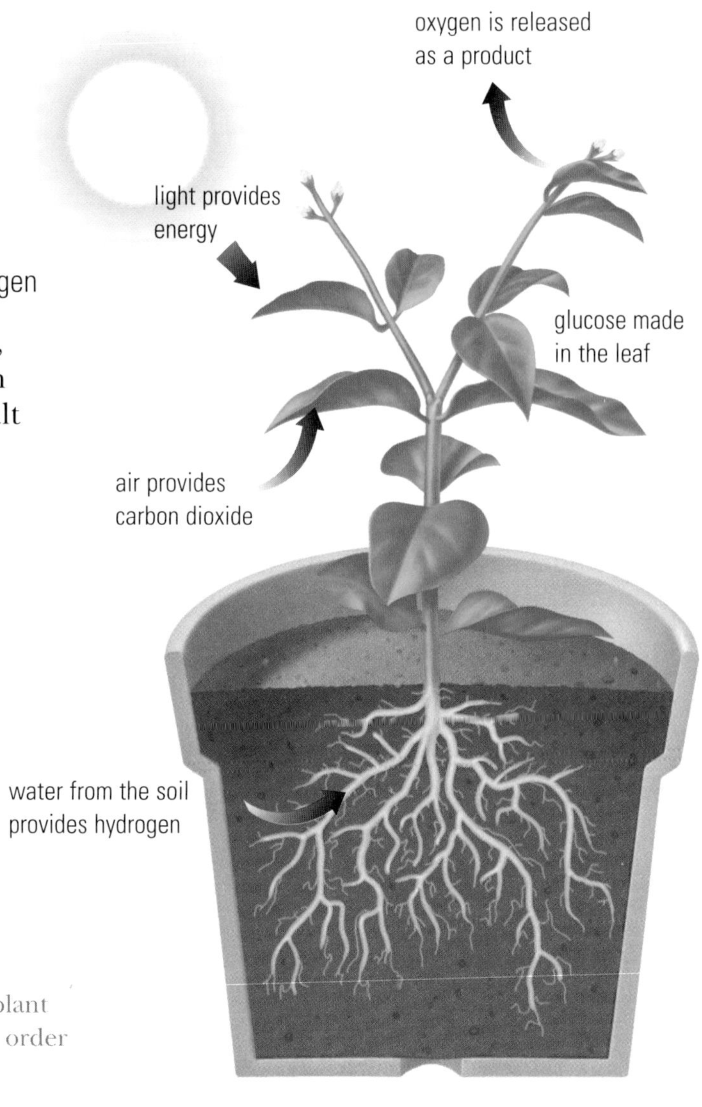

oxygen is released as a product

light provides energy

glucose made in the leaf

air provides carbon dioxide

water from the soil provides hydrogen

Photosynthesis. What does this plant require from its environment in order to perform photosynthesis?

More about Respiration

When you breathe, swallow, or look around, your body is using energy. This energy comes from glucose molecules in your body. Your cells perform respiration in order to "unlock" the energy in glucose so it can be used by your muscles and other body parts.

The word equation for respiration is similar to the one for the combustion of fuels. Keep in mind that respiration, like photosynthesis, is actually a series of chemical reactions. These reactions gradually release the chemical energy of glucose. When respiration occurs, carbon dioxide and water are produced.

glucose + oxygen → carbon dioxide + water + energy

Plants, like animals, must perform respiration all the time in order to use food energy. However, in daylight, plants perform photosynthesis much more rapidly than respiration. During the night, when plants perform respiration only, they release carbon dioxide.

TECHNOLOGY-LINK

Biosphere II

Priestley's experiment was repeated in a 1.2-ha greenhouse in the Arizona desert. On September 26, 1991, the gigantic structure was sealed. It contained 3800 species of plants and animals including four men and four women. Texas billionaire Ed Bass wanted to build and study a model of the Earth's ecosystems. Never had such a large artificial ecosystem been attempted with so many different plants and animals. In Biosphere II, all raw materials and waste products were to be recycled by humans, animals, and plants living together. However, by November 12, 1991, it was disclosed that the scientists in the greenhouse had brought in purified air from the outside to counter high levels of carbon dioxide.

- Use library resources to find out more about the controversial Biosphere II project.

- Why do you think many scientists are now reluctant to accept any of its findings?

- Would you volunteer to take part in an experiment like this one? Why or why not?

Biosphere II under construction

SELF CHECK

5. What is the role of chlorophyll in photosynthesis?

6. (a) What is the source of energy for photosynthesis?

   (b) What is the source of the energy you use in your body?

   (c) How are these sources related?

7. Seeds contain a supply of starch. Starch is made up of thousands of glucose molecules. Explain why a seed is able to germinate and the young plant able to grow even in the dark.

8. Explain how the oxygen you are breathing at this moment could once have been part of a water molecule.

Explaining Global Warming

HAVE YOU EVER NOTICED how warm it can be inside a car, even on cool days? Light from the sun enters through the glass and strikes objects inside the car. The objects absorb some of the light, turning it into heat energy. As they warm up, they also emit energy, but this energy cannot pass through the glass, so it stays inside the car. As a result, the inside of the car becomes warmer than the outside air.

Many of the Earth's atmospheric gases, such as carbon dioxide and water, work much like the glass. The gases trap the heat from the Sun and warm the Earth's surface. A certain amount of these greenhouse gases is essential for the survival of life on Earth. Without greenhouse gases, the average temperature of the planet would fall from 15°C to –18°C.

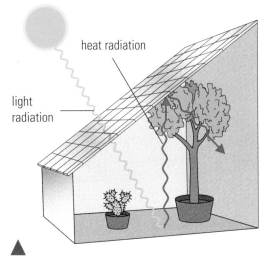

▲

The **greenhouse effect**
The glass panes of a greenhouse allow sunlight to pass through, but prevent heat from escaping. A similar situation occurs in the atmosphere: carbon dioxide in the atmosphere acts like the glass in a greenhouse, trapping heat close to the Earth's surface.

▼

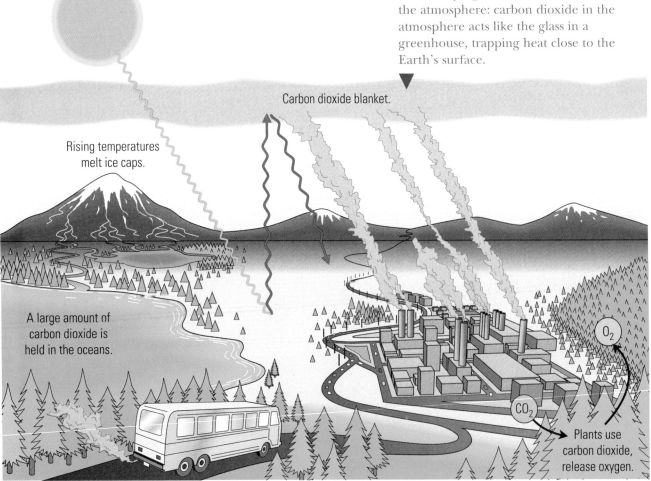

Carbon dioxide blanket.

Rising temperatures melt ice caps.

A large amount of carbon dioxide is held in the oceans.

O_2

CO_2

Plants use carbon dioxide, release oxygen.

Sources of Carbon Dioxide

Carbon dioxide is released during respiration by living things. It is also released by combustion. One estimate suggests that the burning of wood and fossil fuels, such as coal and gas, has caused the amount of carbon dioxide in the atmosphere to triple over the past 40 years. The average global temperature has increased by 1°C over that same time. Scientists have predicted that the Earth's temperature will continue to rise gradually because of an increase in greenhouse gases. This process is called **global warming**. The rising levels of carbon dioxide have changed the balance between photosynthesis and respiration. In doing so, the increased levels of carbon dioxide may alter the world's climate.

A Changing Climate

A warmer climate might appeal to many Canadians—especially in winter. However, increased temperatures are not without their drawbacks. Snow caps would melt and rivers would overflow, causing flooding. Melting snow and ice would also raise the level of the oceans, drastically changing existing coastlines. Dry areas of the country would also be affected. The prairies might become desert-like, while other regions would become wetter.

It is still not certain that global warming is happening, but the potential effects of rising temperatures have been modelled using computer simulations. Even a small increase in average temperature results in major changes, such as flooding.

TRY THIS

Simulating the Greenhouse Effect

The greenhouse effect can be simulated by the following experiment. Find a sunny spot to set up your apparatus. Place equal masses of ice cubes of approximately the same size in two plastic bags. Place one of the bags inside a large, inverted glass jar and allow it to sit in the sun. Place the second bag in the sun, but do not enclose it in glass. Use a graduated cylinder to measure the amount of melting that has occurred after 10 min. (If you have two small thermometers, you can also keep track of the temperature inside each bag.)

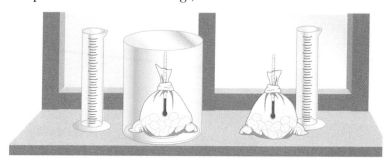

SELF CHECK

9. (a) What is the greenhouse effect?

   (b) What is global warming?

   (c) Give an example of a greenhouse gas and describe its importance to global warming.

10. List two things that may increase the amount of carbon dioxide in the atmosphere.

11. How might global warming affect where people live?

12. Plants use carbon dioxide to make food. If there is more carbon dioxide in the atmosphere, this might result in more food from plants. Why, then, is global warming a problem?

ASK YOURSELF

Would you be willing to reduce your use of carbon dioxide-releasing technology (such as cars) to counteract global warming? Why or why not?

The Future of the Car

THROUGHOUT THE WORLD, about 7 billion tonnes of carbon dioxide are emitted each year as fossil fuels are burned. Consumption of fossil fuels—oil, coal, and natural gas—must be drastically reduced if this carbon dioxide is not to affect the climate through global warming.

Dateline, January 1990: Toronto City Council unanimously adopts a resolution to reduce carbon dioxide emissions. The target is to reduce emissions by 20% by the year 2005.

However, the population of the city is expected to continue to grow. The number of people living in the Toronto area is expected to increase by 20% before the year 2011.

The Atmospheric Fund is given $25 million by the City of Toronto to achieve the reduction of carbon dioxide emissions. A $1.2 million study into reducing energy consumption and finding alternative sources of energy has been completed by consultants.

The Target: Reducing Car Use

The automobile is a major contributor of carbon dioxide emissions. There are nearly 400 million cars in the world. Every year, nearly one billion tonnes of carbon dioxide enter the atmosphere from car engines. To reduce these emissions, people's driving habits must be changed. More people must be willing to leave their cars at home and take public transit, cycle, or walk.

This is not an impossible task. The chart compares Toronto residents with those of other cities. As you can see, 63% of Toronto residents use their car as the principal means of transport, compared with 34% in Stockholm, 16% in Tokyo, and only 3% in Hong Kong. If these cities can reduce the use of cars, so can Toronto.

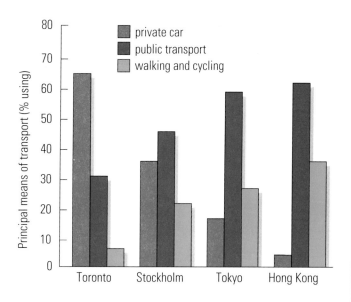

These four cities contain thriving businesses and industries—as well as growing populations.

ASK YOURSELF

Did you change your mind during the debate? Did a particular argument make you stop and think about the proposal again? Outline the steps you took toward making a personal decision on this problem.

The Proposal for Debate

The number of cars allowed into the city each day should be reduced by the following:

- providing freeway lanes for public transit and car-pool vehicles, with heavy fines for single-passenger cars that use those lanes

- increasing the licence fee, to make driving more expensive and less attractive

Point

- The proposal will reduce the number of cars driving into the city each day. Carbon dioxide emissions will drop.

- At the moment, public transit is expensive for taxpayers, but the proposal will encourage people to use the system. The more people use public transit, the more efficient it will be.

Counterpoint

- Businesses will move to cities that have fewer restrictions on the use of cars. What is the point of creating a city that produces much less carbon dioxide, but has no jobs for its citizens?

- How will the city control freeway lanes without hiring people and raising taxes?

What Do You Think?

1. Research the issue. Ask family members, neighbours, and friends how a proposal like this would affect their lives. What problems might they face? What benefits would they expect?

2. Prepare for the debate by studying the points and counterpoints above. From your research, create some more points and counterpoints of your own.

Key Outcomes

Now that you have completed the chapter, can you do the following? If not, review the sections indicated.

- List ways in which plants are important to humans. (13.1, 13.2, 13.5, 13.7)
- Use iodine as an indicator to identify starch. (13.1, 13.3, 13.4)
- Explain the importance of interactions between plants and animals. (13.2, 13.5, 13.6, 13.7 13.8)
- Summarize experimental evidence concerning the connection between photosynthesis and respiration. (13.5)
- Use word equations to identify the raw materials and products of photosynthesis and respiration. (13.5, 13.7)
- Explain the prediction that links carbon dioxide production to global warming. (13.8)

Key Terms

starch	photosynthesis
ecosystem	chlorophyll
food chain	glucose
producer	greenhouse effect
consumer	global warming
decomposer	

Review

1. Match each term in Column A with the statement or definition from Column B that best describes it.

Column A	Column B
glucose	green pigment that absorbs light energy
photosynthesis	chain-like molecule for food storage in plants
starch	
respiration	process that releases food energy
chlorophyll	
	released during photosynthesis
	green plants use light energy to produce food

2. Why are plants important for the survival of life on Earth?

3. (a) Write a word equation for photosynthesis.

   (b) Write a word equation for respiration.

4. Use Joseph Priestley's experiments to explain an important relationship between plants and animals.

5. (a) Describe a test you could perform to tell if starch is present in a sample.

   (b) Describe a test you could perform to tell if carbon dioxide is present in a sample.

6. What is the role of each of the following in photosynthesis?

   (a) chlorophyll   (c) light

   (b) carbon dioxide   (d) water

7. What is the greenhouse effect?

Problem Solving

8. The leaves of two plants were tested for starch. Plant A was placed in a cupboard for 48 h before testing. Plant B was kept in a sunny area for 48 h before testing.

(a) Which plant's leaves would you expect to give a positive test for starch?

(b) What can you infer from this result?

9. An advertising brochure states: "Light, water, and carbon dioxide are needed by plants for photosynthesis, so the more of these raw materials you can give your plants, the better your plants will grow!" Can a plant get too much of a good thing? Design an experiment that tests any one of the claims of this brochure.

10. The leaf shown in the diagram was boiled and tested for starch. Which of the results (A, B, or C) would you expect? Explain your answer.

leaf boiled and tested for starch

A   B   C

11. A series of test tubes was prepared. Each tube contained a different concentration of starch. One drop of iodine was added to each of the test tubes, with the results shown in the diagram. Explain how you could use test tubes like these to help you determine the amount of starch produced by a plant at various times of the day.

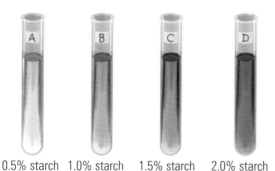

0.5% starch   1.0% starch   1.5% starch   2.0% starch

12. The Earth's atmosphere once contained far less oxygen than it does now. Write a hypothesis to explain why oxygen levels have increased from the early days of the planet.

Critical Thinking

13. A student decides to use soda pop to investigate the importance of carbon dioxide in photosynthesis.

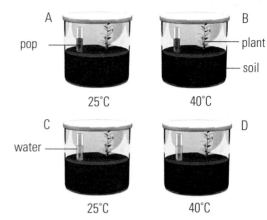

(a) State a hypothesis for this experiment.

(b) What is the source of carbon dioxide in A and B?

(c) Predict, with reasons, which plant would have the highest rate of photosynthesis.

(d) Which experimental setup (B, C, or D) acted as a control for procedure A?

(e) What was the purpose of procedure D?

14. A student sets up an experiment to show the relationship between plants and animals, using bromothymol blue.

(a) What question is the student's experiment designed to answer?

(b) Explain the results.

(c) Predict, with reasons, what would happen to test tubes C and A if they were kept in total darkness.

(d) How would the results of the experiment be affected if the test tubes were not stoppered?

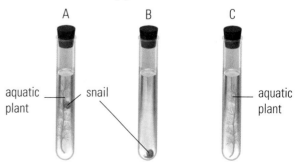

aquatic plant   snail   aquatic plant

remains blue   turns yellow-green   remains blue

CHAPTER 14

The Living Plant

WHEN ANN ROBERTS, a student from North Bay, travelled to Waterloo, she was amazed to see weeping willow trees. Her family had tried to grow a willow, but had not succeeded. What was it about the Waterloo area that was so different from North Bay? Ann also wondered why there were more maple trees than pine trees in the Waterloo area.

To understand why plants grow well in one place and poorly in others, you need to know more about the living plant—how it functions, grows, and reproduces. In this chapter, you will

- learn how plants obtain water and move it to their various parts,
- examine leaf structure and its role in photosynthesis,
- discover how differences in plant structures affect where plants grow best,
- learn how seeds germinate and grow,
- investigate sexual reproduction in plants, and
- examine the effects of competition on plant growth.

 Getting Started

1. Examine the photographs of the jack pine, white spruce, and sugar maple on this page. Discuss with your group where you might expect to find these plants in Ontario. If you don't know, send a representative to other groups to share ideas.

2. On a large piece of paper, trace or draw a rough outline of the province of Ontario. Use this map to record your ideas on where these plants may be most common.

3. Make a list of environmental factors that might explain why these plants grow where they do in Ontario.

Jack pine

White spruce

Sugar maple

DID YOU KNOW?

Chewing gum comes from trees. The chicle tree (*Manilkara zapota*) produces a sticky white sap that is processed and flavoured into gum. What popular gum is named after this tree?

Water Movement in a Plant

IN CHAPTER 13, you learned that water is an essential raw material for photosynthesis. Photosynthesis is how green plants convert light energy into chemical energy, in the form of food. So plants must be able to gather and transport water in order to survive.

How does water make its way from the soil to the leaves of a plant? Blood is carried through your body in tubes called blood vessels. Are there similar structures in a plant? In this investigation, you will examine the movement of water through the stem of a plant. You will also find out if the presence of leaves has any effect on water movement.

Materials

- apron
- safety goggles
- 2 stalks of fresh celery
- single-edged razor blade
- 2 200-mL beakers
- medicine dropper
- water
- red food colouring
- spoon or stir stick
- paper towel
- ruler

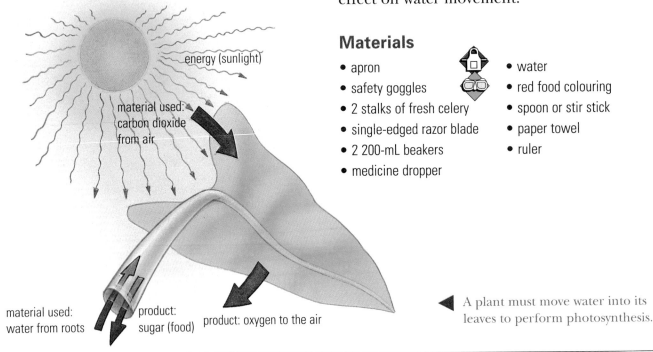

energy (sunlight)

material used: carbon dioxide from air

material used: water from roots

product: sugar (food)

product: oxygen to the air

A plant must move water into its leaves to perform photosynthesis.

Procedure

1 Put on your apron and safety goggles.

2 Obtain two celery stalks that are about the same length. Using a razor blade, cut approximately 1 cm from the end of each stalk.

CAUTION: Be sure the razor blade is clean before you use it. Replace the blade if it appears damaged or very dull. Use care when cutting, and always cut away from yourself.

3 Use your fingers to remove the leaves from one of your celery stalks.

4 Half-fill two 200-mL beakers with water. Add five drops of red food colouring to the water in each beaker and mix well.

5 Place both celery stalks in the water. Leave them in the water for 3 h.

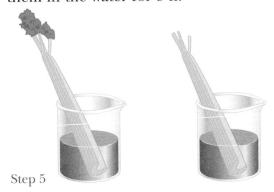

Step 5

6 Make a table in your notebook to record your observations.

Water Movement in Celery	Stalk with leaves	Stalk without leaves
Prediction		
Length of stalk (cm)		
Distance moved:		
1 cm		
2 cm		
3 cm		

✎ (a) Predict which celery stalk will show the greatest movement of water (and dye). Provide a reason for your prediction.

7 After 3 h, remove the celery stalks from the water. Lay both celery stalks on a paper towel. Use a ruler to measure the length of each stalk from the bottom end to where the leaves begin.

✎ (b) Record the length of each stalk in your table.

8 Use the razor blade to cut a cross-section of one celery stalk 1 cm from the bottom end. Examine the cut surfaces of the celery.

✎ (c) Draw a sketch to show where the red dye appears on the cut surface of the stalk.

Step 8

9 Continue cutting the celery stalk at 1 cm intervals until the dye can no longer be seen in the stalk. Repeat with the other celery stalk.

✎ (d) For each cut, record in your table whether the dye was visible in the celery stalk.

✎ (e) Record the total distance the dye moved in each stalk.

✎ (f) Calculate the percentage of the stalk that the dye and water moved up, using this formula:

$$\frac{\text{distance moved by the dye}}{\text{length of stalk}} \times 100\%$$

10 Dispose of the celery as directed by your teacher. Clean your glassware and return it to storage. Wash your hands.

Questions

1. What effect did the leaves have on water movement?

2. (a) Explain why you started with two celery stalks that were about the same length.

   (b) Why is it helpful to calculate a percentage in order to compare the movement of dye in the two stalks?

Apply

3. A gardening book recommends removing some of the leaves from a plant that has been transplanted into a new pot. Based on your observations in this investigation, will removing some leaves help the plant?

Extension

4. Repeat the procedure of this investigation, but this time, place plastic bags over the two celery stalks in the beaker. Predict how this may affect your results.

From the Ground Up

DID YOU EVER FORGET TO WATER a house plant? It doesn't take very long for a plant to wilt. Water is an essential chemical for the plant. But plants outside of the home cannot rely on regular watering. The survival of most plants requires an efficient water-absorbing system as well as a water-transport system.

Water Absorption

Most plants obtain water from the soil in which they grow. The water passes into the plant through the root hairs. **Root hairs** are thin extensions of the surface cells of a root. They penetrate tiny openings in the soil as they grow. As you may recall from your studies of plant cells, every cell is surrounded by a thin layer called the cell membrane. (The cell membrane is itself surrounded by a cell wall.) The cell membrane controls the passage of substances, such as gases and dissolved chemicals, both into and out of the cell. In root cells, the cell membrane allows water and dissolved nutrients such as minerals to enter. Root hairs greatly increase the surface area of the root for absorption of these materials.

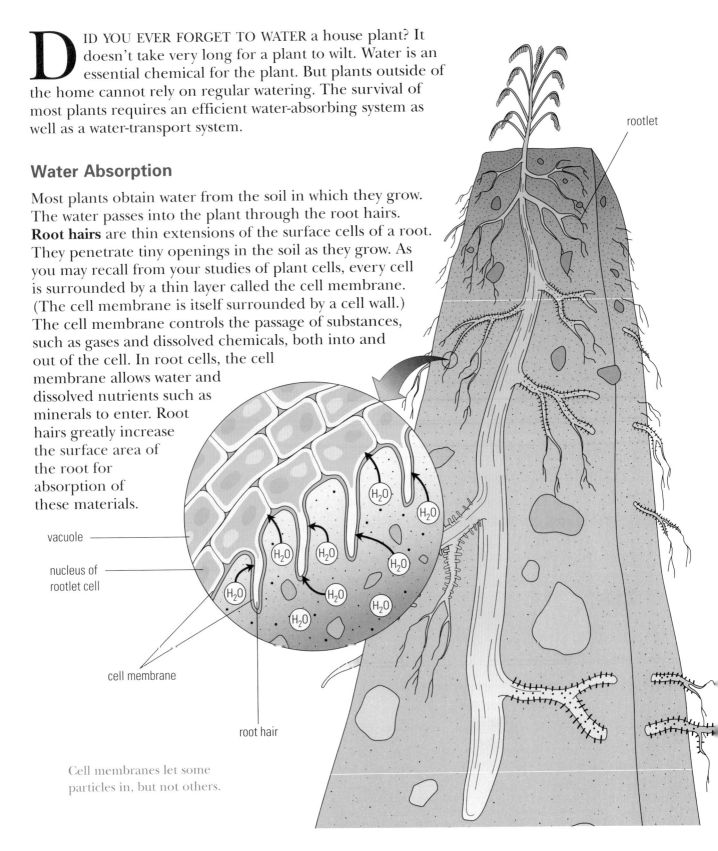

rootlet

vacuole

nucleus of rootlet cell

cell membrane

root hair

Cell membranes let some particles in, but not others.

Tubes for Transport

Every plant cell needs water. In particular, cells in which photosynthesis takes place must have a steady supply of water. Just as you have tubes called blood vessels to transport blood inside your body, plants have tubes called **xylem vessels** to transport water. The xylem vessels are formed from cell walls left behind as columns of cells die in the plant. The cell walls between these cells dissolve, leaving only the outer cell walls for support. Eventually, a xylem vessel, a narrow tube like a straw, forms.

In some plants, water must travel great distances from the roots to the leaves.

Formation of a xylem vessel

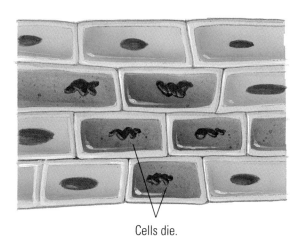

Cells die.

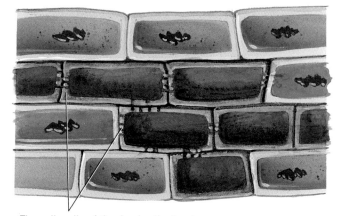

The cell walls of the dead cells dissolve.

Moving Water Around

The transport of water within a plant is not fully understood. Many scientists believe that there are three different forces that help move the water.

Root pressure: Root cells may actively pull in certain minerals. Water from the soil then enters the cells by osmosis. The water that has been drawn into the root produces a pressure that pushes water further up the xylem vessel toward the stem.

Capillarity: Capillarity is the tendency of liquids to cling to the sides of narrow tubes. This tendency helps water to move up inside the narrow xylem vessels.

Transpiration: Water molecules are attracted to each other. (The tendency of molecules to stay together is called cohesion.) As water molecules evaporate from the leaves of the plant, other water molecules are pulled up the xylem vessel, much like a string of beads. The evaporation of water from the exposed parts of a plant is called transpiration. The force produced by the leaves (and other exposed parts) that pulls water up the plant is called transpiration pull. It is considered the most important factor in moving water through a plant.

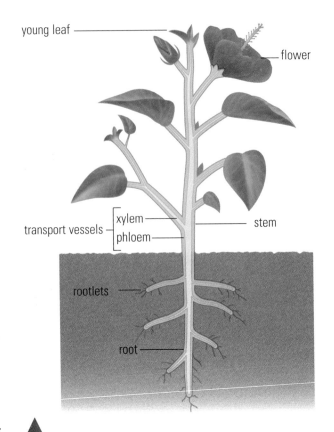

Your heart muscle pumps constantly to move your blood around your circulatory system. How water is moved inside a plant's system of xylem vessels is not yet totally understood. However, many scientists think that at least three different forces are involved.

Transpiration takes place because water molecules are attracted to one another. As each water molecule evaporates from a leaf, the others inside the plant are drawn upward.

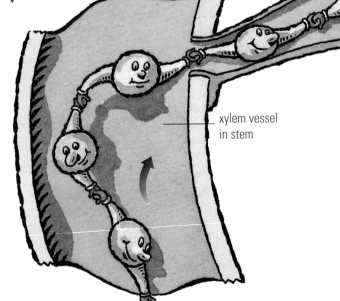

TRY THIS

Capillarity

You can find out more about capillarity by trying this experiment.

Add a few drops of food colouring to a tray of water. Stand glass tubings of different diameters in the water. Measure the distance the water travels up each tube. How does the diameter of the hollow tube affect the distance the water travels?

From the Leaves Down

Plants also have another transport system. A series of tubes called **phloem vessels** move sugars from the leaves to the stems and roots for storage. Phloem vessels also transport nutrients from the roots up to the leaves, as needed. Unlike the xylem vessels, phloem vessels consist of living cells.

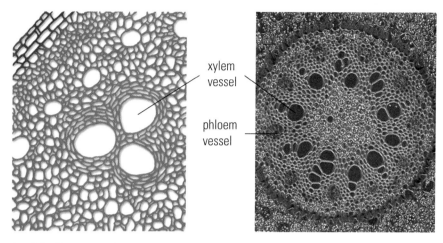

xylem vessel

phloem vessel

In this diagram of a stem (left), you can see how the xylem vessels are arranged. The phloem vessels are found close to each set of xylem vessels. The picture at right shows xylem and phloem vessels in a cactus stem.

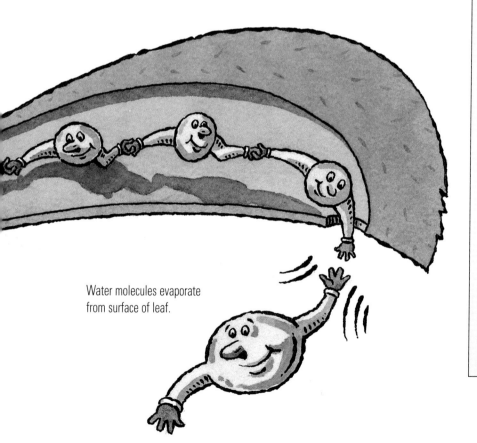

Water molecules evaporate from surface of leaf.

SELF CHECK

1. (a) What structures in a plant help to move water?

   (b) Why is the ability to move water important to the survival of a plant?

2. (a) What structures in a plant help to move nutrients such as sugars?

   (b) Why is the ability to move nutrients important to the survival of a plant?

3. Compare your heart and blood vessels to the transport system in a plant.

4. (a) What are the three forces that help move water through a plant?

   (b) Which of these forces involves an action taken by plant cells? Explain.

   (c) Which of these forces involves a characteristic of water? Explain.

5. To "tap" a sugar maple tree, a thin metal tube is hammered into the tree. The sap from inside the tree flows out of the tube and is collected. The sap tastes very sweet. (When concentrated, the sap is called maple syrup.) Which kind of transport vessel in the tree carries the sap?

6. During Investigation 14.1, you examined the cut surfaces of celery stalks that had transported water mixed with food colouring. The food colouring was concentrated in a series of small "dots." Were these dots xylem or phloem vessels? How do you know?

Examining the Leaf

T HE LEAF IS SOMETIMES REFERRED to as the "factory" for photosynthesis. It is here that the energy of sunlight is used to combine water from the soil and carbon dioxide from the air to make sugars. But leaves are also exposed. By examining leaf structure, you can learn a great deal about how plants survive in different environments.

Protection: The Cuticle

The **cuticle** is a waxy coating that covers the leaf. It acts as a protective layer to prevent water from evaporating from the cells of the leaf.

Photosynthesis: The Palisade

The **palisade** is the layer of cells responsible for most of the photosynthesis in a leaf. These cells are just under the top cuticle. They contain large numbers of chloroplasts— the organelles in which light energy is trapped by molecules of chlorophyll.

Transport: The Veins

The **vein** is a combination of xylem and phloem vessels. Xylem carries water from the roots to the leaf. Phloem carries the sugar and starch made in the leaf to the roots for storage.

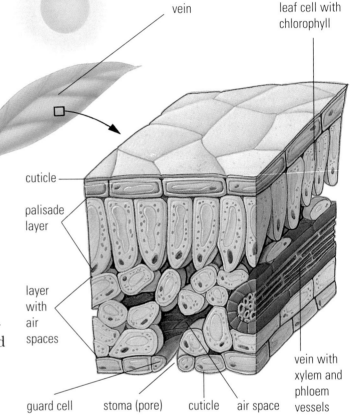

vein

leaf cell with chlorophyll

cuticle

palisade layer

layer with air spaces

guard cell   stoma (pore)   cuticle   air space

vein with xylem and phloem vessels

TRY THIS

Guard Cells and Stomata

Use two long balloons to represent the guard cells that control the opening and closing of the stomata. Grab both balloons at the top with your right hand and grab both balloons at the bottom with your left hand. Apply pressure to the balloons by moving both hands closer together without letting go of the balloons.

- Describe what happens.
- Predict what will happen if some of the air in the balloons is released. Check your prediction.
- Use the balloons to help describe how water pressure affects the opening and closing of stomata.

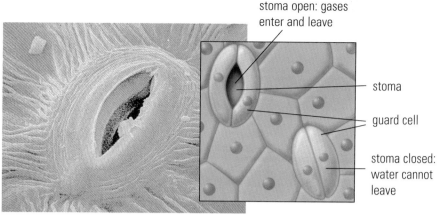

stoma open: gases enter and leave

stoma

guard cell

stoma closed: water cannot leave

The guard cells act like doors. They open to allow gases to move in and out of the leaf. They close to protect cells inside the leaf against the loss of too much water.

Gas Exchange: The Stomata

Remember that for photosynthesis to occur, the plant cells inside the leaf need carbon dioxide from the air. Also, the oxygen gas released by photosynthesis must exit the leaf. There are air spaces between many of the cells in a leaf. These spaces allow free movement of these gases. But how do the gases enter and leave the leaf if it is covered by a waxy cuticle?

There are small openings in the surface of the leaf called **stomata** (singular: stoma). Each of these openings is controlled by a pair of **guard cells**. If there is enough moisture in the air and the leaf, the guard cells swell up and open the stomata. If the air is too dry or the leaf has very little water, the guard cells relax and close the stomata.

Adapted to Survive

Water is extremely important to the survival of plants. Plants have structures such as the cuticle to prevent water loss. Plants in a dry environment need a very thick cuticle. This is an example of an **adaptation**, a structure or behaviour that helps the species of organism survive.

If you examined the leaves of plants from various environments under a microscope, you would see other adaptations that prevent water loss. Plants that grow in dry, sunny areas tend to have fewer stomata and their stomata are all on the underside of the leaf, protected from heat and wind.

Plants that grow in shady areas have less of a problem with water loss due to evaporation. These plants often have thin cuticles and a large number of stomata on both surfaces of the leaf. Shaded plants usually have more cells in their palisade layer than plants growing in very sunny locations. This is because they need to trap all the light they can in order to perform enough photosynthesis.

SELF CHECK

7. Match the function from the left column with the leaf structures in the right column. (Use each structure at least once.)

Function

(a) allows gases to reach cells

(b) transports water from roots to leaves

(c) allows gases to move in and out of leaf

(d) controls movement of gases in and out of leaf

(e) location of photosynthesis

(f) transports sugars and nutrients

(g) protects against evaporation

Structure

cuticle

guard cell

xylem vessel

phloem vessel

air space

stomata

palisade

8. Why is it important to a plant to have air spaces between the cells in the middle of each leaf?

9. How might each of these characteristics or structures differ between an aquatic plant and a plant that lives in a desert?

(a) cuticle

(b) number of stomata

(c) location of stomata

(d) size of air spaces inside leaf

Observations of a Naturalist

Alpine meadow

Tundra

Examine the plants in both pictures above.

 (a) What similarities do you see?

 (b) Speculate about why these plants grow close to the ground.

In many ways, plants that grow in the northern tundra and those that grow in alpine areas share many characteristics. Both areas tend to have poor soil, low air temperatures, little rainfall, and strong, dry winds. Only the top layer of soil is warmed enough to thaw. A layer of ice, called permafrost, remains all year round. In summer, the top layer melts, but little water drains into the frozen ground below. For plants to survive these difficult conditions they require special structures.

 (c) Hypothesize about why an apple tree will not grow in a tundra region.

 (d) Flowers found in alpine meadows and in tundra regions mature rapidly and flower quickly. Why is it important for these plants to grow quickly and flower early in the summer?

Roots and Nutrients

Many types of grasses are found in tundra regions and alpine meadows. Grasses have a fibrous root system. The radish, by comparison, has a more dominant taproot. Fibrous root systems tend to spread outward; taproots grow downward in search for water.

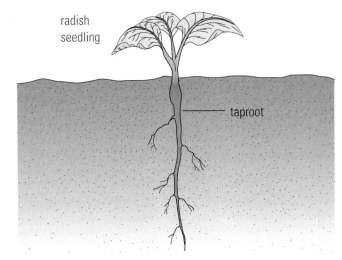

radish seedling

taproot

 (e) Speculate about the advantages of fibrous roots over taproots for plants growing in tundra regions.

 (f) Dandelions grow taproots. What special advantage does the taproot provide the dandelion in moderate climates?

 (g) Make a list of two other plants that have fibrous roots and two that have taproots.

Carefully examine the roots of the carrot and dahlia shown below.

 (h) Classify the roots shown in the diagram as taproots or fibrous roots.

carrot

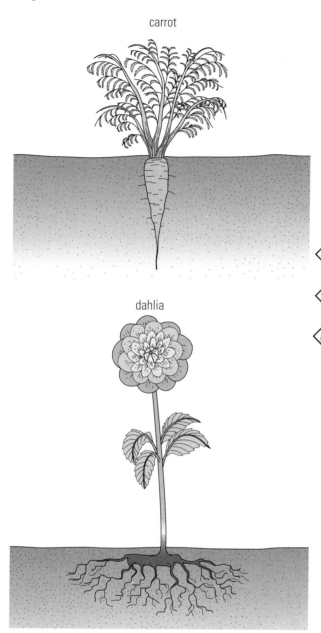

dahlia

Roots and Storage

Roots provide plants with yet another advantage, the storage of food. If food is stored in fruit or the stems, it is exposed to animals. Insects with sucking mouth parts can bore into stems and suck sugars from plants. Not only do plants lose food from their stems, but tissues are often exposed to disease-causing microbes.

Questions

1. How do taproots differ from fibrous roots?

2. List advantages gained from storing food in roots.

3. Identify one adaptation made by plants living in dry climates.

Apply

4. Have you ever cut into a pine tree and noticed how sap begins to flow from the cut? What benefit does the sap provide?

Extension

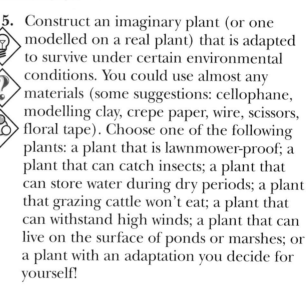 5. Construct an imaginary plant (or one modelled on a real plant) that is adapted to survive under certain environmental conditions. You could use almost any materials (some suggestions: cellophane, modelling clay, crepe paper, wire, scissors, floral tape). Choose one of the following plants: a plant that is lawnmower-proof; a plant that can catch insects; a plant that can store water during dry periods; a plant that grazing cattle won't eat; a plant that can withstand high winds; a plant that can live on the surface of ponds or marshes; or a plant with an adaptation you decide for yourself!

(a) Brainstorm ideas on how your plant can function in its environment. Be prepared to explain your design.

(b) Evaluate your own design, then exchange your plant with that of another group. Evaluate the other group's design.

(c) Give ideas on improving the designs you have evaluated.

Examining Plant Embryos

HOW DOES A PLANT START TO GROW? In this investigation, you will examine seeds.

A **seed** contains a very young plant, called an **embryo**, along with a supply of food. The food, usually in the form of starch, provides nourishment for the young plant until it can perform photosynthesis and make its own food.

CAUTION: Be careful when using Lugol's iodine solution. It is toxic and an irritant. It may stain skin and clothing. Use rubber gloves when cleaning up spills and rinse the area of the spills with water.

Materials

- apron
- safety goggles
- dry bean seeds
- bean seeds soaked in water for 24 h
- dissecting needle
- hand lens or dissecting microscope
- Lugol's iodine solution
- coloured pencils
- corn seeds soaked in water for 24 h
- paper towels
- single-edged razor blade

Procedure

Part 1 *Examining a Bean Seed*

1 Put on your apron and safety goggles.

2 Obtain one dry bean seed and one bean seed that has been soaked in water for 24 h. Use the diagram below to help you identify the various parts of the seed.

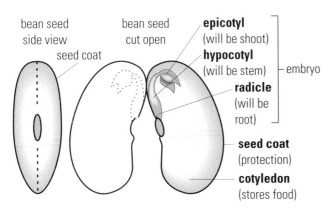

A bean seed

(a) Compare the appearance of the soaked and dry bean seeds.

(b) Suggest a reason for at least one difference you observe.

3 Use your fingers to gently remove the seed coat from the soaked bean seed. Use a dissecting needle to pry the two sections of the seed apart. Find the embryo. Examine the embryo with a hand lens or dissecting microscope.

(c) Draw a diagram of the embryo. Label the cotyledon, the hypocotyl, and the epicotyl.

4 Devise a test to determine which parts of the embryo contain starch. Test the embryo for the presence of starch.

(d) Describe the test you used for starch.

(e) On your diagram of the embryo, use a coloured pencil to mark any areas where you obtained a positive test for starch.

Part 2 *Examining a Corn Seed*

5 Obtain a corn seed that has been soaked for 24 h. Lay the corn seed down with the embryo facing upward. Carefully examine the seed.

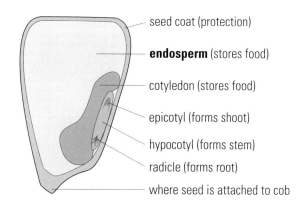

seed coat (protection)

endosperm (stores food)

cotyledon (stores food)

epicotyl (forms shoot)

hypocotyl (forms stem)

radicle (forms root)

where seed is attached to cob

A corn seed

✎ (f) In what ways does the corn seed differ from the bean seed?

6 Note that one side of the corn seed is lighter in colour. This is the location of the embryo.

✎ (g) Describe the appearance of the embryo.

7 Using a razor blade, cut the seed in half lengthwise.

✋ **CAUTION:** Be sure the razor blade is clean before you use it. Replace the blade if it appears damaged or very dull. Use care when cutting, and always cut away from yourself.

cut line

8 Test various areas of the corn seed for starch using the same technique you used to test the bean seed in Part 1.

✎ (h) Sketch the corn seed to show which areas have the greatest amount of starch.

9 Dispose of your materials as directed by your teacher. Wash your hands before leaving the laboratory.

Questions

1. What part of a seed grows into a new plant?

2. (a) Which area of a seed contains the most starch?

   (b) How did you know?

   (c) What function does the starch serve in the seed?

Apply

3. Eventually, the seedling no longer needs the cotyledon. Why?

4. Plant scientists (botanists) classify flowering plants into two major groups, based on the structure of their seeds. The bean is classified as a dicotyledon, and corn is classified as a monocotyledon. On the basis of your observations of the seeds of these plants, explain the meaning of "mono" and "di."

Extension

5. Find out more about the importance of cotyledons by doing this experiment. In a tray of potting soil, plant three rows of bean seeds. In row 1, plant whole seeds. In row 2, plant seeds with one of the cotyledons removed. In row 3, plant seeds with both cotyledons removed. Water the seeds and place your tray in a sunny location where you can observe the plants as they grow. Measure and record the growth rates of your plants.

How Do Environmental Factors Affect Seed Germination?

Y OU CAN THINK OF A SEED as a "plant in a bag." Everything the new plant needs is inside the seed. The protective coat of the seed provides resistance to cold and prevents drying for months or even years. This is why you can buy seeds at a store and wait until spring to plant them. But how does the embryo inside a seed "know" when it is time to start growing—to **germinate?**

In this investigation, you will design your own experiment to determine how various environmental factors affect seed germination.

Materials

- safety goggles
- apron
- combinations of seeds: radish and tomato or bean and lettuce
- other materials, as required

NOT a good time to start growing!

Procedure

1 You will work in a research team with other students. Each team will design an experiment to investigate a particular environmental factor that may affect seed germination.

Possible environmental factors	Possible experiments
How does temperature affect the germination and growth of seeds?	Consider testing a warm environment (room temperature) and a cold temperature.
Do seeds germinate and grow best when exposed to light?	Consider using different light sources (artificial and natural) and a dark area.
Do plants grow well in acidic conditions?	Use different concentrations of acetic acid (vinegar) in water. Make sure that the volume of liquid you add is constant for each trial.
Do plants grow well in basic conditions?	Use different concentrations of dilute sodium hydroxide in water as the base. Make sure that you add the same volume of liquid to each trial.

Here are some suggestions to keep in mind as you plan your experiment:

- Wear safety goggles and an apron, even if your group is not using chemicals, because other groups may be. The entire workplace must be safe.

- Make sure your seeds do not dry out. Use lids on petri dishes.

- Check your seeds for mould growth. Mould will slow growth and eventually kill the seeds. Always use tweezers to handle germinating seeds. Remove any mouldy seeds immediately.

- Filter paper can be used as a divider.

Folded filter paper makes a good barrier.

- Try to measure any changes you observe. Experiments that show the amount of difference are more valuable than those that rely on qualitative observations alone.

2 Work with your group members to develop a procedure. Use a chart like the one below to help you. Discuss your procedure with any other groups in your class that are investigating the same environmental factor. Plan to compare your data at the end of the investigation.

The control we will use for the experiment is:
The independent variable is:
The dependent variable is:
The variables we plan to control are:

3 Present your procedure to your teacher and, upon approval, begin the experiment.

(a) Construct a data table and record your results. If possible, present your data in graph form.

Questions

1. What conclusions did you draw from your experiment?

2. What other experiments might you need to test your conclusions?

3. How did your results compare with those of other groups that investigated the same environmental factor?

4. Make a two-column chart in your notebook. In the left column, list all the factors considered by your class in this investigation. In the right column, note the effects of each factor on the germination of the tested seeds.

5. Can you draw conclusions about the effects of these environmental factors on the germination of seeds from all plants? Why or why not?

Apply

6. Who might be interested in answering the question that you researched? Explain why.

Extension

7. You may have noticed that many of the seedlings you observed in this investigation grew to slightly different lengths.

(a) To find out more about the range of growth for seedlings, use the data in the table below to construct a bar graph.

(b) From your graph, what is the most common length of seedlings? How do you know?

(c) Subtract the shortest length from the longest. This is the range that was observed in this experiment. How could you use this value when comparing this experiment to another?

Length of shoot (mm)	Number of seedlings with shoots of this length
10	1
12	3
14	6
16	14
18	22
20	15
22	7
24	3
26	1

ASK YOURSELF

If your group were to repeat the experiment, what things would you do differently? Why would you change your approach?

Flowers, Seeds, and Fruits

SEEDS ARE THE RESULT of sexual reproduction in plants. **Sexual reproduction** occurs when a female sex cell unites with a male sex cell. The result is a new individual that combines characteristics from both parents. The structures that plants use for sexual reproduction are contained in their flowers.

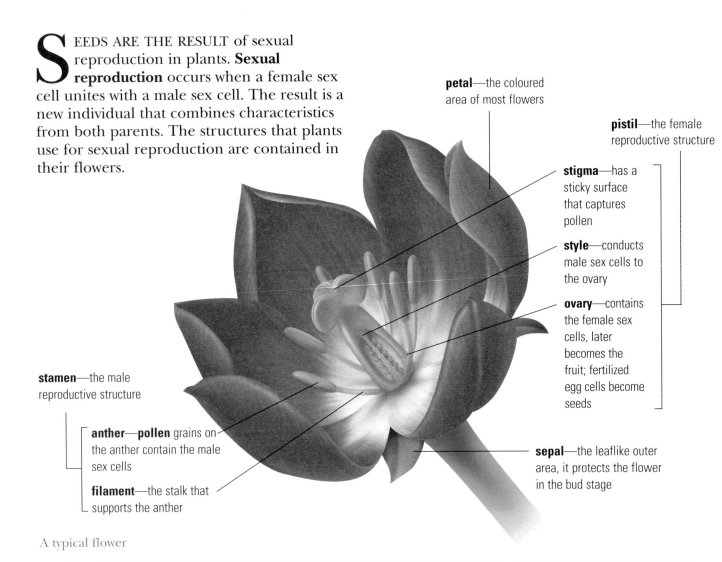

petal—the coloured area of most flowers

pistil—the female reproductive structure

stigma—has a sticky surface that captures pollen

style—conducts male sex cells to the ovary

ovary—contains the female sex cells, later becomes the fruit; fertilized egg cells become seeds

stamen—the male reproductive structure

anther—**pollen** grains on the anther contain the male sex cells

filament—the stalk that supports the anther

sepal—the leaflike outer area, it protects the flower in the bud stage

A typical flower

TRY THIS

Variation among Flowers

Obtain a single flower and examine it closely with a hand lens or under a dissecting microscope. Compare the number of petals, sepals, and stamens on your flower with those of other flowers from the same plant and the other types of flowers being examined by other groups.

- Do all flowers from the same plant have the same number of petals, sepals, and stamens?

- Do flowers from different plants have the same number of petals, sepals, and stamens?

- Remove a few adjoining petals and sepals. Examine the inside of the flower carefully. How many pistils do you see?

- Draw a diagram of your flower. Colour the structures of the female reproductive system with a coloured pencil. Use a different colour to indicate the structures of the male reproductive system.

Pollination

In order for sexual reproduction to take place, the male sex cells must reach the female sex cells. In plants, this process is called **pollination**. During pollination, pollen from an anther is transferred to a stigma. When this occurs within one flower, it is called self-pollination. When it involves pollen from one plant and a stigma from another plant, it is called cross-pollination. Cross-pollination usually occurs when wind, insects, or birds carry pollen from a flower on one plant to another plant.

Shortly after the pollen lands on the stigma, sexual reproduction takes place within the ovary. The result is a fertilized egg. Each egg grows into an embryo. At the same time, the embryo is surrounded by a supply of food and a protective outer layer (the seed coat). A seed has been produced.

▲ Many plants rely on only one or two animals to pollinate them.

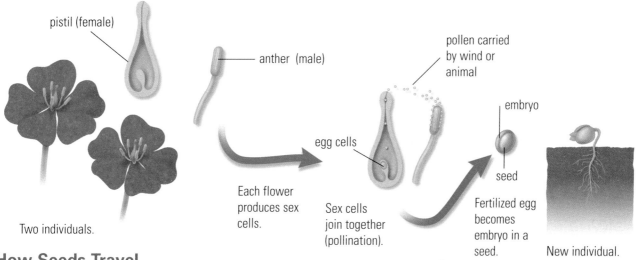

pistil (female)

anther (male)

pollen carried by wind or animal

embryo

egg cells

seed

Two individuals.

Each flower produces sex cells.

Sex cells join together (pollination).

Fertilized egg becomes embryo in a seed.

New individual.

▲ Sexual reproduction in plants

How Seeds Travel

Some seeds are specialized to be carried away, or dispersed by the wind or animals, as shown below. It is usually better for a seed to germinate and grow at some distance from the parent plant. The parent plant may shade the ground nearby, so there may not be enough light for the seedlings. The parent's well-developed root system may also gather nutrients from the soil before the seedling can.

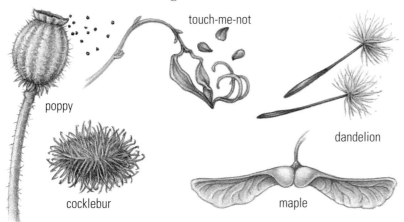

touch-me-not

poppy

cocklebur

maple

dandelion

Plants have many ways to ensure seeds travel far from parents.

SELF CHECK

10. Name the male and female reproductive structures of a plant.

11. In what part of the flower do seeds form?

12. How do insects and birds help with the process of pollination?

13. Bees are attracted to plants to collect sugar-rich nectar. Predict which part of a plant contains the nectar. Give reasons for your prediction.

Competition Between Plants

HAVE YOU EVER NOTICED that few other plants grow under pine trees? Pines and some other plants are able to prevent or slow the growth of other plants. For example, chickpeas, barley, ragweed, and bitter vetch all produce substances that stop the growth of other plants nearby.

Materials

- apron
- safety goggles
- pine needles (or ragweed or bitter vetch leaves)
- scissors
- 100-mL graduated cylinder
- blender
- distilled water
- cheesecloth
- elastic band
- 250-mL beaker

- 2 petri dishes with lids
- wax pencil
- tweezers
- filter paper
- various seeds such as canola, tomato, carrot, lettuce, and radish
- 10-mL graduated cylinder
- clear tape
- hand lens or dissecting microscope

Procedure

1 Put on your apron and safety goggles.

2 Using scissors, cut several needles from a small pine branch. Place the needles in a blender. (Note: ragweed leaves or bitter vetch leaves can be substituted.) Add 50 mL of distilled water to the blender. Put the top on the blender and turn it on for approximately 2 min.

Step 2

 CAUTION: Be certain that no wood is put into the blender.

3 Filter the liquid in the blender from the solid material by pouring the mixture of water and needles through folded cheesecloth into a beaker. Put the beaker aside.

elastic band
cheesecloth

Step 3

4 Use a wax pencil to label the lid of a petri dish "C" for control. Label the lid of a second dish "E" for experimental.

5 Each team will investigate one type of seed. Label the petri dishes with the name of the seeds used by your team.

6 Using tweezers, place filter paper in each of the two petri dishes. Add enough distilled water to the petri dishes to just moisten the filter paper. Replace the lid.

7 Obtain 20 seeds. Use tweezers to place 10 seeds in each petri dish. Spread the seeds out.

Step 7

8 Use a graduated cylinder to measure 4 mL of distilled water. Add this water to the seeds in the dish marked C. The water should just cover the seeds. If you need to add more, measure the amount with the graduated cylinder and be sure to add the same amount of filtrate in step 9.

9 Use the graduated cylinder to measure 4 mL of pine filtrate. Add the filtrate to the seeds in the dish marked E. The filtrate should just cover the seeds.

(a) You used the same graduated cylinder to add the distilled water to C and the filtrate to E. Why is it important to add the water to the control dish first?

Step 9

10 Seal the edges of both petri dishes with clear tape to prevent water loss. Place the dishes in a dark area. You will examine them again in 24 h.

Step 10

11 Prepare a data table like the one below for your observations.

Seed Germination

Treatment	Germination					
	24 h		48 h		72 h	
	number	percent	number	percent	number	percent
control						
experimental						

12 After 24 h, examine your seeds with a hand lens.

(b) Record the number of seeds that have a root (radicle) exposed. These seeds are germinating.

(c) Select 2 seedlings from each petri dish and draw a diagram of their developing roots.

13 Repeat step 12 after 48 h and 72 h.

(d) Record your observations in your data table.

Questions

1. Why was a control used for the experiment?

2. Which seeds are most affected by the pine filtrate?

3. Why were 10 seeds used for each test instead of one seed?

Apply

4. Explain how pine needle filtrate could be used as a herbicide.

Weed Wars

DO YOU KNOW OF A LAWN like the one in the picture below? Weeds can overtake a lawn because they send roots deeper into the soil than the grass, and take up more than their share of the available nutrients. Soon the weeds begin to choke out slower-growing plants.

There are two ways to get rid of the weeds in a lawn. Removing the weeds by hand requires great effort and is time-consuming. The second alternative, spraying the weeds with a herbicide, is often more appealing. It takes a fraction of the time, and tends to take less energy.

A Herbicide—2,4-D

The organic herbicide 2,4-D was introduced in 1944. It is a growth hormone that increases the rate of cell division in broadleaf plants. (Most weeds that grow in fields and gardens, such as the dandelion, are broadleaf plants. Grasses, such as turf grass, rice, wheat, and the other cereal crops, are not broadleaf plants.) 2,4-D works by taking advantage of

what the weeds do best: grow. It speeds up cell division in the weed. Soon the plant's roots can't take in enough nutrients to feed all the cells, and the plant dies of malnutrition. Meanwhile, the cells of the neighbouring slow-growing grass plants have also been dividing faster than usual, but not enough to kill the plants.

Problems of Herbicide Use

Although herbicides like 2,4-D sound wonderful, the use of herbicides is not without its problems. Many herbicides are toxic to some degree, so they must be handled carefully during manufacturing, and then stored using special precautions to prevent leaks. Those who are spraying the herbicide may be able to protect themselves, but there is still a danger to people and animals that pass by. There is also a problem with releasing a substance that kills plants into the environment: after all, a plant that is a weed in one place may be a valuable part of the community in another. How do you keep the herbicide where you are spraying it?

Herbicides can be sprayed over wide areas (top) or on individual plants.

Understanding the Author

1. What are herbicides?

2. Why are herbicides popular?

3. What are some of the potential risks of using chemicals to control weeds?

The Benefits

Opinion of a farmer Herbicides save us a tremendous amount of money every year. If we were to stop using herbicides, consumers would have to pay more for food.

Opinion of a member of the forest industry Some herbicides are effective at removing cheaper softwood trees like spruce and pine, while leaving the more valuable hardwoods, such as oak and walnut. Because the softwood plants no longer compete with the hardwoods, production of valuable wood increases. We use herbicides regularly to select what grows in each area.

Opinion of a chemist If a herbicide is produced carefully, tested thoroughly, and then used according to the instructions, it should pose no threat.

The Risks

Opinion of an organic farmer I do not spray my crops. Yes, I lose more plants to weeds, but when you eat one of my potatoes, that's all you eat.

Opinion of a member of a consumers' group Often, the harmful effects of a herbicide are not immediately visible. We must look to nature for solutions. Some plants prevent the growth of other plants—we should use these natural methods instead of artificial chemicals.

Opinion of a farmer with cancer Can I ever be sure that some of my medical problems were not caused by herbicides? Just because the doctors haven't proved it yet doesn't meant there isn't a link.

What Do You Think?

4. Should the large-scale spraying of herbicides be allowed? Outline your opinions and support them with reasons.

Key Outcomes

Now that you have completed the chapter, can you do the following? If not, review the sections indicated.

- Measure and explain the movement of water in plants. (14.1, 14.2, 14.3)
- Identify plant structures that help transport water and nutrients. (14.1, 14.2)
- Identify leaf structures. (14.3)
- Describe ways that plants are adapted to their environments. (14.3, 14.4, 14.9)
- Identify the parts of a seed. (14.5)
- Identify factors that affect germination. (14.6)
- Identify the structures of a flower. (14.7)

Key Terms

root hair	seed coat
xylem vessel	cotyledon
root pressure	endosperm
capillarity	germinate
transpiration	sexual reproduction
phloem vessel	stamen
cuticle	anther
palisade	filament
vein	petal
stoma (stomata)	pollen
guard cell	pistil
adaptation	stigma
seed	style
embryo	ovary
epicotyl	sepal
hypocotyl	pollination
radicle	

Review

1. Sort the terms in the Key Terms list into the following categories. (The same terms may fit more than one.)

   (a) These terms refer to parts of a leaf.

   (b) These terms refer to parts of a flower.

   (c) These terms refer to parts of a seed.

   (d) These terms refer to water and nutrient transport in plants.

   (e) These terms refer to sexual reproduction in plants.

   (f) You should have one term left that doesn't fit in the above categories. What is it? Write a definition for this term in your own words.

2. (a) List, in order, the structures that carry water from the soil to the leaves of a plant.

   (b) Why is water transport important?

3. Describe the role of root pressure, capillarity, and transpiration in water transport.

4. Explain how guard cells regulate the movement of water and gases in leaves.

5. Explain the importance of the following structures of the leaf.

   (a) a waxy cuticle

   (b) guard cells

   (c) many air spaces

   (d) a layer of cells containing chlorophyll

6. What are the functions of the following parts of a seed?

   (a) the seed coat

   (b) a supply of starch

   (c) the embryo

7. Copy the letters on the diagram of a bean seed in your notebook.

(a) Beside each letter, write the correct label from this list: cotyledon, hypocotyl, epicotyl, embryo, seed coat.

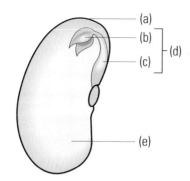

(b) In which structures would you expect to obtain a positive test for starch?

8. Copy the letters on the diagram of a corn seed in your notebook.

(a) Beside each letter, write the correct label from this list: cotyledon, endosperm, radicle, epicotyl, embryo, seed coat.

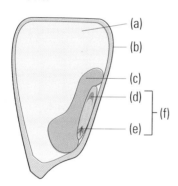

(b) In which structures would you expect to obtain a positive test for starch?

9. (a) What is pollination?

(b) Why is it important to plants?

(c) What roles do wind and animals play in pollination?

10. (a) Why do seeds need to grow at a distance from the parent plant?

(b) What roles do wind and animals play in dispersing seeds?

Problem Solving

11. If you removed the cotyledon of a bean embryo, what would you expect to happen to the growing plant?

Critical Thinking

12. The following experiment was set up to investigate factors that affect water movement in plants.

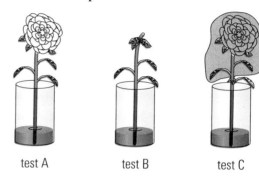

test A   test B   test C

(a) In which test would you expect water to move most rapidly? Give reasons for your prediction.

(b) If red food colouring is used with a white flower, would you expect the flower to change colour? Test your prediction.

(c) If an electrical fan were placed in front of the plants, would you expect the results of the experiment to change? Give reasons for your prediction.

13. A student planted two rows of beans in a garden. Many ragweed plants sprang up near the first row of bean plants. The second row of bean plants grew without any interference from weeds. The student measured the growth rate of both rows of beans and found the plants that grew without weeds grew faster. The student concluded that the ragweed and bean plants must be competing for nutrients.

(a) How could you test this conclusion?

(b) According to the student's conclusion, the slower growth can be explained by competition. Is any other explanation possible?

(c) How would you test your explanation?

Growing Plants

HUMANS DEPEND ON PLANTS FOR FOOD. As the human population has increased, so has the need to produce more food. How can the existing farmland grow more plants? Is there a limit to how much new farmland is available? The best way to start answering these and other questions is to consider how plants grow, what they need to grow, and how best to care for these vital living things.

In this chapter, you will

- measure plant growth,
- discover what plants need to grow,
- diagnose some plant problems, and
- investigate asexual reproduction in plants and its importance to agriculture.

In greenhouses, separate from the environment, scientists discover what plants need to grow. As the picture on the facing page shows, careful control of a plant's environment can produce startling results.

Getting Started

In a Jules Verne novel, *Mysterious Island,* castaways on a deserted island must carefully use all their resources to survive. One castaway has a few wheat seeds in a coat pocket, left over from feeding birds. This wheat becomes an important food source for the next five years. It provides the castaways with flour for bread and feed for livestock.

1. Imagine you have a few grains of wheat. Write down what you think you would need to grow a crop of wheat from these seeds. Your goal is to produce enough wheat to make flour and still have seeds to plant another crop. Arrange the things that you will need in a flow chart that indicates what must be done or found.

2. If you are not sure of some of the details, write down questions that you have. Place question marks in the appropriate places in your flow chart.

3. Add information to your flow chart as you progress through this chapter. You may want to colour-code any additions you make to help you keep track of your progress.

CHALLENGE

Read *Mysterious Island* and find out what the castaways were able to accomplish.

Measuring Plant Growth

I N ORDER FOR THE CASTAWAYS described in the chapter opener to live, they needed the wheat seeds to grow quickly. You discovered in Chapter 14 that plants are adapted to growing best in a particular environment. Can wheat grow on a tropical island? What can you measure to find out if a plant will grow well under certain conditions?

In this investigation, you will measure the growth of plants. In addition, you will consider which parts of the plant contribute most to growth.

Materials

- apron
- 250-mL beaker
- paper towels
- distilled water
- petri dish cover
- 5 germinating seedlings
- permanent marker
- nylon thread
- ruler (mm)
- glass plate or cardboard sheet
- elastic band

Procedure

1 Put on your apron.

2 Prepare a growth chamber by lining a 250-mL beaker with damp paper towel. Add about 20 mL of water to the beaker. Place a petri dish cover over the beaker.

Step 2

3 Select five germinating seedlings that are approximately 4 cm long and reasonably straight. Place them on a dry paper towel to remove excess water.

4 Place a piece of nylon thread on a sheet of paper. Run a permanent marker pen along your thread until the thread has picked up the ink. Use the thread to lightly place a mark every 1 mm along the root of each seedling. Handle the seedlings gently.

✏ (a) Why is it important to use a permanent marker pen?

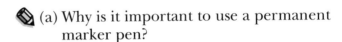

Step 4

5 Cover a glass plate or small piece of cardboard with a paper towel. Use an elastic band to hold the five seedlings in place on the covered plate.

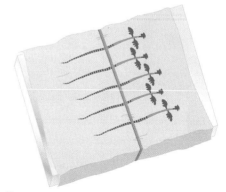

Step 5

6 Place the plate with your seedlings into the growth chamber and leave the chamber in a dark place for 48 h.

Step 6

7 Make a data table like the one below to record your observations. Section 1 is the section closest to the root tip.

Root Growth in Seedlings

Section number	Distance (mm) after 48 h				
	Seedling 1	Seedling 2	Seedling 3	Seedling 4	Seedling 5
1					
2					

8 After 48 h, take one of the seedlings and measure the distance between each pair of ink marks on the root. Remember that your original markings were 1 mm apart.

 (b) Record your measurements in your table.

 (c) Which section of the root showed the most growth?

9 Repeat step 8 for the remaining seedlings.

 (d) Record your measurements in your table.

10 Repeat steps 8 and 9 after 72 h and again after 96 h.

 (e) Note any changes in the root sections that show the most growth.

Questions

1. Make a graph to show which sections of the roots grew the most after 48 h. Plot the average length of each section after 48 h on the y-axis. Plot the section number along the x-axis.

2. Why did you use five seedlings in this experiment instead of only one?

Apply

3. Predict how the growth of seedlings would be affected if nearby soil were sprayed with a chemical that kills cells near the tip of a plant's root.

4. How could you use the techniques from this investigation to compare the effects of two different fertilizers on plant growth?

Extension

5. Remove the root tip from some of the seedlings and compare the growth rate of these seedlings with normal seedlings.

6. Design a method for determining the growth rate of leaves and stems. Plant some of the seedlings remaining from this activity in vermiculite and test your procedure.

7. The type of growth discussed so far makes roots longer; however, roots and stems also grow thicker. In woody plants, stems become thicker as new growth layers are added during the warmer months. Because little growth occurs during the winter months, distinct bands of cells form, called annual rings.

(a) Examine the annual rings in a cross-section of a tree stem and estimate its age. One thin ring and one thick ring equal one year's growth.

(b) Provide a hypothesis to explain the observation that some annual rings are thicker than others.

(c) If you were shown a cross-section of wood from an unknown kind of tree and noticed that it had no annual rings, where would you think this tree grew? Why would you think so?

What Plants Need to Grow

ENVIRONMENTAL CONDITIONS that are just right for some plants may be completely wrong for others. For example, if you gave a cactus plant the same amount of water that a tomato plant needs, the cactus would die. In order to find out more about the conditions plants need, researchers (and gardeners) have performed many experiments on plant growth. In this case study, you will examine some of their results.

More Carbon Dioxide

Plants require carbon dioxide for photosynthesis. They obtain this carbon dioxide from the air. Would providing more carbon dioxide help a plant grow? Examine the diagram that shows lettuces grown in a greenhouse with added carbon dioxide and lettuces grown in a greenhouse in a normal atmosphere.

Lettuces grown in greenhouses. Left, CO_2 was added to the air. Right, air was normal.

(a) Describe any differences between the lettuces grown in different amounts of carbon dioxide.

(b) Provide a hypothesis that explains the differences.

Lights, Action!

Examine the diagram showing two plants of the same species that have been exposed to different amounts of light. The plant on the right received less light than the plant on the left.

bright light   dim light

(c) Describe any differences between the two plants.

(d) Explain any differences you observe, referring to the process of photosynthesis.

Too Bright

Although all plants need sunlight for photosynthesis, different kinds of plants require different amounts of sunlight. For example, geraniums normally grow in relatively dim light, which is why they are useful in shady parts of a garden. The geranium on the right has received too much light.

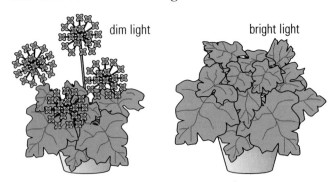

dim light   bright light

(e) Examine the geraniums in the illustration. What are some of the effects of too much light?

(f) Suggest an experimental procedure that would allow you to determine the best amount of light for plant growth.

Aerating Roots

These tomato plants were grown in a solution of water and nutrients (hydroponic gardening). Air was bubbled through the water of the plant on the right.

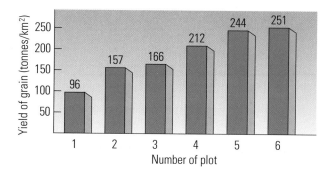 (g) Describe any differences between the two tomato plants.

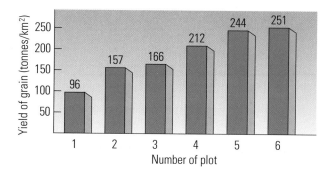 (h) Propose a hypothesis to explain the differences.

Nutrients

Nutrients are substances an organism needs in order to be healthy and to grow. Among the nutrients needed by plants are nitrogen, phosphorus, and potassium. Plant roots absorb these nutrients from the soil. Nitrogen encourages green, leafy growth. Phosphorus helps seeds develop and roots to grow. Potassium stimulates flowering and fruit growth. The diagram below shows the results of an experiment in which different fertilizers were added to wheat.

Plot	Fertilizer
1	none
2	nitrogen only
3	nitrogen and phosphorus
4	nitrogen, phosphorus, and potassium
5	farmyard manure (organic fertilizer)
6	nitrogen, phosphorus, potassium, sodium, and magnesium (complete inorganic fertilizer)

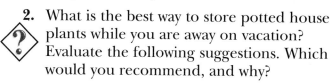 (i) In which plot was the crop yield lowest?

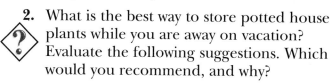 (j) Provide a possible explanation for the low crop yield.

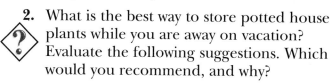 (k) Compare the crop yield for plots 4 and 5. What conclusions could you draw from the data?

Questions

1. (a) What is a nutrient?

   (b) Name one nutrient that plants obtain from soil.

   (c) Describe how this nutrient affects the growth of a plant.

2. What is the best way to store potted house plants while you are away on vacation? Evaluate the following suggestions. Which would you recommend, and why?

   (a) Place the pots in a large pan of water so the roots will stay wet.

   (b) Put the plants in a dark cupboard, so they will not need as much water.

   (c) Put the plants and pots into plastic bags. Keep them in a sunny location.

   (d) Put the plants and pots into plastic bags. Keep them in a bright, but not sunny location.

3. Design an experiment of your own to test the effect of one of the following factors on the growth of plants: gravity, sound, amount of light, colour of light, presence of other plants, temperature, movement, grazing by herbivores, or another factor of your choice. In your design, explain what you would measure to obtain data on the plants' growth.

ASK YOURSELF

Look back at your flow chart from the Getting Started activity at the beginning of this chapter. Add any new information or details you have learned.

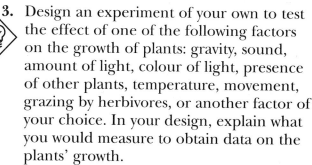

Yield of grain (tonnes/km²) / Number of plot

96 157 166 212 244 251

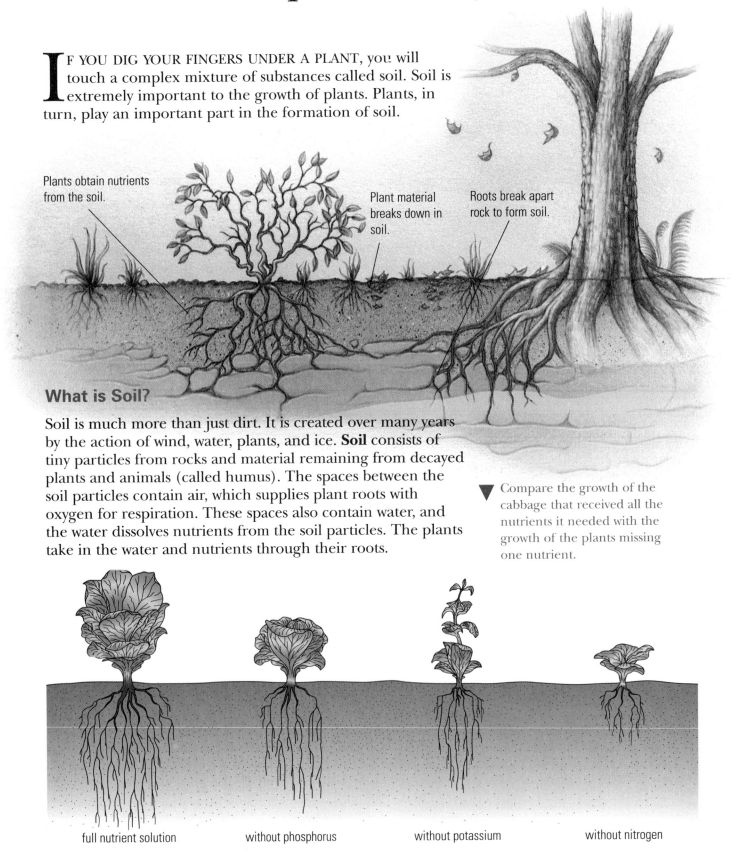

The Importance of Soil

IF YOU DIG YOUR FINGERS UNDER A PLANT, you will touch a complex mixture of substances called soil. Soil is extremely important to the growth of plants. Plants, in turn, play an important part in the formation of soil.

Plants obtain nutrients from the soil.

Plant material breaks down in soil.

Roots break apart rock to form soil.

What is Soil?

Soil is much more than just dirt. It is created over many years by the action of wind, water, plants, and ice. **Soil** consists of tiny particles from rocks and material remaining from decayed plants and animals (called humus). The spaces between the soil particles contain air, which supplies plant roots with oxygen for respiration. These spaces also contain water, and the water dissolves nutrients from the soil particles. The plants take in the water and nutrients through their roots.

▼ Compare the growth of the cabbage that received all the nutrients it needed with the growth of the plants missing one nutrient.

full nutrient solution   without phosphorus   without potassium   without nitrogen

Hydroponics is a technology in which plants are grown in water, with nutrients and air added. To create your own hydroponic garden, fill pots with vermiculite or sand. Plant lettuce seeds in the vermiculite. Obtain a small amount of hydroponic nutrients from a gardening store. Add them to the water as instructed on the label.

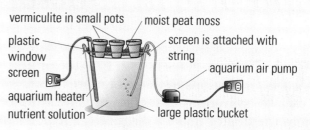

vermiculite in small pots
moist peat moss
plastic window screen
screen is attached with string
aquarium air pump
aquarium heater
nutrient solution
large plastic bucket

The Cycle of Nutrients

If you use a microscope to examine a sample of fresh soil, you will see an incredible number of tiny living organisms. Most of these organisms are decomposers. As they break down dead plant and animal material, they release nutrients into the soil. These nutrients are then picked up by plant roots and used to build new plant material. If this recycling of nutrients did not take place, eventually there would be no nutrients left in the soil for plants to use.

Improving the Soil for Plants

The formation of a thick layer of nutrient-rich soil takes hundreds of years. Each successive generation of plants adds some nutrients to the soil. Roots help break rock into smaller particles. The layer of soil becomes deeper.

When people harvest plants, this process is interrupted. The plants have been removed, so there is no dead plant material to release nutrients. Soil that is not held together by plants may wash or blow away (erosion). Every year, the roots must start at the surface again. The roots cannot break up the lower layers of rock, so the soil cannot deepen. Farming can improve the soil, but much of a farmer's work only repairs or prevents damage. Adding fertilizer replaces missing nutrients; plowing grain stalks back into the soil adds humus; planting trees around fields can reduce wind erosion; mulching prevents the soil from drying out; deep tilling introduces air to the soil; and terracing hillsides prevents water runoff that would increase erosion.

In contour farming, the fields are plowed across the normal flow of water to prevent erosion. How do you think it works?

The Plant Doctor

WHEN A PERSON IS ILL, a doctor asks questions to find out more about symptoms of the illness. The symptoms help the doctor make a **diagnosis**, a hypothesis about the cause of the illness.

Symptoms, the signs of an illness or problem, can also be used to make a diagnosis of plant problems. For example, plants with yellowish leaves may not be receiving enough light. In this investigation, you will diagnose plant problems by using a two-part key. The problem might be a disease due to an infection by a virus or bacterium. Or the problem may be due to an insect pest. Once the problem has been correctly identified, you can find out what to do to cure the problem.

Materials

- unhealthy plants
- diagnosis flow chart (pages 430-433)

Procedure

1 Use the chart on the following pages to analyze the symptoms and identify the disease or problem that is affecting a plant. Provide a diagnosis, and prepare a list of recommended treatments.

(a) Be prepared to present your findings to the class.

(b) Do other groups agree with your findings?

Questions

1. Name two symptoms that would indicate that a plant is suffering from a disease or pest.

2. Why might one symptom not be enough to diagnose what is wrong with a plant?

Apply

3. Diagnose the health of any plants you have at home or school.

Symptom 1

Is the plant drooping?

IF NO →

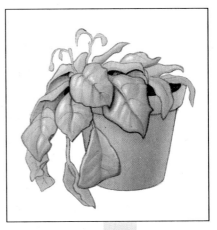

↓ **IF YES**

Touch the soil.
If it is wet
GO TO DIAGNOSIS 1
If it is dry
GO TO DIAGNOSIS 2

Diagnosis 1

The roots are dying of suffocation and rot due to too much water.

Treatment

Let the plant dry out; ensure the roots have proper drainage and air. If the rot is bad, remove the plant from its pot, cut off damaged roots, and plant in fresh soil.

Diagnosis 2

The plant has not been watered properly.

Treatment

Water the plant. Different plants require different amounts of water. Learn the plant's requirements, and keep it watered properly.

Symptom 2

Are the leaves turning yellow?

 **IF NO**

 IF YES

If the plant has been in bright light
GO TO DIAGNOSIS 1

If the plant has been in dim light
GO TO DIAGNOSIS 2

If the level of light is correct for the plant, and it has been fertilized recently
GO TO DIAGNOSIS 3

If the plant has not been fertilized recently
GO TO DIAGNOSIS 4

Diagnosis 1

Too much light has damaged the plant's chlorophyll.

Treatment

Move the plant to a less bright location.

Diagnosis 2

The leaves are not getting enough light to make chlorophyll.

Treatment

Move the plant to a brighter location.

Diagnosis 3

Too much fertilizer in the soil is drawing water out of the roots by osmosis.

Treatment

Rinse the soil with plenty of water, and allow it to drain.

Diagnosis 4

The plant needs magnesium, manganese, or iron to make chlorophyll.

Treatment

Apply a fertilizer that contains these minerals, as directed by the package.

Symptom 3

Are there coloured spots on the leaves?

IF NO

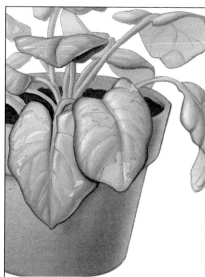

IF YES

GO TO DIAGNOSIS

Diagnosis

A virus may be attacking the plant.

Treatment

Isolate the plant. Remove and dispose of any infected leaves. If you have handled the plant, wash your hands thoroughly before touching other plants. If the spots reappear, you may have to destroy the plant.

Symptom 4

Are there furry patches or black spots on the leaves?

IF NO

IF YES

GO TO DIAGNOSIS

Diagnosis

The spots could be caused by a fungus.

Treatment

Remove the leaves with spots, and dispose of them. If the spots return, dust the plant with a fungicide, following directions on the package. A mixture of water, baking soda (15 mL/L), and a small amount of soap will also kill fungus, if it is sprayed on the leaves.

Symptom 5

Are there holes like windows in the leaves, with a flimsy, transparent covering?

IF NO

Symptom 6

Are there big holes in the leaves, or notches around the outside of the leaves?

IF NO

Symptom 7

Does the plant show none of the previous symptoms, but just looks generally sick — has stunted leaves, or is losing leaves, or droops at the tips?

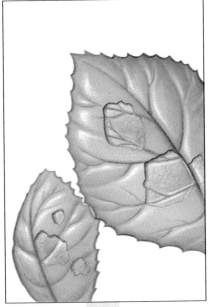

IF YES

GO TO DIAGNOSIS

IF YES

GO TO DIAGNOSIS

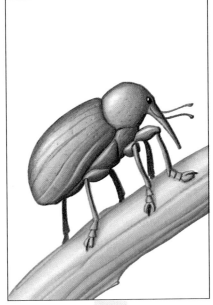

IF YES

GO TO DIAGNOSIS

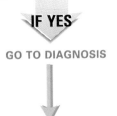

Diagnosis

Leaf miners are eating the leaves from inside. The leaf miners could be the larvae of moths, flies, or beetles.

Treatment

Apply an appropriate insecticide to the soil around the plant, where it can be absorbed by the roots. (Putting insecticide on the leaves will have no effect — the leaf miners are protected by the cuticle of the leaf.)

Diagnosis

The leaves are probably being eaten by caterpillars (the larvae of moths or butterflies) or beetles, such as the weevil.

Treatment

Remove the insects.

Diagnosis

The plant may have a pest infestation. There are many pests that live on the sap in the phloem of plants.

In all cases, isolate the affected plant while you are treating it. Examine the plant closely to identify which pest is on your plant. (You may want to check other plants in the area for the same pest.)

Diagnosis 1

If you shake the plant, and a cloud of small insects fly up, the plant has whitefly.
Go to treatment

Treatment

Let the whiteflies return to the plant. Without disturbing the plant, cover it and its pot with a plastic bag. Put a "no-pest" strip inside the bag, or spray in some pyrethrum powder. Tie the bag closed and leave it overnight. Repeat every five days until the whiteflies are gone.

Diagnosis 2

If you find winged insects on the leaves or buds, the plant has bugs.
Go to treatment

Treatment

You may be able to remove the bugs by hand. If not, dust the plant with diatomaceous earth. Diatomaceous earth contains the sharp, ground-up fossils of small organisms. It kills insects when it cuts open their outer protective layer or damages soft parts of their bodies. Alternatively, spray the plant with a general insecticide.

Diagnosis 3

Small lumps of a white cottony, waxy, or spittle-like substance indicate mealy bugs. They create small tents to protect themselves while they suck sap.
Go to treatment

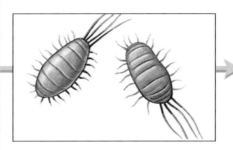

Treatment

Insecticide will not penetrate the protective wax the mealy bugs have made. You can remove the mealy bugs by hand, or dip a cotton swab or small paintbrush in rubbing alcohol and paint each insect with the alcohol. This treatment must be repeated every few days, until no more mealy bugs are seen.

Diagnosis 4

If you notice masses of small, soft insects on growing shoots or on the underside of new leaves, your plant has aphids.
Go to treatment

Treatment

Spray the plant with soapy water. Alternatively, run your fingers over the affected areas of the plant, squeezing just hard enough to kill the aphids. Check every few days for aphids and repeat treatment if necessary.

Diagnosis 5

If you find a web of tiny, fine threads on a leaf or bud, your plant has spider mites. (You will not be able to see the actual mites, they are too small.)
Go to treatment

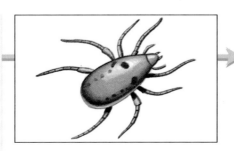

Treatment

There are pesticides specially made for spider mites; follow directions on the package. You may be able to prevent the mites from returning by periodically spraying the plant with water to keep it moist.

Diagnosis 6

If you notice small lumps that look like scales on the stem or leaf stalks, your plant has scale insects.
Go to treatment

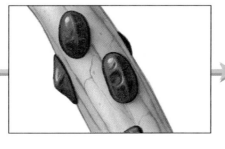

Treatment

Dip a cotton swab or paintbrush in rubbing alcohol, and paint each of the scale insects. Every few days, examine the plant for more scale insects and repeat treatment if necessary.

Producing New Plants Without Seeds

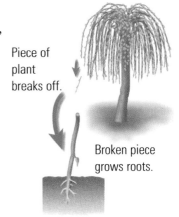

Piece of plant breaks off.

Broken piece grows roots.

A new plant is formed.

I N CHAPTER 14, YOU LEARNED how plants use sexual reproduction to produce seeds. Each seed is a new individual, with a combination of characteristics from both parents. Seeds have the ability to wait until conditions are right for germination to take place. And seeds contain a source of food to nourish the early growth of the new plant.

Many plants also reproduce without using seeds. In the asexual reproduction of plants, a part of the parent plant grows into a new individual. For example, if you take a leaf from an African violet and place it in water, roots and more leaves will eventually grow from the stalk of the leaf. A new individual will be formed.

The new plant produced by asexual reproduction is genetically identical to its parent. If the parent grew well in its environment, the offspring will probably also grow well. Asexual reproduction is a way that successful plants can rapidly reproduce themselves. For this reason, people who grow plants for food or other products often prefer to use asexual reproduction instead of seeds to produce new plants. They can be confident that the new plants will have the same desirable characteristics as the parent.

▲

Asexual reproduction in plants. The part that breaks off could be a leaf, a twig, or a piece of root.

Roots and Stems

Often, a home gardener forgets to remove every carrot or potato from the garden in autumn. The following spring, a new carrot or potato plant pushes up through the soil. Carrots and potatoes are examples of plants that store food in their roots. As the air cools and days become shorter, these plants become less active. The top of the plant dies when temperatures drop below freezing. But the food-containing organ, the root, remains. When the soil warms again in spring, a new plant, or several new plants, will grow—nourished by the food in the root.

Many plants that appear to die back and grow again in spring are actually using this form of asexual reproduction.

▼

Side stem (runner) grows out from the base of the main stem.

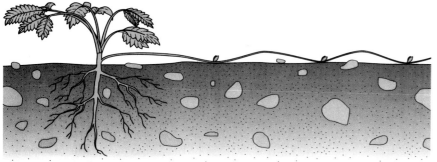

New plants develop from the lateral buds of the runner.

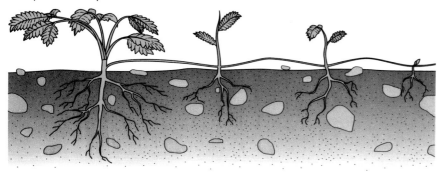

Some plants, such as the strawberry, send out runners along the surface of the soil. Every so often, roots grow downward out of the runner, and leaves begin to form above the ground.

Each eye of a potato can grow into a new plant.

SELF CHECK

6. What is the difference between asexual and sexual reproduction in plants?

7. (a) What are the advantages of asexual reproduction to the parent plant?

(b) What are the advantages to a farmer of using asexual reproduction to produce more plants?

8. A seed contains food for the embryo. What is the source of food for the asexually produced offspring of the following plants?

(a) potato

(b) strawberry

(c) tulip

9. An international organization is collecting seeds of rare and endangered plants, including plants that are the ancestors of food plants used today. The seeds are being stored in a vault in case any of these plants become extinct. Why do you think this organization collects seeds and not other parts of these plants?

TRY THIS

Choosing a Technique for Asexual Reproduction

Several methods of propagating plants using asexual reproduction are available. Certain methods work better for some types of plants. In this activity, work in a group to compare two different techniques for propagating plants.

Choose a plant your group wishes to propagate. (You may find research on the plant useful, to find out how it is propagated commercially or by gardeners.)

• Sketch or photograph the original plant.

• Which parts of the plant grow fastest? Why might they be used for asexual reproduction?

Select two different techniques for propagating your plant. Choose from stem cuttings, leaf cuttings, leaf section cuttings, root division, runners, air layering.

 If a CD-ROM resource is available, you can find out more about each technique by entering its name.

• Keep a daily record of growth, comparing both methods of propagation that you have chosen.

Landscape Design

LANDSCAPING CAN MAKE A dramatic difference to the appearance of a home, school, or other building. However, poorly planned landscaping can create problems. For example, some landscaping plans do not take into account that shrubs and trees continue to grow. Trees with deep roots can crack gas pipes and water pipes. Other problems can occur if plants are chosen for appearance regardless of their ability to grow under local conditions. Plants that cannot survive will need to be replaced. Plants that are too successful may spread and choke out others. The key to good landscape design is to prevent problems while satisfying the needs of the property owner.

Materials

- nursery catalogues

Procedure

1 In a group, discuss landscape problems 1 to 4, shown in the illustrations.

(a) Identify each problem.

(b) Propose a solution for each problem.

Problem 1

Problem 3

Problem 2

Problem 4

2 Your group will be given a diagram that shows a front and a top view of a new school building. Work with your group to prepare a landscape design for the property around the school. Use nursery catalogues to find out what plants grow well in your area. Consider the following hints provided by a professional landscape designer.

Your design should use plants to do the following:

- provide shady sitting areas

- provide a natural area where classes can study

- provide shelter from north winds

- provide fields for sports

- improve the appearance of the building

- keep young children from entering the parking lot

Your design should not include plants that do the following:

- block the view from windows and doors

- block the view for cars and buses entering and leaving the parking lot

- touch or hang over power or telephone lines

- hang over into neighbouring property

3 Do the following and present your design to your class.

(c) Make a large drawing or model of your design, showing top and front views.

(d) Prepare a legend (list) showing the types of plants being used.

(e) State reasons for each of your plant selections.

4 As a class, rate the designs of each group using the criteria from step 2. (You may decide that a combination of designs will work best.)

Questions

1. What was the most important factor to consider when choosing plants to include in your design? Why?

2. (a) Give an example of a design idea that your group discussed and decided not to use.

   (b) Why did you reject this idea?

Apply

3. What types of activities affected your design? Explain.

Extension

4. Redesign the landscape for a section of your schoolyard. In your design, estimate the cost of the plants. Consider who would be responsible for caring for the plants. Present your design to the student council and principal of your school. Make it happen!

5. Create a garden without planting one. There are several computer simulations that allow you to input the dimensions of the garden, soil type, and amount of shade to help you plan what to grow. Some programs even show how the garden changes as shrubs and trees mature.

Agriculture and Food Production

IMAGINE YOUR CLASSROOM with twice the number of students. Would everyone have a place to sit? Now imagine your lunchroom with twice as many people, but with the same amount of food. Without question, the lunchroom would have problems.

The problem facing agriculture is far greater than that of an overcrowded school. More than 5 billion people inhabit this planet. It is estimated that this number will nearly double within 50 years. The most dramatic increases will occur in areas that are already crowded.

Land Shortage

Only about 11% of the Earth's land is suitable for growing crops. Many experts suggest that modern technology will not be able to increase the amount of suitable farmland. For example, the climates of some areas, such as tundra and alpine meadows, are too severe for food plants.

Strategies for Increasing Food Production

One method of increasing the amount of food produced is to increase the amount of land used to grow plants. Adding water to otherwise dry areas, called **irrigation**, has allowed farming in former deserts.

Unfortunately, the irrigation of arid land is not without problems. Most water used for irrigation contains small amounts of salt. During the heat of the day, some of the water evaporates from the surface of the soil, leaving the salt behind. After years of watering, a layer of salt is created. Plants put in this salty soil actually dry up, because the salt draws water from their roots by osmosis.

Improvements in agriculture in the 1960s greatly increased farmers' ability to produce food. Unfortunately, the population has also been growing.

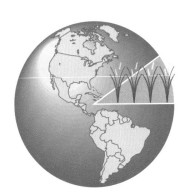

▶ Of the world's 13.1 billion ha of land, only 1.4 billion ha can be used for crops.

Irrigation allows plants to be grown on arid land.

Fertilizers

Earlier in the chapter, you read about using fertilizers to improve plant growth. Nitrogen, phosphorus, and potassium fertilizers were first widely used in the 1960s and 1970s to dramatically increase food production.

However, using fertilizers causes problems as well. Excess fertilizer can seep into lakes and rivers. There, it stimulates the growth of algae. In turn, the algae die and are decomposed by bacteria. The bacteria use up oxygen from the water, and fish begin to die.

Competing with Pests

A staggering amount of food is lost each year due to pests. Pests include rats and insects that eat crops, as well as weeds that compete with the crop plants for nutrients. So another strategy for increasing food production is to reduce the effects of pests. **Pesticides** are substances that kill or harm one or more pests. However, like other technologies, pesticides are not without problems.

Some pesticides also kill beneficial insects, including those needed to pollinate crop plants.

And, pesticides may not continue to work. Scientists have found that many insects are developing a **resistance** to certain pesticides: every application of the pesticide seems to kill fewer of the pests.

How can this type of pollution be the result of farming?

SELF CHECK

10. Why is the need to increase food production such a great concern?

11. During the 1960s food production increased rapidly. What technologies contributed to this increase?

12. What limitations do the following technologies have in providing a solution to feeding the world?

(a) irrigation

(b) fertilizers

(c) pesticides

13. Cotton has become extremely popular as a fabric for clothing. Many countries have encouraged their farmers to switch from growing food plants for their own people to growing cotton to sell to other countries. Do you think this is a good idea? Why or why not? What could you do about this trend?

MATH-LINK

Calculating Population Density

The following data are taken from a United Nations study.

Farmland Available, by Country

Country	Population (millions)	Total area (1000 km²)	Amount of good farmland (1000 km²)
Canada	26	10 000	400
Netherlands	15	34	23
China	1072	9 450	1040
Ethiopia	45	1 209	121

(a) Calculate the number of people per square kilometre (population density) in each country.

(b) Calculate the number of people per square kilometre of good farmland in each country.

Water for Sale

HAVE YOU EVER THOUGHT of the water in a lake or stream as something to be traded or bought? You may need to soon. Your generation may be the Canadians who decide whether to sell some of Canada's fresh water to other parts of the world.

In Search of Plenty

Canada's abundance of water is becoming attractive to other countries for one reason in particular: to help grow food. As you learned in this chapter, most areas with ideal conditions for plant growth are already being used for farming. Yet as the human population has increased, so has the need for more farmland. In 1960, the world's population was about 3 billion. Today, it has almost doubled to 5.3 billion. By 2030, scientists predict, the population will grow to 8.9 billion; by 2050, to 10 billion. Many people face starvation unless more food can be grown.

Irrigation

One way of increasing the amount of food grown has been to use irrigation to bring water to otherwise dry areas. For example, in Uzbekistan, in what was the Soviet Union, massive systems of dams and canals diverted water that used to flow into the Aral Sea. Millions of hectares of land became productive farmland. But huge irrigation projects like this can also be disastrous. The Aral Sea, which was the fourth-largest body of inland water, began to dry up. Scientists predict it will disappear entirely by 2010. The fishing industry on the sea has died—the last fish was caught in 1983. To make matters worse, after a few years, large sections of the irrigated fields became crusted with salt. Crop production, which increased dramatically

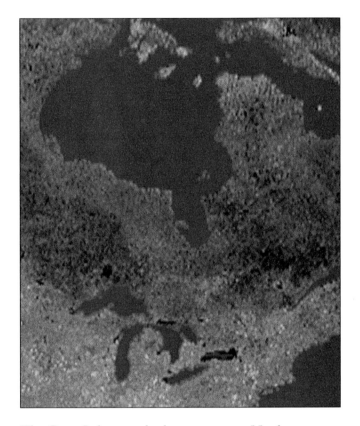

The Great Lakes are the largest group of freshwater lakes in the world. They would become even larger if a huge irrigation project connects them to a new lake in James Bay.

after the irrigation projects began, has since fallen sharply.

Despite these problems, it is still thought that irrigation is an effective way to grow more food. This makes Canada's vast water supply an important resource not only to Canadians, but to the rest of the world. How could Canada's water be transported and sold? Two projects have already been suggested.

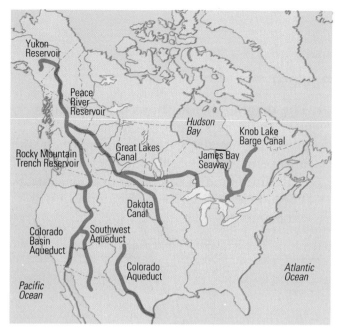

Several huge projects, including canals and aqueducts (red), have been suggested to divert water south.

GRAND Diversion

The GRAND project is a proposal to dam James Bay, slowly converting it into a large, freshwater lake. This new lake would then be connected to the Great Lakes. The water could then be sold south of the border.

Rocky Mountain Trench

Thirsty farms in California could benefit from a proposed trench along the Rocky Mountains. This trench would be a huge freshwater canal, carrying water from the Mackenzie River southward.

Understanding the Author

1. What does the increasing human population of the Earth have to do with selling water?

2. What problems can be caused by irrigation?

3. Describe the two proposals to divert Canada's water. Why have these projects been proposed?

Proposal

James Bay should be dammed and the water diverted south. A trench should be dug along the Rocky Mountains to divert water from the Mackenzie River. The water from both projects should be sold for irrigation in the United States and Mexico.

The Benefits

Opinion of a citizen The sale of fresh water could provide Canada with many economic benefits. We already sell other natural resources, so why not water?

Opinion of California vegetable grower Canada, the United States, and Mexico are part of a free-trade agreement that is designed to benefit all countries. If all that fresh water flows into the Arctic Ocean, it helps no one. Water must be diverted to where it can be used to grow food, and do the most good.

The Risks

Opinion of a wildlife biologist Projects like GRAND will have a major impact on wildlife. Many species of marine organisms will be destroyed. In addition, a channel between the new lake and the Great Lakes will serve as a highway for new predators and parasites. This could change the food chain in the Great Lakes.

Opinion of a climatologist Water that flows north helps warm the Arctic Ocean. Diverting this water southward would change Canada's climate. There could be longer winters and shorter growing seasons in the north.

What Do You Think?

4. Should large-scale irrigation projects be started?

5. Would you be in favour of selling Canada's water? Why or why not?

Key Outcomes

Now that you have completed the chapter, can you do the following? If not, review the sections indicated.

- Measure the growth (15.1)
  of plant roots and
  interpret the result.

- List things that plants (15.2)
  need to grow.

- Use a key to diagnose (15.4)
  and treat plant problems.

- Describe asexual (15.5)
  reproduction in plants
  and its significance
  to agriculture.

- List and explain (15.5)
  three techniques for
  propagating plants.

- Prepare a landscape (15.6)
  design and assess other
  landscape designs.

- Evaluate the limitations (15.7, 15.8)
  of technological solutions
  to agricultural problems.

- Explain why plants are (15.6, 15.7,
  important to people.   15.8)

Key Terms

nutrient

soil

hydroponics

diagnosis

symptom

irrigation

pesticide

resistance

Review

1. The diagram below shows the apparatus used in an experiment to measure plant growth. Copy the letters from the diagram into your notebook. Beside each letter, write the name of the piece of apparatus. Then, briefly describe its function in this experiment.

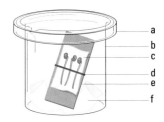

2. Explain why a plant needs to obtain each of the following factors in order to grow and be healthy.

   (a) carbon dioxide

   (b) sunlight

   (c) water

   (d) nitrogen

   (e) phosphorus

   (f) potassium

   (g) oxygen

3. Write the correct version of each of the sentences below in your notebook.

   (a) A geranium exposed to lots of very bright light grew more flowers than a geranium exposed to much dimmer light.

   (b) Tomato plants grew better in an atmosphere with carbon monoxide added to it.

   (c) Bubbles of air in the water around a plant's roots provide a source of carbon dioxide for photosynthesis.

   (d) Adding a fertilizer that contains mostly nitrogen will help produce more flowers on garden plants.

4. (a) What is the difference between sexual and asexual reproduction in plants?

(b) If you had a beautiful rose plant and wished to grow more roses of exactly the same colour, which form of reproduction would you use? Explain your reasoning.

(c) If you had a beautiful rose plant and wished to send offspring from this plant to several friends, which form of reproduction would you use? Explain your reasoning.

5. Identify two common landscaping problems that may arise because of poor planning.

6. When plants are removed from river banks, the water soon becomes cloudy with silt and debris.

(a) Explain what is happening.

(b) How did the plants prevent this from happening?

(c) How could you solve the problem?

7. Make a three-column chart in your notebook with these headings: Technology, Benefit, Risk. Complete your chart for these technologies.

(a) irrigation

(b) fertilizers

(c) pesticides

Problem Solving

8. Suppose you are going to plant a garden in which you hope to grow flowers or vegetables. How could you improve the soil so the plants will grow well?

9. Diagnose what might be wrong with plants that have the following symptoms.

(a) The plant droops, yet the soil feels wet.

(b) There are furry white spots on the leaves.

(c) The leaves are yellowish and are dropping off the plant.

(d) A cluster of tiny green insects swarms on the young plant.

10. These statements were found in a gardening book. For each statement, design an experiment that would allow you to test whether it is true.

(a) To make a tall plant shorter, roots can be developed part-way up the stem of a growing plant.

(b) Removing the top 1 cm of a plant will result in a short, bushy plant.

(c) To keep a plant flowering, cut off all the old flowers that are producing seeds.

Critical Thinking

11. Each kind of plant has adaptations that help it grow better in certain environments than in others.

(a) List some reasons why people try to grow plants in environments to which they are not adapted.

(b) What techniques can be used to help plants grow in otherwise unsuitable environments?

(c) What do you need to know about the plant in order to help it grow?

12. There are many different kinds of plants living on the Earth today. Unfortunately, due to human activities, some plants are becoming extinct before they are even identified and studied. What might this mean in terms of the following?

(a) medicines made from plants

(b) natural ecosystems

(c) future food supplies

ASK YOURSELF

Examine the flow chart you made in the Getting Started activity at the beginning of this chapter. Add any information you have gained since you started. List any questions you still have.

Farming and CO₂ Levels

DR. ROWAN SAGE, a researcher at the University of Toronto, studies how plants such as wheat live and grow under different environmental conditions. Because he looks at whole ecosystems rather than plants alone, his work includes investigating how plants may affect other organisms, including humans.

◀ Dr. Sage and his students are increasing people's understanding about the past and the future of agriculture.

Q. Dr. Sage, I understand that your research involves measuring carbon dioxide levels. What is important about these levels?

A. Experiments involving increasing the amount of carbon dioxide in the air can show whether more carbon dioxide will cause plants to grow more quickly. In fact, the entire planet is undergoing this type of experiment right now. Human activities such as industry and deforestation are increasing the amount of carbon dioxide in the air. Since Canada became a country, the amount of carbon dioxide in the atmosphere has gone from 275 ppm to today's level of 350 ppm. Over the next century, we may be facing double or triple this amount.

Q. What do you think will happen to plants?

A. We know from experiments that increasing the amount of carbon dioxide does increase the amount of photosynthesis a plant can perform. This in turn stimulates the growth of a plant and the number of seeds and fruits it produces. But the situation on a world-wide scale is more complex. For example, some kinds of plants survive better than others when the amount of carbon dioxide in the air is low.

By examining samples of ancient ice from the polar ice caps, we can measure how much carbon dioxide was in the air in the past. We know that this amount has changed many times during Earth's history. I think we will discover that as the levels of atmospheric carbon dioxide changed, so did the productivity of plants in ecosystems. And changes in the productivity of plants would have had significant effects on organisms that depend upon plants.

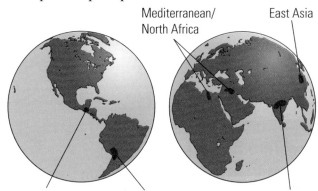

One of the questions Dr. Sage wants to answer is why agriculture began at the same time in these parts of the world.

Q. You have also developed a hypothesis concerning the changing amounts of carbon dioxide in the past and agriculture. Can you explain your ideas?

A. Around 15 000 years ago, the amount of carbon dioxide in the air was 200 ppm, which is relatively low. There is no evidence of agriculture at this time. But shortly after this, the amount of carbon dioxide rose to 270 ppm. This was just before the time when the earliest signs of agriculture appeared. I've hypothesized that the rise in carbon dioxide meant that plants were able to grow more rapidly. Rapidly growing plants produce more food. This made it more likely that agriculture would be successful. For the first time, people could stay in one place and grow enough food.

Q. How are you testing your ideas?

A. We obtained seeds of the early, wild type of wheat from the Germ Plasm Bank in Ottawa. The bank is a storehouse of seeds and plant material—many from plants now extinct in the wild. These seeds are being grown in different amounts of carbon dioxide. We'll measure the growth of these plants to test the hypothesis.

Q. Why should we care about how plants grew thousands of years ago?

A. As I said earlier, we are part of an unplanned experiment in which human activities are increasing the amount of carbon dioxide in the atmosphere. We need to know as much as possible about what may happen to plants because of this change.

Tree Farming

Plant cells can be powerful tools in the forestry industry. Dr. Trevor Thorpe, who studies conifer tree embryos, has found a way to grow up to 200 trees from just one seed. In his laboratory, he takes the embryo from the seed of a particularly strong, healthy tree, and places it in a special sterile nutrient solution. It produces hundreds of tiny embryos. Many of these grow into plantlets, which grow into trees of the same high quality as the parent.

Dr. Thorpe's interest began when studying fruit trees as a young man. He wanted to know why new plants grew from cuttings taken from very young trees, but not from cuttings taken from fully grown trees. To find the answer, he studied how plants function, and now conducts his research by studying trees used in the forestry industry. Dr. Thorpe enjoys satisfying his curiosity, but his research is also useful, and that's a bonus.

Dr. Trevor Thorpe is a professor of botany at the University of Calgary. In his laboratory, he grows new plants from plant cells.

N OW THAT YOU HAVE COMPLETED Chapters 13, 14, and 15, you can assess how much you have learned about Green Plants by trying these questions.
Before you begin, you may find it useful to return to the Chapter Reviews. There, you will find lists of Key Outcomes and Key Terms. Read these to ensure that you understand the main points and the important vocabulary of the chapters. If necessary, look back at the appropriate sections in the text, which are listed with the Key Outcomes.

Write your answers to the questions in your notebook.

True/False

For each of the following, write T if the statement is true. If the statement is false, rewrite it to make it true.

1. During photosynthesis, plants use oxygen and release carbon dioxide.

2. Plants store chemical energy in the form of starch.

3. A green plant kept in the dark will use oxygen and produce carbon dioxide.

4. If a green plant and a small animal are placed in a bell jar in a well-lit room, they will compete for the carbon dioxide in the bell jar.

5. Chlorophyll is necessary for photosynthesis.

6. Xylem vessels carry water from the roots to the leaves of a plant.

7. A plant kept in the dark will have more starch in the leaves than a plant kept in the light.

8. Root pressure alone is responsible for pushing water 100 m up a Douglas fir tree.

9. The cotyledon is the source of nutrients for the growing plant embryo.

Completion

Copy the following sentences, filling in each blank with the word or phrase that correctly completes the sentence. Use the words from this list: hydroponics, stomata, anther, transpiration, nitrogen, zygote, seed, asexual reproduction, tuber, oxygen, carbon dioxide, chlorophyll, xylem, phloem. (You will not need to use all of the words.)

10. The ▮ vessels carry nutrients from the leaf toward the roots.

11. The pores in the leaf that allow for gas exchange are called ▮.

12. The union of pollen and egg cells results in the formation of a ▮.

13. The process of ▮ is identified by the loss of water from a leaf.

14. The growing of plants in water without soil is called ▮.

15. Growing plants from stem cuttings is a form of ▮.

16. A product of respiration is ▮.

17. A product of photosynthesis is ▮.

18. The green pigment found in leaves and stems is ▮.

19. Nutrients for a potato are stored in the ▮.

Matching

Copy the numbers of the descriptions given below. Beside each number, write the word or phrase from the right column that best fits the description. (You will not need to use all of the words.)

20. chlorophyll is found in this organelle
21. control the opening and closing of stomata
22. plants are eaten by insects, which in turn are eaten by birds
23. the pollen reaches the egg cell of a plant, producing a zygote
24. non-cellular covering of leaves, which reduces water loss
25. a force caused by the attraction of water molecules to one another
26. part of the female reproductive structure of the plant
27. the process by which plants and animals use oxygen and glucose to provide cell energy

A food chain
B glucose
C respiration
D chloroplast
E guard cells
F cohesion
G pollination
H pistil
I cuticle
J anther

Multiple Choice

Write the letter of the best answer for each of the following questions. Write only one answer for each.

28. In this diagram of a bean seed, which labelled area holds the greatest amount of starch?

    A 1   D 4
    B 2   E 5
    C 3

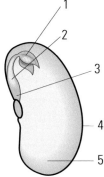

29. Two plants were kept in different conditions. A leaf was removed from each plant, boiled in ethanol, and tested with iodine solution. The following observations were recorded.

Plant	Observation after boiling in ethanol	Observation after iodine added
plant X	pale yellow colour	pale yellow-orange colour
plant Y	pale yellow colour	blue-black colour

Which conclusion is correct?

A Plants X and Y lack nitrogen.
B Plants X and Y lack potassium.
C Plant Y lacks phosphorus, because it turned blue-black.
D Plant X must have been kept in sunlight, because it remained yellow.
E Plant X must have been kept in the dark, because it remained yellow.

30. A student hypothesized that water added to a growing plant is responsible for its increase in mass. The student recorded the mass of water added over a number of days. The following data were collected.

Mass of seed	0.5 g
Water added to plant	250 g
Initial mass of soil	6.5 kg
Final mass of soil	6.4 kg
Final mass of the plant	255 g

Which conclusion is supported by the data?

A Water is not solely responsible for the increase in mass.
B The plant decomposes and adds nutrients to the soil.
C Light is not required for photosynthesis since the seed is under the ground.
D The more water you add to a plant the larger it grows.
E Plants in sunlight grow faster than plants in the dark.

Use the following experimental design to answer the next two questions.

jar A   jar B   jar C

31. Explain why the mouse in jar B becomes distressed before the mouse in jar C.

  A The plant provides the mouse with needed water.

  B The plant provides the mouse with needed oxygen.

  C The plant provides the mouse with needed carbon dioxide.

  D The mouse provides the plant with needed oxygen.

  E The mouse provides the plant with needed chlorophyll.

32. We might expect that

  A the plant in jar A will live longer than the plant in jar C, because the mouse will shade the plant.

  B the plant in jar C will live longer than the plant in jar A, because the mouse supplies oxygen to the plant.

  C the plant in jar C will live longer than the plant in jar A, because the mouse supplies carbon dioxide to the plant.

  D the plant in jar A will live longer than the plant in jar C, because the mouse uses up the oxygen needed by the plant.

  E the plant in jar A will live longer than the plant in jar C, because the mouse uses up the carbon dioxide needed by the plant.

Short Answer

Write a sentence or a short paragraph to answer each of the following questions.

33. What are guard cells and why do they open and close?

34. What is the function of the waxy cuticle that covers leaves?

35. Draw a diagram of a seed and show the location of the plant embryo.

36. What is pollination?

37. List three reasons why plants are important to people.

38. Explain why there are limitations when fertilizers are used to increase crop production.

39. How do plants help prevent erosion?

40. List one advantage and one disadvantage of propagating plants asexually.

41. Give two common landscape problems that arise because of poor planning.

42. Write a word equation for photosynthesis.

43. Write a chemical equation for photosynthesis.

44. Explain the theory that links carbon dioxide production to global warming.

Problem Solving

45. Predict how a plant would be affected if many of its phloem vessels were destroyed by a microorganism.

46. Explain why a leaf of a plant found in the rain forest would have more air spaces in its middle layers than a leaf found in a desert.

47. 10 mL of three nutrient solutions were added to seedlings, and root length was measured over a five-day period. The following data were obtained.

Time (days)	Root length (mm)		
	Solution X	Solution Y	Solution Z
0	2	2	2
1	2	4	4
2	3	6	9
3	4	10	14
4	4	12	18
5	5	15	28

(a) Graph the results by recording days on the x-axis and root length on the y-axis.

(b) Provide a conclusion from the graph.

Challenge

48. Working in a group, design an experiment to test one of the following hypotheses. You must state the materials required and provide a detailed procedure.

(a) If corn seeds are placed in water below 15°C, germination rates will be reduced.

(b) If the root tip is removed, the growth of a seedling will be accelerated.

(c) If dandelion seeds fall on lawns with a low nitrogen content, they are more likely to germinate.

(d) If plants are exposed to green light, then the rate of photosynthesis will decrease.

(e) If plants are cross-pollinated, their offspring will grow larger.

49. Collect pictures of plants adapted for different environments. Make a list of adaptations for each of the plants.

Design and Do

50. Many people who live in apartments would like to own a greenhouse, but are short of space. Your research group is hired to invent a miniature greenhouse for apartments. It must be fairly cheap, easy to put together, and well-designed. The following steps may help you with the planning.

- List the scientific principles that must be considered when building a greenhouse, e.g., Is there enough light? Can there be too much light? Is carbon dioxide desired? (Hint: Sodium bicarbonate in water or dilute vinegar provides an excellent source of carbon dioxide.)

- Draw several different designs. As a group, consider the benefits and problems of each design. Select a design.

- Collect materials and build a model.

- Test the model by comparing plants grown in the model with plants grown in pots outside the model.

- If the design works, build a full-scale apartment greenhouse.

- Prepare a report and present your findings. Include the projected cost of materials and labour, and the final cost of the greenhouse to a customer.

Project Ideas

51. Collect leaves from trees in your area and use field guides to classify them. Prepare a display of the leaves.

52. Visit a modern farm near you. Using a still camera or video camera, prepare a presentation showing some of the agricultural technology that has increased food production and lowered the cost of food.

53. Using a still camera or video camera, prepare a presentation showing some examples of well-planned and poorly planned landscaping. Explain why you chose your examples.

CHAPTER 16

Food and Nutrition

A GREAT DEAL IS WRITTEN ABOUT FOOD and nutrition. However, sometimes one article seems to contradict another article that came out just a few days before. Do you sometimes wonder what to believe?

In this chapter, you will

- examine the nutrients found in food,

- learn about the importance of each nutrient to your body, and

- use laboratory techniques to identify different nutrients.

 Getting Started

1. With your group, collect newspaper and magazine articles about food, nutrition, and health. After you have collected your articles, discuss them. Create a display of the articles. Write a brief summary of each one, including comments or questions your group has about the article. Include the summaries in the display.

2. In your group, discuss some of your beliefs about nutrition, and write them down. The following statements may help you get started. Discuss each statement and then record a T for a statement that you believe is true and an F for a statement that you believe is false. Give a brief reason for each answer.

- People should avoid eating any food that contains cholesterol.

- Taking lots of vitamins will improve your health.

- Teenagers don't have to watch what they eat as much as adults do.

- Food purchased at a fast-food outlet is not as good for you as food prepared from scratch.

Re-examine your beliefs and understanding once you have completed the unit. Have any of your ideas changed?

Examining Carbohydrates

MOST FOOD CAN BE BROKEN DOWN into three groups: carbohydrates, proteins, and fats. These three groups, plus water, make up the bulk of what you eat. Vitamins and minerals are also present in food, but in much smaller amounts. Carbohydrates, proteins, fats, vitamins, and minerals are all nutrients.

You usually can't see individual nutrients in the food you are eating. Most food is a mixture of nutrients. For example, the bowl of vegetable soup you may have for lunch is a mixture of water, carbohydrates, proteins, and fats, with some vitamins and minerals.

Some common sources of carbohydrates. How many of these foods do you regularly include in your diet?

Carbohydrates in Food

Carbohydrates are often described as energy nutrients. They provide quick energy and make up the largest component in most diets. Only plants can make carbohydrates. Animals rely on plants for this energy. Potatoes, bread, corn, rice, and fruit contain large amounts of carbohydrates.

Carbohydrates are also found in the snack foods you are often encouraged to limit. Although carbohydrates are very important in your diet as a source of energy, foods that are high in carbohydrates, such as candies, chips, and nondiet soft drinks, provide only energy and very few other important nutrients. Carbohydrates that are not used immediately are converted into fat. A healthy diet consists of a variety of foods that contain all the required nutrients.

Sugars

Carbohydrates are made of sugar molecules. The molecules can be single, in pairs, or in chains. The base molecules are the simple sugars. A **simple sugar** usually contains carbon, hydrogen, and oxygen atoms in the proportions of 1:2:1. For example, glucose, the most common simple sugar, has the formula $C_6H_{12}O_6$. Glucose is found in all the cells of your body and is your primary source of energy. Fructose, another simple sugar, is found in fruits. Fructose makes an ideal sugar for diet foods because it tastes much sweeter than glucose—a smaller quantity of fructose achieves the same sweet taste. Galactose, yet another simple sugar, is found in milk.

Glucose

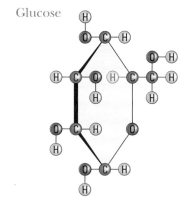

Fructose

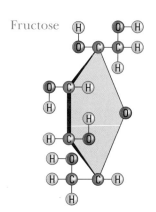

Combining Simple Sugars

Complex sugars are combinations of simple sugars. Maltose, which is used in making beer, is composed of two glucose molecules. Lactose, the most common sugar in milk, is composed of a glucose molecule and a galactose molecule.

Sucrose, also called table sugar, is probably the sugar you are most familiar with. It is a combination of a glucose molecule and a fructose molecule. Sucrose is harvested from sugar cane, sugar beets, and the sugar maple tree and then refined in several forms, the most common being brown and white sugar. Brown sugar is less pure than white sugar. Some of the impurities that remain after refining give brown sugar its colour and sticky feel. The slight difference in taste is due to these impurities.

Starch

You will recall that plants store excess sugar molecules as starch. **Starch** is a carbohydrate made of many sugar molecules linked together in long chains. One starch molecule can contain as many as 6000 glucose molecules. In plants, starches are generally stored in the roots and stems. When a plant needs energy, starches are broken down into sugars, which are used by the plant's cells. Bread, pasta, and potatoes are rich sources of starches.

Sucrose

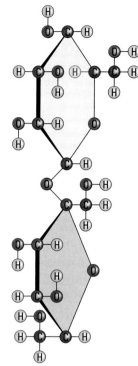

Starch

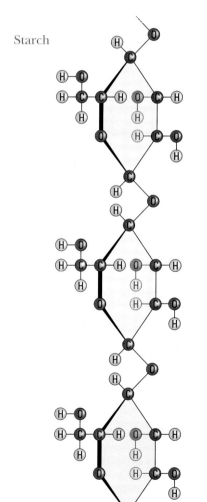

HEALTH-LINK

Identifying Sugars on Food Labels

Did you know that one of the main ingredients in ketchup is sugar? North Americans seem to prefer foods that are sweet.

Collect the ingredient labels from a variety of foods in your homes. Be sure to select as many different foods as possible. Without looking at the ingredients, sort the labels into two groups, foods you think contain sugar and foods you think do not. List the foods in each group. Now examine the ingredients. Make a list of the foods that contain sugar. (Look for the word "sugar" and for any ingredients that end in "ose"—these are also sugars.)

Your group should consider the following questions before presenting your findings to the class.

- Which foods did you not expect to contain sugar? Why?
- Which foods that had sugar added are naturally sweet?
- Did you find any foods that are mostly sugar?
- What advice would you give to those who are trying to reduce the amount of sugar they eat?

Using Preservatives

The energy provided by carbohydrates creates both benefits and problems. The discovery of a long-forgotten bag lunch in your locker at school will remind you that starch, a major component of bread, is an excellent source of energy for a variety of organisms. The greenish threads that cover the old sandwiches are organisms called mould, which are feeding on the starch.

Would you buy bread that had mould on it? Would you buy bread that was dry and tasteless? This is the twin problem the food industry faces. Consumers demand a moist and nutritious bread that retains its flavour and moisture for days. Moisture, like starch, promotes mould growth. Traditional preservatives, such as salt and vinegar, can be used. However, these change the taste of the bread. Calcium propionate may be the ideal preservative. It has little effect on taste, and is nontoxic in low concentrations. In addition, calcium propionate is soluble in water, and so it is ideal for keeping bread moist.

Cellulose

Cellulose, the major component of plant cell walls, is also composed of a great many glucose units. However, because of the way the glucose molecules are linked together, the properties of cellulose are quite different from those of starch. Cellulose cannot be digested by humans. That is, you cannot use it as a source of energy. However, it makes up an important component of your diet. Cellulose is often called **fibre**, or roughage.

Cellulose

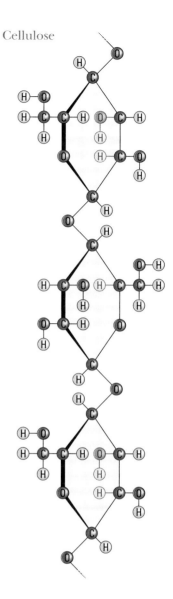

TRY THIS

Keeping Bread Fresh

Put on your apron and safety goggles. Cut a slice of bread that contains no preservatives into two pieces. Add 10 drops of a 1% calcium propionate solution to one of the pieces and place it in a sandwich bag. Place the other piece in a sandwich bag without adding any preservative. Label each bag and store them in a dark cupboard. Examine the bags daily and record your observations. Compare the two pieces. How effective was the calcium propionate?

 CAUTION: Do not open the bags.

• How does the amount of food preservative affect the mould growth on bread? Try to use different concentrations and different volumes of calcium propionate. You may also wish to try vinegar or salt as a preservative for bread.

Cellulose in Your Diet

Do you like vegetables? Some people must be coaxed into eating vegetables such as spinach, turnip, and cauliflower. Vegetables are an important source of cellulose, which is an important part of your diet, despite the fact that it cannot be digested. How can something that offers no energy be an important part of your diet?

The Hazards of Not Eating Cellulose

Foods that enter the digestive system are broken down and absorbed. By the time food gets to the large intestine, only undigested wastes remain. Some of these wastes are poisonous and can be dangerous to cells. People who eat foods with little cellulose encounter two problems.

First, foods with little cellulose produce few solid wastes. Because waste is collecting slowly, there is a longer time between bowel movements, and cells in the large intestine are more likely to be damaged by poisons in the waste.

Second, the large intestine is responsible for absorbing water from foods. The longer food wastes remain in the large intestine, the greater the amount of water that is reabsorbed. If too much water is reabsorbed, the wastes become difficult to remove. This condition is often referred to as constipation. Cell damage can occur if wastes are removed without benefit of water. High-fibre diets ensure that bowel movements occur before too much water is absorbed.

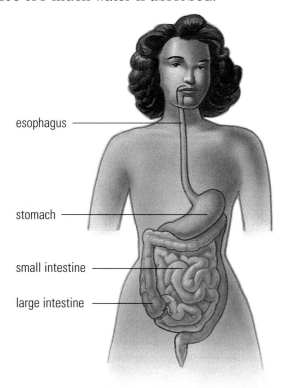

esophagus

stomach

small intestine

large intestine

Wastes accumulate in the large intestine before being eliminated.

SELF CHECK

1. What is the primary function of carbohydrates?

2. Name three simple sugars and indicate where you would expect to find them.

3. Copy and complete the following table.

Name of sugar	Composed of
maltose	
sucrose	
lactose	

4. (a) What happens to carbohydrates that are not immediately used by your body?

   (b) Why might you want to limit your carbohydrate intake?

5. How can you recognize sugars in the ingredients list on food labels?

6. How are starch and cellulose alike? How do they differ?

7. Give two reasons why cellulose is an important part of your diet.

Identification of Simple Sugars

FOOD CHEMISTS USE ANALYSIS techniques to identify nutrients in food products. For example, Benedict's solution is used to check the presence of simple sugars. Unfortunately, some of the larger sugar molecules do not react with Benedict's solution. The colour chart to the right summarizes the amount of sugar present when the sugar reacts with Benedict's solution.

Colour of Benedict's solution	Approximate amount of sugar
Blue	none
Light green	0.5 – 1.0%
Green to yellow	1.0 – 1.5%
Orange	1.5 – 2.0%
Red to red brown	2.0%+

Materials

- safety goggles
- apron
- 400-mL beaker
- hot plate
- thermometer
- wax pencil
- 8 test tubes
- test-tube rack
- distilled water
- 5% fructose solution
- 5% glucose solution
- 5% maltose solution
- 5% sucrose solution

- clear, colourless diet pop
- clear, colourless nondiet pop
- 10-mL graduated cylinder
- Benedict's solution
- medicine dropper
- test-tube brush
- test-tube holder
- assorted candies
- mortar and pestle
- detergent

 CAUTION: Benedict's solution is an irritant and is toxic. Avoid skin and eye contact. Wash all splashes off your skin and clothing thoroughly. If you get any of the chemical in your eyes, rinse for at least 15 min and inform your teacher.

 CAUTION: Do not taste any solution in the laboratory.

Before you begin,

- make sure that all the glassware is undamaged, clean, and well-rinsed, and
- note the location of the eyewash station.

Procedure

Part 1 *Testing for Sugar*

1. Put on your safety goggles and apron.

2. Prepare a water bath by heating about 150 mL of tap water in a 400-mL beaker. Heat the water until it reaches approximately 80°C. Use the thermometer to monitor the temperature.

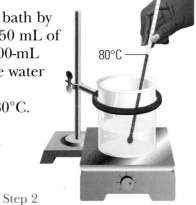

80°C

Step 2

3. Using the wax pencil, label seven test tubes as follows: W (distilled water), F (fructose), G (glucose), M (maltose), S (sucrose), D (diet pop), P (nondiet pop). Place the test tubes in the test-tube rack.

4. Using a 10-mL graduated cylinder, measure 3 mL each of distilled water, fructose, glucose, maltose, sucrose, diet pop, and nondiet pop. Put each liquid into the tube you have prepared for it. Clean and rinse the graduated cylinder after each sample.

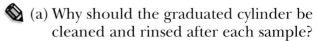 (a) Why should the graduated cylinder be cleaned and rinsed after each sample?

5 Use a medicine dropper to add five drops of Benedict's solution to each test tube.

6 Using a test-tube holder, place the test tubes in the hot-water bath.

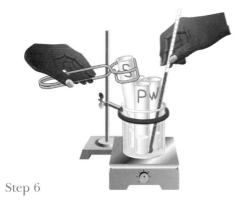

Step 6

7 Observe the test tubes for six minutes.

✎ (b) Make a chart similar to the one below and record your results.

Sample	Initial colour	Final colour	Estimated % sugar
water			
glucose			
fructose			

8 Turn off the hot plate and allow it to cool for at least five minutes.

9 Use a test-tube holder to transfer the test tubes back to the test-tube rack. Dispose of the liquids in the test tubes as directed by your teacher. Wash the test tubes and the graduated cylinder.

Part 2 *Testing for Sugar in Candy*

10 Your teacher will give your group a candy. Using a mortar and pestle, crush the candy.

Step 10

11 Place the crushed candy into a clean test tube. Add 3 mL of distilled water to dissolve the sugar, if any, in the candy.

12 Test the solution for simple sugars. Design your own data table to show if simple sugars are present, and estimate the amount present.

✎ (c) Record your data in your table.

13 Wash your hands.

Questions

1. Which test tube served as a control for the Benedict's test?

2. Which sugars tested do not react with Benedict's solution?

3. Which sugars tested were simple sugars?

4. A student is curious to see if adding a sugar cube to the diet pop would change the results. Predict the effect of dissolving a sugar cube in the pop. Give reasons for your prediction.

Extension

5. Predict which foods might contain simple sugars. Test a variety of foods to check your prediction.

6. Your teacher will use a scoopula to remove a few crystals of each of the sugars listed below from its container and place them in a small paper cup. Use a clean toothpick to transfer crystals of each sugar to your tongue. Make a chart like the one below to record the sweetness of each of the sugars. Use the following ratings:

1 = slightly sweet

2 = moderately sweet

3 = very sweet

Sweetness of Sugars

Type of sugar	Rating
sucrose	
glucose	
fructose	
maltose	
lactose	

Examining Fats

FATS, ALSO CALLED LIPIDS, are an excellent energy source. One gram of fat provides nearly twice as much energy as one gram of carbohydrate. Fats are important nutrients for other reasons: they help the body absorb many important vitamins, serve as body insulation under the skin, protect some of the delicate organs of the body, provide a protective coating around nerves, and are an important component of the cell membrane.

Fats supply energy to the cells of the body. But unlike carbohydrates, they are difficult to digest. That is why fats usually keep you feeling full longer than carbohydrates do.

Many animals prepare for winter by storing energy as fat.

Saturated and Unsaturated Fats

Fats are made up of carbon, hydrogen, and oxygen, the same chemical elements found in carbohydrates. However, the arrangement of these chemicals is different in fats.

A fat molecule to which more hydrogen atoms could be added is said to be **unsaturated**. Oils (plant fats) are unsaturated fats and are liquid at room temperature. Animal fats are said to be **saturated**, because the fat molecules contain close to the maximum number of hydrogen atoms. Animal fats are usually solid or semi-solid at room temperature.

Unsaturated fats are more easily broken down by the cells of your body. Saturated fats tend to be very difficult to break down.

Animal fats, such as lard, provide one important advantage over plant oils. Because animal fats do not break down easily, they permit cooking at higher temperatures than plant oils.

These foods are excellent sources of fat. Which kind of fat does each food contain?

Fat in Your Fries

When potatoes are fried, the potatoes absorb a tremendous amount of fat. When you eat french fries, you eat more than just potato. Here is a way to find out how much fat is in your french fries.

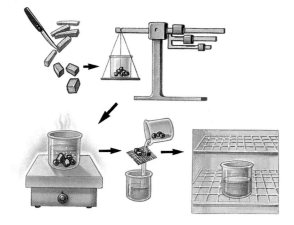

Put on your apron and safety goggles. Determine the mass of an empty 150-mL beaker. Cut a few already fried french fries into pieces approximately 5 cm in length, and place 15 g of the french fries in the beaker. Using a graduated cylinder, add 100 mL of water to the beaker. Place the beaker on a hot plate and bring the water to a boil. After 5 min of boiling, turn off the hot plate, and carefully remove the beaker. Pour the mixture through a strainer into another beaker. Discard the french fries. Place the strained liquid in a refrigerator and examine it 24 h later.

- Devise a procedure for measuring the amount of fat in the beaker. Present the procedure to your teacher for approval and carry it out.

CHALLENGE

Have you ever wondered if one brand of potato chips contains more fat than another? Do pretzels have less fat than nachos? Do diet snacks contain less fat? How much fat is there in pasta? Use the procedure developed in the Try This to prepare a consumer report. Choose the foods you wish to investigate and provide a reason for your study. What will your hypothesis be? What brand names have you chosen? Have your teacher approve your procedure before beginning.

DID YOU KNOW?

People often gain weight during the first few days of dieting. This is because water replaces the fat that has been lost from fat tissue. After a few days, the water leaves the fat cells, and the weight loss begins to show.

The Cholesterol Connection

Cholesterol is formed from fat, and, like fat, it has a bad reputation. Certain forms of cholesterol have been associated with heart disease and circulatory problems. If cholesterol combines with fat, it can block blood vessels. The reduced blood flow can kill the tissue served by the vessel. The build-up of cholesterol in blood vessels that serve the heart muscle is especially dangerous.

Despite cholesterol's bad image, it is also very useful. Cholesterol is one of the chemicals used by your body to make certain hormones. Without cholesterol, the differences between the sexes would be less obvious—the hormones that control sex differences are made from cholesterol.

SELF CHECK

8. Why are fats important in our diet?

9. (a) How do saturated fats differ from unsaturated fats?

   (b) Give one example of a saturated fat and one of an unsaturated fat.

10. How are fats similar to carbohydrates? How are they different?

11. (a) Why does cholesterol have a bad reputation?

    (b) Why is cholesterol important to the body?

Examining Proteins

THE BETTER-KNOWN SOURCES OF PROTEIN include foods such as milk, meat, and fish. However, smaller amounts of protein are also found in vegetables, beans, and rice.

Unlike carbohydrates and fats, proteins are not normally used as an energy source. Proteins form the structures of a cell. Whenever cells are damaged, proteins are needed for repairs. Proteins are also required to make structures for new cells.

These are some sources of protein that may be familiar to you. How many of these do you include in your diet?

The Never-Ending Need for Protein

Consider the amount of protein that your body must be assembling at this very second. Your red blood cells die at a rate of about one million a second. No need to feel uncomfortable though, because red blood cells are *replaced* at the same rate. That means your body needs enough protein to construct one million cell membranes and many millions of cell organelles each and every second.

Amino Acids

Proteins are composed of building blocks called **amino acids**. There are 20 different kinds of amino acids that can be strung together in an almost infinite number of ways. The smallest protein contains eight amino acids, but some of the longer chains have more than 250 000 amino acids.

Breaking Down and Building Protein

The proteins you eat are broken down by your body into amino acids, and then reassembled. When you eat fish protein, for example, you eat the structural components of the fish cells. But you don't end up looking like a fish! Your digestive system breaks apart the fish proteins into amino acids and your cells assemble the amino-acid building blocks into human proteins.

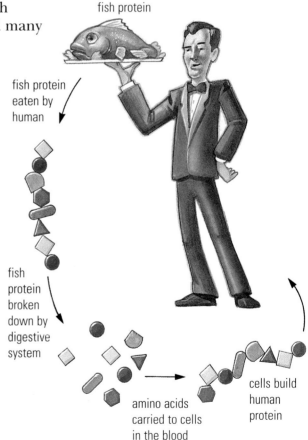

fish protein

fish protein eaten by human

fish protein broken down by digestive system

amino acids carried to cells in the blood

cells build human protein

In this diagram, each amino acid has a different shape. The human protein and the fish protein have the same amino acids, but they are in a different order.

Making Amino Acids

Your body can make all but eight of the 20 different amino acids that are found in various foods. The eight that you cannot make must be included in your diet. These are called **essential amino acids** because they are necessary for growth and repair of body parts, but cannot be made by the body. One amino acid cannot be substituted for another. Each amino acid has unique chemical properties.

Sources of Amino Acids

Fish, eggs, cheese, milk, and meat are excellent sources of the essential amino acids. Did you notice that all these sources come from animals? Plants and their seeds, such as cereal grains, nuts, and beans also supply proteins. However, plants do not provide a complete source of protein. Each plant source is missing some of the essential amino acids, or they are in very low concentrations. It is possible to obtain all the amino acids your body needs without eating animal products, but it requires careful planning. This is why many vegetarians supplement their diet with eggs, milk, and cheese.

DID YOU KNOW?

One of the greatest problems facing our planet is not starvation, but malnutrition. Many people in the poorer nations live on grain diets. They get enough food energy, but not enough essential amino acids.

CAREER-LINK

Dietitian

Do you enjoy helping people? Have you ever considered a career as a dietitian? Dietitians work in hospitals, clinics, diet centres, and health clubs. They help people plan meals that contain the required nutrients in the proper proportions. Some dietitians provide diets for athletes in training. Dietitians also provide invaluable help for those with medical problems.

If you are interested in a career as a dietitian, research the various career opportunities. If you are interested in diets, research the types of diets required by people with special medical needs.

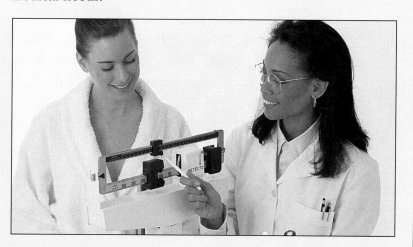

SELF CHECK

12. What is the main way proteins are used by your body?
13. List examples of foods that are considered to be a good source of proteins.
14. What is meant by an essential amino acid?
15. (a) If you eat cereal by itself, would you supply your cells with all of the necessary amino acids?
    (b) How does adding milk to your cereal change the type of amino acids available?
    (c) What are some other combinations of foods that provide a well-balanced diet?

Testing for Fats and Proteins

IN THIS INVESTIGATION, YOU WILL TEST for two important nutrients, fats and proteins. You will identify fats using unglazed brown paper. Because fats allow the transmission of light through the brown paper, the test is often called the translucence test.

Proteins are identified by the Biuret test. Biuret reagent reacts with amino acids, producing colour changes from blue (–), indicating no protein, to pink (+), or violet (++), or purple (+++). You can use the + signs to indicate the relative amount of protein present.

Colour	Symbol
blue	–
pink	+
violet	++
purple	+++

Materials

- safety goggles
- apron
- 10 squares of unglazed brown paper (about 10 cm × 10 cm)
- 5 medicine droppers
- distilled water
- vegetable oil
- 8 test tubes
- wax pencil
- 10-mL graduated cylinder

- test-tube rack
- gelatin solution
- Biuret reagent
- sheet of white paper
- glucose solution
- liquid soap
- egg white
- liquid detergent
- butter
- solutions X, Y, and Z
- test-tube brush

CAUTION: Biuret reagent and iodine are toxic and irritants. Avoid skin and eye contact. Wash all splashes off your skin and clothing thoroughly. If you get any chemical in your eyes, rinse for at least 15 min and inform your teacher.

Procedure

Part 1 *Using the Translucence Test for Fats*

1 Put on your safety goggles and apron.

2 Label a 10-cm square piece of unglazed brown paper C, for control. Place a drop of distilled water on C. Label a second piece of paper E, for experimental. Place a drop of vegetable oil on E.

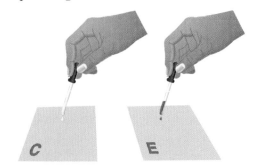

Step 2

3 Wave papers C and E in the air until the drops appear dry. Hold both papers to the light and observe.

 (a) Make a data table and record whether the papers appear translucent.

Part 2 *Using the Biuret Test for Proteins*

4 Obtain two test tubes. Using a wax pencil, label one test tube C and the other E.

5 Add 2 mL of water to C. Add 2 mL of gelatin solution to E. Place the test tubes in a test-tube rack. Rinse the graduated cylinder.

6 Add 2 mL of Biuret reagent to each of the test tubes. Pick up each test tube and tap it gently with your fingers to mix the contents. You may find it helpful to hold a sheet of white paper behind the test tubes when observing the colour.

(b) Make a data table and record any colour change.

Step 6

Part 3 *Testing Unknown Solutions*

7 Test each of the samples provided for the presence of fats and protein.

(c) Make a data table like the one shown below. Record your results in the data table.

Testing for Fats and Proteins

Solution	Translucence test	Biuret reagent colour change
glucose solution		
gelatin solution		
liquid soap		
egg white		

(d) Compare your results with those of other students. Were any of your results different from those of others? Account for any differences you found.

8 Dispose of all solutions as directed by your teacher. Clean any glassware used. Wash your hands.

Questions

1. Why was distilled water used for both the translucence test and Biuret test?

2. Which tested substances contained proteins? Which contained fat?

3. Why might a food chemist test a food for the presence of fat or protein?

Apply

4. It is often difficult to decide whether a solution tested for protein should be given a rating of + or ++. Suggest a method that involves less guesswork. Is there any way to ensure that everyone interprets the results in the same way?

Extension

5. The following procedure can be used to determine how unsaturated an oil is. In general, the more unsaturated the fat, the more easily your body can break it down. You may test various vegetable oils, margarines, and animal fats.

- Put on your apron and safety goggles. Measure 25 mL of oil into a 50-mL beaker. Add 5 drops of iodine to the oil. Use a stirring rod to mix the iodine with the oil. Note the new red-brown color.

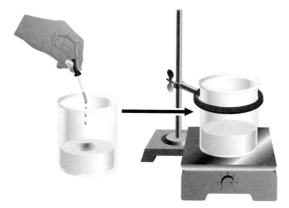

- Use beaker tongs to place the beaker on a hot plate. Turn on the hot plate and record the time it takes for the solution to return to the original colour of the oil. The more unsaturated the fat, the faster it will return to the original colour.

Which of the fats you tested was most unsaturated?

Identifying Nutrients in a Seed

NOW THAT YOU HAVE LEARNED how to test for carbohydrates, fats, and proteins in the laboratory, challenge yourself to find out what nutrients are in a seed. A seed can be thought of as a "packaged plant." It contains the plant embryo and a food source.

CAUTION: Iodine solution, Biuret reagent, and Benedict's solution are all toxic and irritants. Avoid skin and eye contact. Wash all splashes off your skin and clothing thoroughly. If you get any chemical in your eyes, rinse for at least 15 min and inform your teacher.

Materials

- safety goggles
- apron
- 5 corn seeds
- glass microscope slide or plastic cutting board
- 3 medicine droppers
- iodine solution
- mortar and pestle
- sand
- 2 test tubes
- 10-mL graduated cylinder
- distilled water
- Biuret reagent
- Benedict's solution
- 250-mL beaker
- beaker tongs
- hot plate
- test-tube holder
- test-tube brush

Procedure

1 Soak 5 corn seeds in a beaker of water for about 24 h.

2 Remove the corn seeds from the water and place the seeds on a glass microscope slide or plastic cutting board. Your teacher will cut one of the corn seeds along the line shown in the diagram.

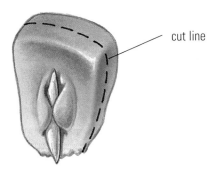

cut line

Step 2

3 Put on your safety goggles and apron.

4 Add a drop of iodine to the cut surface of the corn seed and observe carefully.

✎ (a) Record your observations.

5 Place a pinch of sand and two corn seeds in a mortar. Grind the seeds.

6 Transfer the ground seeds to a test tube.

Step 6

7 Using a graduated cylinder, measure 2 mL of distilled water. Pour the water into the mortar and rinse the mortar.

8 Pour the rinse water into the test tube containing the crushed seeds. Add 2 mL of Biuret reagent. Observe the solution for a colour change. Refer to the previous investigation for indicator colours for Biuret reagent.

(b) Record your observations.

(c) Why was the mortar rinsed?

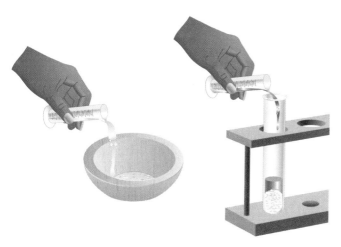

Step 7   Step 8

9 Use the mortar and pestle to grind the two remaining corn seeds with a pinch of sand. Transfer the seeds to a second test tube. Rinse the mortar with 2 mL of distilled water. Add the water to the test tube.

10 Add 1 mL of Benedict's solution to the test tube. Heat the test tube in a hot-water bath for 7 min.

(d) Record your observations.

11 Dispose of all chemicals and clean your glassware as directed by your teacher. Wash your hands.

Questions

1. What nutrient did each of the following test for?

(a) iodine

(b) Biuret reagent

(c) Benedict's solution

2. Suggest a control that you might use for this experiment.

Apply

3. Explain why each of the identified nutrients was present in the corn seed.

4. A student suspects that different nutrients are found in different parts of the corn seed. Design a procedure that would test this hypothesis.

Extension

5. You have been examining various nutrients needed by your body. However, the food you eat also contains materials that are not considered to be essential nutrients. Caffeine is an example. The following table will help you chart your daily caffeine intake. Copy the chart into your notebook, and use it to monitor your caffeine intake over three days.

Measuring Caffeine Intake

Source of caffeine	Amount of caffeine per serving (mg)	Number of servings	Total caffeine from source
coffee, drip filter	145		
coffee, percolated	110		
coffee, instant	75		
tea	65		
cola	35		
hot chocolate	18		
dark chocolate	45		
milk chocolate	10		
cold medicines, tablet or capsule	(check label)		
headache medicine, tablet	(check label)		
TOTAL CAFFEINE INTAKE			

(a) What is your average daily caffeine intake? Compare your average intake with that of other group members. What is your group's average daily caffeine intake?

(b) Research the effect caffeine has on the body, and write a report.

(c) Suggest some ways you could reduce the amount of caffeine you consume.

Taking Your Vitamins and Minerals

YOU HAVE LEARNED ABOUT THE IMPORTANCE of the energy nutrients, carbohydrates and fats, and the structural nutrients, proteins. However, your cells require other essential chemicals to function normally. You also need vitamins and minerals.

Vitamins

Vitamins help your body change food into energy. The table below shows some of the essential vitamins that must be included in your diet.

Some Vitamins

Vitamin	Solubility	Sources	Needed for	Deficiency symptoms
A	fat	green and yellow vegetables, carrots, tomatoes	good vision, normal growth of bones and teeth, healthy skin	poor vision, night blindness, kidney problems
B₁	water	pork, liver, peas, soybeans, grains, vegetables	proper functioning of heart, nerves, muscles	poor appetite, nerve problems, beriberi
B₂	water	lean meat, eggs, milk, liver, fish, poultry, leafy vegetables	healthy skin and hair, good vision, growth, reproduction	poor growth, hair problems, poor vision
C	water	citrus fruits, green vegetables, potatoes	maintaining cells and tissues	low resistance to infections, scurvy
D	fat	fish oils, eggs, milk	strong teeth and bones, growth	weak teeth and bones
E	fat	leafy vegetables, grains, vegetable oils, liver	forming red blood cells	no symptoms
K	fat	leafy vegetables, liver, potatoes	assisting blood clotting, healthy bones	bleeding

Water- and Fat-Soluble Vitamins

Vitamins can be organized into two groups: those that are soluble in water, such as vitamin C and the B-group vitamins; and those that are soluble in fats, such as vitamins A, D, E, and K.

Because the water-soluble vitamins cannot be stored in the body, they must be taken in daily. If you consume too many water-soluble vitamins, the excess is removed in the urine.

In contrast, the fat-soluble vitamins are stored in fat tissue. If you take too many of these vitamins, they can build up in your body and become harmful. For example, vitamin D, which helps regulate calcium and phosphate levels for your teeth and bones, can cause serious problems when it accumulates. An excessive amount of vitamin D has been linked to calcium deposits in kidneys and blood vessels, and is responsible for slowing the growth of some children. Excess vitamin B_6 is linked with nerve damage.

It is wise to avoid an excess of any vitamin, including water-soluble ones.

TECHNOLOGY-LINK

Antioxidants

A great deal of excitement has been generated by a group of vitamins—C, E, and beta-carotene (from which the molecule vitamin A is made). These chemicals are known as antioxidants. Early research suggests that these chemicals can make a group of harmful molecules less dangerous.

Scientists believe that the harmful molecules, known as oxygen-free radicals, play a major role in the development of cancer, and heart and lung diseases. By knocking these molecules out of commission, you might live longer and be healthier.

- Your group, an advertising company, has the contract to design an advertising campaign for antioxidants. Design a poster for antioxidant vitamins as part of your campaign. You must be able to support any claims you make in your poster. Submit the support you have for your claims with your poster.

Vegetables such as Brussels sprouts, cabbage, and broccoli are rich sources of vitamins A and C.

Minerals

Several minerals are also needed in small amounts. Your body requires iron to make the oxygen-carrying pigment in red blood cells. You also need sodium, potassium, copper, iodine, magnesium, phosphorus, calcium, lithium, and zinc. Like vitamins, **minerals** help you obtain the necessary energy from the foods you eat, and help maintain normal body functioning.

Daily requirements for some minerals

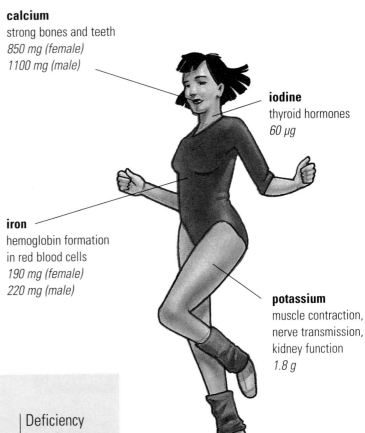

calcium
strong bones and teeth
850 mg (female)
1100 mg (male)

iodine
thyroid hormones
60 µg

iron
hemoglobin formation
in red blood cells
190 mg (female)
220 mg (male)

potassium
muscle contraction,
nerve transmission,
kidney function
1.8 g

Some Minerals

Mineral	Sources	Needed for	Deficiency symptoms
calcium	milk, cheese, grains, beans, hard water	growth and maintenance of bones and teeth, aids blood clotting	soft bones and teeth, osteoporosis
iodine	seafood, table salt	proper working of thyroid gland	swollen thyroid gland, goitre
iron	green vegetables, liver, whole-wheat bread, grains, nuts	needed to transport oxygen through the body	lack of energy, anemia
phosphorus	meats, fish, dairy products, grains	growth and maintenance of bones and teeth, some cell reactions	poor development of bones and teeth
potassium	meats, grains, milk, fruits, green vegetables	needed to make proteins	weak muscles
sodium	table salt, vegetables, canned meat	regulates movement of water between cells and blood	dehydration

Determining Vitamin C Levels in Juices and Drinks

Have you ever read a consumer report? Many products claim to be vitamin-enriched. Here is an opportunity to test for vitamin C in a variety of drinks.

Select drinks such as fresh orange juice, orange juice from concentrate, orange crystals, orange drink, white grape juice, and lemon juice.

- Predict which of the drinks contains the most vitamin C.

 CAUTION: Indophenol is toxic. Avoid skin and eye contact. If you get indophenol in your eyes, rinse thoroughly with cold water and inform your teacher.

You can use indophenol to test the drinks. Indophenol changes colour when it comes in contact with vitamin C. Put on your safety goggles and apron. Add 5 mL of indophenol to a test tube. Using a medicine dropper, add 7 drops of orange juice to the test tube.

Shake the tube and look for a colour change. If no change occurs, continue adding single drops of juice, shaking the tube immediately after adding each drop.

- Record the number of drops required to turn the indicator colourless.
- Repeat the test using the other drinks you have selected to test.
- Devise a method of converting the number of drops added to a measurement in millilitres.

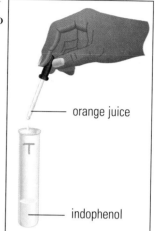

orange juice

indophenol

- Prepare a graph to display your results. (For more information on graphing, see the Skills Handbook on page 514.)
- Which drinks contained the least, or no, vitamin C? Which drinks contained the most?

Debunking the Vitamin Myth

One nutrition report suggests that 33% of Canadians take vitamins regularly to improve their health. Are they wasting their time? In some cases, the answer is yes.

- Do vitamins help relieve stress? The answer is no.

- Does vitamin C prevent colds? Despite some research suggesting that vitamin C may be a factor, the evidence is not conclusive. Much of the scientific community has not accepted the idea.

- Do vitamins in shampoos improve your hair? Again, the answer is no. Only the follicle of the hair is alive. The hair itself is nonliving. Coating the nonliving hair with vitamins will not improve it.

Nutritionists know that people who eat a healthy, well-balanced diet obtain all of the vitamins they need from their food. Vitamin supplements are needed only if your diet lacks certain foods.

16. Why should vitamins be included in your diet?
17. Name one important vitamin, explain its importance, and indicate its source.
18. Name one important mineral and explain why it must be included in your diet.
19. Name two diseases associated with a vitamin shortage.
20. Why could it be harmful to take in large quantities of fat-soluble vitamins?
21. Why do some people take cod liver oil tablets to supplement their diet during the winter months?

The Diet Myth

IN NORTH AMERICA AND EUROPE, a lot of money is spent on showing the "ideal" woman or the "ideal" man. Advertisers lead you to believe that if you use their products, you too can be as "perfect" as the models in their ads. In most of these ads, females are tall and thin, while males appear even taller and muscular. Thin people are portrayed as energetic, exciting, and often very intelligent, qualities that are not known to be related to appearance.

The Tall, Thin Heroine

By showing the heroine as being tall, thin, and athletic, advertisers, the movie industry, and the fashion industry have created a dangerous expectation. Because little can be done to change height, many women, young and old, concentrate on becoming thin. It is not uncommon to find teenage girls obsessed with dieting.

What is also very troubling is the link between dieting and the increase in eating disorders. A recent survey indicates that anorexia nervosa, an eating disorder common among girls and young women aged 10 to 19, has increased more than five times since the 1950s.

Medical evidence shows that people who are obese have a greater risk of getting heart disease, high blood pressure, and diabetes. However, the idea that thinner is healthier is being challenged. A 1994 report, sponsored by the National Institute of Health in the United States, indicated that 95% of people who diet regain any mass they lose. Many people who are trying to be thin go through a cycle of loss and gain, loss and gain. It's called weight cycling, and it may be more dangerous for your health than keeping a constant mass, even if it is above the average for your size.

The American study also pointed out that people on this cycle tend to gain weight back more quickly after each dieting phase. This is especially dangerous, because it subjects the body to repeated and increasing stress.

1504

1919

House of KUPPENHEIMER

1917

1994

1994

The image of the perfect body changes from year to year. However, for the past decade, the "ideal" woman has been very thin, and the "ideal" man very muscular.

This report has not been welcomed by the weight-loss industry. In Canada alone, the weight-loss industry is valued at $300 million every year. Although overeating should not be encouraged, not everyone in Canada can be thin.

The Muscular Hero

A different problem exists for many young males. The image of muscular heroes in movies, sports, and advertising is as appealing to boys as the thin model image is for girls. However, most Grade-9 boys do not have muscular body shapes, and very few are over 2 m tall. Muscle development becomes prominent only after growth has slowed, which for most young males is in the late teen years.

In an attempt to reach the ideal they see in movies and ads, some young men resort to high-protein diets. These diets are intended to increase muscle mass, but most only increase food intake beyond the boy's bodily needs.

For others, anabolic steroids have become a quick but dangerous solution. A recent study estimates that as many as 500 000 North Americans under the age of 18 may be abusing these drugs to improve athletic performance and appearance. The use of anabolic steroids may have many side effects, including mood swings, and, in teenagers, prematurely halted growth. The illegal use of anabolic steroids has given rise to a black market, with sales estimated at as much as $400 million a year.

Understanding the Author

1. In what ways can dieting be harmful?

2. What are the health risks associated with obesity?

3. What are the side effects of the use of anabolic steroids?

4. Who does the author feel is responsible for the "diet craze"?

Statement

The advertisements of the weight-control and diet-food industry must be closely regulated. They should show bodies of different shapes.

Point

- One study estimates that 60% of individuals who are overweight have inherited the tendency to be overweight. We must overcome the idea that these are inactive people who spend their time eating.

- Weight loss, if really needed, should be done with a balance of sensible eating and exercise. The emphasis should be placed on providing a well-balanced diet.

- Eating disorders such as anorexia nervosa may be the result of industry's pressure to make people want to be thin.

Counterpoint

- The diet-food industry is not the only one to advertise that thin is better. The fashion industry, to name one, also uses thin models. Regulating only one industry is not fair.

- Industries that attempt to provide diet meals, diet soft drinks, and the like are providing a service. Without these products, individuals who are overweight might suffer even more.

- Diet food actually promotes healthy eating practices and provides an alternative to fasting and overeating.

What Do You Think?

5. Research the issue further, expand on the points provided, and develop or reflect upon your opinion. Prepare for a class debate.

Key Outcomes

Now that you have completed this chapter, can you do the following? If not, review the sections indicated.

- Describe the importance and function of carbohydrates, fats, and proteins in the body. (16.1, 16.3, 16.4)

- Name common sources of carbohydrates, fats, and proteins in your diet. (16.1, 16.3, 16.4)

- Identify simple sugars, fats, and proteins in the laboratory using the appropriate indicators. (16.2, 16.5)

- Explain the importance of vitamins and minerals in your diet. (16.7)

- Explain how our society's values may influence us to lead unhealthy lives. (16.8)

Key Terms

carbohydrate	unsaturated
simple sugar	cholesterol
complex sugar	protein
starch	amino acids
cellulose	essential amino acid
fibre	
fat	vitamin
saturated	mineral

Review

1. Name the three major groups of nutrients found in foods.

2. Name the indicators used to identify simple sugars and proteins.

3. What is the primary source of carbohydrates for animals?

4. Why should people include fibre in their diet, even though it cannot be digested?

5. Proteins are the structural components of cells. Explain why if you eat fish protein, you do not take on the characteristics of a fish.

6. What are essential amino acids?

7. List two important minerals that are required for normal body function and briefly outline why they are important.

8. Explain why too much vitamin D could be harmful.

9. Differentiate between saturated fats and unsaturated fats.

Problem Solving

10. Classify the following ingredients found on the label of a packaged food: glucose, sucrose, maltose, fructose.

11. Why might some diet foods include fructose rather than sucrose?

12. Benedict's solution was added to three food samples. The observations are provided in the following table.

Food sample	Initial colour of food sample and Benedict's solution	Colour of solution after heating for 5 min
milk	blue	green
distilled water	blue	blue
orange juice	blue	red-brown

Which food sample(s) contain a simple sugar?

13. A student tastes a soft drink and notes a sweet taste; however, when it is tested with Benedict's solution, a positive result is not obtained. Explain the laboratory results.

14. In an experiment, a student tests various foods with different indicators. Based on the results, draw conclusions about the nutrients found in the different foods.

Food type	Benedict's test	Biuret test	Translucence test	Iodine test
potato	red	violet	negative	blue-black
milk	green	violet	slightly translucent	negative
hamburger	negative	purple	translucent	negative

15. Why do many fast food outlets use saturated fats to fry foods?

16. Identify the dangers associated with including a lot of saturated fats in your diet.

Critical Thinking

17. Use the bar graph below to answer the following questions.

   (a) Which food contains the highest percentage of water?

   (b) List the foods in order from the greatest to the lowest percentage of protein.

   (c) Identify the benefits and the disadvantages associated with eating each of the foods shown.

Relative Amounts of Substances Found in Some Foods

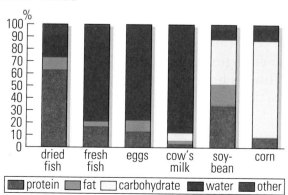

18. Benedict's solution is added to an unknown sample. No colour change is observed, even after the solution is heated in a hot-water bath. A chemical that digests complex carbohydrates is added to the test tube and a color change is noted. Explain the results.

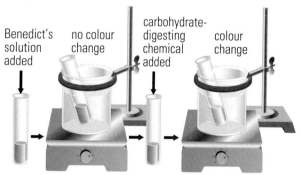

19. Interpret the following laboratory data.

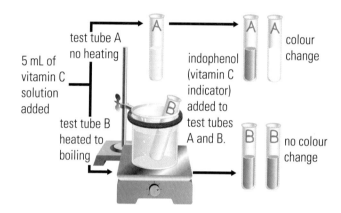

20. Consuming too much or too little of certain nutrients can cause various illnesses. Select one of the following health problems to study: diabetes, rickets, scurvy, hypertension, osteoporosis, pellagra, beriberi, goitre, pernicious anemia, xerophthalmia, kwashiorker.

   (a) What causes the illness you chose?

   (b) What type of person is most likely to have this health problem?

   (c) What effects does it have on a person's body?

   (d) How can it be treated or prevented?

Present the information in whatever form you find most interesting—as a pamphlet of the kind you might find in a doctor's office, as a video interview with a specialist, as a poster, etc.

CHAPTER 17

Food Energy Requirements

HAVE YOU EVER NOTICED HOW MANY ads are aimed directly at people your age? The advertisers hope you will start using their products while you are young. Often, customers continue to use the same products as they grow older, so catching buyers when they are young increases long-term sales of the product.

Scientific knowledge about food and energy can help you evaluate messages from advertisers about what you eat and drink. It can help you make informed decisions about what to buy.

In this chapter, you will

- calculate the energy you can obtain from various foods,

- determine your daily energy requirements,

- evaluate diets for nutritional value,

- learn how food is digested, and

- examine how foods can cause allergic reactions in some people.

Getting Started

Use your knowledge to answer the following questions.

1. Is it better to eat an 85-g chocolate bar or 85 g of pasta?

2. Do teenage males and females require the same amount of food?

3. What information do you find on food labels? Is this information important?

4. Is it possible for two people to maintain the same mass but eat different amounts?

5. How does exercise affect how much you eat?

Re-examine your answers once you have completed the chapter. Write down any changes in your thinking using a pen of a different colour. Categorize the changes as changes in knowledge or changes in attitude. Discuss how both attitudes and knowledge may influence our actions.

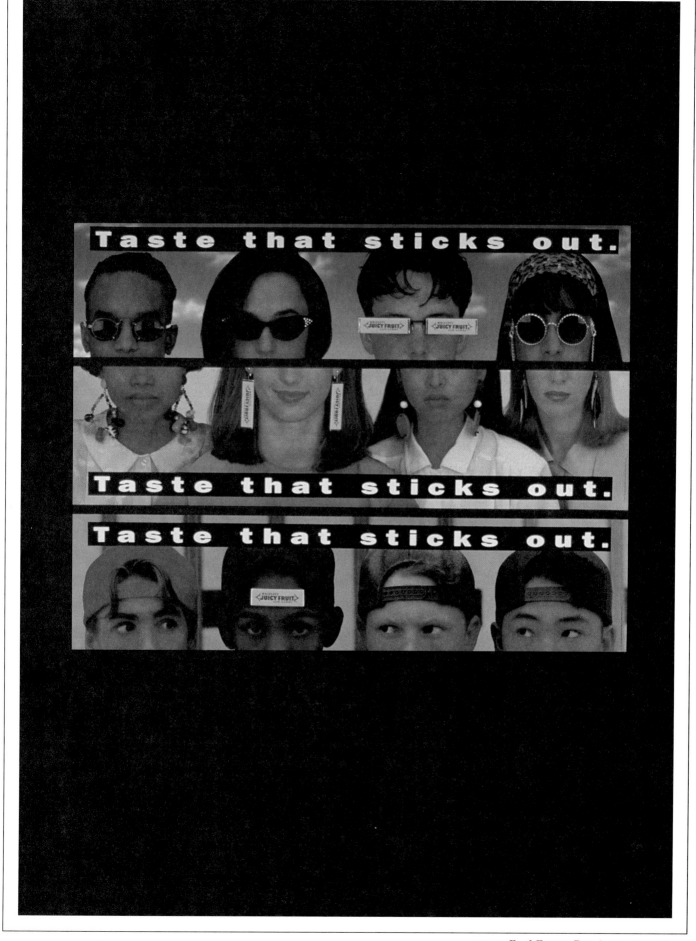

Defining Food Energy

THE TERM ENERGY IS USED OFTEN, but is not easy to describe. You can't see energy, smell it, or find its mass. You know it is present only when it changes form. In your body, chemical energy can be converted by muscle cells into motion. Every time you lift your book, you use energy. However, you use energy even when you don't move. Every breath, every beat of your heart requires energy. Just keeping your body warm takes energy. You need a minimum amount of energy just to keep you alive. The term **basal metabolic rate** describes this minimum amount of energy.

A Unit for Measuring Energy

Energy is measured in **joules** (J) or **kilojoules** (kJ). It takes 4.18 J to raise the temperature of 1 g of water by 1°C. A greater temperature change requires more energy (joules). Also, more energy is required to raise the temperature of a larger mass of water by 1°C. It is important to note that each chemical requires a different amount of energy to increase its temperature by 1°C.

The joule has replaced another unit, the **calorie**. It takes 1 calorie to raise the temperature of 1 g of water by 1°C. Energy values of foods are often given in **kilocalories** (1000 calories), shown on labels as "Calories" (with a capital C). One calorie is equal to 4.18 J, and one kilocalorie (one Calorie) is equal to 4184 J, or 4.18 kJ.

Balancing Energy

A balance between energy input and energy output maintains a healthy body. That is, the amount of energy intake from food should equal the energy output that is used for growth, exercise, and normal metabolic reactions.

If food intake is increased while energy output remains the same, an imbalance will be created. The balance is also lost if energy output is increased while food intake remains the same.

If food intake exceeds energy output, you might expect the person to gain mass. Why? The energy that goes into the body is never lost, it only changes into other forms. The excess energy can be converted into fat or other energy-storage compounds. What do you think will happen if the balance swings the other way, and energy output exceeds food intake?

Daily Energy Requirements (Normal Activity Levels)

Description of person	Energy requirement (kJ per day)
Newborn	2 000
Child (2–3)	6 000
Teenage girl	9 500
Teenage boy	12 000
Office worker	11 000
Heavy labourer	15 000

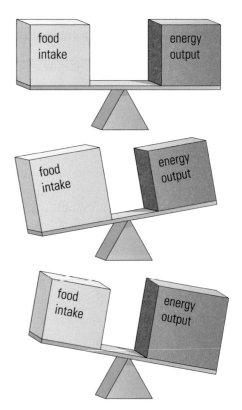

To be healthy, your body needs a balance between food intake and energy output.

energy from food

energy output

- activity
- repair of damaged cells
- maintenance of body temperature
- excess energy stored as fat

Factors that Affect Metabolism

Different people have different energy requirements. Larger people have more cells, so they have greater energy needs. Active people require more energy. Also, different individuals, even if they have the same body mass, can have different rates of metabolism. (**Metabolism** is the sum of all the chemical reactions that occur within the body cells. This includes the reactions that convert the chemical energy from food into other forms of energy.)

A chemical messenger produced in the thyroid gland controls the rate at which the cells of the body convert energy from food into other forms of energy. If the amount of this chemical messenger increases, metabolism increases. A portion of the energy from metabolism is converted into heat energy. Some of this energy is used to warm up the body, and the rest escapes. A person with a low metabolic rate uses the energy from food efficiently. Little energy from food is converted into heat, and therefore less energy escapes from the body. Instead, the energy is converted into energy-storage molecules called fat. A person with a high metabolic rate converts a larger portion of food energy into heat. Less energy from food is converted into fat.

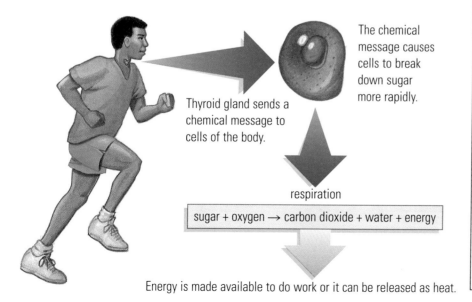

Thyroid gland sends a chemical message to cells of the body.

The chemical message causes cells to break down sugar more rapidly.

respiration

sugar + oxygen → carbon dioxide + water + energy

Energy is made available to do work or it can be released as heat.

Understanding Food Labels

Health and Welfare Canada is a federal agency that regulates the labelling of foods. In 1990, foods with certain *added* nutrients, and those foods for which a *nutritional claim* was made, had to have a label stating the nutrients present. For all other foods, nutritional labelling is voluntary. The Food and Drugs Act regulations state the type of information that companies must include on labels, and how the labels can be presented. Consumer and Corporate Affairs, another federal agency, checks to make sure that proper labelling procedures are followed.

The explanations of the following terms may help you interpret labels.

Enriched means that some, but not all, of the nutrients lost in processing have been added back to the food.

Low-Fat means that a serving must contain less than 3 g of fat, or no more than 15% fat on the basis of dry mass.

Calorie-Reduced means that the food has been modified to give 50% or less of the energy that would normally be found in the food.

Low-Calorie means that the food provides 15 Calories (about 63 kJ) or less per serving.

Sugar-Free means the product is sweetened without natural sugars. The food must not provide more than 1 Calorie (4.18 kJ) per serving.

Light means that the level of at least one component of the food is lower than normal. The "light" nutrient must be identified.

Low-Sodium/Low-Salt means that the food contains no added sodium salts. The product must contain 50% less sodium salts than it would ordinarily contain.

Fortified means that additional vitamins and minerals have been added.

- • *Contains 55% skim m*
- • *Cholesterol free*
- • *Low in saturated fats*
- • *No Preservatives*

INGREDIENTS: SKIM MILK FROM CONCENTRATE (WATER, CONCENTRATED SKIM MILK),

Low Saturated Fats means that the food contains 2 g or less of fat per serving and no more than 15% of this can be saturated fats.

Low-Cholesterol means the food must not provide more than 20 mg of cholesterol per 100-g serving.

Cholesterol-Free means that the food must be low in saturated fats and provide not more than 3 mg of cholesterol per 100-g serving.

Fibre content claims can be made only if the food product contains at least 2 g of dietary fibre per serving.

Evaluating Foods by Reading Labels

The label from a breakfast cereal, shown below, will help you understand what is written on food labels.

The *ingredients* are listed by mass from the largest to the smallest. According to Food and Drug Act regulations, nutrients, vitamins, minerals, and food additives must be listed.

If the product is normally combined with another food product, nutritional information must be given about the food product alone and with the other product.

The major *nutrients*, protein, fat, and carbohydrates, are given in grams per serving.

Sodium and *potassium* amounts are given in milligrams. People with high blood pressure want low-sodium foods.

Claims about *vitamins* must be given as a percentage of the **Recommended Nutrient Intake (RNI)** for Canadians, per serving. The RNI is the recommended amount of a nutrient each person should eat each day.

Claims about *minerals* must also be given as a percentage of the RNI per serving.

Ingredients: whole wheat flour, sugar, wheat germ, yellow corn meal, wheat starch, honey, salt, almonds, golden syrup, vitamins (niacin amide, pantothenate, pyroxidine hydrochlorite, folic acid), mineral (iron), trisodium phosphate, tocopherols.

Nutritional Information

serving size = 30 g = 200 mL = 3/4 cup

	Cereal only	Cereal plus 125 mL 2% Milk
Energy	120 Cal	185 Cal
	505 kJ	765 kJ
Protein	3.1 g	7.3 g
Fat	1.7 g	4.1 g
Carbohydrate	24.0 g	30.0 g
Sugars	10.7 g	16.7 g
Starch	11.8 g	11.8 g
Fibre	1.5 g	1.5 g
Sodium	215 mg	280 mg
Potassium	80 mg	275 mg

Vitamins (% of daily intake)

	Cereal	Cereal and milk
Vitamin D	0	26
Thiamin (B$_1$)	0	3
Riboflavin (B$_2$)	3	16
Niacin	6	6
Vitamin B$_6$	10	13
Folacin	8	11
Vitamin B$_{12}$	0	23
Pantothenate	7	13

Minerals (% of daily intake)

	Cereal	Cereal and milk
Calcium	1	15
Phosphorus	8	19
Magnesium	10	17
Iron	29	29
Zinc	7	12

The *serving size* that energy calculations are based upon must be provided.

The amount of *energy* per serving is provided in both Calories and kilojoules.

SELF CHECK

6. Explain the following terms found on food labels: light, low-sodium, enriched, cholesterol-free, low saturated fats.

7. Explain how product labels can help you differentiate between products. Provide an example.

8. Provide two reasons why an individual might be interested in the ingredients listed on the labels of food products.

9. What is Recommended Nutrient Intake (RNI)?

10. Examine the cereal label.
    (a) Which nutrient is found in the greatest quantity?
    (b) How much is considered a normal serving?
    (c) Identify vitamins that are supplied only by the milk.
    (d) How much calcium is supplied from a normal serving and how much is supplied by the milk?

Measuring Energy in Foods

JUST HOW MUCH ENERGY do you get from each food you eat? In this investigation, you will determine the amount of energy stored in a food using an indirect method. The heat released from burning different foods will be used to heat a water sample. The greater the energy released by burning the food, the more the water will be heated.

Materials

- safety goggles
- apron
- homemade calorimeter
- triple-beam balance
- peanut
- marshmallow
- potato chip
- large cork
- paper clip

- 3 pieces of aluminum foil (large enough to cover the cork)
- 10-mL graduated cylinder
- test tubes
- thermometer (0–110°C)
- retort stand and clamp
- matches
- tongs

Procedure

1 Put on your apron and safety goggles.

2 You will use a calorimeter that has been prepared in advance, as follows:

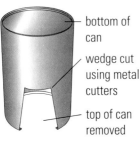

- bottom of can
- wedge cut using metal cutters
- top of can removed

Using metal cutters, remove a wedge from the side of a can at the open end. The wedge must be large enough to allow the cork and the marshmallow to fit through.

- large hole
- smaller vent holes drilled

Drill a large hole in the centre of the bottom of the can. This hole must be large enough to allow a test tube to pass into the can. Drill four small holes around the large hole.

3 In your notebook, make a data table similar to the one that follows. Predict which food will provide the greatest amount of energy.

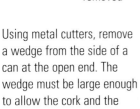 (a) Record your prediction in the # column of your data table.

Food tested	#	Mass of sample (g)	Initial temp. of water (°C)	Final temp. of water (°C)	Change in water temp. (°C)
peanut					
marshmallow					
potato chip					

4 Using a triple-beam balance, determine the mass of the peanut, the marshmallow, and the potato chip.

CAUTION: Never place chemicals (including food) directly on the metal pan of the balance.

(b) Describe how you determined the mass of the three foods.

5 Cover the cork with aluminum foil.

6 Unfold one arm of the paper clip and insert it into the centre of the cork. Bend the rest of the clip so it can support a peanut.

7 Place the peanut on the paper clip.

Steps 6 and 7

8 Using a graduated cylinder, pour 10 mL of water into a test tube.

9 Place the test tube in the calorimeter.

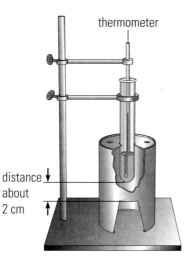

thermometer

distance about 2 cm

Step 9

10 Use a thermometer to take the temperature of the water.

✏ (c) Record the initial temperature of the water in your data table.

11 Check that the cork with the peanut attached to the paper clip fits through the opening of the calorimeter. Make any necessary adjustments.

12 Use a match to light the peanut.

13 Carefully place the cork holding the burning peanut into position inside the calorimeter using a pair of tongs.

peanut on fire

Step 13

14 Once the peanut has burned completely, measure the temperature of the water.

✏ (d) Record the final temperature of the water in your data table.

15 Refer to your data table. Calculate the change in the water temperature.

✏ (e) Record the change in temperature in your data table.

✏ (f) Explain how you determined the change in temperature.

16 Repeat the procedure using the marshmallow and the potato chip in place of the peanut.

✏ (g) Record all values in your data table.

17 Calculate a ratio for temperature change and mass using the following equation.

$$\text{Ratio} = \frac{\text{temperature change}}{\text{mass}}$$

✏ (h) Record the ratio for each food tested.

Questions

1. Compare your predictions with the values obtained for changes in temperature.

2. Compare the ratios for the three foods. Which food had the greatest ratio? How does this value compare with your prediction?

3. Why was it important to record the mass of the foods?

Apply

4. If you wanted a high-energy food, which snack would you choose: peanuts, marshmallows, or potato chips?

Extension

5. Was all of the energy released from the burning marshmallow used to heat the water in the test tube? Explain your answer.

Monitoring Energy Input

I N INVESTIGATION 17.3, YOU LEARNED how to measure the energy stored in food. In this case study, you will compare eating practices by calculating the energy in two different diets.

The word "diet" is often used to refer to specially selected foods, designed for losing or gaining mass. However, a **diet** is, quite simply, the food a person regularly eats and drinks.

The two menus for a full day (below) show very different diets. Matthew and Philip are approximately the same size and are equally active. However, one of the boys is gaining more mass than is typical for his age. Analyze the data carefully in order to determine which diet may be causing a gain in mass. Which foods might cause a gain in body mass? To help you decide, use Energy Available from Selected Foods on page 536.

Matthew's lunch

Philip's lunch

Matthew's Menu	Philip's Menu
Breakfast	**Breakfast**
3 pancakes with syrup	1 poached egg
2 250-mL cups of coffee with cream	250 mL orange juice
2 slices bacon	250 mL skim milk
	2 pieces of toast
Lunch	**Lunch**
90 g hamburger (with bun)	90 g chicken (in sandwich)
60 g hamburger bun	30 g bread (2 slices)
40 french fries	2 250-mL glasses of skim milk
250 mL milkshake	1 apple
Supper	**Supper**
180 g steak	90 g steak
mashed potatoes with butter	1 baked potato
125 mL peas	250 mL peas
1 piece of apple pie	1/2 cantaloupe
355 mL cola	125 mL cottage cheese
	250 mL skim milk

Questions

1. Estimate which menu contains the greater amount of food, by mass.

2. Fats are considered to be the highest-energy food. They supply 3780 kJ for a 100-g serving, as compared with carbohydrates and proteins, which supply 1680 kJ for a 100-g serving. It is recommended that not more than 35% of your energy intake be from fats. Identify foods in both menus that contain a large amount of fat.

3. Compare the energy intake for each meal for both menus.

4. Which menu do you believe would cause a greater gain in mass, other factors being the same? Give your reasons.

Apply

5. Provide suggestions for changing the diet of the boy with the less healthy diet.

6. Evaluate the following statement. (Give reasons why you accept or reject the statement.) "People who gain mass just eat too much. If you want to lose weight, just cut down on what you eat."

Extension

7. Estimate your daily energy input. Record the number in your notebook. Make a daily record of all the foods and beverages that you consume over three days. You should record the type of food and quantity consumed, immediately, in a notebook. Do not rely on your memory.

Sample record:
toast 2 slices, white bread
milk 1 glass
eggs 2, boiled

(a) Prepare a table, like the one that follows, of your food intake for each of the three days. Calculate the energy value of the food you consumed. (Use the chart entitled Energy Available from Selected Foods on page 536.) If some of the foods you eat are not in the chart, make approximations for their energy value by comparing them with similar foods. Indicate the approximation by placing a * beside the food.

Food Intake, Day 1

Food type	Quantity	Energy (kJ/volume) or (kJ/mass)	Total energy (kJ)
toast	2 slices	340/slice	680
milk	1 glass		
eggs			

(b) Add together the amount of energy from all foods for each of the three days.

(c) Calculate the average daily energy intake.

(d) How did your calculated value compare with your estimated value? If there was a difference in the two values, comment on why.

(e) What foods would you recommend to someone who wants to gain body mass? To lose body mass?

(f) Based on your results, do you think you are consuming enough energy for your daily requirements?

DID YOU KNOW?

A Big Mac® contains 2190 kJ, while Dairy Queen's Ultimate Homestyle Burger® has 2950 kJ. The Kentucky Fried Chicken two-piece dinner® has 2457 kJ, while the three-piece dinner® contains 4135 kJ.

Determining Energy Output

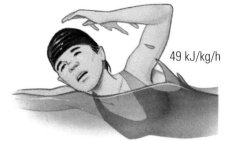

49 kJ/kg/h

A S YOU KNOW, YOUR BODY NEEDS ENERGY even when you are not moving. You need energy to make new red blood cells, repair damaged cells, and maintain a constant body temperature. The more active you are, the more energy you require to maintain the balance between energy input and energy output. The amount of energy required per hour for each kilogram of body mass can be expressed as an "energy factor." The energy factor will increase as activity increases.

Approximate energy factors for some sports. Values can change with the intensity at which the sport is played.

44 kJ/kg/h

38 kJ/kg/h

11 kJ/kg/h

MATH-LINK

Calculating Energy Requirements

How much energy do you use while you are sleeping? The energy factor for sleeping is 4.1 kJ/kg/h. How much energy will a 70-kg person use if the person sleeps for 10 h? This can be calculated by multiplying the energy factor by the body mass in kilograms and again by the amount of time spent sleeping.

Energy required for sleep = energy factor × body mass × time
= 4.1 kJ/kg/h × 70 kg × 10 h
= 2870 kJ

It takes more energy to sit than it does to sleep. The muscles in your back must contract to keep your body upright. Muscle activity requires energy. It has been estimated that 5.2 kJ/kg/h of energy is used while sitting, 6.0 kJ/kg/h is used sitting and writing, and 6.3 kJ/kg/h is used while standing.

*   Why do you think that more energy is used to stand than to sit?

*   Calculate the amount of energy used by a 60-kg person sitting for 10 h. How much energy is used by the same person sitting and typing for 10 h?

*   Calculate the amount of energy required by a 45-kg person to stand for 4 h.

Energy Factors

The table below provides estimates of the amount of energy used for different activities. The speed at which you do a particular activity affects how much energy you use. The estimates below are for moderate speeds, unless otherwise indicated.

21.5 kJ/kg/h

Energy Factors for Various Activities

Type of activity	Energy factor* kJ/kg/h
sleeping	4.1
sitting	5.2
writing	6.0
standing	6.3
singing	7.1
typing, playing cards	9.0
washing car, cooking	10.5
playing piano	11.2
walking (3 km/h)	11.5
bowling	13.6
cycling (3 km/h)	15.8
walking (5 km/h)	16.3
walking (6.5 km/h)	20.7
badminton	21.5
cycling (15 km/h)	25.6
hiking, fast dancing	27.0
tennis, downhill skiing	36.2
climbing stairs, running (9 km/h)	37.7
cycling (20 km/h)	38.2
cross-country skiing	42.0
swimming crawl (46 m/min)	49.1
handball	49.5
running (13 km/h)	62.0
competitive cross-country skiing	73.6

*Approximate values: can change with the intensity of the activity

SELF CHECK

Use the table of energy factors to answer the following questions.

11. Why are the energy factors for cycling and running listed more than once?

12. How much energy would you use in 20 min of continuous swimming? Show your work.

13. Most people cannot work intensely for a long time. However, well-trained cross-country skiers can operate at close to peak performance for three or more hours. Calculate the total amount of energy used in a three-hour period of competitive cross-country skiing. (Assume the cross-country skier has a mass of 50 kg.)

14. How long would you have to bowl to use the same amount of energy as the competitive cross-country skier in question 13?

Digestion

IN THE PREVIOUS SECTION, YOU CALCULATED the amount of energy required for different types of exercise. In this section, you will learn more about how that energy is provided.

Many of the molecules in the food you eat are very large. Unless they are broken down, the body is not able to use them. **Digestion** is the process by which large food molecules are broken down into smaller molecules. The small food molecules are soluble and small enough to enter your body cells. Your body cells use the small molecules for "fuel" and "building blocks."

Enzymes

The diagram below shows a large food molecule being broken into smaller parts. Special proteins, called **enzymes**, help speed chemical reactions in your body. An enzyme "traps" both a large food molecule and a water molecule. The enzyme helps to bring the two molecules closer together. The water molecule then combines with the large food molecule, breaking it into two parts.

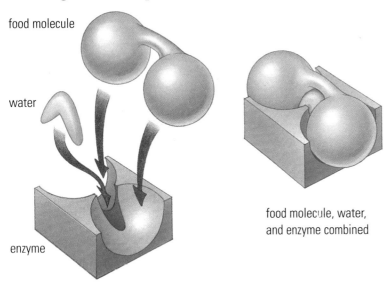

food molecule

water

enzyme

food molecule, water, and enzyme combined

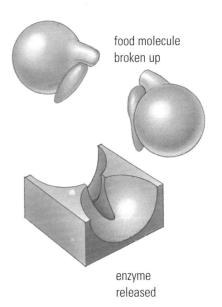

food molecule broken up

enzyme released

 An enzyme splits a food molecule by bringing the food molecule and a water molecule together.

Once the reaction is complete, the enzyme is released, and can be used over and over again. Without enzymes to bring the molecules together, reactions would occur very slowly, if at all. One scientist estimated that complex carbohydrates would remain in your digestive system for up to a month without enzymes to break them down! Some of the molecules that are more difficult to digest, such as fats, might never be digested if it were not for enzymes.

Following Digestion

Your digestive system is designed to both break down and absorb food. Let's follow a turkey sandwich from the mouth to its final stages of digestion. Most of the turkey is meat, a protein. Mixed in with the protein is fat. Starches are found in the bread.

1 The Mouth

Digestion of the turkey sandwich begins in the mouth, when the teeth begin to break up the food. The food is moistened by saliva, which contains water and a starch-splitting enzyme. The enzyme breaks long starch molecules into shorter chains of sugar molecules.

4 The Liver

The liver produces bile, which helps break up large globules of fat into smaller droplets. Bile is stored in the gall bladder, and enters the small intestine through a duct.

gall bladder

pancreas

blood vessel

water molecules

5 The Small Intestine

As the partially digested turkey sandwich enters the small intestine, it meets digestive fluids coming from the pancreas and the gall bladder. These digestive fluids begin the breakdown of fats and complete the digestion of starch and proteins. Once digested, the nutrients are absorbed through the walls of the small intestine (blow-up) and carried by the blood to the body cells.

2 The Esophagus

After the sandwich is swallowed, it passes through the esophagus into a J-shaped tube called the stomach.

3 The Stomach

The stomach starts to digest the protein in the turkey meat. The stomach only begins the breakdown of protein. Pepsin, an enzyme, begins to break long protein molecules into smaller chains.

blood vessel

food molecules

SELF CHECK

15. What are enzymes and why are they important?
16. Define digestion.
17. Summarize digestion that occurs in the mouth, stomach, and small intestine. You may wish to show your answer in the form of a chart or diagram.
18. In what part of the digestive system is food absorbed?
19. ASA can remove the protective mucus coating that lines the stomach. Explain why taking a large number of Aspirin tablets every day might cause digestive problems.

---

6 The Large Intestine

The large intestine removes water from any undigested food (blow-up) and stores wastes until they are eliminated.

Pineapple Power

IN THE LAST SECTION, YOU LEARNED how enzymes speed digestion. In this investigation, you will study enzymes in pineapple juice that can digest the proteins in egg white.

Materials

- safety goggles
- apron
- wax pencil
- 6 test tubes
- test-tube rack
- 10-mL graduated cylinder
- distilled water

- fresh pineapple juice
- 250-mL beaker
- hot plate
- ring stand
- test-tube holder
- hard-boiled egg
- kitchen knife
- ruler

Procedure

1 Put on your apron and safety goggles.

2 Use a wax pencil to label one test tube "P" for pineapple juice and another "W" for water.

3 Using a graduated cylinder, add 15 mL of distilled water to the test tube labelled W. Add 15 mL of pineapple juice to the test tube labelled P.

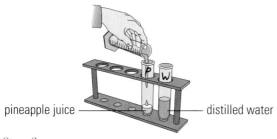

pineapple juice — distilled water

Step 3

4 Set up a hot-water bath. Use a test-tube holder to place the two test tubes in the hot-water bath.

5 Bring the water bath to a boil for 5 min.

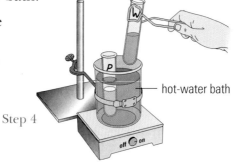

hot-water bath

Step 4

6 Turn off the hot plate and use a test-tube holder to remove the test tubes. Place the test tubes in a rack and allow the solutions to cool for 5 min.

CAUTION: Never handle a hot test tube without using a test-tube holder.

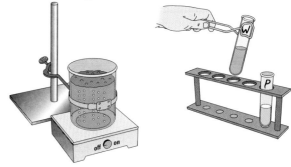

Step 6

7 Remove the shell from a hard-boiled egg. Use a kitchen knife to cut four cubes of egg white. Each cube should measure about 1 cm × 1 cm × 1 cm. Use the ruler to help measure the cubes.

(a) Why should the egg white cubes be the same size?

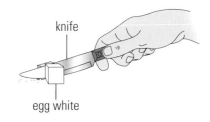

knife

egg white

Step 7

8 Use the wax pencil to number four clean, dry test tubes. Put a cube of egg white in each tube. To each tube, add 10 mL of liquid—distilled water in 1; fresh pineapple juice in 2; boiled pineapple juice in 3; and boiled water in 4. Rinse the graduated cylinder well between measurements.

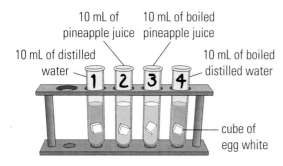

10 mL of pineapple juice   10 mL of boiled pineapple juice
10 mL of distilled water   10 mL of boiled distilled water
cube of egg white

Step 8

9 Make a table in your notebook with columns listing the test tubes and their contents, your predictions, and your observations. Predict what will happen in each tube.

(b) Record your predictions in your table.

10 Store your test tubes where they will not be disturbed. Clean up your work station and wash your hands.

11 View the test tubes during the following class.

(c) Record your observations.

12 Dispose of the contents of the tubes as directed by your teacher. Wash your hands.

Questions

1. Which test tube(s) acted as a control? Explain why.

2. State the independent variable and the dependent variable for this experiment. (To review variables, refer to Exploring Cause and Effect on page 22.)

3. How does boiling affect enzymes?

Apply

4. Two students analyze the data from this investigation and reach different conclusions. Maria thinks the enzymes are changed by heating so they don't work. Estelle thinks a little heating would speed up the reaction, but boiling destroys the enzyme. Suggest an investigation that would determine whether Maria or Estelle is on the right track.

5. Suggest an alternative to the conclusions of Maria and Estelle.

6. Why can you not make gelatin dessert using fresh pineapple juice instead of water?

Extension

7. Set up an experiment to determine the effect of enzyme concentration on the digestion of egg proteins.

   • Provide a hypothesis for your experiment.

   • Identify the independent variable and dependent variable for the experiment.

   • Devise your laboratory procedure and provide a materials list.

   • Submit your laboratory design to your teacher for approval before beginning the experiment.

8. The stomach has a protective wall of mucus that prevents acids or the protein-digesting enzyme from damaging it. In stomach cells, protein-digesting enzymes are stored in an inactive form. Once the enzyme leaves the stomach cell, an acid in the stomach changes the shape of the inactive enzyme, making it active. The active enzyme then begins to digest proteins. Why must protein-digesting enzymes be stored in the inactive form?

When Lunch Threatens Life

I N 1994, A STUDENT DIED on a school camping trip. A jam sandwich, contaminated with peanut butter, was the cause. The student had a severe allergic reaction to the peanut butter. She was unable to receive her medication in time.

Unfortunately, this situation is not a one-time occurrence. Many children have food allergies. Although most are troubled only by an upset stomach if they eat the food they are allergic to, a few are more sensitive and may become very ill, or even die. In 1993, a child died at a Montreal camp after eating a cheese sandwich that had been packed in the same container as peanut butter sandwiches.

Some parents have proposed that peanut butter, one of the main causes of severe allergies, should be prohibited anywhere children gather. Some allergists feel that peanut butter should be banned from children's camps and schools.

Some Ontario schools have removed peanuts and peanut butter from school vending machines. One of those is in

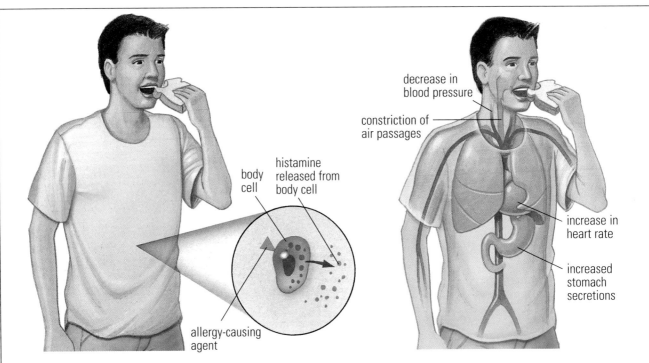

body cell

histamine released from body cell

allergy-causing agent

decrease in blood pressure

constriction of air passages

increase in heart rate

increased stomach secretions

What Is an Allergic Reaction?

- Molecules of the allergy-causing substance attach to a body cell. The cell releases a chemical called histamine into the blood.

- Histamine puts the body's defence system into action.

- Capillaries (tiny blood vessels) expand and white blood cells rush to the allergy-causing invader.

- Fluids rush from the capillaries and blood pressure drops.

- Histamine causes the air passages to constrict; less air moves in and out of the lungs.

- Histamine causes the stomach to increase secretions.

- Adrenaline is released because of stress, and the heart rate increases.

Thornhill. When a Thornhill high school basketball player suffered an allergic reaction because a basketball had some peanut butter on it, the principal took action.

What Are Food Allergies?

Severe food allergies are reactions that involve the respiratory and circulatory system. The reaction is often accompanied by swelling of body parts, "bumps," and itching. These reactions can be brought on by drugs, vaccines, and some foods (for example, peanuts, shellfish, eggs, berries, and milk) if the person is sensitive to these substances.

Symptoms

The reaction can occur very quickly. Weakness, sweating, and difficulty breathing are indicators. Nausea, diarrhea, and a drop in blood pressure may also occur.

Tips for Prevention

Medical advice may range from carrying a kit with adrenaline to taking antihistamines. Those who have severe allergies should wear a medical alert bracelet or necklace and take care to read all food labels.

Understanding the Author

1. What substances commonly provoke allergic reactions?

2. How can you tell if someone is suffering an allergic reaction?

3. During an allergic reaction, the body "thinks" it has been invaded by a toxic substance. Why do you think that restricting the amount of air that enters the body is part of the reaction?

Proposal

Peanuts and peanut butter must be banned from the school lunchroom to protect those who are allergic to peanuts.

Point

- Serving peanut butter infringes on the right of the students who have allergies to eat lunch in the same area as other students.

- Allergies to most other products are not dangerous unless the student actually eats the food. Peanuts are particularly dangerous because even their smell can initiate an allergic reaction.

- Parents can ensure their children avoid other eating places, but the children cannot avoid going to school.

Counterpoint

- Peanuts are nutritious. They provide a good, inexpensive source of protein. How can you ban nutritious foods but allow other food products associated with high blood pressure, heart disease, cancer, and tooth decay?

- Some students have severe allergies to milk products, foods that contain sodium benzoate, or certain cereal grains. Where would the ban on foods end?

- Having a ban in schools only creates a false sense of security. Students will still eat meals in a variety of places that do not have bans on peanuts.

What Do You Think?

4. Your group will prepare a proposal to the school board, either in favour of or opposing a ban on peanuts and peanut butter in your school lunchroom.

Key Outcomes

Now that you have completed this chapter, can you do the following? If not, review the sections indicated.

- Evaluate food labels for different nutrients. (17.2)

- Explain the importance of maintaining a balance between food intake (energy input) and energy output. (17.1, 17.4, 17.5)

- Evaluate diets and calculate energy input. (17.1, 17.3)

- Use a calorimeter to determine the energy stored in various foods. (17.3)

- Compare various forms of exercise and calculate energy output. (17.4, 17.5)

- Explain the importance of enzymes in digestion. (17.6, 17.7)

- Explain how food allergies can be a serious health problem for some people. (17.8)

Key Terms

basal metabolic rate

joule (J)

kilojoule (kJ)

calorie

kilocalorie (Calorie)

metabolism

recommended nutrient intake (RNI)

diet

digestion

enzyme

Review

1. Explain how the order of ingredients on a food label helps you know what you are eating.

2. Why might some people select foods that are low in sodium?

3. How are energy and fat intake related?

4. Give two reasons why an individual might be interested in reading the list of ingredients on a food label.

5. (a) What is a kilojoule?

   (b) What is a Calorie?

6. Which food category (fats, carbohydrates, or proteins) provides the greatest amount of energy?

7. How does your thyroid gland help regulate your metabolism?

8. Match each of the following parts of the digestive system to its function in digestion.

   A mouth

   B stomach

   C small intestine

   D gall bladder

   1. an enzyme breaks down protein molecules into smaller chains

   2. bile is stored here

   3. a starch-splitting enzyme breaks starch molecules into shorter chains

   4. digestive fluids begin to break down fat, and digestion of proteins and carbohydrates continues

Problem Solving

9. List three factors that might explain why two people of equal mass require different amounts of energy.

10. How long would it take a 70-kg man to use the energy supplied by a cola and a cheeseburger if he jogged at a moderate rate? The energy factor for jogging is 37.5 kJ/kg/h. Hint: Use the following equation.

energy output = energy factor × body mass × time

Critical Thinking

11. Use the graph below to interpret the following experimental data.

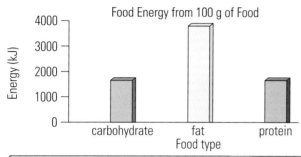

Food Energy from 100 g of Food

Results of Energy Testing

Food type	Mass (g)	Energy (kJ)
cola	204	483
banana split	300	2494
cheeseburger	180	1940

(a) Which food provided the greatest amount of energy per gram?

(b) Explain why this food provided more energy per gram.

12. You are using a calorimeter to find the energy value of a peanut, but the peanut fails to burn completely. How might this affect your results?

13. Compare the ingredients found on the two soup labels below. Which soup would you recommend? Give your reasons.

BRAND X MUSHROOM SOUP

Ingredients: water, skimmed milk, chicken broth, corn starch, mushrooms, salt, vegetable oil, dehydrated onions, MSG, spices

BRAND Y MUSHROOM SOUP

Ingredients: water, 2% milk, chicken broth, corn starch, vegetable oil, dehydrated onions, salt, mushrooms, chicken fat, MSG, spices

14. Using a calorimeter, experimenters obtained the following data.

Energy Values of Various Items

Sample tested	Mass of sample (g)	Initial temp. of water (°C)	Final temp. of water (°C)	Change in water temp (°C)
peanut	5	19	23	4
breakfast cereal	30	19	26	7
cereal box	30	20	32	12

Evaluate each of the following statements. Explain why you accept or reject the statement.

(a) You cannot compare the energy output of the peanut with that of the cereal, because it has a different mass.

(b) You cannot compare the energy value for the cereal box and the cereal because the initial temperature of the water was not the same.

(c) The peanut provides the greatest amount of energy per gram.

(d) Eating the cereal box for breakfast would provide more energy than eating cereal.

15. Use Energy Available from Selected Foods on page 536 to evaluate the following diets.

	Diet A	Diet B
breakfast	no breakfast	• orange juice, fresh (250 mL) • raisin bread (1 slice)
lunch	• cola (200 mL) • macaroni and cheese (250 mL) • brownie (3)	• skim milk (250 mL) • lasagna (1 piece) • apple (1)
4 p.m. snack	• chocolate eclair with custard filling	• raisins (25 mL)

(a) Which diet provides the greater amount of energy?

(b) If both people are very active teenagers, what changes would you recommend to their diets?

Treating Hamburger Disease

DR. GLEN ARMSTRONG, a professor in the Department of Medical Microbiology at the University of Alberta, is testing a new way to treat a potentially deadly bacterial infection that can come from eating undercooked hamburger meat.

◀ Dr. Glen Armstrong leads a team of researchers that studies bacterial diseases.

Q. How did you become interested in the problem of "hamburger disease"?

A. I lead a group of researchers who study microorganisms that cause different kinds of diseases. A few years ago, two children died in Calgary from hamburger disease. The mother of one of my students, who worked in a daycare facility, asked her son whether we could do anything. He came to me and we tackled the problem as a team.

Q. What is hamburger disease?

A. Hamburger disease is an infection in the large intestine caused by a particular form of the bacterium *Escherichia coli*. Normally, the *E. coli* that are found in the human large intestine are not harmful. But this form, *E. coli* type O157, damages the wall of the large intestine and causes pain and bloody diarrhea. Small children and older people get this infection especially easily. The bacteria also release a toxin, or poison, called verotoxin, which can be quite dangerous. In a very few cases, this toxin gets into the bloodstream and attacks the kidneys, doing a lot of damage. In these cases, the victims have to have dialysis, and some patients die.

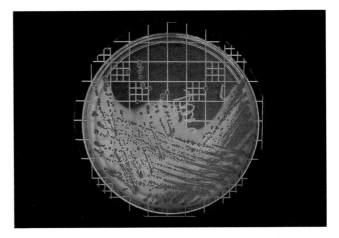

Colonies of *Escherichia coli* bacteria growing in a petri dish. All people have *E. coli* like these in their large intestine. But only a few forms of this bacterium, such as *E. coli* type O157, can make you sick.

Q. How can you get this disease?

A. Cattle carry these bacteria, but the bacteria don't make them sick. Hamburger meat from cattle is sometimes infected. The bacteria are easily killed by heat, but if we eat raw hamburger meat, or meat that hasn't been cooked enough—like a rare hamburger patty—the live bacteria pass into our intestine. Even a small number of them can make us quite sick.

Q. What is unusual about your treatment of this infection?

A. We are testing a treatment that can mop up the toxin. Doctors treat most bacterial infections with antibiotics, like penicillin or streptomycin, but that doesn't work with this disease. When these bacteria are killed by an antibiotic, they release a lot of toxin and that is quite dangerous.

We have found that the toxin binds to molecules of a very specific shape that are found in kidney cells. These molecules are actually complex sugars. What we do is give the patient a complex sugar molecule that looks just like the one in the kidney cells. The toxin then attaches harmlessly to the "decoy" molecule.

Q. Did you always want to be a scientist?

A. I was always curious. When I was a child, I used to take apart all the clocks in the house—I wanted to know how they worked. I guess I always knew I wanted to be some kind of scientist, but it was in university that I realized that I was most interested in biology.

Q. It sounds like you really enjoy your work.

A. I do. I love studying complicated, interesting puzzles, and that's what research is.

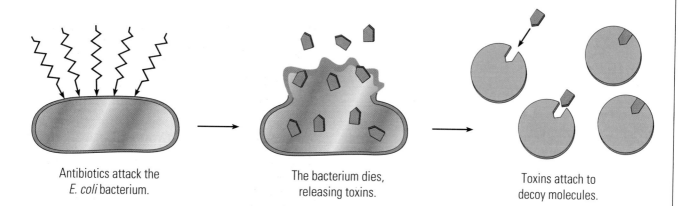

Antibiotics attack the *E. coli* bacterium.

The bacterium dies, releasing toxins.

Toxins attach to decoy molecules.

A Group Effort

Dr. Wendy Johnson is Chief of the National Laboratory for Bacteriology at the Laboratory Centre for Disease Control (LCDC).

In the late 1970s, researchers at Health and Welfare Canada discovered a toxin, called verotoxin, in certain strains of bacteria. In the 1980s, Dr. Johnson joined the team and began to do a "surveillance." She checked many patients with bloody diarrhea to see whether they had anything in common. And that's when she found the link between verotoxin, the strain of *Escherichia coli* type O157, and the symptoms of hamburger disease.

Canadian scientists lead the world in the diagnosis and treatment of this disease.

Techniques that Dr. Johnson's group at Health Canada developed to identify the bacterium are used around the world. According to Dr. Johnson, the reason for our success is the network of scientists across Canada who all contribute to our knowledge of the disease.

NOW THAT YOU HAVE COMPLETED Chapters 16 and 17, you can assess how much you have learned about Food and Energy by trying these questions.

Before you begin, you may find it useful to return to the Chapter Reviews. There, you will find lists of Key Outcomes and Key Terms. Read these to ensure that you understand the main points and the important vocabulary in the chapters. If necessary, look back at the appropriate sections in the text, which are listed with the Key Outcomes.

Write your answers to the questions in your notebook.

True/False

For each of the following, write T if the statement is true. If the statement is false, rewrite it to make it true.

1. Carbohydrates are often described as an energy source.

2. All carbohydrates are sweet.

3. Cellulose, the carbohydrate of plant cell walls, is an important source of energy for people.

4. Saturated fats are more difficult to break down than unsaturated fats.

5. Proteins are composed of amino acids.

6. Vitamins help your body change food into energy.

7. Iron, calcium, and potassium are important minerals in your body.

8. Food energy can be measured in kilojoules.

9. All people who have the same body mass have the same energy requirements.

10. The energy provided by 1 g of fat is greater than that provided by 1 g of protein or carbohydrate.

11. Most fat digestion and the absorption of nutrients occurs in the stomach.

Completion

Copy the following sentences, filling in each blank with the word or phrase that correctly completes the sentence. Use the words from this list: proteins, fats, fibre, cholesterol, saturated, unsaturated, essential amino acid, joules, simple sugars, basal metabolic rate, energy input, pepsin. (You will not need all of the words.)

12. Glucose and fructose are examples of ▧.

13. Carbohydrates, fats, and ▧ are major groups of nutrients.

14. A chemical often associated with heart problems is ▧.

15. Cellulose is an important part of your diet because it provides needed ▧.

16. Animal fats are often called ▧ fats.

17. An amino acid that must be included in your diet is often called an ▧.

18. Your lowest energy requirement is called your ▧.

19. Units for measuring energy are ▧ and calories.

20. A protein-digesting enzyme found in the stomach is ▧.

21. The stomach is responsible for the initial digestion of ▧.

Matching

Copy the numbers of the descriptions given below. Beside each number, write the word or phrase from the right column that best fits the description. (You will not need to use all of the words.)

22. an organ found near the top of the small intestine that produces digestive enzymes

23. a chemical found in coffee, tea, and colas

24. a digestive organ that stores bile

25. a chemical indicator for proteins

26. an indicator for starch

27. used as an indicator for sugars

28. a sweet ingredient of milk

29. helps regulate your basal metabolic rate

30. an example of a simple sugar

31. a chemical that inhibits the growth of moulds or bacteria in food

A pancreas
B fructose
C thyroid gland
D preservative
E lactose
F gall bladder
G caffeine
H Benedict's solution
I iodine
J Biuret solution
K vitamins
L nicotine

Multiple Choice

Write the letter of the best answer for each of the following questions. Write only one answer for each.

32. Which of the following nutrients make up most of the structural components of a cell?

A carbohydrates

B vitamin C

C unsaturated fats

D saturated fats

E proteins

33. Which of the following foods provides a rich source of carbohydrates and a low level of fats?

A potato chips

B pasta

C hamburger

D steak

E eggs

Use the information provided by the analysis of food samples 1–5 to answer the next two questions. A ✓ indicates a positive test. A — indicates a negative test.

| Food sample | Test conducted | | |
	Benedict's test	Brown paper (translucence) test	Biuret test
1	✓	—	—
2	✓	—	✓
3	—	✓	—
4	—	—	✓
5	✓	✓	—

34. The foods were being tested for

A vitamin C, protein, and fat.

B sugar, vitamin C, and starch.

C minerals, vitamins, and cholesterol.

D sugar, fat, and protein.

E starch, sugar, and protein.

35. Protein is found in sample(s)

A 1, 2, and 5.

B 2 and 4.

C 3 and 5.

D 5 only.

E 1 only.

36. The following data were collected on various milk products.

Food	Volume (mL)	Mass (g)	Food energy (kJ)
whipping cream	250	252	3640
whole milk	250	257	660
2% milk	250	258	540
skim milk	250	258	380
buttermilk	250	258	430
evaporated milk	250	356	1490

Four research groups proposed different explanations after examining the data.

Group 1: All milk has the same energy value.

Group 2: The greater the mass of the milk, the greater is the energy.

Group 3: The greater the fat content, the greater is the energy.

Group 4: You can't determine the energy value of different types of milk by looking at the volume used.

Which groups have the most reasonable hypotheses?

A 1 and 3   **D** 1 and 4

B 2 and 4   **E** 2 and 3

C 3 and 4

37. Which of the following foods is a source of protein?

A soda pop

B steak

C butter

D all of the above

E none of the above

Short Answer

Write a sentence or a short paragraph to answer each of the following questions.

38. In what ways does the meaning of "sugar-free" on a label differ from "calorie-reduced"?

39. Why are many Canadians advised to monitor their intake of cholesterol?

40. Why are food preservatives added to bread?

41. List five foods that would provide a good source of each of the following nutrients.

(a) carbohydrates

(b) fats

(c) proteins

(d) vitamin C

42. Plants provide an important source of fibre. Why is fibre recommended in your diet?

43. The following ingredients are found on a food label: dextrose, sucrose, galactose, and glucose. How are these ingredients related?

44. Name two foods that are important sources of vitamins and identify the vitamins in each.

45. Why are some amino acids called essential amino acids?

46. Explain how food allergies can be life-threatening.

47. Why must energy intake be balanced with energy output?

48. In what areas of the digestive system are the following digested?

(a) carbohydrates

(b) fats

(c) proteins

49. List factors that affect your energy needs.

50. What is a kilojoule?

Problem Solving

Use the information in the chart below to answer the next three questions.

Student's Energy Intake During One Day

Food	Serving size	Energy (kJ/serving)	Amount consumed
cheddar cheese	7 g	118	21 g
2% milk	250 mL	540	1000 mL
scrambled eggs	1 egg	400	2
ground beef	1 pattie	1080	2
bacon	1 slice	380	2
peas	250 mL	267	125 mL
apple	1	290	1
french fries	10 pieces	650	20 pieces
lemonade from concentrate	250 mL	420	250 mL
brownie	1 piece	400	2
cola	200 mL	320	200 mL

51. Use the following formula to calculate the student's energy needs while cross-country skiing for two hours.

    Energy requirement = body mass x energy factor x time

    Energy factor for cross-country skiing = 42 kJ/kg/h

    Body mass = 55 kg

52. How much time would the student have to cross-country ski to use all of the energy provided by the food she ate that day?

53. The average teenage female needs 9500 kJ of food energy per day. The student whose diet was studied is average in other ways, but she also goes cross-country skiing for two hours every day. Make suggestions for changes in the student's diet.

Challenge

54. Design a balanced menu for someone requiring 9000 kJ of energy per day. The menu is for one day.

55. Test various dry snack foods for fat content. (Use the procedure developed on page 461.) Prepare a consumer report of your findings.

Design and Do

56. Prepare a questionnaire for grade 9 students to investigate their attitudes about food and energy.

57. Design an experiment to determine how temperature affects the rate of digestion of egg proteins by enzymes from pineapple.

Project Ideas

58. Visit a dietitian and a physiotherapist who specialize in work with athletes. Obtain information about recommended diet and training for the athletes, and prepare a presentation for your class.

59. Use a video camera or still camera to prepare a presentation about snack foods. Select a group on which to concentrate your study. Interview students, adults, and/or young children. Include the information you obtain as a part of your presentation.

Concept Maps

WHEN YOU ARE TRYING TO DESCRIBE objects and events, it is sometimes helpful to write your ideas down so that you can see them and compare them with those of other people. Instead of writing these ideas down in sentences, they can be made into concept maps. A **concept map** is a collection of words (representing concepts) or pictures that you connect to each other with arrows and short descriptions. The map is a drawing of what is happening in your brain.

You may have seen concept maps similar to the one shown above. This concept map, called a food web, shows one way of thinking about animals and what they eat. The arrowhead points to the animal that eats the animal or plant at the other end of the arrow. The arrows describe the relationship between the organisms.

Concept maps can also be drawn of other topics and in other ways. For instance, the relationships between family members can be drawn using a concept map like the one to the right.

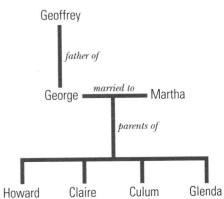

Concept maps can also be drawn to show a series of cause-and-effect relationships. You may find making this kind of map useful during a science investigation.

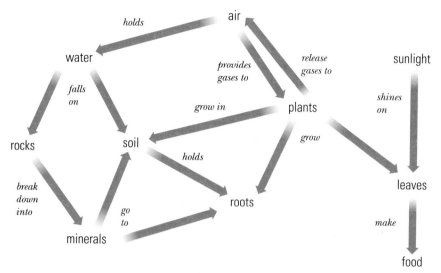

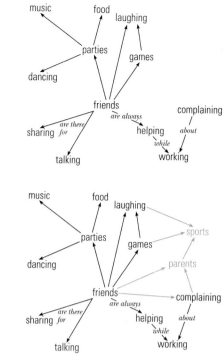

Sometimes concept maps can be used to show how your ideas change and become more complex as you work on a topic. You can see an example of this type of concept map to the right.

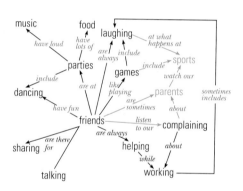

Making a Concept Map

Here are some steps you can take to help you make a concept map.

1. Choose the central idea of your concept map.

2. Write the central idea and all related ideas on small scraps of paper.

3. Move the scraps of paper around the central idea so that the ones most related to each other are near each other. Ask yourself how they are related, and then use that information in the next steps.

4. On a big sheet of paper, write down all of your ideas in the same pattern that you have arranged the scraps. Draw arrows between the ideas that are related.

5. On each arrow, write a short description of how the terms are related to each other.

6. As you go, you may find other ideas or relationships. Add them to the map.

When you gain new ideas—whether from research, from your investigations, or from other people—go ahead and change your concept map. You may want to add new ideas in a different colour of ink, to indicate your new ways of thinking about the ideas.

Concept Maps **503**

Study Skills and Research

UNDERSTANDING ANYTHING—WHETHER IT IS a life-saving technique in the swimming pool, a trumpet solo, or a science lesson—is an active process. The following tips can help you in your learning. You can modify these hints to help you in other school courses and in recreational activities.

Study Tips

- Prepare for class by *reading material ahead of time.* It is also helpful to read or view materials from other sources, such as science magazines, newspapers, and television programs.

- *Take notes.* To make note-taking easier, you may want to make up a shorthand method of recording ideas.

- If you made notes in class, *review* your notes later that day and add comments. Then have a friend or relative quiz you on the material in the notes. Reinforce your understanding by answering the questions in the textbook—even if they are not assigned.

- Use your notes and the textbook to *prepare summaries.* Studying is most effective with pen or pencil in hand, so you can write down the important ideas.

- Draw a *concept map* to help you summarize. (See Concept Maps on page 502.)

- *Practice makes perfect* is as true for science as it is for playing piano and shooting baskets. If you practise your science skills until they become almost automatic, you will have more time to think about how you will use them.

- *Schedule* your study time to avoid that most ineffective of all study methods, "cramming" before tests.

- *Know your strengths and your weaknesses.* Take advantage of all opportunities to get help with areas in which you may have trouble. Use your strengths to help yourself, and others. Try forming a study group and have regular meetings. You may be able to help others in some parts of the course. In turn, you may receive help from them.

- *Teach the material you have learned* to someone who has not yet learned it: a younger student or an adult. Their questions will help you see what areas of the subject you need to learn more about, and what areas you don't completely understand.

Take notes.

Teach what you have learned.

Study Checklist

√ Read material ahead of time.
√ Take notes.
√ Review.
√ Summarize.
√ Draw a concept map.
√ Practise.
√ Schedule study time.
√ Know your strengths and weaknesses.
√ Teach what you have learned.

Research

There is a great deal of information available in our society, but before you can make use of it, you must know how to gather it. This information-gathering skill is known as research.

Research Tips

- Before you begin your research, *make a list of the most important words* associated with your research, so you can search for appropriate topics.

- *Use a variety of resources*—don't rely on one source.

- When deciding if a resource is appropriate, ask yourself: *Do I understand what this resource is telling me?*

- *Check when the resource was published.* Is it up-to-date?

- *Keep organized notes* while doing your research.

- *Keep a list of the resources you used,* so you can make a bibliography when writing your report. (See Reporting Your Work on page 520, for more information.)

- *Review your notes.* After your research, you may want to alter your original problem or hypothesis.

Available Resources

There is no shortage of resources, as a glance at the lists to the right will reveal.

Consultants

(people who can help you locate and interpret information)

teachers

business people

nurses

scientists

public servants

librarians

volunteers

veterinarians

lawyers

senior citizens

parents

doctors

farmers

politicians

members of the media

Places

(sources beyond the walls of your school)

public libraries

shopping malls

parks

colleges

research laboratories

government offices

historic sites

zoos

universities

volunteer agencies

businesses

museums

farms

hospitals

art galleries

References

(sources of packaged information)

encyclopedias

bibliographies

magazines

newspapers

videotapes

slides

data bases

almanacs

year books

maps

charts

radio

films

computer programs

CD-ROMs

dictionaries

biographies

textbooks

pamphlets

television

filmstrips

records

Electronic Source

If you have access to the Internet through a computer and modem, you may have access to all of the resources above, and more.

SKILL BUILDER

Studying

Make a concept map summarizing the information in this section.

Observing

OBSERVATIONS ARE IDEAS AND INFORMATION that you get through your senses. You observe that a rose is red and has a sweet smell. You may also note that it has sharp thorns on its stem. You may count the petals on the flower and the leaves on the stem, and measure the length of the stem.

When people describe the qualities of objects and events, the observations are **qualitative**. The colour of the rose, the odour of the flower, and the sharpness of the thorns are all qualitative observations. Observations that are based on measurements or counting are said to be **quantitative**, since they deal with quantities of things. The length of the stem, the number of petals, and the number of leaves are all quantitative observations.

Scientists have grouped qualitative observations into several categories, based on the kind of qualities of the object or event being described. The following is a list of categories that can be used to qualitatively describe objects or events.

State of Matter: One of three states—solid, liquid, or gas.

Colour: Objects can be described as being any colour or any shade of colour, such as red, orange, yellow, maroon, violet, or puce. Materials that have no colour should be described as colourless.

Smell: Also known as odour. There are many words to describe smells, including pungent, strong, spicy, sweet, and odourless.

Texture: The surfaces of objects can have a variety of textures, including smooth, rough, prickly, fine, coarse.

Taste: Objects can taste sweet, like candy; sour, like lemon; bitter, like baking powder; or salty. Other tastes are combinations of these basic tastes. (In reality, complex tastes depend more on smell than on taste, because our noses are more sensitive than our tongues.)

Shininess: Also known as lustre. Objects with very smooth surfaces that reflect light easily are said to be shiny or lustrous. Kitchen taps, mirrors, even well-polished desktops can be described as lustrous. Objects with dull surfaces are said to be non-lustrous.

Clarity: Some substances let so much light through that letters can be read through them. These substances are said to be clear or transparent. Other substances that allow light through, but not in a way that allows you to see through them, are translucent. Objects that do not let light through are opaque.

Other qualitative descriptions include form (the shape of a substance), hardness, brittleness (how easily the substance breaks), malleability (the ability of the object to be changed into another shape), and viscosity (the thickness of a liquid).

Another important characteristic that can be described qualitatively is the ability of substances to combine with each other. Some qualitative observations of this kind can be found in the Table of Properties on page 532.

SKILL BUILDER

Making Qualitative Observations

For practice in making qualitative observations, try the following activities.

1. Read the paragraph below and identify as many qualitative characteristics as you can. Write down each description in your notebook and include the category you think it belongs to.

It was the middle of October. The autumn air was crisp and tangy, but Shermina was not out to enjoy the clear air. She had to make observations for science class. The teacher had said that the observations could be on any topic, as long as there was a variety that would be interesting to other students. As Shermina walked, she noticed the diversity of colours in the leaves on the trees. Beside the usual yellows and reds, Shermina noticed the range included burnt orange and crimson. The effect of the overlapping hues was pleasing to her eye. She picked up a few of the fallen leaves. One was still quite green and supple, another was completely brown and dried up. Shermina crumpled up the leaves in her fist. When she opened her hand, the broken pieces of the brown leaf slowly floated to the ground. The green leaf popped back to its original shape. The leaf felt smooth between her fingers.

2. Describe an object in your home. Use as many different senses as possible to come up with many different types of observations. Write your descriptions in your notebook.

Measuring

WHICH LINE IS LONGER: **AB** OR **CD**? Use a ruler. You will find that AB and CD are the same length. Our senses can be fooled. That is one of the reasons why quantitative observations are important in science, but it is also the reason measurements must be made carefully.

Standards of Measurement

Units of measurement used to be based on local standards that the community had agreed to. At one time, for example, there was a unit equal to the length of a line of 16 people standing close together. Horse heights are still measured in hands, based on the width of a hand, and measured from the ground to the horse's shoulder.

These standards may sound strange, but the unit of length that replaced most local standards, the metre, was based on an arc on the Earth that ran from the equator, through Barcelona, Paris, and Dunkirk, to the North Pole. The length of this arc, divided by 10 000 000, equaled one metre. That also sounds strange, but it established the first standard that the whole world could use.

The metric system, which includes units such as the metre and the kilogram, has been adopted by Canada. You should be familiar with, and use, the units from this international system. (For more information on the international system of measurement, refer to Appendix 4, Standards in Measurement, on page 530.)

▶ The early standard for the metre was 1/10 000 000 of the distance from the equator to the North Pole.

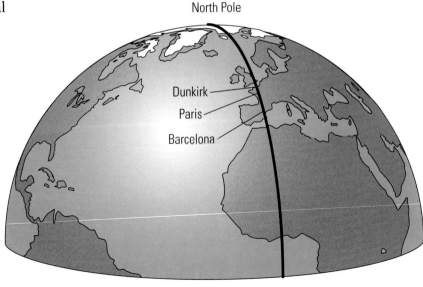

North Pole

Dunkirk
Paris
Barcelona

equator

Problems in Measurement

Many people believe that all measurements are accurate and dependable. But there are many things that can go wrong when measuring. The instrument may be faulty. Another similar instrument may give different readings. There may be limitations that make the instrument unreliable. The person making the measurement may also make a mistake.

Ask your teacher for two thermometers and check the room temperature. Are the readings identical? (You may want to check both thermometers over a range of temperatures—do the two thermometers always give the same readings?) Suppose you use only one thermometer, and it reads 21°C. Is the room temperature really 21°C? That depends on how reliable the thermometer is. If your thermometer is not accurate, the temperature of the room could be 19°C, 23°C, or some other value.

Solving Measurement Problems

When measuring the temperature of a liquid, it is important to keep the bulb of the thermometer near the middle of the liquid. If the liquid is being heated and the thermometer is simply sitting in the container with its bulb at the bottom, you will be measuring the temperature of the bottom of the container, not the temperature of the liquid. There are similar concerns with most measurements. To be sure that you have measured correctly, repeat your measurement at least once. If your measurements are close, calculate the average and use that number. To be more certain, repeat the measurements with a different instrument.

Measurement Checklist

√ Repeat each measurement.
√ Calculate the average.
√ Use more than one instrument.

The Need to Graph

SCIENTISTS AND SCIENCE STUDENTS often create huge amounts of data while doing experiments and studies—maybe hundreds, even thousands, of numbers for every variable. How can this mass of data be arranged so that it is easy to read and understand? That's right—in a graph. The sample table below doesn't have thousands of pieces of data, but it does have enough to become confusing.

Mass and Volume of Rubber Stoppers

Stopper number	Mass (g)	Volume (cm³)	Stopper number	Mass (g)	Volume (cm³)
1	0.8	2.1	11	9.8	17.9
2	1.6	3.8	12	10.5	20.2
3	2.5	4.1	13	11.1	24.1
4	3.9	7.8	14	12.6	24.8
5	4.4	8.8	15	15.7	33.2
6	4.8	10.5	16	29.4	58.4
7	5.0	10.8	17	33.0	67.5
8	7.3	14.6	18	36.8	64.0
9	7.9	15.8	19	42.1	84.7
10	8.9	15.9	20	45.6	95.2

A graph is an easy way to see more precisely what a relationship is, so it can be accurately described in words and mathematics. To the right is a graph that shows the data from the above table.

The graph shows the relationship as a fairly straight line. It could be described by saying that as the mass of the stoppers steadily increased, the volume of the stoppers also steadily increased.

The mass and volume of rubber stoppers is an example of a simple relationship. In more complex relationships, the need for a graph is even stronger. Data are much easier to understand in the organized form of a graph than as numbers in a table.

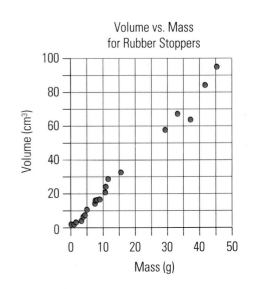

Volume vs. Mass for Rubber Stoppers

Types of Graphs

There are many types of graphs that you can use when organizing your data. The trick is to identify which type of graph is best for your data *before* you start drawing it. Three of the most useful kinds are point-and-line graphs, bar graphs, and circle graphs (also called pie graphs).

When to Use a Point-and-Line Graph

When both variables are quantitative, use a point-and-line graph. The graph to the right was created after an experiment that measured the number of worms on the surface of soil (quantitative) and the volume of rain that fell on the soil (quantitative).

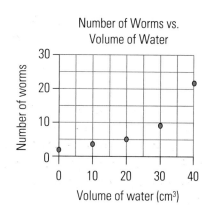

Number of Worms vs. Volume of Water

When to Use a Bar Graph

When at least one of the variables is qualitative, use a bar graph. For example, a study of the math marks of students (quantitative) who listened to different kinds of music (qualitative) while doing their math homework resulted in the graph to the right. In this kind of graph, each bar stands for a different category, in this case a type of music. Notice also that the range on the vertical axis is chosen so that even the smallest bar is still visible.

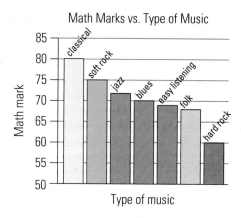

Math Marks vs. Type of Music

When to Use a Circle Graph

Circle graphs and bar graphs are used for similar types of data. If your quantitative variable can be changed to a percentage of a total quantity, then a circle graph is useful. For example, if you surveyed a class to find the students' favourite type of music, you could make a circle graph like the one to the right. In a circle graph, each piece stands for a different category (in this case, kind of music preferred), and the size of the piece tells the percentage of the total that belongs in the category (in this case, the percentage of students who prefer a particular kind of music).

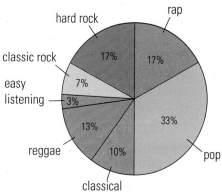

SKILL BUILDER

Choosing a Graph

Copy and complete the table to the right by determining the type of graph (point-and-line, bar, or circle) that is most suitable to show the relationship between the variables in each pair. Explain each of your choices.

Pairs of variables	Most appropriate type of graph
1. Amount of sunlight Number of students late for school	
2. Number of cars owned per person Country of residence	
3. Lipstick colour Number of students wearing each colour	
4. Lizard body temperature Time spent in sunlight	

Making Point-and-Line Graphs

BECAUSE POINT-AND-LINE GRAPHS are common in mathematics, economics, geography, science, technology, and many other subjects, it is useful to become skilled at drawing them. This section should also help you understand point-and-line graphs produced by others.

As an example, the data in the table to the right are used to produce a graph following the steps outlined below.

When making a point-and-line graph, follow these steps:

Light level (cd)	Number of late students
45	16
34	12
27	14
15	9
35	15
12	12
20	12
78	22
65	19
88	24
85	23
92	24
14	8
10	7
7	2
30	11
36	11
47	17
58	23
58	18
46	14

1. Construct your graph on a grid. The horizontal edge on the bottom of this grid is called the x-axis and the vertical edge on the left is called the y-axis. Don't be too thrifty with graph paper —if you draw your graphs large, they will be easier to interpret.

Step 1: Draw the axes.

2. Decide which variable goes on which axis, and label each axis, including the units of measurement. It is common to plot the dependent variable (number of late students) on the y-axis and the independent variable (light level in candelas, cd) on the x-axis.

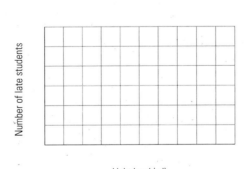

Step 2: Label each axis.

3. Determine the range of values for each variable. The range is the difference between the largest and smallest value. For the light levels in the table, the maximum is 92 cd, and the minimum is 7 cd, so the range is: 92 cd – 7 cd = 85 cd. For the number of late students, the range is 24 – 2 = 22.

4. Choose a scale for each axis. This will depend on how much space you have, and the range of values for each axis. Each line on the grid usually increases steadily in value by a convenient number, such as 1, 2, 5, 10, 20, 50, 100, etc. In the example, there are 10 lines for the x-axis and 6 for the y-axis. To calculate the increase in value for each line, divide the range by the number of lines:

$$\frac{85\ cd}{10\ lines} = 8.5\ cd/line$$

Then, round up to the nearest convenient number, which in this case is 10. The scale on the light level axis should increase by 10 cd every space.

Repeat the calculation for the y-axis:

$$\frac{22\ students}{6} = 3.7\ students/line,\ \text{which is rounded up to 5.}$$

5. Plot the points. Start with the first pair of values from the data table, 45 cd and 16 late students. Place the point where an imaginary line starting at 45 on the x-axis meets an imaginary line starting at 16 on the y-axis.

6. After all the points are plotted, and if it is possible, draw a line through the points to show the relationship between the variables. It is unusual for all the points to lie exactly on a line. Small errors in each measurement tend to move the points slightly away from the perfect line. You must draw a line that comes closest to most of the points. This is called the **line of best fit**—a smooth line that passes through or between the points so that there are about the same number of points on each side of the line. The line of best fit may be a straight line or a curved line.

7. Title your graph.

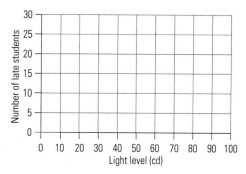

Step 4: Choose a scale for each axis.

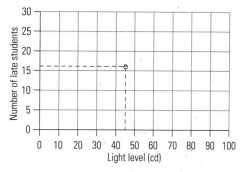

Step 5: Start plotting points.

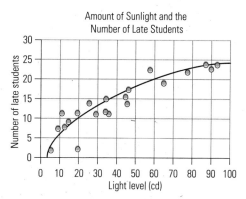

Step 6: Draw a line of best fit.

SKILL BUILDER

Making a Graph

Make labelled point-and-line graphs, with appropriate lines of best fit, for the following sets of data.

(a) Snake heart rate (beats/min)	Air temperature (°C)	(b) Wind speed (km/h)	Average speed of cars (km/h)
11	7	0	100
62	33	10	82
39	24	20	84
31	11	30	73
73	27	40	75
22	4	50	68
80	34	60	72
54	25	70	71

Constructing Bar and Circle Graphs

IF YOU HAVE STUDIED OR EXPERIMENTED with a variable that is divided into categories, then a bar or circle graph is a good way to display the data.

Bar Graphs

Science students did a study of the kind of music students listen to while doing mathematics problems, and got the results listed in the table to the right.

Follow these steps to plot a bar graph of the data in this table.

1. Draw and label the axes of your graph, including units. Some people prefer to have the bars based on the x-axis; others prefer to use the y-axis as the base. In the illustrations, the x-axis was chosen for the base.

2. Develop a scale for the axis of the quantitative variable, just as you would for a point-and-line graph (see page 512). In this example, the y-axis increases by 5s, starting below the lowest value. In the illustration, 50 was chosen as the starting point, so all the bars would be visible.

3. Decide how wide the bars will be, and how much space you will put between them. This decision is based on:

   • How much space you have. Measure the length of the axis on which the bars will be based, and divide that length by the number of bars. This will give you the maximum width of each bar.

   • How you want the graph to look. Decide how much less than the maximum width your bars will be, based on the visual appeal of thick and thin bars.

4. Draw in bars. Start by marking the width of each bar on the base axis. Then, draw in the top of each bar, according to your data table, and the sides. You can shade the bars equally, or make each bar different from the others. It is important, however, to keep the graph simple and clear.

5. Identify each bar. There are several ways to do this. The best choice is the one that makes the graph easy to understand.

Type of music	Math score (%)
easy listening	69
hard rock	60
jazz	72
blues	70
classical	80
folk	68
soft rock	75

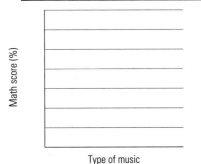

Step 1: Draw the axes.

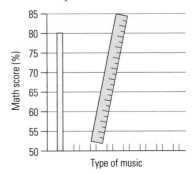

Step 4: Draw the bars.

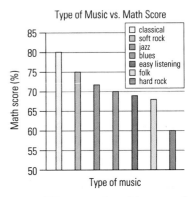

The completed bar graph.

Circle Graphs

If your quantitative variable can be changed to a percentage of a total quantity, then a circle graph is useful. A sample circle graph is worked out below, using the data in the table.

Type of music	Number of students who prefer that type	Percentage of total (% and decimal)	Angle of piece of pie (degrees)
rap	5	17% = 0.17	61.2
pop rock	10	33% = 0.33	118.8
classical	3	10% = 0.10	36.0
reggae	4	13% = 0.13	46.8
easy listening	1	3% = 0.03	10.8
classic rock	2	7% = 0.07	25.2
hard rock	5	17% = 0.17	61.2
TOTAL	30	100% = 1.00	360

1. Convert the values of your quantitative variable into percentages, and then into decimal form. In the sample, each number of students who prefer a type of music was turned into a percentage of the total number of students.

$$\text{Percentage} = \frac{\text{number} \times 100\%}{\text{total}}$$

$$\text{Percentage for rap} = \frac{5 \times 100\%}{30} = 17\% \text{ (decimal version = 0.17)}$$

2. Multiply the decimal version of each percentage by 360° (there are 360° in a circle) to get the angle of each "piece of the pie" within the circle.

$$\text{Angle of piece of pie for rap} = 0.17 \times 360° = 61.2°$$

3. Draw a circle. To make the graph easy to read (and make), the circle should be big. The more pieces there are, the bigger the circle should be.

4. Draw in each piece of pie, using a protractor.

5. Shade each piece of pie using colours or patterns.

6. Label and title the graph. Put the percentages and the name of each category with its piece of pie (perhaps percentage inside and category outside the circle), or include them in a legend. Pick a title for your graph that describes the variables.

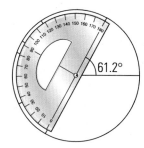

Step 4: Draw the pieces.

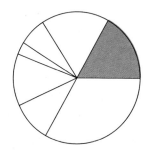

Step 5: Shade the pieces.

Musical Preferences of Students

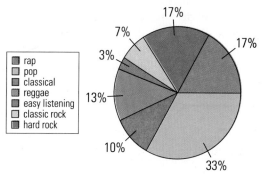

Legend: rap, pop, classical, reggae, easy listening, classic rock, hard rock

The completed circle graph.

Reading a Graph

WHEN DATA FROM AN INVESTIGATION are plotted on a graph, they become much easier to interpret. Any trends or patterns in the data become easier to see. It is easier to tell if the data support your hypothesis. Looking at the data in a graph may also lead you to a new hypothesis. Try the Skill Builders for practice in reading graphs.

SKILL BUILDER

Reading a Graph—Airborne Lead

Until the 1970s, small amounts of lead were added to gasoline to improve the performance of car engines. Eventually, when people became aware of the hazards of lead, leaded gasoline was phased out. Leaded gasoline is no longer in use in Canada.

Lead pollutes the air. In one experiment in Ontario, the amount of airborne lead was measured near expressways and at several other locations. The graph shows the results of this study.

1. In what year was the level of airborne lead highest?

2. Was the amount of lead in the air increasing or decreasing during the time shown in the graph?

3. In any year, is the amount of airborne lead near expressways more than or less than the average of all sites?

4. (a) On the basis of the data, form a hypothesis to explain the presence of lead in the air.

   (b) Why do you think the amount of lead pollution changed over the measuring period?

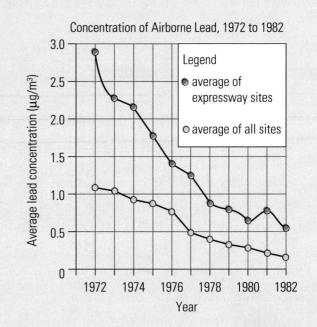

Concentration of Airborne Lead, 1972 to 1982

Legend
● average of expressway sites
○ average of all sites

Reading a Graph—The Growth of Bacteria

All populations have a tremendous capacity for growth when they have sufficient food and space, an ideal environment, and few predators. For example, consider the growth of bacteria in a test tube of nutrient broth. The graph illustrates an experiment in which 1000 bacterial cells were added to a test tube of broth. Each cell divided into two cells every 30 min.

1. How long did it take for the number of bacteria to increase to 100 000?

2. (a) From 0 h to 2.0 h, how many new cells were produced?

   (b) From 2.0 h to 4.0 h, how many new cells were produced?

(c) Does the rate at which new cells are produced increase or decrease with time? Explain your answer.

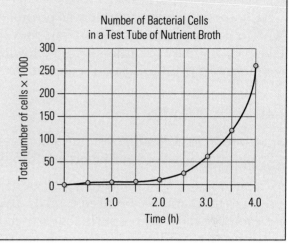

Using Graphs for Predicting

If a graph shows a regular pattern, you can use it to make predictions. For example, you could use the graph to the right, in which mass is plotted against volume, to predict the mass of 5 cm³ of silver. To do this, you would extrapolate the graph, or extend it beyond the measured points, assuming the observed trend would continue.

Some common sense is needed in extrapolation. Sometimes a pattern extends only over a certain range. For example, if you extrapolated the graph of bacterial growth in the Skill Builder above, you would predict that after 24 h there would be 280 000 000 000 000 000 cells. (In scientific notation, that's 2.8×10^{17} cells.) These would have a total mass of about 40 kg. In another day and a half, the cells' mass would be greater than the mass of the Earth. Obviously, something will happen to break the pattern!

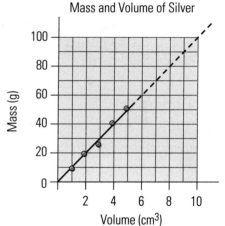

Scientific Drawing

SCIENTIFIC DRAWINGS ARE DONE TO RECORD observations as accurately as possible. They are also used to communicate, which means they must be clear, well-labelled, and easy to understand. Following are some tips that will help you produce useful scientific drawings.

Before You Begin

- *Obtain some unlined paper.* Lines might obscure your drawing or make your labels confusing.

- *Find a sharp, hard pencil* (e.g., 2H or 4H). Avoid using pen, thick markers, or coloured pencils. Ink can't be erased—even the most accomplished artists change their drawings—and coloured pencils are soft, making lines too thick.

- *Plan to draw large.* Ensure that your drawing will be large enough that people can see details. For example, a third of a page might be appropriate for a diagram of a single cell or a unicellular organism. If you are drawing the entire field of view of a microscope, a circle with a diameter of about 10 cm can represent the field.

- *Leave space for labels,* preferably on the right side of the drawing.

- *Observe and study your specimen carefully,* noting details and proportions.

Drawing

- Simple, *two-dimensional drawings* are effective.

- *Draw only what you see.* Your textbook may act as a guide, but it may show structures that you cannot see in your specimen.

- *Do not sketch.* Draw firm, clear lines, including only relevant details that you can see clearly.

- *Do not use shading or colouring* in scientific drawings. A stipple (series of dots) may be used to indicate a darker area. Use double lines to indicate thick structures.

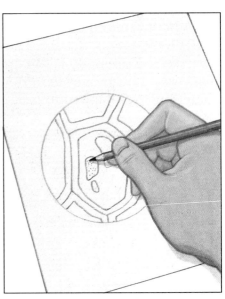

Label Your Drawing

- *All drawings must be labelled fully* in neat printing. Lower-case (small) letters are often used to label names and structures. Avoid printing labels directly on the drawing.

- *Use a ruler.* Label lines must be horizontal and ruled firmly from the structures being identified to the label.

- *Label lines should never cross.*

- If possible, *list your labels in an even column down the right side.*

- *Title the drawing* with capital letters, using the name of the specimen and (if possible) the part of the specimen you have drawn. Underline the title.

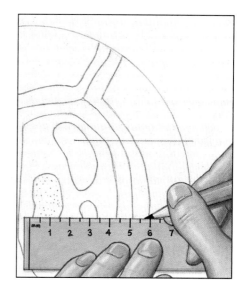

Scale Ratio

- To show the relation of the actual size to your drawing size, *print the scale ratio of your drawing beside the title.*

$$\text{scale ratio} = \frac{\text{size of drawing}}{\text{actual size of the specimen}}$$

For example, if you have drawn a nail that is 5 cm long and the drawing is 15 cm long, then the scale ratio, which in this case is a magnification, is

$$\frac{15\ \text{cm}}{5\ \text{cm}} = 3$$

- *The magnification is always written with a "×" after it.* Beside the title of your drawing of the nail, you would print 3× to show that the drawing is three times the size of the actual specimen.

- *Underline* the title and the scale ratio.

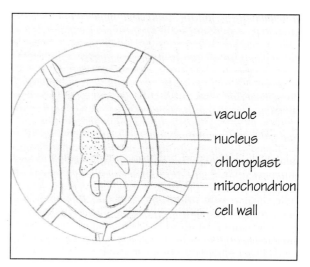

Checklist for Good Scientific Drawing

√ Use blank paper and a sharp, hard pencil.

√ Draw large.

√ Include only relevant details.

√ Do not shade or colour.

√ Draw label lines that are straight, parallel, and run outside the drawing.

√ Include labels, a title, and the scale ratio.

SKILL BUILDER

Drawing a Leaf

Pick a leaf from a plant. You and a friend will draw the leaf, and then evaluate each other's drawings. Make a complete, labelled drawing of the leaf. When your drawing is complete, exchange it with your friend's drawing. Grade your friend's drawing. Note the good points and bad points of the drawing, keeping in mind all the features of a good scientific drawing.

Reporting Your Work

YOU AND A SCIENTIST HAVE many things in common. One of those things is that you must both report on your investigations. But what should be in a scientific report? Should all reports follow a pattern? What things should be in that pattern? In this section are some helpful ideas on how to write a report.

Writing a Report

All investigators use a similar format to write reports, although the headings and order may vary slightly.

Cover Page   Make a cover page. On a blank sheet of paper, write the following:

- the title of your investigation
- your name
- your instructor's name
- the course code
- the due date

On the back of the cover page, make a diagram of the equipment you used in the experiment. Remember to label and title the diagram and write a caption.

The Title   On a fresh page, write the title of your investigation.

Purpose   Make a brief statement about why you did the investigation.

Hypothesis or Problem   Write the hypothesis or describe the invention you were testing in the investigation.

Materials   Make a detailed list of the materials you used. Be specific about sizes and quantities.

Procedure   The most important part of an investigation, when others are trying to determine if it is "good" or "bad" science, is the procedure. Many researchers read only the procedure section in a report, to gain insight into a procedure they could use. To be sure that your work is judged fairly, make sure you leave nothing out!

Observations/Results   Present your observations and results in a form that is easily understood. The data should be in tables, graphs, or illustrations. Each table, graph, or illustration should have a title and a brief statement about what the data mean. If calculations are used, include a sample. The results of the calculations can be shown in a table.

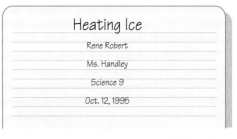

Heating Ice
Rene Robert
Ms. Handley
Science 9
Oct. 12, 1995

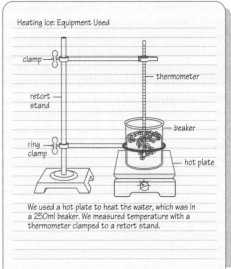

Heating Ice: Equipment Used

clamp — / thermometer / retort stand / beaker / ring clamp / hot plate

We used a hot plate to heat the water, which was in a 250ml beaker. We measured temperature with a thermometer clamped to a retort stand.

Heating Ice

Purpose

Hypothesis

Materials

Procedure

Discussion Justify your method and describe your results. Use theory, or give a theory, to support or interpret your results. If you were assigned questions with an investigation, you would answer them here.

Conclusion Summarize your investigation, as you would if you were writing a book report. Review your hypothesis: Was it correct? Was it incorrect? Explain how you arrived at your conclusion(s). Discuss any errors that may have affected your findings.

Credits and Bibliography The last thing you must do in your report is give credit for the resources you drew on when revising your hypothesis, gathering data, or presenting your results. Failing to do so is considered plagiarism (copying) and could get you in trouble. Whenever you give credit to an author (including yourself from previous reports!) for the use of graphs, tables, diagrams, or ideas, use the following technique:

- Immediately after the information is used, give the last name of the source, the date of the publication in which you found the information, and the page reference. For example:

  It is best to paint the parts of a model airplane before assembling the model (Brown, 1968, p. 15).

- At the end of your report, write the bibliography in alphabetical order of authors' last names. If the quotation comes from a book, use the following format, which includes the publisher's name and the city of publication.

  Brown, John (1968). *Building Model Airplanes.* New York: Octopus Books.

  If the quotation comes from a journal or a magazine, use the following format. Include the volume number of the magazine (usually found on the Table of Contents page), and the page numbers of the article.

  Rodin, Judith (1978). *The Puzzle of Obesity.* Human Nature 3 (2): 38–47.

Heating Ice			
Time (min)	Temperature (°C)	Time (min)	Temperature (°C)
0	0	7	60
1	0	8	80
2	0	9	100
3	0	10	100
4	0	11	100
5	20	12	100
6	40	13	100

Include your tables of data with your report.

Checklist for Writing a Report

Make sure you include the following in your report:

√ Cover page
√ Title of the investigation
√ Purpose
√ Hypothesis
√ Materials

√ Procedure
√ Observations
√ Discussion
√ Conclusion
√ Bibliography

Science Projects

IN ADDITION TO THE INVESTIGATIONS you do in each unit of *Nelson Science 9*, you may decide to conduct your own major project in science. This project may arise out of a Challenge or an Extension, or you may choose to investigate a topic that is of special interest to you. In general, conducting a project means that you will attempt to answer a question or solve a practical problem by carrying out a test that you design.

Planning a Science Project

If you want to do a project, but are not sure what topic to choose, make a list of your interests. Then, list as many observations as you can about each one. Use your list as a jumping-off place for planning your project. Follow the chart below to see how this can work.

Choosing a Topic

Write down as many observations (variables) as you can about one or more of the following topics:

- games you play
- subjects you study
- foods you eat
- clothes you wear
- animals you know about
- plants you have seen
- sports you play
- television programs you watch
- hobbies you have
- materials you find interesting
- chemicals that interest you
- other interests you have

Choosing a Process

House Plants
Observations (Variables)

- Some grow tall.
- Some have wide leaves.
- The amount of green colour differs.
- Some plant leaves dry out easily.
- Some get different kinds of light than others.
- Some plants produce many little "baby" plants.
- Some people add a compost mix to plants.
- The amount of water added differs.
- The air temperature differs.
- The kind of soil differs.

Choosing a Project

After you have explored some project ideas, answering the following questions may help you decide on the best project for you.

- What do I know about the topic already?

- Do I have the time to do the project?

- If I want to work with a partner, do we work well together?

- How difficult will it be to find the materials?

- Do I have appropriate measuring instruments?

- Do I have the space to set up equipment and tests?

- Would my project be ethical? (You should not experiment with live vertebrate animals.)

Designing a Project

For more information on how to design an experiment or a study or how to test an invention, see Science and Invention, pages 24–35.

Conducting Your Project

Once you have designed the project, there are some things to keep in mind while you conduct your project.

- Start early—to give you time in case something goes wrong!

- Make many observations, and keep them all in your notebook. You may also want to make notes of your ideas or thoughts.

- Keep deadlines in mind. Working backward from when your project must be completed, set a schedule for each part.

Question
"What is the effect of different kinds of light on the health of house plants?"

(see Correlational Studies, page 28)

(see Experimenting, page 24)

Correlational Study
Using a light meter, measure the amount of light energy coming from each kind of light source in several people's homes, and also measure the height and mass of all their house plants.

Controlled Experiment
Shine different amounts of light energy on several groups of plants of the same kind, and then measure their height and mass after a certain amount of time.

Practical Problem
"Some plants do not grow as well indoors as outside."

(see Inventing, page 32)

Test of an Invention (your own compost "recipe")
Use several groups of plants. Each group will get the same total amount of sand and compost, but the amount of compost for each group will steadily increase. Measure the height and mass of the plants before and after the test period. Recommend that others use the combination that works best.

Presenting Your Project

After you have completed your project, you may want to display your results in a science fair, or present them to your class. Following are some ideas on how to present your project.

Artistic Impression

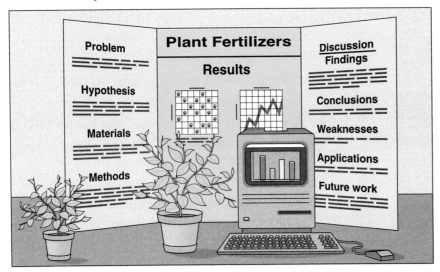

When constructing a display board, there are some things to keep in mind.

- Make sure your board is sturdy, and will not fall down.
- Use a sketch to plan the layout of the display board.
- Collect a variety of display items (photos, sketches, charts, graphs, text).
- Use different sizes of letters for the text on your board. The most important ideas should have the largest letters.
- Place the title in a central location.
- Make all lettering neat and easy to read.
- Simple is best: Use the same kind of lettering throughout. If you are using colours or shapes to highlight important features, use only a few.
- Make sure your diagrams, graphs, and charts are neat.
- Place your results in a prominent position on the board.
- Don't cram things together. Place only the most important information on the display board. If there is lots of space around wording and diagrams, the display will be more attractive.
- Make sure that nothing on your board is blocked by objects that will be in front of the board.

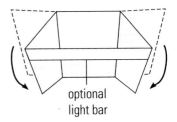

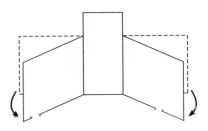

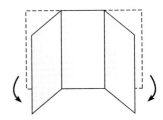

Three different display boards that you can make out of cardboard.

Language Arts

Keep the following in mind when planning the language parts of your presentation.

Written
- Develop a catchy title that is related to the question/problem you investigated.
- Use words that are easy to understand. Check that everything you have written is clear and accurate.
- Use a dictionary—make sure you use scientific terms correctly.
- Check that all spelling and grammar are correct.

Oral
- Plan your oral presentation
- Practise giving your oral presentation to friends or family members. This will allow you to speak with confidence when you make the final presentation.
- If you were part of a group that worked on your project, make sure the presentation is divided equally.
- Prepare for questions by doing some reading—if you are familiar with related science ideas, it will be easier to explain your project.

Hints for an Oral Presentation

Before you attempt to describe your project to your teacher, class, or a science fair judge, prepare a point-form "speech" by answering the following questions:

- What was the goal of your project?
- Why was the topic interesting?
- What methods did you use to carry out your project?
- What were the major results of your project?
- What weaknesses did you notice in the methods you chose?
- What conclusion can you make as a result of your work?
- How might the findings of your project help others?
- On the basis of your results, is there another project that could be done?

It is important not to read your speech when presenting. Reading a speech makes it difficult for your audience to hear you or see your face. It also makes it seem as though you don't really know what you are talking about. But don't memorize every word of your speech. Just practise it several times before your presentation. If you get stuck, you can use your display board as a guide. Another trick is to memorize the eight questions above, or write them on cards, and answer them as you speak.

MAKING A GOOD IMPRESSION

There are ways to make sure you give a good impression while you are speaking.

- Wear clean, neat clothing.
- Stand straight on both feet; don't sway from one foot to the other.
- Look into the eyes of members of your audience, as if you are speaking to each person individually.
- If you have a display, don't block it by standing in front of it during your presentation.
- Be friendly—smile.

Safety in the Laboratory

YOUR SCHOOL LABORATORY, like your kitchen, need not be dangerous. In both places, you avoid accidents when you understand how to use materials and equipment and follow proper procedures.

The activities in this textbook have been tested and are safe, as long as they are done with proper care. Take special note of any instructions following the word "CAUTION" whenever it appears in an activity. These instructions will help you use laboratory equipment and chemicals safely. You should also be familiar with both the WHMIS symbols and the Hazardous Household Product symbols. (See Appendix 2, Safety Symbols, on page 528.)

Follow the safety rules listed below. Your teacher will give you specific information about other safety rules for your classroom and for conducting investigations.

Before You Start

1. Learn the location and proper use of the safety equipment available to you, such as safety goggles, protective aprons, heat-resistant gloves, fire extinguishers, and fire blankets. Find out the location of the nearest fire alarm.

2. Inform your teacher of any allergies, medical conditions, or other physical impairments you may have. Do not wear contact lenses when conducting investigations.

3. Read the procedure of an investigation carefully before you start. Clear the laboratory bench of all materials except those you will use in the investigation. If there is anything you do not understand, ask your teacher to explain. If you are designing your own experiment, obtain your teacher's approval before carrying out the experiment.

4. Wear safety goggles and protective clothing (a lab apron or a lab coat), and tie back long hair. Wear closed shoes in the laboratory, not open sandals.

5. Never work alone in the laboratory.

Working With Chemicals

6. Do not taste, touch, or smell any material unless you are asked to do so by your teacher. Do not chew gum, eat, or drink in the laboratory.

7. Be aware of where the MSDS manual is kept. Know any relevant MSDS information for the chemicals you are working with.

8. Label all containers. When taking something from a bottle or other container, double-check the label to be sure you are taking exactly what you need.

9. If any part of your body comes in contact with a chemical or specimen, wash the area immediately and thoroughly with water. If your eyes are affected, do not touch them but wash them immediately and continuously for at least 15 minutes and inform your teacher.

10. Handle all chemicals carefully. When you are instructed to smell a chemical in the laboratory, follow the procedure shown on the facing page. Only this technique should be used to smell chemicals in the laboratory. Never put your nose close to a chemical.

11. Place test tubes in a rack before pouring liquids into them. If you must hold a test tube, tilt it away from you before pouring in a liquid.

12. Clean up any spilled materials immediately, following instructions given by your teacher.

13. Do not return unused chemicals to the original containers, and do not pour them down the drain. Dispose of chemicals as instructed by your teacher.

Heating

14. Whenever possible, use electric hot plates for heating materials. Use a flame only if instructed to do so. If a Bunsen burner is used in your science classroom, make sure you follow the procedures listed below.

   - Obtain instructions from your teacher on the proper method of lighting and adjusting the Bunsen burner.

   - Do not heat a flammable material (for example, alcohol) over a Bunsen burner. Make sure there are no flammable materials nearby.

   - Do not leave a lighted Bunsen burner unattended.

   - Always turn off the gas at the valve, not at the base of the Bunsen burner.

15. When heating glass containers, make sure you use clean Pyrex or Kimax. Do not use broken or cracked glassware. Always keep the open end pointed away from yourself and others. Never allow a container to boil dry.

16. When heating a test tube over a flame, use a test-tube holder. Hold the test tube at an angle, with the opening facing away from you and others. Move it gently in the flame, to distribute the heat evenly.

17. Be careful when handling hot objects and objects that might be hot. Hot plates can take up to 60 minutes to cool off completely. If you burn yourself, immediately apply cold water or ice, and inform your teacher.

Other Hazards

18. Keep water and wet hands away from electrical cords, plugs, and sockets. Always unplug electrical cords by pulling on the plug, not the cord. Report any frayed cords or damaged outlets to your teacher. Make sure electrical cords are not placed where someone could trip over them.

19. Place broken and waste glass in the specially marked containers.

20. Follow your teacher's instructions when disposing of waste materials.

21. Report to your teacher all accidents (no matter how minor), broken equipment, damaged or defective facilities, and suspicious-looking chemicals.

22. Wash your hands thoroughly, using soap and warm water, after working in the science laboratory. This practice is especially important when you handle chemicals, biological specimens, and microorganisms.

APPENDIX 2

Safety Symbols

BECOME FAMILIAR WITH THE warning symbols that are placed on containers of potentially dangerous materials. You should be able to identify and understand each of the labels shown here.

Hazardous Household Product Symbols

The warning symbols on household products were developed to indicate exactly why and to what degree a product is dangerous.

	poison	flammable	explosive	corrosive
danger				
warning				
caution				

WHMIS Symbols

The Workplace Hazardous Materials Information System (WHMIS) symbols were developed to standardize the labelling of dangerous materials used in all workplaces, including schools. Pay careful attention to any warning symbols on the products or materials that you handle.

 compressed gas

 dangerously reactive material

 oxidizing material

 poisonous and infectious material causing immediate and serious toxic effects

 flammable and combustible material

 biohazardous infectious material

 corrosive material

 poisonous and infectious material causing other toxic effects

Equipment for Investigations

Y OU CAN DO MANY SCIENCE investigations using everyday materials and equipment. In your science classroom, there are other pieces of equipment. Some of these are illustrated here.

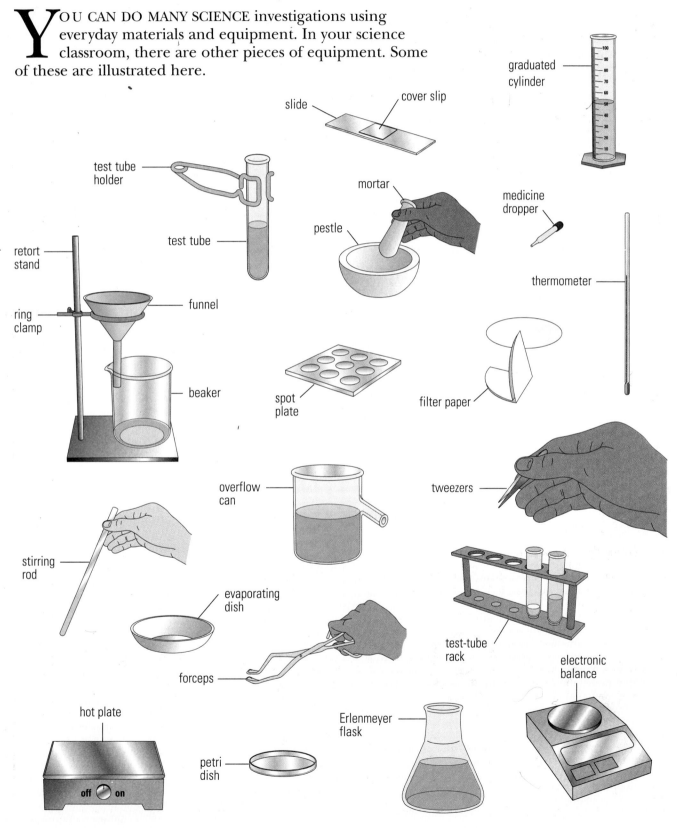

graduated cylinder

slide

cover slip

test tube holder

mortar

pestle

medicine dropper

test tube

retort stand

ring clamp

funnel

thermometer

beaker

spot plate

filter paper

overflow can

tweezers

stirring rod

evaporating dish

test-tube rack

forceps

electronic balance

hot plate

petri dish

Erlenmeyer flask

off on

Standards in Measurement

ABOUT 200 YEARS AGO, a group of scientists met in Paris, France, to design a standard system of measurement. As their basic unit of length, they chose one ten-millionth of the distance from the North Pole to the equator, on a line drawn through Paris. This distance was called a metre. Two lines, a metre apart, were engraved on a metal bar to serve as a standard.

Later, when more accurate measurements of the Earth were possible, scientists abandoned this definition because it was not precise enough. The metre is now defined very accurately as the distance travelled by light in 1/299 792 458 seconds.

In 1960, the metric system was modernized to form the International System of Units. This system is usually referred to as the SI, from the French *Système International d'Unités*. More than 90% of the world's population and more than 100 countries use the SI.

Base Units and Prefixes

There are seven base units, shown in the table below.

The Seven SI Base Units		
Quantity	Unit	Symbol
length	metre	m
mass	kilogram*	kg
time	second	s
electric current	ampere	A
temperature	kelvin	K
amount of substance	mole	mol
light intensity	candela	cd

(*The kilogram is the only base unit that contains a prefix. The gram proved to be too small for practical purposes.)

Larger and smaller units are created by multiplying or dividing the value of the base units by multiples of 10. For example, the prefix deca means multiplied by 10. Therefore, one decametre is equal to 10 metres. The prefix kilo means multiplied by one thousand, so one kilometre is equal to 1000 metres. Similarly, each unit can be divided into smaller units. The prefix milli, for example, means divided by one thousand, so one millimetre is equal to 1/1000 of a metre.

To convert from one unit to another, you simply multiply by a conversion factor. For example, to convert 12.4 m to centimetres, you use the relationship 1 m = 100 cm.

$$12.4 \text{ m} = ? \text{ cm}$$

$$12.4 \text{ m} \times \frac{100 \text{ cm}}{1 \text{ m}} = 1240 \text{ cm}$$

To convert 6.3 g to kilograms, you use the relationship 1000 g = 1 kg.

$$6.3 \text{ g} = ? \text{ kg}$$

$$6.3 \text{ g} \times \frac{1 \text{ kg}}{1000 \text{ g}} = 0.0063 \text{ kg}$$

Any conversions of the same physical quantities can be done in this way. The conversion factor is chosen so that, using cancellation, it yields the desired unit.

Once you understand this method of conversion, you will find that you can simply move the decimal point. Move it to the right when the new unit is smaller and to the left when the new unit is larger.

Metric Prefixes

Prefix	Symbol	Factor by which the base unit is multiplied	Example
giga	G	$10^9 = 1\ 000\ 000\ 000$	
mega	M	$10^6 = 1\ 000\ 000$	10^6 m = 1 Mm
kilo	k	$10^3 = 1\ 000$	10^3 m = 1 km
hecto	h	$10^2 = 100$	
deca	da	$10^1 = 10$	
		$10^0 = 1$	m
deci	d	$10^{-1} = 0.1$	
centi	c	$10^{-2} = 0.01$	10^{-2} m = 1 cm
milli	m	$10^{-3} = 0.001$	10^{-3} m = 1 mm
micro	μ	$10^{-6} = 0.000\ 001$	10^{-6} m = 1 μm

As you can see from the table above, not all the units and prefixes are commonly used. The table to the right shows the quantities that you should be familiar with.

Common Quantities and Units

Quantity	Unit	Symbol
length	kilometre	km
	metre	m
	centimetre	cm
	millimetre	mm
mass	tonne (1000 kg)	t
	kilogram	kg
	gram	g
area	hectare (10 000 m²)	ha
	square metre	m²
	square centimetre	cm²
volume	cubic metre	m³
	cubic centimetre	cm³
	litre	L
	millilitre	mL
time	minute	min
	second	s
temperature	degree Celsius	°C
	degree Kelvin	K
force	newton	N
energy	kilojoule	kJ
	joule	J
pressure	kilopascal	kPa
	pascal	Pa

Table of Properties

THE FOLLOWING TABLE contains some qualitative and quantitative properties of common materials.

Name	Symbol or formula	Melting point (°C)	Boiling point (°C)	Density (g/cm³ or g/mL)	Appearance (at room temperature)	Comments
Elements						
aluminum	Al	660	2467	2.7	shiny, white solid	soft metal with relatively low density; used to make kitchen utensils and bodies of airplanes
carbon (diamond)	C	3500	3930	3.51	colourless solid crystals	hardest known material; gemstone; used for drilling through rock
carbon (graphite)	C	sublimes above 3500°C	—	2.25	grey-black solid	very soft and slippery; used as lubricant
chlorine	Cl_2	−101	−34.6	denser than air	green gas	poisonous; used to kill harmful organisms in water; forms a part of many compounds that, as pollutants, may damage wildlife and human health
copper	Cu	1083	2567	8.92	shiny, reddish solid	soft metal; good conductor of heat
gold	Au	1064	2807	19.3	shiny, yellow solid	very soft metal; highly resistant to tarnishing
hydrogen	H_2	−259	−253	much less dense than air	colourless gas	highly flammable; liquid hydrogen is used as rocket fuel
iron	Fe	1535	2750	7.87	shiny, grey solid	hard metal; strong but brittle; rusts readily
lead	Pb	328	1740	11.3	shiny, blue-grey solid	soft metal; forms poisonous compounds
mercury	Hg	−38.9	357	13.5	shiny, silvery liquid	only liquid metal; forms poisonous compounds
nitrogen	N_2	−210	−196	has a similar density to that of air	colourless gas	will not burn or support burning; makes up 4/5 of air
oxygen	O_2	−218	−183	slightly denser than air	colourless gas	must be present for burning to take place; makes up 1/5 of air
silver	Ag	962	2212	10.5	shiny, white solid	soft metal; best conductor of electricity
sulphur (brimstone)	S	113	445	2.07	yellow solid	used to make dyes, pesticides, and other chemicals; compounds of sulphur in the atmosphere increase the acidity of rain
zinc	Zn	420	907	7.14	shiny, blue-white solid	used in galvanized iron and steel to prevent corrosion

Name	Symbol or formula	Melting point (°C)	Boiling point (°C)	Density (g/cm³ or g/mL)	Appearance (at room temperature)	Comments
Compounds						
aluminum chlorohydrate	$Al_2(OH)_5Cl$	—	—	—	white solid	used in antiperspirants
calcium carbonate (limestone)	$CaCO_3$	decomposes at 825°C	—	2.93	white to grey solid	main ingredient in chalk, marble, cement; used as building stone
copper sulphate (bluestone)	$CuSO_4 \cdot 5H_2O$	decomposes at 150°C	—	2.28	blue solid crystals	used in pesticides
ethanol (ethyl alcohol)	C_2H_5OH	−114.4	78.5	0.79	colourless liquid	used as solvent or fuel; found in wine
glucose	$C_6H_{12}O_6$	146	decomposes before it boils	1.54	white solid	a simple sugar; human body converts most sugars and starches to glucose
glycerol (glycerin(e))	$C_3H_8O_3$	20	290	1.26	thick, colourless liquid	used in antifreeze, hand lotion, plastics
hydrogen peroxide	H_2O_2	−0.4	150.2	1.45	colourless liquid	thick and syrupy when pure; usually sold as a water solution
methanol (methyl alcohol or wood alcohol)	CH_3OH	−97	64.5	0.79	colourless liquid	poisonous if taken internally; used as solvent and fondue fuel
potassium nitrate	KNO_3	334.3	decomposes at 400°C	2.11	white solid	used for pickling meat and in explosives
sodium chloride (table salt)	$NaCl$	801	1465	2.16	white solid	flavour enhancer and preservative
sodium hydrogen carbonate (baking soda)	$NaHCO_3$	decomposes at 270°C; does not melt	—	2.20	white solid	used to make baking powder and environmentally friendly cleaning powder
sodium hydroxide (lye)	$NaOH$	322	1557	2.13	white solid	causes severe burns; used in oven cleaner and drain opener; used to make soap
sucrose (table sugar)	$C_{12}H_{22}O_{11}$	170	decomposes at 186°C	1.59	white solid	made from sugar cane or sugar beets
water	H_2O	0	100	1	colourless liquid	good solvent for non-greasy matter
Solutions						
hydrochloric acid	HCl	varies	varies	varies	colourless liquid	fuming, corrosive acid; a solution of hydrogen chloride in water; properties vary according to concentration
sulphuric acid	H_2SO_4	varies with amount of water present	varies	varies	colourless liquid	corrosive acid; causes severe burns; reacts violently if water is added to it; properties depend on concentration

The Periodic Table

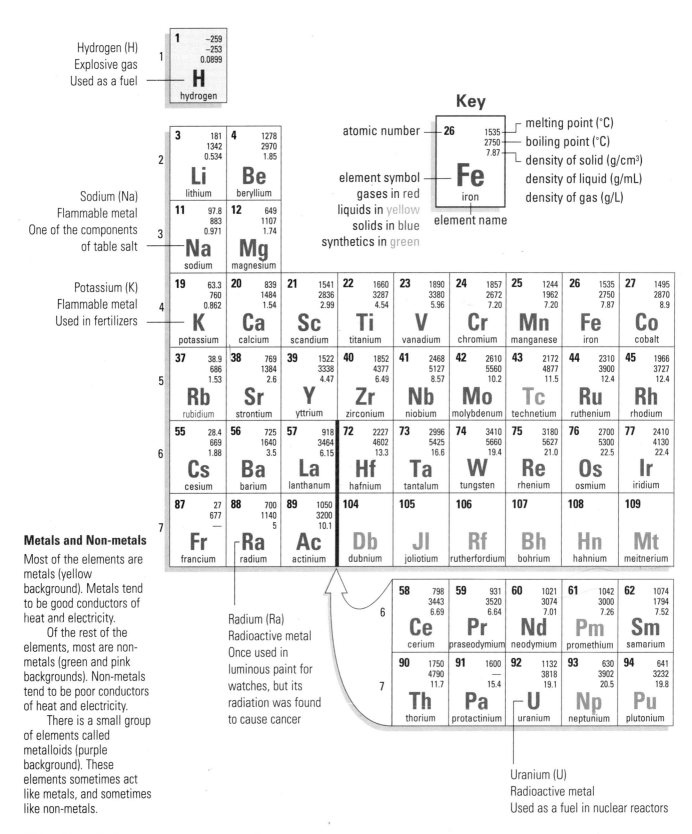

Hydrogen (H)
Explosive gas
Used as a fuel

1	−259
	−253
	0.0899
H	
hydrogen	

Key

atomic number → 26 — melting point (°C)
1535 — boiling point (°C)
2750
7.87 — density of solid (g/cm³)

element symbol → **Fe** — density of liquid (g/mL)
gases in red — density of gas (g/L)
liquids in yellow
solids in blue — iron
synthetics in green — element name

Sodium (Na)
Flammable metal
One of the components
of table salt

Potassium (K)
Flammable metal
Used in fertilizers

Radium (Ra)
Radioactive metal
Once used in
luminous paint for
watches, but its
radiation was found
to cause cancer

Uranium (U)
Radioactive metal
Used as a fuel in nuclear reactors

Metals and Non-metals

Most of the elements are metals (yellow background). Metals tend to be good conductors of heat and electricity.

Of the rest of the elements, most are non-metals (green and pink backgrounds). Non-metals tend to be poor conductors of heat and electricity.

There is a small group of elements called metalloids (purple background). These elements sometimes act like metals, and sometimes like non-metals.

Reactivity

Elements tend to be more reactive the farther they are from the centre of the table, and the closer they are to the bottom left and upper right. Gold (Au) is so unreactive that it can be kept in elemental form fairly easily. On the other hand, fluorine (F) is almost never found in pure elemental form because it is so reactive.

Silicon (Si)
Metalloid
Used in computer chips

Oxygen (O)
Reactive gas
Product of photosynthesis

Helium (He)
Low-density, unreactive gas
Used to fill blimps, balloons

Neon (Ne)
Unreactive gas
Used in electric discharge tubes ("neon lights")

Aluminum (Al)
Low-density metal
Used in aircraft parts, cooking foil

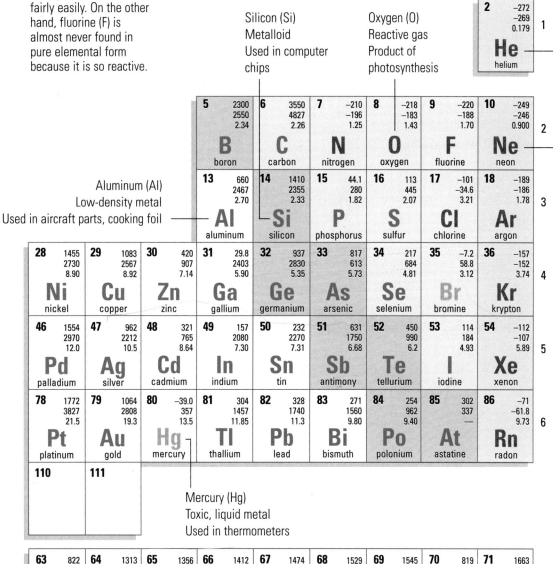

Mercury (Hg)
Toxic, liquid metal
Used in thermometers

Noble Gases

The gases in the column at the far right of the table are very unreactive. As a result, they are found in nature mostly as gases made up of single atoms. Because of this refusal to react, helium (He), neon (Ne), and the others (pink background) are called the noble gases.

Values from *The CRC Handbook of Chemistry and Physics*, 71st Edition

Energy Available from Selected Foods

THE TABLE BELOW LISTS SOME COMMON foods and their energy value. This table will allow you to calculate the amount of food energy that you consume each day. (For a more complete guide, see *Nutrient Values of Some Common Foods*, a supplement to the *Canada Food Guide*, published by Health and Welfare Canada. Energy values in this table were taken from *Nutrient Values*. The classification of foods follows the *Canada Food Guide*. The "measure" for each food is based on a normal serving.)

Food	Measure	Mass (g)	Food energy (kJ)
Milk Products			
cheddar cheese	15 mL	7	118
cottage cheese	250 mL	237	1020
cream	15 mL	16	200
powdered creamer	5 mL	2	40
whipping cream	250 mL	252	3640
milk (whole)	250 mL	257	660
milk (2%)	250 mL	258	540
milk (skim)	250 mL	258	380
buttermilk	250 mL	258	430
milk (evaporated)	250 mL	356	1490
ice cream	125 mL	70	590
ice cream (soft)	125 mL	95	600
yogurt with fruit	125 mL	74	530
eggs (cooked in shell)	1 (medium)	50	330
eggs (scrambled in butter)	1	64	400
eggs (fried)	1	46	350
egg substitute	125 mL	126	790
Meats and Meat Products			
wieners	1	50	520
ground beef	1 patty	90	1080
roast beef (oven-roasted)	2 pieces	90	1570
steak (broiled)	1 piece	90	1330
cod (broiled)	1.5 fillets	90	640
cod (pan-fried with butter)	1.5 pieces	90	960
bacon	1 slice	15	380
ham	2 pieces	90	1410
pork chop	1 chop	98	1090
spareribs	1 rib	90	660
chicken breast (fried)	1 piece	76	650
chicken (roasted)	1 piece	90	510
turkey (roasted)	1 piece	90	720
Vegetables and Related Products			
red kidney beans	250 mL	267	1190
peas	250 mL	263	1260
peas (cooked)	250 mL	169	510
chick peas	250 mL	240	950
asparagus	250 mL	153	130
yellow beans	250 mL	132	130
bean sprouts	250 mL	91	160
beets (sliced)	250 mL	195	240
broccoli	250 mL	164	180
carrots (diced)	250 mL	153	200
cauliflower	250 mL	127	110
celery	250 mL	133	80
corn	250 mL	175	620
corn (creamed)	250 mL	243	760
lettuce	250 mL	78	40
mushrooms (canned)	250 mL	257	180
mushrooms (fresh)	250 mL	257	120
onions	250 mL	222	260
onions (fried)	250 mL	184	1560
parsnips	250 mL	169	440
potatoes (baked in skin)	1 medium	100	380
potatoes (boiled)	1 medium	136	440

potatoes (french fries)	10 pieces	57	650
potatoes (mashed, milk added)	250 mL	206	550
potatoes (mashed, butter added)	250 mL	206	820
spinach (raw)	250 mL	32	40
spinach (cooked)	250 mL	190	180
tomatoes	1	150	35

Fruits and Related Products

apples	1	150	290
apple sauce (canned)	250 mL	269	1020
bananas	1	175	420
cantaloupe	1/2	385	250
cherries	250 mL	137	400
cranberries	250 mL	100	190
grapefruit (white)	1/2	241	190
grapefruit (pink)	1/2	241	210
grapefruit juice	1 can	207	1260
grapes	250 mL	169	420
grape juice (frozen concentrate)	1 can	216	1650
lemon juice (fresh)	250 mL	257	260
lemonade (frozen concentrate)	1 can	219	1800
orange juice (fresh)	250 mL	262	490
orange juice (frozen concentrate)	1 can	213	1510
oranges	1	180	270
peaches (whole)	1	114	150
peaches (sliced)	250 mL	177	290
peaches (canned, with syrup)	250 mL	271	880
pineapple (raw)	250 mL	269	330
pineapple (canned, with heavy syrup)	250 mL	274	860
raisins, seedless	250 mL	174	2120
raisins	25 mL pack	14	170
watermelon	1 slice	236	209

Breads and Wheat Products

bread, white enriched	1 slice	30	340
bread, 60% whole wheat	1 slice	30	300
raisin bread	1 slice	25	270
bread, French or Vienna	1 slice	34	410
cinnamon bun	1	50	660
commercial hard roll	1	40	520
hotdog bun	1	50	570
hamburger bun	1	60	690

Desserts

brownies	1	20	400
chocolate chip cookie	1	10	210
chocolate marshmallow cookie	1	19	310
pancakes	1	27	250
apple pie	1 piece	160	1720
cherry pie	1 piece	160	1620
lemon meringue pie	1 piece	140	1490
pumpkin pie	1 piece	150	1330
popcorn with salt and oil	250 mL	9	170
potato chips	10 chips	20	480
chocolate eclair with custard filling	1 piece	110	1320

Combination Plates

cabbage rolls with meat	2 rolls	206	1090
chili con carne	250 mL	264	1470
chop suey with meat or poultry	250 mL	163	790
chow mein with chicken	250 mL	184	780
egg rolls (with pork)	2 rolls	146	2000
Irish stew	250 mL	211	1240
fish stew	250 mL	237	600
lasagna	1 slice	180	1100
macaroni and cheese	250 mL	231	2080
meat loaf	1 slice	70	110
pizza, cheese	1 piece	75	740
pizza, sausage	1 piece	105	1030
spaghetti with meat balls	250 mL	260	1460
tourtiere (pork pie)	1 piece	139	1890

Beverages

cola (non-diet)	200 mL	197	320
ginger ale (non-diet)	200 mL	195	260
coffee (instant)	250 mL	235	20
tea (instant)	250 mL	224	0

Glossary

A

adaptation
a structure or behaviour that helps a species of organism to survive

additive colour mixing
the process of adding light colours together to produce other colours

alloy
a mixture (solution) in which a metal is the solvent; bronze is an example

amino acids
molecules that are strung together to make proteins; each of the 20 amino acids has unique chemical properties (see *essential amino acid, protein*)

anaphase
the phase of mitosis when the chromosomes split, and single strands of genetic information move to opposite ends of the cell

angle of incidence
the angle between an incident ray of light and its normal

angle of reflection
the angle between a reflected ray of light and its normal

anther
part of the stamen, the male structure, in the flower of a plant; holds pollen grains

asexual reproduction
the division of a parent cell into two daughter cells (see *binary fission, budding, cloning, fragmentation, spore formation, vegetative reproduction, mitosis*)

atom
the smallest particle of an element

Atomic Theory
a theory that includes four statements: 1. all matter is made up of tiny particles, called atoms; 2. atoms of any one element are like one another and are different from atoms of other elements; 3. atoms may combine with other atoms to form larger particles, called molecules; 4. atoms are not created or destroyed by any ordinary means

B

basal metabolic rate
the minimum amount of energy needed to keep the body alive

binary fission
the form of asexual reproduction in which the organism splits into two equal-size offspring

bioluminescence
the process, similar to chemiluminescence, by which some living creatures make themselves luminous

boiling
the rapid change of state from liquid to gas (see also *evaporation*)

boiling point
the characteristic temperature at which a liquid changes rapidly to form a gas (also called *condensation point*)

brittle
a physical property of some substances; brittle objects shatter easily; glass is an example

budding
the form of asexual reproduction in which the offspring begins as an outgrowth of the parent

C

calorie
a unit measuring energy; it takes 1 calorie to raise the temperature of 1 g of water by 1°C; 1 calorie = 4.18 J

cancer
the name for a broad group of diseases associated with the uncontrolled, unregulated division of cells

capacity unit
a unit of volume measurement; usually used for liquids; examples are litres (L) and millilitres (mL) (see *cubic unit*)

capillarity
the tendency of liquids to cling to the sides of a narrow tube; helps water to move up inside the narrow xylem vessels of plants

carbohydrate
one of the three major nutrient groups; made of sugar molecules, either single, in pairs, or in chains

cell
the smallest living thing; the separate unit that all living things are composed of

cell membrane
holds the contents of a cell in place and regulates the movement of materials into and out of the cell

cell specialization
multicellular organisms have cells that come in a variety of sizes and shapes, each designed to carry out a special function

cell theory
the theory that all living things are composed of cells and that all cells come from pre-existing cells

cell wall
surrounds the cell membrane of a plant cell, protecting and supporting the cell

cellulose
the major component of plant cell walls; composed of a great many glucose molecules linked together (see *fibre*)

chemical change
a change in which the original substance is changed into a different substance that has different properties; also called chemical reaction

chemical formula
the combination of symbols that represent the elements that form a particular compound; indicates which elements are in the compound and in what proportion they are present

chemical reaction
a chemical change in which reactants become products

chemical test
a distinctive chemical reaction that allows an unknown substance to be identified

chemiluminescence
the process of changing chemical energy into light energy with little or no change in temperature

chemistry
the study of matter and its changes

chlorophyll
a green pigment that is used by plants to trap light energy; located in the chloroplasts of plant cells

chloroplast
plastid that contains the green pigment chlorophyll, used in photosynthesis

cholesterol
a substance that is formed from fat; has been associated with heart disease and circulatory problems; used by the body to make certain hormones

chromosome
threadlike structure formed of the genetic material, deoxyribonucleic acid; found in the nucleus of plant and animal cells

cloning
the technological process by which identical offspring are formed from a single cell or tissue

colloid
a mixture in which pieces of solid or drops of liquid are suspended, but the pieces or drops are so small that if conditions remain the same they will not settle out of the mixture; fog is an example

combustion
burning; a reaction in which a substance reacts rapidly with oxygen to release energy

communicable disease
a disease that can spread from one person to another (also called *contagious disease*)

complementary light colours
any two light colours that add together to produce white light

complex sugar
a combination of simple sugars; examples are sucrose and lactose

compound
a pure substance that contains two or more elements in a fixed proportion

compound light microscope
employs two lenses and a light source to make objects appear larger

concave mirror
a mirror with the reflecting surface on the inside of the curve

concept map
a collection of words or pictures (representing concepts) that are connected to each other by arrows and short descriptions to show the relationships between them

condensation
the change of state from a gas to a liquid (also called *liquefaction*)

condensation point
the characteristic temperature at which a substance changes from its gas state to its liquid state (also called *boiling point*)

conjugation
the form of sexual reproduction in which two cells come together and exchange small bits of genetic information

consumer
an organism that must eat other organisms to obtain food energy

contagious disease
a disease that can spread from one person to another (also called *communicable disease*)

controlled experiment
a test of a hypothesis in which one variable (the independent variable) is purposely and steadily changed to find the effect on a second variable (the dependent variable), while all other variables are kept constant

convex mirror
a mirror with the reflecting surface on the outside of the curve

correlational study
a test of a hypothesis in which two variables are studied to find any relationship between them; the variables are allowed to change naturally

cotyledon
the food storage area in a seed

cubic unit
a unit of volume measurement; examples are cubic metres and cubic centimetres (see *capacity unit*)

cuticle
the waxy coating that covers leaves; acts as a protective layer to prevent water from evaporating from the cells of the leaf

cytoplasm
the area of the cell in which nutrients are absorbed, transported, and processed

daughter cells
the two cells that result from asexual reproduction of a parent cell

decomposer
an organism (such as fungi and some bacteria) that breaks down the complex molecules in dead organisms

density
the amount of matter per unit volume of that matter; expressed as grams per cubic centimetre (g/cm^3) or, for very large objects, kilograms per cubic metre (kg/m^3)

deoxyribonucleic acid (DNA)
the genetic material (see *gene, chromosome*)

dependent variable
in an experiment or test of an invention, the variable measured to study the effect of changing another variable (the independent variable); sometimes called the *effect variable*

depth of field
the amount of an image that is in sharp focus when it is viewed under a microscope

diagnosis
a hypothesis about the cause of an illness

diet
the food a person regularly eats and drinks

diffuse reflection
occurs when light hits an irregular surface, from which the light scatters in many directions

diffusion
the gradual spreading of a substance from an area where the substance is highly concentrated to an area where its concentration is lower

digestion
the process by which large food molecules are broken down into smaller molecules; these small food molecules are soluble and small enough to enter body cells

dissolve
when a substance (a solute) mixes so thoroughly with another substance (the solvent) that the parts of the mixture can't be distinguished

dry mount
a microscope slide prepared using no water

ductile
a physical property of some substances; a ductile substance can be pulled into wires; examples are copper, gold, and aluminum

ecosystem
a community of living things and their physical and chemical environment

electric discharge
the process of emitting light as electricity passes through a gas

element
a pure substance that cannot be broken down into a simpler substance

embryo
in plants, the collection of cells, found in a seed, that will grow to form an adult plant

emulsion
a type of colloid in which tiny liquid droplets are mixed in another liquid; milk is an example

endocytosis
the process by which a cell extends its cytoplasm to engulf large particles

endoplasmic reticulum
organelle composed of parallel membranes; carries materials throughout the cell

endosperm
a food storage area in some seeds

enzyme
a protein that helps speed a chemical reaction in the body; enzymes make the reaction more likely by bringing the reactants together; enzymes are not changed in reactions; an example is pepsin, an enzyme produced by stomach cells that helps digest protein

epicotyl
part of the embryo of a seed; becomes the top of the shoot of the seedling

essential amino acid
one of eight amino acids that cannot be made by the human body, and so must be included in the diet

evaporation
the slow change of state from liquid to gas over a wide range of temperatures (see also *boiling*)

fat
one of the three major nutrient groups; in humans, used to store excess energy from food; made up of carbon, hydrogen, and oxygen, the same chemical elements found in carbohydrates, but in a different arrangement; difficult to digest (also called *lipid*)

fibre
component of the human diet that cannot be digested (another name for *cellulose*)

field of view
the area you can see while looking through a microscope

filament
part of the stamen in the flower of a plant; supports the anther

filter
a device that allows part of a mixture to pass through (the filtrate), but traps another part (the residue); filter paper

filtrate
the substance that passes through when a mixture is filtered (see *residue*)

filtration
a process used to separate particles from either a gas or a liquid; traps the part of the mixture that cannot pass through the filter (see *residue, filtrate*)

flagellum
a whiplike tail, present in some animal cells; used for movement

fluorescence
the process of emitting light while receiving energy from another source

focal length (f)
the distance from the vertex to the principal focus of a mirror or lens

food chain
describes the movement of energy and matter from one group of organisms to other groups; the first organisms in any food chain are plants

fossil fuel
a substance that is used because it burns readily; formed from organisms that lived millions of years ago and were buried in sediments; coal, oil, natural gas, and gasoline are all examples

fragmentation
the form of asexual reproduction in which a part of an organism breaks off from the parent and forms a new organism

freezing
the change of state from a liquid to a solid. (If this change occurs at temperatures above 0°C, the term *solidification* is often used.)

freezing point
the characteristic temperature at which a substance changes from its liquid state to its solid state

freezing rain
super-cooled liquid precipitation that solidifies instantly as it strikes the ground

gene
one of the units that make up a chromosome; these units determine the specific traits of an individual

germination
when the embryo inside a plant seed begins to grow

global warming
a prediction that the Earth's temperature will rise gradually because of an increase in greenhouse gases such as carbon dioxide

glucose
an energy-rich simple sugar; formed by plants in photosynthesis and used by humans as the principal source of cellular energy

Golgi apparatus
organelle that stores and packages protein molecules

greenhouse effect
warming of the Earth's surface, caused by carbon dioxide and other atmospheric gases, which trap energy from the Sun

guard cell
one of a pair of cells that controls the opening and closing of a stoma in the leaf of a plant; used to control water loss

hail
solid, layered precipitation that forms in a cycle of rising and falling through warm and cold regions of the atmosphere

hardness
a measure of the resistance of a solid to being scratched or dented; diamonds are hard, chalk is soft

heterogeneous mixture
a mixture in which more than one phase is visible; examples are wood, breakfast cereal, people

hydrocarbon
a name for the molecules that make up fossil fuels; when a hydrocarbon burns in enough oxygen, the products are carbon dioxide and water

hydroponics
a technology in which plants are grown with their roots in water, with nutrients and air added

hypocotyl
part of the embryo of a seed; becomes the stem of the seedling

hypothesis
an attempt to explain observations made in the natural world; describes a possible relationship between two variables

image
the likeness of an object, formed by an optical device

impermeable
describes membranes that do not permit passage of a substance (see *permeable, selectively permeable*)

incandescence
the process of emitting light due to high temperature

incident ray
a ray of light that travels toward a reflecting surface such as a mirror

independent variable
in an experiment or test of an invention, the variable that is steadily changed to study the effect on another variable (the dependent variable); sometimes called the *cause variable*

irrigation
adding water to otherwise dry areas; a method used to increase the amount of food produced

joule (J)
a unit measuring energy; it takes 4.18 J to raise the temperature of 1 g of water by 1°C

kilocalorie (Calorie)
1000 calories; 1 kilocalorie = 4184 J, or 4.18 kJ

kilojoule (kJ)
1000 joules

knowledge
in science, information that has been communicated to others and agreed upon by a large number of people

Law of Conservation of Mass
scientific law stating that in a chemical reaction, the total mass of the reactants is always equal to the total mass of the products

light
a form of energy you can detect with your eyes

line of best fit
in graphing, a smooth line that passes through or between the graphed points so that there are about the same number of points above and below the line; may be a curve or a straight line

liquefaction
The change of state from a gas to a liquid (also called *condensation*)

luminous
describes objects that emit light

lunar eclipse
occurs when the Earth is located between the Sun and the Moon so the Moon is in the Earth's shadow

lysosome
a saclike structure that contains proteins that can break down large molecules and other cell parts; formed by the Golgi apparatus

magnification
the comparison of the actual size of an object with the size of its image

malleable
a physical property of some substances; a malleable substance can be hammered into thin sheets; gold is an example

mass
the amount of matter an object has; measured in kilograms (kg)

matter
anything that has mass and takes up space

melting
the change of state from solid to liquid

melting point
the characteristic temperature at which a substance changes from its solid state to its liquid state

metabolism
the sum of all the chemical reactions that occur within body cells; includes the reactions that convert the chemical energy from food into other forms of energy

metaphase
the phase of mitosis in which chromosomes containing double strands of genetic information line up in the middle of the cell

mineral
a kind of nutrient; used to obtain the necessary energy from foods, and to help maintain normal body functioning; examples are sodium, calcium, iodine, zinc

mitochondrion
oval-shaped organelles; the centre of cell respiration

mitosis
the division of genetic information during cell division

mixture
in chemistry, a mixture contains at least two pure substances (see *heterogeneous mixture, solution, colloid, emulsion, suspension*)

model
a mental picture, a diagram, or some other means of representing a thing or a process

molecule
a combination of atoms; can contain two atoms or many thousands of atoms

mutation
a change in a cell's genetic information

nonluminous
describes objects that do not emit light

normal
a line drawn at 90° from a reflecting surface at the point where a ray of light has struck the surface

nucleus
the control centre of the cell; stores the genetic information that tells the cell what to do and when (see *chromosomes, genes*)

nutrient
a substance needed by an organism to be healthy, to grow, or to reproduce

opaque
describes materials that either absorb or reflect light; they do not allow any light to pass through them

organ
a body structure with a specific function; made up of several different kinds of tissue

organelle
any structure found in the cytoplasm of a cell that has a specific form and function

organ system
a group of organs that have related functions

osmosis
the diffusion of water through a selectively permeable membrane

ovary
part of the pistil, the female structure, in the flower of a plant; contains the female sex cells that combine with male sex cells during sexual reproduction

palisade
the layer of cells situated just under the top cuticle of a leaf; palisade cells contain many chloroplasts and are responsible for most of the photosynthesis in a leaf

paper chromatography
separation of solutes from a solvent using paper; relies on the fact that some solutes will move more easily through the paper than others

Particle Theory of Matter
a theory that consists of five statements: 1. all matter is made up of tiny particles; 2. all particles of one substance are the same, and different substances are made of different particles; 3. there are spaces between the particles; 4. the particles are always moving—the more energy they have, the faster they move; 5. there are attractive forces among particles that are stronger when the particles are closer together (see also *Atomic Theory*)

passive transport
materials moving into and out of a cell without the use of energy (see also *active transport*)

penumbra
the lighter part of a shadow, where some light reaches

permeable
describes membranes that permit passage of a substance

pesticide
a substance that kills or harms one or more pests

petal
the coloured part of most flowers; one of several structures that surround the reproductive structures of the flower

phloem vessel
a tube of live cells that transports sugars and other nutrients among the leaves, stem, and roots of a plant

phosphates
fertilizers that encourage the growth of plants; contain the elements phosphorus and oxygen

phosphorescence
the process of emitting light for some time after receiving energy from another source

photosynthesis
the process by which plants make sugar and oxygen from light, water, and carbon dioxide

physical change
a change in which the substance involved remains the same substance, even though it may change state or form

physical properties
the characteristics of a substance; examples are state, hardness, and density

pigment
a chemical that absorbs certain colours of light, but reflects others

pinhole camera
a box used to view images; has a hole at one end and a viewing screen at the other end

pistil
the female reproductive structure in the flower of a plant, composed of the stigma, style, and ovary

plastid
specialized organelle associated with the production and storage of food; chemical factories and storehouses for food and colour pigments

point of incidence
the spot where a ray of light strikes a reflecting surface

pollen
contains the male sex cells of a plant that combine with the female sex cells during sexual reproduction; located on the anther

pollination
in plants, the process of male sex cells (contained in pollen) reaching the female sex cells (contained in a stigma)

precipitate
a solid, insoluble material that forms in a liquid solution

precipitation
droplets or crystals of water that fall to Earth, including *rain*, *snow*, *freezing rain*, *sleet*, and *hail*

primary light colour
one of the three light colours (red, green, or blue) that, when added together, produce white light

primary pigment
a pigment (magenta, yellow, or cyan in colour) that absorbs only one of the primary light colours

principal axis
the line that passes through the principal focus and the vertex of a curved mirror

principal focus (F)
in a concave mirror, the point where rays of light parallel to the principal axis, and reflected from the mirror, intersect; in a convex mirror, the point behind the mirror from which reflected rays of light parallel to the principal axis appear to come from

prism
a solid, transparent piece of glass or plastic that can split white light into the visible spectrum

producer
an organism (such as a green plant) that converts solar energy into chemical energy that it can use as food

product
in chemistry, a substance that results from a chemical reaction

prophase
the phase of mitosis in which the individual chromosomes become visible

protein
one of the three major groups of nutrients; most cell structures are made of protein; used by the body to build and repair; composed of building blocks called amino acids

pure substance
contains only one kind of particle (molecule or atom); examples are sugar and aluminum foil

qualitative
an observation based on the aspects of an object or event that are detected by our senses; qualitative observations include things such as texture, smell, and taste

quantitative
an observation based on a measurement of an object or event

radicle
part of the embryo of a seed; becomes the root of the seedling

rain
liquid precipitation that falls as droplets of water

reactant
in chemistry, a substance that reacts to form another substance or substances, called products

real image
one of two types of image; a real image can be placed onto a screen (see *virtual image*)

recommended nutrient intake (RNI)
the recommended amount of a nutrient each person should eat each day

reflected ray
a ray of light that travels away from a surface, such as a mirror, after bouncing off that surface

Reflection, Law of
the angle of incidence equals the angle of reflection for light rays hitting a regular surface, such as a mirror

refrigerant
a substance that readily changes state from gas to liquid and from liquid to gas, used in cooling devices

regular reflection
the reflection of light off a smooth, shiny, regular surface that produces an image

residue
the substance trapped when a mixture is passed through a filter (see *filtrate*)

resistance
a condition in which pests become less vulnerable to the effects of a pesticide; every application of the pesticide kills fewer of the pests

respiration
process by which cells combine sugar molecules with oxygen to form carbon dioxide, water, and energy; happens in the mitochondria of plant and animal cells

ribosome
organelle that puts proteins together

root hair
a thin extension of the surface cell of a root; used to gather water and nutrients from the soil

root pressure
used to transport water within the xylem vessels of plants; water pressure is raised when root cells actively pull in minerals, causing water from the soil to enter the cells by osmosis

saturated
in nutrition, a fat molecule that contains close to the maximum number of hydrogen atoms; animal fats are saturated fats and are usually solid or semi-solid at room temperature (see *unsaturated*)

saturated solution
a solution in which no more solute will dissolve

scanning electron microscope
a device that reflects electrons from the surface of an object being studied; produces a three-dimensional image

scientific law
a general statement that sums up the conclusions of many experiments

secondary light colour
a colour (magenta, yellow, or cyan) produced when two of the primary light colours are added together

secondary pigment
a pigment (red, green, or blue in colour) that absorbs two primary light colours, and reflects the other

seed
the result of sexual reproduction in plants; consists of a container, an embryo, and a supply of food for the embryo

seed coat
the protective jacket of a seed; contains the other parts of the seed

selectively permeable
describes membranes that allow certain substances to enter or leave, but not other substances

sepal
one of several leaflike outer structures at the base of a flower; protects the flower in the bud stage

settling
a method of separation that depends on the different densities of the substances in a mixture; denser substances will tend to settle to the bottom of a container, and less dense substances will float to the top

sexual reproduction
reproduction that requires two parents; in multicellular organisms, when a sex cell from a male organism unites with a sex cell from a female organism, forming a fertilized egg that can grow to become a new individual that combines characteristics from both parents (see also *conjugation*)

shadow
an area where light has been blocked by an opaque object

simple sugar
the base molecule that combines to form carbohydrates; usually contains carbon, hydrogen, and oxygen atoms in the proportions of 1:2:1; examples are glucose and fructose

sleet
solid precipitation that falls in the form of ice pellets

snow
solid precipitation that falls in the form of water crystals

soil
consists of tiny particles from rocks and material remaining from decayed plants and animals (called humus); the spaces between the soil particles contain air and water

solar eclipse
occurs when the Moon is between the Sun and the Earth so the Earth is in the Moon's shadow

solidification
the change of state from a liquid to a solid (if this change occurs at temperatures below 0°C, the word *freezing* is often used)

solute
a material that dissolves in a solvent to form a solution

solution
a mixture in which the parts cannot be distinguished; made up of a solvent and one or more solutes; if a solution is gaseous or liquid it is transparent, if it is solid, it is the same throughout

solvent
a material into which a solute dissolves to form a solution

spontaneous generation
the theory, now abandoned, that nonliving things can be transformed into living things without any external causes

spore formation
the form of asexual reproduction in which the organism undergoes cell division to produce smaller, identical cells, called spores, that are usually housed within the parent cell

stamen
the male reproductive structure in the flower of a plant, composed of the anther and the filament

starch
a carbohydrate made of many sugar molecules linked together in long chains; used by plants to store food

stigma
part of the pistil, the female structure, in the flower of a plant; has a sticky surface that captures pollen

stoma (pl., stomata)
a small opening in the surface of the leaf that gases can pass through; the stoma is controlled by a pair of guard cells

style
part of the pistil, the female structure, in the flower of a plant; conducts male sex cells to the ovary of the flower

sublimation
the change of state directly from a gas to a solid, or from a solid to a gas, without going through the liquid state

subtractive colour mixing
the process of mixing pigments to obtain new colours; so called because each of the pigments absorbs (subtracts) different colours of light

surface area
the total area of all the faces of an object

suspension
a mixture in which the particles are not mixed as completely as a solution, but are mixed better than a heterogeneous mixture; a suspension appears to be one phase, but actually contains suspended solids that cause a cloudy appearance; the pieces of solid in a suspension are large enough that they will eventually settle out; pineapple juice is an example

symptom
a sign of an illness or problem; can be used to make a diagnosis

telophase
the phase of mitosis in which the two halves of the cell reorganize to form daughter cells

theory
a hypothesis or a set of related hypotheses that is supported repeatedly by experimental results

tissue
in the body, a group of cells of similar shape and function

translucent
describes materials that allow light to pass through, but scatter the light so a clear image cannot be seen through them

transmission electron microscope
a device that uses a beam of electrons instead of light to form an image; capable of much higher magnification than a light microscope

transparency
a measure of how much light can pass through an object (see *transparent, translucent, opaque*)

transparent
describes materials that allow light to pass through them easily so a clear image can be seen through them

transpiration
the evaporation of water from the exposed parts of a plant; because water molecules are attracted to each other, as each molecule evaporates, other water molecules are pulled up the xylem vessel, like a string of beads—this process is considered the most important factor in moving water through a plant

turgor pressure
water pressure that pushes the cytoplasm of a plant cell against the cell wall; keeps plants rigid

umbra
the darker part of a shadow, where no light reaches

unsaturated
in nutrition, a fat molecule to which more hydrogen atoms could be added; oils (plant fats) are unsaturated fats and are liquid at room temperature (see *saturated*)

vacuole
a space in cells filled with water, sugar, minerals, and proteins; animal cell vacuoles tend to be much smaller than those of plant cells

vaporization
the change of state from a liquid to a gas (also called *evaporation* or *boiling*)

variable
something that can change (vary) (see *dependent variable* and *independent variable*)

vein
in a plant, a combination of xylem and phloem vessels

vegetative reproduction
the form of asexual reproduction in which a section of a plant is used to grow a new plant

vertex (V)
the point at the middle of a curved mirror

virtual image
one of two types of image; a virtual image can be seen only by looking through or at the optical device (see *real image*)

viscosity
a physical property; refers to how easily a liquid flows—the thicker the liquid, the higher the viscosity

visible spectrum
the band of colours visible to the human eye; has six main colours (red, orange, yellow, green, blue, violet) that are called the spectral colours

vitamin
a nutrient that helps the body change food into energy; some are fat-soluble and some are water-soluble; examples are vitamins A, B, and C

volume
how much space an object fills; measured in cubic units (cubic metres, m^3) or capacity units (litres, L)

W

water cycle
the series of changes of state of water in nature

wet mount
a microscope slide prepared using water or another fluid

word equation
a short way of representing a chemical reaction; it lists the reactants and the products

X

xylem vessel
a tube used by plants to transport water; formed from cell walls left behind after a column of cells has died

Z

zygote
in sexual reproduction, the fertilized egg formed when two sex cells unite

Index

tree farming, 445
turgor pressure, 320
twins, identical or fraternal, 364
Tyndall effect, 130

ultraviolet (UV) radiation, 110, 190-191
    ultraviolet light, 259
umbra, 214-215
unsaturated fats, 460

vaccine research, 337
vacuole, 299
vaporization, 73, 74
    and the particle theory, 103
    requires heat, 86
variables, 22, 24, 25, 28
vegetables in the diet, 457
vegetative reproduction, 359
veins, in plants, 406
vertex
    of a concave mirror, 241, 243
    of a convex mirror, 241, 245
video arcade, 228, 233
video camera, 228
virtual images, 218, 237, 247, 248
virtual reality, 219, 274
viruses, 332
viscosity, 47, 48, 507
visible spectrum, 260-261
    and human vision, 266

vitamin C in drinks, testing for, 471
vitamins, 454, 468-469, 471
volume
    calculating, 52-53
    combining volumes, 94-95
    defined, 44
    measuring, 53, 54-55
    relating to mass, 56-57

warming curves, 78, 80, 102
water, 46
    absorption by plants, 402
    changes of state, 71, 72, 73, 74
    changes of state and weather, 82-83
    cooling curve, 81
    movement in plants, 400-401, 403-405
    pollution of, 132, 133, 134-135, 192-195
    sale of fresh water, 440-441
    use of, 53
    warming curve, 78, 80, 102
water cycle, 82
water mixtures and the environment, 132-135
water treatment, 146, 147
water vapour, cobalt chloride test for, 161
water-soluble vitamins, 469
wax candle, combustion of, 154, 167
weather
    and changes of state, 82-83
    and flight safety, 84-85
weeds, 418

weight cycling, 472
weight loss, 472-473
Wenman, Dr. Wanda M., 337
wet mount, 300
wheelchairs, mirrors for people in, 239
white blood cells, 305
WHMIS symbols, 528
wood frogs, freezing, 338
word equations for chemical reactions, 164-165
Wright, Jim, 198-199
writing a report, 520-521

xylem vessels, 403, 404, 405, 406

yellow light for safety, 266

zebra mussels, 67
zinc, reaction with hydrochloric acid, 162-163, 165
zygote, 359, 364

Credits

Front Matter: 22 Sinclair Stammers/Science Photo Library; **28** Kevin Forest/The Image Bank; **34** Ford Motor Company; **36** M. Tcherevkoff/The Image Bank; **40** left, First Light; centre 1, Ron Watts/First Light; centre 2, John P. Kelly/The Image Bank; right, Comnet/First Light

Unit Openers:
Unit 1, **40** G. Brad Lewis/Tony Stone Images; inset, Comstock;
rock in the liquid state—molten lava; [inset] a model of a molecule of DNA hints at a model for matter

Unit 2, **121** NASA/Science Photo Library/Photo Researchers; inset, Paul Dance/Tony Stone Images;
the environment around Cape Canaveral is in the foreground as the space shuttle takes off; [inset] antacid tablets perform their familiar chemical reaction

Unit 3, **205** Pekka Parviainen/Science Photo Library; inset, Malcolm Fielding/Science Photo Library;
the most important source of light, the Sun, sets over a coastal island; [inset] night lights enliven a city

Unit 4, **285** Professor P. Motta/Science Photo Library; inset, Andy Walker/Science Photo Library;
a close view (scanning electron microscope) of red (smooth) and white (hairy) blood cells on the lining of the heart; [inset] a human embryo at the early stage—four cells

Unit 5, **375** James Martin/Tony Stone Images; inset, Nick Gunderson/Tony Stone Images;
a botanical garden in Java gives a sense of the variety and importance of green plants; [inset] wheat, just one of the green plants that people depend on

Unit 6, **451** Anthony Blake/The Image Bank; inset, Alan Becker/The Image Bank;
food, in its incredible variety; [inset] wheelchair athletes furiously burn their stores of food energy

Chapter 1: 45 William Sallaz/The Image Bank; **46** top left, © 1993 Ontario Ministry of Culture, Tourism and Recreation; top centre, Charles Thatcher/Tony Stone Images; top right, Al Handan/The Image Bank; bottom, Trevor Wood/Tony Stone Images; **47** top left, William Rivell/The Image Bank; top right, Goldleaf Studios; bottom left, Science Photo Library; bottom right, Alcatel, Canada Wire; **49** Jane Shemitt/Science Photo Library; **51** Jeremy Jones; **61** Jeremy Jones; **62** top, Bettman Archive; bottom, Jeremy Jones; **65** Harry Fox/Oxford Scientific Films

Chapter 2: 70 Ontario Ministry of Culture, Tourism and Recreation; **71** Ontario Ministry of Culture, Tourism and Recreation; **72** David Taylor/Photo Researchers; **73** top left, G. Rossi/The Image Bank; top middle, Don King/The Image Bank; top right, Jeremy Jones; bottom left, Jeremy Jones; bottom middle, Steve Niedorf/The Image Bank; bottom right, Jeremy Jones; **74** Patrick Cocklin/Tony Stony Images; **75** Charles Mahaux/The Image Bank; **80** sequence 1, John Turner/Tony Stone Images; 2, Steve Barnett/Creative Stock; 3 John Beatty/Tony Stone Images; **81** top sequence 1, John Turner/Tony Stone Images; 2, Steve Barnett/Creative Stock; 3, John Beatty/Tony Stone Images; bottom, Canadian Sports Images; **83** Bill Ivy/Ivy Images; **84** top, Environment Canada; bottom, Steven Wilkes/The Image Bank; **85** David Brownell/The Image Bank; **87** top, Parks Canada, St. Lawrence Island National Park; bottom, Bill Ivy/Ivy Images; **88** top, Mark Tomalty/Masterfile; middle, Clint Clemens/First Light; bottom, Gabe Palmer/Masterfile

Chapter 3: 92 middle and right, McLaughlin Planetarium; **93** NASA; **113** © 1994 Paramount/Motion Picture and TV Archive

Canadian Science and Invention: 114 top and bottom, Dusanka Filipovic

Chapter 4: 122 Virginia Division of Tourism; **123** Simon Fraser/Science Photo Library; **125** Canadian Sports Images; **129** top, Jeremy Jones; bottom, David Keevil; **130** circle, University of Guelph, Department of Food Science; bottom, Tim Maylon/Science Photo Library; **131** Charles Krebs/Tony Stone Images; **132** Michael Salar/The Image Bank; **133** left, Kaz Mori/The Image Bank; right, Bill Ivy/Ivy Images; **136** Michael Melford/The Image Bank; **138** Victor Last/Geographical Visual Aids; **145** Imperial Oil

Chapter 5: 151 Jeremy Jones; **155** Tom McCarthy/Photo Edit; **161** Metro Toronto Police; **164** top and bottom, Jeremy Jones; **165** sequence of 3, Jeremy Jones; **166** top, Courtesy of Ontario Ministry of Natural Resources; middle, Jake Rajs/The Image Bank; bottom, AP/Canapress; **167** Gary S. Chapman/The Image Bank; **168** left, Bill Ivy/Ivy Images; right, A. & J. Verkaik/Skyart; **170** top and bottom, Benson & Hedges Inc. Symphony of Fire; **171** Canada Wide Features; **173** Terry Vine/Tony Stone Images

Chapter 6: 174 © 1994 MGM/Motion Picture and Television Archive; **175** Canapress; **176** Mary Evans Picture Library; **179** Richard Megna/Fundamental Photographs; **181** Mazda; **183** Jeremy Jones; **189** Jeremy Jones

Canadian Science and Invention: 198 Wright Environmental Management

Chapter 7: 206 Joanna McCarthy/The Image Bank; **207** Benson & Hedges Inc. Symphony of Fire; inset, Tim Maylon/Science Photo Library; **208** top, Gerald Brimacombe/The Image Bank; bottom, Astrid & Hanns-Frieda Michler/Science Photo Library; **209** top, A. & J. Verkaik/Skyart; bottom, Joe Azarra/The Image Bank; **211** Joe Van Os/The Image Bank; **212** left, Stephen Derr/The Image Bank; middle, Pekka Parviainen/Science Photo Library; right, Martin Bond/Science Photo Library; **213** A.J. Hirsch; **216** Rev. Ronald Royer/Science Photo Library; **219** Frank Whitney/The Image Bank; **222** Vince Hill, David Williamson; **223** Vince Hill, David Williamson; **224** top, Ivor Sharpe/The Image Bank; bottom, Grant Faint/The Image Bank; **225** top left and right, Bill Ivy/Ivy Images; bottom, Chris Thomaidis/Tony Stone Images

Chapter 8: 229 Dennis Brack/The Image Bank; **230** Pekka Parviainen/Science Photo Library; **234** Courtesy of Pulp & Paper Research Institute of Canada, Pointe-Claire, Quebec; **235** left, Gary Russ/The Image Bank; right, Colleen Warnock; **240** Jeremy Jones; **242** Jeremy Jones; **244** Jeremy Jones; **246** Tony Freeman/Photo Edit; **250** top, Charles Gupton/Tony Stone Images; bottom left, Jeremy Jones; bottom right, Martin Nix; **251** left, G.V. Faint/The Image Bank; right, Dick Hemingway; **252** left, David Nunuk/First Light; top, NASA; inset, NASA; **253** NASA; **255** Yuri Dojc/The Image Bank

Chapter 9: 256 Adam Hart-Davis/Science Photo Library; **257** Ontario Ministry of Culture, Tourism and Recreation; **258** Alfred Pasieka/Photo Researchers; **259** John Wiley and Sons; **260** Phil Jude/Science Photo Library; **263** Andy Sacks/Tony Stone Images; **266** Matsushita Electric of Canada Limited; **267** Michael Newman/Photo Edit; **270** Jeremy Jones; **272** Boden/Ledingham/Masterfile; **273** CNRI/Science Photo Library; **274** left, Liquid Image Corporation; right, Nintendo of Canada; **277** Antonio Rosario/The Image Bank

Canadian Science and Invention: 278 top, Scott Winter; bottom, Institute for Space Research, University of Calgary; **279** Dr. Debbie Hearn

Chapter 10: 287 background, Profs. P.M. Motta, K.R. Porter & P.M. Andrews/Science Photo Library; inset top, Walter Bibikow/The Image Bank; inset bottom, Martin Dohrn/Science Photo Library; **288** top, Joanna McCarthy/The Image Bank; sequence top, Biophoto Associates/Photo Researchers; left Philippe Plailly/Science Photo Library; circle, Guiliano Colliva/The Image Bank; bottom, Bill Ivy/Ivy Images; **289** top left, Peter Hendrie/The Image Bank; top right, Chalfant/The Image Bank; centre, Gower Medical Publications/Biophoto Associates/Photo Researchers; bottom, Joe Deveney; **300** John Burbridge/Science Photo Library; **302** top, Sinclair Stammers/Science Photo Library; inset, D.P. Wilson/Photo Researchers; **303** top, Geoff Thompkinson/Science Photo Library; top inset, Dr. Ann Smith/Science Photo Library/Photo Researchers; middle, Takeshi Takahara/Photo Researchers; middle inset, Biophoto Associates/Photo Researchers; bottom, Alexander Tsiaras/Science Photo Library; **304** top, CNRI/Science Photo Library; bottom, CNRI/Science Photo Library; **305** top, Dr. Gopal Murti/Science Photo Library; bottom, Dr. Gopal Murti/Science Photo Library; **309** Elena Roorail/Photo Edit; **310** Alexander Tsiaras/Science Photo Library; **313** top left, Biophoto Associates/Photo Researchers; top right, David Philips/Photo Researchers; bottom left, Biophoto Associates/Photo Researchers; bottom right, Biophoto Associates/Photo Researchers